Collectables

PRICE GUIDE 2007

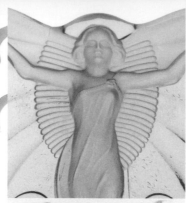

Collectables
PRICE GUIDE 2007

Judith Miller
and Mark Hill

A DORLING KINDERSLEY BOOK

LONDON, NEW YORK,
MELBOURNE, MUNICH AND DELHI

A joint production from DORLING KINDERSLEY
and THE PRICE GUIDE COMPANY

THE PRICE GUIDE COMPANY LIMITED

Publisher Judith Miller

Collectables Specialist Mark Hill

Publishing Manager Julie Brooke

Assistant Editor Sara Sturgess

Digital Image Co-ordinator Ellen Sinclair

Sub-editors Jessica Bishop, Dan Dunlavey, Karen Morden, Carolyn Malarkey

Design and DTP Tim & Ali Scrivens, TJ Graphics

Photographers Graham Rae, Bruce Boyajian, John McKenzie, Byron Slater, Steve Tanner, Heike Löwenstein, Andy Johnson, Adam Gault

Indexer Hilary Bird

Workflow Consultant Bob Bousfield

Business Advisor Nick Croydon

DORLING KINDERSLEY LIMITED

Publishing Director Jackie Douglas

Managing Art Editor Christine Keilty

Managing Editor Julie Oughton

DTP Designer Adam Walker

Production Rita Sinha

Production Manager Sarah Coltman

While every care has been taken in the compilation of this guide, neither the authors nor the publishers accept any liability for any financial or other loss incurred by reliance placed on the information contained in *Collectables Price Guide 2007*

First published in 2006 by
Dorling Kindersley Limited
80 Strand, London WC2R 0RL

A Penguin Company

The Price Guide Company (UK) Ltd
Studio 21, Waterside
44–48 Wharf Road
London N1 7UX
info@thepriceguidecompany.com

2 4 6 8 10 9 7 5 3 1

A CIP catalogue record for this book is available from the British Library.

ISBN-13: 978 1 4053 1570 8
ISBN-10: 1 4053 1570 9

Printed and bound in Germany by GGP Media GmbH

Discover more at
www.dk.com

CONTENTS

List of consultants 6
What's Hot 7
How to use this book 12

ADVERTISING
Coca-Cola 13
Other Advertising 14

AGATE 17

ART DECO 18

BANKNOTES 22

BEADS 24

BICYCLING 26

BLACK CAT
COLLECTABLES 27

BONDS &
SHARES 28

BOOKS
Modern First Editions 29
Paperback Books 39
Children's Books 48
Annuals 51

CAMERAS 52

CERAMICS
Beswick Animals 56
Beswick Characters 63
Briglin 67
Carlton Ware 68
Clarice Cliff 71
Coalport 81
Susie Cooper 82
Crowan Pottery &
Harry Davis 83
Crown Devon 84
Royal Doulton 85
Royal Doulton
Figurines 86
Royal Doulton
Characters 91

Royal Doulton
Animals 94
Fornasetti 95
Hazle Ceramics 96
Louis Hudson 97
Hummel Figurines 98
Italian Ceramics 103
Josef Originals 106
Lladró 108
Lotus Pottery 111
Midwinter 112
Moorcroft 115
Myott 117
Poole Pottery 119
Postmodern 129
Bernard Rooke 130
Rosenthal 132
Royal Copenhagen 134
Ruskin 137
Rye Potteries 138
Scandinavian 139
Shelley 147
Studio Pottery 148
Swid Powell 154
Teapots 156
Tremaen 157
Troika 158
Wade &
Wade Heath 164
Wedgwood 166
West German
Ceramics 168
Other Factories 175

CHARACTER
COLLECTABLES 181

CHOCOLATE
MOULDS 187

COINS 193

COMICS 198

COMMEMORATIVES
210

COSTUME &
ACCESSORIES
Costume 214
Handbags 218

COSTUME
JEWELLERY
Costume Jewellery 225
Bakelite Jewellery 240
Acme Studio 247

CRUISE LINER
MEMORABILIA 248

DISNEYANA 250

DOLLS 255

EYEWEAR 262

FIFTIES 266

FILM & TV
Dr Who 270
Other Film & TV 272

GLASS
1930s
Pressed Glass 274
British Cut Glass 280
Cloud Glass 281
Czech Glass 283
Dartington 286
Depression Glass 288
Langham 289
Mdina &
Isle of Wight 290
Murano 293
Scandianvian Glass 296
Schott 307
Spheres 308
Studio Glass 311
Wedgwood 315
Whitefriars 316
Other Makers 322

MAGAZINES 325

MARBLES 327

MECHANICAL
MUSIC 331

MILITARIA 333

NATURAL
HISTORY 335

PENS & WRITING
EQUIPMENT 338

PERFUME
BOTTLES 351

PEZ
DISPENSERS 354

PLASTICS &
BAKELITE 358

POSTERS
Railway Posters 364
Cruise Liner Posters 368
Airline Posters 370
Tourism Posters 371
Skiing Posters 373
Food Related Posters 374
Product Posters 377
Wartime Posters 379
Theatre Posters 382
Film Posters 383

POT-LIDS 384

POWDER
COMPACTS 390

RAILWAYANA 396

ROCK & POP 406

ROYAL
COMMEMORATIVES
416

CONTENTS

SCRAPS	**424**	Olympics	476	Corgi	513	**WINE**
		Tennis	478	Dinky	516	**& DRINKING** 569
SIXTIES &		Other Sports	479	Tri-ang	522	
SEVENTIES	**425**			Other Diecast	525	**WEIRD &**
		STAINLESS		Trains	531	**WONDERFUL** 573
SMOKING		**STEEL**	**480**	Tinplate Sandpails	533	Glossary 574
COLLECTABLES	**440**	**STAMPS**	**484**	Other Tinplate Toys	535	Index to Advertisers 576
				Lead Figures	539	Key to Illustrations 576
SMURFS	**447**	**TAXIDERMY**	**485**	Star Wars Toys	547	Directory of Specialists 581
				Chess	548	Directory of Auctioneers 584
SPORTING		**TECHNOLOGY**	**489**	Other Toys & Games	552	Clubs, Societies &
MEMORABILIA		**TEDDY BEARS**	**493**			Organisations 587
Fishing	455			**TRIBAL ART**	**554**	Collecting on the
Football	459	**TOOLS**	**506**	**WATCHES**		Internet 589
Golf	463			Wristwatches	559	Internet Resources 589
Horse Racing	474	**TOYS & GAMES**		Swatch Watches	566	Index 590

LIST OF CONSULTANTS

Beads

Stefany Tomalin
Author & Collector

Books

Roddy Newlands
Bloomsbury Auctions, London

Ceramics

Beth Adams
Alfies Antiques Market, London

Judith Miller
The Price Guide Company (UK) Ltd

Coins, Banknotes & Bonds

Rick Coleman
Bloomsbury, London

Comics

Phil Shrimpton
phil-comics.com

Chess & Natural History

Luke Honey
Bloomsbury Auctions, London

Dolls

Susan Brewer
britishdollshowcase.co.uk

Glass

Ashmore & Burgess
ashmoreandburgess.com

Dr Graham Cooley
graham.cooley@metalysis.com

Mark Hill
The Price Guide Company (UK) Ltd

Andy McConnell
Author & Collector

Marcus Newhall
Researcher & Collector

Val & Chris Stewart
cloudglass.com

Railwayana

Tony Hoskins
GWRA Railwayana Auctions

Sporting

Rachel Doerr
Lyon & Turnbull, Edinburgh

Graham Budd
Graham Budd Auctions

Teddy Bears

Leanda Harwood
leandaharwood.co.uk

Tools

Tony Murland
Toolshop Auctions, Needham
Market

We are very grateful to our friends
and experts who gave us so much
help – Patrick Bogue, Ian
Broughton, Beverley Adams, James
Bassam, Dave Cameron & Vincent
Charlton, Peter Card, Andrew Hilton,
Mark Laino, Geoffery Robinson,
Pepe Tozzo, Ron & Ann Wheeler,
Richard Wallis and Nigel Wiggin.

WHAT'S HOT

The world of collectables has continued to change dramatically over the past year. New areas have been revealed, knowledge about existing areas has deepened through extensive research, and the vogue for 'retro' style has continued. The phenomenon of online trading has continued to be the single most important factor to change the way collectables are bought and sold. A few quick clicks of a mouse are now enough to start anyone on the road to amassing a collection of...well, absolutely anything that takes their fancy. The world, in short, has become our oyster.

GLITTERING TREASURES

Since the publication of my first Collectors' Guide on Costume Jewellery in 2004, I have watched what was already a growing market go from strength to strength.

Signed pieces by those such as Trifari, Kenneth Jay Lane and Coro have remained highly sought after. Prices for some of their most characteristic designs have even shown notable price rises over the past year. Within those names, prices for some pieces or the work of certain designers, such as Alfred Philippe at Trifari have really rocketed. For example, a Trifari 'Crane' pin designed by Philippe sold for over £4,500 earlier in the year proving that costume jewellery is now big business and can command even higher prices than comparable items of precious jewellery. However, well designed and well made unsigned pieces, and those from the 1960s and '70s, can still offer excellent value for money – but now may be the best time to buy as prices are creeping upwards. Look out for novelty forms and designs that are typical of their era, as these tend to be the most desirable. The same is true for Bakelite and plastic jewellery, with its stylised forms and bright

colours being as popular today as when it was first made in the 'Jazz Age' of the 1920s and '30s.

I've also seen what can only be described as a 'globalisation' of the market. Boundaries that once stopped a collector in one market from learning about, and collecting, the hot trends that gripped other nations have fallen away. With access to dealers' stores and auctions through the internet, collectors are no longer limited by what they find in local antiques and collectables fairs, and shops and auctions. As costume jewellery, like many collectables, is small and light in weight, it can be packed easily and sent anywhere in the world.

Of course, as well as making even more collectables available, it has also meant that prices for items from overseas have levelled off. Whereas before, these pieces might fetch a much higher price due to their scarcity abroad, this has now changed as collectors globally are able to bid on equal terms.

A 1980s Kenneth Jay Lane umbrella pin, set with coloured glass rhinestones. **Worth £40-60. LJ**

A Coro floral "duette" pin in vermeil silver, with enamelling and rhinestones. **Worth £120-180. CRIS**

A 1950s large Briglin studio pottery cylinder vase with handpainted and sgraffito flower pattern. **Worth £60-90 FD**

it may be an undiscovered treasure. Wise collectors are investing in books showing the marks used by these potters, and are learning how to recognise their styles. Unrecognised pieces can be sold for sums as low as a few pounds, so never pass over the £5 bargain table at a collectors fair!

But its not just vintage pieces that are attracting increasing levels of interest. Work produced by today's potters and ceramic designers is often arguably undervalued when it comes up for sale again on the 'secondary' market. Once again, a knowledge of the marks and styles used by today's masters, this time combined with an awareness of their current work and career, could mean a future, modern masterpiece lands on your lap. It's generally wrong to look at this market purely as an investment, so always ask yourself if you will still love the piece after it has been staring at you from the shelf for ten years.

POTTY FOR POTS

One area that my collectables specialist Mark Hill and I both think is just about to boom is postwar and contemporary studio ceramics. Although top names such as Bernard Leach and Lucie Rie are well known to specialist collectors, with people often paying a thousand pounds or more to own examples of their work, there were a whole host of other potters working at the same period who have been largely ignored. This is often due to a lack of knowledge or understanding, particularly over the marks they used to sign their works or how they fit into the history of 20th century ceramic design. Research can show where they studied, or who they were taught by, with the intrinsic quality of a piece being the first clue that

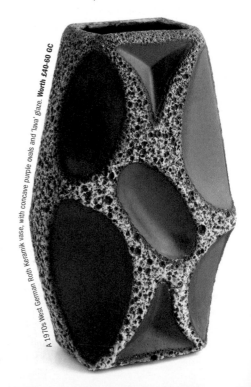

A 1970s West German Roth Keramik vase, with concave purple ovals and 'lava' glaze. **Worth £40-60 GC**

MAKE A STATEMENT

It's usually the 'look' of a piece that initially catches your eye and leads to you taking it home. You may not know much about it, but it just 'speaks' to you on some level. As more and more people come to the world of collectables looking for 'statement' pieces to add character to their homes, the style and eye appeal of a piece are becoming increasingly important factors to desirability and value. Nowhere is this more apparent than in the recent developments regarding West German and Italian ceramics of the 1960s and '70s. Exported all over the world and highly fashionable in their day, until recently they were laughed at and exiled to attics, or even thrown away, as new styles and fashions were introduced. Those that survived the experience languished, forgotten, in junk shops, often fetching no more than a couple of pounds. However, their immense

A 1970s Whitefriars Tangerine 'Banjo' vase **Worth** £500-800 GC

decorative appeal, combined with research that has revealed their importance to 20th century ceramics design, has meant that new group of fans has begun to collect them. As a result, prices have begun to rise, and look set to continue doing so.

STUPENDOUS STYLING

It's not all about new markets however, and the retro style continues to yield high prices. Modern classics such as Whitefriars' Textured range continue to attract an ever-increasing number of buyers, particularly for pieces that combine typical colours and patterns with forms that are characteristic of the style.

Produced slightly more recently, the eccentric forms and bright colours used during the late 1970s and 1980s by the so-called 'Postmodern' designers are becoming more popular again. As these pieces

A Postmodern Peter Shire handpainted ceramic studio teapot. **Worth** £450-550 GM

are still considered too much of an 'eye full' for most people, we think that it may take a little more time for most to adjust to a style that many of us still literally consider as 'yesterday's' fashion. Nevertheless, the world of collecting is full of examples of areas that were highly fashionable once, were then forgotten, only to be re-discovered and become sought after once again.

INDIVIDUAL STYLE

One area that nobody can dictate to you is your personal style. The recent 'retro' trend sported by models all over the world, and an increased desire to stand out from the crowd, has had a major effect on this. As a result the market for vintage clothing has boomed, particularly for those pieces that sum up the style of the era they were made in. One increasingly popular area is eyewear, from sunglasses worn on holiday to the glasses we wear every day. After all, when people meet you, what is it they look at the most? Your face! We change our clothes every day, but rarely our glasses. However, this is gradually changing.

Many of today's designers are either being inspired by, or adopting, the styles of the past. This has made original designs hotly sought after, particularly if they sum up a particular period in their shape and colouring, with the styles of the 1950s and '60s leading the field. Collectors and fashionistas alike compete over outrageous styles, and 'new-old' stock from now defunct opticians. Of course, some frames do not fit neatly into the look of any style or decade and yet are enormously appealing, having what can only be described as 'specs appeal'!

A 1950s Dunhill 'Aquarium' lighter, showing a duck. **Worth £2,000-3,000** WW

CHANGING HABITS

Smoking was once seen as both a fashionable and a healthy activity, incredible as this sounds to us today. From the 1920s to the 1950s many fine, and eccentric, accessories were produced and are being hunted by collectors today. Typical examples are Dunhill lighters. While those in precious metals, often with ingenious features such as inset watches, now fetch large sums of money, nobody could have predicted the rise of the plastic 'Aquarium' lighter. The couple of hundred pounds that these fetched only a few short years ago seemed high, but the thousands of pounds that they fetch now make them well worth tracking down. Of course, many were sold or thrown away, which has added to their rarity.

A pair of 1950s triple-laminated Raybert 'Baccara' frames, with hand-cut 'flame' rims. **Worth £100-150** VE

TREASURES IN YOUR HOME

With the range of what is being collected diversifying all the time, you often need look no further than your own home to find collectables that can be valuable.

Beswick's charming animal and character figurines have long been popular, and many have seen enormous price rises over the past two years. In the main part, these have been for rare variations in terms of colour, form, or even small details such as the positioning of a dog's tail. Small differences such as these can make a big difference to value. It's the same with the ever-popular Clarice Cliff ceramics, where different patterns in different colours

have their own, often widely varying values. This makes a fully illustrated, full-colour guide like this all the more useful.

Increased trade over the internet has also led to more information being posted on message boards, websites and, of course, auction descriptions. While this generally serves as a benefit to the market, it is important to remember that not everyone is an expert. Anyone can contribute to this global community of collectors, but they may not always be right and the importance of a trusted book must never be under-estimated. Having worked with so many different collectibles over the years, I realise that a personal connection is one of the key aspects of starting a collection, and explains why the collectables field is so broad. It is that variety – and the chance I'll find a piece I've been searching for – that makes every collectors' fair a potential treasure trove.

Judith Miller.

A Clarice Cliff 'Blue Chintz' pattern Etzarre Stamford shape teapot, **Worth £450-550 GHOU**

A Beswick piebald 'Girl On A Pony' figure, **Worth £3,500-4,500 PSA**

HOW TO USE THIS BOOK

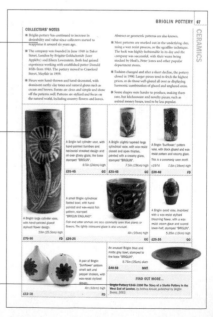

Category Heading
Indicates the general category as listed in the table of contents on pp.5–6.

A Closer Look at...
Here, we highlight particularly interesting items or show identifying features, pointing out rare or desirable qualities.

Subcategory Heading
Indicates the subcategory of the main category heading and describes the general contents of the page.

The Source Code
The image is credited to its source with a code. See the "Key to Illustrations" on pp.576-580 for a full listing of dealers and auction houses.

The Caption
Describes the item and can include the maker, model, year of manufacture, size and condition.

The Price Guide
All prices are shown in ranges and give you a "ball park" figure close to what you should expect to pay for a similar item. The great joy of collectables is that there is not a recommended retail price. The price given is not necessarily that which a dealer will pay you. As a general rule, expect to receive approximately 30 per cent less. When selling, pay attention to the dealer or auction house specialist to understand why this may be, and consider that they have to run a business as well as make a living. When buying, listen again. Condition, market forces and location of the place of sale will all affect a price. If no price is available, the letters NPA will be used.

Collectors' Notes
Provides background information on the designer, factory or make of the piece or style in question.

The Object
All collectables are shown in full colour, which is a vital aid to identification and valuation.

Find out more...
To help you seek further information, these boxes list websites, books, and museums where you can find out more.

COLLECTORS' NOTES

■ Coca-Cola has international appeal, and is the best-selling drink in most countries in the world. This, combined with an instantly recognisable logo and early, aggressive marketing campaign, makes it one of the most widely collected brands in the world.

■ The formula for the 'pick-me-up' drink was developed by Dr John Pemberton in 1886 and was originally sold as 'Pemberton's French Wine Coca'. Asa Griggs Candler took control of the company in 1887 and it was Candler who started the trend for aggressive advertising leading to the company's vast array of advertising merchandise and its market position today.

■ As there is a seemingly endless variety of memorabilia, collectors tend to focus on one area, such as trays, postcards or bottles, or artwork by artists such as Haddon Sundblom and Hamilton King.

■ Pre-1900s advertising is extremely rare and is often the most desirable. As a result, fakes are found so it is advisable to familiarise yourself with the company's changing logos and designs, which will help to date and authenticate pieces.

A Coca-Cola advertising pocket mirror, marked "From the painting, copyright 1906, by Wolf & Co., Phila., Bastian Bros. Co., Roch., N.Y., Duplicate Mirrors 5¢ Postage, Coca-Cola Company, Atlanta, Ga.".

This is an early, desirable piece of advertising memorabilia. This image can also be seen on a 1907 serving tray and calender, both of which are even more desirable.

1907　　　　　　　　　　2.75in (7cm) high

£250-350　　　　　　　　　　　　　**SOTT**

A 'The Prize Winning Coca-Cola – Drink Coca-Cola Delicious & Refreshing 5¢' watch fob, in mint condition.

Reproductions of these are being made, so buy from a reputable dealer.

1.75in (4.5cm) wide

£200-300　　　　**LDE**

A Coca-Cola green glass seltzer soda siphon, reading "Coca-Cola Bottling Co. Sharon PA, 28oz Capacity" and "Lynbrook Cold Beer".

12.25in (31cm) high

£150-250　　　**PWE**

A Coca-Cola diecast toy truck, retaining original decals on either side and on the tailgate, all over surface rust and scratches.

20in (51cm) long

£100-200　　　**JDJ**

A 1940s Coca-Cola sign, by Kay Displays Inc.

Kay Displays Inc. worked with Coca-Cola from 1934 and designed some of Coca-Cola's most sought-after signs. Their patriotic signs produced during US participation in WWII are the most desirable. The company closed in 1951.

27.25in (69cm) long

£120-180　　　**SOTT**

A 1941 Tournament of Roses souvenir programme, sponsored by Coca-Cola, with information about pandas inside.

1941　　　　　6in (15cm) high

£50-80　　　**LDE**

A Coca-Cola 'Hi-Fi Club' membership card.

The Hi-Fi Club was a 1960s dance club for teenagers sponsored and promoted by Coca-Cola. Although membership was free, a membership card was required to gain entrance to the dances, which were held in schools and similar venues. Each dance held a competition, the prizes from which are very popular with collectors today.

4in (10cm) wide

£60-70　　　**LDE**

A 1980s Coca-Cola sweatshirt, size large.

£18-22　　　**BR**

COLLECTORS' NOTES

■ Babycham was developed in the late 1940s by Francis Showering, who ran a small brewery and mineral water company with his brothers in Shepton Mallet, Somerset. He experimented with fermenting fruit juices and found that pear juice (perry) worked better than apple juice (cider). He entered the resulting sparkling drink under the name 'Champagne de la Poire' into many agricultural show competitions, all of which it won, becoming known as 'Baby Champ'.

■ Babycham was officially launched in 1953 and was the first alcoholic drink, and the second brand ever, to be advertised on national TV. Around this year the famous deer became associated with the drink, being suitably light, sparkly and feminine, with its bright 1950s colours and bow. The drink was aimed at women at a time when they were becoming more dominant in society and it became very successful.

■ Sales declined against competition from 'alcopops' and gained an unfashionable image during the 1980s and 90s, but the brand was relaunched in 1996. Vintage advertising featuring the deer is becoming increasingly collectable, in mint condition, but is still largely affordable. It represents an important development in the British drinks industry. Look for large, scarcely seen models and other objects, as most glasses are very common.

A Beswick Babycham ceramic advertising figurine, modelled by Arthur Hallam, model 1615B, with small eyes.

10cm (4in) high

£22-28   **PSA**

A Babycham plastic advertising figurine, on detachable stand.

This form can be hung from a bar shelf or a glass with its front legs.

8.5in (22cm) high

£45-55   **DIM**

A Babycham figural advertising bottle top.

This is the rarest form of these figurines as fewer were made and its thin legs were easily broken.

6.25in (16cm) high

£45-55   **DIM**

A Babycham plastic fawn advertising figurine.

This is the medium size of the three sizes made. The larger and smaller ones are worth around £5-8 more or less respectively.

2.25in (6cm) high

£15-25   **DIM**

A rare Babycham advertising glass, with twisted stem.

5.5in (14cm) high

£10-15   **DIM**

A Babycham advertising glass, with transfer decoration and gilt rim.

This form came both with and without a gilt rim and colour transfer, and both versions are worth roughly the same value.

A Beswick ceramic Babycham large advertising ashtray.

11in (28cm) wide

£35-45   **DIM**

A Babycham advertising glass, with transfer decoration and gilt rim.

4.25in (10.5cm) high

£3-4   **DIM**

A Carlton Ware Guinness toucan ceramic table lamp, the base reading 'How Grand to be a Toucan, Just Think What Toucan do. If He Can Say as You Can, Guinness is Good for You', together with original shade, printed mark.

The shade is very rare and shows designer Gilroy's other zoo animals that featured in Guinness campaigns.

Lamp 975in (25cm) high

£120-180   **CHEF**

A Carlton Ware Guinness toucan ceramic advertising figurine, the base with printed wording and printed mark.

9in (23cm)

£220-280   **SWO**

A Carlton Ware Guinness toucan advertising ceramic lidded jar.

4.75in (12cm) high

£70-90   **BAD**

Three Carlton Ware Guinness toucan wall-mounted ceramic advertising plaques, with printed mark including "Registered Australian Design" wording.

Fakes of these popular Carltonware items, made from the 1930s-50s, are often found. They are usually not marked on the back and the red and yellow on the beak is clearly demarcated, rather than being blended together into a near orange. The reference to Australia refers to Carltonware's 1930s registration of their designs in Australia in an attempt to prevent Japanese factories copying their designs under the South East Asia Treaty Organisation.

Largest 9.75in (25cm)

£280-320   **SWO**

A Spillers Homepride Fred kitchen companion, the hat being a cullender, the head forming a bowl, the body to hold salt and pepper shaker, the feet as pastry cutters, together with a set of four measuring spoons, a rolling pin and spoon.

c1979   *14in (35.5cm) high*

£70-90   **RBC**

A Jolly Green Giant plastic advertising figure, modelled as the 'Little Sprout' character with a leafy hat and tunic.

6in (15cm) high

£10-15   **MTS**

A PG Tips chimp plastic advertising figure.

£10-15   **MTS**

A 1930s 'Michelin' tyres black and white Bakelite advertising ashtray.

5in (12.5cm) high

£60-70   **HH**

A Huntley & Palmers 'Orient' biscuit tin, in the form of a piece of luggage, scratched.

The 'travel labels' actually show biscuit names rather than destinations.

1899   8in (20cm) wide

£30-50   **ROS**

A Huntley & Palmers bell-shaped biscuit tin, inscribed "Where Ye Doe Ringe I Sweetly Sing".

6.75in (17cm) high

£70-100   **GORL**

A Huntley & Palmers yellow and tan octagonal biscuit tin, commemorating the company's founding in 1826, overall in good condition, some corrosion to inside base.

£12-18   **SAS**

A CLOSER LOOK AT A BISCUIT TIN

Huntley & Palmer of Reading are perhaps the most sought-after and collected name in biscuit tins, mainly made in the first half of the 20thC.

The artwork on this later tin was taken from a design by Kate Greenaway (1846-1901), the popular children's book illustrator and author.

It became notorious after a grocer spotted the addition and the tin was withdrawn and reissued without the dogs - since then it has become legendary although is not as rare or valuable as many claim.

A disgruntled employee added a pair of fornicating dogs in the shrubbery on the right of the tin which was not initially noticed, and the tin was released on sale.

A Huntley & Palmer biscuit tin, printed with an idyllic tea party scene.

1980   8in (20cm) diam

£25-35   **ROS**

A Fillerys Toffees tin, depicting two astronauts and two spaceships on a planet surface, in excellent condition.

It is the space themed artwork as well as the condition that make this tin valuable.

5.25in (13.5cm) wide

£15-20   **SAS**

An unusual Cadbury's chocolate stoneware advertising milk jug, inscribed in white slip 'Cadbury', together with a metal whisk, the wooden handle inscribed 'Cadbury Bourneville'.

The milk jug may refer to the Cadbury promise that a 'glass and a half' of milk are added to each half pound of chocolate bar.

Jug 6.5in (16.5cm) high

£30-50   **LFA**

A 1950s Coty glass advertising dish, with transfer-printed design and gilt rim.

This will also appeal to perfume bottle collectors.

6in (15cm) long

£40-60   **DIM**

An oval pressed brass and brown agate pillbox.

3.25in (8cm) wide

£70-100   AB

A small rectangular double-opening box, made from clear, green- and white-veined agate and silver-plated metal, with ball clips.

This could have been used for pills, snuff or tobacco.

3.25in (8.5cm) wide

£60-70   AB

A small lidded pillbox, made from green-, white- and brown-veined agate and silver-plated metal.

1.5in (3.5cm) wide

£20-30   AB

A carved agate and brass bow-fronted box, with bevelled interior panels and engraved brass fittings, on agate ball feet.

Agate was popular during the 19thC due to its durability, variety of colours and suitability for carving or setting into mounts. Agate jewellery is hotly sought-after. Shaped agate-walled boxes, particularly with bow walls, are very rare due to the wastage generated by creating the curve and the time taken to achieve it.

3.75in (9.5cm) widest

£600-800   AB

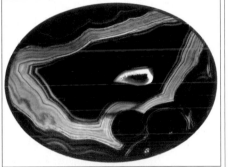

An oval one-piece agate bowl, with small foot.

9.25in (23.5cm) wide

£200-250   AB

A silver-plated melon or cheese scoop, with a carved tapering agate handle and slightly curved blade.

7in (18cm) long

£30-40   AB

A display piece of four joined agate spheres, carved from four separate pieces.

2.25in (5.5cm) high

£70-100   AB

COLLECTORS' NOTES

■ Cutting away the fussiness and ornament of the prevailing Art Nouveau style with its clean lines and extreme modernity, Art Deco revolutionised and dominated Western style, affecting nearly all levels of society, from the mid-1920s until WWII. There is consequently a wide array of items available for today's collector.

■ Art Deco style is suited to today's homes. Look for clean lines and minimal surface decoration. Where decoration appears, it is often geometric or stylised, breaking away from the traditional representations of patterns found in the 19th and early 20th century.

■ Colours vary from dramatic monochrome black, white and silvers to bold reds, oranges and greens. Consider material as well as form and colour. As new technologies developed, materials such as plastics were used. Aluminium, chrome and enamel are also typical.

■ Themes range from architecture, inspired by the new skyscrapers, to speeding cars and trains and desired luxury. Lamps and figurines - often dancing or sporty ladies - are popular areas. Consider marks, decoration and materials, and look for signs of age, wear and construction, as reproductions are very common.

An Art Deco patinated spelter figure of a female dancer, with her leg raised, mounted on an onyx socle.

12in (30.5cm) high

£350-450 **GHOU**

An Art Deco patinated spelter figure of a lady, dancing on the face of the moon, mounted on a cream onyx socle.

11in (28cm) high

£300-400 **GHOU**

An Art Deco patinated spelter figure of a female dancer, modelled holding an onyx ball mounted on an onyx socle.

12.5in (31.5cm) high

£350-450 **GHOU**

An Art Deco patinated spelter (zinc alloy) figure-match striker, after Josef Lorenzl, modelled as a scarf dancer upon a marble socle.

Spelter figurines were made in imitation of more expensive bronze and ivory figurines designed by notable names such as Ferdinand Preiss, Demetre Chiparus and Josef Lorenzl. Spelter figurines tend to be less well detailed and formed, hence their greater affordability, then and now.

11in (28cm) high

£220-280 **GHOU**

An Art Deco patinated spelter figure of a lady, with her leg, mounted on an onyx socle.

13in (33cm) high

£220-280 **GHOU**

An Art Deco patinated spelter figure of a female dancer, in period dress and hat, mounted on an onyx socle.

10.5in (26.5cm) high

£180-220 **GHOU**

An Art Deco style cold-painted plaster figure of a maiden with hound.

Although painted plaster figures were produced during the Art Deco period itself, they were also produced afterwards. Such reproductions fetch considerably less.

19.25in (49cm) long

£35-45 **DN**

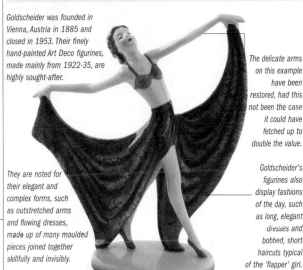

A CLOSER LOOK AT AN ART DECO FIGURINE

Goldscheider was founded in Vienna, Austria in 1885 and closed in 1953. Their finely hand-painted Art Deco figurines, made mainly from 1922-35, are highly sought-after.

The delicate arms on this example have been restored, had this not been the case it could have fetched up to double the value.

They are noted for their elegant and complex forms, such as outstretched arms and flowing dresses, made up of many moulded pieces joined together skillfully and invisibly.

Goldscheider's figurines also display fashions of the day, such as long, elegant dresses and bobbed, short haircuts typical of the 'flapper' girl.

An Art Deco Goldscheider ceramic figurine, impressed marks, restored arms.

British company Myott also made some superb figurines for Goldscheider in the 1940s and a limited number were also produced after WWII. Always examine an example closely for mould lines and other production 'shortcuts', which can indicate a piece made after WWII.

8.75in (22.5cm) high

£300-500   **WW**

An American Manning-Bowman bird's-eye maple mantel clock.

The light, finely grained appearance and luxurious appeal of bird's eye maple made it a highly popular wood used during the Art Deco period.

11.25in (28.5cm) wide

£350-450   **DETC**

An American Revere Clock Co. electric clock of truncated pyramid form, with am/pm indicator and half hour strike, mechanism by Telechron.

Telechron are noted for their movements, see the example on p.362 for more information.

c1925   13.5in (34.5cm) wide

£250-350   **DETC**

An American desk or mantel clock on a stand, with an illuminated pressed glass fish, the movement by Sessions.

c1935   11.5in (29cm) wide

£150-250   **DETC**

An opaque green glass wall clock, depicting a couple pursuing different activities at 12, 3, 6 and 9 o'clock.

c1930   14in (35.5cm) wide

£300-400   **DETC**

An early 20thC Winterhalder and Hofmeier clockwork calendar, the chromed case with octagonal bezel, the silvered dial with an outer ring of weekdays in black and Sundays in red, on a wood stand.

6in (15cm) high

£180-220   **CHEF**

An American Art Deco original artwork for the book cover for 'The Baccarat Club' by Jesse Louisa Rickard, the artwork by Wenck.

1929   7.5in (19cm) high

£40-70   **DD**

A 1930s American Art Deco theatrical advertisement for 'The Bijou Theater' in New York, designed by Chappell.

This advertisement plays on the ritzy glamour and skyscraper-filled modernity of the Big City.

8in (20cm) high

£15-20 DD

An Art Deco stamp, with geometric design.

Images of speeding vehicles are typical of Art Deco designs. With the brightly coloured geometric design, the paintings of Robert Delauney are suggested.

c1928 1.5in (4cm) high

£15-20 DD

A 1920s American Art Deco stationery box graphic.

1.5in (29cm) high

£30-40 DD

An American Art Deco geometric picture frame, black glass and mirror, containing a photo of Joan Crawford.

c1930 11.5in (29cm) high

£300-400 DD

A pair of Art Deco chrome and bakelite candelabra-style boudoir lamps.

c1935 16.5in (42cm) high

£300-400 DETC

A 1930s Art Deco polished chrome Chase bud vase.

The Chase Brass & Copper Company was founded in Waterbury, Connecticut in 1876 and produced metalwares for the home from the 1930s. The strong Art Deco styling, most often in chrome, was hugely popular. Production of homewares ceased at the outbreak of WWII.

9in (23cm) high

£40-50 DD

A 1930s English Art Deco 'Bunting' designer radiant heater, in the form of a yacht, the two chrome tin sails acting as heat reflectors, the mast as heating rod.

29in (73.5cm) high

£180-220 GORL

A pair of 1930s Art Deco Chase Corp. copper bookends, designed by Walter von Nessen.

5in (12.5cm) high

£200-300 DETC

An Art Deco silver-plated tea set, consisting of teapot, water jug, sugar bowl and milk jug, each of cubist form with bakelite handles and finials, maker's and registration marks to underside.

£200-300 ROS

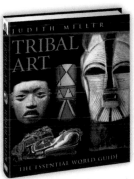

COLLECTORS' NOTES

■ Notaphily, the collecting of paper money, first became popular in the 1960s and grew in the 1970s when it became a separate collecting area from coins.

■ Notes are often decorated with vignettes and detailed scenes that are not only decorative but are designed to foil counterfeiters. These vignettes often form the basis of a collection with themes including famous people, wildlife, battles or other historical events. Other collecting themes include special or significant serial numbers, wartime currency or notes from a specific country or period.

■ As banknotes are produced in limited editions, they tend to accrue in value steadily, so collectors can often see a return on their investment quite quickly compared with many other collecting areas.

■ Condition has a huge effect on value, and notes in mint condition are highly sought-after. Store banknotes flat in plastic wallets and take care when handling them.

A scarce Hong Kong & Shanghai Banking Corporation 500 dollars note, dated 1st February 1965, light wear to edges.

1965

£300-400 BLO

An Italian Regie Finanze-Torino 100 lire note, unissued, printed in black on one-side with arms at left centre, in extremely fine condition.

1746

£100-150 BLO

A Maltese Banco Anglo Maltese 50 pounds note, dated "18--", unissued, printed in black on one side with St. George slaying dragon at upper left, worn down left edge of counterfoil otherwise in extremely fine condition.

£350-400 BLO

A Spanish Aramburu Hermanos 500 reales de vellón, dated "18--", unissued, printed in black on one side with brown and green panel across centre and arms at upper centre, in about uncirculated condition.

£30-40 BLO

A rare Government of Tonga Treasury four shillings note, dated 16th January 1933, with a couple of short edge tears and three small holes in body, otherwise in fine condition.

£80-120 BLO

An English Treasury one pound note, with John Bradbury printed signature, in very fine condition.

1914-16

£120-180 BLO

An English Treasury one pound note, with Sir Norman Fenwick Warren Fisher printed signature, in very fine condition.

1919-22

£50-70 BLO

A Bank of England five pounds note, dated 2 June 1950, with Percival S. Beale printed signature, with light pencil marks top right and short tear bottom edge.

£40-60 BLO

A CLOSER LOOK AT A BANKNOTE

A Central Bank of Ireland 100 pounds note, dated 19.7.1947, with Joseph Brennan and J.J. McElligott signatures, inked letters right side, pinholes, few edge nicks plus short tear bottom edge, good early date.

1947

£200-300 BLO

Prior to 1900 there were approximately 100 banks in Ireland that produced their own banknotes.

By the 1960s, this number had been reduced to just six.

This is an early example, issued in Dublin.

It has been hand-signed by William James Alexander, one of the directors of the bank.

A rare Irish Alexanders Bank, Dublin two pounds note, dated 7 September 1819, issued for partnership, good to very fine condition.

1819

£600-800 BLO

An Irish Central Bank of Ireland, fifty pound notes, dated 01.11.1982, in fine condition.

1982

£80-120 BLO

A Scottish Royal Bank of Scotland plc., five pounds note, new issue with Jack Nicklaus on back, uncirculated.

2006

£4-5 BLO

COLLECTORS' NOTES

■ Beads were one of the first forms of personal decoration. The earliest examples found used materials taken from nature, such as shells, stones, seeds and feathers. Beads and jewellery often held great social and cultural importance and a study of the object often leads to a greater understanding of the people producing and wearing them.

■ Bead collecting tends to falls between jewellery and tribal art, and as a result is often overlooked as a collecting area in its own right. Given their wide range

of materials, ages and countries of origin they make an ideal collecting field to suit a wide range of budgets and tastes. Examples here are mainly African trade beads.

■ Although glass is a common material, almost none was made in Africa. It was either produced from recycled bottles or older beads, or was produced in Europe, particularly Venice, and then exported to Africa.

■ Many types are copied today, so make sure you know if you are buying an antique or modern example.

A necklace of fused recycled 'powderglass' 'king' beads, by the Krobo people of Ghana, African or Venetian for the African market, with polychrome decoration, strung with a Moroccon silver clasp.

Necklace 15in (38cm) long

Beads £4-5 (each)   VC

A strand of 1920s-30s Bohemian glass 'wedding' beads, for the African market.

21.5in (54.5cm) long

£70-90   VC

A strand of 1930s-50s Venetian millefiori glass beads.

15in (38cm) long

£40-60   VC

A strand of Neolithic African beads, including agate and cornelian, excavated in Djenné, southern Mali.

Strand 21in (53.5cm) long

£30-40   VC

Three turned agate beads.

The agate was probably mined in Africa, shipped to India for shaping and then exported back to Africa for sale.

Largest 4in (10cm) long

£4-8 (each)   VC

Two 20thC Ethiopian silver-plated brass pendants, decorated with Coptic symbols.

These pendants are worn by the Jewish Falasha people of the Gondar region of Ethiopia. They often combine Jewish and Christian symbols such as the Star of David and a cross.

Largest 2.5in (6.5cm) high

£50-60 (each)   VC

Six 20thC Ethiopian silver telsum charms.

0.75in (2cm) wide

£5-6 (each)   VC

A large seven-layer chevron glass bead, Venetian for the African market.

c1600s   1in (2.5cm) wide

£50-60   **VC**

Five Venetian glass 'Rosetta' beads, with five layers of polychrome glass.

These beads can be found with varying numbers of layers. With bevelled edges they are known as chevron beads.

0.5in (1.5cm) wide

£4-5 (each)   **VC**

Five late 19th/early 20thC millefiori glass beads, Venetian for the African market.

Largest 1.5in (4cm) long

£5-10   **VC**

A CLOSER LOOK AT KIFFA BEADS

Traditionally there is very little glass-making in Africa, so these beads are produced using an inventive method.

As this process is very time consuming, they were not made in great quantities. The beads are still made today, but do not show the complex and clearly delineated patterns of older examples.

Clear glass is crushed to a fine powder between stones and then mixed with saliva to form a core for the bead. Coloured glass power is added over this core with a needle in complex patterns. The beads are then fired in a tin can or on a pottery sherd over hot coals.

The triangular beads were used as forehead pendants, and are the result of a T-shaped frame used to support the bead during production.

A collection of late 20thC African 'kiffa' glass beads.

Kiffa beads, also known as murakad, are named after the city of Kiffa in Mauretania, where they were first discovered by a Westerner.

Largest 0.75in (2cm) long

£8-15 (each)   **VC**

Three 18thC Venetian miniature chevron glass beads, each with seven layers.

The process of producing these chevron beads was invented in Venice about 500 years ago. These tiny glass beads demonstrate the level of skill found in 18thC Venetian glass makers. The sides have been bevelled to show the various layers when the beads are strung on a necklace.

Largest 0.25in (0.5cm) wide

£10-15 (each)   **VC**

Four late 19th/early 20thC millefiori glass 'elbow' beads, Venetian for the African market.

These beads are named for their bent shape.

2in (5cm) long

£10-25 (each)   **VC**

A late 19th/early 20thC millefiore glass 'elbow' bead, Venetian for the African market, with West African gold pendant mount.

2.5in (6.5cm) long

£50-70   **VC**

FIND OUT MORE...

The Bead Society of Great Britain, www.beadsociety.freeserve.co.uk.
The Bead Study Trust, www.beadstudytrust.org.uk.
http://bead-database.org, online interactive bead database.
http://beadcollector.net/openforum/index.html, US online discussion forum.

A Swedish Itera plastic bicycle.

This was the first all-plastic bicycle and was made in Gothenburg, Sweden with component parts from Sturmey-Archer. It proved to be a huge failure and was only made for one year. Many considered it ugly and the material meant that the frame flexed when ridden.

c1982   68in (172.5cm) long

£100-150   **GAZE**

A penny-farthing bicycle, with solid rubber wheel rims and a lever-operated brake on front wheel, in good working condition.

Also known as a 'high-wheeler' or 'ordinary bicycle', the penny-farthing was produced mainly in the US and UK in the mid-to late 19thC. As the design pre-dated geared bicycles, the front wheel became increasingly large in order to achieve higher speeds. The arrival of the geared Rover 'safety' bicycle, with the now typical diamond-shaped frame, in c1885 saw the decline of the penny-farthing.

c1885   57in (145cm) high

£1,800-2,200   **ATK**

A Manchester Components Company 'Manchester' acetylene gas bicycle lamp.

1898

£80-120   **TCA**

A Joseph Lucas 'Silver King' oil lamp.

1938

£60-80   **TCA**

A Doulton Lambeth brown stoneware tyg, applied in white with figures on bicycles.

5.5in (14cm) high

£220-280   **SAS**

A 'Bicycling' pearlware nursery plate, the centre printed in blue with a gentleman riding a 'boneshaker', inscribed with four lines of verse.

c1820   6.25in (15.5cm) diam

£650-750   **SAS**

A Powell & Hanmer Cycle & Motor lamps advertising poster.

1905

£300-400   **TCA**

A French Hurtu 'Tubes Renforcés Rationnels' stone-lithographed advertising poster, with slight roll creases.

53.75in (136.5cm) high

£250-350   **JDJ**

COLLECTORS' NOTES

■ The black cat has been a powerful, often negative, symbol for centuries and features in traditional folklore, usually connected to witchcraft and evil.

■ Although predominately considered a sign of bad luck, some countries see them as favourable symbols. In the UK, a black cat crossing your path is considered a sign of good things to come. However the opposite is believed in other countries, such as the US.

■ This negative association probably began in ancient Babylonian and Hebrew mythologies which equated cats curled in hearths with serpents.

■ Black cats as familiars are also associated with witches; their dark colouring making them perfect for remaining unseen at night and in the 1930s the Wiccan religion adopted the black cat as an official symbol. This connection means that black cats are commonly featured in Hallowe'en memorabilia.

■ Despite its negative connotations, the black cat has been used in product advertising and as company logos, such as the Eveready Battery.

A 1930s German black cat painted composition candy container, with "GERMANY" printed on base.
4.75in (12cm) high

£120-180　　　　　　　**SOTT**

A 1960s Japanese black cat ceramic figure, marked "JAPAN".
5in (12.5cm) high
£15-25　**PKA**

A homemade Felix-style black cat wood doorstop.
10.5in (27cm) high
£20-30　**PKA**

One of a pair of small black cat ceramic bud vases.
3.25in (8cm) high
£15-25　**PKA**

A one of a pair of small black cat ceramic bud vases.
3.25in (8cm) high
£15-25　**PKA**

A 1930s black cat hand-made wooden trump indicator, for a game of cards.
3.5in (9cm) high
£60-80　**PKA**

A Japanese black cat small hand-painted ceramic posy or trinket holder, marked "JAPAN".
3in (7.5cm) wide
£15-25　**PKA**

A set of three black cat numbered game pencils, with carved and turned wooden bases.
4.75in (12cm) high
£60-70　**PKA**

An English Channel Tubular Railway Preliminary Co. Ltd. certificate for five founders shares, with vignettes of English and French coasts and train in tube on seabed, text in English and French, in very fine condition.

1892

£100-150   **BLO**

An English Great North of England Railway Co. certificate for one share, with a chain link at left with names of towns on the proposed route, in very fine condition.

1836

£150-200   **BLO**

A scarce English Middlesbrough & Guisbrough Railway Co. certificate for one share, with a large vignette of locomotive pulling coal wagons passing mine, cut-cancelled at bottom right corner, not effecting print, in very fine condition.

1857

£400-500   **BLO**

An English Wharfdale Railway Co. certificate for one share, with a vignette of the famous 'Craven Heffer', large red seal, in very fine condition.

The Craven Heffer was an extremely large cow, which made vast profits for its owner by being exhibited around the country.

1846

£70-100   **BLO**

An English Whitehead Aircraft (1917) Ltd., certificate for cumulative participating ordinary shares, with a vignette of airfield with biplanes either side, large underprint of biplane, in very fine condition.

1918

£120-180   **BLO**

A Chinese Kiangsu Province Water Conservancy Construction Loan bond for 10 yuan, with a large vignette of a river scene, mountains and Sun Yat Sen, with coupons six to 26, folded, otherwise in very fine condition.

1934

£120-180   **BLO**

An Irish Waterford, Wexford, Wicklow & Dublin Railway Co. certificate for one share, ornate design with coat of arms at top, green seal, in very fine condition.

1847

£100-150   **BLO**

A scarce Great East Asia War Special Loan of the Imperial Government of Japan treasury bond for 1,000 yen, vignette of building at right, equestrian statue at left, with coupons two to 18, two punch holes in top margin.

1943

£220-280   **BLO**

BOOKS

COLLECTORS' NOTES

■ True first editions, as far as collectors are concerned, are from the first printing, or impression, of the first edition. To identify one, look for the number '1' in the series of numbers on the copyright page.

■ Some publishers state clearly that a book is a first edition, or use letters. Check that the publishing date and copyright date match, and learn about different publishing styles indicating first editions.

■ 'First' numbers are limited – values usually rise as desirability increases. Very famous, iconic titles will always be prized, but a classic title published at the height of an author's career will often be worth less than an early and less well-received work as these are usually produced in much smaller numbers.

■ Condition is another key indicator of value. Dust jackets are very important – values of modern titles can fall by 50 per cent or more without them.

■ Authors' signatures are a bonus, while dedications are slightly less desirable unless the person is famous or connected with the author. A good tip is to buy (preferably) signed copies of up-and-coming authors nominated for major prizes, like the Booker, before the winner is announced.

■ There are many perennially popular authors such as Iris Murdoch, Agatha Christie and Ian Fleming, but fashion does play a significant role. Books made into successful, popular films usually increase in value as interest surges.

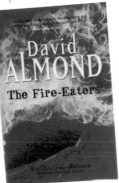

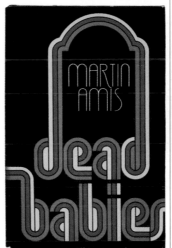

Martin Amis, "Dead Babies", first edition, presentation copy from the author, original boards, dust jacket.

David Almond, "The Fire-Eaters", first edition, published by Hodder, signed by the author.

John Banville, "Nightspawn", first edition, original boards, dust jacket, tanned at upper edge and spine.

2003

£20-30   **BIB**

1975

£450-550   **BLO**

1971

£200-250   **BLO**

Saul Bellow, "The Victim", first English edition, original boards, spine faded, tanned and rubbed.

Pat Barker, "The Eye in the Door", first edition, original boards, dust jacket.

Julian Barnes, "The Lemon Table", first edition, published by Jonathan Cape, signed by the author.

This was the author's second book.

Tim Bowler, "Starseeker", first edition, published by Oxford Press.

1993

£70-100   **BLO**

2004

£18-22   **BIB**

1948

£100-150   **BLO**

2002

£7-10   **BIB**

William Boyd, "A Good Man in Africa", first edition, original boards, dust jacket a little creased at spine ends.

1981

£220-280   **BLO**

Michael Bracewell, "Perfect Tense", first edition, published by Jonathan Cape.

£8-12   **BIB**

Ray Bradbury, "Fahrenheit 451", first English edition, original boards, dust jacket.

1954

£400-500   **BLO**

Ray Bradbury, "Dark Carnival", first English edition, some isolated foxing, original cloth covers and dust jacket.

Even though the dust jackets of this work were supposed to have been price clipped by the publisher before circulation, this copy seems to have escaped that fate, remaining unclipped.

1948

£450-550   **BLO**

Bruce Chatwin, "In Patagonia", first edition, original boards, dust jacket.

1977

£280-320   **BLO**

Tracy Chevalier, "The Virgin Blue", first edition, published by Penguin.

1997

£20-30   **BIB**

Lee Child, "Echo Burning", first edition, published by Bantam Press.

2001

£7-10   **BIB**

James Clavell, "King Rat", first English edition, peripheral foxing near beginning, original boards, dust jacket slightly bumped in one corner.

£50-70   **BLO**

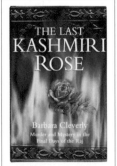

Barbara Cleverly, "The Last Kashmiri Rose", first edition, original cloth, dust jacket.

2001

£80-120   **BLO**

Jim Crace, "Six", first edition, published by Viking, signed by the author.

2003

£18-22   BIB

Rachel Cusk, "The Lucky Ones", first edition, published by Fourth Estate.

2003

£15-20   BIB

Linda Davies, "Into the Fire", first edition, published by Harper Collins.

1999

£12-18   BIB

Jill Dawson, "Wild Boy", first edition, published by Sceptre, signed by the author.

2003

£12-18   BIB

Len Deighton, "The Ipcress File", first edition, original boards, dust jacket.

1962

£280-320   BLO

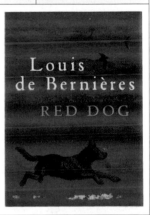

Louis De Bernières, "Red Dog", first edition, published by Secker & Warburg.

2001

£7-10   BIB

Louise Doughty, "Dance with Me", first edition, published by Touch Stone.

1996

£6-8   BIB

Sebastian Faulks, "A Trick of the Light", first edition, faint water-staining to edges of front endpapers, original boards, dust jacket, a little creased at edges.

1984

£180-220   BLO

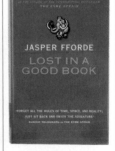

Jasper Fforde, "Lost in a Good Book", first edition, published by Hodder & Stoughton, signed by the author.

The signature is in upper case, which is rare for this author.

2002

£30-50   BIB

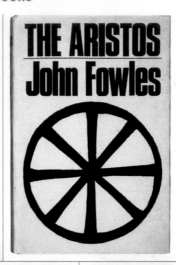

John Fowles, "The Aristos", first edition, original boards, price clipped dust jacket, slightly tanned at spine.

Price clipping refers to the price found on the bottom corner of the dust jacket being cut off. This was normally done by the buyer, and very rarely by a publisher if the price changed between printing and releasing a book. Unclipped examples are more desirable.

Frederick Forsyth, "The Day of the Jackal", first edition, ink ownership signature on title page, original boards, dust jacket very slightly rubbed at edges and with a couple of small tears, price clipped.

1971

£80-120   **BLO**

1965

£350-450   **BLO**

John Fowles, "The Collector", first edition, original brick red boards, dust jacket, a little tanned at spine and edges.

1963

£350-450   **BLO**

Michael Frayn, "Spies", first edition, published by Faber & Faber, signed by the author.

2002

£15-20   **BIB**

Nicci French, "Land of the Living", first edition, published by Michael Joseph, signed by both authors.

2002

£18-22   **BIB**

Terry Pratchett & Neil Gaiman, "Good Omens", first edition, published by Gollancz, signed by Terry Pratchett.

1990

£30-40   **BIB**

Damon Galgut, "The Good Doctor", first edition, published by Atlantic, Booker prize listed.

Works by literary award winning authors are often more sought-after.

2003

£10-15   **BIB**

Alex Garland, "The Coma", first edition, published by Faber & Faber, signed by the author.

2004

£15-20   **BIB**

William Golding, "Lord of the Flies", first edition, second impression, small ink ownership inscription on front endpaper, original cloth, dust jacket, very small chips to head of spine.

1954

£180-220   **BLO**

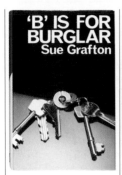

Sue Grafton, "'B' is for Burglar", first edition, original boards, dust jacket.

1985

£250-350   BLO

James Graham (Jack Higgins), "A Game for Heroes", first edition, original boards, dust jacket.

1970

£180-220   BLO

Caroline Graham, "The Killings at Badger's Drift", first edition, margins a little browned, original boards, dust jacket.

1987

£70-100   BLO

Caroline Graham, "The Envy of the Stranger", first edition, signed on title page.

1984

£50-80   BLO

Henry Green, "Nothing", first edition, published by Hogarth Press, London, spine slightly faded and bumped, in like dust jacket, spine a trifle darkened, back panel dusty, top edge and corners slightly rubbed.

1950

£40-50   PB

Abdulrazak Gurnah, "Paradise", first edition, published by Hamish Hamilton, Booker prize listed.

1994

£15-25   BIB

Shirley Hazzard, "The Great Fire", first edition, published by Virago, signed by author.

2003

£20-30   BIB

Zoë Heller, "Notes on a Scandal", first edition, published by Viking, signed by the author.

2003

£70-90   BIB

Jack Higgins, "In the Hour Before Midnight", first edition, original boards, gilt spine, dust jacket a little tanned and a little creased at upper edge.

1969

£120-180   BLO

Tobias Hill, "The Cryptographer", first edition, published by Faber & Faber, signed by the author.

2003

£10-15 BIB

Robin Hobb, "The Farseer I: Assassin's Apprentice", first edition, original boards, dust jacket.

1995

£70-100 BLO

Robin Hobb, "The Tawny Man III: Fool's Fate", first edition, published by Voyager, signed by the author.

2003

£10-20 BIB

Wendy Holden, "Pastures Nouveaux", first edition, published by Headline, signed by the author.

2001

£12-18 BIB

John Irving, "The Water-Method Man", first US edition, published by Random House, New York.

1972

£300-400 BRB

Howard Jacobson, "Who's Sorry Now", first edition, published by Jonathan Cape, signed by the author.

2002

£20-30 BIB

P.D. James, "The Black Tower", first edition, original boards, dust jacket, designed by Errol Le Cain.

£80-120 BLO

Kazuo Ishiguro, "The Remains of the Day", first edition, original boards, dust jacket.

Books that have been made into successful films, such as this one, tend to be more sought-after.

1989

£120-180 BLO

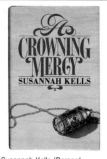

Susannah Kells (Bernard Cornwall), "A Crowning Mercy", small ink name on front pastedown, first edition, original boards, dust jacket.

1983

£100-150 BLO

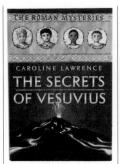

Caroline Lawrence, "The Secrets of the Vesuvius", first edition, published by Orion, signed by the author.

2001

£10-15 BIB

Andrea Levy, "Small Island", first edition, published by Review, signed by the author.

2004

£20-30 BIB

Toby Litt, "Exhibitionism", first edition, published by Hamish Hamilton, signed by the author.

2002

£10-20 BIB

Gabriel García Márquez, "No One Writes to the Colonel", ink ownership signature on title, original boards, dust jacket, small clean tear to one corner.

1971

£120-180 BLO

Alistair MacLean, "H.M.S. Ulysses", first edition, signed by the author, original boards, dust jacket, slightly rubbed and browned at extremities.

1955

£400-500 BLO

Gabriel García Márquez, "One Hundred Years of Solitude", first American edition, later state with row of numbers on p.424, original cloth, dust jacket, second state without exclamation mark at end of second paragraph on front flap.

1970

£120-180 BLO

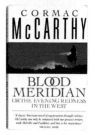

Cormac McCarthy, "Blood Meridian or The Evening Redness in the West", first English edition, original cloth, dust jacket.

1989

£100-150 BLO

Cormac McCarthy, "Outer Dark", first English edition, original cloth, dust jacket slightly edge-worn at spine.

1970

£180-220 BLO

George McDonald Fraser, "Black Ajax", first edition, published by Harper Collins, signed by the author.

1997

£12-18 BIB

Patrick O'Brian, "The Mauritius Command", first edition, original boards, dust jacket.

1977

£400-500 BLO

George MacDonald Fraser, "Flash for Freedom", first edition, published by Barrie & Jenkins.

1971

£70-90 BIB

Ian McEwan, "First Love, Last Rites", first edition, original boards, dust jacket.

1975

£350-450 BLO

Magnus Mills, "The Restraint of Beasts", first edition, published by Flamingo.

1998

£15-25 BIB

V.S. Naipaul, "Half a Life", first edition, published by Picador, signed by the author.
2001

£25-35 BIB

Patrick O'Brian, "The Nutmeg of Consolation", first edition, original cloth, dust jacket.
1991

£150-200 BLO

Patrick O'Brian, "The Surgeon's Mate", first edition, original boards, dust jacket.

This is the scarcest Jack Aubrey title. The success of the 2003 film 'Master and Commander' has increased interest in the series.

1980

£700-1,000 BLO

Maggie O'Farrell, "My Lover's Lover", first edition, published by Review.
2002

£10-15 BIB

James Patterson, "Hide and Seek", first edition, published by Harper Collins.
1996

£15-20 BIB

Ellis Peters, "Dead Man's Ransom", first edition, original cloth, dust jacket, slightly faded at spine.

1984

£70-100 BLO

Ellis Peters, " A Nice Derangement of Epitaphs", first edition, original cloth, dust jacket, torn and repaired internally but with no loss, slight edge creasing.

1965

£70-100 BLO

DBC Pierre, "Vernon God Little", first edition, published by Faber & Faber.

2003

£60-80 BIB

Ian Rankin, "Knots & Crosses", first edition, ex-library copy, with stamps on title and rear pastedown, some creases.

1987

£250-300 BLO

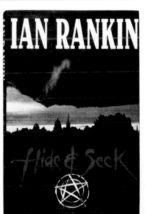

Ian Rankin, "Hide & Seek", first edition, original boards, dust jacket, slightly rubbed.

1991

£200-250 BLO

Ian Rankin, "The Flood", first edition, Edinburgh, original boards, dust jacket.

1986

£650-750 BLO

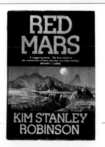

Kim Stanley Robinson. "Red Mars", first edition, original boards, dust jacket, a little creased at upper edges.

1992

£150-200 BLO

Arundhati Roy, "The God of Small Things", first edition, published by Flamingo.

1997

£25-35 BIB

Salman Rushdie, "Midnight's Children", first American edition, original cloth-backed boards, dust jacket, very slight edge creasing near spine head, uncut.

1981

£120-180 BLO

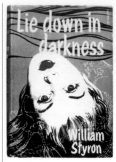

William Styron, "Lie Down in Darkness", first edition, dust jacket torn at lower edge, original boards, dust jacket, a little rubbed at extremities.

1952

£50-80   **BLO**

A CLOSER LOOK AT A MODERN FIRST EDITION

This is Swift's third book, and only 750 copies of the first edition were printed.

The addition of a signed postcard adds to the interest.

Graham Swift won the Booker Prize for Fiction in 1996 for 'Last Orders'.

A copy without a signed postcard would be worth around £200.

Graham Swift, "Learning to Swim", first edition, original cloth, dust jacket, signed postcard from the author loosely inserted.

1982

£350-450

BLO

Graham Swift, "Waterland", first edition, original boards, dust jacket.

1983

£150-200   **BLO**

Amy Tan, "The Bonesetter's Daughter", first edition, published by Flamingo.

2001

£12-18   **BIB**

William Trevor, "The Day We Got Drunk on Cake", first edition, original boards, dust jacket, very slightly tanned.

This is the author's first collection of short stories and is a sought-after title.

1967

£550-650   **BLO**

Jeanette Winterson, "The Passion", first American edition, New York, original cloth-backed boards, first edition, dust jackets.

1987

£30-40   **BLO**

Percival Christopher Wren, "Sinbad the Soldier", first English edition, half-title, original cloth, dust jacket, slightly foxed on flaps, slight edge ware but with no loss.

1935

£150-200   **BLO**

John Wyndham, "The Kraken Wakes", first edition, original boards, dust jacket slightly rubbed at extremities.

1953

£100-150   **BLO**

COLLECTORS' NOTES

■ Early paperbacks were inspired by the popular fiction found in magazines from the 1920s and 30s onwards. Intended as 'throwaway' reads, the name 'pulp' fiction derives from the cheap pulped paper or newsprint used in the manufacture of the original magazines.

■ The golden years for paperback books stretch from the years following WWII to the 1960s. During this period thousands of 'pulp' titles, aimed at the mass market, were produced for adults. Typical genres include crime, science fiction and addiction and many collectors limit their collections to such specific areas.

■ It is the colourful or kitsch designs on the covers, particularly on books printed from the late 1940s, that catch the attention of many of today's collectors.

Many feature graphics in the distinctive style of an era, or scantily clad ravished dames. During the 1950s, some titles were outlawed and destroyed due to their obscene content or cover. Surviving examples can attract a cult following.

■ Condition is key in determining value and the cover in particular should be free of damage such as tears, stains and fading. Mint examples are worth more.

■ Some titles and editions are rarer than others, the earliest examples are usually more collectable. A well known pulp fiction author – such as Hank Janson or Ben Sarto – can add appeal, but the value more typically lies in the cover artwork. Look for notable artists such as Reginald Heade or F. W Perle.

Fredric Brown, "Murder Can Be Fun", published by Boardman Books.

1952

£20-40   **PCC**

John Eagle, "The Hoodlums", published by Avon, New York.
1953
£7-10   **PCC**

Carol Carnac, "Murder As A Fine Art", published by the Crime Club.
£3-5   **ZDB**

Ashley Carter, "Against All Odds", A Star Book, the paperback division of W.H. Allen & Co Ltd.
1982
£3-5   **PCC**

Philip Chambers, "Bullets to Baghdad", published by Sexton Blake Library, Fleetway Publications Ltd, cover artwork by Jacoby.
1960
£3-5   **ZDB**

James Hadley Chase, "The Dead Stay Dumb", published by Corgi Books, first published in 1947.
1980
£3-5   **ZDB**

David Dodge, "A Drug On The Market", published by Corgi Books, first published 1949.
1953
£5-8   **PCC**

Hal Ellson, "Stairway To Nowhere", published by Pedigree books.

Titles involving delinquency, particularly amongst the young, can be sought after. This is especially true if the image is dramatic and illustrates the style of rebels of the period, typified by James Dean, as this cover does.

Harlan Ellison, "Gentleman Junkie", Pyramid Books, New York.

1975

£7-10   MBO

1959

£40-60   PCC

Arthur Farmer, "Sin Ship", Private Edition Books, North Hollywood.

£10-15   MBO

Henry Gregor Felsen, "Hot Rod", published by Bantam Books.

1951

£7-10   MBO

Jack Finney, "The Body Snatchers".

1957

£10-15   PCC

Steve Fisher, "Hot Spot", published by Pedigree Books.

1959

£12-18   PCC

Pierre Flammeche, "When Passion Rules", published by Archer Press, with cover by Reginald Heade.

£20-40   PCC

Erie Stanley Gardener, "Perry Mason Solves The Case Of The Golddiggers Purse", published by Pocket Books, first paperback edition, first published in 1949.

1952

£5-8   PCC

Darcy Glinto, "Snow Vogue", published by Robin Hood Press.

£20-40   PCC

Harry Grey, "The Hoods", Signet Books, The New American Library, 7th print, with quote from Mickey Spillane on the cover.

This book formed the basis for the Sergio Leone's 1984 film "Once Upon a Time in America".

1959

£18-22   **MBO**

Evan Hunter, "The Blackboard Jungle", published by Panther Books.

In 1955, the book was made into a film starring Sidney Poitier, Glenn Ford and Anne Francis. It was nominated for 3 Oscars.

1960

£5-8   **PCC**

Hank Janson, "The Unseen Assassin", published by Alexander Moring Ltd.

£20-40   **PCC**

John D. MacDonald, "Deadly Welcome", published by Pan Books Ltd.

1964

£3-5   **ZDB**

A CLOSER LOOK AT A PAPERBACK BOOK

Richard Matheson (b.1926), is an American author and screenwriter, best known for his science fiction, fantasy and horror novels.

This is Matheson's first novel. First titles are often printed in smaller quantities than later works, making this example harder to find and more sought-after.

Many of Matheson's books have reached the silver screen, this title was filmed in 1974 and starred Alain Delon.

Matheson's second novel 'Fury on Sunday' is also sought-after.

Richard Matheson, "Someone Is Bleeding", published by Banner Books, L.Miller & Sons Ltd.

1953

£100-150   **PCC**

Spike Morelli, "You'll Never Get Me", published by Archer, Reginald Heade cover.

1952

£30-50   **PCC**

Peter O'Donnell, "Modesty Blaise: The Night of Morning Star", published by Pan Books.

1984

£5-8   **ZDB**

Geoffrey Pardoe, "Traffic In Souls", published by E. Halle Ltd.

1959

£10-15   **PCC**

Ben Sarto, "Miss Otis Has A Daughter", published by Modern Fiction.

1948

£20-40   **PCC**

Robert Selman, "Once Upon a Crime", a Sundown Book, published by W. Foulsham Ltd.

1950

£10-15   **PCC**

Georges Simenon, "The Witnesses", published by Four Square Books.

1958

£3-5   **ZDB**

Mickey Spillane, "The Long Wait", published by Dragon Books, No.29 by Arthur Barker Ltd, first published in 1951.

Spillane (b.1918) has been one of the most popular writers in the US despite being criticised for the then high levels of violence and sex included in his novels. His most famous creation was the hard-boiled detective Mike Hammer.

1958

£5-8   **PCC**

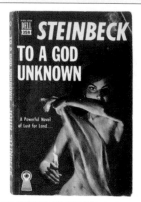

Mickey Spillane, "The Big Kill", published by Corgi Books.

1962

£3-5   **ZDB**

John Steinbeck, "To A God Unknown", published by Dell Publishing Company, first published 1933.

1958

£5-7   **MBO**

Michael Storme, "Dame In My Bed", published by Archer Press, with Reginald Heade cover.

1951

£30-50   **PCC**

Jim Thompson, "A Hell Of A Woman", published by Banner Books.

1954

£100-150   **PCC**

Edgar Wallace, "When The Gangs Came To London", published by Arrow Books.

1957

£3-5   **ZDB**

Piers Anthony, "Var The Stick", Corgi Sci Fi, published by Corgi Books.
1975

£3-5　　　　　ZDB

Robert Bassett, "Witchfinder General", published by Pan Books.
1968

£5-8　　　　　ZDB

Ray Buckland, "Ancient & Modern Witchcraft", HC Publishers Inc, New York.

Both the colourful and lurid cover art and the topic make this a desirable title.
1970

£12-18　　　　MBO

Randall Conway, "Out Of This World", published by John Spencer & Co. Ltd.

£12-18　　　　ZDB

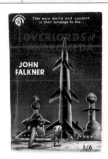

Reed De Rouen, "Split Image", a Digit Book.
1963

£3-5　　　　　ZDB

Philip K. Dick, "A Maze of Death", Pan Science Fiction, published by Pan Books Ltd.
1973

£3-5　　　　　ZDB

John Falkner, "Overlords of Andromeda", published by Panther Books.
1955

£8-12　　　　ZDB

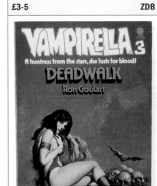

Hank Janson, "One Against Time", published by Alexander Moring Ltd., with cover artwork by Reginald Heade.

The Reginald Heade cover, the combination of a science fiction theme and a busty female, and the popularity of author Hank Janson make this more valuable.

Ron Goulart, "Vampirella 3: Deadwalk", published by Sphere Books.
1977

£5-8　　　　　PCC

£20-40　　　　PCC

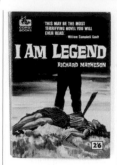

Richard Matheson, "I Am Legend", published by Corgi Books.
1960

£12-18   **PCC**

Frederik Pohl & C. M. Kornbluth, "The Space Merchants", A Digit Book.

£3-5   **ZDB**

John Rankine, "Space 1999: Astral Quest", An Orbit Book, published by Futura Publications Ltd.
1975

£3-5   **ZDB**

Clifford D. Simak, "Time and Again", Magnum Books, published by Methuen Paperbacks Ltd.
1977

£3-5   **ZDB**

W.J. Stuart, "Forbidden Planet", first UK edition.

This is the novelisation of the 1956 film, whose characters and setting were inspired by Shakespeare's The Tempest. The presence of Robbie the robot on the cover adds desirability.

Guy N. Smith, "The Slime Beast", published by New English Library.
1976

£5-8   **ZDB**

1956

£20-30   **PCC**

E.C. Tubb, "The Terra Data", published by Arrow Books.
1985

£3-5   **ZDB**

Jules Verne, "Journey To The Centre of the Earth", published by Digit Books.
1959

£3-5   **ZDB**

"Worlds of Fantasy No.8", includes "Martian Terror" by Ray Mason, by John Spencer & Co Ltd.

£10-15   **ZDB**

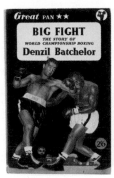

Denzil Batchelor, "Big Fight", published by Pan Books Ltd.

1956

£3-5   ZDB

Justin Cartwright, "The New Avengers: Fighting Men", published by Futura Publications Ltd.

1977

£3-5   ZDB

Leslie Charteris, "The Saint In New York", published by Hodder & Stoughton.

1964

£3-5   ZDB

L.P. Easton, "Target..Rome", published by Badger Books.

£3-5   ZDB

Ian Fleming, "The Diamond Smugglers", published by Pan Books.

This was one of Fleming's few non-fiction books.

1965

£10-15   ZDB

John Gardner, "James Bond: For Special Services", Coronet Books, published by Hodder & Stoughton.

1995

£3-5   ZDB

Marco Garon, "Silent River", published by Curtis Books.

Mark Garon was one of the pseudonyms of Dennis Hughes. Silent River is from a series of books featuring the character Rex Brandon, who bears similarities to Tarzan.

1951

£40-60   PCC

Marco Garon, "Leopard God", published by Curtis Books.

1952

£40-60   PCC

George G. Gilman, "Edge No. 48: School for Slaughter", published by New English Library.

1985

£3-5   ZDB

Billie Holiday with William Dufty, "Lady Sings The Blues", published by Ace Books.

1960

£5-8   ZDB

William Hope Hodgson, "The Night Land: Volume II", published by Pan/Ballantine.

1973

£5-8   ZDB

Wilhelm Johnen, "Duel Under The Stars", published by Kimber Pocket Editions.

1958

£3-5   ZDB

Robert K. Lander, "With Flame And Sabre", published by Badger Books.

£3-5   PCC

Wilfred McNeilly, "Danger Man: No Way Out", published by Consul Books.

1966

£3-5   ZDB

Alistair Revie, "That Kind Of Girl", a Digit Book.

1963

£5-8   ZDB

Edgar Rice Burroughs, "Tarzan's Quest", published by Four Square Books Ltd.

1960

£5-8   ZDB

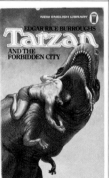

Edgar Rice Burroughs, "Tarzan And The Forbidden City", published by New English Library.

1976.

£3-5   ZDB

Kenneth Robson, "Doc Savage 1: The Man Of Bronze", published by Corgi Books.

1975

£5-8   ZDB

Richard Sapir & Warren Murphy, "The Destroyer 34: Chain Reaction", published by Corgi Books.

1980

£3-5   **ZDB**

Russell Thorndike, "Doctor Syn", published by Arrow Books, first published by Rich & Cowan in 1915.

1966

£10-15   **ZDB**

Russell Thorndike, "The Courageous Exploits of Dr Syn", published by An Arrow Adventure, first published by Rich & Cowan in 1939.

1959

£10-15   **ZDB**

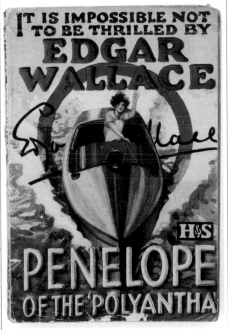

Russell Thorndike, "The Further Adventures of Doctor Syn", published by Arrow Books, story first published in 1936.

1966

£10-15   **ZDB**

Russell Thorndike, "Doctor Syn Returns", published by Arrow Books.

1959

£10-15   **ZDB**

Edgar Wallace, "Penelope Of Polyantha", published by Hodder & Stoughton.

Wallace was one of the scriptwriters on the original King Kong film from 1933.

£10-15   **ZDB**

F. van Wyck Mason, "The Barbarians", published by Panther Books.

1958

£3-5   **ZDB**

"Affinity", published by the British Reader's Digest, June 1947.

£20-40   **PCC**

FIND OUT MORE...

The Mushroom Jungle – A History of Postwar Paperback Publishing, *by Steve Holland, published by Zeon Books, 1997.*

Huxford's Paperback Value Guide, *by Sharon & Bob Huxford, published by Corgi Books, 2003.*

Michael Bond, "More About Paddington", first edition, original cloth and dust jacket, chipping at head and foot of spine.

This is the second book featuring children's favourite Paddington Bear, the first was published the previous year.

1959

£250-350 BLO

Eoin Colfer, "Artemis Fowl", first edition, published by Viking, signed by the author and with a signed compliment slip.

2001

£100-150 BIB

Richmal Crompton, "William And The Monster", published by Armada Paperbacks.

1965

£3-5 ZDB

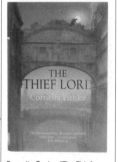

Cornelia Funke, "The Thief Lord", first English edition, published by Chicken House, signed by the author.

2002

£50-70 BIB

Jamila Gavin, "The Blood Stone", first edition, published by Egmont.

2003

£12-16 BIB

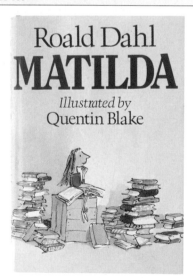

Roald Dahl, "Matilda", first edition, published by Jonathan Cape, London, signed by the author in the year of publication.

Signed copies of Dahl's books are scarce and the fact it was signed in the year of publication makes it more desirable.

1988

£1,500-2,500 BRB

Debi Gliori, "Deep Trouble", first edition, first printing, published by Doubleday, signed by the author.

2004

£10-20 BIB

Mary Hoffman, "Stravaganza - City of Masks", first edition, published by Bloomsbury.

2002

£10-15 BIB

Brian Jacques, "Redwall", first edition, double page map, with "Tales of Redwall" bookmark loosely inserted, original boards, dust jacket, a mint copy.

1986

£250-350   **BLO**

Brian Jacques, "Salamandastron", first edition, published by Hutchinson, London.

1992

£350-450   **BIB**

Capt. W.E. Johns, "Biggles and the Lost Sovereigns", first edition, published by the Brockhampton Press.

1964

£80-120   **BIB**

Roy McKie and P.D. Eastman, "Snow", first edition review copy, published by Random House, New York.

1962

£200-250   **BRB**

Ian Ogilvy, "Measle and the Wrathmonk", first edition, published by the Oxford Press, signed by the author.

2004

£10-15   **BIB**

Terry Pratchett, "The Amazing Maurice and His Educated Rodents", first edition, published by Doubleday, signed by the author.

2001

£15-20   **BIB**

A CLOSER LOOK AT A CHILDREN'S BOOK

This first edition would have been published in much smaller numbers than his later, better known titles such as the 'His Dark Materials' trilogy.

Although not as well known as J.K. Rowling, Pullman's children's books also tend to be very popular with adults and his more recent works has won a number of awards.

A film of the first book from the 'His Dark Materials' trilogy in planned. Its release will increase the author's profile and should raise interest in collecting his books

Count Karlstein is one of Pullman's earliest novels and his first children's novel.

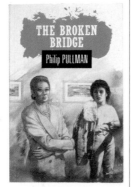

Philip Pullman, "The Broken Bridge", first edition, published by Macmillian, original pictorial wrappers, unattached sticker signed by the author loosely inserted.

1990

£350-450   **BLO**

Philip Pullman, "Count Karlstein", first edition, original cloth, dust jacket, slight edge wear to upper margin with small tear at front, no loss or disruption to image.

1982

£700-900   **BLO**

Philip Pullman, "I Was a Rat! ... or The Scarlet Slippers", first edition, illustrations by Peter Bailey, original pictorial boards.
1999

£120-180   **BLO**

Philip Reeve, "Predator's Gold", first edition, published by Scholastic, signed by the author.
2003

£15-20   **BIB**

J.K. Rowling, "Harri Potter a Maen yr Athronydd", first Welsh edition of The Philosopher's Stone, published by Bloomsbury, signed by the author.
A first edition copy of the English language version can be worth over £10,000.
2003

£20-25   **BIB**

Paul Stewart and Chris Riddell, "Stormchaser", first edition, original boards, dust jacket.
This is the particularly scarce second book in the seven book series.
2000

£400-600   **BLO**

Malcolm Saville, "Spring Comes To Nettleford", paperback published by Armada.
1971

£3-5   **ZDB**

Margery Sharp, "The Rescuers", first edition, published by Collins, London.
1959

£150-250   **BRB**

G.P. Taylor, "Shadowmancer", first special edition, published by Faber & Faber.
This special edition contains a previously unpublished final chapter.

E.B. White, "Charlotte's Web, first edition, published by Harper & Brothers, New York.
1952

2003

£12-18   **BIB**

£800-1,200   **BRB**

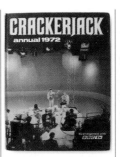

Tourtel, Mary, "Rupert Annual", published by the Daily Express.

1944

£85   **BIB**

Tourtel, Mary, "Rupert Annual", published by the Daily Express.

1958

£50   **BIB**

"Crackerjack Annual", published by Stafford Pemberton.

1972

£4-6   **MTS**

"The Official Dallas Annual", published by Grandreams.

1982

£4-5   **MTS**

"Girl!, Girl!, Girl! Annual", published by Purnell.

1970

£10-15   **MTS**

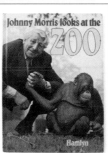

Enid Blyton, "Enid Blyton's Annual", date unknown, very scarce.

£70-100   **BIB**

"Johnny Morris looks at the Zoo Annual", published by Hamlyn.

1977

£6-8   **MTS**

"Pinky and Perky Picture Story Book", published by the Amex Co. Ltd.

£7-9   **MTS**

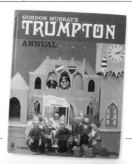

"Roy Rogers Cowboy Annual", published by World Distributors.

c1955

£8-12   **MTS**

"Gordon Murray's Trumpton Annual", published by Purnell.

1969

£10-14   **MTS**

CAMERAS

COLLECTORS' NOTES

■ Interest in photography began to spread from c1840, although it was still a costly exercise involving expensive rigid wood and brass-bodied cameras and complex mixing of chemicals. By the 1880s with the development of pre-prepared 'dry' photographic plates and advances in camera design, the market was opened to many more.

■ Leica cameras, first developed in 1913, are perhaps the world's most collectable, with a truly global market. Values vary from around £100 up to tens of thousands of pounds. Most examples are still useable today, or can be repaired, due to Leitz's fine quality engineering. Accessories, such as lenses, can also have a value of their own.

■ Each Leica camera bears a unique serial number on the top plate and this will identify the model and year of manufacture. Variations or unusual engravings can add value, but beware as fakes are known. Condition

is of paramount importance, with scratches, dents and damaged mechanisms affecting value seriously. Leica Collectors always prefer to buy in mint condition.

■ Miniature and 'spy' cameras are an interesting and developing collecting area. Many used ingenious and finely engineered mechanisms. Those in novelty or disguised forms, or of particularly fine quality, are generally the most desirable. The addition of original boxes will add value.

■ Look for fine quality construction and well-known brand names, such as Voigtlander, Canon, and Zeiss Ikon. Mass-produced cameras that survive in large numbers, such as Kodak's 'Box Brownie' are usually of low value. Condition is again important, but perhaps less so than in the often rarified world of Leica collectors. Look out for variations in terms of colour and features, such as lenses, as these can add value.

A Dallmeyer teak 'wetplate' sliding box camera, with brass fittings, rack and pinion focusing, a 'Hermagis, Paris' brass lens, focusing screen back and wooden double-plate cassette.

'Wetplate' rigid box cameras are amongst the earliest cameras used. The photographic plate was made up at the location with chemical liquids, hence the name. Dallmeyer is a desirable brand known for its quality. Although this example is of the rarer, wider stereo format, it is fitted with a mono lens board.

c1865

£2,200-2,800 ATK

A French mahogany and brass sliding half-plate box camera, the brass lens with pull-tube focusing, tightening screw, two Waterhouse stops and cap, the interior with card inner-liner, the base of laminated oak and mahogany.

c1860   9.5in (24cm) long

£800-1,200 EG

A 19thC Watson mahogany and brass tailboard half-plate camera, with stereo sliding lens board.

The lens board slides horizontally, allowing stereo shots to be taken.

c1890

£400-500 COLC

A Thornton-Pickard 'Imperial Perfecta' mahogany and brass quarter-plate folding camera, with black bellows.

Bellows were introduced c1851, but took over from rigid boxes from the late 1860s, enabling cameras to have greater lens movement and to be folded down compactly.

c1913

£250-300 ATK

A late 19thC London Stereoscopic Co. mahogany and brass quarter-plate camera, with Waterhouse stop and brass rectiliniar lens.

£300-400 COLC

A French Compagnie Française de Photographie 'Le Photosphère' silver-plated brass camera, with Zeiss Krauss Protar 8/124 lens, hemispherical shutter and wooden plate holder.

This rare and early camera was based on a November 1888 patent held by Napoleon Conti. It was produced in four sizes until the mid-1890s. The reflecting viewfinder could be fitted on either of the adjacent sides of the body.

c1889

£700-900 ATK

A CLOSER LOOK AT A FAKE LEICA CAMERA

A Leica Ia 'Near Focus' camera, with Elmar 3.5/50mm lens, top and base plate restored professionally, with lens cap and camera case.
1929

£850-950   ATK

This is a fake Leica camera, probably made in Russia or Eastern Europe, but it is still of some interest to certain collectors.

The original gold-plated Leica 'Luxus' was an earlier model with a different top plate configuration and crocodile leather body covering. Only around 95 authentic examples were made from c1930-31.

The top plate is not engraved in Leica's standard manner and the serial number on this example dates it to 1942-44.

The quality of the manufacture, materials and plating is very poor, especially when compared to an authentic Leica camera.

A late 20thC 35mm camera in the style of a Leica II with bronze finish, with f=3.5/50mm lens marked "Leitz Elmar".

These were made as Leica prices rose – an authentic example fetched £39,600 at Christie's in 1994.

5.5in (14cm) wide

A Leica IIIc chrome camera, with later Summaron 3.5/3.5cm lens from 1957.
1949

£450-550   ATK

£20-30   PC

A Leica IIf chrome camera, with earlier Summar f=5cm/1.2 lens from 1936, contained in a black leather case.
1952   *5.25in (13.5cm) wide*

£200-300   GORL

A Leica M5 chrome camera, with two lugs and orginal carrying strap.
1972

£250-350   ATK

A Leica R4 black camera, with an Elmarit-R f=2.8/35 lens with caps and a Canadian Elmarit-R f=2.8/135 lens with two caps and a Leitz filter.
1981

£250-350   ATK

A Leica R5 black camera, with Leitz 35-70 and 75-200 lenses, a Leitz extender R2x lens, an instruction book and a Leica R4 manual.
1988

£350-450   SWO

A French Aiglon nickel-plated cast metal subminiature camera, with wire viewfinder.

1934

£80-120　　　　　　　　　　**ATK**

A Japanese Suzuki Optical Co. 'Echo 8' novelty 'spy' camera, with Echor f=3.5/15mm lens, shaped as a Zippo lighter and useable as a lighter and a camera.

c1951

£550-750　　　　　　　　　　**COLC**

A Italian Officine Galileo Di Milano 'Gami 16' 16mm film subminiature camera, with Esamitar f=1.9/25mm lens, spring motor drive, optical light meter, rangefinder, chain, accessories and box.

To wind the film on and charge the shutter spring, the hinged front cover is opened and closed. This powers the film movement and shutter to work for three exposures. The shutter should not be charged when the camera contains no film as this can damage the shutter mechanism.

1955

£350-450　　　　　　　　　　**ATK**

An Austrian C.P. Goerz brown 'Minicord' twin lens reflex 16mm film subminiature camera, with Helgor f=2/2.5cm lens.

c1951

£150-200　　　　　　　　**ATK**

A German Ising 'Puck' subminiature camera, with Cassar f=2.8/5cm lens and maker's case.

1948

£100-150　　　　　　　　**ATK**

A late 1940s Czechoslovakian Meopta 'Mikroma' 16mm film subminiature camera, with Mirar f=3.5/20mm lens and brown luxury leather-covered body, in original box.

This camera was designed before WWII, but only produced after 1946.

£80-120　　　　　　　　**ATK**

A German Minox chrome 'Minox A' miniature camera, with Complan f=3.5/15mm lens.

1956

£60-80　　　　　　　　**ATK**

A Japanese Riken Optical 'Steky Model II' 16mm film subminiature camera, with Stekinar f=3.5/25mm lens, lens cap and original case.

c1951

£80-120　　　　　　　　**ATK**

A Japanese Tailyodo Koki 'Epochs' subminiature camera, with Talent f=3.5/20mm lens, the body also marked "Made in Occupied Japan".

1948

£200-300　　　　　　　　**ATK**

CAMERAS

A CLOSER LOOK AT A KODAK CAMERA

The condition is excellent, with no damage to the enamelling or wear to the matching brown leather covering.

It was offered for Christmas in 1930 and was made into 1931.

An American Art Deco Eastman Kodak Co. chrome-plated and enamelled metal Kodak folding 1A 'Gift Camera', with matching wooden box.

The camera on its own in a standard black finish is much more common, and worth up to £30.

It was part of a series of cameras produced between 1928 and 1931 that were aimed at fashionable women. They were all designed by Dorwin Teague in the prevalent Art Deco style of the period.

The enamelled design on the camera and matching box was by Walter Dorwin Teague, the notable Industrial designer.

1930-31

£800-1,200   DD

A German Ernemann Ernamox camera outfit, with Ernostar f=1.8/8.5cm lens, a Vertex f=4.5/6cm lens, cable release, film pack, dark slide, lens cap and instructions, in maker's fitted leather case.

c1925

£550-650   EG

A German Ihagee chrome VP Exakta, Model A, Version 5.1, two screws damaged.

£150-200   ATK

A German 'Patent Klapp-Reflex No. 1920' folding camera, with a Tessar f=3.5/165mm lens, and rotating back, lacks folding foot.

£250-300   ATK

A French J.Richards 'Le Glyphoscope' bakelite-bodied stereoscopic camera, with Zeiss Tessar f=4.5/35mm lens, metal backs and original case.

c1914-20   6in (15cm) wide

£25-35   F

A German Zeiss Ikon Contessa 35 camera, with Zeiss-Opton Tessar f=2.8/45mm lens and Synchro-Compur shutter.

1953

£70-100   ATK

A German Zeiss Ikon 'Bob' camera, with Nettar f=6.3/75mm lens, instructions and maker's box.

c1934-41

£25-35   EG

FIND OUT MORE...

McKeown's Price Guide to Antique & Classic Cameras 2005-2006, edited by James & Joan McKeown, published by Centennial Photo Services, 2004.

Cameras, by Brian Coe, published by Marshall Cavendish, 1978.

COLLECTORS' NOTES

■ The family-run Beswick pottery firm was set up by James Wright Beswick in 1894. Animal figures were made before 1900, but early pieces are hard to identify as the Beswick backstamp was only generally used from 1934; this was also when shape numbers began to be impressed in the base of figures.

■Names of note include long-serving mouldmaker and modeller Albert Hallam, who joined Beswick in 1926 aged 14, and decorating manager and art director James Hayward, who designed almost 3,000 decorations and patterns, and was instrumental in developing glazes. Arthur Gredington is probably Beswick's most famous designer. He is known for designing and making both realistic and stylized animal models.

■ Many models are available in different colourways and matte or gloss finishes. The value of a piece is often dependent upon the rarity of the colourway or finish, so invest in a specialist guide for detailed information. Certain ranges are prized, such as the Spirit horse collection, introduced in 1981 by Graham Tongue, and the accurately modelled Connoisseur range.

■ The firm was sold to Royal Doulton in 1969, but Beswick animals continued to be produced. In 1989 most animal models in production became 'Doulton Animals' and the pieces were issued with DA numbers. In 1999 Royal Doulton moved their range of animals, excepting limited editions, to the Beswick backstamp. The factory closed in 2002, and prices on the secondary market have consequently risen.

A Beswick 'King Eider Duck', 1521, designed by Colin Melbourne, from the Peter Scott Wildfowl series.

1958-71　　　*4in (10cm) long*

£100-150　　　**GORW**

A Beswick 'Mallard' small duck, 1518, designed by Arthur Gredington, first version.

The second version, made from 1962-71 is worth about two-thirds of this earlier version.

1958-62　　　*4.5in (11.5cm) wide*

£100-150　　　**GORW**

A Beswick large 'Goldeneye Duck', 1524, designed by Colin Melbourne, from the Peter Scott Wildfowl series.

1958-71　　　*6.5in (16.5cm) wide*

£120-180　　　**GORW**

A Beswick medium 'Pochard Duck', 1520, designed by Arthur Gredington, from the Peter Scott Wildfowl series.

1958-71　　*4.5in (12cm) long*

£120-180　　　**GORW**

A Beswick 'Shoveler' duck, 1528, designed by Colin Melbourne, from the Peter Scott Wildfowl series.

1958-71　　　*3.5in (9cm) long*

£120-180　　　**GORW**

A Beswick 'Tufted Duck', 1523, designed by Colin Melbourne, from the Peter Scott Wildfowl series.

1958-71　　　*2.75in (7cm) long*

£100-150　　　**GORW**

A Beswick 'Widgeon Duck', 1526, designed by Colin Melbourne, from the Peter Scott Wildfowl series.

1958-71　　　*3.5in (9cm) long*

£80-120　　　**GORW**

A Beswick 'Grouse (pair)', 2063, designed by Albert Hallam.
1966-75   5.5in (14cm) high
£350-450   PSA

A Beswick 'Leghorn Cockerel', 1892, designed by Arthur Gredington.
1963-83   9in (23cm) high
£120-180   PSA

A Beswick 'Great Tit', 3274, designed by Martyn Alcock.
1990-95
£200-250   PSA

A Beswick 'Lapwing' figure, 2416A, designed by Albert Hallam, first version with split tail feathers.
The second version with the tail feathers together, made until 1982, is worth about 25 per cent less.
1972-unknown   5.5in (14cm) high
£220-280   PSA

A Beswick 'Lesser Spotted Woodpecker', 2420, designed by Graham Tongue.
1972-82   5.5in (14cm) high
£200-300   PSA

A Beswick 'Whitethroat', 2106A, designed by Graham Tongue, first version with mouth open and green mound base.
1967-73
£120-180   PSA

A Beswick 'Penguin', 2357, designed by Albert Hallam, from the Fireside Model series.
As well as being unusually large, this figure would have been expensive in its day, meaning fewer are likely to have been sold.
1971-76   12in (30.5cm) high
£700-800   PSA

A Beswick 'Courting Penguins', 1015, designed by Arthur Gredington.
This model was produced in this traditional black and white colourway as well as a slightly more desirable blue version.
1945-65   5.5in (14cm) high
£180-220   PSA

A Beswick 'Penguin Chick Sliding', 2434, designed by Graham Tongue.
1972-76   8in (20cm) long
£300-400   PSA

CERAMICS

A Beswick 'Huntsman (on rearing horse)', 868, designed by Arthur Gredington, style two, with brown horse.

This is the most common colourway for this model. Chestnut, Rocking Horse Grey and Palomino can be worth upto five times more.

1952-95   *10in (25.5cm) high*

£220-280   **SWO**

A rare Beswick 'Huntsman', 1501, designed by Arthur Gredington, style two standing, on painted white horse.

The different versions of model 1501 below show how much difference to the value the colour of the horse can make.

1958-71   *8.25in (21cm) high*

£800-1,200   **PSA**

A Beswick 'Huntsman (on a rearing horse)', 868, designed by Arthur Gredington, style two, on painted white horse, restored, with crazing.

Made for a much shorter period than the brown version, this painted white model is much more sought-after. The value could have nearly doubled if it had not been restored.

1965-71

£450-550   **PSA**

A Beswick 'Huntsman', 1501, designed by Arthur Gredington, style two standing, on brown horse.

This colourway was produced for the longest period and is the least valuable.

1957-95   *8.25in (21cm) high*

£200-250   **SWO**

A Beswick 'Huntsman', 1501, designed by Arthur Gredington, style two standing, with Palomino horse.

As with many other horse models, the Rocking Horse Grey is more desirable and worth about 25 per cent more than this colourway.

1965-71   *8.25in (21cm) high*

£250-300   **LAW**

A Beswick 'Huntswoman', 982, designed by Arthur Gredington, style one with horse and rider jumping.

Note the similarity to the the 'Girl on Jumping Horse' model on the next page. The horse and base are the same.

1942-67   *10in (25.5cm) high*

£400-500   **SWO**

A Beswick 'Huntswoman', 1730, designed by Arthur Gredington, style two standing, on grey horse.

1960-95   *8.25in (21cm) high*

£350-450   **SWO**

A Beswick 'Lifeguard', 1624, designed by Arthur Gredington, style one with trumpet.

1959-77   *9.5in (24cm) high*

£500-600   **PSA**

A Beswick 'H.M Queen Elizabeth II On Imperial', 1546, designed by Mr. Folkard.

The model of the horse was also available on its own as no. 1557. They are generally worth less than this model, apart from the Rocking Horse Grey and Painted White colourways.

1958-81

£400-500   **PSA**

A CLOSER LOOK AT A BESWICK HORSE AND RIDER

A Beswick 'Girl on Jumping Horse', 939, designed by Arthur Gredington.

1941-65   9.75in (24.5cm) high

£300-400   **PSA**

The pony was available on its own as Girl's Pony (1483) from 1957 to 1967.

Most other colours found are worth about 50 per cent of this example.

There are two variations to the shape as well, one with the girl down and one with her looking straight ahead. There is no difference in value.

The similar brown and white Skewbald version is the most common, and is worth about a tenth of this black and white version.

A Beswick 'Girl On A Pony', 1499, designed by Arthur Gredington, on rare Piebald (black and white) colourway pony.

1957-65

£3,500-4,500   **PSA**

A rare Beswick 'Cowboy on a Rodeo Horse' matt finish trial piece, made by Royal Doulton and decorated at the Beswick factory in the 1970s, unmarked.

£1,000-1,500   **PSA**

A Beswick 'Psalm with Ann Moore Up', 2535, designed by Graham Tongue, from the Connoisseur Horses series.

1975-82

12.75in (32.5cm) high

£350-450   **PSA**

A Beswick 'Boy On Pony', 1500, designed by Arthur Gredington, with Palomino pony.

The brown colourway is over twice as valuable, and other colours worth more than four times as much, as this Palomino example.

1957-76   5.5in (14cm) high

£280-320   **PSA**

A Beswick 'Cantering Shire', 975, designed by Arthur Gredington, in brown.

1943-89   8.75in (22cm) high

£40-60   **PSA**

A limited edition Beswick 'Przewalski's Wild Horse' figure, designed by Amanda Hughes-Lubeck, from an edition of 1,000 made exclusively for Sinclairs, boxed with certificate.

2005   6.25in (16cm) high

£120-180   **PSA**

A Beswick 'Shire Mare', 818, designed by Arthur Gredington, in Rocking Horse grey, first version without harness, slight restoration to one ear.

Unusually for an equine model, the rocking horse grey version is not one of the most valuable. Blue and iron grey are much rarer.

c1940-62

£500-600   **PSA**

CERAMICS

A Beswick 'Aberdeen Angus Cow', 1563, designed by Arthur Gredington, matt version.

The gloss version was introduced in 1959 and was retired at the same time as this matt example. The gloss version is worth about a third less.

1985-89	4.5in (11cm) high
£200-300	**PSA**

A Beswick 'Ayrshire Bull Ch. "Whitehill Mandate"', 1454B, designed by Colin Melbourne, second version with thick leg and tail.

1957-90	5.25in (13.5cm) high
£300-400	**GORW**

A Beswick 'Ayrshire Cow Ch. Ickham Bessie', 1350, designed by Arthur Gredington, matt version.

The gloss version was issued from 1954 and is worth about 25 per cent less than this matt version.

1985-89	5in (12.5cm) high
£200-280	**PSA**

Left: A Beswick 'Highland Calf', 1827D, designed by Arthur Gredington.

1962-90	3in (7.5cm) high
£50-80	**GORW**

Right: A Beswick 'Highland Cow', 1740, designed by Arthur Gredington.

1961-90	5.25in (13.5cm) high
£150-200	**GORW**

Left: A Beswick 'Fresian Calf', 1249C, designed by Arthur Gredington.

1956-97	2.75in (7cm) high
£60-80	**GORW**

Right: A Beswick 'Fresian Cow Ch. "Claybury Legwater"' 1362A, designed by Arthur Gredington.

1954-97	4.5in (12cm) high
£100-150	**GORW**

A Beswick 'Fresian Calf', 1249C, designed by Arthur Gredington, matt version.

1987-89	2.75in (7cm) high
£150-200	**PSA**

A Beswick 'Wessex Saddleback Sow "Merrywood Silver Wings 56tH"', 1511, designed by Colin Melbourne.

1957-69	2.75in (7cm) high
£400-500	**PSA**

A Beswick 'Middle White Boar', 4117, from the Rare Breeds series, boxed.

2001-02	4in (10cm) high
£30-50	**PSA**

A Beswick 'Nigerian Pot Bellied Pygmy Goat', G223, designed by Amanda Lughes-Lubeck.

1999-	5.25in (14cm) high
£18-22	**PSA**

A Beswick 'Greyhound "Jovial Roger"' figure, 972, designed by Arthur Gredington.

1942-90   *6in (15cm) long*

£40-50   **PSA**

A Beswick 'Whippet "Winged Foot Marksman of Allways"', 1786A, designed by Arthur Gredington, first version with tail curled between legs.

Designs were often changed to remove delicate, protuding parts, such as this dog's tail, which would have been prone to damage during manufacture. Today, earlier versions are usually more sought-after, as they are the original design, and are harder to find especially in undamaged condition. Compare this version to the second version to the right.

1961-unknown   *4.5in (12cm) long*

£120-180   **PSA**

A Beswick 'Whippet "Winged Foot Marksman of Allways"', 1786B, designed by Arthur Gredington, second version with tail attached to leg.

Unknown-1989   *4.5in (12cm) long*

£80-120   **PSA**

A Beswick large 'Corgi', 1299B, designed by Arthur Gredington.

The black version (1229A) available from 1953-82 is worth about twice this version.

1953-94   *5.5in (14cm) long*

£40-60   **PSA**

A Beswick 'Caught It', 2951, unknown designer, from the Playful Puppies series.

This figure was produced by Royal Doulton from 1934-85 as HN1097, which is worth about the same as the Beswick version.

1986-89   *2.75in (7cm) wide*

£30-40   **PSA**

A Beswick 'Endon Black Rod' smooth-haired terrier gloss figure, No. 964.

£300-400   **PSA**

A Beswick 'Bull Terrier Romany Rhinestone' white figure, 970.

£50-100   **PSA**

CERAMICS

A Beswick 'Cheetah On Rock' figure, 2725, designed by Graham Tongue, with satin finish, from the Connoisseur series.

1981-89   6.5in (16.5cm) high

£180-220   **PSA**

A Beswick 'Seated Leopard', 841, designed by Arthur Gredington.

1940-c1954   6.25in (16cm) high

£400-500   **PSA**

A Beswick 'Lion On A Rock', 2554A, designed by Graham Tongue, satin finish, from the Connoisseur series.

This figure was also produced as 2554B in a gloss finish and without the base. It is worth about a third less than this example.

1975-84   8.25in (21cm) high

£100-150   **PSA**

A Beswick 'Siamese Cat', 1882, designed by Albert Hallam, from the Fireside Model series, seal point colourway.

The copper lustre version, made only for export is the most desirable at nearly double the value of this colourway.

1963-89   9.5in (24cm) high

£70-90   **PSA**

A Beswick 'Siamese Cat – Climbing', 1677, designed by Albert Hallam.

1960-97   6.5in (16.5cm) high

£15-25   **PSA**

A Beswick 'Marlin', 1243, designed by Arthur Gredington, restored.

1952-70   5.5in (14cm) high

£300-400   **PSA**

A Beswick 'Barracuda', 1235, designed by Arthur Gredington.

1952-68   4.75in (12cm) high

£300-400   **PSA**

FIND OUT MORE...

Beswick Animals, *by Diana & John Callows and Marilyn & Peter Sweets, published by Charlton Press, 8th edition, 2005.*

COLLECTORS' NOTES

■ Founded in 1894 to produce ornamental vases and other decorative objects, the John Beswick factory became known for its high quality character figures from the late 1940s. Talented ceramic artist Arthur Gredington joined the company to model finely realised animals, such as portraits of famous horses. In 1947, he began to mould characters from Beatrix Potter tales at the suggestion of Lucy Beswick, wife of the managing director, who had been inspired by a trip to the famous writer's home.

■ Albert Hallam gradually took over from Gredington during the 1960s and continued to expand the range of Beatrix Potter characters. In 1968, he launched a 'Winnie the Pooh and the Blustery Day' series, based on the Disney cartoon. In 1975, Graham Tongue succeeded Hallam as head modeller and produced classic Beatrix Potter characters in new poses as well as introducing 'double figures' such as 'Tabitha Twitchet and Miss Moppet'.

■ Beswick's cartoon figures are becoming increasingly popular. Characters from David Hand's Animaland were produced from 1949 to 1955 and are extremely sought-after today. Introduced in 1968 following the release of the Disney cartoon, Winnie the Pooh has also become a favourite. A second series of Winnie the Pooh characters were introduced in 1996.

■ Discontinued Beatrix Potter figures, and examples with early moulds or colour variations, attract the highest prices. Early and rare variations often have the desirable gold Beswick mark, used before 1972. Other popular ranges include Brambly Hedge, introduced in 1983, and the Snowman, produced between 1985 and 1994.

A Beswick 'Rupert Bear' figure, 2694, designed by Harry Sales, style one, from the Rupert Bear series.

This was the first figure released from the Rupert Bear series and the most desirable of the four of Rupert himself.

1980-86

£180-220   **PSA**

A Beswick 'Pong Ping' figure, 2711, designed by Harry Sales, from the Rupert Bear series.

1981-86   *4.25in (11cm) high*

£60-80   **PSA**

A Beswick 'Algy Pug' figure, 2710, designed by Harry Sales, from the Rupert Bear series.

1981-86   *4in (10cm) high*

£80-120   **PSA**

A Beswick 'Rupert Snowballing' figure, 2779, designed by Harry Sales, from the Rupert Bear series.

1982-86   *4.25in (11cm) high*

£220-280   **PSA**

A Beswick 'Bill Badger' figure, 2720, designed by Harry Sales, from the Rupert Bear series, style one.

1981-86   *2.75in (7cm) high*

£120-180   **PSA**

A Beswick 'A Good Read' figure, 2529, designed by David Lyttleton, from the Kitty MacBride series.

1975-83   *3.5in (9cm) high*

£60-80   **PSA**

A Beswick 'Winnie The Pooh' figure, 2193, designed by Albert Hallam, from the Winnie The Pooh series.

These figures are based on the Walt Disney cartoons, rather than the original illustrations by E.H. Shephard, although these did form the inspiration for the cartoons. All the figures are therefore marked "© Walt Disney Prod." on the base.

1968-90	*2.5in (6.5cm) high*
£30-40	**PSA**

A CLOSER LOOK AT A BESWICK CHARACTER FIGURE

Although virtually unknown today, the limited series of 'Animaland' animated short films was successful enough at the time for Beswick to release this series of animal figures based on the characters.

Hand previously worked for Walt Disney on projects including Bambi and Snow White & the Seven Dwarves.

The Animalands series was the first from Beswick to be based on a cartoon.

All the figures from the Animaland series are sought-after today.

A Beswick 'Loopy Hare' figure, 1156, designed by Arthur Gredington, from the David Hand's Animaland series.

1949-55	*4.25in (11cm) high*
£280-320	**PSA**

A Beswick 'Tigger' figure, 2394, designed by Graham Tongue, from the Winnie The Pooh series.

1971-90	
£35-45	**PSA**

A Beswick 'Rabbit' figure, 2215, designed by Albert Hallam, from the Winnie The Pooh series.

1968-90	*3.25in (8.5cm) high*
£30-40	**PSA**

A Beswick 'Owl' figure, 2216, designed by Albert Hallam, from the Winnie The Pooh series.

1968-90	*3in (7.5cm) high*
£25-35	**PSA**

A Beswick 'Dusty Mole' figure, 1155, designed by Arthur Gredington, from the David Hands Animaland series.

1949-55	*3.5in (9cm) high*
£100-150	**PSA**

A Beswick 'Oscar Ostrich' figure, 1154, designed by Arthur Gredington, from David Hand's Animaland series.

1949-55	*3.74in (9.5cm) high*
£220-280	**PSA**

A Beswick Beatrix Potter figure 'Amiable Guinea-Pig', style one, designed by Albert Hallam, printed brown mark.

1967-83

£70-90　　　　　　**WW**

A Beswick Beatrix Potter 'Anna Maria' figure, BP3b, modelled by Albert Hallam.

1974-83　　*3in (7.5cm) high*

£60-80　　　　　　**PSA**

A Royal Albert Beatrix Potter 'Babbity Bumble' figure, BP5, modelled by Warren Platt, boxed.

1989-93　　*2.75in (7cm) high*

£120-180　　　　　　**PSA**

A Beswick Beatrix Potter 'Benjamin Bunny', BP3, modelled by Arthur Gredington, first version with shoes and ears out.

1973-74　　*4in (10cm) high*

£180-220　　　　　　**GOR**

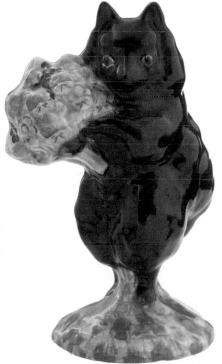

A Beswick Beatrix Potter 'Cecily Parsley' figure, BP2, modelled by Arthur Gredington, first version with head down, boxed.

1965-72　　*4in (10cm) high*

£100-150　　　　　　**PSA**

A Beswick Beatrix Potter 'Hunca Munca' figure, BP1, modelled by Arthur Gredington, style one.

1951-54　　*2.75in (7cm) high*

£180-220　　　　　　**PSA**

A rare Beswick Beatrix Potter 'Duchess' figure, BP2, modelled by Graham Orwell, style one holding flowers.

Duchess with flowers was the first Beatrix Potter figure to be retired and tended to be unpopular when on sale.

1955-67　　*3.75in (9.5cm) high*

£800-1,200　　　　　　**WW**

A Beswick Beatrix Potter 'Mr Alderman Ptolemy' figure, BP3b, modelled by Graham Tongue, boxed.

1974-85　　*3.5in (9cm) high*

£35-45　　　　　　**PSA**

A Beswick Beatrix Potter 'Mr Benjamin Bunny' figure, BP2, modelled by Arthur Gredington, first version with pipe out, boxed.

1971-72　　*4.25in (11cm) high*

£120-180　　　　　　**PSA**

A Beswick Beatrix Potter 'Mr Jackson' figure, BP3a, modelled by Albert Hallam, first variation with green body, boxed.

1974   2.75in (7cm) high

£120-180   **PSA**

A Beswick Beatrix Potter 'Mrs Tiggy-Winkle' figure, BP2, modelled by Arthur Gredington, first version, second variation, boxed.

1972   3.25in (8.5cm) high

£70-100   **PSA**

A Royal Albert Beatrix Potter 'Old Mr Pricklepin figure, BP6, modelled by David Lyttleton.

This figure was also released with backstamp BP3 and, although earlier, is less desirable than this edition.

1989

£300-400   **PSA**

A Beswick Beatrix Potter 'Pig-Wig' figure, BP3a, modelled by Albert Hallam, boxed.

Although all versions are sought-after, the first version with backstamp BP2, is the most desirable. It can be easily identified by the grey coloured body.

1973-88   4in (10cm) high

£80-120   **PSA**

A Beswick Beatrix Potter 'Simpkin' figure, BP3b, modelled by Alan Maslankowski, boxed.

This is the only backstamp that this figure was released with.

1975-83   4in (10cm) high

£180-220   **PSA**

A Beswick Beatrix Potter 'Sir Isaac Newton' figure, BP3b, modelled by Graham Tongue.

The size and colour of this figure does vary, but the value is the same.

1974-84   3.75in (9.5cm) high

£100-150   **PSA**

A Beswick Beatrix Potter 'Susan' figure, BP3b, modelled by David Lyttleton, boxed.

Look for this figure with the Royal Albert backstamp, it can be worth upto six time more than this one.

1983-85   4in (10cm) high

£100-150   **PSA**

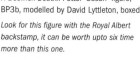

A Beswick Beatrix Potter 'Timmy Tiptoes' figure, BP2, modelled by Arthur Gredington, first version with red jacket.

1955-72   3.75in (9.5cm) high

£70-100   **PSA**

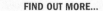

A Beswick Beatrix Potter figure 'Tommy Brock', BP3a, modelled by Graham Orwell, first version with spade handle out, first variation with small eye patches.

1973-74   3.5in (9cm) high

£80-120   **WW**

FIND OUT MORE...

Beswick Collectables, by Diana & John Callows and Hank Corley, published by The Charlton Press, 9th edition, 2005.

COLLECTORS' NOTES

■ Briglin pottery has continued to increase in desirability and value since collectors started to reappraise it around six years ago.

■ The company was founded in June 1948 in Baker Street, London by Brigitte Goldschmidt (later Appleby) and Eileen Lewenstein. Both had gained experience working with established potter Donald Mills from 1945. The pottery moved to Crawford Street, Mayfair in 1959.

■ Pieces were hand-thrown and hand-decorated, with dominant earthy clay tones and natural glazes such as cream and brown. Forms are clean and simple and show off the patterns well. Patterns are stylized and focus on the natural world, including country flowers and leaves.

Abstract or geometric patterns are also known.

■ Most patterns are marked out in the underlying clay, using a wax resist process, or the sgraffito technique. The look was highly fashionable in its day and the company was successful, with their wares being stocked by Heal's, Peter Jones and other popular department stores.

■ Fashion changed and after a short decline, the pottery closed in 1990. Larger pieces tend to fetch the highest prices, as do those well-glazed all over or displaying harmonic combination of glazed and unglazed areas.

■ Some shapes were harder to produce, making them rare, but kitchenware and novelty pieces, such as animal money boxes, tend to be less popular.

A Briglin large cylinder vase, with hand-painted glazed stylised flower design.

10in (25.5cm) high

£70-90   **FD**

A Briglin tall cylinder vase, with hand-painted bamboo and horizontal streaked design and all-over glossy glaze, the base stamped "BRIGLIN".

9.5in (24cm) high

£35-45   **GC**

Λ Briglin slightly tapered large cylindrical vase, with wax-resist closed and open thistles, painted with a creamy glaze, stamped "BRIGLIN".

7.5in (19cm) high

£35-45   **GC**

A Briglin 'Sunflower;' pattern vase, with black glazed and wax-resist pattern and creamy glaze.

This is a commonly seen motif.

c1974   7.5in (19cm) high

£30-40   **FD**

A small Briglin cylindrical footed bowl, with hand-painted and wax-resist fish pattern, stamped "BRIGLIN ENGLAND".

Fish and other animals are less commonly seen than plants or flowers. The lightly iridescent glaze is also unusual.

4in (10cm) high

£20-25   **GC**

A Briglin ovoid vase, inscribed with a wax-resist stylised blooming flower, with a wax-resist cream glaze and scored lower-half, stamped "BRIGLIN".

5.25in (13cm) high

£25-35   **GC**

A pair of Briglin 'Sunflower' pattern small salt and pepper shakers, with wax-resist stylized design.

4in (10cm) high

£12-18   **FD**

An unusual Briglin blue and matte grey bowl, stamped to the base "BRIGLIN".

9.75in (25cm) diam

£40-50   **MHT**

FIND OUT MORE...

Briglin Pottery 1948-1990 The Story of a Studio Pottery in the West End of London, by Anthea Arnold, published by Briglin Books, 2002.

COLLECTORS' NOTES

- Carlton Ware was initially the trade name of Wiltshaw & Robinson Ltd, Stoke on Trent, which was established in 1890. Carlton Ware became the official company name in 1958.

- Inspired by Wedgwood's popular Fairyland Lustre range, designed by Daisy Makeig-Jones, Carlton Ware produced a range of lustrous and fanciful decorative wares. Popular with collectors today, the patterns were often influenced by Oriental, Egyptian and Persian designs, and were laid on rich, deeply coloured grounds.

- Another popular line was the 1930s moulded range decorated with flower, leaves and fruit against pastel grounds. Certain motifs and colours are scarce, as are some combinations. For example, Buttercup is easy to find in yellow, but much scarcer in pink.

- The company also produced some striking designs in the 1950s and '60s, such as the 'Orbit' range. These later ranges, while not as valuable as the 1920s lustre pieces are growing in popularity and value.

- Carlton Ware fakes are on the market, so examine pieces closely and check the backstamp is appropriate for the item and its period of manufacture.

A Carlton Ware 'Lacecap Hydrangea' pattern tall vase, pattern no. 3967, designed by Violet Elmer, enamelled and gilded on a red lustre ground, printed script mark, minor enamel loss.

This pattern can also be found on a pale green ground. Elmer was also responsible for the 'Bell', 'Explosions' and 'Fantasia' patterns for Carlton Ware.

c1937   8.5in (21.5cm) high

£400-500   **WW**

A Carlton Ware 'Honest' pattern sleeve vase, pattern no. 3278, shape no. 217.	A Carlton Ware Rouge Royale 'Mikado' pattern baluster vase.	A 1930s Carlton Ware 'Hydrangea' pattern vase, with embossed decoration.	A Carlton Ware baluster vase, signed Geo. Roberts and dated 1922, painted with blue-tits amid blackberry canes, gilt rims, brown printed mark.
6in (15cm) high	12.5in (32cm) high	5in (12.5cm) high	8.25in (21cm) high
£50-80 BAR	**£60-80** CA	**£80-120** BEV	**£80-120** BONR

A Carlton Ware Chinoiserie small round bowl, the inside decorated with a Chinese river landscape.

£25-35   **LFA**

A Carlton Ware 'Swallow and Cloud' pattern ginger jar and cover, pattern no. 3073, with printed and painted marks.

8in (20cm) high

£200-300   **WW**

A Carlton Ware Chinoiserie jardinière, decorated with Oriental figures in a landscape, printed mark.

During the 1920s and '30s Carlton Ware produced a wide range of patterns on the Oriental theme, known collectively as Chinoiserie. The first pattern was 'Kang Hsi' in c1916. Certain motifs and decorations were copied across the different patterns, sometimes making it difficult to tell one pattern from another. Look for characteristics, such as two lovebirds in flight as seen on the Mikado pattern, and study the pattern on larger pieces to see it in full.

6in (15cm) high

£50-70   **WW**

A CLOSER LOOK AT A CARLTON WARE BOWL

This pattern was designed at the height of the West's fascination of all things Egyptian, following Howard Carter's discovering of Tutankhamen's tomb in Egypt in 1922.

Egyptian Fan' was also produced on mottled red, and dark blue ground.

The delicate, protruding feet and handles are easily damaged – undamaged examples such as this one command a premium.

Although the form is not particularly Egyptian, it displays the pattern well due to its large surface and ornate form.

A Carlton Ware 'Egyptian Fan' pattern pedestal bowl, pattern no. 3698, printed and painted in colours and gilt, printed mark.

Look for the range of commemorative 'Tutankhamen' wares produced by Carlton Ware not long after the tomb's discovery, as they are sought-after by collectors.

12.5in (31.5cm) wide

£550-650   **WW**

A Carlton Ware 'Tutankhamen' pattern bowl, printed and enamelled in colours and gilt, printed marks.

5.5in (14cm) diam

£220-280   **WW**

A Carlton Ware 'Heron and Magical Tree' pattern bowl, pattern no. 4160, designed by Rene Pemberton, shape no. 1577, painted script mark.

c1938   10.5in (26.5cm) wide

£280-320   **WW**

A Carlton Ware 'Hollyhocks' pattern circular bowl, pattern no. 3973, printed and painted marks.

10in (25cm) diam

£80-120   **L&T**

A Carlton Ware 'Bird of Paradise' pattern square serving dish, decorated with a paradise bird, printed and painted marks.

9.75in (24cm) wide

£180-220   **L&T**

A Carltonware 'Cubist Butterfly' pattern square dish, pattern no. 3195.

Also produced on a red, blue and green ground.

11.25in (28.5cm) wide

£70-90   **BAD**

A Carlton Ware 14-piece coffee set, each piece with a green ground and scrolling bands, the saucers in brown.

£40-60 **SWO**

A 1950s Carlton Ware hand-painted 'Windswept' pattern asymmetric mustard pot.

4in (10cm) wide

£10-15 **BAD**

A rare 1960s Carlton Ware 'Orbit' pattern gravy boat and tray.

The Orbit pattern, together with the Windswept pattern also on this page, are typical of 1960s design, with the bold use of colour using a limited palette, and simple, stylized decoration, clearly influenced by the space race.

Tray 6in (15cm) diam

£50-70 **BAD**

A Carlton Ware Walking ware 'seated' soup bowl and cover.

The popular Walking Ware range was developed by Roger Mitchell and Danka Napiorkowska in 1974 and comprised a complete tea service. The range expanded to include 'running' and 'sitting' and pieces were also produce at the Mitchell's own Lustre studio. Today the range is produced by the Price Kensington pottery.

5.5in (14cm) high

£35-45 **BAD**

A Carlton Ware 'Lucy May' novelty tea pot, modelled as a bi-plane, printed Carlton Ware mark.

c1985 *6in (15cm) high*

£80-120 **WW**

A Carlton Ware 'Red Baron' novelty teapot, modelled as a bi-plane.

Part of a series of novelty teapots, including the green 'Lucy May' seen on this page and a blue 'Blue Max'. Fakes are being produced but do not have the name or the plane motifs on the nose.

8.25in (21cm) long

£100-150 **BAD**

A Carlton Ware 'Humpty Dumpty' musical jug, printed mark, paint wear, movement not working.

8in (20cm) high

£120-180 **WW**

A Carlton Ware 'Glacielle Ware' figure, modelled as a seated terrier, unmarked.

Glacielle Ware range was developed at Carlton Ware in the 1920s by a former Sevrès potter. Due to its high retail price it proved unpopular with the buying public and was withdrawn from production after six months.

7.25in (18.5cm) high

£120-180 **WW**

A Carlton Ware earthenware moulded model of an English blue roan spaniel.

4.25in (11cm) high

£40-60 **BIG**

FIND OUT MORE...

Collecting Carlton Ware, by David Serpell, published by Krause Publications, 1999.

Collecting Carlton Ware, by Francis Joseph & Francis Salmon, published by Kevin Francis Publishing, 1994.

COLLECTORS' NOTES

■ Clarice Cliff (1899-1972) was born in the potteries town of Tunstall, Staffordshire. She joined A.J Wilkinson's of Burslem in 1916, after studying and working for a local pottery from 1912. The pottery was impressed with her skill and soon promoted her to a position of more influence and artistic control.

■ In 1925, managing director Colley Shorter gave Cliff her own studio. It was based in the newly purchased Newport Pottery, which had a large stock of defective blank wares, many in old-fashioned shapes. Cliff was encouraged to experiment, and to hide the faults in the blanks, covered them in brightly coloured and thickly applied patterns. This new range, named 'Bizarre', was launched in 1928 and proved so successful that the entire pottery was moved over to its production. The similar 'Fantasque' line was launched in 1928.

■ Over time, both the 'Bizarre' and 'Fantasque' range developed, with patterns becoming more elaborate, abstract and bold. By 1935 both the ranges had been phased out.

■ Cliff continued designing when the pottery restarted after WWII, but her designs were not as popular with the public. Cliff sold the pottery to Midwinter after Shorter, by now Cliff's husband, died in 1963.

■ Today, collectors look for Art Deco patterns in Cliff's trademark bright colours, which are thickly applied with visible brushstrokes. Large plates, jugs and vases are popular as they display the pattern well. Atypical patterns and muted colours are less desirable.

■ Fakes and reproductions do exist, so always buy from a reputable source. Crude painting, as opposed to Cliff's hallmark visible brushstrokes, smudges, and thickly applied and uneven glazes could indicate a fake.

A Clarice Cliff Bizarre 'Acorn' pattern vase, shape 602.

This pattern is quite hard to find as it was only made during 1934.

1934   *6.75in (17cm) high*

£180-220   **GHOU**

A Clarice Cliff Banded ware 'Bonjour' shape Honeyglaze teapot and sugar bowl, printed registration mark only, No.776243.

Introduced 1937

£60-80   **CHEF**

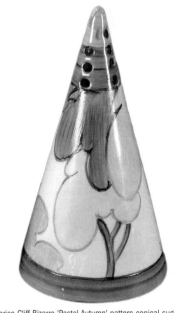

A Clarice Cliff Bizarre 'Pastel Autumn' pattern conical sugar sifter.
1930-34   *5.5in (14cm) high*
£800-1,000   **GHOU**

A Clarice Cliff Fantasque 'Red Autumn' pattern side plate.

Red was the first version of this pattern to be released.

1930-34   *5.5in (14cm) wide*

£200-300   **GHOU**

A Clarice Cliff Fantasque Bizarre 'Berries' pattern tankard coffee pot and cover.

1930-32   *7.5in (19cm) high*

£500-600   **GHOU**

A Clarice Cliff Fantasque Bizarre 'Berries' pattern Leda shape plate.

1930-32
9in (23cm) diam

£280-320   **GHOU**

CERAMICS

A Clarice Cliff Bizarre 'Blue W' pattern octagonal side plate.

1929-30

5.75in (14.5cm) diam

£350-450   **GHOU**

A Clarice Cliff Bizarre 'Orange Bridgwater' pattern Bonjour shape preserve pot and cover.

1934   *4in (10cm) high*

£350-450   **GHOU**

A Clarice Cliff Bizarre 'Yellow Branch and Squares' pattern bowl.

Introduced 1930   *7.5in (19cm) diam*

£350-450   **GHOU**

A Clarice Cliff Fantasque Bizarre 'Bobbins' pattern vase, shape 342.

1931-33   *8in (20cm) high*

£650-750   **GHOU**

A Clarice Cliff 'Cabbage Flower' pattern Bizarre vase, shape 602.

1934   *6.75in (17cm) high*

£350-450   **GHOU**

A Clarice Cliff Fantasque Bizarre 'Orange Chintz' sandwich tray, printed mark.

Introduced 1932   *11.5in (29cm) wide*

£150-250   **WW**

A Clarice Cliff Bizarre 'Blue Chintz' pattern Stamford teapot, cover restored.

This popular pattern was also produced in orange and in green, the latter is rare.

Introduced 1932   *5in (12.5cm) high*

£400-600   **GHOU**

A Clarice Cliff Fantasque 'Circle Tree' pattern octagonal plate, printed marks.

1920-30   *9.5in (24cm) wide*

£450-550   **SWO**

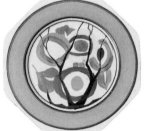

A Clarice Cliff Fantasque 'Circle Tree' pattern octagonal plate.

1929-30   *9.5in (24cm) diam*

£450-550   **GHOU**

CERAMICS

A CLOSER LOOK A CLARICE CLIFF SUGAR SIFTER

A Clarice Cliff Fantasque 'Comets' pattern plate.

1929-30   8.75in (22cm) diam

£350-450   **GHOU**

A Clarice Cliff 'Crocus' bowl, with printed mark in green.

7.75in (19.5cm) diam

£50-80   **GORL**

A Clarice Cliff Bizarre 'Autumn Crocus' pattern Bonjour shape preserve pot and cover.

1928-63   4in (10cm) high

£220-280   **GHOU**

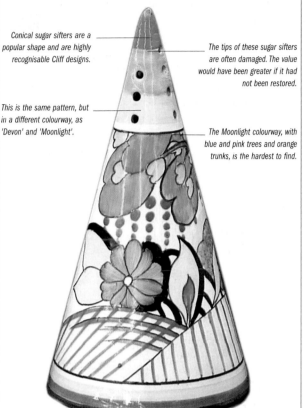

Conical sugar sifters are a popular shape and are highly recognisable Cliff designs.

The tips of these sugar sifters are often damaged. The value would have been greater if it had not been restored.

This is the same pattern, but in a different colourway, as 'Devon' and 'Moonlight'.

The Moonlight colourway, with blue and pink trees and orange trunks, is the hardest to find.

A Clarice Cliff Bizarre 'Cornwall' pattern conical sugar sifter, tip restored.

Introduced 1933   5.5in (14cm) high

£600-800   **GHOU**

A Clarice Cliff 'Autumn Crocus' pattern Bizarre candlestick, early painted green mark, shape 310.

1928-63   3in (7.5cm) high

£250-350   **GHOU**

A Clarice Cliff 'Blue Crocus' pattern conical salt pot, lacks factory mark.

Introduced 1935   3.25in (8.5cm) high

£100-150   **GHOU**

A Clarice Cliff Bizarre 'Cubist' pattern plate.

1929-30   8.75in (22cm) diam

£300-400   **GHOU**

A Clarice Cliff Bizarre 'Delecia' ware stepped candlestick, shape 391.

The Delecia range was originally just decorated with a thin wash of colour, which was then covered in enamel colour diluted with turpentine and allowed to run randomly over the piece. The effect was later combined with patterns such as Poppy, Citrus and Nasturtium.

3.5in (9cm) high

£200-300 GHOU

A Clarice Cliff 'Diamonds' partial pattern Bizarre circular ashtray.

4.5in (11.5cm) diam

£180-220 GHOU

A Clarice Cliff Fantasque Bizarre 'Farmhouse' pattern conical jug.

1931   6in (15cm) high

£650-750 GHOU

A Clarice Cliff 'Feathers and Leaves' pattern Fantasque fluted side plate.

6in (15cm) diam

£150-250 GHOU

A Clarice Cliff Fantasque Bizarre 'Coral Firs' pattern conical sugar sifter.

1933-38   5.5in (14cm) high

£500-600 GHOU

A Clarice Cliff Bizarre 'Blue Firs' pattern conical cup and saucer.

Rarer than the Coral version, the blue colour caused problems during firing and the colourway was only produced during 1933.

1933   Cup 2.25in (5.5cm) high

£500-600 GHOU

A Clarice Cliff 'Football' pattern Bizarre biscuit barrel and cover with wicker swing handle, shape 335.

Introduced in 1929   6in (15cm) high

£1,000-1,500 GHOU

A Clarice Cliff 'Fruitburst' pattern Fantasque Bizarre plate.

10in (25.5cm) diam

£300-400 GHOU

A Clarice Cliff Fantasque Bizarre 'Orange Gardenia' pattern plate.

Introduced 1931
10in (25.5cm) diam

£300-400 GHOU

A Clarice Cliff Bizarre 'Gibraltar' pattern plate.
Introduced 1931
9in (23cm) diam

£550-650   **GHOU**

A Clarice Cliff Fantasque Bizarre plate 'House and Bridge', painted in colours, printed mark.
1931-35   9in (22.5cm) diam

£280-320   **WW**

A Clarice Cliff Bizarre 'Honolulu' pattern biscuit barrel, shape 336.
'Rudyard' is an alternative colourway of this pattern.
Introduced 1933   6.5in (16.5cm) high

£800-1,200   **GHOU**

A Clarice Cliff Fantasque Bizarre 'Orange House' pattern octagonal plate.
This is a rarer version of the 'Green House' pattern.
Introduced 1930
8.5in (21.5cm) wide

£700-1,000   **GHOU**

A Clarice Cliff Bizarre 'Latona Floral' pattern Dover jardinière.
1929-30   6in (15cm) high

£700-1,000   **GHOU**

A Clarice Cliff Bizarre 'Latona Pink Tree' pattern stepped vase, shape 369.
1929-30   7.75in (19.5cm) high

£800-1,200   **GHOU**

A Clarice Cliff 'Liberty' Havre shape bowl, printed and painted marks.
The name 'Liberty' refers to the fact that the paintresses were at liberty to decorate these banded bowls in any colours they liked. These simple designs were usually produced to bulk out orders as they were quick and easy to produce.
1929-34

£120-180   **CHEF**

A Clarice Cliff Fantasque Bizarre 'Limberlost' pattern Daffodil shape bowl, shape 475.
1932   12.5in (31.5cm) wide

£400-500   **GHOU**

A Clarice Cliff 'Lorna' pattern single-handled Lotus jug.

1936   11.5in (29cm) high

£500-600   **GHOU**

CERAMICS

A Clarice Cliff Bizarre 'Luxor' pattern Drum shape preserve pot and cover.

1929-30   2.75in (7cm) high

£350-450   **GHOU**

A Clarice Cliff Fantasque Bizarre 'Melon' pattern octagonal plate.

1930-32   8.5in (21.5cm) wide

£400-500   **GHOU**

A Clarice Cliff Fantasque 'Melon' pattern bowl.

This orange colourway is the most common, it was also produced in pastel, red, green and blue.

1930-32   8.5in (21.5cm) diam

£250-350   **GHOU**

A Clarice Cliff Bizarre 'Mondrian' pattern side plate.

There are a number of colour variations to this pattern, it is also very similar to Cubist and Orange Blue Squares.

Introduced 1929   5.75in (14.5cm) diam

£350-450   **GHOU**

A Clarice Cliff Fantasque Bizarre 'Moonlight' pattern Bonjour shape sugar sifter.

Introduced 1932   5in (12.5cm) high

£550-650   **GHOU**

A Clarice Cliff Bizarre 'New Flag' pattern beehive preserve and cover, printed mark.

1929   4in (10cm) high

£250-350   **WW**

A Clarice Cliff 'Moonlight' pattern jug, shape 563, with printed marks and facsimile signature.

Introduced 1932   9in (23cm) high

£350-450   **SWO**

A Clarice Cliff Fantasque Bizarre 'New Fruit' pattern square ashtray.

This pattern is also referred to as 'Apples'.

1931-32   4.75in (12cm) diam

£200-250   **GHOU**

A pair of Clarice Cliff Bizarre 'My Garden' vases, shape 685, one with crack to rim.

'My Garden' is a range of shapes, each with the same moulded flower decoration and painted in a range of colours. The range was not very original and is not particularly sought-after today.

Introduced 1934

£60-80   **DNT**

A Clarice Cliff Fantasque Bizarre 'Blue Newport' pattern conical sugar sifter.

1934   5.5in (14cm) high

£400-500   **GHOU**

A Clarice Cliff Bizarre 'Oranges and Lemons' pattern circular ashtray.

1931-32   5in (12.5cm) diam

£180-220   **GHO**

A Clarice Cliff 'Original Bizarre' vase, shape 265.

c1928   6in (15cm) high

£450-550   **GHOU**

A Clarice Cliff 'Original Bizarre' Isis shape vase.

c1928   9.5in (24cm) high

£450-550   **GHOU**

A Clarice Cliff Bizarre 'Delecia Pansies' pattern conical sugar sifter, restored.

1932-34   5.5in (14cm) high

£250-350   **GHOU**

A CLOSER LOOK AT A CLARICE CLIFF GLOBE VASE

Patina ware can be recognised by its textured surface, which was created by splattering the biscuit body with coloured slip.

Other Patina ware patterns include Country, Garden, Coastal, Tulip and Daisy. The shape is echoed in the design of the tree's foliage.

This textured surface meant that traditional geometric patterns would not be suitable and a range of freehand designs were created to suit the finish.

The unusual globe shaped vase displays the pattern well.

A Clarice Cliff Bizarre 'Patina Tree' pattern globe vase, shape 370.

1932-33   6in (15cm) high

£1,200-1,800   **GHOU**

An early Clarice Cliff 'Persian' pattern plate, printed and painted mark, impressed 1927 date mark.

1927   9in (23cm) diam

£800-1,000   **GHOU**

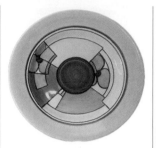

A Clarice Cliff Bizarre plate.

This is possibly a variation of 'Orange Picasso Flower'.

10in (25.5cm) diam

£350-450 GHOU

A Clarice Cliff 'Red Picasso Flower' pattern vase, shape 356.

This pattern was originally known as Red Flower.

4.5in (11.5cm) high

£1,000-1,500 GHOU

A Clarice Cliff Bizarre 'Orange Picasso Flower' pattern vase, shape 361.

1930 8.25in (21cm) high

£700-900 GHOU

A Clarice Cliff Fantasque Bizarre 'Poplar' pattern beehive honey pot and cover.

1930 3in (7.5cm) high

£350-450 GHOU

A Clarice Cliff Bizarre 'Rhodanthe' pattern wall charger.

Introduced 1934 18in (45.5cm) diam

£600-800 GHOU

A Clarice Cliff Bizarre 'Rudyard' pattern poppy bowl, rim restored.

The poppy bowl was probably a 1920s Newport factory shape that was used for Bizarre and phased out in the early 1930s.

1933-34 12in (30.5cm) diam

£550-650 GHOU

A Clarice Cliff Bizarre 'Sliced Fruit' pattern Coronet shape jug.

1930 7in (18cm) high

£250-350 GHOU

A Clarice Cliff Bizarre 'Rhodanthe' pattern vase, shape 358.

Introduced 1934 8in (20cm) high

£300-400 GHOU

A Clarice Cliff Fantasque Bizarre 'Secrets' pattern Havre shape bowl, printed mark.

7.5in (18.5cm) diam

£100-150 WW

A Clarice Cliff 'Sliced Circle' pattern Bizarre plate.

1929   10in (25.5cm) diam

£500-600   **GHOU**

A Clarice Cliff 'Stile and Trees' pattern pedestal bowl, printed mark.

c1937   12in (30.5cm) diam

£120-180   **WW**

A Clarice Cliff Fantasque Bizarre 'Summerhouse' pattern octagonal bowl.

This pattern is also used for the 'Café au Lait' range.

1931-33   8.5in (21.5cm) diam

£350-450   **GHOU**

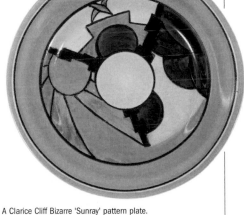

A Clarice Cliff Bizarre 'Sunray' pattern plate.

1929-30   9in (23cm) diam

£650-750   **GHOU**

A Clarice Cliff Bizarre 'Sunray' pattern candlestick, shape 310.

1929-30   3in (7.5cm) high

£450-550   **GHOU**

A Clarice Cliff Fantasque 'Green Sunrise' pattern vase, shape 341, rim restored.

1929   5.5in (14cm) high

£450-550   **GHOU**

A Clarice Cliff Bizarre 'Tennis' pattern Havre shape bowl.

1930   8in (20cm) diam

£450-550   **GHOU**

A Clarice Cliff Bizarre 'Tralee' pattern Gaiety shape basket.

1935-36   14in (35.5cm) high

£400-500   **GHOU**

A Clarice Cliff Bizarre 'Tennis' pattern plate.

c1930   10in (25.5cm) diam

£600-700   **GHOU**

CERAMICS

A Clarice Cliff Fantasque Bizarre orange 'Trees and House' pattern Leda plate.

Orange is by far the most common colourway for this pattern, although it was initially produced in red.

Introduced 1930

8in (20cm) diam

£400-500 GHOU

A Clarice Cliff Fantasque 'Umbrellas and Rain' pattern Meiping vase, restored.

Introduced 1929

12in (30.5cm) high

£400-500 GHOU

A Clarice Cliff 'Viscaria' pattern Leda plate.

This is the pink colourway of the Rhodanthe pattern.

1934-36　9in (23cm) wide

£100-150 GORL

A rare Clarice Cliff Fantasque 'Triangular Flowers' pattern vase, shape 342, printed gold backstamp.

7.75in (19.5cm) high

£1,500-2,000 GHOU

A Clarice Cliff Fantasque Bizarre 'Windbells' pattern wall plate.

1933-34　10in (25.5cm) diam

£450-550 GHOU

A Clarice Cliff Bizarre circular ashtray, shape 503, painted with bands in shades of orange, blue, green and black.

4.5in (11.5cm) diam

£70-90 GHOU

A Clarice Cliff ashtray, shape 902, the top decorated with a house and a tree.

4in (10cm) diam

£60-80 CA

A Clarice Cliff Fantasque Bizarre 'Windbells' pattern conical sugar sifter, tip restored.

1934-35　5.5in (14cm) high

£450-550 GHOU

FIND OUT MORE...

www.claricecliff.com – *The Clarice Cliff Collectors' Club website.*

www.claricecliff.co.uk

Comprehensively Clarice Cliff, by Greg Slater and Jonathan Brough, published by Thames & Hudson, 2005.

Clarice Cliff – The Bizarre Affair, by Leonard Griffin and Louis K. & Susan Pear Meisel, published by Thames & Hudson, 2000.

A CLOSER LOOK AT A PADDINGTON BEAR FIGURE

Coalport first started making Paddington Bear figures and nurseryware in 1976.

In 2001, Coalport reintroduced the range with over 14 new figures.

A total of 42 figures, as well as eight other pieces, were produced until the range was discontinued in 1988.

Paddington Bear was created by Michael Bond and was first published in 1958 with illustrations by Peggy Fortnum.

A Coalport 'Paddington Bear and the Marmalade' figure, version one.

A Coalport 'Paddington Bear in the Snow' figure, version one.

Invest in a specialist price guide that lists the relative prices of potentially valuable variations and versions, such as the book listed below.

Introduced 1976　　*5in (12.5cm) high*

£60-80　　　　　　　　　　　　**PSA**

Introduced 1976　　　　　　　　*5in (12.5cm) high*

£70-100　　　　　　　　　　　　**PSA**

A Coalport 'Paddington Bear Waiting for a Train' figure, version one.

A Coalport 'Paddington Bear Eats an Apple' figure, version one.

A Coalport 'Paddington Bear Hitchhikes' figure, version one.

A Coalport 'Paddington Bear the Chimney Sweep' figure, version one.

Intro. 1976　*3in (7.5cm) high*

Intro. 1976　*3.5in (9cm) wide*

£30-50　　　　　　**PSA**

£30-50　　　　　　**PSA**

Intro. 1976 5in (12.5cm) high

£60-80　　　　　　**PSA**

Intro. 1976　　*4in (10cm) high*

£60-80　　　　　　**PSA**

A Coalport 'Paddington Bear Reads a Book' figure, version one.

A Coalport 'Paddington Bear at the Seaside' figure, version one.

Intro. 1976　　*4in (10cm) wide*

£60-80　　　　　　**PSA**

Introduced 1976

2.5in (6.5cm) wide

£35-45　　　**PSA**

FIND OUT MORE...

The Charlton Standard Catalogue of Coalport Collectables (*1st Edition*), by Alf Willis, published by Charlton Press, 2000.

CERAMICS

COLLECTORS' NOTES

■ Susie Cooper (1902-95) ranks alongside Clarice Cliff as one of the key 20thC British ceramics designers. She began working as a paintress at A.E. Gray & Co. Ltd in 1922 before founding her own company in 1929. In 1931 she worked from the Crown Works at Woods & Sons in Burslem, initially using their shapes before designing her own from 1932. The Crown Works closed in 1979.

■ Her highly recognisable 1920s-30s Art Deco shapes and patterns are the most sought-after and are typified by stylized flowers or geometric patterns in bold colours. Her gentle floral designs from the late 1940s and 1950s are popular but do not fetch as high prices. In 1950, Cooper acquired a bone china factory and began to produce in bone china. These tend to be the least valuable, but reflect design tastes of the period well and represent an affordable entry point to her designs.

A Susie Cooper Falcon shape teapot, with a printed star pattern and moulded "42" and painted "1680" to base.

c1939   8.25in (21cm) high

£70-90   **BAD**

A Susie Cooper Productions Kestrel shape coffee set, comprising coffee pot, three cups, five saucers and a milk jug, with ochre and black banded pattern.

c1933   *Teapot 7.5in (19cm) high*

£150-250   **ING**

A Susie Cooper 'Printemps' pattern milk jug, marked "2205" and impressed "42" on the base.

4.25in (11cm) high

£50-70   **BAD**

A Susie Cooper Productions 'Patricia Rose' pattern jug.

6.25in (16cm) wide

£40-50   **BAD**

A 1930s-50s Susie Cooper 'Dresden Spray' pattern 29-piece part dinner service, comprising: dinner, dessert, side plates and soup bowls, tureen and cover.

£180-220   **SWO**

A Susie Cooper Production platter, with foliate design and graduated pink rim.

£30-40   **BAD**

A Susie Cooper printed 'Wild Strawberry' pattern Quail shape bone china trio set.

c1958   *Plate 6.5in (16.5cm) diam*

£40-60   **BAD**

COLLECTORS' NOTES

■ Harry Davis (1910-86) learnt pottery at the Broadstone Pottery, near Poole, where he worked from 1926-33. He then joined Bernard and David Leach at St Ives where he honed his legendary skills at throwing and became their chief thrower. He met his wife May (1914-95) there and taught her to throw in 1936.

■ Davis and his wife moved to Ghana just before WWII to head pottery at the Achimota art school and returned to the UK in 1946 when they set up the Crowan Pottery near Praze in Cornwall. They produced mainly domestic wares of very fine quality, typically with a green/beige or brown brushed glaze, often using wax-resist techniques. Prices are rising as interest in his skilled work grows.

■ In 1962 they closed the Crowan Pottery and moved to New Zealand where they founded Crewenna Pottery, which produced similar wares to Crowan and ran until 1972. They then moved to Peru and established a pottery at Izcuchaca at which they worked until 1979 when they returned to New Zealand. They lectured and worked there until their deaths.

A Crowan Pottery milk jug, by Harry Davis, with CP monogram.

2.25in (5.5cm) high

£20-25   **GROB**

A Crowan Pottery milk jug, by Harry Davis, with CP monogram.

2.75in (7cm) high

£15-25   **GROB**

A Crowan Pottery teapot, by Harry Davis.

Crowan's pottery is marked with an impressed 'CP' square seal near the base.

5.25in (13.5cm) high

£40-60   **GROB**

A Crowan Pottery cup and saucer, by Harry Davis, with CP monogram.

Saucer 4.5in (11.5cm) diam

£10-15   **GROB**

A Crowan Pottery dish, with unglazed exterior, and CP monogram.

4in (10cm) diam

£7-10   **GROB**

A Crowan Pottery soup bowl, by Harry Davis, with unglazed exterior, and CP monogram.

6in (15.5cm) diam

£8-12   **GROB**

A Crowan Pottery bowl, decorated by May Davis with a wax-resist design, with CP monogram.

1.5in (3.5cm) high

£20-25   **GROB**

CERAMICS

A Crown Devon Lustrine 'Summer' pattern lustre vase, by S. Fieldings & Co.

Simon Fielding formed S. Fielding & Co. in the early 1870s. It was renamed the Devon Pottery in 1912, but is better known by its trade name Crown Devon.

9.5in (24cm) high

£80-120   **BAD**

A Crown Devon lustre ginger jar, painted by D. Cole, with enamelled ship at sea pattern, signed by the artist.

7in (17.5cm) high

£100-150   **BAD**

A Crown Devon 'Orient' pattern coffee pot and cover, pattern 2115, printed and painted marks.

8.25in (21cm) high

£280-320   **WW**

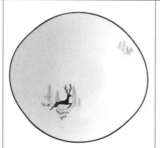

A 1930s Crown Devon earthenware vase, of ovoid form decorated with orange, yellow and silver grey lozenges.

7.5in (19cm) high

£40-60   **BIG**

A Crown Devon 'Stockholm' pattern Karen shape bowl, designed by Bill Kemp.

The green colourway is known as Greenland.

Introduced 1955   8.75in (22.5cm) diam

£30-40   **BAD**

A Crown Devon 'Stockholm' Karen shape sugar sifter, with designed by Bill Kemp, leaping gazelle.

Introduced 1955   4.25in (12cm) high

£50-70   **BAD**

A 1950s Crown Devon 'Oceania' pattern moulded and painted salt pot.

5.5in (14cm) high

£7-10   **MTS**

A late 1970s Crown Devon 'Curry' storage jar, with wooden lid and printed decoration.

4.25in (11cm) high

£10-15   **MTS**

A Crown Devon 'Memphis' vase, by Colin Melbourne, with signature and impressed "CM", restored.

Sculptor and designer Colin Melbourne worked with a number of potteries, perhaps most significantly with Beswick, where he produced his CM range. Other potteries include Midwinter, Royal Norfolk and Bossons. He was head of Ceramics at the Burslem School of Art from 1958-86 and he formed the Drumlanrig Melbourne design consultancy with Lord Queensberry in 1954. His work is sought-after today.

8.25in (21cm) high

£20-30   **GAZE**

A Doulton Lambeth stoneware teapot and cover, by Hannah Barlow, incised with dogs hunting a deer.

Hannah Barlow is one of Doulton's most popular of stoneware artists and is renowned for her animal designs.

4.5in (11cm) high

£650-750 WW

A Doulton Lambeth stoneware milk jug, by Hannah Barlow, incised with grazing deer, silver mount to rim.

3.5in (8.5cm) high

£550-650 WW

A Royal Doulton 'Huntsman' series water jug, D2778.

7in (18cm) high

£40-60 PSA

A Royal Doulton 'Titanian' glaze Egyptian tea caddy, D4263.

This range was released in 1924 to commemorate the opening of Tutankhamun's tomb.

1924-c1930   5in (13cm) high

£60-80 PSA

A Royal Doulton 'Flambé Veined' oviform vase, decorated with high-temperature glazes, printed mark and number "1619".

11.5in (29cm) high

£150-200 DN

A limited edition Royal Doulton 'Treasure Island' jug, designed by Charles J. Noke and Harry Fenton, from an edition of 600, with printed factory mark.

1934   7.75in (19.5cm) high

£600-800 GHOU

A Royal Doulton 'Lobster Man' large toby jug, D6617, designed by David B. Biggs.

1968-71

£60-80 KCS

A Royal Doulton coffee can and saucer, with a hand-painted floral design.

4.5in (11.5cm) diam

£35-45 BAD

A Royal Doulton hand-painted bud vase, impressed "7349" and printed "DS4971".

3.75in (9.5cm) high

£35-45 BAD

CERAMICS

COLLECTORS' NOTES

■ Doulton had produced figurines during the 19th century, but the first Doulton figurines as we recognise them were launched in 1913 by the company's Art Director Charles Noke.

■ Many people choose to collect by type such as 'fair ladies', children or literary and historical characters. Ranges such as 'Dickens' and 'The Lord of the Rings' remain popular. Others collect by period or artist. Leslie Harradine, Mary Nicoll, Bill Harper and Peggy Davies – who spent 40 years with Royal Doulton and produced about 250 different figures – all have their own distinctive style and a significant following.

■ Over 4,000 different models and colour variations are known to exist. A figure may have been produced in a number of different colourways, and each variation has an allocated 'HN' number. Each colourway is often worth a different amount, usually depending on rarity and length of production time.

■ Pieces without a 'Made In England' reference mark on the base are usually pre-1920 and can be rare and valuable. Figurines discontinued before WWII are also sought after, as are those produced for short periods of time. Figurines produced continuously for long periods like 'The Balloon Man', or those that are still in production today tend to be less desirable.

■ Condition directly contributes to value. Chips, cracks and restoration reduce value considerably, so examine all examples carefully. Take care when handling or cleaning – use a small soft brush to dust figurines and avoid getting water inside pieces.

A Royal Doulton 'A Country Lass' figurine, HN1991A, designed by Leslie Harradine.

This was first released as 'Market Day' HN1991 from 1947-55, which can be worth 20 per cent more than this example.

1975-81   7.25in (18.5cm) high

£80-120   **L&T**

A Royal Doulton 'Autumn' figurine, HN2085, designed by Margaret Davies, style two from The Seasons series.

1952-59   7.5in (19cm) high

£100-150   **L&T**

A Royal Doulton 'A Winters Walk' figurine, HN3052, designed by A. Hughes, from the Reflections series.

This figure was released one year earlier in the US.

1988-95   12.25in (31cm) high

£80-120   **L&T**

A Royal Doulton 'Boudoir' figurine, HN2542, designed by E.J. Griffiths, from the Haute Ensemble series.

1974-79   12.25in (31cm) high

£120-180   **L&T**

A Royal Doulton 'Carmen' figurine, HN2545, designed by E.J. Griffiths, from the Haute Ensemble series.

The original figurine named Carmen was designed by Leslie Harradine, and released in 1928. The early version can be worth upto four times this example.

1974-79   11.5in (29cm) high

£80-120   **L&T**

A Royal Doulton 'Cherry Blossom' figurine, HN3092, designed by P. Parsons, from the Reflections series.

This figurine was released a year earlier in the US.

1987-89 12.75in (32cm) high

£60-100   **L&T**

A limited edition Royal Doulton 'Eastern Grace' blue flambé figurine, HN3683, designed by Pauline Parsons, from an edition of 2,500.

Also available in red flambé and in traditional colours. The flambé versions are more desirable.

1995   12.5in (31.5cm) high

£150-200   **PSA**

A CLOSER LOOK AT A FIGURINE

This shape was also released in pink as HN1741, and was produced for one less year. It is usually of a similar value to HN1740.

Lawleys By Post commissioned the re-release of this figurine in 2000 in a limited edition of 2,000. It is worth about 20 per cent of this version.

Leslie Harradine was a prolific designer of 'Fair Lady' figurines and collectors often specialise in examples of his work.

The style of this figure is unusual: 'Fair Ladies' are usually full-length figures, either standing or seated.

A limited edition Royal Doulton 'Eliza Farren, Countess Of Derby' figurine, HN3442, designed by Peter Gee, from an edition of 5,000, with certificate, issued for the Royal Doulton International Collectors Club.

1993   *8.75in (22cm) high*

£80-120   **PSA**

A Royal Doulton 'Gladys' figurine, HN1740, designed by Leslie Harradine.

1935-49   *5in (12.5cm) high*

£300-400   **SWO**

A Royal Doulton 'Enigma' figurine, HN3110, designed by R. Jefferson, from the Reflections series.

1987-95   *12.75in (32cm) high*

£80-120   **L&T**

A Royal Doulton 'Genevieve' figurine, HN1962, designed by Leslie Harradine.

1941-75   *7in (18cm) high*

£80-120   **PSA**

A Royal Doulton 'Lori' figurine, HN2801, designed by Margaret Davies, from the Kate Greenaway series.

1976-87   *5.75in (14.5cm) high*

£60-90   **L&T**

A Royal Doulton 'Midsummer Noon' figurine, HN2033, designed by Leslie Harradine.

The blue version released 1939-49 is the most desirable version, worth upto double this one.

1949-55 5in (12.5cm) high

£150-250   **PSA**

A Royal Doulton 'Penelope' figurine, HN1901, designed by Leslie Harradine.

The lavender and green version, released as HN1902 in 1939 was only issued until 1949 and can be worth over three times as much.

1939-75   *7in (18cm) high*

£80-120   **L&T**

CERAMICS

A Royal Doulton 'Ruth' figurine, HN2799, designed by Margaret Davies, from the Kate Greenaway series.

1976-81   6in (15cm) high

£70-100   **L&T**

A limited edition Royal Doulton 'Sophie Charlotte, Lady Sheffield' figurine, HN3008, designed by P. Gee, from the Gainsborough Ladies series, from an edition of 5,000, with certificate.

1990   10in (25.5cm) high

£60-80   **PSA**

A Royal Doulton 'Spring' figurine, HN2085, designed by Margaret Davies, style four, from The Seasons series.

1952-59 7.75in (19.5cm) high

£80-120   **L&T**

A Royal Doulton 'Strolling' figurine, HN3073, designed by A. Hughes, from the Reflections series.

This figure was released two years earlier in the US.

1987-95 13.5in (34.5cm) high

£80-120   **L&T**

A Royal Doulton 'Sweet Anne' figurine, HN1318, designed by Leslie Harradine, style one.

The most valuable version of this figure is HN1631, only issued between 1934-38 and in a green, red, pink and yellow colourway.

1929-49   7.5in (19cm) high

£100-150   **L&T**

A Royal Doulton 'Top O' The Hill' figurine, HN1834, designed by Leslie Harradine, style one.

Introduced 1937   7in (18cm) high

£50-80   **L&T**

A Royal Doulton 'Vivienne' figurine, HN2073, designed by Leslie Harradine.

1951-67   7.75in (19.5cm) high

£60-80   **PSA**

A Royal Doulton 'Water Maiden' figurine, HN3155, designed by Adrian Hughes, from the Reflections series.

1987-91   12in (30.5cm) high

£60-100   **L&T**

A Royal Doulton 'Cavalier' figurine, HN2716, designed by Eric J. Griffiths, style two.

1976-82   10in (25.5cm) high

£80-120   **L&T**

A Royal Doulton 'Ko-Ko' figurine, HN2898, designed by William K. Harper, from The Gilbert & Sullivan series.

1980-85   11.5in (29cm) high

£120-180   **PSA**

A Royal Doulton 'The Carpenter' figurine, HN2678, designed by Mary Nicoll.

Nicoll is known for her portrayal of traditional British crafts and pastimes, with other designs including 'The Clockmaker', as well as marine characters.

1986-92   8in (20cm) high

£150-200   **PSA**

A Royal Doulton 'The Laird' figurine, HN2361, designed by Mary Nicoll.

At some point the base was made larger and the HN number was changed to HN2361A. The value is the same for either version.

1969-   8in (20cm) high

£60-80   **L&T**

A Royal Doulton 'Lambing Time' earthenware figurine, HN1890, designed by W.M. Chance, style one.

1938-81   9.25in (23.5cm) high

£120-180   **PSA**

A Royal Doulton 'Aragorn' figurine, HN2916, designed by David Lyttleton, from the Middle Earth series.

1981-84   6.25in (16cm) high

£40-60   **PSA**

A Royal Doulton 'Bilbo' figurine, HN2914, designed by David Lyttleton, from the Middle Earth series.

1980-84   4.5in (11.5cm) high

£30-50   **PSA**

A Royal Doulton 'Gandalf' figurine, HN2911, designed by David Lyttleton, from the Middle Earth series.

1980-84   7in (18cm) high

£40-60   **PSA**

A Royal Doulton 'Owd Willum' figurine, HN2042, designed by Leslie Harradine.

1949-73   6.75in (17cm) high

£120-180   **L&T**

A Royal Doulton 'The Bedtime Story' figurine, HN2059, designed by Leslie Harradine.

1950-96   4.75in (12cm) high

£80-120   **L&T**

A CLOSER LOOK AT A ROYAL DOULTON FIGURINE

Sculptor Phoebe Stabler is perhaps best known for her association with Carter, Stabler and Adams, which became Poole Pottery, through her husband Harold Stabler.

It was the first Doulton figurine to feature a 'street vendor'. Later additions include the Old Balloon Seller, the Carpet Vendor and The Potter.

This figure, which was designed in 1911, was also produced by Poole as 'The Lavender Woman' in a different colourway.

The shape was first issued as HN10 in 1913, one of the earliest from the HN series. All the variations are desirable, the last HN2034 (1949-51) is the least valuable, at less than half this version.

A Royal Doulton 'Madonna of the Square' figurine, HN613, designed by Phoebe Stabler, impressed "Phoebe Stabler", printed Doulton mark, restored neck.

1924-36   8in (20cm) high

£450-550   **WW**

A Royal Doulton 'The Patchwork Quilt' figurine, HN1984, designed by Leslie Harradine.

1945-59   6in (15cm) high

£100-150   **L&T**

A Royal Doulton 'Pierrette' figurine, HN643, designed by Leslie Harradine, style one.

This is one of a number of colourways; only one was produced after WWII. They are all sought-after.

1924-38

£1,000-1,500   **PSA**

A Royal Doulton 'Ruth The Pirate Maid' figurine, HN2900, designed by W.K. Harper, from The Gilbert & Sullivan Series.

1981-85   11.75in (30cm) high

£200-300   **PSA**

A Royal Doulton 'Schoolmarm' figurine, HN2223, designed by Margaret Davies.

1958-81   6.75in (17cm) high

£120-180   **L&T**

A Royal Doulton 'The Wardrobe Mistress' figurine, HN2145, designed by Margaret Davies.

1954-67   5.75in (14.5cm) high

£200-300   **PSA**

FIND OUT MORE...

Royal Doulton Figurines, by Jean Dale, published by Charlton Press, 10th Edition, 2005.

COLLECTORS' NOTES

■ Royal Doulton have been producing animal character figures since the 1880s. Ranges have included Aesop's Fables, The Wind in the Willows and Beatrix Potter.

■ In 1969 the firm acquired the Beswick factory and benefited from Beswick's expertise in creating ceramic character animals. Modellers and designers Albert Hallam, Graham Tongue and Harry Sales helped further Royal Doulton's reputation for producing fine quality, collectable pieces.

■ Brambly Hedge mouse figures, based on the books by Jill Barklem, have remained popular since their introduction in 1983. Their poses were carefully designed so that different figures would appear to react well with each other when grouped together. Look out for rare models or colour variations. The first Brambly Hedge range was retired in 1997, but a new collection was introduced in 2000.

■ Bunnykins figures were first produced in 1939 and early figures are rare. The range was relaunched in 1972 with DB pattern numbers, and Harry Sales expanded the range in the early 1980s to appeal more to adult collectors. In 1987 the Royal Doulton International Collectors' Club issued a figure exclusively for its members and this 'Collector Bunnykins' DB54 is one of the most prized pieces.

■ Early discontinued models are sought-after, and figures are withdrawn regularly from the range, increasing value. Though limited editions have increased in size, demand often outstrips supply for many new Bunnykins figures as soon as they are launched.

A Royal Doulton Brambly Hedge 'Basil' figure, DBH14, style one, designed by Harry Sales.

1985-92   3.25in (8.5cm) high

£70-100   **PSA**

A Royal Doulton Brambly Hedge 'Clover' figure, DBH16, designed by Graham Tongue.

1987-97   3.25in (8.5cm) high

£20-30   **PSA**

A Doulton Brambly Hedge 'Mrs Toadflax' figure, DBH11, designed by Harry Sales.

The contents of the bowl varies in colour, but this does not affect the value.

1985-95   3.25in (8.5cm) high

£30-50   **PSA**

A Royal Doulton Brambly Hedge 'Old Mrs Eyebright' figure, DBH9, designed by Harry Sales.

1984-95   3.25in (8.5cm) high

£30-50   **PSA**

A Royal Doulton Brambly Hedge 'Old Vole' figure, DBH13, designed by Harry Sales.

1985-92   *3.25in (8.5cm) high*

£120-180   **PSA**

A Royal Doulton Brambly Hedge 'Primrose Entertains' figure, DBH22, designed by Graham Tongue.

1990-95   3.25in (8.5cm) high

£50-70   **PSA**

A Royal Doulton Brambly Hedge 'Wilfred Entertains' figure, DBH23, designed by Graham Tongue.

1990-95   3.25in (8.5cm) high

£50-70   **PSA**

CERAMICS

A limited edition Royal Doulton 'Arabian' Bunnykins, DB315, designed by Caroline Dadd, from an edition of 1,000 commissioned by UKI Ceramics, boxed with certificate.

2004

£60-80   **PSA**

A CLOSER LOOK AT AN EARLY BUNNYKINS

Bunnykins figures are based on the drawings of Sister Mary Barbara Vernon, the daughter of Royal Doulton's Stoke-on-Trent manager at the time.

The first six figures are believed to have been designed by Charles Noke as they are similarities to his animal figures.

These first figures bear little resemblance to Barbara's drawings, which may explain why they were redesigned by Walter Hayward when the range was relaunched in 1972.

Production was interrupted by WWII meaning this version was only made for a short period of time. This makes them among the the rarest Bunnykins today.

A lively trade on the internet has seen more of these early figures come to light, meaning prices have dropped slightly, particularly for Billy and Mother.

A Royal Doulton earthenware 'Billy' Bunnykin, D6001, designed by Charles Noke.

1939-40   *4.5in (12cm) high*

£350-450   **PSA**

A Royal Doulton 'Daisie Bunnykins Spring Time' Bunnykins, DB7, modelled by Albert Hallam based on a design by Walter Hayward.

1972-83   *3.5in (9cm) high*

£80-120   **PSA**

A limited edition Royal Doulton 'Detective' Bunnykins, DB193, designed by Kimberley Curtis, from an edition of 2,500 exclusively for UKI Ceramics, boxed with certificate.

1999   *4.75in (12cm) high*

£50-70   **PSA**

A limited edition Royal Doulton 'Dutch' Bunnykins, DB274, from an edition of 2,000 from the Bunnykins of the World series, boxed with certificate.

2003

£50-70   **PSA**

A Royal Doulton 'Irishman' Bunnykins, DB178, designed by Denise Andrews, from a limited edition of 2,500 exclusively for UKI Ceramics, boxed with certificate.

1998

£80-120   **PSA**

A limited edition Royal Doulton 'Judy' Bunnykins, DB235, designed by Kimberley Curtis, from an edition of 2,500 exclusively for UKI Ceramics, boxed with certificate.

2001

£40-60   **PSA**

A limited edition Royal Doulton 'Juggler' Bunnykins, DB164, designed by Denise Andrews, from a limited edition of 1,500 exclusively for UKI Ceramics, boxed.

1996   *4.5in (12cm) high*

£100-150   **PSA**

A limited edition Royal Doulton 'Mandarin' Bunnykins, DB252, designed by Caroline Dadd, from an edition of 2,500 exclusively for UKI Ceramics, boxed with certificate.

This one of 15 Bunnykins of the World, a range produced exclusively for UKI Ceramics.

2001   4.25in (11cm) high

£40-60   **PSA**

A rare Royal Doulton earthenware 'Mary' Bunnykins, D6002, designed by Charles Noke.

1939-40   6.5in (16.5cm) high

£800-1,000   **PSA**

A limited edition Royal Doulton 'Matador' Bunnykins, DB281, designed by Caroline Dadd, from an edition of 2,000, boxed with certificate.

2003   4.75in (12cm) high

£50-60   **PSA**

A limited edition Royal Doulton 'Mexican' Bunnykins, DB316, designed by Caroline Dadd, from an edition of 1,000 exclusively for UKI Ceramics, boxed with certificate.

2004

£50-70   **PSA**

A limited edition Royal Doulton 'Mr Punch' Bunnykins, DB234, designed by Kimberley Curtis, from an edition of 2,500 exclusively for UKI Ceramics, boxed with certificate.

2001   4.75in (12cm) high

£40-60   **PSA**

A Royal Doulton 'Parisian' Bunnykins, DB317, from an edition of 1,000 for UKI Ceramics, boxed with certificate.

This was the last of the Bunnykins of the World series.

2005

£60-80   **PSA**

A limited edition Royal Doulton 'Rugby Player' Bunnykins, DB318, from an edition of 1,000, boxed with certificate.

2005

£50-70   **PSA**

A limited edition Royal Doulton 'Samurai' Bunnykins, DB280, from an edition of 2,000 exclusively for the UKI Ceramics series Bunnykins of the World, boxed with certificate.

2003

£60-80   **PSA**

A limited edition Royal Doulton 'Witch's Cauldron' Bunnykins, DB293, designed by Caroline Dadd, from an edition of 1,500 exclusively for UKI Ceramics, boxed with certificate.

2004

£60-80   **PSA**

FIND OUT MORE...

Royal Doulton Collectables, by Jean Dale and Louise Irvine, published by The Charlton Press, 4th edition, 2006.

A Royal Doulton 'Cocker Spaniel Setter with Pheasant' medium figure, HN1138, designed by Frederick Daws.

The large size version of this figure, HN1137, can be worth up to twice as much as this medium-sized version.

1937-85   *5.25in (13.5cm) high*

£180-220   **PSA**

A Royal Doulton 'Collie, Seated' flambé figure, HN105 or 106, restored.

Introduced 1912   *7.5in (19cm) high*

£200-250   **PSA**

A CLOSER LOOK AT A ROYAL DOULTON FIGURE

The flambé glaze, inspired by Oriental glazes, was developed by Doulton over a number of years and was in production from 1904.

This shape was also produced in grey earthenware, which is particularly rare; and in the Sung glaze, which can be worth about 15 per cent more than this version.

The elephant was produced in three sizes, this being the largest and the most valuable. Both the small and medium versions are worth about 20 per cent less.

Animals were added to the flambé range within a few years, with the first shapes being moulded by Noke.

A rare Royal Doulton 'Elephant' large flambé figure, HN1121, designed by Charles Noke, with trunk down and curled, signed.

c1938-57   *13in (33cm) high*

£2,000-2,500   **PSA**

A Royal Doulton 'Stalking Tiger' flambé figure, HN225, designed by Charles Noke.

1912-68   *9.5in (24cm) long*

£200-300   **PSA**

A 1990s Royal Doulton 'Siamese Kittens' flambé figure, designed by Jan Granoska.

The flambé version of this figure seems to have only been made as a prototype.

£120-180   **PSA**

A Royal Doulton 'Tiger on a Rock' figure, HN2535, style three, designed by Charles Noke.

These powerful, big cat sculptures were a speciality of Art Director Noke and are popular with collectors.

1940-60   *9in (23cm) long*

£550-650   **PSA**

A Royal Doulton 'Drake Resting' large flambé figure, HN977 or 1192, signed by Charles Noke.

c1929-61 *7.25in (18.5cm) high*

£150-200   **PSA**

A Royal Doulton 'Guinea Fowl' flambé figure, signed by Charles Noke.

1912-67   *3.25in (8.5cm) high*

£250-300   **PSA**

COLLECTORS' NOTES

- The designs of Italian Piero Fornasetti (1913-88) have become increasingly popular over the past five years. His first exhibition was in Milan in 1933 and he went on to become a notable interior decorator during the 1940s and '50s, and designed many ceramic, glass and furniture items as well.

- Fornasetti's love of surface ornamentation set him apart from his contemporaries in the mid-century Modern movement who aimed to unite form and function over surface decoration. Disregarded by his contemporaries, his work was popular with the buying public in the 1950s, and began to undergo a renaissance in the 1980s.

- Motifs are typically taken from the Classical Roman and Greek world and include elements of architecture and statuary. Others include suns, moons, playing cards and fish, and many have a integral sense of humour or wit. Patterns are applied by lithographed transfers, typically in black, or gold, on a white background. Stronger, primary colours are known but are less common.

- Always look for the Fornasetti transfer-printed mark, that includes a painter's hand or brush on the reverse of ceramics, as reproductions and fakes are known. Also examine pieces carefully as wear, particularly to the gilt surface, is common and devalues a piece. Aim to buy complete sets, as finding a replacement, especially in similar condition, can be very hard.

- Pieces produced until Fornasetti's death in 1988 are considered vintage. Many designs are still being produced today as re-editions, or otherwise are being released by the company that still exists, run by his son Barnaba. Always aim to buy from an experienced dealer or consult reference works to ensure the piece is vintage.

Two German Eschenbach 'Strumenti Musicali' porcelain plates, designed by Piero Fornasetti, numbered "1" and "2".
1955-56   8.25in (21cm) diam
£100-150   GAZE

A set of eight late 1960s to early 1970s 'Adam' transfer-printed plates, designed by Piero Fornasetti.
Note the clever positioning of Adam's naked body over the set to avoid 'embarrassment'.
£120-180   P&I

One of set of 12 plates, designed by Piero Fornasetti, all with black ink mark on reverse.
10in (25.5cm) diam
£450-550 (set)   SK

A 'match man' transfer-printed dish or ashtray, designed by Piero Fornasetti.
5.5in (14cm) high
£70-100   HLM

A 'match dog' transfer-printed dish or ashtray, designed by Piero Fornasetti.
5.5in (14cm) high
£70-100   HLM

A pair of bathroom covered jars, designed by Piero Fornasetti, with gilt and black transfer-printed design.
7in (18cm) high
£70-100   ROS

A chocolate mug and cover, designed by Piero Fornasetti, with gilt and black portrait medallion transfer-printed pattern.
£30-50   GAZE

A 'Pumpkin' white ceramic lidded pot, designed by Piero Fornasetti, with hand-painted gilt decoration, lid cracked.
13in (33cm) long
£20-30   GAZE

COLLECTORS' NOTES

- Hazle Boyles founded her pottery in 1990, drawing on her previous careers as an interior designer and as a Craft, Design & Technology teacher. It was while teaching that she began to develop her low-relief clay models.

- The company's main product is the 'A Nation of Shopkeepers' series of flatback models of shops, often based on existing historic buildings throughout the UK. This popular range is predominately hand-painted, with the use of decals being phased out completely.

- Look for limited production models; some were produced in editions as few as five, and event pieces from the 10th and 15th anniversary celebrations. Also desirable are examples signed 'Hazle Boyles' on the front, as this was only used between 1990-92. In 1993, it was replaced with the simplified 'Hazle', which can be signed by senior painters as well as Hazle herself.

A CLOSER LOOK AT A HAZLE CERAMICS WALL PLAQUE

The plaque takes its title from the Charles Dickens' book of the same name. The design is based on the Old Curiosity Shop, Portsmouth Street, London, which claims to be the inspiration for the book.

It was launched at a Dickens' Event in 2003 where it was signed on the flatback by Hazle Boyles and Cedric Charles Dickens, great grandson of the famous author.

The shape was also used to portray a modern-day version of the shop, which was produced from 1999-2005.

Date codes were introduced in 1995, starting with 'a'. This example is marked 'i' for 2003.

A limited edition Hazle Ceramics 'The Old Curiosity Shop' wall plaque, from an edition of 30, together with a certificate of authenticity.

2003   *7in (17.5cm) wide*

£300-400   **JEG**

A limited edition Hazle Ceramics 'Chinese Restaurant' wall plaque, from an edition of 100 from the Hazle 2000 series.

Based on a Boot's the Chemist building in Nottingham, built in 1877.

2003   *9in (22.5cm) high*

£300-400   **JEG**

A Hazle Ceramics 'The Florist' wall plaque.

Based on a building in Maldon, Essex. This is the early version signed "Hazle Boyles", which is worth up to 50 per cent more than the later "Hazle" version.

1990-92   *8in (20.5cm) high*

£100-150   **RA**

A Hazle Ceramics 'Post Office' wall plaque.

Based on a building on Colchester. The blank was decorated as 'Corner Shop' from 1991-97 and as 'Post Office' from 1998.

7.75in (19.5cm) high

£80-120   **RA**

A limited edition Hazle Ceramics 'Royal Regalia' wall plaque, from an edition of 300.

Based on a building in Windsor. The first 100 pieces produced were used as part of a five-piece Jubilee Parade set, issued in 2002 to celebrate Queen Elizabeth II's golden jubilee.

8in (20cm) high

£100-150   **JEG**

A limited edition Hazle Ceramics 'A Pet is for Life' wall plaque, from an edition of 800.

Based on a 16thC farmhouse in Epping, currently used as a master saddlers.

1997-2001

6.5in (16.5cm) high

£200-250   **JEG**

FIND OUT MORE...

www.hazle.com, official company website.

COLLECTORS' NOTES

■ The Louis Hudson pottery was founded in Trethevy, near Bodmin, Cornwall in 1971. In the early 1970s he produced a range of art pottery, much of which bears a striking resemblance to Troika. These pieces are gaining in popularity today.

■ His pieces typically feature heavy geometric mouldings reminiscent of runes or hieroglyphics. They usually have bands of patterns – often circular or arched, sometimes echoing the shape of the piece itself. The textures and muted earthy tones of his work reflect Cornish ceramics of the period.

■ He worked in stoneware and developed a range of glazes using natural minerals. His stoneware glazes, which are buff green and beige colour, are still commonly used today.

■ His pieces are usually marked with his initials in lowercase. Look out for a tiny "lh" impressed close to the base.

■ Hudson left the pottery to become a truck driver in 1983. The pottery became Presingoll in 1998 and relocated to Bodmin, Cornwall. It is now owned by Hudson's brother, and produces tableware.

A Louis Hudson lamp base, with typical moulded runic symbols and circular design, hand-painted on base "Trethevy".

The similarity to Troika, in terms of form, is striking.

12.5in (31.5cm) high

£40-60　　　　　　**GC**

A Louis Hudson lamp base, with moulded circular boss to top and semi-circular motifs to base, with impressed "lh" monogram.

10.5in (27cm) high

£40-60　　　　　　**GC**

A Louis Hudson wheel-shaped lamp base with moulded circular designs to one side and runic/hieroglyphic designs to the reverse.

Hudson's larger pieces, such as lamp bases, are the most sought-after. The wheel shape is fairly common, but is a hallmark form, so is still sought after.

8.75in (22cm) high

£25-35　　　　　　**GC**

A tall Louis Hudson lamp base, with runic symbols and circular designs and "lh" monogram impressed by base.

11.75in (30cm) high

£40-60　　**GC**

A tall cylindrical Louis Hudson vase with protruding band of moulded runic symbols, impressed "lh" stamp to base.

9.5in (24cm) high

£60-80　　**GC**

A small Louis Hudson rectangular vase, with two moulded semi-circles of runes and lines.

6in (15cm) high

£25-30　　**GC**

A small Louis Hudson rectangular vase with three bands of runic patterns and semi-circular linear pattern.

5in (13cm) high

£20-25　　**GC**

COLLECTORS' NOTES

■ Inspired by drawings of children by a nun, Sister Berta Hummel, Goebel's 'Hummel' figurines were first produced in 1935. Over the years, more than 500 different figurines have been released. Marks on the base help identify the name and the period in which a particular piece was made.

■ Since 1935, there have been many changes to the Hummel trademark. Early pieces, denoted by 'Crown' marks and marks with a large bee motif, can be particularly valuable. From 1950, the bee design became smaller in size and its position was altered to sit inside the V shape. The bee motif was dropped after 1964, in favour of text, and a large 'G' dominated the mark from 1972.

■ Unusual and rare variations are sought-after and can fetch high prices. Look for variations in colour of certain parts of clothing. Early Hummel examples from the 1930s-50s are also popular. Larger examples – above 6in (15cm) in size – are also more valuable.

■ The dates for pieces shown here relate to the period each piece was produced in, using its mark, and often its size, to help date it. Buyers should remember that some designs are still in production today.

■ The bisque chips and cracks easily, so examine figurines carefully for damage or repair, as this will reduce value. Pieces can bruise when stored against each other, so care must be taken in display.

A Hummel 'Little Gardener' figure, No. 74, marked "Germany" in black.

1940-59   4.25in (11cm) high

£30-50   **AAC**

A Hummel 'A Stitch in Time' figure, No. 255.

1964-72   6.25in (17cm) high

£50-70   **AAC**

A Hummel 'Sister' figure, No. 98, marked "Germany" in black, no decimal.

1940-59 5.75in (14.5cm) high

£40-60   **AAC**

A Hummel 'School Girl' figure, No. 81/2/0, marked with an incised circle and "Germany" in black.

1940-59   4.25in (11cm) high

£35-45   **AAC**

A Hummel 'The Weary Wanderer' figure, No. 204, full bee mark, some restoration to the back of the head, stamped "204".

Look for the rare variation with blue coloured eyes as they can be worth over £1,000.

c1949

6in (15.5cm) high

£70-90   **EAB**

A Hummel 'Valentine Gift' figure, No. 387, exclusive special edition for the Hummel Collectors' Club, crazing under base.

1977-79 5.75in (14.5cm) high

£50-70   **AAC**

A late 1930s Hummel 'Happiness' figure, No. 86, marked "Germany" in black, repaired.

4.75in (12cm) high

£18-22   **AAC**

CERAMICS

A Hummel 'Little Gabriel' figure, No. 32/0, incised circle, marked "Western Germany" in black, damage.

1958-72   5in (12.5cm) high

£25-35   **AAC**

A Hummel 'Mother's Helper' figure, No. 133, incised circle, marked "Germany" in black.

1940-59   5in (12.5cm) high

£60-80   **AAC**

A Hummel 'Signs of Spring' figure, No. 203/2/0, incised circle, marked "Western Germany" in black.

1958-1972   4in (10cm) high

£40-60   **AAC**

A Hummel 'Friends' figure, No. 136/I, incised circle.

1958-72   5in (12.5cm) high

£60-80   **AAC**

A Hummel 'Doll Mother' figure, No. 67, marked with an incised circle and "Germany" in black.

1940-59   4.75in (12cm) high

£70-90   **AAC**

A Hummel 'Farewell' figure, No. 65/I.

1958-72   4.75in (12cm) high

£50-70   **AAC**

A Hummel 'Favorite Pet' figure, No. 361.

All examples carry a 1960 copyright date, although the model was not released for sale until the 1964 New York City World's Fair. Examples with earlier stamps can be found and are often worth significantly more.

c1964   4.25in (11cm) high

£120-180   **MAC**

A Hummel 'Angel Serenade' figure, No. 214D.

1958-72   3in (7.5cm) high

£18-22   **AAC**

A Hummel 'Book Worm' figure, No. 8, base chip.

1972-79   4in (10cm) high

£25-35   **AAC**

CERAMICS

A Hummel 'Street Singer' figure, No. 131.

1960-72   4.75in (12cm) high

£35-45   **WDL**

A Hummel 'Baker' figure, No. 128, crazing and some rubbing.

1958-72   4.75in (12cm) high

£30-40   **AAC**

A Hummel 'Soldier Boy' figure, No. 332, with blue cap badge, painter's signature for 1994.

1994   6in (15cm) high

£70-90   **WDL**

A Hummel 'Village Boy' figure, No. 51.

c1972   4.75in (9.5cm) high

£50-70   **EAB**

A larger Hummel 'Doctor' figure, No. 127.

1991-99   5.25in (13cm) high

£45-55   **WDL**

A Hummel 'Lost Sheep' figure, No. 68 2/0, marked with painter's signature.

1991-99   4.75in (12cm) high

£22-28   **WDL**

A Hummel 'Little Hiker' figure, No. 16/2/0, marked with an incised circle and "Germany" in black.

1940-59   4.25in (11cm) high

£30-50   **AAC**

A Hummel 'Chimney Sweep' figure, No. 12/2/0, base crazing.

1972-79   4in (10cm) high

£18-22   **AAC**

A Hummel 'Merry Wanderer' figure, No. 11, slight scratch to the umbrella, stamped "11".

c1964-72   4.5in (11cm) high

£50-70   **EAB**

A Hummel 'The Builder' figure, No. 305.

1964-72   5.5in (14cm) high

£35-45 AAC

A Hummel 'Good Hunting' figure, No. 307.

1972-79 5.25in (13.5cm) high

£70-90 AAC

A Hummel 'The Artist' figure, No. 304, some crazing.

1972-79 5.25in (13.5cm) high

£40-60 AAC

A Hummel 'Little Pharmacist' figure, No. 322, painter's signature for 1998.

1991-99   6in (15cm) high

£60-70 WDL

A Hummel 'Begging His Share' figure, No. 9, with hole in cake.

1958-64   5.5in (14cm) high

£40-60 AAC

A Hummel 'Grandpa's Boy' figure, No. 562, wrong colour trousers, mark since 1991, painter's signature from 1994.

1991-99   4.5in (11cm) high

£50-70 WDL

A Hummel 'She Loves Me, She Loves Me Not' figure, No. 174, incised crown mark, marked "Made in U.S. Zone Germany" in black in an oval, repaired.

1945-50   4.25in (11cm) high

£30-50 AAC

A Hummel 'Apple Tree Boy' figure, No. 142/3/0, some rubbing.

1958-72   4in (10cm) high

£25-35 AAC

A Hummel figurine 'Playmates', No. 58 2/0, painter's signature for 1998.

1991-99   3.75in (9.5cm) high

£35-45 WDL

A Hummel 'Culprits' figure, No. 56/B, full bee mark appearing below the tips of the 'V'.

Later examples are painted with the boys eyes downcast towards the dog, there is no significant difference in value between these two versions.

1972-79   *6.75in (17cm) high*

£100-170   **AGO**

A Hummel 'Bird Duet' figure, No. 169.
1972-79   *4in (10cm) high*

£40-60   **AAC**

A CLOSER LOOK AT A HUMMEL FIGURE

The Merry Wanderer was one of the original 46 figures released in 1935.

This figure was made in a range of sizes, the larger sizes are generally more valuable.

The jumbo 32in figure, often used as a promotional figure, is the most sought-after.

It was modelled by master sculptor Arthur Moeller.

A Hummel 'Merry Wanderer' large figure, No. 7/II.
1972-79   *9.5in (24cm) high*

£200-300   **AAC**

A Hummel 'Volunteers' figure, No. 50/2/0, marked "Germany" in black, chip to base.

1940-59   *5in (12.5cm) high*

£30-50   **AAC**

A Hummel 'Smart Little Sister' figure, No. 346.

1964-72   *4.75in (12cm) high*

£45-55   **AAC**

A Hummel 'Forest Shrine' figure, No. 183, base crazing.

1972-79   *9in (23cm) high*

£80-120   **AAC**

A Hummel 'Guardian Angel' holy water font, No. 29/0, incised circle, marked "Western Germany" in black, discontinued.

1958-72 5.75in (14.5cm) high

£50-80   **AAC**

COLLECTORS' NOTES

■ Italian ceramics of the 1950s-70s are growing in popularity along with West German ceramics. They are typified by bright colours reminiscent of the Mediterranean and the use of sgraffito – where a design is engraved into the surface using a stylus. However, even less is currently known about most Italian ceramics than their West German cousins.

■ The most commonly found examples have a strong aqua blue glaze, often with a green tinge. The surface is decorated with bands of impressed symbols including crosses and ovals. These are from the Rimini Blu range, designed by Aldo Londi (1911-2003) in 1953 and today are still produced by Bitossi of Montelupo, Italy. A large number of different, modern shapes, some based on the baluster form were produced, as well as characteristic rectangular vases. A wide range of highly stylized, and often humourous, animal forms was also made. These tend to be the most valuable and desirable today.

■ Bitossi use an impressed shield-shaped mark but most examples found tend to be stamped or painted 'Made in Italy' and bear a series of numbers. These were made to be exported, with Hutcheson & Sons Ltd of London responsible for the UK market and Raymor for the US, during the 1960s.

■ Raymor, known first as Richards Morgenthau, were founded by Irving Richards (1907-2003) and his partners, and had showrooms on Fifth Avenue, New York, and Chicago. They became known throughout the 1950s-70s for bringing affordable modern designs to the public, such as Russel Wright's 'American Modern' ceramics range. Italy was also a focus and they imported pieces by Fantoni and others, which are often found with Raymor labels.

■ Look for large undamaged examples with eye appeal. The market is still emerging and will undoubtedly develop over the next few years as more information is discovered. Colourful designs that take more skill to create are more likely to be of value in the future.

A 1960s-70s Bitossi 'Rimini Blu' vase, designed by Aldo Londi, impressed "727/21 Made in Italy", with Hutcheson & Sons importer's label.

8.5in (21.5cm) high

£40-60   GC

A 1960s-70s Bitossi 'Rimini Blu' large baluster vase, designed by Aldo Londi, decorated in the 'Spagnolo' pattern, with "Made in Italy" paper label.

14in (35.5cm) high

£50-70   GC

A 1960s-70s Bitossi 'Rimini Blu' large rectangular vase, designed by Aldo Londi, with bands of impressed symbols, the base with painted marks "727/30 TTR".

12in (30.5cm) high

£50-70   GC

A 1960s-70s Bitossi 'Rimini Blu' lampbase, designed by Aldo Londi, with plain bands and bands of impressed symbols.

10.5in (26.5cm) high

£50-70   GC

A 1960s-70s Bitossi 'Rimini Blu' lampbase, designed by Aldo Londi, impressed with bands of symbols.

6in (15cm) high

£25-35   GC

A 1960s-70s Bitossi 'Rimini Blu' large round bowl, designed by Aldo Londi, with bands of impressed symbols, the base with painted marks "501/24 Tiny".

9in (23cm) diam

£40-60   GC

CERAMICS

A pair of 1960s-70s Bitossi 'Rimini Blu' small dish candlesticks, designed by Aldo Londi, impressed with bands of symbols, both bases impressed "Italy".

4.25in (10.5cm) diam

£30-40   **GC**

A 1960s-70s Bitossi 'Rimini Blu' hippopotamus figurine, designed by Aldo Londi, and decorated in the 'Spagnolo' pattern.

8.25in (21cm) long

£40-60   **GC**

A 1960s-70s Bitossi 'Rimini Blu' cylindrical cat, designed by Aldo Londi, with disc-shaped face, impressed with bands of symbols.

15.75in (40cm) long

£120-180   **GC**

A 1950s-60s Italian tapering bullet-shaped vase, hand-painted with random multicoloured, textured squares outlined with black lines on a pastel blue ground, the base painted "Italy 6679".

Along with many other examples marked simply "Italy" and a number, the makes are not yet know.

8.75in (22.5cm) high

£20-30   **GC**

A 1960s-70s Bitossi 'Rimini Blu' bird figurine, designed by Aldo Londi, inscribed by hand to mimic feathers.

6in (15cm) long

£40-60   **GC**

Λ 1960s-70s Bitossi 'Rimini Blu' stylized hen sculpture, designed by Aldo Londi, impressed with bands of symbols.

8.75in (22cm) high

£60-90   **GC**

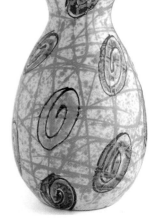

A 1950s-60s Italian factory tapering vase, hand-painted with random multicoloured, textured squares outlined with black lines on a pastel pink ground, the base painted "Italy 6807".

8.25in (21cm) high

£20-30   **GC**

A 1950s-60s Italian factory gourd-shaped vase, hand-painted with random cross hatched lines and multicoloured spots, the base painted "013 Italy 5/11".

5.5in (14cm) high

£15-25   **GC**

A 1950s-60s Italian factory baluster vase, hand-painted in glossy glazes with random grey lines and multicoloured swirls, the base painted "Italy 7965".

8in (20cm) high

£20-30   **GC**

A 1950s-60s Italian factory tapering cylinder vase, incised and hand-painted with a central floral band, scored cross hatched areas and lines, and green bands, the base painted "Italy 6648".

A 1950s-60s Italian factory baluster vase, hand-painted with white, red, yellow and blue glazed stripes and circles, each with black outlines, the base painted "Italy".

8.5in (21.5cm) high

£35-45　　　　　**GC**

A 1950s-60s Italian factory small waisted vase, with satin finish, hand-painted zig-zag, dash and circle design on a white ground, the base painted "Italy 7456".

6in (15cm) high

£15-25　　　　　**GC**

This incised or scored technique, speckled textured background and thickly laid on coloured glaze is typical of these types of Italian ceramics of the period, as are the bright, Mediterranean colours.

8in (20cm) high

£15-25　　　　　**GC**

A 1950s-60s Italian factory cylindrical jug, brightly hand painted with stylized suns and linear, crennelated designs in bands, inscribed "M" or "W" on the base.

11.5in (29cm) high

£25-35　　　　　**GC**

A 1950s-60s Italian factory baluster vase, with hand-painted design of stylized Mediterranean houses on a textured matte beige ground, the base painted "Italy".

10in (24.5cm) high

£50-70　　　　　**GC**

A 1950s-60s Italian factory vase, with hand inscribed and hand-painted stylized Africans, glossily glazed over a brown ground with incised lines, the base painted "Italy 7894".

7.75in (19.5cm) high

£30-50　　　　　**GC**

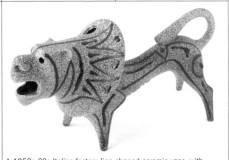

A 1950s-60s Italian factory ceramic dish, hand-painted with a tree and house design, with a volcanic base.

West German factories such as Ruscha were also producing similar ceramics decorated with exotic scenes at this time. West German examples tend to be marked on the back with inscriptions and pattern names.

11.5in (29.5cm) wide

£18-22　　　　　**MTS**

A 1950s-60s Italian factory lion-shaped ceramic vase, with mottled stone-effect glazed decoration and painted multicoloured lines, the underbelly marked "RR ITALY".

12.25in (31cm) long

£30-50　　　　　**MTS**

CERAMICS

COLLECTORS' NOTES

■ Josef Originals was founded in Arcadia, California by Murial Joseph George in 1945 and went on, like so many US potteries in the post war period, to become both successful and prolific. The spelling of the name came about when 'Joseph' was misspelt on the first labels, which could not be amended.

■ The 'Birthday Doll' collection was the first range released, with George herself designing this, and the vast majority of the figurines, until her retirement. Ladies, girls, and a few animals dominated production until around 1960 when production moved to Japan. The range was then expanded to include household objects such as laundry sprinklers and planters.

■ Production moved again to Taiwan and then Korea, and in 1982 Murial Joseph George retired. The company was sold to Applause in 1985, which continues to produce the much-loved 'Birthday Doll' range today. These more modern figurines are of little interest to collectors and usually fetch under £12.

■ The lady and girl figurines produced in California before 1960 are the most desirable and valuable and can fetch over £80. These are followed in popularity by figurines produced from the 1960s to c1985, with the later Korean examples being the least valuable. Household wares are popular and also appeal to kitchenalia collectors.

■ Learn how to spot early examples made in California. Labels will often help to date a piece, as they can indicate the country of manufacture. Look out for large figurines with complex moulded details such as roses or a butterfly. Damage affects value considerably, so examine protruding parts, such as arms, the neck or a birthday number, for signs of repair.

A Josef Originals large figurine, with violet dress and a basket of flowers.

A 1960s Japanese Josef Originals 'Charmaine' figurine, the base inscribed/stamped "A Josef Original C".

7in (18cm) high

£50-70   **DAC**

A Josef Originals 'Sylvia' figurine, with blue dress highlighted with gold-coloured glitter.

This is a large and well-painted vintage figurine and has comparatively complex features such as the arms, sleeves, hairstyle, basket, and gilt detailing to her dress.

8.75in (22cm) high

5.75in (14.5cm) high

£70-100   **DAC**   **£40-50**   **DAC**

A Josef Originals 'Russia' figurine.

A Josef Originals figurine, with pink dress, decorated with gold-coloured bows and rhinestones.

A Josef Originals 'Spring' figurine, with butterflies, original card swing tag.

4in (10cm) high

4.5in (11.5cm) high

6in (15cm) high

£25-35   **DAC**   **£30-40**   **DAC**   **£40-50**   **DAC**

CERAMICS

A Josef Originals yellow girl figurine, for November.

3.75in (9.5cm) high

£18-22 DAC

A CLOSER LOOK AT A JOSEF ORIGINALS FIGURINE

Hairstyles can help date a figurine.

Small black eyes are another feature of examples produced until the early 1980s.

She has a Coralene edged dress, showing she dates from before 1960. The easily worn Coralene is also largely intact.

The sprinkled gilt highlights are again a sign of an early date before 1960.

A Josef Originals 8th birthday figurine, the base incised "Josef Originals C".

c1950 5in (12.5cm) high

£15-20 DAC

A Josef Originals small figurine of a girl, in a yellow dress and bobble hat, made in California.

c1950 3.5in (9cm) high

£25-35 DAC

A Josef Originals 14th birthday figurine.

This series is popular as children were given one every year as a present. Higher numbers towards 20 can be more valuable, probably as many girls had grown out of them by then.

6in (15cm) high

£25-35 DAC

A Josef Originals graduation present figurine, of an angel in a pink graduation gown and hat, with gilt detailing.

4.25in (10.5cm) high

£25-35 DAC

An unusual Josef Originals bust, with waisted stem.

The rhinestones are an early feature, and the faux pearls make her more desirable.

6in (15cm) high

£30-40 DAC

FIND OUT MORE...

Josef Originals: Charming Figurines, by Dee Harris, Jim & Kaye Whittaker, published by Schiffer Publishing, 1999.

Josef Originals: A Second Look, by Jim & Kaye Whittaker, published by Schiffer Publishing, 2000.

CERAMICS

COLLECTORS' NOTES

■ Founded in 1953 in Almacera, Spain, by three brothers, Lladró has produced over 4,000 designs since its inception. Over 1,200 are still available, with figurines being retired annually. The Nao company was established in 1968 as part of the Lladró group.

■ Pastel colours and a high gloss glaze are typical. The scarcer matte glaze is prized. A third 'Gres' finish, similar to stoneware, is often used for large pieces. Early pre-production pieces have a plain creamy finish and are sought-after and valuable, as are early pieces from the 1950s-70s. Limited editions, retired designs, or pieces with a short production period can fetch higher prices due to their comparative rarity.

■ Fakes are known to exist, so check the base for marks. Pieces from the 1950s are rare and usually have incised marks. Standardized impressed and incised marks were used from c1960. From 1971 the familiar blue stamp was used, but lacked the accent over the 'o' until 1974, when the version still used today was introduced.

■ Examine pieces carefully for damage or repair, as this reduces value considerably. Consider the facial expression, which should be full of character and individuality, something Lladró is known for. Lladró never use black to mark out eyes, brows and lids, a fact that can help identify fakes.

A Lladró large bust modelled as a young girl, in pastel tones of brown, grey and cream, printed mark to underside.

16.5in (42cm) high

£150-200   **ROS**

A Lladró 'Little Jester' figurine, 5203M, designed by Juan Huerta.

1984-92   7.75in (19.5cm) high

£150-200   **KCS**

A Lladró 'Baby with Pacifier' limited edition figure, 5102G, designed by Salvador Debón.

1982-85   6.5in (16.5cm) high

£150-200   **KCS**

A Lladró 'Reclining Angel' figure, 4541, designed by Fulgencio García.

Intro. 1969   2.5in (6cm) high

£30-50   **AAC**

A Lladró 'Angels Wondering' figure, 4962G/M, with matte finish, designed by Salvador Debón.

1977-91
    5.5in (14cm) high

£40-60   **AAC**

A Lladró 'Soldier on Stand' figure, 1163G, designed by Vincento Martinez.

1971-78   *12in (30.5cm) high*

£280-320   **KCS**

A CLOSER LOOK AT A LLADRÓ FIGURE

Based on the TV cartoon character 'Sport Billy', this figure is from a range featuring Billy playing a range of sports, as well as a 'Lilly Football Player' figure for his companion, 'Sport Lilly'.

A Lladró 'Soccer Player Puppet' figure, 4967, designed by Juan Huerta.

1977-85   8.25in (21cm) high

£150-250   KCS

A Lladró 'Hang On!' figure, 5665, designed by Francisco Catalá.

1990-95   6in (15cm) high

£80-120   AAC

A Lladró 'Olympic Puppet' figure, 4968G, designed by Juan Huerta, commemorating the Madrid Olympics, with stand.

1977-83   9.75in (25cm) high

£700-900   KCS

This is one of Lladró's 'puppet' figures, which differ from their traditional, more natural figures. They can be overlooked as they bear such little resemblance to other Lladró examples.

They are particularly sought-after in the US, where the cartoon was fairly popular, although collectors often favour the more traditional figures.

Production was limited to only one year, making these figures harder to find.

A Lladró 'Billy Football Player' figure, 5135G, designed by José Roig, for the US Market, production limited to one year.

c1982   9in (23cm) high

£250-300   KCS

A Lladró 'Boy with Dog' figure, 4522, designed by Vincente Martínez.

1970-77   7.5in (19cm) high

£120-150   KCS

A Lladró 'Pick of the Litter' figure, 7621, an 'event' piece, designed by Salvador Debón.

1993   7.5in (18cm) high

£120-180   AAC

A Lladró 'Behave!' figure, 5703, designed by Juan Huerta.

1990-94   6in (15cm) high

£80-120   AAC

CERAMICS

A Lladró 'New Playmates' figure, 5456G, designed by Antonio Ramos.

1988-2004   *4.75in (12cm) high*

£120-180   **KCS**

A Lladró 'Study Buddies' figure, 5451, designed by Regino Torrijos.

Introduced 1988   *4in (10cm) wide*

£100-120   **AAC**

A Lladró 'Bedtime Buddies' figure, 6541, designed by José Javier Malavia.

1998-2004   *3.5in (9cm) high*

£60-80   **AAC**

A Lladró 'Dog' figure, 4583G, designed by Fulgencio Garcia.

1969-81   *7in (18cm) high*

£120-180   **BIG**

A Lladró 'Dog' figure, 4583G, designed by Fulgencio Garcia.

1969-81   *7in (18cm) high*

£120-180   **BIG**

A Lladró 'Sea Lore' pipe, 5613, designed by Julio Ruiz.

1989-93   *3in (7.5cm) high*

£250-350   **KCS**

FIND OUT MORE...

Collecting Lladró: Identification & Price Guide, by Peggy Whiteneck, published by Krause, 2003.

Lladró Authorised Reference Guide, by Lladró, published by Lladró US Inc., 2000.

www.lladro.com – official company website, with searchable 'historic' catalogues.

A Lladró 'Dog in Basket' figurine, 1128G, designed by Juan Huerta.

1971-85 7.25in (18.5cm) high

£250-300   **KCS**

A Lladró 'Heaven's Lullaby' figurine, 6583, designed by Antonia Ramos.

Introduced 1998

£120-180   **KCS**

COLLECTORS' NOTES

- The Lotus Pottery was founded in 1958 at Old Stoke Farm, Devon, by Leeds College of Art graduates Michael and Elizabeth Skipworth. It was initially known as the Loversall Pottery, becoming known as Lotus Pottery after their move to Stoke Gabriel, near Totnes, Devon.

- Their most typical and popular colourway was a grey/green colour, usually in a daisy motif, on a deep sage green ground. Other colours include speckled blue-on-blue, blue-on-white, known as 'Loire' and introduced in 1974, white-on-red and a speckled green colour. The natural motifs and colourways saw great success, particularly during the 1970s.

- Shapes tend to be rounded with clean lines and limited, or no, moulded decoration. Many pieces are stamped with an 'LP' mark, but many are not, particularly if the stamp would have interrupted the form or decoration. Larger pieces, decorative items and those in typical patterns with stylised shapes tend to be the most popular and valuable. The pottery declined during the 1980s and finally closed in 1999.

A Lotus Pottery tapering sugar sifter, with sponged daisy motif.

5.5in (13.5cm) high

£8-12   DSC

A Lotus Pottery tapering salt shaker, with sponge-printed daisy motif.

3.25in (8cm) high

£3-5   DSC

A Lotus Pottery waisted vase, with sponged daisy motif.

8in (20cm) high

£25-35   DSC

A Lotus Pottery large bull figure, with printed daisy motifs.

These bulls were made in different sizes from 5in (13cm) to 13in (33cm) long. Decoration varies and includes moulded 'hair' on the head, a fern leaf, rings and daisies. Colours vary from grey-green to olive-green and a deep blue. They are not usually marked, and are among Lotus' most desirable shapes.

13in (33cm) long

£50-80   DSC

A Lotus Pottery small bull figure, with sponged interlocking ring design.

6in (15.5cm) long

£20-30   DSC

A Lotus Pottery bird figure, with sponged daisy motif.

This is a scarce shape.

6.25in (16cm) high

£30-40   DSC

A Lotus Pottery bun-shaped sugar sifter, with sponged daisy motif.

3.25in (8cm) diam

£8-12   DSC

COLLECTORS' NOTES

■ W.R. Midwinter was founded in 1910, moving to Burslem, Staffordshire in 1914. Art Deco style tableware such as tea sets dominated production until WWII. The company's turning point came in the late 1940s, when the factory began to modernise. By 1950, Roy Midwinter had risen through the company to become Sales and Design Director and he encouraged new, young designer Jessie Tait, who had joined in 1946, to develop her designs.

■ Inspired by innovative modern ceramic designs by US designers such as Eva Zeisel and Russel Wright, Midwinter's 'Stylecraft' shape and range was launched in 1953, with a variety of modern patterns designed by Tait. Some were hand-painted. This was followed by the 'Fashion' range in 1955, which saw even more

modern and clean-lined shapes being introduced. The ranges were aimed at, and popular with, young homemakers.

■ Look for patterns that sum up the style and feeling of the day as these are usually the most popular. Period textiles were often an inspiration. Abstract patterns and highly stylized floral, fruiting or foliate designs are typical, usually executed in bright colours. More traditional floral designs tend to be less sought-after.

■ Characteristic pieces that combine a typically modern shape with a modern pattern are ideal. Tea cups, saucers and plates are generally worth less than vases, teapots, coffee pots and cake stands, which are harder to find as less were made. Look out for designs by notable designer Terence Conran, as these are also popular.

A Midwinter Fashion shape 'Alpine Pink' pattern transfer-printed plate.

This pattern was also produced in blue.

1960	6in (15.5cm) diam

£3-6 — FFM

A Midwinter 'Bella Vista' pattern hand-painted two-tiered cake stand, with chrome supports.

c1960	9.5in (24cm) high

£25-35 — AGR

A Midwinter Fashion shape 'Cannes' pattern plate, designed by Sir Hugh Casson, with printed and enamelled decoration.

This is a later version of the 1954 'Riviera' pattern.

1960	8.5in (22cm) diam

£10-20 — FFM

A Midwinter Fashion shape 'Cassandra' pattern transfer-printed salt and pepper pots.

1957	2.75in (7cm) high

£10-15 — FFM

A Midwinter Pottery Handcraft period 'Clay Stain' pattern vase, designed by Jessie Tait.

Produced after the restrictions of WWII, the Handcraft range was produced by a team including Jessie Tait. Much like Poole's Delphis range, the painters were given a free rein with the designs that were produced in underglaze crayons.

c1947	10.25in (26cm) high

£100-150 — GGRT

A Midwinter Stylecraft shape 'Cottage Ivy' pattern hand-painted milk jug, designed by Jessie Tait.

1953	2.25in (5.5cm) high

£15-20 — FFM

A 1970s Midwinter Stonehenge shape 'Day' pattern transfer-printed trio set, possibly designed by Eve Midwinter.

	Plate 6.75in (17.5cm) diam

£12-18 — FFM

A Midwinter Fashion shape 'Happy Valley' pattern plate, designed by Jessie Tait.

See p113 for a later example of this pattern.

1959	6in (15.5cm) diam

£8-12 — FFM

A Midwinter Fashion shape 'Happy Valley' pattern coffee pot, designed by Jessie Tait, with blue transfer-printed decoration on white glaze.

This is the later version of Happy Valley, see the previous page for the original version.

c1961   8.5in (22cm) high

£25-45   **FFM**

A Midwinter 'H.M.S. Queen Mary' novelty teapot and cover, the base with impressed and printed marks.

c1940   9.5in (24cm) wide

£250-350   **WW**

A 1950s Midwinter Pottery 'Lustre' vase, designed by Jessie Tait.

7.5in (19cm) high

£70-100   **GGRT**

A Midwinter Fashion shape 'Melody' pattern transfer-printed trio set, by an unknown designer.

1958   Plate 6in (15.5cm) diam

£35-45   **FFM**

A unusual Midwinter Stylecraft shape 'Mimosa' pattern transfer-printed trio set, by an unknown designer.

Introduced 1953 Plate 6in (15.5cm) diam

£15-20   **FFM**

A Midwinter Stylecraft 'Petula' pattern cup and saucer, with transfer-printed decoration.

Saucer 5.5in (14cm) diam

£15-25   **GROB**

A Midwinter Fashion shape 'Pierrot' pattern transfer-printed plate, designed by Jessie Tait.

1955   6.25in (16cm) diam

£25-35   **FFM**

A Midwinter Fashion shape 'Plant Life' pattern transfer-printed trio set, designed by Terence Conran.

This is the later version of the original 1954 design.

c1960   Plate 6in (15cm) diam

£40-50   **FFM**

A 1950s Midwinter Stylecraft shape 'Primavera' pattern hand-painted large meat plate, designed by Jessie Tait.

14in (35.5cm) wide

£40-60   **GAZE**

A Midwinter Fashion shape 'Quite Contrary' pattern transfer-printed plate, designed by Jessie Tait.

1959   6in (15.5cm) diam

£5-8   **FFM**

A CLOSER LOOK AT A MIDWINTER DINNER SERVICE

Casson was inspired after a holiday in the south of France to design this pattern.

The pattern was reissued on the Fashion shape in the 1960s with the name 'Cannes' and with more solid coloured turquoise pieces.

There are a number of different scenes, all based on a similar theme, reflecting the increase in holidays abroad in the 1950s.

Aimed at young newly wed couples in post-war Britain, Roy Midwinter produced starter sets of four dinner settings with other, larger pieces available singularly.

A Midwinter Stylecraft shape 'Red Domino' pattern hand-painted plate, designed by Jessie Tait.

1953   8.5in (21.5cm) diam

£10-20   **FFM**

A Midwinter Stylecraft shape 'Riviera' pattern part dinner service, designed by Hugh Casson, comprising a gravy boat, ladle and stand plate, two narrow dishes, three egg cups, cheese dish and cover, two lidded tureens, two large meat plates, six large dinner plates, water jug, six soup bowls, four dessert bowls, two plates, two breakfast cups and saucers, a coffee cup and a teapot lid.

c1954

Jug 6.25in (16cm) high

£400-600 (set)   **GAZE**

A Midwinter 'Salad Ware' transfer-printed large plate, designed by Terence Conran.

c1956

£20-30   **GAZE**

A Midwinter Stylecraft shape 'Shalimar' pattern plate, designed by Jessie Tait, with printed and enamelled decoration.

1953   9.5in (24.5cm) diam

£15-25   **FFM**

A Midwinter Stylecraft shape 'Silver Bamboo' pattern hand-painted teapot, designed by Jessie Tait, damage to inside of lid.

1953   5in (13cm) high

£15-25   **FFM**

A Midwinter Fashion shape 'Wild Geese' pattern transfer-printed plate, originally designed in 1954 by Sir Peter Scott.

1960   9.5in (24.5cm) diam

£12-18   **FFM**

A Midwinter Stonehenge shape 'Wild Oats' pattern transfer-printed milk jug, designed by Eve Midwinter.

1974 4in (10cm) high

£5-8   **FFM**

COLLECTORS' NOTES

■ William Moorcroft (1872-1945) began working at James McIntyre's Staffordshire ceramics factory in 1898. His first major designs were the 'Aurelian' and 'Florian' ranges, with their often symmetrical and Moorish-inspired floral and foliate designs, which exemplified the prevalent Art Nouveau style in ceramics.

■ Moorcroft split from McIntyre's in 1912, founding his own company with backing from London retailer Liberty & Co., who had previously sold his designs with great success. His success grew, with the company being awarded the Royal Warrant in 1929. Stylized floral designs executed in a tube-lined process with rich and deep glaze colours became the company's hallmarks.

■ Tube-lining uses liquid clay piped on to the surface of the body forming enclosed 'cells' that are filled with

liquid glaze. William died in 1945 and his son Walter took over, continuing many of his father's designs, as well as introducing designs of his own. Here, the designer of the pattern is given, if known.

■ Early ranges, including 'Florian', 'Claremont' and 'Eventide', and limited production ranges tend to be the most valuable. However, more modern and even contemporary ranges by designers such as Sally Tuffin and Rachel Bishop are also becoming sought-after.

■ Pieces can be dated to a period from the shape, size, pattern, colours and type of marks on the base. Damage affects value considerably, so inspect a piece very carefully. Patterns produced for long periods of time tend to be the least valuable, particularly if on small sized pieces.

A 1980s Moorcroft 'Anemone' pattern baluster vase, designed by William Moorcroft, die-stamped "Moorcroft made in England" on the base and signed "WM" in green slip.

10.25in (26cm) high

£150-250   **BEL**

A Moorcroft 'Anemone' pattern shallow dish, signed to the base and with paper label.

9.5in (24cm) diam

£150-200   **MAX**

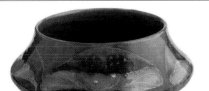

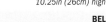

An early Moorcroft 'Claremont' pattern bowl, designed by William Moorcroft, typically decorated in shades of blue, green and red, with painted signature and date.

Claremont is a highly desirable range, registered in 1903 and named, and initially sold, by Liberty. It was produced for nearly 40 years. Later pieces have bolder rendering and stronger colours. This is also an unusual shape.

1914   7in (18cm) wide

£1,800-2,200   **GORL**

A Moorcroft 'Eventide' pattern baluster vase, designed by William Moorcroft, with a landscape design of trees against an ochre ground, cracked.

Landscape themes were popular in the 1920s and '30s. Eventide was launched in 1923.

c1925   9in (23cm) high

£750-850   **GORL**

A Moorcroft 'Coral Hibiscus' pattern baluster vase, designed by Walter Moorcroft, die-stamped "Moorcroft made in England", with a circular Moorcroft paper label.

'Hibiscus' was designed c1949 and 'Coral Hibiscus', with a single-coloured flower, was introduced in 1968.

8.25in (21cm) high

£100-200   **BEL**

A Moorcroft 'Leaf & Berries' pattern bowl, with a blue foot, impressed facsimile mark "Potter to HM The Queen".

1929-49   9in (23cm) diam

£200-400   **SWO**

A Moorcroft 'Flambé Leaves and Fruit' pattern shouldered vase.

c1928-45   4.25in (11cm) high

£400-600   **GHOU**

A Moorcroft 'Magnolia' pattern jardinière, designed by Walter Moorcroft, impressed and signed in green.

This pattern was introduced in 1976, initially in pink on blue and later also in pink on ivory, yellow and green backgrounds.

7in (18cm) high

£180-220   **MAX**

A CLOSER LOOK AT A MOORCROFT VASE

This range was designed by Philip Gibson, and was launched in 1999 to great acclaim.

The designs were complex to produce, particularly the long, flowing lines of the trout's body and the freehand dots used to create the trout's scales.

Although there are always two trout, a new design was created for each shape meaning there is more variation in design between shapes than in any other range.

The range was also expensive to produce, leading to a high retail price. The skill needed to decorate it, the low numbers produced and the great appeal of the design is likely to make it a Moorcroft classic.

A Moorcroft 'Trout' pattern squat vase, with two trout chasing a dragonfly, marked "Moorcroft Made in Stoke on Trent England" in green, the artist's mark "LB", "Copyrighted in 98" and a black "GP" stamp.

1999   *8in (20cm) wide*

£300-400   **BEL**

A pair of Moorcroft 'Meknes Night and Day' large vases, designed by Beverley Wilkes, dated "11-9-2002" and "24-3-2003".

15.5in (39.5cm) high

£800-1,200   **GHOU**

A Moorcroft ovoid 'Orchids' pattern vase, designed by William Moorcroft, with a design of multi-coloured flowers against a deep green ground, incised facsimile signature and impressed "Potter to HM The Queen".

c1935   *5in (12.5cm) high*

£200-300   **GORL**

A 1930s Moorcroft 'Pomegranate' pattern vase, of flared cylindrical form, with triple handles, impressed and signed in green.

7.5in (19cm) high

£500-600   **MAX**

A Moorcroft 'Pomegranate' pattern posy vase, designed by William Moorcroft, painted initials and impressed marks including "M32", cracked.

2.75in (7cm) high

£180-220   **GORL**

A small Moorcroft 'Spring Flowers' pattern vase, designed by William Moorcroft, with a colourful array of flowers against a deep blue ground.

4.25in (11cm) high

£150-200   **GORL**

FIND OUT MORE...

Moorcroft, by Paul Atterbury, published by Richard Dennis, 1998.

COLLECTORS' NOTES

■ Ashley Myott bought the Alexander Pottery in 1898 and renamed it Myott, Son & Co. In the late 1920s Myott expanded its range of tablewares to encompass the then new Art Deco style and introduced a range of hand-painted decorative wares. Collectors are currently most interested in this range.

■ Decorators did not sign or date their work, and a fire at the Myott factory in 1949 destroyed records and pattern books. The lack of information may explain why interest in, and values for, Myott have not risen as much as for its contemporary Clarice Cliff. However, this is changing rapidly.

■ Pieces from this popular later Art Deco period can be identified by a gold-stamped mark that was used from 1930-42. Other backstamps include the printed pattern number and an impressed number that relates to the production process.

■ The two main indicators to value are the shape and the pattern. Shapes to look out for include the 'Beaky' jugs and the 'Wedge', 'Cone' and 'Owl' vases, which can be worth up to £1,500. Red is rarely used, however browns and oranges are common, as are blues and greens. The brown and orange paint tends to flake, so check the condition carefully as this will reduce the value. Other damage also affects value, particularly on more common pieces.

A Myott hand-painted 'Round' jug, pattern no. B.A.G.100, with rare swirl decoration.

5.75in (14.5cm) high

£150-200   **NAI**

A Myott hand-painted medium 'Round' jug, pattern no. B.A.G.101.

6.5in (16.5cm) high

£250-300   **NAI**

A Myott large 'Round' jug, pattern no. B.A.G.91.

7in (17.5cm) high

£250-350   **NAI**

A Myott hand-painted large 'Danté' jug, pattern no. 9804.

£120-160   **NAI**

A set of three Myott hand-painted 'Danté' jugs, pattern no. B.A.G.1.

Individually, the large version would be worth £120-160, the medium version would be worth £100-140 and the small version would be worth £80-120. These jugs were never originally sold or available as sets.

£350-450 (set)   **NAI**

A Myott hand-painted large 'Classic' jug, unnumbered.

This pattern is only found on this shape

£80-120   **NAI**

A Myott hand-painted 'Balloon Tree' pattern 'Classic' jug, pattern no. 1143F.0.

£120-180   **NAI**

A Myott hand-painted large 'Pinchtop' jug, pattern no. 8509.

8in (20cm) high

£80-120   **NAI**

A Myott hand-painted 'Doric' jug, pattern no. 9410.

7.25in (18.5cm) high

£80-120   NAI

A Myott hand-painted large 'Conical' jug, pattern no. 8496, with moulded decoration.

8in (20cm) high

£80-120   NAI

A Myott hand-painted medium 'Squareneck' jug, pattern no. 8952.

8.5in (22cm) high

£150-200   NAI

A Myott hand-painted 'Scroll' jug, pattern no. 9041.

£350-450   NAI

A Myott hand-painted 'Top Hat' vase, pattern no. 974?, decorated a with rare landscape scene.

Landscapes are much less common than stylized flowers or geometric patterns.

8.5in (21.5cm) high

£200-250   NAI

A Myott hand-painted 'Wavy Rim' vase, pattern no. P9647, with honey glaze and streaked flowers, marked with Reg'd design no. 779153.

The overhanging sections are very easily damaged.

6.75in (17cm) high

£230-350   NAI

A Myott hand-painted small dressing table candleholder, pattern no. 8834.

£30-50   NAI

A Myott hand-painted 'Torpedo' vase, pattern no. 8980.

This shape is one of the most sought-after.

8.5in (22cm) high

£400-500   NAI

A Myott hand-painted 'Diamond' vase, unnumbered.

6in (15.5cm) high

£180-220   NAI

CERAMICS

COLLECTORS' NOTES

■ Carter & Co. Pottery of Poole began producing domestic ware in 1921, through their subsidiary company, Carter, Stabler & Adams. Pieces by key designer Truda Adams (later Carter), typically hand-painted with Art Deco or floral designs, are desirable.

■ After WWII, Alfred Burgess Read became chief designer. He worked with thrower Guy Sydenham and painter Ruth Pavely to create effectively unique hand-thrown and hand-decorated pieces. Read's Swedish-inspired 1950s Contemporary range, with its bold stripes and wavy lines, is prized by collectors.

■ In 1958 Robert Jefferson became resident designer. With Sydenham and Tony Morris he developed the Delphis range, bridging the gap between commercial ware and studio pottery. Typifying the 1960s and '70s with its bright colours and organic, abstract designs, Delphis has become popular with collectors today.

■ The Craft Section, set up in 1966, increased production of studio pottery and other decorative ranges such as Aegean, Ionian and Atlantis. Aegean, introduced in 1970, featured a dark colour palette and a variety of decorating techniques.

■ Poole Studio Pottery underwent a renaissance in the mid-1990s. Look out for pieces by Sir Terry Frost, Sally Tuffin, Janice Tchalenko and Charlotte Mellis.

A Poole Pottery 'KS' pattern vase, by Eileen Prangnell, impressed "Poole England", painted artist cipher and "KS", small nick to base rim.

1924-37   6in (15cm) high

£100-200   WW

A Poole Pottery 'ED' pattern vase, shape 267, painted by Phyllis Ryall, with water staining.

Water staining is common, as these vases were bought to be used. Perfect examples are very sought-after.

1928-37 5.75in (14.5cm) high

£40-60   KCS

A Poole Pottery 'HE' pattern vase, shape 203, painted by Ruth Pavely, with the early swastika mark.

This pattern is better known as the 'Bluebird' pattern and was designed by Truda Adams. Popular paintress Pavely used a swastika painter's mark from 1922 until 1937 when she changed it, presumably due to its adoption by Nazi Germany. Pieces bearing this mark are more desirable those with the mark she used afterwards.

1922-37

£200-300   KCS

A 1930s Carter, Stabler & Adams Poole Pottery vase, with floral decoration.

6.5in (16.5cm) high

£30-50   GOR

A Poole Pottery 'CO' pattern trial vase, shape 969, pattern designed by Truda Carter, painted by Hilda Hampton, with hexagonal trial mark.

Trial pieces are more desirable than standard pieces and may show extreme or very subtle variations on the standard line.

1930-34

£120-180   KCS

A pair of Poole Pottery 'BF' pattern sprig vases, shape 443, painted by Hazel Allner

These traditionally decorated vases were first made in the early 1920s. These later examples would have been made alongside more modern designs developed after WWII.

1946-57

7in (18cm) high

£100-150   KCS

A Carter, Stabler & Adams Poole Pottery 'EN' pattern vase, shape 380, painted by Margaret Holder.

This example only has painted decoration on the lower half of the vase. Examples that are fully covered with the pattern are more valuable.

1925-34   6.5in (16.5cm) high

£80-120   **KCS**

A Poole Pottery 'PC' pattern vase, shape 803, painted by Sheila Jenkins.

This is a rare shape to find as it has moulded, banded decoration.

1949-61 5.75in (14.5cm) high

£50-60   **KCS**

A 1930s Poole Pottery 'BN' pattern vase, shape 596, painted by Myrtle Bond (1927-42).

This is a rare shape and also displays the pattern well due to its size.

9in (23cm) high

£120-180   **KCS**

A Carter, Stabler & Adams Poole Pottery 'Bluebird' pattern earthenware cylindrical vase, painted by Anne Hatchard.

1922-37   10in (25.5cm) high

£60-80   **CA**

A rare and early Poole Pottery 'VE' pattern red earthenware jam pot, shape 288, painted by Dorothy James.

This rare 'Jazz' pattern is desirable. A more standard patterned jam pot would be worth upto £40. The red earthenware body was used from 1922 until 1934 when it was changed to a white body.

1924-34   4in (10cm) high

£60-80   **KCS**

A Poole Pottery 'V' pattern jam pot, shape 286, painted by Marjorie Cryer.

1934-37   4in (10cm) high

£40-60   **KCS**

A Poole Pottery 'AP' pattern bowl, shape 432, painted by Vera Mills.

1936   8in (20cm) wide

£80-120   **KCS**

A rare Carter, Stabler & Adams Poole Pottery 'RP' pattern red earthenware footed bowl, shape 495, painted by Ruth Pavely, with impressed mark.

1922-34 9.25in (23.5cm) wide

£100-150   **KCS**

A Poole Pottery 'MD' pattern red earthware trial shallow bowl, shape 413, painted by Eileen Prangnell.

It is rare to find this pattern with a bird included.

1924-37   8in (20cm) diam

£150-200   **KCS**

A 1950s Poole Pottery 'Freeform' plain carafe, shape 690, designed by Guy Sydenham.

10.5in (26.5cm) high

£100-150   **KCS**

A 1950s Poole Pottery 'Freeform' 'PJ.B' pattern vase, shape 703, the shape designed by Guy Sydenham and Alfred Read, the pattern designed by Alfred Read.

7.75in (19.5cm) high

£80-120   **GAZE**

A 1950s Poole Pottery 'PL.T' pattern waisted vase, shape 669 designed by Guy Sydenham and Alfred Read, the pattern by Read, printed mark and painted monogram.

7.75in (19.5cm) high

£150-250   **LFA**

A 1950s Poole Pottery 'PL.C' pattern Contemporary vase, shape 686 by Claude Smale and Guy Sydenham, the pattern designed by Alfred Read, impressed "98", painted marks.

9.75in (24.5cm) high

£100-150   **GAZE**

A Poole Pottery 'ROC' pattern cucumber dish, shape 555, the shape designed by John Adams c1935, the pattern designed by Ruth Pavely in 1954.

c1955   *16in (40.5cm) wide*

£30-40   **C**

A Poole Pottery 'UIL' pattern tray, shape 361, the shape designed by Alfred Read and Guy Sydenham, the pattern designed by Ruth Pavely and Ann Read, with pre-1959 back stamp.

1956-58   *7in (18cm) wide*

£25-35   **NPC**

A Poole Pottery 'Poole Whaler 1783' deep dish plate, painted by Gwen Haskins, from a design by Arthur Bradbury.

Being based in a coastal town, ships have featured on a number of pieces. Ship plates were introduced in the 1930s and can still be commissioned from the pottery today.

1950   *15in (38cm) diam*

£550-650   **C**

A Poole Pottery display plaque, designed and first painted by Ann Read in 1956.

14in (35.5cm) wide

£400-600   **C**

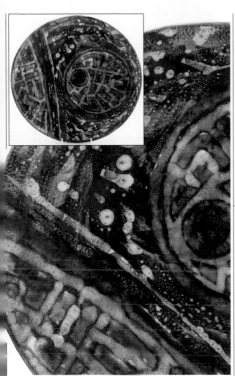

A Poole Studio Pottery small pin tray, painted in an abstract architectural green and blue design.

5in (12.5cm) wide

£70-100 C

A Poole Studio Pottery hand-thrown dish, by Guy Sydenham, with an orange ship's wheel design, marks to base.

12in (30.5cm) diam

£280-320 C

A Poole Studio Pottery charger, by Tony Morris, finished in an abstract architectural design in blue and green on a white ground, impressed "Poole Studio" to back and Tony Morris monogram to back.

1962-82　　　　　　　　*13.5in (34.5cm) diam*

£1,800-2,200 C

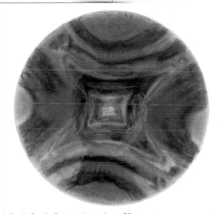

A Poole Studio Pottery plate, shape 58.

1964-66　　　　　　　　*13in (33cm) diam*

£350-450 KCS

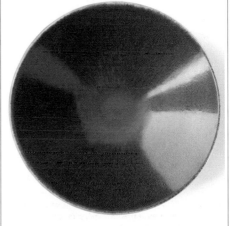

A Poole Studio Pottery bowl, decorated by Thelma Bush.

1966　　　　　　　*5in (12.5cm) wide*

£100-150 KCS

A Poole Studio Pottery plate, designed by Robert Jefferson.

1964-66　　　　　　　*8in (20cm) diam*

£80-120 KCS

CERAMICS

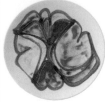

A 1960s Poole Pottery Delphis plate, painted in a swirl of colours, unknown artist.

A late 1960s Poole Pottery Delphis plate, with rare white background.

A late 1960s Poole Pottery Delphis plate, shape 4, with textured decoration.

Textured decoration is unusual, adding to the value.

A 1960s Poole Pottery Delphis shield dish, shape 91.

10.5in (26.5cm) diam

8in (20cm) diam

10.5in (26cm) diam

12in (30.5cm) long

£120-180   **C**

£60-80   **KCS**

£80-120   **KCS**

£70-90   **KCS**

A Poole Pottery Delphis bowl, painted by Thelma Bush.

The Delphis range developed out of the Studio line and this early example shows the range's heritage – the colours and design are both from the Studio line and were not officially part of the Delphis range.

1967-68   *5.5in (14cm) wide*

£120-180   **KCS**

A CLOSER LOOK AT A POOLE POTTERY CHARGER

This large charger is typical of later examples from the Delphis range.

Despite each piece being hand-painted, this symmetrical, stylized floral decoration is commonly found on later Delphis pieces.

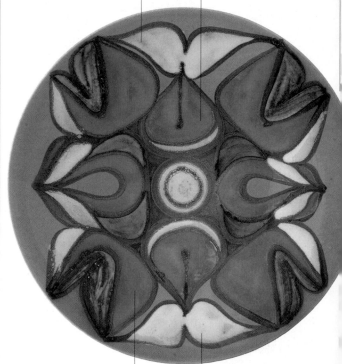

In 1971, the colour palette was refined to yellow, orange, green and red.

The large size format is ideal for displaying the pattern.

A Poole Pottery Delphis charger, painted by Cynthia Bennett.

1971-77

16in (40.5cm) diam

£200-300   **KCS**

A Poole Pottery Delphis shield dish, painted by Carol Cutler, shape 91.

Carol Cutler is one of Poole's most sought-after Delphis paintresses. The stylized 'alien face' is typical of her work.

1969-75   *12in (30.5cm) long*

£70-90   **KCS**

A Poole Pottery Delphis small vase, shape 31, painted by Carol Kellett (née Cutler), with blue and green decoration.

This vase has been decorated with two linking Cs, which are typical of Cutler's work. The use of blue and green together is unusual.

A Poole Pottery 'Delphis' vase, shape 90, painted by Jean Millership.

This is a rare shape.

1966-69   8in (20cm) high

£250-300   **KCS**

c1969

£40-60   **KCS**

A Poole Pottery Delphis vase, factory and painters mark to base.

5.5in (14cm) high

£15-25   **JN**

A rare Poole Pottery 'Delphis' hand-potted vase, shape 83, by Christine Tate.

1964-70   6in (15cm) high

£60-80   **KCS**

A rare Poole Pottery 'Delphis' carved vase, painted by Irene Kirton.

Carved decoration and the use of purple are both rare.

1968-69 15.5in (39.5cm) high

£350-450   **KCS**

An early and unusual Poole Pottery Delphis carved vase, painted by Geraldine O'Meara.

This is a very early Delphis vase, O'Meara only worked at Poole for one year. The use of carved decoration in two directions is rare.

1966   9in (23cm) high

£120-160   **KCS**

An early Poole Pottery 'Delphis' textured vase, painted by Angela Wyburgh.

The use of blue and green indicates this is from the start of the Delphis range and the textured finish is desirable. Wyburgh is a sought-after artist and her pieces are rising in value.

A Poole Pottery 'Delphis' vase, shape 84, painted by Ingrid Hammond.

This is a rare shape.

1971-73   9in (23cm) high

£100-150   **KCS**

A late 1960s Poole Pottery Delphis vase, shape 83, unmarked.

The use of deep red indicates this is an early example from the Delphis range.

5.75in (14.5cm) high

£45-60   **KCS**

c1968

15.5in (39.5cm) high

£350-450   **KCS**

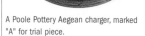

A Poole Pottery Aegean large bowl, pattern number 58.

13.5in (34.5cm) diam

£80-120 FD

A unique 1970s Poole Pottery Aegean charger, by Ros Sommerfelt.

Sommerfelt is a sought-after Aegean range paintress.

13in (33cm) diam

£300-400 KCS

A Poole Pottery Aegean charger, marked "A" for trial piece.

1974-75 12.5in (31.5cm) diam

£100-150 KCS

A 1970s Poole Pottery Aegean 'Yacht' pattern plate, shape 4.

Leslie Elsden was responsible for the creation of the Aegean range. He also designed this, one of a series of 'Yacht' patterns.

10.5in (20cm) diam

£40-60 KCS

A Poole Pottery Aegean sweet dish, shape 82.

17.25in (44cm) long

£20-40 GAZE

A Poole Pottery Aegean vase, shape 84, potted by Alan White and painted by Julie Wills.

1972-78 9in (23cm) high

£150-200 KCS

A 1970s Poole Pottery Aegean vase, shape 85, with sgraffito decoration, and 'mosaic' band.

16in (40.5cm) high

£200-250 KCS

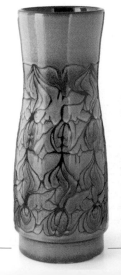

A Poole Pottery Aegean grey vase, by Carol Kellett (née Cutler), based on shape 84.

The use of grey is rare and the pattern is unusual.

1976-78

£300-500 KCS

A late 1970s Poole Pottery 'Aegean' vase, hand-potted by Alan White, with sgraffito decoration.

Alan White is considered one of Poole's best potters. The use of sgraffito to create a 'silhouette' design is common to the Aegean range.

15.75in (40cm) high

£150-200 KCS

A rare Poole Pottery Atlantis A20/3 vase, by Carol Kellett (née Cutler), marked with artist's cipher and "Poole, England".

Developed by Guy Sydenham out of the Craft Section, the Atlantis range was launched in 1969. The 'studio' style pieces were produced in muted colours on red, grey or black bodies that were often carved. Many pieces were produced by Sydenham himself.

1972-77   5.5in (14cm) high

£200-300   **FD**

A Poole Pottery Atlantis A14/1 bowl, thrown and painted by Catherine Connett.

1973-76

£30-45   **GAZE**

A Poole Pottery Ionian small stoneware bowl, with a stylized design.

This short-lived range was produced between 1974-75 and was an elaborate variation on the Aegean range. It is comparatively rare and sought-after today.

1974-75   5.75in (14.5cm) diam

£20-30   **FD**

A CLOSER LOOK AT A POOLE POTTERY VASE

The Olympus range was only produced for one year and is gaining in popularity.

The shapes and patterns were designed by Ros Sommerfelt and all feature a band of decoration, the themes usually being fruit, flowers, seeds or the seashore.

Ros Sommerfelt began working in 1970 as a paintress on the Delphis range and also painted the Aegean range. She was also responsible for developing the Beardsley and Dorset ranges.

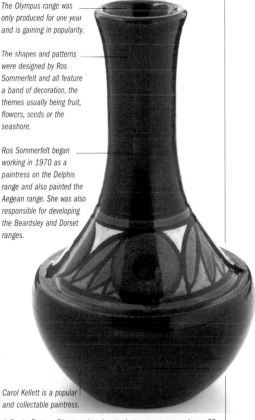

Carol Kellett is a popular and collectable paintress.

A Poole Pottery Atlantis A14/1 bowl, thrown and painted by Catherine Connett.

1973-76

£70-80   **GAZE**

A Poole Pottery Ionian vase, carved with sunrise motif, printed marks.

1974-75   12.5in (32cm) high

£200-300   **WW**

A Poole Pottery Olympus hand-potted stoneware vase, shape 63, painted and potted by Carol Kellett (née Cutler).

1975-76   6in (15cm) high

£60-80   **KCS**

CERAMICS

A Poole Studio Pottery bottle vase, hand-potted and decorated by Alan White, with seal to bottom.

The tradition of studio-type wares began in the 1920s and proved particularly successful in the 1960s when it spawned successful ranges such as Delphis and Aegean. The Poole Studio was re-established in 1995 and produces unique pieces, such as this, as well as limited editions. White has added his seal to this vase, which was reserved for special pieces.

c1995   8in (20cm) high

£150-200   **KCS**

A Poole Studio Pottery 'HX' pattern vase, by Karen Brown.

Based on the traditional patterns from the 1920s and '30s, these vases are made to order. Karen Brown first worked in the Traditional Decoration department when she joined Poole in 1973.

2004   10in (25.5cm) high

£150-180   **KCS**

A Poole Studio Pottery 'HX' pattern vase, by Sue M. Pottinger, made to order.

2004   10.25in (26cm) high

£150-180   **KCS**

A Poole Studio Pottery 'Old Harry Rocks' Athens vase, from the 'Isle of Purbeck' series designed by Karen Brown.

Introduced in 1997, the Athens vase was made exclusively for the Poole Collectors' Club.

10.5in (26.5cm) high

£80-120   **CHEF**

A limited production Poole Studio Pottery 'Fish' vase, designed by Sally Tuffin.

This vase was only made from one year.

1996   8in (20cm) high

£120-150   **KCS**

A Poole pottery terracotta owl plate, thrown and glazed by Alan White.

c1996   12in (30.5cm) diam

£150-200   **C**

A 1990s Poole Studio Pottery Egyptian plate, designed and painted by Nicola Massarella, with "NN15" date mark.

8in (20cm) diam

£70-100   **KCS**

A late 1990s Poole Studio Pottery limited edition plate, designed by Tony Morris and painted by Nicola Massarella, from an edition of 100.

14in (35.5cm) diam

£350-450   **KCS**

A Poole Pottery 'Seagull' pattern dish, designed by Sally Tuffin, dated "10/06/1998".

Made in three sizes, this, the largest size dish is the rarest and the most valuable.

1998   14in (35.5cm) diam

£220-280   **KCS**

FIND OUT MORE...

Poole Pottery, by Leslie Hayward, published by Richard Dennis, third edition 2002.

COLLECTORS' NOTES

■ The Postmodern movement, led by architects such as Ettore Sottsass, developed at Studio Alchimia during the late 1970s and boomed with the Memphis Group in the 1980s. Ceramics were an integral part of the movement. Typical styles include the use of traditional architectural and historical references and forms, bright colours, geometric designs, the use of unusual materials and a certain type of wit in combining these themes.

■ Bitossi in Italy produced many of these designers' works, and some have been re-issued since. Production is kept to a small amount, keeping prices relatively high. However, as the movement is not currently considered fashionable, bargains can still be found. In its time the movement was highly popular and representative, and is arguably yet to reach its peak on the secondary market. See p154-155 for Postmodern ceramics by Swid Powell.

An Italian Bitossi 'Vaso Calice' hand-painted ceramic goblet vase, designed by Ettore Sottsass.

This is a contemporary re-issue of Sottsass' 1960 design.

18.25in (46.5cm) high

£180-220   **GM**

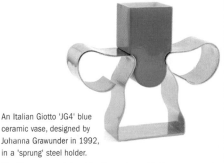

An Italian Bitossi 'Vaso Ossidante Turch' blue and oxidised copper glazed vase, designed by Ettore Sottsass, with unglazed white band under the rim and signed underneath.

This vase has been recently re-issued.

8.75in (22cm) high

£100-200   **GM**

An Italian Giotto 'JG4' blue ceramic vase, designed by Johanna Grawunder in 1992, in a 'sprung' steel holder.

The Giotto range, designed by Grawunder and Sottsass was intended to be made inexpensively in the Far East, opening this style of design up to more people. However, the deal never took off and very few examples were made, making them rare today.

c1992   9.25in (23cm) high

£500-800   **GM**

A Peter Shire hand-painted and handmade ceramic studio teapot, signed on the base "P.X. SHIR.E 1996".

1996   9in (23cm) wide

£450-550   **GM**

A 1990s Italian Bitossi 'E-Vaso' double vase, designed by Paola Palma and Carlo Vannicola in 1990, the central urn-shaped vase sliding out of the main body.

This was available in a range of colours including black and white, and burgundy and white. This green 'verdigris' glazed finish recalls weathered bronze garden urns.

9.75in (24.5cm) high

£100-150   **GM**

A set of German Ritzenhoff 'Dinner For Two' transfer-printed dinner plates, designed by Alessandro Guerriero in 1990, with original card box.

Note the use of (neo) classical sculpture as imagery.

Largest 12.75in (32cm) wide

£70-100   **GM**

CERAMICS

A Bernard Rooke brown tapered lamp base, with applied bosses, stamped "ROOKE MADE IN ENGLAND".

7.5in (19cm) high

£50-70 GC

A Bernard Rooke stoneware lamp base, impressed "ROOKE".

7in (18cm) high

£40-60 JN

A Bernard Rooke cast lamp base, decorated with applied hand-made insect and foliage decoration.

Bernard Rooke (b.1938) founded his pottery in South London in 1960. Outgrowing his premises, he moved to Suffolk where he continues to produce pottery and paintings today. Lampbases are commonly found as they were popular with the public, particularly during the 1970s and 1980s, due to their practical use in homes. Look out for very large, floor standing pieces, which can be worth £100-150, and those with added hand-made and applied decoration. A rougher feel and surface often indicates an earlier example.

16.5in (42cm) high

£80-120 FD

A Bernard Rooke tapering stoneware lamp base, impressed "ROOKE".

14in (35.5cm) high

£60-80 JN

A Bernard Rooke lamp base, impressed "ROOKE".

10.75in (27cm) high

£50-80 GC

A 1970s Bernard Rooke Studio pottery lampbase, with abstract decoration and rust-coloured glaze.

Moulded or impressed runic designs in natural clay are typical of the 1970s - for similar examples see the work of Louis Hudson, Peter Ellery at Tremaen and certain pieces by Jersey Pottery.

£80-100 MHT

A Bernard Rooke small lampbase, with beige background, brown moulded boss and two side 'panels'.

The smooth beige glaze and rough, moulded or impressed, brown decoration typifies much studio pottery produced in England around the 1970s.

7.5in (19cm) high

£35-45   GC

A Bernard Rooke stoneware oval lamp base, impressed "ROOKE".

7in (18cm) high

£40-60   JN

A Bernard Rooke circular stoneware pilgrim bottle, impressed "ROOKE".

6.5in (16.5cm) high

£40-60   JN

A Bernard Rooke large stoneware vase, decorated with owls, other birds and foliage, incised monogram.

12in (30.5cm) high

£80-120   JN

A 1980s Bernard Rooke studio ceramic frog and lily vase, incised "BR".

£25-35   GAZE

A large Bernard Rooke pottery bowl, of textured abstract form.

7in (18cm) diam

£80-120   GAZE

COLLECTORS' NOTES

- Rosenthal was founded as a porcelain decorating company in 1879, and began producing its own ceramics in 1891. Products were first marked with the company name in 1907. Quality has always been high and after WWII it began working with many notable designers, producing innovative designs, many under its higher end 'Studio Linie' brand.

- Danish designer Bjørn Wiinblad (b.1918) began designing for the company in 1957 and continues today. He is known for his poster, glass and theatrical designs as well as his ceramic designs for his own studio and Nymølle. For examples of these, please see p146. Most patterns are transfer-printed and focus on his core themes of legends, fairy tales or stories.

A 1970s/80s German Rosenthal Studio Linie vase, from the 1001 Nights series designed by Bjørn Wiinblad, with printed Rosenthal backstamp in green and Wiinblad's facsimile signature to base.

6in (15cm) high

£80-120   **RWA**

A 1970s/80 German Rosenthal Studio Linie vase, from the 1001 Nights series designed by Bjørn Wiinblad, with printed Rosenthal backstamp in green and Wiinblad's facsimile signature to base.

8in (20cm) high

£100-150   **RWA**

A 1990s German Rosenthal Studio Linie vase, from the '1001 Nights' series, designed by Bjørn Wiinblad, with printed round Rosenthal mark and Wiinblad's facsimile signature to base.

Produced from 1976-96, this was one of Wiinblad's most popular designs for Rosenthal, particularly in blue. Large vases, such as this, were expensive at the time making them rare today.

9.5in (24.5cm) high

£200-250   **RWA**

A 1970s/80s German Rosenthal Studio Linie vase, by Bjørn Wiinblad, decorated with a female figure, with Henning Hansen retailers sticker, with printed Rosenthal mark.

14.25in (36cm) high

£100-150   **RWA**

A German Rosenthal Studio Linie porcelain bottle vase, designed by Bjørn Wiinblad, with gold transfer pattern of a Chinaman in a landscape, the base with printed mark.

10.75in (27cm) high

£80-120   **L&T**

A German Rosenthal 'Romanze' ceramic vase, designed by Bjørn Wiinblad, with gold transfer floral pattern, printed marks and signature.

6.25in (16cm) high

£60-70   **TCM**

A German Rosenthal 'Romanze' ceramic dish, designed by Bjørn Wiinblad, with gold transfer floral pattern, with printed marks and signature.

£60-80   **TCM**

A German Rosenthal Studio Linie figural candlestick, designed by Bjørn Wiinblad, with circular impressed stamp to base.

More valuable blue and white hand-made designs, similar to this, were also produced at Wiinblad's personal studio in Denmark.

13in (33cm) high

£50-70   **GAZE**

A 1950s German Rosenthal white glazed vase, with printed design of stylized penguins, printed marks "Inka 3372/29".

£12-18 **GAZE**

A CLOSER LOOK AT A ROSENTHAL PLATE

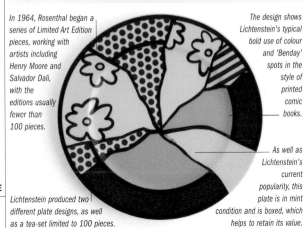

In 1964, Rosenthal began a series of Limited Art Edition pieces, working with artists including Henry Moore and Salvador Dali, with the editions usually fewer than 100 pieces.

The design shows Lichtenstein's typical bold use of colour and 'Benday' spots in the style of printed comic books.

As well as Lichtenstein's current popularity, this plate is in mint condition and is boxed, which helps to retain its value.

Lichtenstein produced two different plate designs, as well as a tea-set limited to 100 pieces.

A limited edition German Rosenthal wall plate, designed by Roy Lichtenstein, from an edition of 3,000, boxed.

12in (30.5cm) diam

£250-350 **JN**

A German Rosenthal 'Jet Rose' pattern pot, designed by Raymond Loewy, with printed marks and signature.

Raymond Loewy (1893-1986) is one of the best known Industrial designers of the 20thC and was responsible for the contoured Coca-Cola glass bottle in 1955 among other great achievements.

3.25in (8cm) high

£15-20 **TCM**

A German Rosenthal 'Pollo' Studio Linie porcelain vase, designed by Tapio Wirkkala, boxed.

Wirkkala is better known for his textured glass designs for littala.

4.75in (12cm) high

£40-50 **GAZE**

A 1960s German Rosenthal 'Studio Linie' tall cylindrical porcelain vase, designed by Hans Balimann, with intricate gold design on a black ground.

9.5in (24cm) high

£70-100 **JN**

A 1980s German Rosenthal Studio Linie 'Flash' cheese dish and cover, designed by Dorothy Hafner.

This is a well-known Postmodern design due to its use of colour, pattern and form.

7.5in (19cm) wide

£10-15 **GAZE**

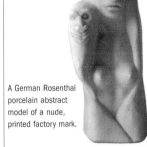

A German Rosenthal porcelain abstract model of a nude, printed factory mark.

4.75in (12cm) high

£80-120 **DN**

CERAMICS

COLLECTORS' NOTES

■ Founded by Franz Heinrich Müller in 1775, the Royal Copenhagen Porcelain Manufactory gained the patronage of Queen Juliane Marie in 1779 after severe financial problems.

■ Müller's obsession with finding the secret of hard paste porcelain lead to the company being prized by collectors for its fine, Meissen-inspired pieces. Today, collectors also look to its later works of stoneware and porcelain art ceramics. With designers such as Axel Salto and Nils Thorsson, works from the 1950s and '60s are typical of post war Scandinavian design with inspiration often being taken from the local landscape and nature. Decoration tends to be in muted, earthy or cool colours, with stylized natural or geometric designs.

■ Pieces are usually marked with the factory's three wavy line or crown marks, together with initials or a number for the painter, which can help to date a piece. Examples by popular designers are desirable, as are hand-painted pieces and those of a larger size.

A Danish Royal Copenhagen bottle with stopper, no. 4494, decorated with moulded low-relief quince and Danish crown and three line logo to each side.

£40-50   **MHT**

A Danish Royal Copenhagen crackle glaze vase, the baluster shape with flared rim decorated with iron red foliage and gilt highlights, printed and painted marks.

8.5in (21.5cm) high

£70-90   **CHEF**

A Danish Royal Copenhagen 'Tenera' bottle vase, designed by Kari Christensen.

c1969-74   9in (22.5cm) high

£40-60   **RWA**

A Danish Royal Copenhagen 'Baca' bottle vase, designed by Nils Thorsson, with tribal design in brown glaze, marked to base with printed Royal Copenhagen Crown mark, Nils Thorsson monogram, shape number 3259 and date code.

Nils Thorsson (1898-1975) worked for Royal Copenhagen from 1912 until his death. He was their most prolific and important designer and became Artistic Director.

c1969-74   9in (22.5cm) high

£70-100   **RWA**

A Danish Royal Copenhagen 'Fayance' bottle vase, designed by Nils Thorsson, painted "712/3529" and "S", and impressed "3259".

8.75in (22.5cm) high

£60-80   **GAZE**

A Danish Royal Copenhagen 'Fayance' bottle vase, designed by Nils Thorsson, painted "712/3529", impressed "3259", painted "S" and printed mark.

8.75in (22.5cm) high

£60-80   **GAZE**

A Danish Royal Copenhagen 'Fayance' pillow vase, designed by Bengt Jacobsen, painted "436/3121", impressed "3259", painted marks.

7.5in (19cm) high

£70-100   **GAZE**

A Danish Royal Copenhagen 'Tenera' pillow vase, decorated with stylized fruit and foliage, painted and printed marks.

7.5in (19cm) high

£80-120   **CHEF**

A CLOSER LOOK AT A ROYAL COPENHAGEN ANNUAL MUG

Royal Copenhagen have produced a commemorative mug every year since 1967.

They are available in two sizes, this being the larger. The smaller version is 3in (7.5cm) high.

The larger version has a metal disc set into the base for presentation inscriptions. The disc was silver until 1980 when it was replaced with pewter and then later a shiny base metal.

Examples from the first years of production are the most desirable and could be worth double.

A Danish Royal Copenhagen 'Tenera' fayance vase, designed by Kari Christensen, the compressed bottle form with hand-painted abstract design, printed and painted marks.

8.25in (21cm) high

£50-70   **CHEF**

A Danish Royal Copenhagen large annual mug for 1975, designed by Bodil Buch, decorated with an abstract design and dated 1975, with silver plaque set into base for inscription, printed marks.

4.5in (11.5cm) high

£80-120   **CHEF**

A Danish Royal Copenhagen Aluminia moon vase, by Kari Christensen, with beehive and three waves mark.

The Aluminia faïence factory acquired Royal Copenhagen in 1882, explaining the use of two names and marks.

5.25in (13.5cm) high

£20-30   **GAZE**

A Danish Royal Copenhagen 'Tenera' mug, by Inge-Lise Koefoed, with blue glazed design, marked to base with printed Royal Copenhagen backstamp, painted pattern number 454, shape number 3113, Inge-Lise Koefoed monogram and decorators mark.

c1986-89   5.5in (14cm) high

£60-70   **RWA**

A Danish Royal Copenhagen large annual mug for 1976, designed by Anne Marie Trolle, with silver plaque in base with Danish hallmark "AMT 9255 DM", printed, painted and impressed marks.

c1976   4.5in (11.5cm) high

£15-25   **TCM**

A Danish Royal Copenhagen 'Fayance' large square-form dish, marked "156/2885", painted mark "4".

10.5in (26.5cm) wide

£30-40   **GAZE**

A Danish Royal Copenhagen Aluminia 'Tenera' wall relief, by Beth Breyen, with stylized bird design, with painted marks and printed Aluminia backstamp, Beth Breyen monogram and decorators mark "BA".

c1961   11.75in (30cm) high

£70-90   **RWA**

CERAMICS

A CLOSER LOOK AT A ROYAL COPENHAGEN VASE

Scandinavian ceramic and glass design is often influenced by nature, as can be seen in this rough, organic and bark-like texture.

Axel Salto (1889-1961) studied painting before working for Bing & Grøndahl from 1923-25 and Royal Copenhagen from 1933.

Salto, Jais Nielsen and Knud Kyhn (well-known for his stoneware models of animals), were particularly skilled at working with stoneware.

As was often typical of Royal Copenhagen, the surface decoration is kept to a minimum allowing the form and the solfatara glaze to come to the fore.

A Danish Royal Copenhagen stoneware budding vase, by Axel Salto, with brown and fawn solfatara glaze.
c1957

3.5in (9cm) high

£1,000-1,200   RWA

A 1950s/60s Danish Royal Copenhagen Aluminia Marselis vase, by Nils Thorsson, with incised under-glaze stylized leaf design, marked with printed Marselis Aluminia beehive mark, Nils Thorsson monogram and pattern number 2648.

10.75in (27.5cm) high

£120-180   RWA

A 1950s/60s Danish Royal Copenhagen (Aluminia) Marselis vase, by Nils Thorsson, with incised under-glaze diamond design, marked to base with printed Marselis Aluminia beehive mark, Nils Thorsson monogram and pattern number "2634".

6.5in (17cm) high

£100-150   RWA

A rare Danish Royal Copenhagen stoneware vase/pot, by Kari Christensen, with incised line decoration, marked to base with printed backstamp, incised CK monogram, painted "22162" and three wavy lines.

Kari Christensen was one of the 'Tenera' range designers and it is very unusual to find pieces other than her 'Tenera' designs.

c1965

5.25in (13.5cm) high

£100-150   RWA

A 1950s/60s Danish Royal Copenhagen Aluminia Marselis vase, by Nils Thorsson, with incised under-glaze leaf design, marked to base with printed Marselis Aluminia beehive mark and Nils Thorsson monogram.

10.75in (27.5cm) high

£120-180   RWA

A Danish Royal Copenhagen stoneware vase, designed by Jørgen Mogensen, in unusual celadon glaze with relief owl decoration, with printed Royal Copenhagen backstamp, painted pattern no. 21488 and three wavy lines and JM monogram.

c1957   7in (17.5cm) high

£180-220   RWA

A 1930s Danish Royal Copenhagen studio bowl, designed by Carl Halier, with stag design in celadon glaze, marked to base with "CH" monogram and three blue wavy lines.

8.7in (22cm) diam

£120-180   RWA

COLLECTORS' NOTES

■ The Ruskin Pottery was founded in 1898 at Smethwick, near Birmingham, by Edward Richard Taylor. The pottery was named in honour of art critic and artist John Ruskin and was run by William Howson Taylor, Edward's son. Production followed the ethics of the Arts & Crafts movement and represented John Ruskin's ideals closely.

■ The company is best known for its complex and varied glazes, which were inspired, like many of the shapes used, by Chinese pottery. Lustre, crystalline, mottled, flambé and high-fired glazes were produced in a profusion of colours. The company achieved international success and won a prize at the St Louis Exhibition in 1904.

■ The pottery closed upon William's death in 1935 and all records and glaze formulas were destroyed. Experts continue to puzzle over the specific formulae of the glazes. The size of the piece, the colours used and the complexity of the glaze are key factors for value. Prices for Ruskin pottery have risen over the last five years.

A Ruskin high-fired small onion pot, with mottled red, green, cream and yellow graduated glazes, and circular paper label to base

c1905   *3.75in (9.5cm) high*

£1,000-1,500   **GAZE**

A Ruskin high-fired green 'snake skin' glaze vase, impressed marks to base dated, also marked "West Smethwick".

1908   *7.25in (18.5cm) high*

£450-550   **GAZE**

A Ruskin vase, with bright blue dripped and mottled matte glaze, impressed "Ruskin" to base.

7in (18cm) high

£150-200   **JN**

A Ruskin high-fired flambé ware vase, impressed marks to base, dated, with paper label.

1912   *9in (23cm) high*

£1,800-2,200   **GAZE**

A Ruskin water jug, with a high-fired mottled cream and red glaze.

8in (20cm) high

£800-1,200   **PSA**

A Ruskin stoneware footed bowl, with a mottled pale blue/green glaze to the exterior graduating to a mottled sandy glaze to the interior, impressed "Ruskin".

7.75in (20cm) diam

£100-150   **WW**

COLLECTORS' NOTES

■ The coastal town of Rye has been home to potteries since the Middle Ages. 20thC production was focused on a small number of potters in the town. These included Walter and Jack Cole at the Rye Pottery, who trained a number of other key names including Dennis Townsend, who later founded the Iden Pottery, and David Sharp.

■ Sharp is a particularly noteworthy name and worked for Rye Pottery from 1947-53 before founding Cinque Port Pottery with George Gray in 1956. Styles were typically avant garde for their time. Look for striped, zig-zag and 'atomic' motifs and designs in bright colours. Gray left in 1964 and set up his own pottery in the 'Monastery' in Rye.

■ Sharp then went on to founded his own eponymous pottery, which still continues today. He died in 1993. Prices for Rye pottery have plateaued after peaking a few years ago, however it is likely that they will rise again given the importance of the designs, particularly Sharp's earlier examples.

A Rye Pottery green glazed ovoid jug, with serrated rim and applied serrated handle, incised marks.

6.75in (17cm) high

£40-60   L&T

A Rye pottery sang-de-boeuf glazed flattened ovoid jug, with applied arched handle.

6.75in (17cm) high

£30-50   L&T

A 1950s Rye Pottery elliptical vase, with hand-painted striped design and folded rim, with impressed marks.

The form and decoration is typical of Sharp at Rye.

8in (20cm) wide

£120-180   CHS

A Rye Pottery footed vase, hand-painted with blue stripes, squiggles and stars, with impressed and painted marks.

5in (12.5cm) high

£15-20   GAZE

A Rye Pottery hand-painted duck money bank, by David Sharp, signed on the base "David Sharp Rye A England".

Along with house name plaques, such animals are typical of David Sharp's later production.

11in (27.5cm) long

£35-45   MTS

A late 1960s Cinque Ports Monastery vase, with hand-painted rectangular design, marked "R18".

9.75in (24.5cm) high

£25-35   GC

A 1960s-70s Cinque Ports Pottery hand-painted flower pot.

6in (15cm) diam

£15-20   FD

A Cinque Ports Pottery decorated ovoid footed bowl, with printed Cinque Ports mark.

1960-64   *5in (13cm) high*

£40-60   AGR

COLLECTORS' NOTES

■ Scandinavian ceramics proved to be both popular and influential as styles became more modern from the early 20thC onwards. The 1930s and 1950s-'70s were particularly important periods, with many innovative and influential designs being created. In all instances, aim to buy pieces that best represent the movement's core themes, and preferably those by notable designers.

■ Major factories included Sweden's Gustavsberg and Finland's Arabia. Key designers were Wilhelm Kage and Stig Lindberg at Gustavsberg and Ulla Procope and Kaj Franck at Arabia. Both introduced and popularised modern forms, colours and patterns, exemplified in one aspect by Lindberg's colourful faience designs and on the other by Kaj Franck's cooler, more classical and functional pieces.

■ Also look to other, smaller factories such as Saxbo and Palshus for good examples of the design ethic of the time, particularly in terms of form and strong colours. Although lines are generally clean and modern, a strong functional aspect pervades all designs. Nature also provided strong inspiration, with asymmetric, bud-like forms. Whimsical designs were also popular and often took animal forms, furthering this natural inspiration.

■ Unique Scandinavian hand-made studio ceramics are an interesting sector of the market. Names such as Arne Bang, during the 1930s and '40s, and Connie Walther are hotly sought-after. Stig Lindberg and others also experimented with studio ceramics, and their miniature vases, usually with fine and complex glazes, are desirable with surprisingly high values, given their small size.

A Swedish Gustavsberg 'Argenta' vase, designed by Wilhelm Kage, decorated in silver with a fish, painted marks with anchor.

6.25in (16cm) high

£120-180   **WW**

A Swedish Gustavsberg 'Argenta' charger, designed by William Kage, decorated with stylised fish in silver, with painted mark including Kage's signature, hairline to rim.

Argenta ware was introduced as a luxury range in 1930 at the Stockholm 'Stockholmsutstallingen', the major exhibition of art and industrial design. It was produced into the 1950s in a variety of shapes.

18in (46cm) diam

£350-450   **WW**

An early 1950s Swedish Gustavsberg vase, designed by Stig Lindberg, with a silver basket of flowers, with painted marks and paper label.

10.5in (26.5cm) high

£250-350   **SWO**

A Swedish Gustavsberg 'Karneval' faïence slab vase, designed by Stig Lindberg, with hand-painted figure of a lute-playing centaur on front and sunflowers on the back, with painted Gustavsberg studio hand, model number "230.1", and star monogram for decorator Giovanni Pugno to base.

c1958-62   *8in (20.5cm) high*

£150-200   **RWA**

A Swedish Gustavsberg 'Karneval' faïence slab vase, designed by Stig Lindberg, with hand-painted fantasy figure caged girl on front and a bird on the back, with painted Gustavsberg studio hand, original Stig Lindberg label, model number "R.199", and monogram for unknown decorator to base.

c1958-62   *7in (17.5cm) high*

£100-150   **RWA**

A Swedish Gustavsberg 'Bohus Bersa' dish, designed by Stig Lindberg, with stylized leaf transfer decoration.

This varied and popular range of oven-to-tableware was designed by Lindberg in 1960 and was produced until 1974.

12.25in (31cm) long

£50-60   **MHT**

CERAMICS

A CLOSER LOOK AT A MINIATURE VASE

Miniature vases were made by many Scandinavian factories as part of their hand-made 'studio' ranges.

Gustavsberg's studio pieces were marked with an inscribed hand motif. The style of this and the placement of the artist's name changed each year and helps to date them.

Both Stig Lindberg and Berndt Friberg designed miniatures for Gustavsberg, they were signed "Stig L", and "Friberg" respectively.

They differ from standard production in their comparatively traditional forms and fine, highly detailed, subtly coloured glazes.

A 1950s Swedish Gustavsberg faïence dish, designed by Stig Lindberg, with hand-painted lattice pattern.

This is typical of Lindberg's modern faïence designs from this period. They influenced many potteries outside of Scandinavia, such as England's Poole Pottery.

8in (20.5cm) wide

£150-200   **GGRT**

A Swedish Gustavsberg Studio miniature vase, by Stig Lindberg, with dark red glaze.

Although the presence of the inscription "Stig L" does not guarantee that that piece was by Lindberg personally, it is highly likely.

c1980   3in (8cm) high

£150-200   **RWA**

A 1950s Swedish "Gustavsberg small leaf tray, designed by Stig Lindberg, marked to back with painted Gustavsberg studio hand, "G/86, 30, Sweden" and decorator's mark for Franca Pugno.

4.75in (12cm) long

£50-80   **RWA**

A 1950s Swedish Gustavsberg indigo vase, by Karin Björquist, with hand-painted blue decoration, marked to base with painted Gustavsberg studio hand, Karin Björquist monogram and decorator's mark.

Björquist was inspired by her predecessors Kage and Lindberg, as can be seen in the style of decoration, and guided Gustavsberg's designs through the 1960s and '70s. Her work is arguably yet to be fully appreciated.

9.5in (24cm) high

£80-120   **RWA**

A 1960s Swedish Gustavsberg Granada vase, designed by Lisa Larson.

The cylinder was a popular form for ceramics during the 1960s – for transfer-printed wares it allowed easy application of the transfer and maximised display of the pattern.

9in (23cm) high

£80-120   **RWA**

A 1960s/70s Swedish Gustavsberg vase, designed by Britt-Louise Sundell, with brown mottled glaze and band of white rings, marked to base with original Gustavsberg "B.-L SUNDELL" label and Gustavsberg paper label.

9.5in (24cm) high

£80-120   **RWA**

A 1960s/70s Swedish Gustavsberg large bowl, designed by Britt-Louise Sundell, with dark green mottled glaze and white ring decoration, marked to base with original "Gustavsberg B.-L SUNDELL" label and Gustavsberg paper label.

11.75in (30cm) diam

£70-100   **RWA**

A Swedish Gustavsberg Studio miniature globe vase, designed and possibly made by Stig Lindberg, with dark red mottled glaze, signed on the base.

c1978   3.5in (8.5cm) diam

£180-220   **RWA**

A Swedish Gustavsberg Studio miniature vase, designed and possibly made by Stig Lindberg, signed on the base.

This is a typical inscribed mark found on such miniature vases.

2.25in (5.5cm) high

£40-60   GAZE

A Swedish Gustavsberg Studio pottery miniature vase, designed and possibly made by Berndt Friberg, with caramel striated glaze, signed on the base.

Friberg (1899-1981), was awarded a gold medal at the Milan Triennale in 1948 along with Stig Lindberg. Note the subtlety of the glaze and the delicacy of the rim on this high quality, hand-made miniature.

2.25in (6cm) high

£100-150   GAZE

A Swedish Gustavsberg Studio thin-walled footed bowl, designed and possibly made by Berndt Friberg, with green and brown shiny glazes, marked to base with incised Gustavsberg studio hand, "Friberg" and "42".

c1942   5in (12.5cm) wide

£220-280   RWA

A 1960s/70s Swedish Gustavsberg horse, designed by Stig Lindberg, with green glaze, marked to base with printed Gustavsberg anchor mark and 'Sweden'.

4.5in (11.5cm) high

£100-150   RWA

A 1960s/70s Swedish Gustavsberg horse, designed by Stig Lindberg, with speckled brown glazes and white to mane and tail, marked to base with printed Gustavsberg anchor mark and "Sweden".

5.25in (13.5cm) high

£120-180   RWA

A Swedish Gustavsberg bulldog, designed by Lisa Larson, from the Kennel series.

This popular range of stylised dogs included a white poodle, a black and white bull terrier and a boxer.

1972-83

£40-60   RWA

A 1950s Swedish Gustavsberg stoneware cat, designed by by Stig Lindberg, with darkened sgraffito decoration.

7.5in (19cm) long

£150-200   FD

CERAMICS

A Swedish Rorstrand hand-painted tall cylindrical 'Sarek' vase, designed by Olle Alberius.

12in (30.5cm) high

£50-60   MTS

A 1950s/60s Swedish Rorstrand vase, designed by Carl-Harry Stålhane, with shiny brown glaze, marked to base with incised "R" with three crowns, "C.H.S.", "Sweden" and "S A E".

4.5in (11.5cm) high

£70-100   RWA

A 1950s Swedish Rorstrand tall vase, designed by Gunnar Nylund, with brown and coffee-coloured glaze, horizontal shallow flutings and unglazed vertical flutings to base, marked to base with incised "R", three crowns, "Sweden" and "GN", stamped "5".

Rorstrand was founded in 1926 at Rorstrand, Stockholm and has been part of the Rorstrand-Gustavsberg group since 1988. The 20thC saw the employment of many innovative designers working in porcelain and stoneware. After training at Bing & Grøndhal, Nylund (1904-97) joined as art director in 1931, until 1958. He then freelanced at Nymølle and worked with glass at Strombergshyttan.

11.25in (28.5cm) high

£80-120   RWA

A 1960s Swedish Rorstrand squat stoneware vase, designed by Carl-Harry Stålhane, with grey and brown glaze, marked to base with incised "R" with three crowns, "Atelje, C.H.S. – c" and "Sweden".

5.5in (14cm) diam

£80-120   RWA

A 1950s Swedish Rorstrand bowl, designed by Gunnar Nylund, in coffee-coloured glaze with brown glazed incised decoration and unglazed vertical fluting around base, marked to base with incised "R" with three crowns, "Sweden" and "GN".

6.5in (16.5cm) high

£40-60   RWA

A Swedish Rorstrand miniature tri-lobed bowl, designed by Gunnar Nylund, hand-incised "Sweden GN ASH" to base.

2.25in (5.5cm) high

£60-80   GAZE

A Swedish Rorstrand bowl, designed by Carl-Harry Stålhane, with spiral relief pattern.

Stålhane worked for Rorstrand from 1939-73, leaving to start his own studio. His harmonically formed stoneware pieces with their subtle glazes inspired many period studio pottery designs and are much loved.

8in (20cm) long

£60-80   GAZE

A Swedish Rorstrand heavy brown mottled and petrol blue dish, by Gunnar Nylund, scored "R Sweden GN KN' on the base.

8in (20.5cm) diam

£70-90   GAZE

A Swedish Rorstrand cube-shaped candle holder, designed by Sylvia Leuchovius, with painted mark and impressed initials.

2.5in (6.5cm) high

£15-25   TCM

A 1970s Danish Søholm stoneware wall plaque, with abstract design under a heavy high-fired glaze, marked to back with impressed Søholm factory mark and pattern number 3559, painted with paintress mark "K".

The underglaze crazing and slight warping is normal and does not indicate a faulty 'second'. Søholm Stentoj is based on the island of Bornholm, Denmark.

13.5in (34cm) wide

£70-100 **RWA**

A CLOSER LOOK AT A SØHOLM TILE

Although it is unsigned, it is likely to be by Noomi Backhausen due to the strong linear decoration and heavily moulded pattern.

The inclusion of a bird also indicates it is by Backhausen, who designed for the company from 1966-90.

Like so many tiles and studio pieces produced by Søholm, it is thick and very heavy for its size.

Ceramic wall plaques were popular during the 1960s and '70s and were also produced by other Scandinavian and West German ceramics companies.

A Danish Søholm Stoneware wall relief, unsigned but almost certainly designed by Noomi Backhausen, with bird design partly glazed in matt and shiny black, brown and red, marked on back with impressed Søholm factory mark, pattern number 3592.1 and date "14 Juli 1981" and painted paintress mark "K".

c1981 13.5in (34cm) wide

£80-120 **RWA**

A 1970s Danish Søholm stoneware wall relief, designed by Noomi Backhausen, with flower design, marked to front left-hand bottom corner with incised "Noomi", marked to back with impressed "Søholm" factory mark, impressed pattern number "3573", painted paintress mark "A".

15.25in (39cm) high

£40-60 **RWA**

A Danish Søholm moulded blue gloss glaze lamp base, with low relief abstract decoration, the base inscribed "Søholm Denmark S Tenty 1018".

10.5in (26.5cm) high

£30-40 **PSI**

Søholm DANMARK Noomi

A 1970s/80s Danish Søholm studio large stoneware vase, designed by Noomi Backhausen, with heavy applied relief decoration in brown glazes, painted marks to base 'Søholm Danmark Noomi'.

10.25in (26cm) high

£100-150 **RWA**

A Danish Søholm miniature lampbase, with printed marks to base.

4.75in (12cm) high

£15-20 **GAZE**

A Danish Søholm Stentoj earthenware bowl, with glazed stylised floral decoration, painted marks to base for "Søholm Stentoj, Denmark".

11.75in (30cm) long

£18-22 **GAZE**

A 1950s Finnish Arabia oxblood glazed ginger jar, designed by Francesca Mascitti-Lindhl.

4in (10cm) high

£30-40   **GAZE**

A 1940s/50s Swedish Höganäs miniature vase, designed by John Andersson, with blue glaze.

2.5in (6.5cm) high

£60-80   **RWA**

A Swedish Höganäs stoneware vase, designed by John Andersson, with blue glaze, marked to base with printed "Höganäs Keramik" back-stamp with centre entwined "AJ".

Höganäs was founded in 1797 and Berndt Friberg worked there as a thrower from 1915-18.

c1956-67   5in (12.5cm) high

£70-90   **RWA**

A 1960s/70s Danish Laholm Keramik tall vase, with floral design.

11.25in (28.5cm) high

£25-35   **RWA**

A 1950s Danish Nymølle tall vase, designed by Gunnar Nylund, with matt blue glaze, marked to base with painted "Nymöelle Denmark. N" with three hearts/crowns, "G Nylund".

This is similar in form and decoration to many Palshus pieces.

13in (33cm) high

£100-150   **RWA**

A Swedish Rolf Palm Studio bottle vase, with mottled brown glaze.

Rolf Palm works from his own studio in Mölle.

5.75in (14.5cm) high

£100-150   **RWA**

A 1950s Danish Palshus teapot, by Frode Bahnsen, with blue haresfur glaze and wicker handle, marked to base with impressed "Palshus Denmark", monogram for Frode Bahnsen and pattern number T3.

Sculptor Frode Bahnsen (1923-83) is also well-known for his coin and medal designs. The 'haresfur' glaze is a sought-after hallmark of the factory, particularly in this deep blue.

8in (20.5cm) high

£150-200   **RWA**

A 1950s Danish Palshus stoneware vase, designed by Per Linnemann-Schmidt, with olive haresfur glaze, marked to base with incised "Palshus Denmark", "PL-S" and "PR6VF".

4.25in (11cm) high

£150-200   **RWA**

A Norwegian Porsgrund porcelain vase, the white ground with transfer-printed blue birds and flowers, blue and green printed marks, including an anchor and numbered "M231" and "D.78084".

5.5in (14cm) high

£20-30   **GAZE**

A 1930s-40s Danish Saxbo teapot, with cane handle and cobalt blue semi-matte glaze.

Saxbo was founded by Nathalie Krebs in 1930 and closed in 1968. Krebs developed the glazes and Eva Stæhr-Nielsen developed the shapes. Oriental style glazes and simple, clean-lined shapes are typical of the factory's production.

6.5in (16.5cm) long

£150-200   **FD**

A 1950s Danish Palshus 'Torpedo' vase, designed by Per Linnemann-Schmidt, with blue haresfur glaze.

8.5in (21.5cm) high

£200-250   **RWA**

A Danish Saxbo miniature footed dish, with silvery green glaze, hand inscribed on base "Saxbo Denmark 73 (S) ⅄ E.S.E.N. X".

£30-40   **GAZE**

A Danish Saxbo square-sided vase, designed by Eva Stæhr-Nielsen, with impressed panels on front and back in shiny brown glazes, marked to base impressed Saxbo Zing Yang mark, number "228" and "6" and incised E.ST.N. monogram.

c1951-68   3.25in (8cm) high

£80-120   **RWA**

A Swedish Upsala-Ekeby vase, by Mari Simmulson, with leaf design.

Estonian-born Simmulson (b.1911) worked for Upsala Ekeby from 1949-72.

9in (23cm) high

£40-60   **RWA**

A Swedish Upsala Ekeby vase, designed by Ingrid Atterberg, with swirling design.

Atterberg (b.1920) worked for Upsala Ekeby from 1944-63 and won a gold medal for her designs at the Milan Triennale in 1957. It is rare to find the original label on these pieces.

c1951-56   8.25in (21cm) high

£50-80   **RWA**

A Swedish Upsala Ekeby pot, designed by Ingrid Atterberg, with swirling decoration.

c1951-56   5in (12.5cm) diam

£40-60   **RWA**

CERAMICS

A 1960s Danish Conny Walther studio chamotte dish, with brown and fawn glaze, marked to the base with impressed "CW" Conny Walther own studio mark (partially hidden by sticker).

Chamotte is a type of high-fired clay.

11in (28cm) wide

£80-120 RWA

A CLOSER LOOK AT BJØRN WIINBLAD

These are from Wiinblad's studio, which made unique hand-made and hand-decorated pieces, rather than being produced by one of the factories he designed for, such as Nymølle and Rosenthal.

These are more intricately decorated than most studio pieces, but are in Wiinblad's typical 'flat' linear style and match the theme of the story.

The historic, story-based choice of subject matter is typical of Wiinblad.

They are from the estate of Guy Badse, Wiinblad's secretary and rumoured lover – without this provenance; they would be worth around £300-400 each.

A Danish Bjørn Wiinblad studio 'King Solomon' and 'Queen of Sheba' pair of candleholders, from the estate of Wiinblad's secretary Guy Badse, dated.

1979 & 1987

35cm (14in) high

£500-600 (each) RWA

A 1960s Danish Conny Walther studio large chamotte stoneware vase, with a brown running glaze along top edge and down front, hairline firing crack on base, marked to the base with impressed "CW" Conny Walther own studio mark.

7in (8cm) high

£180-220 RWA

A 1960s Danish Conny Walther studio squat vase, with brown running glaze and partially exposed body, base marked with impressed "CW".

5in (12.5cm) diam

£60-80 RWA

A 1960s Danish Conny Walther stoneware bowl, with applied, glazed motif and glazed interior.

5.25in (13.5cm) high

£60-90 RWA

Five from a set of 12 Danish Nymølle ceramic 'Month' plaques, designed by Bjørn Wiinblad.

Wiinblad worked at Nymølle from 1946-56 and then again when he acquired the financially troubled company in 1976 until its closure in the 1990s.

6in (15cm) diam

£50-70 (set) GAZE

A Danish Nymølle circular dish, designed by Bjørn Wiinblad, number 3029-1285, with T.H. Torntoft of Aarhus retailer's paper label.

8.75in (22.5cm) diam

£15-25 GAZE

A 1960s Danish Bjørn Wiinblad Studio pair of male and female centaur candleholders, in a heavy brown glaze.

These are unmarked, which is quite common for these figures. The choice of glazes is unusual for Wiinblad, who usually worked with more ornamented and enriched designs. Wiinblad also designed for German pottery Rosenthal, see pages 132-133.

13.75in (35cm) high

£800-1,000 RWA

A CLOSER LOOK AT A SHELLEY FIGURE

A Shelley three-piece nursery tea set, designed by Mabel Lucie Attwell, comprising a teapot and cover, a milk jug and a sugar bowl, each forming the shape of a mushroom and painted in green, orange and yellow, painted marks and Rd. no.724421.

5in (12.5cm) high

£300-400 **L&T**

Book illustrator Mabel Lucie Attwell joined Shelley in 1926 and designed a range of popular nursery ware, that even reached the nurseries of Princesses Elizabeth and Margaret, and later Prince Charles.

The range included teapots, cups and saucers, and sugar bowls, but the figures are the most desirable and among the rarest today.

They typically featured rosy cheeked children or playful elves, which appealed to adults and delighted children.

Fakes are found, so check the marks and the quality of the paintwork carefully. Also check for damage as many were broken.

A Shelley 'I's Shy' figure, by Mabel Lucie Attwell, printed mark in green.

6in (15cm) high

£1,000-1,500 **LFA**

A Shelley 'Harrogate' crested cup and saucer.

Saucer 6in (15cm) diam

£20-30 **BAD**

A Shelley 'Syringa' pattern teapot, marked "W12070".

8in (20cm) wide

£100-150 **BAD**

A Shelley 'Mode' shape teapot and cover, pattern no. P11754, in shades of green and gold, printed and painted marks.

High Art Deco shapes such as Mode, Eve and Vogue are popular. The combination of green, gilt and black is also a typical Art Deco colour combination.

5in (13cm) high

£250-350 **WW**

A Shelley 'Melody' pattern chintz preserve pot and cover, pattern no. 13453.

c1930 *3.5in (9cm) high*

£70-90 **BEV**

A Shelley Harmony Ware ginger jar and cover, printed factory mark.

The Harmony Ware range was available on a wide variety of shapes. The colour was applied by hand and the piece was then spun to blend the colours together. Some pieces just show bands of colour, others, such as this, combine drips and bands. Colour combinations abound.

9in (23cm) high

£250-350 **WW**

A Shelley Harmony Ware ginger jar and cover.

5in (13cm) high

£100-150 **BAD**

CERAMICS

COLLECTORS' NOTES

■ Much mid- to late 20thC studio pottery, away from the recognised Modernist designs of Lucie Rie, Hans Coper and others, is becoming increasingly sought-after. Encompassing the 'look' of the period it was produced in, many potteries also approached the subject in a unique manner, producing highly individualistic designs.

■ Much work is still comparatively inexpensive and arguably 'yet to be discovered'. Always look for quality in terms of period feel, form, glaze and overall design. Larger pieces are often scarcer as most potteries were

based in tourist areas, such as the West Country, and sold primarily to tourists, who usually preferred smaller, less expensive objects.

■ Always look for marks as these will help identify the potter. Investing in a book showing potters' marks is essential – there are still bargains to be had, both among currently unrecognised potteries and with those pieces whose marks have not been recognised by the seller. Learn about key potters, such as the Leach family, Michael Cardew and Janice Tchalenko, where they worked and who they trained.

An Ashtead Pottery 'Corn Girl' figure, designed by Allan C. Wyon, with printed marks to base.

1927   8in (20cm) high

£150-200   **WW**

An unusual Ashtead Pottery figure, designed by Phoebe Stabler, design M38, with printed marks to base.

The Ashtead Pottery was founded by Sir Laurence Weaver in Ashtead, Surrey in 1923 and aimed to provide employment for ex-servicemen from WWI. Figurines and commemorative works are found, many designed by notable designers such as Phoebe Stabler. Weaver's death, the Depression and competition from foreign imports led to the pottery's demise in 1935.

6.25in (16cm) high

£450-550   **WW**

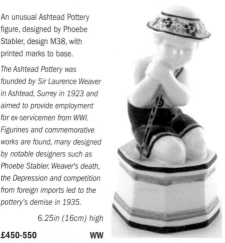

A Michael Cardew brown pottery jug, with incised decoration.

9.5in (24cm) high

£800-1,000   **JN**

An Abuja Pottery large Africa-style pot with lid, by Michael Cardew.

After studying under Bernard Leach and founding the Winchcombe pottery in 1926, Cardew founded the Wenford Bridge Pottery in Cornwall in 1939. Cardew then taught pottery on the Gold Coast, West Africa from 1942-48 and again from 1950-65, when he founded and ran the Abuja Pottery in Nigeria. The origins, size, design and shape of this pot make it desirable, as does the fact that it is by Cardew.

20in (51cm) high

£1,800-2,200   **JN**

A Michael Cardew Wenford Bridge circular brown splashed pottery bowl.

7in (18cm) diam

£180-220   **JN**

A Michael Cardew Wenford Bridge studio pottery dish, with piecrust top.

9.75in (25cm) wide

£180-220   **GAZE**

A Winchcombe pottery jug, with mottled brown glaze and printed mark.

4.25in (10.5cm) high

£20-30   **MHT**

A Carn Pottery rectangular vase, with inset glossy red glazed panel, the base marked "Carn Nancledra".

5.75in (14.5cm) high

£30-40 **MTS**

A CLOSER LOOK AT A COMPTON POTTERY PLAQUE

The Compton Potter's Art Guild was founded in 1899 in the village of Compton just outside Guildford, Surrey, using clay found in the grounds of their house. It was active until the mid-1950s.

The founder was Mary Watts, wife of eminent Victorian painter George Frederick Watts. She employed local villagers, teaching them skills and providing extra income.

The angel design of this plaque is very similar to the plaques on the inside of the Watts memorial chapel – designed by Mary Watts and built from 1895-1904 to commemorate G.F. Watts.

This piece is likely to have been produced after Mary's death.

A Compton Pottery wall plaque, modelled as a angel, unmarked.

Some Compton pieces were designed by notable Arts & Crafts designers such as Archibald Knox and Alfred Gilbert and sold in prestigious retailers such as Liberty's.

9.75in (24.5cm) wide

£180-220 **WW**

A 1980s Carn Pottery trapezoidal vase, with tulip and abstract design, the base marked "Carn Pottery, Nancledra, Penzance, Cornwall".

11in (28cm) high

£40-50 **FD**

A tall Carn Pottery rectangular vase, with lined tulip design and deeply moulded flanges, the base marked "CARN POTTERY".

Carn Pottery was founded in 1971 by John Beusmans and continues to produce today. Vintage shapes have risen in desirability and price over the past five years. Look out for large pieces, fan-shaped vases and plaques. Some pieces are additionally signed by Beusmans in pencil.

11in (27.5cm) high

£60-80 **MTS**

A Carn Pottery flat cat, the base marked "Carn Pottery/Penzance/Cornwall" on three separate lines.

9.25in (23cm) high

£40-60 **MTS**

A Carn Pottery hollow cat figure, finished in blue.

4.75in (12cm) high

£20-30 **MTS**

A Joanna Constantinidis studio pottery bowl, with impressed marks to base.

£70-100 **GAZE**

A 1980s Dartington (Dart) Pottery hand-painted flared vase, stamped "DP".

8in (20cm) high

£30-40 **MTS**

A CLOSER LOOK AT A DARTINGTON POTTERY TEAPOT

Ex-Leach student and RCA tutor Janice Tchalenko (b.1947) provided the pottery's main creative impetus from 1983. She has also worked for Poole Pottery, Royal Doulton and even Next.

This teapot cost £46.55 in 1989, so was expensive at the time. Fewer would have been made and sold, making it comparatively scarce today.

Although the form is very traditional, the bright colours and abstract design are typical of both Tchalenko's designs and the 1980s.

Dart Pottery has become increasingly sought-after – particularly one-offs, limited editions and pieces designed by Tchalenko.

A 1980s Dartington (Dart) Pottery teapot, designed by Janice Tchalenko.

8.75in (22cm) long

£50-70 **MTS**

A 1980s Dartington (Dart) Pottery jug, designed by Janice Tchalenko.

The Dartington Pottery, Devon, often known as the 'Dart Pottery', originated in the 1930s when Bernard and David Leach founded the first pottery at Shinner's Bridge. Marianne de Trey joined in 1947 and remained until 1983 when the pottery was sold to three potters. It gained prominence during the 1980s and continues to produce today.

6in (15cm) high

£40-50 **MTS**

A David Frith large studio pottery charger, decorated in pale blue and copper, impressed seal mark.

Frith (b.1943) has worked in Wales since 1963 and is one of Britain's most respected living potters, most notable for his reduction glazes. His pottery was known as the David Frith Pottery until 1975 when it became the Brookhouse Pottery.

16.25in (41.5cm) diam

£100-150 **CHEF**

A Hastings Pottery purple and silver lustred dish, with imprinted double fish mark to base.

7.75in (19.5cm) long

£10-15 **MHT**

A St Ives bowl, made by Amanda Brier, with cut decoration and glazed in green.

Brier was strongly influenced by noted potter David Leach, son of Bernard Leach.

5.5in (14cm) high

£60-90 **AGR**

A St Ives studio pottery 'Z' bowl, with impressed seal to base.

£180-220 **GAZE**

A rare Jersey Pottery dish, with early 'Channel Islands' three lions circular mark.

The Jersey Pottery was founded in 1946, but only began to gain prominence, primarily as a tourist destination, after 1954 when it was acquired by the Jones family.

1946-54   9.5in (24cm) wide

£50-70   **FD**

A 1970s Langley hand-painted vase, designed by Glynn Colledge, with flared rim and stylized leaf and fruit pattern.

8in (20cm) high

£50-70   **GC**

An early 1950s St Ives Pottery beige-glazed jug, made by David Leach, with impressed marks.

David Leach (1911-2005), son of notable potter Bernard, learnt pottery under Shoji Hamada. This piece pre-dates his work at Lowerdown, which he founded in 1955.

7in (18cm) high

£100-150   **AGR**

A 1970s Langley small vase, designed by Glynn Colledge, with waisted neck and hand-painted stylized leaf and fleur-de-lys motifs.

6.75in (17cm) high

£40-60   **GC**

A 1970s Langley tall waisted vase, designed by Glynn Colledge, with hand-painted column and stylized leaf design.

Colledge is more commonly associated with Denby from 1950 onwards. However, Denby acquired Lovatt & Lovatt (who made Langley) in 1959 meaning Colledge also designed for Langley.

11.25in (28.5cm) high

£70-90   **GC**

An Eric Leaper long orange speckled tray, with incised signature.

17in (43cm) wide

£30-50   **JN**

An Eric Leaper multicoloured speckled tray, with incised signature.

12in (30.5cm) wide

£30-50   **JN**

An Eric Leaper speckled rectangular tray, with incised signature.

Eric Leaper (1921-2002) founded his first (not entirely successful) pottery in Swanage, Dorset in the late 1940s before moving to Newlyn in Cornwall in 1954. Here, he enjoyed greater success and he became known for his bold, brightly coloured and contrasting glazes, which stood out against the more muted colours used by his contemporaries.

10.5in (26.5cm) wide

£40-60   **JN**

An Eric Leaper circular multicoloured speckled charger.

10.5in (26.5cm) diam

£30-50   **JN**

A hand-painted pottery clown wall plaque, incised "LICINIO" on the reverse.

13.5in (34.5cm) high

£50-80 | **CHS**

A CLOSER LOOK AT A LUCIE RIE SAUCEBOAT

Lucie Rie (1902-95) became one of the earliest leading figures of Modernist studio pottery, along with Hans Coper, winning many awards including an OBE in 1968.

This piece typifies her work in terms of its clean, flowing form and subtly speckled, coolly coloured glaze highlighted by a rim in a contrasting colour.

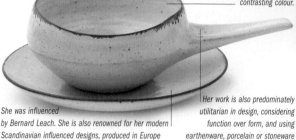

She was influenced by Bernard Leach. She is also renowned for her modern Scandinavian influenced designs, produced in Europe before WWII and in Britain after 1949.

Her work is also predominately utilitarian in design, considering function over form, and using earthenware, porcelain or stoneware as a medium.

A Lucie Rie stoneware sauceboat and saucer, with impressed "LR" seal to underside.

£1,000-1,500 | **ROS**

A Llangollen, Wales tall vase, with green lustre glaze and incised linear column design.

11.75in (30cm) high

£30-40 | **GC**

A John Maltby studio pottery figure of a penguin with fish, mounted a wooden block, moulded monogram.

Maltby's work is typically highly stylised and has been compared with Picasso's due to this stylisation and its colouring. After training as an artist, he studied pottery under David Leach at Lowerdown, founding his own pottery in Crediton, Devon in 1964.

10.75in (27.5cm) high

£280-320 | **GAZE**

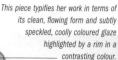

A 1980s Promenade Pottery heart-shaped vase, inscribed "Promenade Pottery Brighton" on base.

9.5in (23.5cm) high

£20-30 | **MTS**

A 1980s Promenade Pottery diamond-shaped vase, inscribed "Promenade Pottery Brighton" on base.

Promenade Pottery was run by Mark Jamieson (b.1950), who had studied art and sculpture in Belfast and graphic design and illustration at Brighton University. The pottery existed for 20 years around the 1980s, and produced shaped, lightweight slip-cast wares for tourists and for retailers such as Liberty's. Colours and shapes tend to be typically 1980s.

9.5in (23.5cm) high

£20-30 | **MTS**

A 1970s Purbeck Pottery stoneware ashtray, with thick green glassy glaze in centre and impressed "Purbeck England" stamp to base.

Purbeck was founded in Dorset in 1966 and produced functional designs by Robert Jefferson, previously of Poole Pottery, made from clay mined in the Purbeck Hills.

4.25in (11cm) wide

£10-15 | **MHT**

A Phil Rogers white salt-glazed vase, with iron and cobalt brushwork.

Rogers (b.1951) opened his first pottery in 1977, moving to his current location at Cefn Faes farm in Wales in 1984. He is known for his stoneware and salt glazes made from local minerals and wood ash and has pieces in the collection of the Victoria & Albert Museum, London. He is also a Fellow of the Craft Potters Association.

13in (33cm) high

£300-400 GAZE

A pair of early Torquay Pottery blue ground jugs, with moulded and painted design of a parrot in a tree.

Torquay ware covers the production of a number of potteries around Torquay, Devon founded from the 1850s, but more so from the 1880s. Made from red bodied earthenware, the most commonly found pieces are motto ware for tourists, bearing a picture of a flower, house, animal or tree along with a motto. Arts & Crafts style pieces, such as these, were primarily produced by Aller Vale, the Torquay Terracotta Company and Watcombe.

10in (25.5cm) high

£120-180 B&H

A pair of early Torquay Pottery blue ground baluster vases, with three handles, and moulded and painted parrot decoration.

12in (30.5cm) high

£80-120 B&H

A Tremar coffee pot, with band of impressed runic letters around the base, with "TREMAR UK" impressed stamp.

Runic symbols were popular motifs for many studio potters from the 1970s – also see the work of Louis Hudson and Peter Ellery at Tremaen.

9.75in (25cm) high

£20-30 GC

A Charles Vyse stoneware footed bowl, covered in a blue glaze, with incised marks.

Vyse (1882-1971) developed an interest in Oriental ceramics and glazes from 1920 onwards after moving next to a collector in Chelsea, London in 1919, hence the Chinese form and colour of this bowl.

5in (13cm) diam

£120-180 WW

A 1970s Isle of Wight Pottery large pottery vase, by Jo Lester, with flared lip and lost wax circle and diamond pattern and island shaped stamp to base.

Isle of Wight Pottery, founded by Lester (b.1912) in 1953 is becoming increasingly sought-after by collectors, particularly after the recent publication of a book on the island's pottery. Lester himself retired in the mid-1980s.

12.75in (32.5cm) high

£50-70 GC

A near spherical studio pottery vase, comprising leaves of blue glazed pottery, with slim opening to top, with impressed mark.

6.75in (17cm) high

£30-40 PSI

FIND OUT MORE...

British Studio Potters Marks, by Eric Yates-Owen, published by A&C Black, 1999.

COLLECTORS' NOTES

■ Swid Powell was founded in New York in 1983 by Nan Swid and Addie Powell. Both had previously been employed by furniture makers Knoll International to produce a range of architect-designed functional objects for the home. These included transfer-printed ceramics and metalware, such as candlesticks and salt and pepper shakers. In c1994 it became known as Nan Swid Design, with Swid also designing for other manufacturers and notable labels. The company closed c2000.

■ The company produced works by some of the major designers of the day, many of whom were also architects and leaders of the prevalent 'Postmodern' style. They included eminent names such as Michael Graves, Ettore Sottsass, Zaha Hadid and Robert Venturi.

■ These Postmodernists rejected the functional and plain ideals of the Modern movement, begun in earnest during the first decades of the 20thC. They introduced historical, cultural and Pop motifs and references, as well as a feeling for colour and surface pattern. No longer was design dictated purely by function.

■ Quality was very high, with ceramics being finely transfer-printed. All ceramics bear a facsimile signature of the designer on the back, underneath the company name and the pattern name. They were expensive and were aimed at the growing numbers of style-conscious urban professionals. They also influenced many other less costly, lower quality wares during the 1980s and '90s.

■ The market is still emerging, as the style had fallen out of fashion. Despite its importance to 20thC design, it is yet to come to the attention of larger numbers of collectors. The nearest equivalent is Italy's Alessi, who also employed similar design ethics, but has enjoyed more appeal amongst collectors. Aim to buy examples in the best condition possible as many were were worn or damaged through use.

An American Swid Powell 'Medici' pattern transfer-printed teacup and saucer, designed by Ettore Sottsass in 1984.

Ettore Sottsass is perhaps the best known and most prolific Italian Postmodernist. After taking part in the radical and experimental Alchimia design group, he helped found the more successful and influential Memphis group. He then went on to design products and buildings, on his own behalf and for many other notable companies.

Saucer 5.75in (14.5cm) diam

£100-150   **GM**

An American Swid Powell 'Medici' pattern transfer-printed soup bowl, designed by Ettore Sottsass in 1984.

9.25in (23.5cm) diam

£80-120   **GM**

An American Swid Powell 'Medici' pattern transfer-printed dinner plate, designed by Ettore Sottsass in 1984.

12in (30.5cm) diam

£80-120   **GM**

An American Swid Powell 'Notebook' pattern transfer-decorated ceramic dinner plate, designed by Robert Venturi in 1984.

An American Swid Powell 'Medici' pattern transfer-printed side plate, designed by Ettore Sottsass in 1984.

9.25in (23.5cm) diam

£80-120   **GM**

An American Swid Powell 'Beam' pattern transfer-printed dinner plate, designed by Zaha Hadid in 1988.

12in (30.5cm) diam

£80-120   **GM**

Venturi took this design from the front cover of a school notebook. As well as the black being typically 1980s, the pattern's unexpected use on dinnerware makes a strong Postmodern statement.

12in (30.5cm) diam

£100-150   **GM**

A CLOSER LOOK AT A SWID POWELL PLATE

Robert Venturi (b.1925) is a Philadelphia-based architect who was one of the founding fathers of the late 20thC Postmodern movement, criticising the plain and functional Modern principle of design.

The pattern is known as 'Grandmother' and is an ironic statement about a grandmother's favourite old chintzy tablecloth updated with black lines and stylization. It was based on a tablecloth belonging to the grandmother of one of Venturi's associates.

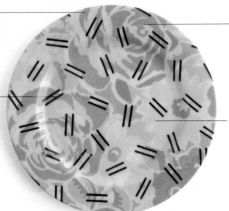

It also relates to one of Venturi's principles that we consider the styles of our immediate (our mother's) past as being bad taste, but after the 'buffer' of one generation, our grandmother's styles can be appealing.

It represents the Postmodern style as it brings in colourful surface decoration that has historical and cultural references – ideals that Modernists had baulked at and rejected.

An American Swid Powell transfer-decorated 'Grandmother' pattern ceramic plate, designed by Robert Venturi in 1984.

9in (23cm) high

£70-100   **GM**

An American Swid Powell transfer-decorated 'Grandmother' pattern ceramic mug, designed by Robert Venturi in 1984.

3.75in (9.5cm) high

£20-30   **GM**

An American Swid Powell 'Black Stripes' pattern transfer-printed mug, designed by Robert and Trix Haussmann in 1984.

Although considered strictly Postmodern, the design is very similar to the Op Art movement of the 1960s, championed by those such as painter and printmaker Bridget Riley.

4in (10cm) high

£100-150   **GM**

An American Swid Powell 'Broken' pattern transfer-printed dinner plate, designed by Robert and Trix Haussmann in 1984.

12in (30.5cm) diam

£100-150   **GM**

An American Swid Powell 'Volumetric' pattern transfer-printed dinner plate, designed by Steven Holl in 1986.

12in (30.5cm) diam

£80-120   **GM**

An American Swid Powell 'Planar' pattern transfer-printed dinner plate, designed by Steven Holl in 1986.

12in (30.5cm) diam

£80-120   **GM**

An American Swid Powell 'Calla Lily' pattern transfer-printed plate, designed by Robert Mapplethorpe in 1984 after one of his photographs, with original card box.

1984 12in (30.5cm) diam

£350-450   **GM**

FIND OUT MORE...

Swid Powell, by Sarah Nolan and Annette Tapert, published by Rizzoli, 1990.

A Grimwades Art Deco form cube-shaped teapot, with dragon decorated band and gilt trim.

c1930   4in (10cm) wide

£50-70   **BAD**

A Grimwades 'Royal Winton' yellow teapot, with a floral handle and finial, marked with patent number "301262".

£70-100   **BAD**

A Price Bros. 'Ye Olde Inn' cottageware teapot and cover.

The purple/orange/green colourway is rarer than other colourways.

c1930s

£60-80   **JF**

A Till majolica teapot and cover, of baluster form with weeping widow finial, in brown green and mustard glazes.

£80-120   **ROS**

A Wade transfer-printed 'Paisley' pattern chintzware-style teapot.

c1930   9.75in (25cm) wide

£60-70   **BAD**

A Price & Kensington Potteries 'Ye Olde Cottage' teapot, marked.

Price Brother was formed in 1896, becoming Price Bros. Ltd in 1903. In 1962 the company amalgamated with Kensington Pottery Ltd (established c1922) becoming Price & Kensington. They are known for their production of cottageware.

9in (22.5cm) wide

£35-45   **JL**

A German teapot, with moulded and floral swag decoration and gilt highlights.

£40-60   **JL**

An English sepia transfer-printed teapot, depicting Bragham Castle, impressed "Made in England", one chip.

9in (22.5cm) wide

£40-50   **JL**

An early 20thC Whieldon-type cabbageware teapot and cover, naturalistically modelled and glazed in shades of green.

Master potter Thomas Whieldon (1719-95) is associated with the production of tortoiseshell ware and agateware that was decorated with green, brown or blue translucent glazes applied with a mottled effect.

5.5in (14cm) high

£180-220   **ROS**

COLLECTORS' NOTES

■ The Tremaen Pottery was founded in Marazion, Cornwall by artist Peter Ellery in 1965. Ellery was inspired by the landscape around him, as well as by his training, and took an unusual approach to studio pottery. His first designs were hand-pressed into moulds before being decorated in a painterly and abstract manner, and then fired.

■ Many of his forms are taken directly from the large rounded pebbles found on Cornish beaches. Patterns tend to include runic-type symbols, geometric linear decoration or abstract painterly designs. Examples incorporating cow parsley plants or Cornish harbour scenes are scarce and highly desirable to the growing number of collectors.

■ Many pieces are marked with an impressed logo, as seen on this page, or a rectangular label. Not all pieces are marked, and labels may have been removed or fallen off, so always look out for his characteristic forms and patterns.

■ Despite being successful enough to gain 12 employees and move to a larger pottery in Newlyn in 1967, the 1970s proved difficult for Tremaen. Designs became less innovative and focused on novelty forms for the tourist market. In 1988, Ellery left to focus on painting and the pottery closed some years afterwards. Early and characteristic works, such as those seen here, are rising rapidly in value.

A Tremaen lampbase, with moulded runic symbols and beige and brown glazes.

Runic symbols were a popular decorative motif during the 1950s-70s and were also used by potters Louis Hudson and designer Aldo Londi for his 'Rimini Blu' range for Bitossi in Italy – see p103-105.

9.5in (24cm) high

£60-80   **GC**

A Tremaen 'pebble form' lampbase, with impressed Chinese-style symbols, the base with blue "Tremaen Pottery Newlyn" sticker.

11.5in (29cm) high

£50-70   **GC**

An unusual Tremaen white glazed small lampbase, with moulded runic symbols highlighted with a green glaze wash.

8.5in (21.5cm) high

£40-60   **GC**

A large Tremaen 'Cow Parsley' lampbase, with gold foil "Tremaen Pottery Cornwall" sticker to brown baize covered base.

To create this very rare design, Ellery pressed real cow parsley seed-heads into the wet clay to obtain a life-like imprint. The cow parsley was then burnt off in the kiln, leaving a dark brown mark and impressed life-like pattern. This is also a very large size, making it even rarer.

14.25in (36cm) high

£100-150   **GC**

A Tremaen creamy blue-green glazed lampbase, with raised, trailed abstract pattern in a gun-metal grey glaze, with impressed Tremaen triple-lined stamped mark.

8.75in (22cm) high

£50-70   **GC**

A Tremaen 'pebble' vase, with flat base and small opening, with impressed Tremaen mark.

This is an interesting example for two reasons. Firstly, its decoration is both typical of Ellery's painterly style and of the beach stone the vase was modelled from. Secondly, the rough interior indicates it is an early piece, assembled by hand-pressing the clay into moulds.

c1968   8in (20cm) high

£50-80   **PC**

A Tremaen 'pebble form' vase, with abstract storm-like dripped, brushed and scraped pattern, the base with blue "Tremaen Newlyn" sticker.

12.25in (31cm) high

£60-80   **GC**

COLLECTORS' NOTES

■ The Troika Pottery was founded in 1963 by sculptor and painter Lesley Illsley, potter Benny Sirota and architect Jan Thompson, who left the trio in 1965. The pottery's first location was at Wells Pottery in Wheal Dream, St Ives. It moved to Newlyn in 1970 due to expansion.

■ Early pieces are functional domestic ware, most often with a glossy, shiny glaze. The instantly recognisable matte, textured finish was not commonly produced until c1974. New shapes were introduced c1965 and again in 1970, when the pottery expanded. Most pieces were made using moulds to give uniform shapes and sizes.

■ Painted marks on the base of a piece will help you find out more. Pieces produced from 1963-67 will usually contain the wording 'St Ives' with a stylized trident mark. This mark was phased out during 1967, leaving just 'St Ives'. When the pottery moved to Newlyn, the 'St Ives' mark was dropped. 'Newlyn' never appears on any piece. The pottery closed in 1983.

■ The pottery was successful, selling to tourists during the holiday seasons, but also selling to major London department stores Selfridges, Liberty and Heal's, as well as to other companies for export across the world. Look for shapes that are most characteristic of Troika, such as the 'wheel' or 'Doublebase'. Wall plaques, dishes, ashtrays and domestic wares are rare.

■ Marks may also contain a decorator's monogram or initials. These can be hard to read, so refer to illustrated guides to identify a decorator correctly. Some are as yet unknown. Dates shown here are for the working dates of decorators, or the date range of the pottery mark. The work of some decorators, such as those who became Head Decorators, can be more valuable.

■ Values appear to have reached a plateau over the past year and it seems that the recent rises will not continue unabated. Exceptionally rare pieces or those with great eye-appeal will still fetch considerably more than they would have, even a few years ago, but there now appears to be an upper limit to what collectors will pay.

A Troika Pottery white slab vase, decorated by Honor Curtis, with a brown circle.

1966-74   4.5in (11.5cm) high

£150-200   JN

A Troika Pottery white slab vase, with painted "A" monogram, for an unknown decorator, with a brown circle.

4.5in (11.5cm) high

£180-220   JN

A 1960s-70s Troika Pottery blue slab vase, with black circle motif and painted marks to base.

4.5in (11.5cm) high

£180-220   JN

A Troika Pottery slab vase, decorated by Linda Taylor, with geometric and oval patterns, painted factory mark, minute chip to leading edge.

c1970-72   7in (18cm) high

£250-300   DN

A 1960s Troika Pottery dark brown slab vase, incised with a stylized flowerhead, painted marks to base.

4.5in (11.5cm) high

£120-180   JN

A Troika Pottery blue slab vase, decorated by Louise Jinks, with circles and rectangles.

Louise Jinks worked as Head Decorator from 1979-81.

1976-81   6.5in (16.5cm) high

£250-350   JN

A 1970s Troika Pottery 'Coffin' vase, with all-over brown textured finish, decorated with green and ivory geometric forms, painted marks to base.

'Coffin' vases were introduced after the pottery had moved to Newlyn in 1970, so should never be found with St Ives marks. They are amongst the most common Troika shapes, especially in smaller sizes.

A late 1970s Troika Pottery rectangle vase, decorated by Tina Doubleday, incised with geometric devices, painted factory and decorator's marks.

9in (22.5cm) high

£220-280   **DN**

A 1970s Troika Pottery rectangle vase, by an unknown decorator, with geometric symbols.

8.75in (22cm) high

£220-280   **KCS**

A 1970s Troika Pottery rectangle vase, with a blue glaze and geometric motifs, painted marks, cracked.

8.75in (22cm) high

£120-180   **SWO**

7in (18cm) high

£120-180   **BIG**

A 1970s Troika Pottery 'Coffin' vase, with blue glaze and stylized symbols, painted marks including "Troika Cornwall" to base.

7in (18cm) high

£100-150   **GAZE**

A 1970s Troika Pottery cube vase, with incised geometric motifs and painted marks to base.

Despite its small size, the decoration on this example is very fine and detailed, almost resembling a stylized house, and buildings with the sun to one side.

A Troika St Ives Pottery rectangle vase, decorated by Sylvia Vallence, with gold and black bands and a circle on each face, with painted marks to base, firing crack to rim.

1967-69   *13in (33cm) high*

£350-450   **SWO**

6in (15cm) high

£220-280   **SWO**

A 1970s Troika Pottery cube vase, of square form, with incised motifs, painted marks to the base.

5.75in (14.5cm) high

£220-280   **SWO**

A Troika St Ives Pottery lidded jar, with stylized petal motifs, with printed 'Troika, St Ives, England' mark to base.

As well as being early, these lidded jars are quite rare.

1967-70 5.25in (13.5cm) high

£500-600 SWO

A Troika Pottery cylinder vase, with a blue glaze and two decorative bands, painted marks to base.

14.25in (36.5cm) high

£280-320 SWO

A Troika Pottery white chimney vase, decorated by Alison Brigden, with panels of heavy, stylized geometric designs to the front and back, with painted "Troika Cornwall" mark.

Brigden was Head Decorator from 1981-83, taking over from Louise Jinks.

1976-83 7.5in (19cm) high

£500-600 JN

A Troika Pottery small cylinder vase, decorated by Honor Curtis, marked "Troika Cornwall".

Honor Curtis decorated at Troika from 1968-73. From 1968-69, she used the initials "HP", the "P" from her maiden name, Perkins. From 1975, Curtis worked for Troika again, but only part-time from home.

1970-73 5.5in (14cm) high

£80-120 GAZE

A Troika Pottery small cylinder vase, decorated by Avril Bennett, painted "Troika, Cornwall" and decorator's monogram.

1973-79 5.75in (14.5cm) high

£100-150 GAZE

A Troika Pottery tall cylinder vase, decorated by Avril Bennett, with painted "Troika Cornwall" marks.

1973-79 14in (35.5cm) high

£350-450 JN

A Troika St Ives Pottery cylinder vase, decorated by Marilyn Pascoe, with painted "Troika, St Ives England" and painter's monogram.

c1969 8in (20cm) high

£120-180 GAZE

A 1970s Troika Pottery cylinder vase, painted star motifs on the body, painted marks to base.

7.75in (19.5cm) high

£150-200 SWO

A CLOSER LOOK AT A TROIKA WHEEL VASE

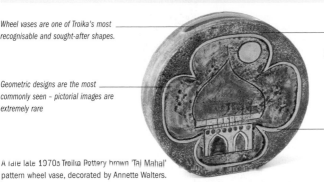

Wheel vases are one of Troika's most recognisable and sought-after shapes.

Artist Paul Klee's paintings were an inspiration for many designs – it is interesting to note that he travelled widely in North Africa where these domed minarettes are common.

Geometric designs are the most commonly seen – pictorial images are extremely rare

This pattern is even rarer in blue.

A late late 1970s Troika Pottery brown 'Taj Mahal' pattern wheel vase, decorated by Annette Walters.

8in (20cm) high

£600-700   KCS

A 1970s Troika Pottery small wheel vase, by an unknown decorator, with painted "Troika N" mark to base, small chip.

This is another extremely unusual design, at first glance resembling an image of Christ on the Cross perhaps in a church's stained glass window.

4.75in (12cm) high

£120-180   GAZE

A 1970s Troika Pottery wheel vase, with moulded and coloured decoration, with painted 'Troika Cornwall' and decorator's mark to base.

6.5in (16.5cm) high

£180-220   SWO

A Troika Pottery medium-sized wheel vase, decorated by Colin Carbis, with painted 'Troika Cornwall' mark and decorator's monogram.

Carbis worked as a caster and fettler at Troika from 1976-77. When decorating he using the initials "CC" or "CJC".

1976-77   6.5in (16.5cm) high

£250-350   JN

A Troika Pottery wheel vase, decorated by Honor Curtis, with incised and moulded design and painted target, with painted decorator's marks to base.

1970-73   4.5in (11.5cm) high

£150-200   JN

A Troika Pottery wheel vase, decorated by Penny Black, with moulded inverted triangular design, with painted marks to base.

1970-76   4.75in (12cm) high

£100-150   GAZE

A Troika Pottery wheel vase, decorated by Honor Curtis, modelled in low relief in shades of blue and brown on grey/green ground, painted marks.

1968-73   8in (20cm) high

£350-450   WW

CERAMICS

A 1970s Troika Pottery wheel vase, decorated in low relief with geometric motifs, in shades of blue and white on a grey/green ground, painted marks to base.

4.5in (11.5cm) high

£80-120   **WW**

A Troika Pottery small wheel vase, decorated Simone Kilburn, the base with painted "Troika" mark and decorator's monogram, chip to rim.

1975-77   4.75in (12cm) high

£60-80   **GAZE**

A CLOSER LOOK AT A TROIKA WHEEL VASE

This is an extremely early and, despite its small size and simple decoration, a comparatively rare example.

The presence of the 'trident' mark on the base dates this piece to 1965-67, as wheel vases were introduced in c1965 and the trident mark was phased out in 1967.

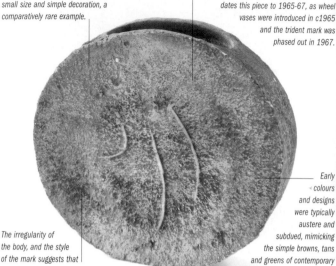

Early colours and designs were typically austere and subdued, mimicking the simple browns, tans and greens of contemporary Scandinavian pottery, which was popular at the time.

The irregularity of the body, and the style of the mark suggests that this was handmade, rather than moulded.

A Troika St Ives Pottery small wheel vase, with three low relief curving lines and mottled green textured glaze, the base with painted 'Troika St Ives' and trident marks.

1965-67   *4in (10cm) high*

£300-400   **GAZE**

A Troika Pottery wheel lamp base, decorated by Honor Curtis, with painted "Troika Cornwall" marks and decorators' monogram.

1970-74   8.25in (21cm) high

£180-220   **DN**

A Troika Pottery square lamp base, decorated by Alison Brigden, the base with painted "Troika Cornwall" marks and decorator's monogram.

1977-83   9in (22.75cm) high

£250-350   **JN**

A Troika Pottery wheel-shaped lamp base, decorated by Penny Black, with typical geometric designs, the base painted "Troika".

1970-76   10.5in (26cm) high

£400-500   **SWO**

A Troika Pottery square lamp base, decorated by Alison Brigden, the base with painted "Troika Cornwall" marks.

The circular design is reminiscent of a spaceman's helmet, a recurring design motif of the 1960s and '70s.

1977-83   11.5in (29cm) high

£400-600   **JN**

A 1970s Troika Pottery large 'Doublebase' lamp base, with painted marks including an "EW" monogram for an unknown decorator.

Despite the unknown decorator, this is a large example of the sought-after 'Doublebase' shape.

17in (43cm) high

£600-800   **JN**

A Troika Pottery 'Doublebase' vase, decorated by Teo Bernatowitz, with typical stylized geometric decoration, the base with painted marks and decorator's monogram, slight hairline crack to top inside corner.

Bernatowitz only worked for Troika for around 18 months. His monogram combining the rounded part of a lower case 'b' on the stem of a capital 'T' is commonly mistaken for Tina Doubleday. Doubleday's monogram is more like a capital 'D'.

c1974   13.75in (35cm) high

£550-650   **GAZE**

A Troika St Ives Pottery teapot and cover, with bamboo

The early circular design was commonly used on domestic wares, which are generally earlier and much scarcer than vases and most other decorative wares.

1963-70   6.75in (17cm) diam

£350-450   **WW**

A Troika St Ives Pottery blue mug, with orange circles on black.

Early pieces tend to have bands of shiny glaze in addition to the rougher glazes. The banded circular design on this mug was one of the earliest used and is found later on cylinder and 'urn' vases.

1965-67   4.5in (11.5cm) high

£100-150   **JN**

A rare Troika St Ives Pottery D-plate, of rounded square form, having embossed flower head and leaf designs, impressed trident mark to base.

D-Plates were one of the earliest shapes made at Troika from 1963. The shiny glaze is also typical of early pieces, before textured designs dominated from c1974 onwards.

1963-70   7in (18cm) diam

£300-500   **B&H**

A Troika Pottery square dish, decorated by Louise Jinks, with geometric moulded patterning, with painted marks to base including decorator's monogram.

The runic-like moulded decoration seen here was a common motif for 1970s potteries such as Louis Hudson, Tremaen and even some Bernard Rooke designs.

1976-81   6.5in (16cm) wide

£180-220   **JN**

A CLOSER LOOK AT A TROIKA MASK

The bases of these masks are frequently damaged, as are the fragile corners.

Look for examples with detailed and crisp mouldings, as the moulds wore down over time.

Only a very few masks were made compared to other shapes, and they were expensive, meaning few are found today.

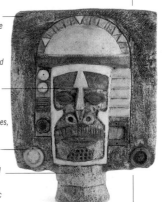

It shows the influences of Paul Klee and Aztec designs in the colours and also the geometric stylization.

A 1970s Troika Pottery mask, modelled in low relief with stylized face to both sides, painted marks to base.

The reverse has a simpler mask design comprising of oval and geometric designs that could to have been inspired by Cycladic or African tribal masks and sculptures.

10in (25.5cm) high

£2,000-3,000   **WW**

FIND OUT MORE...

'Troika Ceramics of Cornwall', by George Perrott, published by Gemini Publications, 2003.

www.cornishceramics.com – includes a regularly updated, illustrated list of decorators' marks, and more.

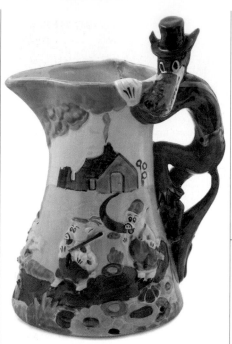

A Wade Heath jug, pattern no. 3397, marked with Reg'd design 787794 for 1933 and "VV" painters initials.

Compare this to the similar Myott jug on p119 of the Myott section in last year's book. Which came first...?

7.75in (19.5cm) high

£40-50 NAI

A Wade green-glazed moulded jug, no. 567.

8.75in (22cm) high

£20-30 GAZE

A Wade 'Zena' figurine, designed by Jessie Hallen, factory marks.

Jessie Hallen was responsible for the majority of Wade's 1930s lady figurines, inspired by Doulton's Fair Ladies. In 1930 she was given her own studio within Wade's Manchester Pottery and eventually had studios in all three of the Wade potteries.

8.75in (22cm) high

£120-180 SWO

A Wade Heath 'Big Bad Wolf & The Three Little Pigs" musical jug.

This was inspired by the Disney animation The Three Little Pigs, featuring the wolf as the villain. It was released in 1933.

c1933 10.25in (26cm) high

£300-500 NAI

A 1940s Wade Harvest Ware vase.

9in (21.5cm) high

£40-50 GAZE

A Wade panda bear plaque, size 195.

From the Wade Extravaganza, held at Alton Towers in 1998. It was produced in other colours for other events.

1998 8in (20.5cm) high

£50-70 CA

A 1940s Wade cockatoo spirit container.

5in (12.5cm) high

£40-60 GAZE

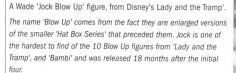

A Wade 'Jock Blow Up' figure, from Disney's Lady and the Tramp'.

The name 'Blow Up' comes from the fact they are enlarged versions of the smaller 'Hat Box Series' that preceded them. Jock is one of the hardest to find of the 10 Blow Up figures from 'Lady and the Tramp', and 'Bambi' and was released 18 months after the initial four.

1962-65

£150-200 WW

An early Wade Mambo dish, later renamed Zamba.

Africa and African art were another huge influence on 1950s design, perhaps aided by the reduction of cost in international air travel and films such as African Queen released in 1951.

c1957   9.5in (24cm) wide

£50-70   **NPC**

A set of five Wade Mambo plates.

c1957   4.25in (11cm) wide

£50-60   **NPC**

A Wade Harmony Ware 'Shooting Star' pattern fruit bowl, shape 440, with tripod base.

The space race between the USSR and US at this time had a significant influenced on design, such as the shooting stars on this bowl.

c1957-62   9in (23cm) wide

£60-70   **NPC**

A 1950s Wade Harmony ware 'Carnival' pattern bowl, with pierced rim.

12.25in (31cm) wide

£60-80   **NPC**

A 1950s Wade Harmony Ware 'Carnival' pattern fruit bowl, shape 440, with pierced rim and tripod base.

9in (23cm) long

£15-20   **GAZE**

A Wade 'Quack-Quacks' pattern nursery mug, by Robert Barlow.

3in (7.5cm) high

£12-18   **CHS**

A Wade Harmony Ware 'Parasols' pattern fruit bowl, with pierced rim.

1957-62   12.25in (31cm) wide

£80-100   **NPC**

A rare Wade Harmony Ware 'Parasols' pattern catherine wheel dish, with metal handle.

7in (18cm) wide

£50-70   **NPC**

COLLECTORS' NOTES

- New Zealand born architect and designer Keith Murray (1892-1981) was approached by Wedgwood in 1932, after a short but successful period designing glass for Stevens & Williams. His first ceramic designs were released in Spring, 1933.

- The simple, Modernist shapes show his architectural background, and decoration is integral to the design, rather than being painted or otherwise applied. Ribbing, fluting and incised lines are typical on these moulded wares. Some shapes, such as a bulbous footed vase with a flared rim, and complete desk inkwells, are scarce.

- Colours were cool and classical, suiting the clean lines of Modernist and Art Deco interiors, and included matte, glossy and celadon green, 'Moonstone' white, yellow, pale blue and the very rare 'black basalt'.

- The type of printed mark on the base will help to date a piece to a period (see below). Murray's designs were produced into the early 1950s, but were slowly discontinued thereafter, with only a few remaining in the 1960s. Today, they are highly sought-after, but always examine pieces closely for damage.

A Wedgwood green centrepiece charger, designed by Keith Murray, with 'signature' mark.

The printed facsimile 'signature' was the first mark and was used from 1933.

1933-40

£180-220   **GAZE**

A 1940s Wedgwood circular green comport and a set of six circular plates, designed by Keith Murray, with printed 'KM' marks.

The printed 'KM' mark was introduced in 1940.

Comport 9in (23cm) diam

£120-180   **JN**

A Wedgwood banded matte green tankard, designed by Keith Murray, with printed 'signature' mark.

1933-40   *4.75in (12cm) high*

£50-70   **CHEF**

A 1940s Wedgwood gloss green glazed footed vase, designed by Keith Murray, with printed 'KM' mark.

8in (20cm) high

£220-280   **D**

A Wedgwood 'Moonstone' white glazed urn vase, shape no. 3805, designed by Keith Murray, crack to base.

11.25in (28.5cm) high

£280-320   **GAZE**

A 1940s Wedgwood 'Moonstone' white ribbed plate, with printed 'KM' mark.

14in (35.5cm) wide

£500-700   **SCG**

A 1940s Wedgwood ribbed matte blue vase, shape no. 3870, designed by Keith Murray, with printed 'KM' mark.

6in (15cm) high

£220-280   **CHEF**

A CLOSER LOOK AT A WEDGWOOD BOWL

The Daventry pattern was designed by Makeig-Jones around 1926, at the height of the Fairyland Lustre range's popularity.

The success of the range inspired Carlton Ware to produce their 'Lustre' range – the influence can clearly be seen in the Chinoiserie pattern shown here.

A Wedgwood Fairyland Lustre 'Daventry' pattern vase, designed by Daisy Makeig-Jones, on a ruby lustre ground, printed mark, minor wear.

12in (30cm) high

£280-320   **WW**

Bowls offer excellent value for money as both the inside and outside are decorated, unlike vases, making a great visual impact.

The market for Fairyland Lustre has risen dramatically, with great interest from the US market, particularly for those in bright, mint condition.

A Wedgwood Fairyland Lustre 'Daventry' pattern octagonal bowl, designed by Daisy Makeig-Jones, on a ruby lustre ground, printed and painted marks.

c1928   *8in (20cm) diam*

£1,000-2,000   **WW**

A Wedgwood 'The Mayor' transfer-printed and hand-painted plate, D6283.

10.5in (26.5cm) diam

£50-60   **BAD**

A Wedgwood 'The Admiral' transfer printed and hand-painted plate, D6278.

This would appeal to collectors of Nelson memorabilia, particularly considering the centenary of the Battle of Trafalgar in October 2005.

10.5in (26.5cm) diam

£50-60   **BAD**

A Wedgwood 'The Huntsman' transfer-printed and hand-painted plate, D6282.

10.5in (26.5cm) diam

£50-60   **BAD**

A Wedgwood lidded box, with hand-painted stylized quasi-Moorish floral design, marked "C.5456s".

6.25in (16cm) wide

£40-50   **BAD**

A 1960s-70s Wedgwood 'Design 63' cylindrical container or vase, with printed black and green diamond pattern, lacks cork stopper.

8.75in (22.5cm) high

£10-15   **BAD**

CERAMICS

COLLECTORS' NOTES

■ Although West German ceramics from the 1950s have been a recognised collecting field for some years, their later, very different 1960s and '70s younger siblings have largely been ignored. Over the past few years, this has begun to change and interest is growing.

■ Much research is still to be done, and the lack of official company records, which were not kept or were destroyed, makes it hard. Handling as many identified pieces, preferably with labels, is the best way of learning. The name and period of manufacture can be gained from considering the shape, colour of clay used, colour and type of glaze and the marks on the base.

■ The most desirable designs are known as 'fat lava' by collectors and are brightly coloured with thick, dripped, and cratered textured glazes that look like molten or dried lava, or the moon's surface. Many of these were complex to produce and are rare. Shapes that were typical of their time are also desirable. Simple, glossy glazes in dull colours on simply moulded bodies are generally less desirable.

■ Many of the more sought-after 'wild' glazes were only produced in limited numbers, with the 'tamer' designs being exported widely in much larger numbers. Size is important, with large, floor standing vases being sold in smaller quantities at the time, making them rare today. Many collectors collect by shape, glaze or company.

■ Always buy in the best condition possible, as many perfect examples can still be found on the market. Most companies closed, or discontinued their decorative ranges, from the mid-1970s to early 1990s as tastes changed and less expensive imports from the Far East affected them.

A 1970s West German Scheurich vase, with repeated 'sliced onion' like moulded design and cream glaze, the base marked "285-18 W. Germany".

7in (18cm) high

£15-20   **DTC**

A 1970s West German Scheurich vase, with repeated 'sliced onion' like moulded design and brown glaze, the base moulded "285-15 W. Germany".

6in (15cm) high

£15-20   **DTC**

A 1970s West German Scheurich vase, with repeated 'sliced onion' like moulded design, the base marked "285-30 W. GERMANY".

This is one of the most commonly seen patterns and can be found in a wide variety of sizes and colours.

11.75in (30cm) high

£35-45   **DTC**

A West German Scheurich tapering cylinder vase, with dripped purple lava-type glaze over painted green bands on a matte brown ground, the base moulded "205-32 W.Germany".

12.5in (31.5cm) high

£30-50   **GC**

A 1970s West German Scheurich vase, the base marked "202-22 W.Germany".

9in (23cm) high

£18-22   **L**

A West German Scheurich vase, with alternating bands of volcanic textured orange and brown glaze, the base moulded "205/32 W.Germany", with paper label.

Note the shape of the rim and neck, which is a typical Scheurich feature.

12.5in (32cm) high

£35-45   **GC**

A West German Scheurich large floor vase, with creamy brown mottled and textured top and base, and orange band with brown lava-type glaze dripped design, the base moulded "517-30 W.Germany".

On Scheurich pieces, the first figure indicates the shape number, the second the size in centimetres.

A West German Scheurich vase, with matte brown lava 'tartan' pattern effect glaze over a glossy red ground, the base moulded "200-28 W.Germany", and with paper label.

11in (28cm) high

£25-35   **GC**

A West German Scheurich vase, with orange lava glaze dripped over a glossy ultramarine blue glazed body, the base moulded "200-22 W.Germany".

8.75in (22.5cm) high

£25-35   **GC**

11.75in (30cm) high

£30-50   **GC**

A late 1970s West German Scheurich large floor standing vase, with a painted design of a stylised flower stem and random brushstrokes in brown, the base moulded "Scheurich-Keramik 291-45 W.Germany".

17.75in (45cm) high

£100-150   **GC**

A West German Scheurich vase, with handle, with green, orange and black glossy glazed bands, the base moulded "401-28 W.Germany".

Like many of Scheurich's handled jug vases, this shape can also be found without a handle.

11in (28cm) high

£15-20   **GC**

A 1970s West German Scheurich jug vase, with handle and wavy and straight line design, the base marked "408-40 W.Germany".

This is typical of 1970s Scheurich production in its colour, form and decoration. The base markings and label are also typical of the maker.

15.75in (40cm) high

£40-60   **DTC**

A West German Scheurich jug vase, with handle, unmarked.

This is one of the harder to find Scheurich jug forms.

15.5in (39.5cm) high

£30-40   **GAZE**

A West German Scheurich ovoid jug vase, with handle, with wide central band hand-painted with a green and black volcanic textured glazed stylised flower, with creamy brown top and base, the base moulded "484-30 W.Germany".

11.75in (30cm) high

£30-40   **GC**

An enormous West German Scheurich floor standing vase, with a wide band of hand-painted and carved yellow diamonds and circles between two bands of textured black and white glaze, the base moulded "553-52 W.Germany".

20in (51cm) high

£120-180   **GC**

A huge West German Scheurich floor vase, with a 'stained glass window' design of different coloured cells bordered by raised black glaze lines, with matte black top and 'volcanic' textured brown areas, the base moulded "517 45 W.Germany".

17.25in (44cm) high

£100-150   **GC**

A West German Scheurich vase, the bronze glaze overlaid on the flanges with drips of purple lava glaze, the base moulded "267-25 W.Germany".

The thin, raised areas of glaze damage has occurred when bubbles have burst as the piece has been moved and handled.

9.75in (24.5cm) high

£30-50   **GC**

A West German Scheurich square floor bottle, moulded with the 'Montignac' pattern of a bull and a stag with hand-painted detail, dripped brown lava glaze, the base moulded "281-30 W.Germany".

This pattern is inspired by the French Lascaux caves, which contain some of the best prehistoric cave paintings known.

11.5in (29.5cm) high

£70-100   **GC**

A huge West German Bay Keramik floor jug vase, with handle, with all-over dripped glossy yellow lava-type glaze, the base moulded "BAY 218-50 W.Germany".

The Contura label is likely to be for a distributor or a retailer.

19.25in (49cm) high

£120-180   **GC**

A huge West German Bay Keramik floor vase, the body and rim with rows of moulded berry-like bosses, with textured cream and brown brushed glazed waisted neck, the base moulded "BAY 44 50 W.Germany".

19.25in (49cm) high

£80-120   **GC**

A West German Bay Keramik vase, with thick cream glaze dripped over the matte black glazed body, the base moulded "BAY 630 40 W.Germany".

15.75in (40cm) high

£40-60   **GC**

A West German Bay Keramik globe vase, with semi-iridescent glossy speckled blue, brown and cream glazes with painted circular and wavy line patterns, the base moulded "64 17 BAY W.Germany".

6.5in (16.5cm) high

£35-45   **GC**

CERAMICS

A CLOSER LOOK AT A CARSTENS VASE

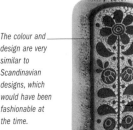

It is a very large, floor standing size.

This label indicates Carsten's high-end 'Luxus' range, many designed by Dieter Pieter, Trude Carstens or Gerda Heuckeroth.

The colour and design are very similar to Scandinavian designs, which would have been fashionable at the time.

The Luxus range was more expensive and less were made, making examples harder to find today.

A West German Carstens 'space capsule' tapered vase, with central band printed with orange and white glazed shapes, the top half with mottled bronze and brown gloss glaze, the bottom half with textured brown glaze, the base moulded "1253-15 W.Germany".

6.25in (16cm) high

£30-40   **GC**

A West German Dümler & Breiden vase, with moulded pebble design in red and yellow over a glossy blue-green glazed ground, the base impressed with the factory motif and "613/22 Germany".

8.75in (22cm) high

£50-70   **GC**

A West German Carstens 'Luxus' range floor vase, with moulded brown glazed stylised flower design on a textured cream glazed ground, the base moulded "7690-50 W.Germany".

20in (51cm) high

£120-180   **GC**

A West German Dümler & Breiden square footed vase, from the 'Relief' range, with dripped snow-like textured white glaze over a satin finish royal blue glazed body, the base impressed with a factory motif and "RELIEF 84/36 Germany".

14.25in (36.5cm) high

£50-70   **GC**

A West German Dümler & Breiden vase, with tapering orange top section with moulded runic designs and paper label, the base impressed with factory motif and "10 30 Germany".

Runic designs were also popular with studio potters of the period.

11.5in (29.5cm) high

£60-90   **GC**

A West German Dümler & Breiden two-handled pot, from the 'Relief' range, in glossy glazes, moulded with circular bosses and impressed on the base with factory motif and "RELIEF 90/15 Germany".

10.25in (26cm) high

£40-60   **GC**

A fine and large West German ES-Keramik amphora-type vase, with 'Bombay' red and blue-grey lava glaze over a blue-grey ground, unmarked.

ES Keramik was the name used by Emonds & Söhne.

10.5in (26.5cm) high

£80-120   **GC**

A West German ES-Keramik jug vase, with tall neck and handle and dripped matte red and blue-grey lava effect glaze over a blue-grey ground, unmarked, with shield-shaped foil label.

11.25in (28.5cm) high

£60-80   **GC**

A West German Fohr baluster vase, the satin finish glazed purple body overlaid with a dripping, glittering bronze coloured glaze, the base moulded "W.Germany 312-20".

8in (20.5cm) high

£40-60　　　　　　　　　GC

A CLOSER LOOK AT A WEST GERMAN BOWL

The bright colour with the black lava glaze bubbling through it is a typical hallmark of Otto Keramik pieces from the 1970s.

The craters show where the glaze has bubbled through and popped - this example has a good range of sizes and dense clustering.

Otto Keramik is still in business today, producing tamer designs.

The bases of Otto Keramik pieces are most often covered in felt.

A West German Otto Keramik small bun-shaped bowl, with matte black glaze bubbling through the thick matte yellow lava glaze, unmarked, with felt base.

3.25in (8.5cm) high

£40-60　　　　　　　　　GC

A West German Jasba ovoid vase, with moulded knobbly, pebble-like effect and orange glaze brushed over a matte black glazed body, the base impressed "N 9001125", with English language gold foil label.

9.75in (25cm) high

£40-60　　　　　　GC

A West German Jopeko octagonal jug, with yellow and black mottled glossy lava-type glaze dripped over a smooth black speckled purple glazed ground, the base impressed "1305".

6in (15.5cm) high

£30-40　　　　　　GC

A West German Jopeko small footed circular vase, with light covering of smooth lime green glaze on a black ground, the base with textured matte black glaze, indistinctly marked.

The combination of smooth, bright glazes and a black lava glaze is typical of Jopeko.

6in (15.5cm) high

£30-50　　　　　　GC

A 1970s West German Otto Keramik cylinder vase, the glossy red glaze with matte cratered textured black glaze bubbling through, unmarked, with felt base.

9.5in (24cm) high

£40-40　　　　　　GC

A West German Roth Keramik rectangular section oval vase, with moulded red gloss glazed concave areas between bubble textured black glazed strands, with paper label, the base moulded "W.Germany 310".

Roth Keramik are based in Ebernhahn, and this design, found in yellow, purple and red with black, is one of their best known and loved by collectors. Look out for the taller jug vases with ring handles, as these can fetch over £100 in large sizes.

6.25in (16cm) high

£30-50　　　　　　GC

A West German Roth Keramik shaped vase, moulded with concave purple glossy glazed ovals between white and black textured bubbled strands, the base moulded "W.Germany".

10.25in (26cm) high

£40-60　　　　　　GC

A West German Ruscha rounded rectangular footed vase, with dripped and graduated brown, lime green and purple lava type glazes, unmarked.

9.75in (25cm) high

£40-60   GC

A CLOSER LOOK AT A WEST GERMAN VASE

This design was by Cari Zalloni, who went on to found the fashionable Cazal eyewear company.

It is part of a range of differently shaped vases with similar glazes and decoration.

It was designed in the early 1960s and forsees the Op Art movement, championed by Bridget Riley.

Steuler Keramik pieces are often marked on the base with a moulded 'S' and 't' monogram within a shield.

A West German Steuler Keramik 'Zyklon' pattern rectangular vase, the base moulded and numbered "215/25".

9.75in (24.5cm) high

£30-40   GC

A West German Ruscha footed vase, with small, flared rim, with 'Vulcano' orange-red lava glaze over a black ground, the base moulded "805".

The form and even finish of this vase recall antique Oriental ceramics and also the works of some modern ceramicists. 'Vulcano', developed in 1959, is one of the most sought-after and famous West German glazes of the period.

7in (18cm) high

£60-90   GC

A West German Schlossberg rectangular section vase, the textured cream glazed body with moulded ovals filled with glossy blue, the base moulded "296/25".

9.75 (24.5cm) high

£60-90   GC

A West German Schlossberg rectangular vase, with glossy orange drips over a glossy brown lava-type glaze, the base moulded "298 25".

As well as the company name, the label reads "Handarbeit", which indicates the piece is 'hand-made'.

9.75in (24.5cm) high

£50-70   GC

A West German Spara Keramik gourd vase, with gloss green and black glaze, the base stamped "SPARA 266/15".

The form of this vase closely resembles many antique Chinese forms.

6in (15cm) high

£25-35   GC

A West German Ü-Keramik square section jug, with inset handle and dripped and mottled glaze, the top with small off-centre opening, unmarked.

11.75in (30cm) high

£50-80   GC

A West German Ü-Keramik vase, with dripped cream satin finish and speckled orange-red gloss glazes, the base indistinctly impressed, with gold foil label.

10.25in (26cm) high

£30-40   GC

FIND OUT MORE...

Fat Lava West German Ceramics of the 1960s & 70s, by Mark Hill, *www.markhillpublishing.com, 2006, ISBN: 978-0-95528-650-6.*

A Lorna Bailey 'The Dingle Porthill' pattern jug, with factory stamps to base including impressed "78" and a painted signature.

Contemporary designer Lorna Bailey's pieces are inspired by the work of Clarice Cliff in terms of their colour and stylization.

5.5in (14cm) high

£40-60   **JN**

A Danish Bing & Grøndahl porcelain model of a rabbit standing, no. 2443, designed by Dahl-Jensen.

5in (12.5cm) long

£30-40   **LOB**

A Bretby Art Deco vase, with faint impressed marks to base.

This form is similar to many designs from the sought-after Art Deco 'Futura' range by US manufacturer Roseville. If you want to be ahead of the game in spotting treasures others may not recognise, invest in a copy of 'Collectors' Guide: Art Deco' by Judith Miller, published by DK in 2006.

7.25in (18.5cm) high

£80-120   **BAD**

A Broadhurst Bros 'Rushstone' pattern ironstone trio set, designed by Kathie Winkle.

c1965   *Saucer 6.5in (16.5cm) diam*

£10-15   **GROB**

A 1930s Burleigh ware small milk jug, with hand-painted leaf and streaked design on typical yellow ground.

Bright colours and handles moulded into animal or floral/natural forms are typical features of Burleigh pieces.

3.25in (8cm) high

£70-90   **BAD**

A Burleigh ware small milk jug, with hand-painted yellow leaf-like moulded form.

3.25in (8cm) high

£40-50   **BAD**

A Royal Cauldon Arcadian Ware 'Arabian' pattern vase, designed by Frederick Rhead, with a hand-painted Art Deco stylized foliate and fruiting design, the base with printed mark.

11.25in (28cm) high

£200-250   **WW**

A Burleigh ware pedestal bowl, designed by Harold Bennett, with tube-lined decorated of a windmill scene, the base with printed mark and facsimile signature.

10.75in (27cm) diam

£100-150   **WW**

Two Polish Cmielow ceramic animals, comprising an elephant and a monkey, the bases unmarked.

Monkey 5in (13cm) long

£10-15 (each)   **PSI**

CERAMICS

A Denby 'cottontail' yellow glazed deer figurine, with hollow body.

The hollow body contains cotton wool, which is pulled through a hole leaving him with a constant bushy white tail. Rabbits were also available.

5in (12.5cm) high

£45-55   **DIM**

A CLOSER LOOK AT A BUST OF A GIRL

Essevi was founded by ceramic designer Sandro Vacchetti, who had previously been a key designer at Lenci.

Each hand-painted piece is effectively unique, and is signed and dated on the base by the artist. Note the charming look and delicate handling of her make-up and rosy cheeks.

Like Goldscheider, Lenci is known for its elegant, finely made and valuable Art Deco figurines of ladies. At Essevi, Vacchetti continued his work on similar designs.

This example had some chips and wear, had it been in perfect condition, it could have fetched around 25 per cent more. Had it been an elegant lady figurine, rather than a young girl it could have fetched around double this value.

An Italian Essevi bust of a young girl, modelled wearing a flower encrusted bonnet, the base with painted factory marks and dated "14-9-38", some minor chips.

1938   8.25in (21cm) high

£350-450   **DN**

A 1920s-30s Fielding's Crown Devon 'Summer' pattern Lustrine vase.

9.5in (24cm) high

£80-120   **BAD**

A 1950s-60s Fielding's Crown Devon clown-shaped cookie jar, marked "1050".

10.5in (26.5cm) high

£60-80   **BAD**

A Crown Ducal vase, pattern 4794, designed by Charlotte Rhead, with flowers and foliage in shades of blue and purple, the base with printed mark and facsimile signature.

8in (20cm) high

£300-500   **WW**

A Crown Ducal 'Byzantine' ovoid ribbed vase, pattern 2681, designed by Charlotte Rhead, with printed marks to the base.

Charlotte Rhead (1885-1947) was the daughter of noted ceramic designer Frederick Rhead. She is best known for her tube-lined work where the pattern is applied with liquid slip, like icing on a cake. Currently, her work is largely underappreciated and probably undervalued.

10.5in (26.5cm) high

£150-200   **GHOU**

A Royal Dux porcelain figure of a seated naked maiden.

8.5in (21.5cm) high

£250-350   **GHOU**

An Icelandic Glit baluster vase, with applied chippings and a volcanic textured, lava-like glaze, glazed in graduated blue, creamy yellow, red and dark brown, the base impressed "GLIT".

Glit was founded around 1958 by Ragnar Kjartansson. The pottery uses real Icelandic lava chippings in the glazes to give texture to their production. Glit is also Icelandic for 'brocaded'.

9.75in (24.5cm) high

£20-30   **GC**

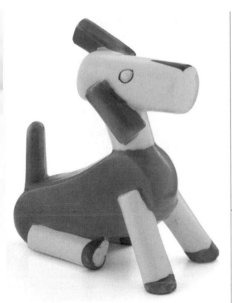

A rare 1930s W. Goebels 'Cubist' or Modernist style hand-painted dog figurine, with early crown mark, impressed "K.T. 735B".

4.25in (11cm) high

£350-450   **DIM**

A pair of Gouda 'Bertino' pattern hand-painted vases, signed "2669/Bertino/GD/4648/Gouda Holland" on the base.

8in (20.5cm) high

£180-220   **DRA**

A 1960s Gouda 'Flora' hand-painted vase, the base marked "Flora HOLLAND 911".

5.25in (13.5cm) high

£18-22   **MTS**

A Sampson Hancock & Sons Ivoryware hand-painted coffee can and saucer.

4.25in (10.5cm) diam

£20-25   **BAD**

A Sampson Hancock & Sons Coronetware 'Cherry Ripe' hand-painted candle sconce night light, with handle to rear.

Hancock's was founded in 1858 and went through a number of name and location changes before its closure in 1937. During the late 1920s and '30s, the pottery produced a number of wares decorated with flowers to compete against Moorcroft.

6in (15cm) high

£120-180   **BAD**

A Sampson Hancock & Sons Art Deco 'Ivoryware' hand-painted candleholder.

4.25in (11cm) high

£25-35   **BAD**

A 1980s Honiton Pottery plane ashtray, design by Julie Galuszka.

This was part of 'The Julie Range' produced by Honiton Pottery (1881-1997), which included cars, planes and boats on a variety of dishes and two lampbases.

6.25in (16cm) wide

£18-22   **MTS**

A Hornsea 'Summit' black and white cruet set, designed by John Clappison, on a black dish.

c1960   5.25in (13.5cm) high

£8-12   **TCM**

A Hornsea Pottery 'Classic' range amphora vase, designed by John Clappison, with grey vertical stripes, the base impressed "828".

7.75in (19.5cm) high

£18-22   GAZE

A 1960s Irish Kilrush Pottery white waisted vase, with dark brown glazed textured finish.

7.5in (19cm) high

£18-22   L

An Irish Kilrush Pottery vase, with brushed and incised decoration.

Little is currently known about the Irish company Kilrush. Their products are often mistaken for West German or Italian ceramics of the 1950s-70s, due to their similar colours and designs.

c1955   *8.25in (21cm) high*

£30-40   MA

A Langley 'Jamaica' pattern hand-painted teapot.

6in (15cm) high

£30-35   GROB

A J. & G. Meakin Studioware 'Habitat' pattern hand-painted teapot.

The form is similar to some of noted industrial designer Russel Wright's designs for American companies Iroquois and Steubenville.

£25-35   GAZE

A Royal Norfolk 'Petra' range vase, designed by Colin Melbourne, with facsimile signature to base and impressed "112" mark.

6in (15.5cm) high

£40-60   GC

A 1930s Noritake gilt ring holder, with attached tray.

3.5in (9cm) diam

£30-40   BAD

A 1980s Next Interiors vase, designed by Janice Tchalenko, with random pink and beige glazes, with printed mark to the base.

Janice Tchalenko has become a notable studio potter and ceramics designer and is renowned for her own studio pieces, as well her as design work for Poole Pottery and Dartington Pottery. Few realise that she designed a now collectable range for Next, which shows her hallmark colourful and abstract approach to glaze decoration.

6in (15cm) high

£10-15   MHC

A 1920s-30s Noritake Lustreware figural bird toastrack.

5.5in (14cm) wide

£70-90   KCS

A CLOSER LOOK AT A NORITAKE PUNCHBOWL

Vibrant colours and liberal applications of gilt decoration are hallmarks of the company and appeared on the earliest Western-style pieces.

Its large size also makes this piece comparatively rare, as smaller pieces would have been more affordable and so more common at the time. It is also in excellent, unworn condition.

The decoration is skillfully hand-painted – values depend on the complexity, success and eye-appeal of these designs.

This is a large and very well detailed piece made to imitate expensive French and German porcelains, and would have been expensive in its day.

A Noritake punchbowl and stand, with hand-painted scene and gilt decoration.

The Japanese export company that became known as Noritake was founded in 1876 by Baron Ichizaemon Morimura to take advantage of new trade links between Japan and the US. After a visit to the Paris World's Fair, Morimura saw an opportunity for making Western-style pieces as well as exporting Japanese-style pieces. He founded a factory to make them in 1904, with the first exports beginning in 1910.

1910-30   12in (30.5cm) wide

£350-450   KCS

A Portmeirion 'Tivoli' pattern sugar sifter.

This pattern was designed by Portmeirion owner and ex-textile designer Susan Williams-Ellis after a visit to Copenhagen's famous Tivoli Gardens in 1964. Plain cylindrical shapes are typical 1960s forms and display the transfer pattern well.

6.75in (17cm) high

£10-15   MTS

An American Schmid International 'Think' head-shaped condom holder, designed by Tarck, with transfer printed design.

With its early thought provoking message, this piece was used in bars.

1959   8.5in (21.5cm) high

£80-120   HLM

A pair of 1920s SylvaC twin-handled cups, no.4699, decorated with mythical winged beasts, the handles modelled as rams, in shades of brown, impressed marks, paper retail label to one, one handle restuck.

Before the development of its highly collectable animal figurines, SylvaC made many such decorative pieces, including vases and clocks.

5.25in (13cm) high

£70-100   WW

An Italian Tendentze 'Tatzine' conical teacup and saucer, with stylised face transfer to handle, designed by Andrea Branzi in 1986.

Branzi (b.1938) is a noted Postmodern architect and designer. Tendentze has been part of Alessi since 1989.

c1987   3.5in (8.5cm) high

£80-120   GM

A late 1980s Italian Tendentze transfer-printed table centrepiece, designed by Riccardo Dalisi, with line drawing of a masked man.

15in (38cm) diam

£150-200   GM

A Wilkinson's 'Oriflamme' range Buber lustre brown glazed vase.

c1920   4.5in (11.5cm) high

£80-120   BAD

CERAMICS

A 1930s Royal Winton Beehive hand-painted milk jug.

Grimwade's Royal Winton brand is better known for its highly collectable floral 'chintz' transfer-printed wares.

5in (13cm) long

£30-40   **BAD**

A CLOSER LOOK AT A PUZZLE JUG

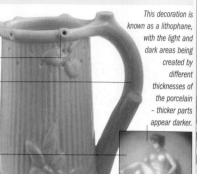

Puzzle jugs emit water from the holes on the rim, soaking the unaware user when he or she tries to pour out the liquid inside.

The 'puzzle' is how to stop this happening – here, covering a hole on the inside of the handle with a finger makes a seal, meaning the liquid can be poured safely.

This example also holds a surprise – when the base is held to the light a reclining nude is seen in the base.

This decoration is known as a lithophane, with the light and dark areas being created by different thicknesses of the porcelain – thicker parts appear darker.

A mid-to late 19thC German white porcelain 'puzzle jug', with moulded naturalistic motifs, the base with a lithophane of a reclining naked woman.

These puzzle jug 'amusements' were popular from the Middle Ages onwards, but saw a second peak in the 19thC. The lithopane is typically Victorian.

7in (17.5cm) high

£60-80   **DWG**

An Art Deco Royal Winton 'Ducks' sugar sifter, with chrome plated top.

c1930   6.25in (16cm) high

£80-120   **BAD**

A Royal Worcester 'British Friesian Bull – Terling Trusty' bone china figurine, model number RW3746, designed by Doris Lindner, mounted on an original hardwood stand.

This model was released in 1962 in a limited edition of 500 pieces, as part of the 'Prize Cattle' series. It is currently very desirable.

1962   8in (20cm) high

£500-600   **BIG**

An Art Deco Czechoslovakian hand-painted vase, printed "40" and impressed "10218".

Stylized floral motifs such as this were often taken from printed pattern books produced during the Art Deco period. These books also inspired many textile designs.

10in (25.5cm) high

£50-70   **BAD**

A 1980s Bassett's Liquorice Allsort sweet jar, the base unmarked.

4.25in (11cm) high

£10-15   **MTS**

A pair of Modernist-style handmade and painted soup bowls and saucers, with red striped decoration.

This unusual design may have been inspired by the Russian Constructivist and Suprematist ceramic pieces designed during the 1920s-30s by those such as Kasimir Malevich and Nikolai Suetin.

5.25in (13cm) diam

£40-60   **GAZE**

A Batman mirror, licensed to Creative Accessories Ltd, Bellmore NY, by DC Comics 1987.

c1987   18in (46cm) high

£12-18   **NOR**

A Batman & Robin moulded plastic 'talking' alarm clock, marked "1974 Janex Corp".

c1974   7in (17.5cm) high

£40-50   **NOR**

A Batman bat logo machine-cut perspex clock, by Creative Accessories Ltd.

13.75in (35cm) wide

£30-40   **NOR**

A Batman & Robin Melmac printed plate, with "National Periodical Publications Inc" wording.

7.25in (18.5cm) diam

£15-20   **NOR**

A Batman 'Super Plants' ceramic planter, printed "©National Publications 1975" and impressed "JAPAN".

From a set of four 'Super-Hero Planters' featuring Superman, Batman, Wonder Woman, and Shazam! (Captain Marvel – see page 183 for an example). These 'pot' plant holders were perhaps used to grow 'Super Plants'.

3.25in (8cm) high

£10-15   **NOR**

A 44-card set of Topps Batman 'Blue Bat' series cards, in original case, marked "1966 ©National Periodical Publications Ltd".

Topps issued five sets of Batman cards in 1966, three of which had painted illustrations. They are differentiated by the colour of the bat logo which can be found in blue, red and black. They are all about the same value and are the most common of the 1966 cards.

1966   3.75in (9.5cm) wide

£20-30   **NOR**

A 55 card set of Topps Batman 'Black Bat' series cards, in original case, marked "1966 ©National Periodical Publications Ltd".

1966   3.75in (9.5cm) wide

£18-22   **NOR**

A box of Topps Batman deluxe reissue edition cards.

In 1989 Topps reissued the three painted series of cards from 1966. They can be confused with the originals, but have a glossy front and the backs are printed with "reissue 1982".

1989   3.5in (9cm) wide

£7-10   **NOR**

An American 'Adventures of Batman, Chapter 4: Poison Peril' Super 8 reel, boxed, Columbia Pictures Home Movie.

1943   5in (13cm) wide

£15-25   **NOR**

An American Toy Biz Co. Superman action figure, '©1989 Superman DC Comics".

It is rare to find a figure with the cape. A carded example is worth around £120.

c1989

£30-40   NOR

A Burger King Superman figural cup holder.

This was produced as a promotional give-away for stores.

1988   4.25in (10.5cm) high

£6-8   NOR

A Superman the Movie promotional double-walled plastic mug and cup set, by Dawn, Passaic NJ, marked "©1978 DC Comics".

c1978   4.25in (10.5cm) high

£8-12   NOR

A large Superman screen-printed glass.

This is a very unusual shape and size.

1971   6.75in (17cm) high

£10-15   NOR

A Pepsi Collectors' Series Superman screenprinted glass.

6.25in (16cm) high

£10-15   NOR

An American Superman laminated card, 78-record single 'Supercase', "©DC Comics Inc 1976".

7.75in (19.5cm) high

£22-28   NOR

A rare Superman Thermos flask, "©1967 National Periodical Publications Inc.", in great condition.

This rare Superman Thermos will appeal to collectors of Thermos and those wanting to complete a set with a lunchbox.

7.25in (18.5cm) high

£60-70   NOR

A pair of Superman licensed plastic child's rollerskates, "©1975 DC Comics".

7in (18cm) long

£8-12   NOR

An early Superman printed Valentine card.

1940   4.25in (11cm) high

£10-15   NOR

An American Popeye WWII propaganda postcard, marked "© King Features Syndicates".

1942 5.5in (14cm) high

£22-28 LDE

An American Popeye jointed wood doll, with transfer-printed and carved decoration, the foot printed "Made in USA".

5in (13cm) high

£100-150 MG

A 1940s unmade-up Captain Marvel Club 'Shazam' printed tin pin.

There is another, scarcer version of this pin where the superhero is looking off to one side.

1in (3cm) wide

£20-30 LDE

A Captain Marvel 'Shazam!' 'Super-Hero Planter', "©National Publications 1975" and impressed "JAPAN".

A number of comic book publishers have characters called Captain Marvel. This version was created by Fawcett Publications in 1939. The character was then licensed to DC Comics in 1972 but the name had been copyrighted by Marvel. To get around the issue, DC marketed the character under the trademark 'Shazam!'

c1975 3.25in (8cm) high

£6-8 NOR

An Amazing Spider-Man promotional 7-Eleven Slurpee cup, marked "©1975 Marvel Comics Group".

5in (12.5cm) high

£3-5 NOR

A box of Marvel Superhero 'Adventure Cookies', with Spider-Man promotional money bank, unopened.

1991 9.75in (25cm) high

£8-12 NOR

A Barbie as Wonder Woman Collector Edition doll, by Mattel, mint, boxed.

This Barbie doll will be popular with Barbie collectors as well as Wonder Woman fans. The planned 2007 film by Joss Whedon should help to increase interest in the character.

1999 13.5in (34.5cm) high

£30-40 NOR

A pair of Wonder Woman plastic scissors, for Dyno MDDSE corp, made in Hong Kong.

1978 5in (13cm) high

£5-7 NOR

A Corgi Magic Roundabout 'Dylan' plastic figure.

The Magic Roundabout was originally a French children's programme (Le Manège Enchanté), created by Serge Danot in 1963. It was shown in the UK by the BBC who commissioned Eric Thompson (father of actress Emma Thompson) to provide an English voiceover which he based not on the original script but soley on the visuals. The show proved a huge hit with both adults and children and numerous interpretations exist to the 'true' meaning of the show.

2in (5cm) high

£10-15   RBC

A Magic Roundabout 'Florence' plastic figure.

8.25in (21cm) high

£10-15   MTS

A Corgi Magic Roundabout 'Dougal' plastic figure

3in (7.5cm) long

£7-10   RBC

A Magic Roundabout printed tin kaleidoscope, by Green Monk Combex, dated.

1968   9in (23cm) high

£20-25   MTS

A Deans Playtime 'My Magic Roundabout Pop-Up Book'.

1975   9.25in (23.5cm) wide

£15-20   RBC

A box of Magic Roundabout Crackers, by Tom Smith & Co Ltd., Norwich, England, each containing a tissue party hat, balloon, a 'character' badge and a snap, box marked "BBC TV 1971".

A complete and unused box of crackers, such as this, is very rare.

Box 16.75in (42cm) wide

£100-150   MTS

A 1970s Magic Roundabout printed paper party plate.

7.5in (19cm) diam

£2-3   MTS

A Magic Roundabout printed plastic lampshade.

8.75in (22cm) high

£30-40   MTS

CHARACTER COLLECTABLES

A Snoopy soft toy.

Charlie Brown's beagle Snoopy first appeared in the Peanuts comic strip on October 4th, 1950, two days after the very first strip. Initially a silent, supporting character, Snoopy came into his own when writer Charles Schultz began to draw thought balloons for the character. From the 1960s the strip focused more on Snoopy and his various alter-egos which included a WWI flying ace. Today he is arguably one of the most recognisable comic strip characters in the world.

c1950   8in (20cm) high

£12-18   **RBC**

A 1970s Snoopy 'Another Determined Production' vase.

5in (12.5cm) wide

£10-15   **MTS**

A Snoopy painted wood money box, marked "©1958, 1966".

6in (15cm) high

£20-25   **RBC**

A 1990s Snoopy electric hairdryer, by Clariol Appliances, marked "© 1958, 1966".

9.5in (24cm) high

£15-20   **RBC**

A 1970s Peanuts diecast car, with Snoopy driving and Woodstock as a passenger.

4.25in (11cm) long

£60-80   **RBC**

An American Peanuts Belle Fun & Fashion Dress-Up doll, by Knickerbocker, with Woodstock figure, mint and boxed, marked "© 1958, 1965".

Belle, a little seen character in the Peanuts strip, is Snoopy's sister. She is mostly known through merchandise rather than the comic strip, leading occasional readers to mistake her for Snoopy's girlfriend.

Box 10.25in (26cm) high

£40-60   **RBC**

A Snoopy 'Tea for Two' transfer-printed mug, marked "FOREIGN".

3.25in (8.5cm) high

£8-12   **RBC**

A Peanuts cartoon graphic printed silk tie.

£18-22   **S&T**

A 'Bendy' foam Kermit the Frog Muppet figure, with indistinct marks.

c1970   *8.5in (21.5cm) high*

£22-28   **RBC**

A 1970s 'Bendy' foam Miss Piggy Muppets figure, in karate outfit.

8in (20cm) high

£15-20   **RBC**

A CLOSER LOOK AT A PAIR OF LONE RANGER DOLLS

These examples are in mint, original condition. As they would have been bought to play with, most examples show wear, damage or missing parts

The painted composition is in excellent condition and shows no signs of cracking or crazing on the face.

They retain their clothing, accessories and moreover their weapons, which is very unusual.

These large size figures would have been relatively expensive when originally made, meaning fewer would have been sold.

A rare pair of 1930s Dollcraft Novelty Lone Ranger and Tonto composition dolls, clothed.

The Lone Ranger and Tonto were based on characters created by George W. Trendle and developed by writer Fran Striker. They first appeared on radio in 1933, beginning a hugely successful run of nearly 3,000 episodes. The series moved to television in 1949 and the duo also appeared in comic books, novels and movie serials.

c1938   *20in (51cm) high*

£600-700   **SOTT**

A Fozzie Bear Muppets soft toy, by Fisher Price Toys, copyright 1976, with moulded rubber hat and plastic eyes.

c1976   *12in (30.5cm) high*

£25-35   **RBC**

A Little Miss Chatterbox, by Holland Studio Craft Ltd, copyright 1998.

2.75in (7cm) high

£8-12   **RBC**

A Li'l Abner 'Shmoo' moulded brass pin.

The selfless Shmoo first appeared in Al Capp's L'il Abner comic strip in August 1948. The perfect herd animal, the Shmoo delighted in being eaten and tasted of different meats depending on the cooking method. A vast amount of licensed Shmoo merchandise was created, particularly in the late 1940s and early '50s and is still desirable today.

1.5in (4cm) high

£20-30   **LDE**

A Li'l Abner 'Kigmy' brass hollow pin.

In 1949, Al Capp followed up his popular Shmoo character with the Kigmy (Kick-Me) creature, which was similar in shape to the selfless Shmoo and loved to be kicked. Capp stated that he was inspired by two ethic groups who were 'kicked around' by American society: the African Americans and Jews, but the L'il Abner readership did not take to the new character and it was soon dropped. Despite the Kigmy's short run, merchandise including kickable inflatable toys was produced, but in smaller amounts than for the Shmoo.

c1949   *1in (2.5cm) wide*

£20-30   **LDE**

COLLECTORS' NOTES

■ Metal moulds used to form chocolate into novelty or themed shapes began to be widely used from the late 1800s, growing in popularity and reaching their apex during the 1920s and 1930s. Makers at this time were centred in Germany, but also in France and the US. Use began to tail off during the 1950s.

■ Stamped numbers indicate the catalogue number, enabling moulds to be ordered from makers' catalogues. Makers included Anton Reiche of Dresden, H.Walter of Berlin, Sommet of Paris and Eppelsheimer of New York. Many moulds are unmarked, but their style and manufacture can help to identify makers. Walter, for example, was the only maker that stamped its mould numbers on the inside.

■ Some makers used a symbol, such as Sommet's stylised fish and Eppelsheimer's spinning top. Marked, and particularly dated, examples are more desirable in general. Materials can also help with

dating. Tin-plated copper came first, used until the late 1890s, followed by tin-plated steel (the most commonly found material), and finally nickel-plated steel and nickel silver, both of which have a different feel and shiny silvery appearance.

■ Reiche is considered one of the best and most prolific mould makers. Founded in 1870, over 50,000 designs were produced. The company exported to the US via T.C Weygandt of New York, from 1885 until 1939, when WWII broke out. The factory was destroyed during the war, to re-open in Communist East Germany in 1950 and then to close finally in 1972.

■ Look for good levels of detail and large sizes. Popular themes include transport, characters and Christmas and Easter themes. Unusual details or forms can add value. Clips do not count towards value as they are never the original clips, which were interchanged by the original chocolatiers many times over.

An early American Eppelsheimer tin-plated copper chocolate mould, no.4743.

Examine the edges for tell-tale copper brown colouring to recognise copper moulds.

8.5in (21.5cm) high

£60-80   DF

An American Eppelsheimer chocolate mould, no.4723, of a standing bunny with a basket on his back.

8.5in (21.5cm) high

£50-70   DF

An American Eppelsheimer tin-plated copper chocolate mould, no.8200, in the form of a bunny with a basket on his back.

It is the enormous size of this mould, the notable maker's name, marked date and its extreme rarity that make it this valuable. Used as a shop display piece, the eventual pure chocolate bunny would have weighed in at over 30lbs.

1937   37.5in (95cm) high

£10,000-12,000   DF

A German Anton Reiche standing rabbit chocolate mould, no.24458.

6.75in (17cm) high

£50-70   DF

A German Anton Reiche small seated rabbit chocolate mould, no.6770, with maker's mark.

3.25in (8.5cm) high

£20-30   DF

A German Anton Reiche seated bunny chocolate mould, no.26968.

1930   7in (18cm) high

£50-70   DF

CHOCOLATE MOULDS

A 1930s American Eppelsheimer standing bunny with basket chocolate mould, no.8192.

This mould also bears the stamp "Repaired Eppelsheimer & Co N.Y. Jan 1937". Note the bright tin-plated parts which help the chocolate come out of the mould easier.

6in (15cm) high

£40-60   DF

A rare German Anton Reiche bunny pushing a pram chocolate mould, no.21888S, with indistinct date stamp.

1926-36   5in (13cm) high

£100-150   DF

A rabbit playing a saxophone chocolate mould, no.9.

4.75in (12cm) high

£40-50   DF

A German Walter seated rabbit chocolate mould, no.1521.

Seated bunnies are the most commonly found mould shape.

5.5in (14cm) high

£30-40   DF

A German Walter bunnies around a basket chocolate mould, impressed inside the mould "5306".

6.25in (16cm) high

£120-180   DF

A rare rabbit riding on a dolphin chocolate mould, no.4005.

4.25in (11cm) high

£80-120   DF

A German Anton Reiche 'egg boat' chocolate mould, no.6399, with date mark.

1925   5.25in (13.5cm) long

£60-80   DF

A 1920s American Jaburg Bros. solid nickel silver chocolate mould.

5.25in (13.5cm) long

£35-45   DF

A German Anton Reiche double bunny and basket chocolate mould, no.25523, with date mark and Weygandt importers and date stamp.

This mould appears life-size in a 1930s Anton Reiche catalog.

1935   10.5in (27cm) wide

£150-250   DF

An unmarked cockerel chocolate mould, with chocolate remains.

The oils in the chocolate helped to preserve the mould. Today many collectors use mineral oil.

4.25in (11cm) high

£25-35   **DF**

A French Letang Fils stork chocolate mould, no.4209.

7.5in (19cm) high

£70-100   **DF**

A small seated cat chocolate mould, stamped "641" and "48".

3.25in (8cm) high

£35-45   **DF**

A German Anton Reiche seal chocolate mould, no.26483, with date stamp and additional indistinct French "Georges Diltoer Agent Générale" stamp.

1935   4.5in (11.5cm) high

£80-120   **DF**

A CLOSER LOOK AT A SOMMET CHOCOLATE MOULD

On Sommet moulds, a figure in a diamond is the date mark – here it is "49" for 1949.

Sommet used a stylized fish or dolphin as their maker's mark.

This mould is large and has a 'lid' on the base showing that it could also be used for ice cream – this is borne out by the additional "1L" stamp.

Sommet were the only makers to have overlapping sides.

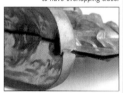

A French Sommet prancing horse chocolate and one litre ice cream mould, no.1436.

1949   9in (23cm) high

£200-300   **DF**

A French Letang Fils manta ray fish chocolate mould.

These brackets are typical of Letang who were the only maker to use them, even though they do not appear on all of their moulds.

5.5in (14cm) long

£50-70   **DF**

An unusual four-part tortoise chocolate mould.

The shell was moulded separately from the base, which would then be filled with chocolates and served.

8.5in (21.5cm) long

£180-220   **DF**

An American Eppelsheimer standing Santa Claus chocolate mould, no.8003.

4.75in (12cm) high

£70-100 DF

A modern Chinese reproduction Santa Claus chocolate mould.

Compared to vintage moulds, new moulds use different materials, have no wear or makers' stamps, are lighter and display less detail.

4.75in (12cm) high

£2-3 DF

A standing Santa Claus in a long coat chocolate mould, no.171.

This is a common form for Santa but values can vary depending on the size and number and type of items he is holding.

7.75in (19.5cm) high

£80-120 DF

A small German standing Santa Claus in a long coat with clasped hands chocolate mould, unmarked.

4.25in (11cm) high

£60-80 DF

A German Anton Reiche standing Santa Claus in a short coat chocolate mould, no.21123S, with date stamp.

This more rounded, more American, form is another commonly found shape for Santa Claus.

1925   5in (12.5cm) high

£60-80 DF

A German Hornlein Santa Claus in a Jaguar chocolate mould, no.1013.

This amusing mould shape came in different sizes, like many chocolate moulds.

11.75in (30cm) long

£150-250 DF

A German Walter 'Bad Boy' Santa Claus chocolate mould, no.131 or 180.

This is the less rare mould of the popular pair.

6.5in (16.5cm) high

£180-220 DF

A German Walter 'Good Girl' Santa Claus chocolate mould, stamped "Germany 180A".

This is much rarer than the 'Bad Boy' mould.

7in (17.5cm) high

£450-550 DF

A German Anton Reiche 'postcard' type chocolate mould, with Santa clutching a Christmas tree and sack, no. 519, with date stamp.

Look for fine details and complex scenes. Reproductions often have badly finished edges and less detail and are also not as inventive in subject matter.

1936   5.75in (14.5cm) high

£300-400 DF

An Anton Reiche for the American market 'W.C. Fields' chocolate mould, no. 25628.

5in (13cm) high

£100-150 DF

A Charlie Chaplin chocolate mould, no.17959.

6in (15.5cm) high

£80-120 DF

A German Walter for the American market Popeye mould, no.9034, with US distributor's stamping.

7.25in (18.5cm) high

£200-300 DF

A 1950s Dutch Vormenfabriek 'Puss in Boots' chocolate mould, no.16301, stamped "JKV Tilburg".

5in (13cm) high

£40-60 DF

A German Anton Reiche Felix the Cat chocolate mould, no.13006.

5in (13cm) high

£280-320 DF

A 1950s Dutch Vormenfabriek 'Donald Duck' chocolate mould, no.16358.

5in (13cm) high

£50-70 DF

A 1930s German Anton Reiche 'Mickey Mouse' mould, no.27396, with stamped maker's mark.

As licensing laws did not restrict European makers at this time, they were able to produce moulds such as this.

3.25in (8cm) high

£220-280 DF

A German Anton Reiche 'Polly on the Potty' chocolate mould, no.16767, with date stamp.

1935

£40-80 DF

4.75in (12cm) high

CHOCOLATE MOULDS

A German Anton Reiche sword in scabbard chocolate mould, no.10013.

14.75in (37.5cm) long

£80-120 DF

A large rifle chocolate mould, unmarked.

14.75in (37.5cm) long

£100-150 DF

A small key chocolate mould, stamped "5".

6.25in (16cm) long

£40-60 DF

A German Anton Reiche radio chocolate mould, no.28448, with date stamp.

1933 *3.5in (9cm) high*

£40-60 DF

A German Anton Reiche Halloween pumpkin chocolate mould, no.21836S, with date stamp.

1926 *3.25in (8.5cm) long*

£100-150 DF

A French 'Ets Metro Anvers' locomotive chocolate mould.

6.25in (16cm) long

£50-70 DF

A post war Dutch Vormenfabriek fire engine chocolate mould, no.16247.

4in (10cm) long

£30-40 DF

A large German Anton Reiche 'Zeppelin' chocolate mould.

The exceptionally large size, rarity and popularity of the subject matter make this a valuable mould.

30.5in (78cm) long

£3,200-3,800 DF

FIND OUT MORE...

Chocolate Molds: A History & Encyclopedia, *by Judene Divone, Oakton Hills Publications, 1987.*

The Chocolate Mould, *by Henry & Laure Dorchy, 2000.*

Collectors' Guide to Antique Chocolate Molds, *by Wendy Mullen, published by Hobby House Press, 2002.*

COLLECTORS' NOTES

- Due to the sheer range of types available, most coin collectors concentrate on one area such as the ancient world, commemoratives, error coins, or examples from one specific period and/or place.

- Beware of facsimile collectors coins, which are common. Although not necessarily made to deceive, it can be hard to tell them from the genuine article. The abundance of facsimiles may lower the value of rare coins.

- When buying commemoratives, note the edition number. Those produced in large numbers will appreciate less than strictly limited issues.

- As condition is very important, coins should be handled as little as possible. Always hold coins by the edges or wear gloves, and invest in a good quality album and mounts to display and store your collection. Do not clean coins, as collectors generally prefer coins with an 'original' appearance. Cleaning might reduce values by half or more.

A Paxs type penny of Winchester, minted by William I, in good to very fine condition with light gold and grey tones.

1066-87

£400-500   DLO

A rare class D groat, minted by Edward III, fourth coinage with normal 'R', reversed 'N', with some original colour, one of the finest known examples.

1327-77

£450-550   BLO

A rosette-mascle groat of Calais, minted by Henry VI, with reverse with plain cross, in very fine condition, struck on a large flan.

1422-61

£80 120   BLO

A light coinage ryal of Bristol mint, minted by Edward IV, in extremely fine condition, slightly small flan.

During the reign of Edward IV, the face value of his coinage became less than that of the metals they were made from. To counter this the amount of metal in the coins was reduced by approximately 20 per cent. This is known as light coinage.

1461-70

£1,000-1,500   BLO

A scarce groat, minted by Henry VII, with profile portrait, in extremely fine condition, dark grey tones.

1485-1509

£320-380   BLO

A third coinage groat, minted by Henry VIII, second bust, light grey tones, in extremely fine condition, rare as such.

1509-47

£700-800   BLO

A sixpence, minted by Elizabeth I (1558-1603), the obverse with a bust in plain dress with rose, toned, weak impression around forehead, very fine condition.

1562

£150-200   BLO

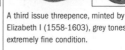

A third issue threepence, minted by Elizabeth I (1558-1603), grey tones, in extremely fine condition.

1571

£70-100   BLO

A third coinage shilling, minted by James I, the obverse with sixth bust, in extremely fine condition, scarce in this condition.

1603-25

£300-400   **BLO**

A type 3a3 halfcrown of Tower mint under Parliament, minted by Charles I, rainbow-toned, in good condition.

1625-49

£120-180   **BLO**

A lozenge-shaped halfcrown of Newark mint (beseiged), minted by Charles I (1625-49), in fine condition, weak area of strike.

1646

£750-850   **BLO**

A shilling, minted by Oliver Cromwell (1649-58), in extremely fine condition, with superb blue and gold toning, scarce as such.

1658

£1,000-1,500   **BLO**

A second bust shilling, minted by Charles II (1660-85), in good condition.

1668

£70-90   **BLO**

A guinea, minted by James II (1685-88), in good condition.

1687

£1,200-1,800   **BLO**

A CLOSER LOOK AT A GOLD COIN

The obverse and reverse of this coin were designed by John Roettier (1631–c1700), the notable German-English engraver known for the veracity of his portraits.

Five guineas was equal to £5 5p and was a significant amount of money at the time of issue. Fewer coins of this large denomination were therefore produced.

This coin contains over an ounce of gold, giving it an intrinsic value as well.

Due to the large gold content, the edge was milled to deter clipping or filing of the coin.

A five guineas coin, minted by Charles II (1660-85), the obverse with second bust, in very fine condition, with some edge bruising, a die crack at base of King's hair.

1679

£4,000-5,000   **BLO**

A plain crown septimo, minted by Anne (1702-14), with second bust portrait, in good condition with some light field scratches.

1707

£320-380 BLO

A guinea, minted by George III (1767-1820), with fourth bust portrait, in very fine condition.

1774

£250-350 BLO

A scarce proof halfcrown, minted by George IV (1820-30), lightly garnished shield, in as struck condition, some obverse abrasions.

1820

£550-650 BLO

A scarce shilling, minted by George IV (1820-30), in as struck condition, with full radiant lustre.

1825

£120-180 BLO

A scarce halfpenny, minted by William IV (1830-37), in as struck condition, with rainbow and chocolate tones.

1837

£200-250 BLO

A rare plain-edged proof sovereign, minted by William IV (1830-37), with second bust portrait, once mounted with trace of solder to left of bust, some edge bruising.

1831

£600-800 BLO

A penny, minted by Victoria (1837-1901), with young head portrait, in as struck condition, 20 per cent red-brown lustre.

1858

£100-150 BLO

A shilling, minted by Victoria (1837-1901), die no.54, with young head portrait, in as struck condition, with full radiant lustre.

1865

£150-200 BLO

A wreath crown, minted by Edward VII (1902-10), in as struck condition, with full radiant lustre.

1928

£220-280 BLO

An American Connecticut penny, with "ET LIB" on the reverse, in fair condition, date illegible.

1787

£10-20 BLO

A Canadian two dollar gold coin, from Newfoundland, in as struck condition with full lustre, rare as such.

1885

£450-550 BLO

A scarce Republic of China dollar coin, with bust of Sun Yat-sen, the reverse with a junk with birds above and a rising sun, in extremely fine condition, with much lustre.

1932

£200-250 BLO

A CLOSER LOOK AT A CURAÇAON FIVE REAL

The island of Curaçao was an open port and traders from Europe and Latin America met to exchange goods.

As a result a variety of different currencies were in circulation as small change.

Coins were often in short supply so larger coins were cut into sections to create smaller values.

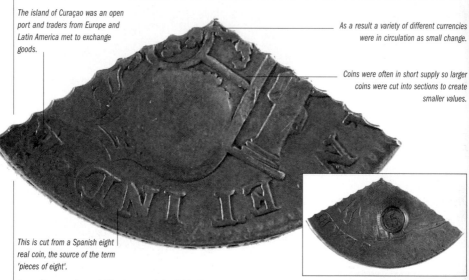

This is cut from a Spanish eight real coin, the source of the term 'pieces of eight'.

A rare Curaçao five real, ND countermark for 1818, '5' in circle struck on crenellated cut third of an 1809 Spanish colonial eight real coin, in fair condition, mark in extremely fine condition.

£1,800-2,200 BLO

A Filipino shipwrecked peso, light corrosion of surfaces and adherences in ear, probably in as struck condition before being wrecked.

1897

£70-90 BLO

A French gold proof 100 franc coin, with bust of Marie Curie 1934/1984, in mint condition.

This was produced in a low mintage of only 5,000 gold coins.

£150-200 BLO

A scarce German five reichmarks, from the Weimar Republic, in extremely fine condition.

1913

£70-90 BLO

A German States 24 Mariengroschen, from Brunswick, with bust of George II of England, in good condition, with superb rainbow tones.

1705

£70-90 **BLO**

An Guatemalan half real, die countermark struck on Peru Peso 1893, coin and mark in extremely fine condition.

1894

£45-55 **BLO**

A Hong Kong 50 cents, in very fine condition, with light grey to blue tones.

1891

£60-80 **BLO**

A Hungarian ducat, in extremely fine condition.

1765

£150-200 **BLO**

An Indian Kushan gold stater, from the Kidarite Kingdom, Kushan Empire, the obverse with King standing left, the reverse with Ardoksho seated facing, in fine condition.

c360-380 AD

£80-120 **BLO**

An Indian gold mohur, in extremely fine condition.

1841

£450-550 **BLO**

A Maltese 30 tari, with bust of Emmanuel de Rohan, in good condition, with uneven toning, scarce as such.

1795

£200-250 **BLO**

A Scottish thirty shilling coin, minted by Charles I, grainy as though from the ground, slightly off centre, in good-to-fine condition.

1625-49

£150-200 **BLO**

A rare Maltese four tari, minted by Jean de Valette, period of Turkish siege, toned, in very fine condition with areas of flat strike.

c1565

£700-1,000 **BLO**

COLLECTORS' NOTES

■ Although not currently reaching the level of US comics such as Superman and Batman, interest in UK comics has increased significantly in recent years, fuelled primarily by nostalgia. Examples from the 1930s into the 1970s are sought-after, with the 1930s, as with the US market, considered the 'golden age'.

■ Two of the best-known UK comics are The Dandy and The Beano, both published by D.C. Thomson & Co., Ltd. The Dandy was the first to launch in 1937 and featured Korky the Cat and Desperate Dan, who still appears in The Dandy today. As of issue 3007, it became the longest running comic in the world.

■ The Beano was launched the following year and had Big Eggo on the cover. Popular characters include Dennis the Menace, the Bash Street Kids and Minnie the Minx,

although these appeared later in the early to mid-1950s.

■ Being the most popular titles, The Beano and The Dandy also account for the two highest prices paid for UK comics so far. In 2004, a first issue of The Dandy in very clean condition, and more importantly retaining the 'Express Whistler ' free gift, sold at auction for just over £20,000. The previous year The Beano issue one sold for over £12,000.

■ Other popular titles are Eagle, featuring the heroic Dan Dare, The Hotspur, war-themed comics such as Commando, and Classics Illustrated. As the market is lead by male buyers, girl's titles such as Bunty and Misty appeal to a smaller portion of the market and are usually more affordable. All prices given here are for examples in very good condition.

"The Beano Comic", No. 204, Apr. 24th, 1943, published by D.C. Thomson & Co., Ltd.

With desirable WWII propaganda cover featuring Big Eggo defeating Adolf Hitler.

1943

£40-60   **PCOM**

"The Beano Comic", No. 65, Oct. 21st, 1939, published D.C. Thomson & Co., Ltd.

War-time comic production was limited as paper was used in munitions manufacture. Readers were encouraged through adverts to recycle their comics meaning issues between 1939-45 are particularly hard to find.

1939

£100-150   **PCOM**

"The Beano", No. 649, Dec, 25th, 1954, published by D.C. Thomson & Co., Ltd.

These festive Christmas covers are sought-after.

1954

£10-20   **PCOM**

"The Beano", No. 1000, Sept. 16th, 1961, published by D.C. Thomson & Co., Ltd.

This attractive single panel cover, celebrating the 1,000th issue, makes this a desirable comic.

1961

£25-40   **PCOM**

"The Beano", No. 1268, Nov 5th, 1966, published by D.C. Thomson & Co., Ltd.

Fireworks issues often had the brightest, most artistic covers and consequently are popular with collectors today.

£10-15   **PCOM**

"The Beano", No. 1534, Dec. 11th, 1971, published by D.C. Thomson & Co., Ltd.

1971

£6-8   **VM**

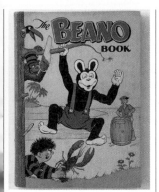

"The Beano Book", published by D.C. Thomson & Co., Ltd.

1954

£100-150 BIB

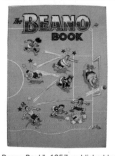

"The Beano Book", 1957, published by D.C. Thomson & Co., Ltd.

1957

£60-80 PCOM

A CLOSER LOOK AT A BEANO ANNUAL

The first annual was issued in 1940 and was titled The Beano Book.

They were printed without a date on the cover until 1966.

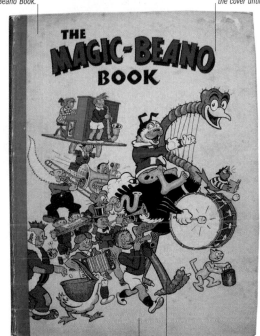

The title 'Magic Beano' was only used from 1943-50, after which it reverted to its original title.

These early editions are sought-after, particularly in very good condition.

"The Magic-Beano Book", 1948, published by D.C. Thomson & Co., Ltd.

£200-300 PCOM

"The Beano Book", 1963, published by D.C. Thomson & Co., Ltd.

These annuals had laminated covers from 1961 onwards and are hard to find without lamination breaks down the spine grooves.

1963

£40-80 PCOM

"The Beano Summer Special", 1966, published by D.C. Thomson & Co., Ltd.

Summer Specials were introduced in the early 1960s and are still published today. Virtually tabloid in size they were often folded along the centre to aid delivery and storage. Consequently, flat copies in good condition are very sought-after today.

1966

£20-40 PCOM

"Dennis the Menace Book", 1960, published by D.C. Thomson & Co., Ltd.

Dennis the Menace got his own bi-annual book in 1956, which was released yearly from 1987.

1960

£25-35 PCOM

"The Dandy Comic", No. 121, Mar. 23rd, 1940, published by D.C. Thomson & Co., Ltd.

1940

£25-45   **PCOM**

"The Dandy Comic", 331, Nov. 9th, 1946, published by D.C. Thomson & Co., Ltd.

1946

£15-25   **PCOM**

"The Dandy Comic", No. 1310, Dec. 31st, 1967, published by D.C. Thomson & Co., Ltd.

It is believed that the print runs were reduced in the 1960s due to competition from television. As a result, 1960s issues can be harder to find than those from the 1950s.

1967

£4-10   **PCOM**

"The Dandy Book", 1955, published by D.C. Thomson & Co., Ltd.

The Dandy Monster Comic changed to the Dandy Book in 1953. Korky the Cat usually featured on the front cover spot with a Desperate Dan strip on the back.

1955

£35-55   **PCOM**

"The Dandy Book", 1963, published by D.C. Thomson & Co., Ltd.

Although this is the 1963 annual, it was actually published in the autumn of the previous year. This system was used for all D.C. Thomson annuals. This can be confusing when examples are inscribed "Xmas 1962" for the 1963 edition.

1963

£30-45   **PCOM**

"The Dandy Summer Special", 1968, published by D.C. Thomson & Co., Ltd.

1968

£10-20   **PCOM**

"The Dandy's Desperate Dan", 1954, published by D.C. Thomson.

Despite being The Dandy's longest running character, appearing from issue one until today with only a brief rest in 1997, he has only had five of his own annuals. This is the first issue and is usually found in worn condition.

1954

£80-120   **PCOM**

"The Dandy Monster Comic", 1942, published by D.C. Thomson.

The Dandy annual was titled the Dandy Monster Comic until 1951 when it became The Dandy Book. It became The Dandy Annual with the 2003 issue.

1942

£350-500   **PCOM**

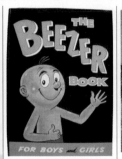

A CLOSER LOOK AT A MAGIC FUN BOOK ANNUAL

The Magic Comic was a short-lived title that ran for 80 issues and two annuals before its demise in 1941.

Launched just two months before WWII began, paper rationing had a huge impact on its production.

Several character from Magic were saved and moved to The Beano and as a result of this move, The Beano annual was titled The Magic-Beano Book from 1943 to 1950.

"The Beezer Book", 1960, published by D.C. Thomson & Co., Ltd.

Beezer was issued from 1959 to 1993, however the Beezer annual continued to be issued until 2003.

"The Beezer Summer Special", 1973, published by D.C. Thomson & Co., Ltd.

This was the first issue of the Summer Special. Note the now classic Raleigh Chopper bike on the cover.

As one of only two editions with this title, and the print run was low, this is a rare and sought-after issue.

"The Magic Fun Book", No. 1, 1941, published by D.C. Thomson.

1960	*1973*	*1941*
£15-25 PCOM	**£5-10** PCOM	**£500-750** PCOM

"Black Bob - The Dandy Wonder Dog", 1957, published by D.C. Thomson & Co., Ltd.

Black Bob made his first appearance in The Dandy in 1944. He had his own titled annual eight times between 1950 and 1965.

1957

£15-25 PCOM

"Commando", No. 1, Jul. 1941, published by D.C. Thomson & Co., Ltd, in good condition.

Commando is one of the most popular English military comics produced and is still issued today. The early issues are the hardest to find, with this being the most sought-after.

1940

£150-300 BPAL

"The Hotspur", No. 103, Aug. 17th, 1935, published by D.C. Thomson & Co., Ltd.

1935

£4-8 BPAL

"Scoop", No. 7, Mar. 4th, 1978, published by D.C. Thomson & Co., Ltd.

£2-4 BPAL

"The Topper Book", 1957, published by D.C. Thomson & Co., Ltd.

A collectable title, Topper annuals were first issued in 1955, making this an early example. The landscape format was used through the 1950s.

1957

£20-30 PCOM

"Classics Illustrated – Robin Hood", No. 7, first issued in Dec. 1942.

The publication history of the Classics Illustrated series is extremely complicated with the values for each of the various editions differing widely. Consult a specialist guide or dealer if you are unsure.

£10-20   BPAL

"Classics Illustrated – The Black Arrow", No. 31, first issued Mar. 1956.

£8-12   BPAL

"Classics Illustrated – Knights of the Round Table", No. 108, first issued in Jun. *1953*

£10-15   BPAL

"Super-Detective Library – Meet the Saint in the Case of the Contraband People", No. 1, Mar. 1953, published by Amalgamated Press.

"Super Detective Library – Sherlock Holmes", No. 78, published by Amalgamated Press.

£30-60   BPAL

1953

£100-150   BPAL

"War Picture Library – Fight Back to Dunkirk", No. 1, Sep. 1st, 1958, published by Fleetway Publications.

£15-25   BPAL

"War Picture Library – Cold Steel", No. 40, published by Fleetwood Publications.

£10-15   BPAL

"Super-Detective Picture Library – John Steel Special Agent", No. 177, 1960, published by Fleetway Publications.

£8-12   BPAL

"Air Ace Picture Library – Target Top Secret", No. 1, Jan. 18th, 1960, published by Fleetway Publications. *1960*

£10-20   BPAL

"Eagle", No. 26, October 6th, 1950, published by Hulton Press.

£15-25   VM

"Eagle", Vol. 3, No. 46, Feb. 20th, 1953, printed by Hulton Press.

£4-6   BPAL

"Eagle", No. 31, November 10th, 1950, published by Hulton Press.

£15-25   VM

"Eagle", Vol. 8, No. 34, Aug. 23rd, 1957, published by Hulton Press.
1957

£4-6   BPAL

"Eagle", Vol. 8, No. 28, July 12th, 1957, published by Hulton Press.

£10-15   VM

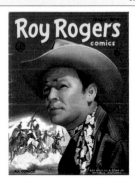

"Roy Rogers Comics", Vol. 1, No. 8, published by WDL.

£5-10   BPAL

"The Searchers", No. 15, 1956, published by Dell Published Co.

£10-15   BPAL

"Wow!", Jun. 6th, 1982, published by IPC Magazines Ltd.

£2-3   BPAL

COLLECTORS' NOTES

- Comics have long since ceased to be just for kids and many are now collectors' items. Rarity and condition are crucial to value, as are age and featured characters. Collectors may focus on one era, or may prefer to collect the complete run of a title.

- The first issue of a title is usually the most desirable, with values dropping considerably for subsequent issues. Other sought-after issues often feature the first appearance or death of a character. Historical topicality, such as the appearance of of the first nuclear explosion, can also increase value.

- The most prized comics date from the Golden Age (1938-c1955). This era began with the publication of

Action Comics No.1, featuring Superman, and a mint condition copy of this issue could now fetch up to £200,000! A host of rival publications and characters followed. Superman and Batman are generally the most sought-after today from this period.

- Spider-Man is probably the most desirable of the Silver Age (c1956-c1969) characters, which also include X-Men and The Fantastic Four. Marvel titles of that period are currently more popular than titles from the other big publisher, DC Comics.

- Mainstream comics, even early examples, have large print runs. However, scarcities, such as the 1984 first issues of Teenage Mutant Ninja Turtles, exist.

"All Star Comics", No.3, Winter 1940, published by DC Comics, fine to very fine condition (7), off-white to white pages, featuring the origin and the first appearance of the Justice Society of America.

The Justice Society of America was the first superhero team and was initially put together as a marketing ploy to increase the exposure of a number of characters. The title was cancelled in 1951 with issue 57 and many fans mark this as the end of the Golden Age of Comics and the decline of superhero titles. DC Comics issued a reprint of this issue in 1974 with the cover titled "Famous First Edition". Beware of later versions with their covers removed being offered as the original version.

1940

£7,000-10,000   **MC**

"The Amazing Spider-Man", No.4, Sept. 1963, published by Marvel Comics, fine to very fine condition (7), off-white pages, featuring the first ever appearance of the Sandman.

£500-600   **MC**

"The Amazing Spider-Man", No.8, Jan. 1964, published by Marvel Comics, near mint condition (9.4), off-white pages.

£2,500-3,000   **MC**

"The Amazing Spider-Man", No.17, Oct. 1964, published by Marvel Comics, near mint condition (9).
1964

£800-1,200   **MC**

"The Amazing Spider-Man", No.39, Aug. 1966, published by Marvel Comics, very fine to near mint condition (9).
1966

£250-300   **MC**

"The Amazing Spider-Man", No.6, Nov. 1963, published by Marvel Comics, fine to very fine condition (7), featuring the first appearance of The Lizard.

£400-500   **MC**

"The Amazing Spider-Man", No.9, Feb. 1964, published by Marvel Comics, near mint condition (9.4), off-white pages, featuring the origin and first appearance of Electro.

£3,000-4,000   MC

"The Avengers", No.2, Oct. 1963, published by Marvel Comics, very fine to near mint condition (9), off-white pages.

1963

£500-600   MC

"The Avengers", No.57, Oct. 1968, published by Marvel Comics, near mint condition (9.6), cream to off-white pages, featuring the first appearance of the Silver Age Vision.

£350-450   MC

"Batman", No.6, Aug/Sep. 1941, published by DC Comics, very fine to near mint condition (9).

£2,500-3,500   MC

"Batman", No.7, Oct./Nov. 1941, published by DC Comics, very fine condition (8), white pages, features a Bullseye cover, with artwork by Bob Kane.

£1,200-1,800   MC

"Captain America Comics", No.1, Mar. 1941, published by Marvel Comics, fine condition (6), red ink not printed, cream to off-white pages, featuring the origin and first appearance of Captain America, with cover artwork featuring Hitler and by Joe Simon.

A correctly printed copy of this comic, in similar condition, would be worth approx. £4,000-6,000.

£7,000-10,000   MC

"The Defenders", No. 1, Aug. 1952, published by Marvel Comic Group, near mint condition (9.4), off-white to white pages.

£180-220   MC

A CLOSER LOOK AT A DETECTIVE COMICS ISSUE

This issue features the first appearance of Robin, the Boy Wonder.

The idea of a young sidekick was originally disliked, but this issue sold double the usual amount of issues and the character remained.

This is one of the top three most sought-after Batman era Detective Comics issues.

The character of Robin was created by Bill Finger and Bob Kane, who were also responsible for the creation of Batman.

"Detective Comics", No.38, published by National Periodical Publications, very fine condition (7.5), off-white pages.

£12,000-16,000   MC

"The Fantastic Four", No.4, May 1962, published by Marvel Comics, near mint condition (9.4), off-white pages, featuring the first appearance of the Sub-Mariner.

£8,000-12,000 MC

"The Fantastic Four", No.48, Mar. 1966, published by Marvel Comics, very fine to near mint condition (9), off-white pages, featuring the first appearance of Galactus.

£500-600 MC

"The Fantastic Four", No.50, May 1966, published by Marvel Comics, near mint condition (9.2), off-white to white pages, featuring the first Silver Surfer cover.

£450-550 MC

"The Incredible Hulk", No.5, Nov. 1974, published by Marvel Comics, near mint condition (9.2), graded.

£2,000-2,500 MC

"The Incredible Hulk", No.181, published by Marvel Comics, near mint condition (9.6), off-white pages, featuring the first full story with Wolverine.

This issue is worth significantly more than any other issue from the second series due to the introduction of Wolverine, a firm fan favourite and X-Men regular.

£2,000-2,500 MC

"More Fun Comics", No.54, published by National Periodical Publications, very fine condition (8), featuring classic Specter cover artwork.

£5,000-6,000 MC

A CLOSER LOOK AT RED RAVEN COMIC

"Superman", No.5, published by National Periodical Publications, near mint condition (9.4), off-white pages.

£10,000-15,000 MC

This was the first and only issue of this title, the name was changed to "The Human Torch" with issue two.

This cover is the first signed cover art work by the hugely influential and prolific comic book artist, Jack Kirby.

Although the title only lasted one issue, Red Raven was the first superhero character to debut with his own title. Captain America is often thought to be the first, with" Captain America Comics" debuting in March 1941.

The character of Red Raven was resurrected in issue 44 of the X-Men, May 1968 and has made odd appearances since.

"Red Raven", No.1, Aug. 1940, published by Timely Publications, very fine to near mint condition (9), off-white pages.

£10,000-15,000 MC

"Crypt of Terror", No.19, Jun.-Jul. 1950, published by E.C. Comics, very fine condition (8.5).

Called Crime Patrol until issue 16, only three issues of this title were produced before the name was changed again to Tales from the Crypt.

£700-900   MC

"Dark Mysteries", No.21, Apr. 1955, published by Merit Publications, very fine to near mint condition (9), off-white to white.

£250-350   MC

"The Haunt of Fear", No.11, Jan.-Feb. 1952, published by E.C. Comics, near mint condition (9.2), off-white pages.

£350-450   MC

"The Haunt of Fear", No.18, Mar./Apr. 1953, published by E.C. Comics, near mint condition (9.4), white pages.

£700-1,000   MC

"Haunted Thrills", No.5, Oct. 1952, published by Ajax/Farrell Publications, near mint condition (9.6), off-white pages.

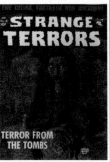

£700-1,000   MC

"Shock SuspenStories", No.14, published by E.C. Comics, near mint condition (9.6), off white to white pages.

£700-800   MC

"Spook", No.24, Mar. 1953, published by Star Publications, near mint condition (9.4).

This issue was cited with others by Dr. Fredric Wertham in his book Seduction of the Innocent, which partially blamed comics for juvenile delinquency.

£600-700   MC

"Strange Terrors", No.4, Sep. 1952, published by St. John Publishing Co., very fine condition (8), cream-off-white pages, with cover artwork by William Ekgren.

£400-500   MC

"Tales From The Crypt", No.24, Jun./Jul. 1952, published by E.C. Comics, very fine to near mint condition (9), off-white pages.

£450-550   MC

COMICS

"Tales To Astonish", No.27, Jan. 1962, near mint condition (9.4), off-white to white, featuring the first appearance of the Ant-Man.

£700-1,000   MC

"The Thing!", No.8, Sep. 1952, published by Captiol Stories, near mint condition (9.2).

The Thing! was particularly notorious for the level of gore and violence included, before the Comic Code Authority was formed.

£550-650   MC

A CLOSER LOOK AT A HORROR COMIC

The title Vault of Horror started with issue 12, and was previously called War Against Crime.

Together with Crypt of Terror, also by E.C. Comics, Vault of Horror was the first horror comic produced.

"The Vault of Horror", No.18, Apr./May 1951, published by E.C. Comics, near mint condition (9.4).

£700-1,000   MC

"The Vault of Horror", No.22, Dec. 1951/Jan. 1952, published by E.C. Comics, near mint condition (9.2).

£300-400   MC

E.C. Comics are particularly well known for their gory, violent crime and horror comics and were particularly affected by the introduction of the Comic Code Authority in 1954.

The cover art work was painted by Johnny Craig who was responsible for the covers for the entire run and introduced a naturalistic approach to the series.

"The Vault of Horror", No.12, Apr./May 1950, published by E.C. Comics, near mint condition (9.4).

£10,000-15,000   MC

"The Vault of Horror", No.23, Feb./Mar. 1952, published by E.C. Comics, near mint condition (9.4).

£700-1,000   MC

"Weird Terror", No.7, Apr. 1953, published by Allen Hardy Associates, very fine to near mint condition (9), off-white to white.

£400-500   MC

"Witchcraft", No.5, Oct./Nov. 1952, published by Avon Periodicals, very fine condition (8.5), off-white pages.

This was the penultimate issue of this title. The cover artwork is by award-winning illustrator Frank Kelly Freas (1922-2005).

£700-1,000   MC

"Mad", No.15, Sep. 1954, published by E.C. Comics, very fine to near mint condition (9).

£700-1,000   **MC**

"Mad", No.16, Oct. 1954, published by E.C. Comics, near mint condition (9.6).

£1,000-1,500   **MC**

"Famous Funnies", No.209, Dec. 1953, published by Eastern Color, near mint condition (9.4), cream-off-white pages, with cover artwork by Frank Frazetta.

£1,000-1,500   **MC**

"Mad", No.19, Jan. 1955, published by E.C. Comics, very fine to near mint condition (9).

£350-450   **MC**

"Mad", No.20, Feb. 1955, published by E.C. Comics, very fine to near mint condition (9), artist file copy.

£200-300   **MC**

A CLOSER LOOK AT A COMIC

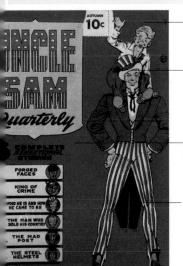

Even before the US joined WWII, a number of patriot superheroes appeared to defend the world against evil.

Uncle Sam first appeared in "National Comics", No. 1, issued July 1940. His own title ran for eight issues until 1943 and he would not appear again until 1973.

Issue one came with two cover variations, this, darker one with the price and a lighter one without the price. The values are the same.

The superhero version of Uncle Sam as created by the renowned comic artist and writer Will Eisner, who also did the cover artwork for this issue.

"Mad", No.21, Mar. 1955, published by E.C. Comics, near mint condition (9.4), off-white to white pages.

£700-1,000   **MC**

FIND OUT MORE...

Official Overstreet Comic Book Price Guide, by Robert M. Overstreet, published by House of Collectibles, 2006, 36th Edition.

www.dccomics.com, official DC Comics website.

www.marvel.com, official Marvel Comics website.

"Uncle Sam Quarterly", No.1, Autumn 1941, published by Quality Comics Group, near mint condition (9.6).

1941

£7,000-10,000   **MC**

A 'John Wesley in Memoriam' octagonal pottery plate, by Challinor, printed in black, gilt rim, small rim chip.

c1791

£100-150   **SAS**

A rare pair of 'Colonial Native Life' nursery plates, manufactured for D. Brandon of Kingston, Jamaica, the centres printed with amusing scenes depicting a man going to work, and a dancer, inscribed with two lines of pidgin English verse, each with a reverse printed with Brandon retailer's mark.

A marriage announcement in the Daily Gleaner of 4th June 1867 described the late David Brandon of Kingston as a merchant.

c1840   *7.5in (19cm) diam*

£500-600   **SAS**

A 'Temperance' nursery plate, the floral and foliate moulded border enamelled in colours, the centre printed in black.

c1840   *7in (18cm) diam*

£30-40   **SAS**

A Joseph Livesey commemorative jug, founder of the Temperance movement.

6.5in (16.5cm) high

£80-100   **RCC**

A Thomas Mellor Esq. commemorative jug, MP for Ashton-under-Lyne.

4.75in (12cm) high

£40-60   **RCC**

A George Peabody 'The Poor Man's Friend' commemorative mug.

4.5in (11.5cm) high

£70-90   **RCC**

A late 19thC small bust of William Booth, founder of the Salvation Army.

3.5in (9cm) high

£65-75   **RCC**

A William Gladstone in memoriam bone china mug, with transfer of Hawarden Castle.

c1898   *3.25in (8cm) high*

£80-120   **H&G**

A Preston Guild commemorative bowl, featuring a portrait of the Guild Mayor and Mayoress, Mr and Mrs Astley-Bell.

A celebration of the Preston Guild Merchant has been held every 20 years, with a few exceptions, since at least 1542. The most recent was held in 1992. A variety of memorabilia has been produced to commemorate these events ranging from badges, to pottery and silverware.

1922   *6in (15cm) high*

£40-60   **RCC**

A Spode Copeland Munich Agreement commemorative plate, featuring portraits of Neville Chamberlain, Joseph (his father) and Austen (his older half-brother).

1938   10.5in (26.5cm) diam

£70-100   **RCC**

A Winston Churchill brown glazed pottery character jug, by Shorter.

c1941   6in (15cm) high

£70-100   **SAS**

A Spode limited edition In Memoriam 'The Churchill Plate', by Thomas Goode, from an edition of 5,000.

10.5in (26.5cm) diam

£80-100   **RCC**

A Spode for Thomas Goode limited edition Winston Churchill In Memoriam lidded vase, from an edition of 125.

The fine quality of the work, the sought-after manufacturer and the small limited edition help to make this vase so desirable.

1965   14in (35.5cm) high

£1,200-1,500   **RCC**

A Price Kensington Harold Wilson gurgling jug, the handle in the form of a pipe.

c1970   7.5in (19cm) high

£70-90   **RCC**

A Price Kensington Edward Heath gurgling jug, the handle in the form of a boat.

c1970   7.5in (19cm) high

£70-90   **RCC**

A Caverswall mug commemorating the Convening of the First European Parliament.

1979   3.75in (9.5cm) high

£20-30   **RCC**

A pair of slippers after Luck and Flaw, depicting Ronald and Nancy Reagan.

£40-60   **SAS**

A Russian parian bust of Vladimir Ilyich Lenin.

c1935   9.5in (24cm) high

£200-250   **H&G**

A Nelson In Memoriam pearlware plate, with allegorical panels and yellow rim, named and dated.

Interest in Nelson memorabilia is always strong but the 200th anniversary of his death at Trafalgar in 2005 helped to raise its profile.

1805   8.25in (20.5cm) diam

£600-800   **SAS**

An English Boer War commemorative plate, featuring a portrait of Major General John French, with moulded border and gilt trim.

c1900   9in (23cm) diam

£60-80   **RCC**

A cylindrical creamware tankard commemorating the 1813 French Defeat by the Russians, entitled 'Specimen of Russian Chopping Blocks', printed in black and enamelled in colours with a gruesome scene.

The inspiration for this cartoon was published by Hannah Humphrey on 8th January 1813.

4.75in (12cm) high

£800-1,000   **SAS**

An English Boer War commemorative plaque, featuring an unusual portrait of Robert Baden-Powell, with gilt trim.

c1900   8in (20cm) high

£80-100   **RCC**

An English Lord Kitchener commemorative jug.

3.5in (9cm) high

£70-80   **RCC**

A Grimwades 'United We Stand' earthenware bowl, commemorating WWI.

c1916   5in (12cm) diam

£60-90   **H&G**

A French Sarreguimes 'Après Quatre Années de Trachées' (After Four Entrenched Years) WWI commemorative plate, featuring a smiling soldier with two pretty ladies.

1918

£80-90   **RCC**

A Royal Doulton model of a bulldog, no. 6627, seated wearing a helmet with a khaki glaze.

c1918   6.5in (16cm) high

£450-550   **SWO**

A Chelson China bone china mug, commemorating the signing of peace after WWI.

c1919   3in (7.5cm) high

£60-90   **H&G**

A Wilkinson Ltd. 'Marechal Foch – Au Diable le Kaiser' character jug, designed by Francis Carruthers Gould, issued by Soane & Smith Ltd., with printed marks, certificate and invoice for December 1918.

c1918   *12.5in (31cm) high*

£200-300   **SAS**

A Wilkinson Ltd. 'Lloyd George – Shell Out' character jug, designed by Francis Carruthers Gould, issued by Soane & Smith Ltd during WWI, with printed marks.

c1918   *10.5in (26cm) high*

£250-350   **SAS**

A CLOSER LOOK AT COMMEMORATIVE CHARACTER JUG

Initially intended to be one of a series of 12 character jugs commemorating key figures from WWI, Churchill's jug was dropped from production after he resigned over the disastrous Gallipoli landings at the Dardanelles in 1915.

It was to be released in a limited edition of 350 but it is thought that the edition was never completed.

The range was originally designed by Sir Francis Carruthers Gould (1844-1925), a caricaturist and politician, in 1915. This jug was remodelled by Clarice Cliff and subsequently issued in 1941 at a price of five guineas.

The entire range is very popular with collectors, with this scarce, late addition to the range being particularly sought-after.

A Wilkinson Ltd. 'Winston Churchill' limited edition pottery character jug, designed by Clarice Cliff, depicting the First Sea Lord seated on a British Bulldog holding a warship, inscribed "May God Defend the Right" and "Going into Action".

See the Royal Memorabilia section for an example of the 'HM King George V – Pro Patria' character jug.

c1941   *12.5in (31cm) high*

£1,800-2,200   **SAS**

A Wilkinson Ltd. 'Earl Haigh – Push and Go' character jug, designed by Francis Carruthers Gould, issued by Soane & Smith Ltd during WWI, with printed marks.

c1918   *10.5in (26.5cm) high*

£800-1,000   **SAS**

A Wilkinson Ltd. 'Marechal Joffre – Ce que J'offre' character jug, with certificate, designed by Francis Carruthers Gould, issued by Soane & Smith Ltd during WWI, with printed marks.

c1918   *10.25in (25.5cm) high*

£280-320   **SAS**

A Wilkinson Ltd. character jug 'Lord Kitchener – Bitter for the Kaiser', designed by Francis Carruthers Gould, issued by Soane & Smith Ltd during WWI, with printed marks.

c1918   *10.5in (26cm) high*

£450-550   **SAS**

A Wilkinson Ltd. 'President Wilson – Welcome Uncle Sam' character jug, designed by Francis Carruthers Gould, issued by Soane & Smith Ltd during WWI, with printed marks.

c1918   *10.5in (26.5cm) high*

£500-600   **SAS**

COSTUME & ACCESSORIES

COLLECTORS' NOTES

■ Vintage fashion attracts interest from both collectors and those looking for a unique or classic look, away from the proliferation of 'high street' styles. As such, values have risen sharply, particularly in the past decade. However every budget is catered for, particularly away from the top fashion houses pieces.

■ Important names such as Christian Lacroix, Chanel, Dior and Yves Saint Laurent will generally always attract high prices, particularly for 'couture' garments made to exacting standards in small quantities for specific personal orders, or examples of classic collections. Always consider the label design, as many designers such as Versace have had long established 'diffusion' lines that were originally less expensive and more mass-produced.

■ Aim to look for iconic classics, such as Chanel's famous tweed suit or dresses in Dior's revolutionary 'New Look' of the 1950s. The 1950s and 60s are two particularly 'hot' decades, although the 1980s is rapidly gaining ground, particularly Punk, minimal and 'power dressing' designs by those such as Vivienne Westwood, Giorgio Armani and Lagerfeld at Chanel.

■ Always consider the shape, construction, material, pattern and colour. Pieces by top houses will usually be very well made, using fine quality materials. Look at fashion books to learn how to recognise the key looks of the decade you wish to collect or wear. Stained or torn pieces should be ignored unless very rare (or intended!), and thoroughly examine a piece before buying as repairs can be expensive and unsightly.

A Bill Blass couture floor-length silk satin gown, with wide waist band, and fine tulle covering the entire skirt and forming a halter overlaying the strapless bodice, approx size 12.

£250-350   **FRE**

A Bill Blass couture silk evening ensemble, with coordinating woven tapestry iridescent silk bustle skirt and burgundy silk cinch-waist jacket, size 12.

£250-350   **FRE**

A fine Chanel evening gown and matching jacket, in silk chiffon with translucent green sequins, the silk dyed in very pale vertical stripes in pink, yellow and green and creating an ombre effect, with a sewn insert creating a gathered area at left side and split at hem, the jacket with no closure and quilted with tiny embroidered 'plus' signs with loose threads and stand-up collar, size 40.

2000

£550-650   **FRE**

A Chanel silk and wool evening skirt ensemble, with a collarless wool blend metallic-flecked tweed jacket and a cranberry iridescent silk long skirt and camisole, size 44.

£300-500   **FRE**

A Chanel off-white cotton and linen beaded skirt suit, with red woven lines and glass beads and matching knitted and beaded cotton camisole, lined in silk.

£300-500   **FRE**

A Christian Dior oversized knitted sweater coat, in dark grey heather wool and cream coloured contrasting fringe knit pattern, marked size small.

£200-300   FRE

A vintage 1970s Gucci fur wrap calf length coat, with a thin leather tie-belt, with a full fox collar, lined in brown signature "Gucci" acetate, approx. size 4.

£450-550   FRE

A CLOSER LOOK AT A CHANEL DRESS

This dress is based on Coco Chanel's classic tweed suit released in 1954.

The houndstooth tweed in strongly contrasting colours is typical of the look and in its day was revolutionary, bringing a functional fabric to high fashion.

The modern and tailored profile, rounded, almost collarless, neck and the bold buttons are other hallmarks of the style.

The matching handbag with its hallmark Chanel gold metal chain and form has a value of its own, fetching around £400.

A Christian Lacroix chartreuse cropped jacket, with gold iridescent lace overlay and gold and rhinestone buttons, size 42.

£70-100   FRE

An Andre Laug couture embroidered metallic rayon dress, with silk cording, beaded and embroidered cuff trim, waist and fold-over neckline, approx. size 12.

£200-300   FRE

A Chanel orange and white houndstooth tailored sleeveless dress and matching handbag, with faux pearl buttons and four pockets, short stand-up collar, falling to below the knee, with a large camelia brooch in same fabric, size 42.

£800-1,200   FRE

A Thierry Mugler tailored grey woven silk skirt suit, the jacket with sculptural silhouette and futuristic pin-tuck pleated details, two snap closure and no lapels, with a straight matching skirt, size 46.

£80-120   FRE

A 1970s Emilio Pucci 'Queen Anne's Lace' pattern pink and black printed silk jersey gown, with banded V-neck and gathered under the centre/bust, approx size 8.

Although the use of a banded bust collar and hem is typical of Pucci, the length and particularly the style of the print are very unusual.

£300-400   FRE

A 1960s-70s Emilio Pucci printed silk dress.

This is more typical of Pucci in terms of the printed pattern and the form. Always look for the 'Emilio' signature within the print.

£180-220 HP

A Mary Quant 'Ginger' label black and white short dress, size 11.

Quant's more mass-produced 'Ginger Group' clothing was aimed at a less wealthy buyer.

c1967   34.25in (87cm) long

£60-80 GAZE

An Oscar De La Renta couture lace evening tuxedo suit ensemble, consisting of a long black lace coat, with satin ribbon trim at waist, matching black lace tuxedo trousers, and a cream silk chiffon ruffled halter blouse. approx size 12.

£500-600 FRE

An Oscar De La Renta couture powder blue felt coat, with large fox collar, in a heathered wool or wool blend with a felted surface, with a single button and additional hook closure on the large full dyed fox collar, size 12.

£350-450 FRE

A late 1960s 'Paperdelic' four-piece paper cloth beach outfit.

Packet 10in (25.5cm) high

£18-22 NOR

A CLOSER LOOK AT A CAMPBELL SOUP DRESS

Although it feels like paper, this dress is made from 80 per cent cellulose and 20 per cent cotton, and made a Pop Art statement about disposability as it was meant to be thrown away after use.

The design is taken from Andy Warhol's iconic Pop Art soup can artworks, which summed up 1960s popular and consumer culture.

The simple sleeveless A-line shape of the dress is also typically 1960s.

It was mass-produced but proved unpopular, meaning few were sold and making survivors rare today.

A late 1960s Campbell's Soup 'The Souper' paper dress, designed Andy Warhol, labelled with care instructions, in bright, clean and undamaged condition.

£700-1,000 SDR

A 1960s Castaways 'Disposable Dress', sealed in its original bag, made from printed paper.

Paper clothing, meant to be thrown away after use, enjoyed a brief period of popularity in the late 1960s. Although it allowed fashionable ladies to buy up to the minute shapes in up to the minute patterns, it was not terribly practical and somewhat uncomfortable. Original packaging is rare.

10in (25.5cm) high

£20-30 NOR

A 1960s denim bikini, with dungaree-style top.

£35-45 SM

A 1950s Estrava bikini, made from Tootle fabric decorated with an Emilio Pucci fish design.

Pants 12.5in (31.5cm) wide

£100-150 SM

A 1970s printed cotton bikini, with ships and sea decoration, unmarked.

Pants 15in (38cm) wide

£70-100 SM

A pair of Levi's 501 'red line' jeans, size W32 L33.

Red Line jeans have a red line down each side of the selvage on the inside leg seams and this feature helps to date the jeans. Red lines were discontinued in 1983, which is also the cut off date for Levi's jeans to be considered as 'vintage'.

£50-70 BR

pair of vintage Bronks jeans, by Oshkosh B-Gosh, size 34.

shKosh B'Gosh introduced Bronks jean in 1951. Vintage examples an be rare and sought-after.

200-300 BR

A hand-painted silk tie, by Jones of New York, with stylized decoration.

£7-10 BR

A modern gentleman's tie, made to a 1950s design using unused, original 1950s printed 'showgirl' silk.

5.25in (13.25cm) long

£120-180 SM

A 1950s printed cotton cravat, with rock 'n' roll design.

When seeing the combination of this traditional form of neckwear with the avant garde pattern of rock'n'rollers, surely the practical, yet slightly caddish, cravat is due for a revival?

40in (101cm) long

£40-50 SM

A 1950s Gossard black lace and stretch 'all in one' corset.

£60-80 SM

COLLECTORS' NOTES

■ Handbags have been an essential accessory for 100 years, but have now also become hotly sought-after collectables, charting changing styles and fashions. Values depend on a number of factors: quality of materials and manufacture, the maker, condition of the bag and its date and style.

■ Always look for high quality materials. Some, such as lizard or snakeskin, can be scarcer than others and can add to the value. Details such as straps and metal clasps should also be made from good quality materials that will withstand usage. Examine stitching and construction carefully as a well-made piece is likely to indicate a good maker and have a higher value.

■ Makers' names are important, with those such as Hermes, Gucci, and Judith Leiber leading the field. However, many bags by unknown makers are also desirable, if they are of a good quality and design. Look for bags made for fine retailers in prestigious locations, such as Bergdorf Goodman, as this is likely to indicate a good example.

■ Date and style are important. Look for examples that sum up the fashions of the period in terms of the materials, colour and overall design. These are likely to appeal to collectors, as well as followers of fashion keen to acquire a particular period look.

■ Condition is vital, as so many collectors buy their bags to use, as well as to build a collection. Style icons such as Kate Moss and popular TV characters such as Carrie Bradshaw from 'Sex In The City' have widened the popularity of vintage style. Bags in truly mint condition will command a premium, so examine edges, corners, linings and metal fittings for signs of wear or damage.

■ Bags have always been widely exported and imported, and today this continues with a lively trade over the internet. Online auction sites such as eBay, vintage fashion shops and charity shops are ideal places to look for examples – but always keep an eye on fashion magazines to try to spot the 'next big thing'.

A late 1950s American Murray Kruger rectangular calfskin-covered box purse, decorated with faux airline travel stickers, with typical blue leather fitted interior and matching change purse.

The 1950s saw a boom in air travel as the number of airlines grew and prices fell, encouraging tourism. However, flying was still comparatively expensive and was synonymous with glamour and 'life in the fast lane'.

A 1950s American Holzman black calfskin handbag, with Lucite handles and satin lining.

Holzman were known for their sculptural handles, as on this example.

A 1950s Nettie Rosenstein black box calfskin handbag, made in Florence, Italy.

12.25in (31cm) wide

9.5in (24cm) wide

13in (33cm) wide

£300-500   MGL | £150-300   MGL | £250-350   MGL

A late 1950s Gucci handbag, with ruched black silk covering and gilt clasp.

7.5in (19cm) wide

£100-150   LB

A 1950s Nettie Rosenstein black silk box purse, with an unusual clasp.

American fashion designer Rosenstein is also well known for her costume jewellery. Note how this aspect of her designs are included here in the costume jewellery style of the clasp.

9.5in (24cm) wide

£250-350   MGL

A 1950s American Bienen-Davis enamelled and pleated box purse, with mirror inside lid and original purse.

Bienen-Davis produced very fine quality bags.

8.75in (22cm) wide

£80-120   MGL

A 1940s American Bogan black calfskin handbag, the accordion top with recessed base and green satin lining, retains original patent tag.

c1949   8in (20.5cm) wide

£250-350   MGL

A 1950s Nettie Rosenstein brown crocodile handbag, made in Florence, Italy.

10.5in (26.5cm) wide

£450-650   **MGL**

A CLOSER LOOK AT A HANDBAG

This unique, custom-made bag was designed and made by Martin van Shaak, who designed opulent bags for wealthy New York socialites.

The cast metal poodle clasps are unusual – the poodle was a popular motif during the 1950s, evoking the elegance of Paris.

Van Shaak did not use a shop, but preferred to visit his clients personally. His bags were always very well made from fine and expensive materials.

The exterior is covered with alligator skin and the interior is lined with red leather – all parts are in excellent condition.

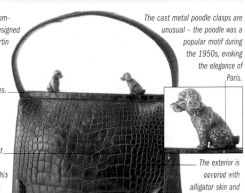

A 1950s alligator bag, with poodle clasps, the interior signed "Martin van Schaak".

8.5in (21.5cm) wide

£450-550   **MGL**

A 1950s British L. & M. Edwards tapestry bag, with Lucite handle and change of cover.

This bag has a detachable cover, which can be replaced with other patterned or plain examples that were often made at home. This is a typical design feature of many 1950s handbags.

9in (23cm) wide

£50-80   **MGL**

A 1950s rare, reversible woven plaid bag, with black trim and interior, unsigned, with glove holder vinyl strap.

The shape, pattern, presence of a glove holder in the strap and reversible design are all hallmarks of 1950s handbag design.

14.5in (5.5cm) wide

£50-80   **MGL**

An unusual 1950s woven basket bag, with applied fabric rosebuds and flowers, with Lucite details and velvet ribbon.

10in (25.5cm) wide

£40-60   **FAN**

An early 1950s American 'Dorset Rex 5th Avenue' woven metal strips box bag, with Lucite lid and red fabric lining.

Although not as collectable as Lucite-bodied or beaded bags, woven metal bags are growing in desirability.

6in (15cm) wide

£80-120   **DJI**

A 1950s Nettie Rosenstein lizard skin box bag, the lizard covering with gold wash, made in Florence, Italy.

8.25in (21cm) wide

£200-250   **MGL**

An unsigned 1960s bag, with psychedelic swirling pattern, plastic handle and matching purse.

10in (25.5cm) wide

£50-80 **MGL**

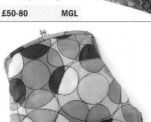

An American 1960s Ingber bag, of classic psychedelic pattern and typical form.

11.5in (29cm) wide

£50-80 **MGL**

A 1960-1970s Emilio Pucci velvet handbag, with waterfall front and geometric design.

Designer Emilio Pucci's iconic 1960s-70s swirling or geometric designs in bright, often acid, colours have legions of fans, ensuring high prices.

7.5in (19cm) wide

£450-650 **MGL**

A 1960s Emilio Pucci box handbag, with black, purple and blue swirled velour fabric, leather interior, gold metal handles and clasp.

This bag is worth less as the hallmark Pucci design only covers a part of the bag.

7.5in (19cm) wide

£150-200 **RR**

An 1960s American Kadin faux cowhide or pony skin handbag.

12in (30.5cm) wide

£120-150 **MGL**

A 1960s American Ronay faux pony skin bag, unsigned.

c1960   16in (40.5cm) wide

£150-200 **MGL**

A 1960s American Ronay faux-leopard skin handbag, with leather covered handle.

15.75in (40cm) wide

£150-200 **MGL**

A 1960s American Enid Collins handbag, in beige canvas decorated with a bird pattern with applied plastic cabochons.

9.5in (24cm) wide

£70-100 **LB**

A 1960s American Enid Collins handbag, beige canvas with a bowl of fruit and floral design highlighted with gold and clear plastic cabochons.

Enid Collins was based in Texas and signed her bags with an EC monogram or her name and an internal label. Instantly recognisable and much sought-after, her wood box bags are the most desirable.

10.25in (26cm) wide

£120-180 **LE**

A CLOSER LOOK AT AN HERMÈS KELLY BAG

The Kelly bag was named after film star and style icon, Grace Kelly, Princess of Monaco who favoured this style of bag.

It has been ultra-fashionable since its introduction in 1956, being a 'holy grail' for both collectors and fashionistas.

They are crafted from the finest materials by luxury brand Hermès – always look for complete examples with their padlock, keys and key cover, as here.

A 1960s black box calf 'Kelly' handbag, by Hermès, with lock, keys and clochette.

In 2005 a Hermès 'Etrusque' crocodile Kelly bag sold for over £7,000 at auction in New York.

The Kelly bag can be found in many different finishes and leathers, some rarer and more expensive than others. Beware of fakes which are common – they use lower quality materials and display poorer detailing, stitching and finishing.

11.25in (28.5cm) wide

£1,200-1,800

MGL

£180-280   **MGL**

A 1960s Judith Leiber black patent leather handbag.

This bag is valuable due to its notable maker and because the patent leather is still extremely crisp and clean.

8.5in (21.5cm) wide

A 1960s unsigned classic black crocodile bag, with gilt chain shoulder strap and clasp.

The form and chain in particular are inspired by Chanel's iconic 2.55 bag, which celebrated it's 50th anniversary in 2005.

10.25in (26cm) wide

£150-250   **LB**

A 1960s American Bobbie Jerome black velvet structured bag, with brown Lucite circle handles and satin interior.

15.25in (38.5cm) wide

£100-150   **MGL**

A 1960s yellow leather faux crocodile handbag, with gilt clasp.

8.75in (22cm) wide

£70-100   **LB**

A 1960s unsigned patent white and gold-finished leather handbag, with gilt metal handle and clasp.

9.5in (24cm) wide

£100-150   **LB**

A 1960s American Gaylene red corduroy and black leather cylinder bag, with matching black purse.

12in (30.5cm) wide

£150-200   **MGL**

COSTUME & ACCESSORIES

A 1970s Gucci black handbag, with shoulder strap.

10.25in (26cm) wide

£250-350 **MGL**

A 1970s-80s dark brown crocodile bag, by Gucci, in as new condition.

This bag is so valuable, as it is extremely unusual to find such bags in truly mint, unused condition.

10in (25.5cm) wide

£1,200-1,800 **MGL**

A 1960-70s Gucci black lizard handbag, with bamboo handle.

This bag is rarely found in lizard skin and the handle has a pleasing patina built up through careful use, giving it a good finish and colour.

10.5in (26.5cm) wide

£400-600 **MGL**

A 1980s French Charles Jourdain purple leather shoulder bag, with gilt frame and clasp.

8.75in (22cm) wide

£50-90 **LB**

A 1980s black crocodile backpack, possibly by Ralph Lauren.

11.75in (30cm) wide

£50-90 **LB**

A 1970s American Morris Moskiwitz multicoloured, sculpted chenilled bag, signed "MM", of doctor's bag form with leather piping and trim.

14in (35.5cm) wide

£180-280 **MGL**

A 1970s Carpet Bags of America brown and black chenille carpet bag.

8in (20.5cm) wide

£50-70 **MGL**

A unusual 1970s Judith Leiber leather tote bag, with needlework of whale and floral designs to exterior, unsigned.

This is an extremely unusual bag for Leiber, who is more famous for her jewelled 'minaudieres' in novelty shapes.

16in (40.5cm) wide

£400-500 **MGL**

A 1970s Chanel cocoa colour lambskin clutchbag, with lizard trim, with retractable chain strap.

11.5in (29cm) wide

£500-800 **MGL**

COLLECTORS' NOTES

■ Lucite bags are one of the most popular areas of handbag collecting. Lucite is a form of early plastic and can be found in clear, opaque, 'pearlised' and mottled finishes. The components for each bag were moulded individually and assembled and decorated by hand. Production declined sharply in the late 1950s as injection moulding led to less expensive imports and the fashion for leather bags returned.

■ The majority were made in the US in the 1950s and exported widely. Names such as Rialto, Wilardy and Llewelyn are among the most popular due to their fine quality and variety of superb designs. Black and pearlised white and grey are the most common colours. Others colours such red, blue and yellow are rarer and often more valuable.

■ Look for extra exterior detailing, such as inset rhinestones or moulded or carved patterns, in appealing and period designs. Unusual shapes also command a premium. Some have fabric lining, but those with rigid fitted interiors are more desirable.

■ Avoid storing Lucite bags in high temperatures or strong sunlight as this can lead to the plastic degrading completely, or to 'fogging' where the plastic becomes misty. Examine bags for signs of 'crazing' as this indicates irreversible degrading. If the interior has a strong chemical smell, avoid the bag as this is an indication that the plastic has started to deteriorate.

A 1950s Florida mottled grey Lucite hexagonal handbag.

c1953   *9.5in (24cm) wide*

£150-180   **DJI**

An early 1950s Myles Originals clear Lucite handbag, with internal copper and silver threads.

7in (18cm) wide

£150-180   **DJI**

A 1950s Wilardy Lucite handbag, decorated with shells, pearls and tiny grey beads in floral patterns.

6in (15cm) wide

£250-350   **DJI**

A late 1950s Wilardy pearl white Lucite handbag, with pleated design and black fabric lining.

10.5in (26.5cm) wide

£250-350   **DJI**

A Wilardy grey swirl Lucite handbag.

This bag has been nicknamed 'the rocket' because of its shape.

c1953   *9in (23cm) wide*

£250-350   **DJI**

A late 1950s Wilardy pearl white pearlised Lucite handbag, with gold and rhinestone clasp.

This bag is from the collection of Will Hardy who started the Wilardy range.

7.5in (19cm) wide

£250-350   **DJI**

An unsigned rectangular Lucite handbag, by Shoreham, the glitter plastic shell with grey and silver confetti and rhinestones at the base of the handle.

The unusual, flat shape and high level of decoration make this bag more sought-after.

c1955   *8in (20.5cm) wide*

£400-550   **DJI**

A CLOSER LOOK AT LUCITE HANDBAG

American maker Wilardy is one of the most respected and sought-after names in vintage Lucite handbags.

Blue is a rare colour, making this example more desirable and valuable.

The handle has an attractive twist and the clean-lined oval box shape is popular with collectors.

The lid has a design of small shells and beads imitating pearls, set into a ground of small grey beads to look like sand on a beach.

A 1950s Wilardy blue pearl Lucite handbag, with pattern of shells, pearls and beads on top.

c1955

7in (18cm) wide

£450-550

DJI

c1952

8in (20.5cm) wide

£700-1,000

DJI

A 1950s Wilardy black Lucite oval handbag, with bands of inset rhinestones.

The almost Art Deco appearance and the inset rhinestones make this an especially appealing bag.

An early 1950s Weisner black Lucite handbag, with a thick band of inset pearls and rhinestones at the base.

8in (20.5cm) wide

£220-320

DJI

A 1950s Charles Kahn of Miami, Florida, shiny satin white Lucite handbag, with moulded criss-cross design on the clear lid.

8in (20.5cm) wide

£120-180

DJI

A mid-1950s Rialto of New York pearl white Lucite handbag, with 'aurora borealis' and milk glass rhinestone decoration.

Aurora borealis stones are so named as they contain and reflect numerous colours, just like the polar sky phenomenon.

c1955

6.25in (16cm) wide

£450-650

DJI

An early 1950s Wilardy Lucite handbag, of tambourine design, inset with rhinestones.

6.25in (16cm) wide

£450-650

DJI

A Wilardy pearl white Lucite handbag, the lid with gold and rhinestone decoration.

This is a rare shape, designed to fit around and 'hug' the hips.

c1958

7.75in (19.5cm) wide

£300-500

DJ

COSTUME JEWELLERY

COLLECTORS' NOTES

■ The general costume jewellery market has enjoyed significant growth recently, and demand for vintage pieces has continued to rise. Named pieces and high-quality jewellery from the 1930s-1940s are sought after. Many people buy to wear, so even unsigned pieces can command high prices if they are particularly attractive, unusual or fashionable.

■ Trifari is one of the most collectable names. Among the most coveted pieces are the Jelly Belly figural pins, crown pins and designs by Alfred Phillippe. Other names to look out for include Miriam Haskell, Coro, Joseff, Chanel and Schiaparelli.

■ Kenneth Jay Lane jewellery has been worn by high-profile figures such as Jackie Kennedy Onassis, Audrey Hepburn and Diana, Princess of Wales, but has remained affordable to most. Inspired by a diverse range of traditional styles from around the world from Art Deco to Asian, pieces made before the late 1970s are the most sought after.

■ Coro's prodigious and diverse output caters to most income brackets and tastes. Designs by Adolph Katz and the double-pin Coro Duettes are particularly prized.

■ Fakes and forgeries have become more common, especially at the upper end of the market. Learn to recognise makers' styles and marks. The latter also helps with dating a piece.

A 1970s Kenneth Jay Lane umbrella pin, cast in gold-tone metal with pavé-set clear crystal rhinestones and red, blue and green glass stones and drops.

2.5in (6.5cm) long

£50-70 JJ

A 1980s Kenneth Jay Lane umbrella pin, cast in gun metal and set with polychrome and clear glass stones of various cuts, including round and baguette.

2.5in (6.5cm) long

£40-60 JJ

A Kenneth Jay Lane coach pin, gold-tone metal set with green, blue and red rhinestones, amethyst-coloured glass drops and sapphire blue glass cabochons.

3in (7.5cm) wide

£50-70 ABIJ

A 1970s Kenneth Jay Lane 'Catwalk' or 'Runway' chain necklace and pendant, in gilt base metal with smaller ruby red and larger dark emerald green glass beads.

A 1980s Kenneth Jay Lane Buddha pendant necklace, cast in gold-tone metal with a serpent above the Buddha, embellished with mother-of-pearl and emerald green glass cabochons, and with diverse metal and faux stone pendants.

Pendant 5.5in (14cm) long

£80-120 JJ

Kenneth Jay Lane (b.1930) began his career in design in the Art Department of Vogue magazine in the mid-1950s. After designing shoes and jewellery for others, he set up his own company, K.J.L., in 1963. Early pieces are the most sought-after and are distinguished by their "K.J.L." mark, which changed to "Kenneth Jay Lane" or "Kenneth Lane" in the late 1970s. He is still designing today.

29in (73cm) long

£200-250 JJ

A 1970s Kenneth Jay Lane twin ram's head bangle, in gold-tone metal set with clear, ruby red and emerald green rhinestones.

3in (7.5cm) long

£80-120 ABIJ

A pair of 1970s Kenneth Jay Lane pendant hoop earrings, in antique gold-tone metal with purple-red glass drops and cabochons, clear rhinestones.

2.5in (6.5cm) long

£60-90 ABIJ

A 1940s Coro clown pin, in vermeil sterling silver with tiny polychrome rhinestone highlights.

3in (7.5cm) long

£60-90   ABIJ

A 1930s Coro hobo pin, cast in gold-tone metal with polychrome rhinestone highlights.

1.25in (3cm) high

£40-50   JJ

A Coro 'Oriental' pin, comprising a Buddha-like figure cast in vermeil sterling silver and embellished with carved 'fruit salad' stones and clear crystal rhinestones.

Established in 1901, Coro came to prominence under the design directorship of Adolph Katz who joined in 1924. The company was hugely prolific and produced jewellery for every pocket. Look for pieces from the Corocraft and Vendome ranges, which were aimed at the high-end market. Vendome became a subsidiary company in 1953, see p.234 for examples.

A 1940s Coro circus girl-on-a-trapeze pin, cast in vermeil sterling silver, set with blue, pink and clear crystal rhinestones.

3in (7.5cm) long

£70-100   JJ

c1945   1.5in (3.75cm) high

£200-300   JJ

A 1930s Coro umbrella pin, cast in gold-washed metal with a girl, dog and palm tree, all under an arch of wheatsheaves, and with green and red enamelling and clear rhinestone highlights.

1.5in (4cm) wide

£50-60   JJ

A Corocraft umbrella pin, cast in vermeil sterling silver, set with pink and clear crystal rhinestones.

1938   2.5in (6.5cm) long

£120-150   JJ

A 1960s Coro green enamelled artichoke pin.

2in (5cm) long

£20-30   ABIJ

A 1950s Corocraft peach pin, in brushed vermeil with European crystal rhinestone accents.

2in (5cm) long

£50-70   ABIJ

Two 1940s Coro squirrel-under-umbrella pins, one cast in silver, the other in vermeil silver with selective black enamelling.

2.75in (7cm) long

£40-50 each   JJ

An early 1950s Coro 'Duette' owl clip, in sterling silver set with faceted green glass eyes and pavé-set clear and green crystal rhinestones.

1.5in (4cm) long

£150-200　　　　　　　　　　　　JJ

A CLOSER LOOK AT A CORO DUETTE PIN

The double pin mechanism was invented by Louis Cartier in 1927.

Initially of Art Deco design, Coro found great success with their figural pins featuring birds, other animals or characters, such as this Dutch couple.

Coro began making their own version, the Duette, in 1931.

The highly versatile double pin could be worn as a single piece, or divided into two and worn on either side of a neckline, for example.

A 1940s Coro Dutch couple 'Duette' pin, in rose vermeil sterling silver set with ruby red, aquamarine and clear crystal rhinestones.

2in (5cm) wide

£400-500　　　　　　　　　　　CRIS

A late 1940s/early 1950s Coro floral 'Duette' pin, in vermeil sterling silver, with jade green enamelling and clear crystal rhinestone highlights.

2.5in (6.5cm) long

£120-180　　　　　　　　　　CRIS

A late 1950s Coro 'Space Age' starburst pendant necklace, in yellow gold-tone metal with turquoise rhinestone highlights.

2.25in (5.5cm) diam

£15-25　　　　　　　　　　MILLB

A late 1940s Coro bolo-style necklace, in white metal with a rosette set with green and red rhinestones.

20in (51cm) long

£30-40　　　　　　　　　　MILLB

A 1950s/60s Coro foliate motif necklace, in silver-tone metal.

7.5in (19cm) long

£15-25　　　　　　　　　　MILLB

A 1950s Trifari pin, with a lozenge-shaped pendant, in silver-tone metal encrusted with brilliant clear rhinestones.

3in (7.5cm) long

£50-80 ABIJ

A 1940s Trifari bow pin, in rhodium-plated metal with pavé rhinestones and two rows of graduated faux pearls.

Gustavo Trifari founded his own jewellery-making business c1912 after training as a goldsmith at his uncle's company. Alfred Phillippe joined as chief designer in 1930 and was responsible in part for the company's success, insisting on the use of top quality materials and using setting techniques usually seen only on precious jewellery. Trifari continue to produce sought-after pieces today.

2.5in (6.5cm) long

£70-100 ABIJ

A 1940s Trifari feather pin, in rhodium-plated metal with clear and blue rhinestones and faux pearls.

2.75in (7cm) long

£40-50 ABIJ

A 1960s Trifari pin, in brushed gold-tone metal set with clear rhinestones and moonstone-coloured glass cabochons.

2.25in (6cm) long

£40-60 ABIJ

A late 1940s Trifari pin, in gold-tone metal with swirling rows of black and red rhinestones.

1.5in (4cm) diam

£30-50 ABIJ

A 1950s Trifari foliate and berry pin, in matte-finish, brushed gold-tone metal with graduated white faux pearls.

3in (7.5cm) long

£60-80 ABIJ

A 1990s Trifari flamingo pin, in gold-tone metal with pink rhinestones and pink enamelling, from their limited-edition 'Safari' range.

3.25in (8.5cm) long

£50-80 ABIJ

A 1990s limited edition Trifari alligator pin, from an edition of 350 from the 'Safari' range, cast in textured gold-tone metal and set with jade and emerald green and red glass stones, and with pavé-set clear rhinestones, with original packaging.

3.5in (9cm) long

£50-100 ABIJ

A pair of 1970s Trifari pendant earrings, in gold-tone metal with channel-set clear rhinestones and faux yellow and black onyx.

2.75in (7cm) long

£20-30 ABIJ

An Accessocraft necklace, with beads of pearlized brown plastic and clear Lucite with white inclusions, and with rings of clear rhinestones as spacers.

c1970   *16in (40.5cm) long*

£50-70   **ABIJ**

A CLOSER LOOK AT A CHANEL PIN

Coco Chanel founded her fashion house in 1914 in Paris, after initially designing and selling hats.

She drew inspiration from many historical influences, including Russian icons, Byzantine mosaics and the Venetian Republic.

The horn of plenty or cornucopia, a symbol of food and plenty dates to the 5thC BC, and is a common decorative device.

Gold-toned metal and faux pearls are classic Chanel, perfectly complementing the signature Chanel suit.

A 1970s/80s Chanel 'Horns of Plenty' pin, cast in gold-washed metal with faux pearls and tiny clear crystal rhinestones.

3in (7.5cm) long

£400-500   **JJ**

An Avon New Millennium clock pin, of polished silver-tone metal casting with sapphire rhinestone star centres and a plastic clockface.

2000   *1.75in (4.5cm) high*

£8-12   **MILLB**

A 1970s Avon pendant cross necklace, cast in gold-tone metal and with a ruby red glass cabochon.

Cross 7.5cm (3in) long

£20-25   **JJ**

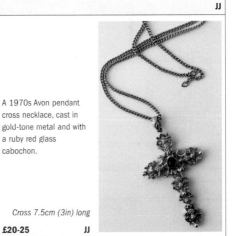

An early 1970s Hattie Carnegie flower pin, cast in gold-tone metal with green and pink enamelling, and pink nylon petals.

5in (13cm) long

£20-30   **JJ**

A 1930s/40s Hattie Carnegie umbrella ring bowl, cast in gold-tone metal with clear crystal rhinestone highlights.

2in (5cm) high

£20-30   **JJ**

A Chanel pink reindeer pin, from their Winter Collection 2001.

2in (5cm) wide

£50-80   **PC**

A 1940s Denbe by J.J. Denberg of New York necklace and bracelet, in rhodium-plated metal set with clear and ruby red rhinestones.

Necklace 16in (40.5cm) long

£100-120 ABIJ

A pair of Mitchell Maer for Dior floral motif earrings, with clear rhinestones in rhodium-plated settings.

One of a number of designers licensed by Dior, Maer produced pieces for Dior's collections for four years from 1952. Maer was responsible for some of Dior's most sought-after designs. Other designers working with Dior include Henry Scheiner, Kramer and Josette Gripoix.

1952-56 *1.25in (3cm) diam*

£150-250 FM

A late 1970s Florenza stylized floral motif pendant necklace, in gold-tone metal set with turquoise and amethyst glass cabochons.

Pendant 3in (7.5cm) long

£15-25 ABIJ

A pair of 1960s Florenza clover motif earrings, in gold-tone metal with aurora borealis rhinestones and jade green glass beads set against a black enamelled ground.

1in (2.5cm) wide

£25-35 JJ

A 1950s Leo Glass bracelet, in silver-tone metal with blue glass stones.

6.75in (17cm) long

£50-70 ABIJ

A pair of 1990s Dinny Hall 'Diffusion Line' silver clip earrings.

0.75in (2cm) diam

£50-60 PC

A 1990s Dinny Hall gold and white topaz pendant cross necklace.

Necklace 9.5in (24cm) long

£70-100 PC

A 1950s Har fortune-telling genie pin, in gilt base metal with round-cut clear and star-cut sapphire blue rhinestones.

Little is known about Har other than the fact that they operated in New York during the 1950s. This mystery seems to add to the desirabilty of their exotic designs, often showing Oriental influences.

2.5in (6.5cm) long

£500-700 SUM

A 1950s Har exotic pendant necklace, with a silver-tone metal chain, aurora borealis rhinestones, and other fantasy stones.

Pendant 4in (10cm) wide

£280-320 SUM

A 1950s Har rabbit-on-a-carrot pin, cast in gold-tone metal with green and red enamelling and crystal rhinestones.

1.5in (4cm) high

£80-120　　　**JJ**

A 1950s Har swirling wheat-sheaves pin, in brushed gold-tone metal.

2.25in (5.5cm) diam

£20-25　　　**MILLB**

A pair of 1970s Miriam Haskell pendant hoop earrings, in antiqued gilt metal, and each with a faux pearl drop.

2.75in (7cm) long

£70-100　　　**ABIJ**

A 1940s/early 1950s Miriam Haskell umbrella pin, cast in vermeil sterling silver and set with polychrome glass beads and faux pearls.

1.5in (4cm) long

£80-120　　　**JJ**

A 1960s Hollycraft floral motif necklace, with a gilt metal chain and castings, the latter set with pink and clear crystal rhinestones.

Established as the Hollywood Jewelry Manufacturing Company in 1938 and operating until the mid-1970s, Hollycraft's 1950s pieces and Christmas tree pins are some of its most collected pieces. Unusually, all examples are marked, adding to their collectability.

15in (38cm) long

£180-220　　　**JJ**

A 1940s Harry Iskin of Philadelphia pin and pair of matching earrings, in vermeil sterling silver with blue glass stones.

Pin 2.75in (7cm) long

£30-40　　　**ABIJ**

A 1960s Jewelerama floral pin, of antiqued white metal casting with a pewter-tone refractive disc centre.

2.5in (6.5cm) long

£15-25　　　**JJ**

A late 1950s Kramer choker, with textured yellow metal leaves edged with faux pearls.

15in (38cm) long

£30-50　　　**MILLB**

A pair of 1980s Karl Lagerfeld stylized plant-form earrings, in gold-washed metal, each with a faux pearl highlight, with original packaging.

1in (2.5cm) long

£30-40　　　**MILLB**

COSTUME JEWELLERY

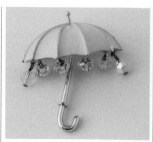

A Lanvin hinged bangle, of gilt metal casting with Classic key motif border against red enamelling.

c1970s/80s *8in (21cm) wide*

£70-100 LB

An early 1970s Lisner necklace, in burnished gold-tone metal with foliate green rhinestones.

16.5in (42cm) long

£50-70 ABIJ

A 1940s Lisner umbrella pin, cast in gold-washed metal with yellow enamelling and clear, faceted glass bead drops.

2in (5cm) long

£25-35 JJ

A Lucinda house pin, in black and white plastic.

2.5in (6.5cm) long

£15-20 JJ

A pair of 1980s Lunch At The Ritz 'Happy Hour' earrings, in gold-tone metal with black beads and enamelling.

5in (12.5cm) long

£120-160 JJ

A 1930s Marvella lion-tamer pin, in gold-washed metal with white and red enamelling.

2in (5cm) wide

£25-35 JJ

A 1940s Mazer Brothers bow pin, in vermeil sterling silver set with clear and polychrome rhinestones, and with a prong-set, ruby-coloured glass stone centre.

2.25in (5.5cm) long

£100-150 ABIJ

A 1970s Mimi Di N (Niscemi) flower pin, cast in gold-tone metal with pavé-set rhinestones.

2.25in (6.5cm) long

£60-80 ABIJ

A 1960s Napier 'ethnic' necklace, bracelet and earrings parure, with gold findings and diverse polychrome beads and stones of various cuts, including blue aurora borealis rhinestones.

Necklace 60in (152.5cm) long

£60-80 ABIJ

A CLOSER LOOK AT A SCHIAPARELLI PIN

Schiaparelli's love of colour is evident here, with the use of aurora borealis against the deeper green and blue stones.

Pieces dating from the 1940s and later are more easily found, making them popular with collectors. Earlier pieces are extremely scarce and therefore valuable.

Abstract designs are common, as are bold flora and fauna, influenced by her connection with the Surrealist movement.

Not all pieces are signed and copies do exist, so be sure to buy from a reputable source.

A 1950s Elsa Schiaparelli pin, in gilt metal with prong-set glass stones in shades of blue and green, and with small aurora borealis rhinestone highlights.

3.5in (9cm) long

£300-400   **SUM**

A 1960s Mary Quant flower ring, in green and clear plastic, together with its original box, not shown.

1.5in (3.5cm) diam

£100-150   **LB**

A 1970s Robert Originals elephant pendant necklace, cast in gold-tone metal and with small, purple rhinestone highlights.

Pendant 3in (7.5cm) wide

£15-25   **ABIJ**

A 1960s Sandor floral pin, in orange and yellow enamelled base metal.

2in (5cm) diam

£30-40   **JJ**

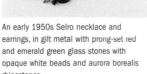

A 1950s Elsa Schiaparelli necklace, with three strands of contrasting-coloured glass beads and faux pearls.

16in (40.5cm) long

£100-150   **ABIJ**

An early 1950s Selro necklace and earrings, in gilt metal with prong-set red and emerald green glass stones with opaque white beads and aurora borealis rhinestones.

Necklace 17in (43cm) long

£240-280   **JJ**

A 1990s Swarovski sun motif pin and pair of earrings, cast in gilt metal pavé-set with clear Swarovski crystal rhinestones.

Pin 2.25in (7cm) wide

£100-150   **RITZ**

A 1960s Vendome necklace, of brushed gold-tone metal set with magenta, white and blue crystal rhinestones.

16in (40.5cm) long

£40-50   **ABIJ**

A 1950s Vendome necklace and earrings, made with glass beads in various shades of coral, and clear crystal rhinestones.

Necklace 15in (38cm) long

£80-120   **JJ**

A CLOSER LOOK AT A VIVIENNE WESTWOOD NECKLACE

Vivienne Westwood opened her first shop with partner Malcolm McLaren in 1970. McLaren also famously managed the Sex Pistols who wore her designs at their first gig.

Royal motifs are commonly part of Westwood's witty designs, subverting symbols of the British establishment. This was a common theme of the punk movement of which Westwood was a key player.

The use of gold-tone metal with clear rhinestone highlights are also typical of her work.

As with other high fashion designers, Westwood's vintage accessories are much more affordable than her highly sought-after and iconic costumes, making them accessible to a larger number of collectors.

A 1980s Vivienne Westwood pendant orb necklace, in gold-tone metal with rhinestone highlights.

Pendant 1.25in (3.5cm) long

£180-220   **LB**

A Warner 'night and day' flower pin, in gold-tone metal with an open-and-shut mechanism.

This 'night and day' flower pin has two settings; open (day), as here, and night (closed). Warner's mechanical pins such as this one are relatively rare and have been rising in value.

c1960   2.25in (5.5cm) long

£80-120   **LB**

A Warner 'sun and rain' umbrella pin, in gold-tone metal set with floral motifs of coloured and clear crystal rhinestones.

c1960   3in (7.5cm) long

£30-40   **JJ**

A 1980s Vivienne Westwood triple-strand faux pearl choker, the clasp and royal orb in silver-tone metal pavé-set with clear crystal rhinestones.

13.5in (34.5cm) long

£80-120   **REL**

A 1960s Whiting & Davis coiled snake bangle, in gold-tone, expandable metal mesh, with a solid punched and engraved head.

12in (30.5cm) circ

£30-40   **JJ**

A 1950s unsigned elephant pin, cast in gold-tone metal and set with turquoise and ruby red glass stones.

2.25in (6cm) wide

£30-40　　　　　　　　　CRIS

A 1950s unsigned cat pin, cast in textured gold-tone metal with blue and green enamelling and green glass cabochon eyes.

1.5in (4cm) high

£20-25　　　　　　　　　CRIS

A 1950s unsigned bassett hound pin, cast in gold-tone metal with pavé set clear crystal rhinestones.

£15-20　　　　　　　　　CRIS

An unsigned English 'jelly belly' penguin pin, in silver-mounted clear glass with diamanté highlights.

c1910　　2.25in (5.5cm) high

£100-250　　　　　　　　LYNH

A 1950s unsigned French bird-on-a-branch pin, cast in gold-tone metal and set with turquoise glass beads.

A 1940s unsigned 'jelly belly' fish pin, in vermeil sterling silver with a Lucite body.

Jelly belly pins were originally conceived by Alfred Phillippe, Trifari's chief designer, who used smooth Lucite pebbles to form the bodies of whimsical animal, bird or insect-shaped pins. The value depends on the motif used, and original Trifari examples are more desirable than unsigned ones.

2in (5cm) long

£20-30　　　　　　　　　CRIS

3.5in (9cm) long

£150-200　　　　　　　　ABIJ

A 1950s unsigned Siamese goldfish pin, cast in gold-tone metal with selective dark blue enamelling.

2.5in (6.5cm) wide

£30-40　　　　　　　　　CRIS

A late 1950s unsigned butterfly pin, in gold-tone metal with dark blue and green enamelling and pavé-set clear crystal rhinestones, and ruby-red glass cabochon eyes.

3.25in (8cm) wide

£25-35　　　　　　　　　CRIS

A late 1930s unsigned beetle pin, cast in rhodium-plated metal with a large blue glass cabochon abdomen and green glass cabochon eyes.

2in (5cm) long

£70-100　　　　　　　　CRIS

A 1950s Austrian fruit pin, with gilt metal stalks, pale green enamelled glass leaves, and foil-backed red glass cherries.

Always marked "Austria", these fruit pins were made by a number of factories across Austria and occasionally have matching earrings. Fruits commonly found include strawberries, cherries, pears and bunches of grapes and are formed from brightly coloured glass that is foil-backed to reflect the light and enhance the richness of the colours.

1.75in (4.5cm) wide

£60-80   **ECLEC**

A 1940s unsigned Alpine motif chatelaine pin, cast in gold-washed metal and set with red, blue and turquoise glass stones.

Chalet 1.75in (4.5cm) wide

£60-80   **JJ**

A 1950s unsigned floral pin, in textured gold-tone metal, with pavé-set clear crystal rhinestones.

3in (7.5cm) wide

£35-45   **CRIS**

A 1930s unsigned floral, fruit and foliate basket pin, cast in rhodium-plated metal and set with baguette-cut red glass stones.

2.5in (6cm) wide

£80-100   **CRIS**

A 1950s unsigned pair of floral scatter pins, in white metal set with clear crystal rhinestones.

1in (2.5cm) long

£40-50   **JJ**

A 1940s unsigned scrolling bow pin and pair of earrings, in rose-vermeil sterling silver with large, prong-set aquamarine glass stones.

Pin 1.25in (3.5cm) long

£120-180   **CRIS**

A 1940s unsigned crown pin, in vermeil sterling silver with fleur-de-lis finials, sapphire blue, ruby red and emerald green glass teardrops, and small clear crystal rhinestones.

2in (5cm) wide

£70-90   **CRIS**

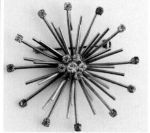

A late 1950s unsigned 'Space Age' starburst pin, in white metal with rhinestone highlights.

2.25in (5.5cm) diam

£15-25   **MILLB**

A mid-1950s unsigned hyacinth pin and pair of earrings, in antiqued gold-tone metal set with amber, citrine and red faceted glass stones.

Pin 3.25in (8cm) long

£70-90   **CRIS**

A 1940s unsigned Aborigine pin, cast in gold-tone metal.

2.25in (5.5cm) long

£60-70 JJ

An unsigned watch pin, resembling the Tin Man from 'The Wizard of Oz', in gold-tone metal with articulated arms and legs, and rhinestone highlights.

Despite being unsigned, the addition of a watch and the pin's whimsical form add to the value.

2.5in (6cm) long

£250-300 LB

A late 1950s unsigned clown-on-a-bicycle pin, cast in gold-tone metal with selective red, blue and green enamelling, and glass cabochon eyes.

3in (7.5cm) high

£15-25 CRIS

A 1940s unsigned 'Manneken Pis' style umbrella pin, probably a souvenir piece, cast in vermeil silver, with enamel highlights.

1.5in (4cm) long

£100-150 JJ

An unsigned umbrella pin, with a tree and two sheltering figures, in polychrome painted plastic.

c1920 1.75in (4.5cm) high

£30-40 JJ

A late 1920s courting couple pin, with articulated revolving umbrella, in polychrome plastic.

2.25in (5.5cm) long

£50-60 JJ

A 1930s unsigned dog-walking-dog pin, cast in gold-washed metal set with rectangular, navette and round-cut clear crystal rhinestones.

5in (12.5cm) wide

£100-150 JJ

A 1940s theatrical dancing couple pin, cast in base metal and enamelled in red, green and gold.

3in (7.5cm) long

£40-50 ECLEC

A pair of 1950s earrings, with clusters of turquoise glass stones banded by, and set in, gold-tone castings.

1in (2.5cm) long

£20-30   **CRIS**

A pair of 1950s Czech Republic earrings, with large purple glass cabochons and pale blue rhinestone highlights.

1in (2.5cm) long

£20-30   **CRIS**

A pair of 1950s crescent moon earrings, cast in gold-tone metal and set with peridot glass stones.

1.25in (3cm) long

£20-30   **CRIS**

A pair of 1950s plastic poodle earrings.

Poodles are a common 1950s decorative theme, echoing the chic Paris of the time, and seen as the epitome of good taste.

1in (2.5cm) long

£15-20   **ECLEC**

A pair of 1940s triangular-pendant gold-tone metal earrings.

2.25in (5.5cm) long

£40-50   **ECLEC**

A pair of 1920s unsigned pendant earrings, with carved, shell-shaped, clear crystal drops.

3in (7.5cm) long

£120-160   **ECLEC**

A 1960s unsigned necklace, with rows of mauve-coloured plastic beads and a gold-tone metal clasp.

15.75in (40cm) long

£30-40   **ECLEC**

A 1960s mother-of-pearl necklace, with faux pearl centre.

14.25in (36cm) long

£30-40   **ECLEC**

An Austrian silver necklace, set with clear crystal rhinestones and pendant polychrome glass beads.

13in (33cm) long

£120-180   **ECLEC**

An early 1940s American silver necklace, set with mother-of-pearl and clear crystal rhinestones.

16.5in (42cm) circ

£60-80   **ECLEC**

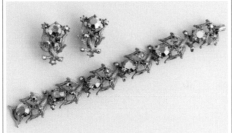

A 1920s French unsigned necklace, with cut crystal beads of graduated size and jade green glass spacers.

15.75 (40cm) long

£150-200   **CRIS**

A 1950s unsigned bracelet, in japanned black metal with opaque white glass floral motifs, with clear rhinestone centres.

7.5in (19cm) diam

£70-90   **CRIS**

A 1920s unsigned silver bracelet, set with three faceted, emerald-green crystal stones.

7.25in (18.5cm) long

£100-120   **CRIS**

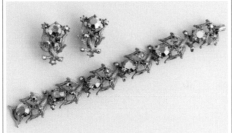

An unsigned bracelet and pair of earrings, in gold-tone metal with prong-set aurora borealis rhinestones.

Bracelet 7in (18cm) long

£70-80   **CRIS**

A 1980s unsigned leopard bracelet, in textured gold-tone metal with ruby red crystal rhinestone eyes.

This was probably made by Sphinx for Saks of Fifth Avenue.

6.75in (17.5cm) circ

£25-35   **CRIS**

A 1950s unsigned expandable bracelet, in textured gold-tone metal set with emerald green, ruby red and clear crystal rhinestones.

6.5in (17cm) circ

£80-100   **CRIS**

A late 1940s unsigned copper bangle, with comedy and tragedy masks.

Although unsigned, this bangle was made by Francisco Rebajes who worked almost exclusively in copper. A signed example would be worth twice as much.

6.5in (16.5cm) circ

£100-150   **CRIS**

A 1940s wooden bracelet, with a copper clasp and a carved wooden horse's head set on a disc of caned leather and wood.

Disc 2in (5cm) diam

£80-100   **CRIS**

FIND OUT MORE...

DK Collectors' Guide: Costume Jewellery, by Judith Miller, published by Dorling Kindersley, 2003.

COLLECTORS' NOTES

■ Bakelite jewellery became popular in the 1920s, allowing ladies of all incomes, particularly during the difficult years of the Depression, to share in the glamourous fashions of the era. Victorian ideals had downplayed the use of jewellery, but the Jazz age saw no need for such restraint, and flamboyant women adorned themselves with brightly coloured pieces.

■ Colour, form, size and the type and level of decoration are the main indicators to value. In general, the brighter the colour, the more valuable a piece will be. Strong cherry reds, bright oranges and vibrant greens are particularly sought-after. Although less typical, black can make a bold statement, particularly with large pieces with similarly bold Art Deco designs.

■ Plastics were also ideal for carving. Geometric patterns are sought after, as are other highly stylized motifs. Many are based on flowers, leaves or other natural forms. The most desirable forms tend to be either deep and dramatic, or intricate and detailed.

■ Always consider how a piece was made as this will also indicate value. Look closely at the decoration as hand-carving adds value. Machine carving tends to be shallower and more regular. Examine pieces for cracks, which often show up as thin dark lines, or filed down areas of damage, which reduce value.

■ Although many different plastics, such as cast phenolics, were used, they are commonly grouped under the term 'bakelite', a term which is used here.

A 1930s heavily carved and pierced yellow cast phenolic bangle, with stylized flowers.

3in (7.5cm) diam

£400-600   **MG**

A 1930s carved and pierced bakelite bangle, with a 1960s appearance.

3in (7.5cm) diam

£300-400   **MG**

A hand-carved yellow bakelite bangle, carved with stylized feathers.

3in (7.5cm) diam

£150-200   **MG**

A wide carved green bakelite ribbed bangle.

The same carved ribbing was also used on small dressing table accessories, such as lidded pots for rings.

3in (7.5cm) diam

£80-120   **MG**

A 'creamed corn' carved cast phenolic bangle, with curving and twisting pattern

3.25in (8.5cm) diam

£70-100   **MG**

A 1930s hand-carved tortoiseshell-patterned bangle, carved with stylized roses.

2.75in (7cm) diam

£400-600   **MG**

A 1950s turquoise green Lucite bangle, made from a single curled piece.

3.25in (8.5cm) diam

£180-220   **MG**

A heavily carved and pierced cherry red cast phenolic bangle.

Pieces in bright colours, and particularly cherry red, are often more desirable. Strong levels of carving and piercing are sought-after features.

3in (8cm) diam

£1,000-1,500   **MG**

A CLOSER LOOK AT A PLASTIC BANGLE AND MATCHING EARRINGS

These are known as 'Philadelphia' bangles, possibly after the city they were first sold in. Summing up the bright colours of the Jazz Age, they are rare today.

The coloured cast phenolic sections had to be carefully cut, assembled and laminated together and finally worked to give a seamless surface finish. This took many hours of work.

A 'Philadelphia' laminated bangle and matching earrings.

Other examples are found with carved 'fins'. Although plastics were generally used to create more affordable pieces, high quality pieces such as these were expensive in their day.

A 'Philadelphia' bracelet sold for over £9,000 at auction in 1998, demonstrating their rarity and great desirability.

3.25in (0.5cm) long

£1,200-1,800 **MG**

A large laminated yellow and black zig-zag bakelite bangle.

3in (8cm) diam

£800-1,200 **MG**

A 1980s light wood-effect bangle, engraved with black stained bands , with 'df' gilt decal for Diane von Furstenburg.

Diane von Furstenburg is famous for designing the 'Wrap Dress', which she launched in 1976 with the slogan "Feel like a woman – wear a dress". This style of dress is currently enjoying a revival.

3.5in (9cm) diam

£30-40 **BB**

Three yellow cast phenolic bangles, with wood corners.

Wood applied to bakelite bodies is more unusual and more valuable than the more commonly found bakelite mounted on wood.

£400-600 (each) **MG**

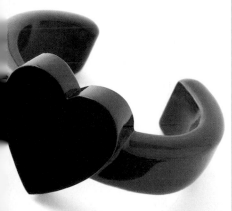

A black bangle, with heart, made from a single piece of bakelite.

This bangle was carved from a single very thick piece of plastic rather than being bent into shape or made from assembled separate pieces. Bangles were rarely carved in this way as the amount of waste material this generated was uneconomical. This factor and the heart design makes this piece valuable.

3in (8cm) diam

£1,000-1,500 **MG**

A late 1920s large mottled red bakelite bangle.

Despite being made in the 1920s, this bangle has a 1960s look. The shape, size and colour combine to make it desirable.

3.5in (9cm) high

£1,000-1,500 **MG**

A 1930s reverse-carved and painted clear Lucite bangle.

Lucite was invented in 1931 by chemists at DuPont. It was often carved and painted with designs.

3in (8cm) diam

£400-600 **MG**

A translucent dark-green bakelite hinged bracelet.

The textured pattern on this bangle is reminiscent of snake skin. Snakes are popular motifs.

3in (7.5cm) diam

£400-600   MG

A 1940s chocolate brown bakelite bracelet, with razor blade effect.

This bracelet is from the Donald Alvin collection.

3in (8cm) diam

£450-650   MG

A CLOSER LOOK AT A CARVED PLASTIC BRACELET

The size and 'depth' of the leaves indicates the use of large and thick pieces of plastic.

The plastic is coloured to imitate jet, which was commonly used in the Victorian era for mourning jewellery.

It is heavily influenced by Victorian jewellery in its colour and design.

The hand carved, curving leaves are naturalistic and finely detailed.

An articulated black bracelet, hand-carved with a curling motif and two leaves.

2.75in (7cm) diam

£550-750   MG

A Czechoslovakian 'apple juice' bakelite and Czech glass bracelet.

Note the Egyptian styling. Egypt was a major influence on Art Deco design, fuelled by Howard Carter's discovery of Tutankhamen's tomb in 1922.

2.75in (7cm) diam

£150-200   MG

A hand-carved green 'apple juice' bakelite bracelet.

Transparent 'apple juice' bakelite comes in a range of colours. It was made by injecting a form of Lucite with pigment. It is most often carved and is highly sought-after today.

2.5in (6.5cm) high

£400-600   MG

An Art Deco 'apple juice' and black bakelite stretch-open articulated bracelet.

3in (8cm) diam

£400-600   MG

A red 'over-dye' yellow bakelite horse racing or hunting themed charm bracelet, with brass insets.

The red colour is an 'over-dye', a secondary process which involves the shaped bakelite being washed with colour. The 'over-dye' is often worn away through use, revealing the true colour of the bakelite beneath. The theme of this bracelet adds to the value.

7in (18cm) long

£220-280   EL*

A very deeply carved and pierced cherry red Catalin brooch, with leaves and flowers.

This is very deeply carved and pierced piece, with a well composed, and typically highly stylized design, hence its high value.

3in (7.5cm) high

£1,000-1,500   MG

A carved cherry red Catalin stylized leaf bar brooch,

2.75in (7cm) wide

£70-100   ELI

A large and deeply hand-carved cherry red leaf brooch.

3.75in (9.5cm) long

£400-600   MG

A carved cherry red Catalin 'pinwheel' design flower brooch.

Catalin is a trade name for a form of cast phenolic resin, known for its strong colours and shiny surfaces.

2.25in (6cm) diam

£100-150   ELI

A carved red Catalin clip, with stylized floral or foliate pattern.

This lighter level of carving and shaping, with no piercing, is the most commonly found.

2in (5cm) high

£50-80   ELI

A 1940s cherry red bakelite 'bleeding heart' and cherry brooch with original beads.

The 'bleeding heart' has great sentimental appeal for collectors. It is unusual to find these with their original beads intact as they easily crack or break off and are replaced.

3in (8cm) high

£350-550   MG

A hand-carved burgundy cast phenolic stylized flower and leaf design oval brooch.

3in (7.5cm) long

£150-200   MG

A burgundy bakelite and carved wood stylized pineapple brooch.

3in (8cm) high

£70-100   MG

A transparent tortoiseshell Lucite brooch, with carved geometric pendant on metal.

3.25in (8.5cm) high

£150-200   MG

COSTUME JEWELLERY

A rare Lucite hand-shaped brooch, with enamelled metal flower.

This design is strikingly similar to a Schiaparelli hand brooch, and the flower resembles an orchid brooch by Chanel.

3.5in (9cm) long

£700-1,000   **MG**

A CLOSER LOOK AT A PORCELAIN AND LUCITE BROOCH

The curving pieces of Lucite resemble scarves twirling around the dancer as she moves.

Josephine Baker (1906-75) was a famous nightclub dancer of the 1920s. She performed her popular Banana Dance routine at the Folies Bergère in Paris.

The face is hand-painted and made from porcelain.

The design of the head mimics African masks, which were seen as exotic and were very influential on art of the time.

A very rare painted porcelain and bent Lucite brooch, in the form of Josephine Baker's head.

3in (8cm) high

£450-650   **MG**

A large carved and painted Lucite Indian's head brooch, with metal pin fixing to reverse.

The placing of the pin fixing is unusual here, as it is so visible.

3.25in (8.5cm) high

£120-180   **MG**

A 1950s French large Lucite cicada bug brooch, hand painted on the exterior and interior.

5in (13cm) high

£400-600   **MG**

A pair of reverse-carved and injected oval bakelite dress clips, with flower motif.

Dress clips were popular from the 1920s to the 1950s. They were worn at the neckline of a dress to highlight the outfit.

2in (5cm) high

£300-500   **MG**

A pair of bakelite-on-wood dress clips, with flower and leaf design.

This combination of bakelite on wood is more commonly found than wood on bakelite.

2.25in (6cm) high

£80-120   **EL**

A 1920s black hand-carved bakelite peacock necklace and pendant.

The skill that has gone into carving the detailed and delicate pendant makes this valuable.

3in (7.5cm) diam

£1,000-1,500   **MG**

A CLOSER LOOK AT A BAKELITE NECKLACE

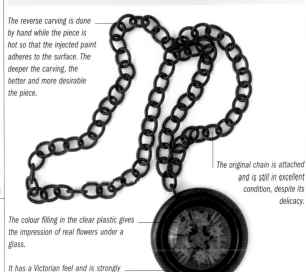

The reverse carving is done by hand while the piece is hot so that the injected paint adheres to the surface. The deeper the carving, the better and more desirable the piece.

The original chain is attached and is still in excellent condition, despite its delicacy.

The colour filling in the clear plastic gives the impression of real flowers under a glass.

It has a Victorian feel and is strongly reminiscent of a locket.

A 1930s Prystal and black bakelite necklace, with reverse-carved and injected pendant.

Prystal is a synthetic clear crystal-like plastic material developed in Italy during the 1930s.

Pendant 2.25in (6cm) diam

£450-650   **MG**

A 1920s sterling silver and red bakelite pendant, with original red bakelite chain.

A design has been cut out of the, now tarnished, sterling silver allowing the red bakelite beneath to show through.

Pendant 3.75in (9.5cm) high

£400-600   **MG**

A mottled orange and black Catalin pendant, swivelling open to reveal a mirror.

This Art Deco necklace with small vanity mirror conjures up images of glamourous flapper girls 'powdering their noses' at wild parties.

2.75in (7cm) high

£450-650   **MG**

A 1920s necklace with red and black Catalin cube pendants and metal chain.

8in (20cm) diam

£300-400   **MG**

A 1940s Napier green bakelite and white metal necklace and earrings.

7in (18cm) diam

£300-400   **MG**

A 1950s two-tone bakelite necklace.

Geometric patterns and combinations of colours are very popular. Here, amber transparent and opaque yellow bakelite has been laminated together to form the beads.

6.25in (16cm) diam

£400-600   **MG**

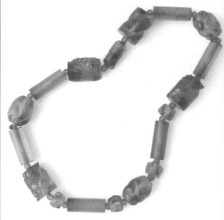

A green and beige carved bakelite necklace, with metal fittings.

8in (20cm) long

£150-200   MG

A hand-carved 'apple juice' bakelite necklace, with cylindrical and barrel beads.

7in (18cm) diam

£400-600   MG

A 1950s multi-coloured laminated Lucite ring.

The size of this ring makes it a very showy and desirable item. It is layered with multiple colours so that it changes appearance when seen from different angles.

1.5in (4cm) high

£15-25   MG

A laminated square yellow and brown-streaked bakelite ring.

1.25in (3cm) high

£100-150   MG

A hand-carved 'creamed corn' bakelite stylized rose and triangle ring.

1in (2.5cm) high

£40-60   MG

A green and yellow carved cog ring.

1in (2.5cm) high

£15-25   MG

A hand-carved 'creamed corn' bakelite stylized curving leaf ring.

1in (2.5cm) high

£50-80   MG

A hand-carved green bakelite and stylized leaf ring.

1in (2.5cm) high

£40-60   MG

FIND OUT MORE...

DK Collectors' Guide: Costume Jewellery, *by Judith Miller, published by Dorling Kindersley, 2003.*

COLLECTORS' NOTES

- Acme Studios is an American product design company and was founded in 1985 by Adrian Olabuenaga and his wife Lesley Bailey. It produces writing instruments, stationery, personal accessories and other items, all with a strong design focus. It has since worked with many important late 20thC designs and designers and has exported its products around the world.

- Brooches and jewellery were amongst the first items offered, with the 'Memphis Designers For Acme' range, comprising over 100 designs by 14 notable Postmodern designers, being released in 1985. The following year, the 'Architects for Acme' range was released. Designers included Ettore Sottsass, Michele De Lucchi, Peter Shire and Marco Zanini.

- All represent the Postmodern movement strongly, with references to architecture rendered in bright colours being typical. All pieces are of high quality and are marked on the reverse. In recent years, the tools and dies used to make certain jewellery ranges have been destroyed and the ranges withdrawn from general sale. As interest in Postmodernism of the 1980s and early 1990s grows, these are likely to become desirable collectables of the future.

A 1980s Acme Studios 'Circulus' enamelled metal brooch, designed by Ettore Sottsass, from the 'Memphis Designers For Acme' range.

One of these brooches is in the permanent collection of the Brooklyn Museum, New York.

2in (5cm) high

£120-180   **QU**

An Acme Studios 'Madras' enamelled metal pin, designed by Ettore Sottsass, from the 'Architects For Acme' range.

2in (5cm) high

£120-180   **BWH**

A pair of ACME Studios 'Aristotele' enamelled metal earrings, designed by Michele de Lucchi, mounted on an original card, from the 'Memphis Designers For Acme' range.

Like many designs, this was also made as a pin and a 'bolo' tie pull.

2in (5cm) high

£100-150   **MTS**

An Acme Studios 'Optima' enamelled metal brooch, designed by Ettore Sottsass, from the 'Memphis Designers For Acme' range.

2.75in (6.5cm) high

£150-200   **BWH**

An Acme Studios 'Grids 4' enamelled metal brooch designed by Cesar Pelli in 1986, from the 'Architects For Acme' range.

2in (5cm) wide

£100-150   **BWH**

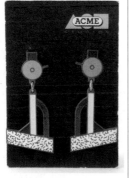

A pair of Acme Studios 'Tahiti' enamelled metal earrings, designed by Ettore Sottsass, mounted on an original card, from the 'Memphis Designers For Acme' range.

These take the form of Sottsass' notable 'Tahiti' table lamp design of 1981.

Earrings 1.75in (4.5cm) high

£150-200   **BWH**

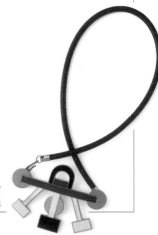

An ACME Studios 'Euphoria' enamelled metal pendant on original necklace, designed by Ettore Sottsass, from the 'Memphis Designers For Acme' range.

Pendant 3in (7.5cm) wide

£180-220   **MTS**

COLLECTORS' NOTES

■ 19thC items, such as pottery plates, specially made to commemorate famous trading ships have long appealed to collectors and now give an insight into a lost era. Objects that were actually used on the ships are equally popular, particularly if connected to a well-known historical figure.

■ Ocean Liner memorabilia from the golden age of luxury sea travel is also very popular. Many collectors concentrate on a single ship or line, or a specific category such as menus or advertisements. Objects relating to the best-known shipping companies, such as Cunard, White Star Line, Union Castle, P&O and Canadian Pacific, are highly sought after and items showing the ship or logo are particularly prized. The most collectable cruise ship items are associated with the 'Titanic'.

■ Not all souvenirs were made to be used or sold on a particular ship and some commemorative items were produced many years after a ship took its last voyage.

A pearlware plate, commemorating the steam ship 'The Robert Bruce', within a border of flowers of the Union.

In 1819, The Robert Bruce ran the first regular route that called at the Isle of Man from the mainland. She was transferred to the Liverpool-to-Dublin run in 1820 but after only a few months she caught fire and was sunk to extinguish the flames.

c1819

£350-450 SAS

A pink lustre-banded earthenware plate, printed in grey with a cartouche of two sailing vessels, hairline crack.

c1820　　　8.5in (21.5cm) diam

£25-35 SAS

A 'Transatlantic Steam Ship Company' ironstone plate, the centre printed in puce with a paddle steamer under sail, rim chip.

The Transatlantic Steamship Company operated in the North Atlantic from 1838 running only one ship, the Liverpool. The company was disbanded in 1840 and the ship was sold to P&O who renamed her the Great Liverpool.

c1838　　　8.5in (21.5cm) diam

£150-200 SAS

A steam passenger list from the North German Lloyd Line 'Rhein' steamship, sailing from New York to Bremen on 30th May 1874, exhibits minor soiling.

1874　　　8.5in (21.5cm) high

£70-100 AAC

A 'Victoria and Albert Yacht' commemorative pink lustre banded soup bowl, decorated with coloured enamels with the named paddle steamer.

The first vessel to carry the name 'Victoria and Albert, she was designed by Sir William Symonds and was launched in 1843. She made over 20 voyages with the royal couple aboard and was renamed Osbourne in 1854. She was broken up in 1868.

c1854

£120-180 SAS

A Victorian stevenograph bookmark, commemorating Captain H.R.H. Alfred, Duke of Edinburgh.

In 1867, Prince Alfred visited the island of Tristan da Cunha while on a world tour aboard the royal yacht Britannia. The main settlement on the island was named Edinburgh of the Seven Seas in his honour.

c1867　　　9.25in (23.5cm) long

£70-90 COB

A pair of HMS Raleigh leaves, each painted with a warship under sail, framed.

The HMS Raleigh was an iron frigate built at Chatham in 1873. The ship enjoyed a long overseas commission and in 1899 led the last squadron of Naval ships to put to sea under sail.

8.75in (22.5cm) wide

£80-100 SAS

An interesting Continental porcelain plaque, the green body overlaid in white with a ship thought to be the Kaiserin Augusta.

Kaiserin Augusta was a luxurious German North Atlantic liner of 1906. After WWI she was surrendered to the British and subsequently became the Canadian Pacific's 'Empress of Scotland'. She was scrapped in 1930.

c1900   8in (20cm) wide

£40-60   **SAS**

A small Titanic commemorative jug, by Carlton China, inscribed on the reverse.

Despite its small size and plain decoration, its connection to the most famous of cruise liners makes it desirable.

1912   2.25in (5.5cm) high

£150-200   **SAS**

A White Star Line silver-plated wine bottle stopper.

c1930   3.25in (8.5cm) high

£150-200   **F**

A 1930s Clyde-Mallory Lines cruise line brochure, for trips to and from Miami to Havana.

9.5in (23.5cm) high

£50-75   **DD**

An S.S. Normandie commemorative ceramic dish.

c1935   5in (13cm) diam

£60-80   **COB**

A 1930s pack of P&O playing cards.

3.5in (9cm) long

£20-25   **COB**

A 1950s pack of Orient Line S.S. Orcades playing cards.

3.5in (9cm) long

£12-15   **COB**

An RMS Queen Elizabeth menu, for Sunday, October 20th, 1968.

This was used during the liner's final voyage.

1968   10.5in (16.5cm) high

£10-15   **COB**

A 1950s P&O 'Arcadia' eggcup, marked "Mappin & Webb" and "Mappin Plate".

3.25in (8.5cm) high

£12-18   **DH**

DISNEYANA

COLLECTORS' NOTES

■ Walter Elias Disney (1901-66) founded a pioneering animation studio in 1922 with his brother Roy. Mickey Mouse was developed in 1928, and the film 'Snow White & The Seven Dwarfs' in 1937 had an enormous impact on cinema. Values for the vast amount of memorabilia produced around his characters and films is largely based on the character, the type, the date it was made and the condition and rarity.

■ Memorabilia began to be produced from c1930 onwards, and it is memorabilia from the 1930s that is generally the most valuable today. Marks are important and help to date a piece. Early marks may include George Borgfeldt's name, as he was the first to receive a license from Disney to produce his characters. Star salesman and marketeer Kay Kamen was another early name. He signed a deal with Disney in 1939 that was cut short by his death in 1949.

■ Before 1939, most pieces were marked "Walt Disney Enterprises" or, more rarely, "Walter E. Disney". British-made pieces of the 1930s may also feature "Walt Disney Mickey Mouse Ltd". From 1939-84, the marking changed to "Walt Disney Productions" and after 1984 the marking "© Disney" or "© Disney Enterprises" tended to be used.

■ Characters such as Mickey Mouse will have a broad and lasting appeal amongst the widest variety of generations of collectors. Earlier, more short-lived and obscure characters, such as Horace The Horse, will be less desirable to many, despite being rare. However, the small group of collectors who do collect rare characters will often pay large sums for good examples. Certain characters have also changed in appearance over time. Mickey Mouse lost his toothy grin in the early 1930s and became rounder, and less rodent-like by the 1950s.

A 1930s Steiff Mickey Mouse small soft toy, in excellent and clean condition, complete with Steiff ear button and foot stamp.

7in (17.5cm) high

£600-700   **SOTT**

A 'Bendy' foam Mickey Mouse figure, marked "©WD".

c1970   *7in (18cm) high*

£10-15   **RBC**

A Walt Disney Production Mickey Mouse Disneyland nodder, labels.

6.5in (16.5cm) high

£25-45   **PA**

A 1980s Walt Disney Minnie Mouse 'Bendy' foam figure, marked "1981 (c) Walt Disney Co.", original cotton and lace bib.

Damage reduces value dramatically.

8in (20cm) high

£10-15   **RBC**

An R. Dakin & Company Walt Disney Productions soft vinyl Mickey & Minnie.

8in (20cm) high

£60-80   **NOR**

A 1960s-70s Donald Duck painted wood money bank.

The paintwork is still in surprisingly good condition.

13.5in (34cm) high

£40-50   **MEM**

A 1980s Donald Duck painted wood money bank, with lock and key, marked "© Disney".

11.75in (30cm) high

£40-50   **MEM**

A CLOSER LOOK AT MICKEY & MINNIE MOUSE TOYS

Dean's introduced character memorabilia in 1930, but gaining the right to make the first ever Mickey Mouse dolls from Walt Disney in 1930 was a real coup.

The design with printed teeth is the earliest; in 1934 a softer version without 'scary' looking teeth was introduced.

It is very rare to find Minnie, let alone a pair together, and both are in mint condition, being very clean with unfaded printed facial features and clothes.

A pair of rare Dean's Rag Book Mickey & Minnie 'Evripose' fabric and velvet wire-framed dancing dolls, with printed Regd No.750611 for late 1929.

These toys were voted the 'Boom' toy of the year in February 1930.

c1931

A smaller 6in (15cm) high Mickey with a clip can be found. Known as a 'jigger' and costing two shillings at the time, he could be attached to the arm of a gramophone where he would dance around as the music played.

12.5in (32cm) high

£500-700   **TCT**

A 1980s 'Bendy' foam Donald Duck figure, marked "1984 copyright Walt Disney Co.", with original fabric bowtie.

8in (20cm) high

£10-15   **RBC**

A 1980s Thumper moulded plastic figure, marked "©Disney China".

4.5in (11.5cm) high

£8-12   **RBC**

A 1980s Flower moulded plastic figure, from 'Bambi', marked "©Disney China".

4.5in (11.5cm) high

£8-12   **RBC**

A 'Lady' hand-painted ceramic figurine, from 'Lady and the Tramp', marked "Disney Japan".

4in (10cm) high

£10-15   **TSIS**

A 1950s-60s Walt Disney Snow White hand-painted ceramic figurine, marked "©Walt Disney Prod. Japan".

7.25in (18.5cm) high

£35-45   **RBC**

A 1960s Walt Disney Productions plastic Goofy on a tricycle toy.

5in (13cm) high

£10-15   **NOR**

A Bambi hand-painted ceramics figural flower pot, impressed "Bambi Walt Disney ®".

9.5in (24cm) wide

£30-40 TM

A Marx Toys plastic and soft vinyl Pinnochio 'Pip Squeek' figure, mint in box.

1970 5in (12.5cm) high

£6-7 MEM

A 1970s Walt Disney Productions Pluto battery-operated 'Mystery Action' figure, in mint condition with original box.

'Mystery Action' was a term used frequently in the 1950s and 1960s by Japanese makers to describe the moving or flashing elements on their toys.

10.75in (27.5cm) high

£20-30 MEM

An American Walt Disney Mickey Mouse Club wind-up fireman toy, by Durham, in mint condition with unopened box.

Box 11in (28cm) high

£40-50 MEM

An AHI Walt Disney Productions Mickey Mouse in car toy, in mint condition in blister pack.

It is rare to find these toys still unopened in their blister packs. The 'Fast Wheels' were made to compete with Corgi's 'Whizz Wheels' and Mattel's 'Superfast' Hot Wheels models.

1977 5in (13cm) high

£6-7 MEM

An AHI Walt Disney's Productions Donald Duck in car, in mint condition in unopened blister pack.

1977 5in (13cm) high

£6-7 MEM

A Herbert George & Co. 'Donald Duck' black Bakelite camera, for Walt Disney Productions.

The survival of the original card box is very rare, and makes the camera many times more desirable. This is due also to its appealing and colourful graphics. Without the box, a used camera usually fetches under £30.

c1946 4.75in (12cm) wide box

£120-180 MEM

An Ensign Ltd. Mickey Mouse battery-powered toy lantern set, consisting of a viewer, 11 sets of slides, spare battery and bulbs, with "Walter E. Disney" licensing wording, all in original labelled boxes.

The use of the wording "Walter E. Disney" implies licensed merchandise made in Britain during the 1930s and its appearance is rare.

c1935 Box 10.5in (26.5cm) wide

£120-180 GORL

A set of 1950s Mickey Mouse Picture Cubes, each wooden cube covered with printed paper, "Walt Disney Productions Made in West Germany".

Box 7in (18cm) wide

£10-15 NOR

A 1950s-60s American 'Donald Duck' lithographed tin paint box, by Transogram Co. Inc, marked "© Walt Disney Productions.

8in (20cm) wide

£20-30 **SOTT**

A 1950s Walt Disney Productions Snow White hand-painted ceramic mug.

From the lightweight, white, granular ceramic used and style of the hand-painted design, this was probably made in Japan.

3.75in (9.5cm) high

£15-25 **NOR**

A 1930s Donald Duck hand-painted jug, the base impressed either "Walter Disney" or "Walt E. Disney".

6in (15.5cm) high

£50-70 **NOR**

A 1960s-70s Walt Disney Productions Mickey Mouse plastic cup, with 'blinking' eyes.

4in (10cm) high

£18-22 **NOR**

A 1960s Walt Disney Production Jiminy Cricket plastic cup, with 'blinking' eyes.

4in (10cm) high

£8-12 **NOR**

A 1950s Walt Disney Productions child's lampshade, in excellent clean condition.

8.5in (21.5cm) high

£10-15 **MA**

A 1950s American box of Walt Disney Productions Mickey Mouse '100 Sunshine Straws', unopened and complete.

It is the rarity of the unopened nature of this box, as well as the colourful and comparatively early artwork on the box, that makes this valuable.

8.75in (22cm) long

£35-45 **TRA**

A 1950s American box of Walt Disney Productions Donald Duck 'Sunshine Straws' unopened and complete.

8.75in (22cm) high

£35-45 **TRA**

An American Warren Biggs Co. calendar card for July 1947, with Walt Disney's Donald Duck with Mrs. Jumbo and Dumbo.

1947 *9in (23cm) high*

£20-30 **LDE**

An American Warren Biggs Co. calendar card for December 1947, with Walt Disney's Mickey, Minnie, Huey and Duey.

1947   *9in (23cm) high*

£20-30   **LDE**

A CLOSER LOOK AT A FANTASIA SCARF

Fantasia memorabilia is rarer than that for other Disney films as the world was at war when the film was released in 1940.

The film is deemed one of Disney's high points and has many fans who are eager to collect original items relating to the film.

It is very large and in excellent, clean ____ condition with no tears or stains and original, bright colours, which is unusual for items made for children to wear.

It is also unusual as it does not feature ____ Mickey Mouse, but shows other characters such as Mademoiselle Upanova, cupids and Melinda the Centaurette, who is featured in the Pastorale Symphony part of the film.

A rare 1940s Walt Disney Productions 'Fantasia' rayon scarf.

30.25in (77cm) wide

£120-180   **NOR**

A 1950s-60s Walt Disney Productions 'Disneyland' rayon and silk-mix handkerchief, the corner signed or printed "Hillegas".

16.5in (42cm) wide

£10-15   **NOR**

A late 1960s-70s Walt Disney Productions Jungle Book printed cotton handkerchief, featuring Shere Khan.

9in (23cm) high

£8-12   **NOR**

A rare 'Yoo Hoo' Mickey Mouse badge, printed with "©1930 Walter E. Disney All Rights Reserved For Great Britain", but made in the 1960s.

3.5in (9cm) diam

£60-80   **LDE**

An Ingersoll Mickey Mouse child's wristwatch, with articulated metal strap, inoperative.

Ingersoll began producing these watches in 1933, this example dates from the late 1930s and has its original strap with moulded and painted Mickey Mouses. Value, particularly for less expensive later examples from the 1950s-60s, is dependant on whether the watch works, as the movements were typically of poor quality and are hard to find in working order.

£100-150   **SAS**

A Walt Disney World Minnie Mouse plastic wallet.

3.75in (9.5cm) wide

£7-10   **NOR**

COLLECTORS' NOTES

■ Bisque dolls can be identified by looking for impressed or incised marks, which indicate a mould number and sometimes a maker, on the nape of the neck. The facial characteristics of a doll can also act as a guide to makers. Armand Marseille (AM) was one of the most prolific makers, with production peaking from c1900-30. Their '390' doll is one of the most commonly seen. Look for well-painted, lively and characterful features, and clean bisque. Cracks and mismatched bodies devalue a doll, and the presence of original clothes adds value.

■ Composition and fabric dolls are also widely collected. Always examine the painted surface of composition dolls as damage to the surface or cracks will devalue a doll. Composition is a mixture of plaster, wood pulp, glue and other ingredients that can

be moulded. It was used from c1900 to the 1950s when it was superseded by the more economical and versatile plastic. Early fabric dolls from the early to mid-19thC can be rare as most have been worn or fallen apart. Many were home-made, or sewn together and stuffed using self assembly kits bought from shops.

■ Plastic dolls have risen in value dramatically over the past decade as the generation who remember them as children has begun to collect. Examples in clean, un-played with condition, complete with their original clothes, boxes and tags (ie; in shop-sold condition) are the most valuable. Look out for examples that also retain their original hairstyles. Madam Alexander, Pedigree, Terri Lee and American Character Doll Co. are among the many collectable makers.

A German Armand Marseille bisque doll, with sleeping blue eyes, open mouth, blonde wig and jointed body in original white dress and underclothes, marked "A8M 996".	A German Armand Marseille bisque doll, with sleeping blue eyes, blonde wig and composition body with wooden limbs dressed in cream nightwear, marked "1894".	A German Armand Marseille doll, with sleeping brown eyes, brown wig and composition body dressed in cream nightdress, marked "390".	A German Armand Marseille child doll, with fixed blue eyes, pierced ears, long blonde wig and jointed composition body, dressed in a white and red dress and under-clothes, marked "1894", one foot detached.
22.5in (57cm) high	*15.25in (39cm) high*	*21in (53cm) high*	*17in (43cm) high*
£120-180 SAS	**£120-180** SAS	**£120-180** SAS	**£80-120** SAS

A German Heinrich Handwerck girl doll, with brown sleeping eyes, pierced ears, open mouth with four teeth, mohair wig, jointed body, wearing a pink dress with hat and shoes, marked "109/11 3/4", some wear.	A German Schoenau & Hoffmeister bisque child doll, with blue sleeping eyes, blonde wig and jointed composition body wearing a cream dress with matching bonnet, underclothes and black leather shoes.	A German Schoenau & Hoffmeister child doll, with sleeping blue eyes, brown wig and wood and composition body wearing a lilac dress, marked "1923".
c1900 *22in (55cm) high*	*1909* *24in (61cm) high*	*23.25in (59cm) high*
£450-550 LAN	**£120-180** SAS	**£150-200** SAS

An American Kellogg's 'Papa Bear' printed fabric doll.

These promotional cloth dolls were given away by Kellogg's as kits to be cut out, sewn and stuffed at home. 'Papa Bear' was only made in 1925, with the other characters from the Goldilocks story being produced only in 1926.

1925   13.25in (33.5cm) high

£40-50   **HGS**

An American Kellogg's 'Goldilocks' printed cloth doll, with "©1926 Kellogg Co. Battel Creek Mich." printed fabric label.

12.75in (32.5cm) high

£40-50   **HGS**

An 1920s American Kellogg's Nursery Rhymes 'Little Bo Peep' cloth doll.

14.25in (36.5cm) high

£40-50   **HGS**

A late 19thC Judy printed cloth doll.

15.25in (38.5cm) high

£40-50   **HGS**

A late 19thC American Arnold Printworks 'Our Soldier Boys' printed fabric doll.

This self-assembled cloth doll kit was advertised in 'The Youth's Companion' in October 1894, together with a variation holding a sword.

c1894   8in (20cm) high

£30-50   **HGS**

A rare set of ten American Arnold Printworks printed fabric skittles, weighted at base area with heavy beads.

The complete set of different, characterful faces and the complexity of printing makes this set especially appealing.

1904-05   9.75in (24.5cm) high

£200-300   **HGS**

A Steiff German soldier felt doll, with button and original tag.

This complexly made cloth doll is both very hard to find, and in mint condition, with its tag and with no wear or damage, which makes it exceptionally rare. It is unlikely that a boy would have wanted such a cloth doll, and the same certainly rings true for girls. Despite this, its great rarity and fine condition make it highly desirable to collectors today.

c1930s   8.5in (22cm) high

£2,500-3,500   **TCT**

A Käthe Kruse fabric boy doll, with painted hair and face, dressed in a pair of trousers, jacket and shoes.

16in (40cm) high

£450-550   LAN

An Italian Lenci pressed felt girl doll, with brown painted side-glancing eyes, blond mohair wig, jointed felt and cloth body, some damage to dress, lacks shoes.

13.75in (35cm) high

£100-150   SAS

A Norah Wellings fabric boy doll, with moulded felt face, painted features, and velvet hands and legs, marked "Norah Wellings made in England" on wrist.

c1950   11in (28cm) high

£70-100   RBC

A late 1930s American Effanbee Playmate Anne Shirley composition doll, with original clothes, card tag and box.

21.25in (54cm) high

£160-200   MEM

An Effanbee 'Skippy' composition soldier doll, with side-glancing eyes, military outfit and cap, fine crazing and minor chipping to face paint.

'Skippy The All American Boy' was a 1920s newspaper character drawn by Percy Crosby. He was a playmate for the popular Patsy doll.

14in (35.50cm) high

£180-220   JDJ

A Campbell Kid composition and cloth-bodied doll, with composition hands, dressed in original checker board dress and shoes.

11.75in (30cm) high

£70-100   MEM

An American Madame Alexander Sonja Henie composition doll, complete with original hairstyle, tagged dress and leatherette ice skates.

Sonja Henie (1912-69) was a Norwegian champion figure skater who won 10 consecutive world championships from 1927. Moving to the US, she turned professional in 1936. During the 1950s she performed in shows, TV programmes and films.

1939-42   15in (38cm) high

£150-200   MEM

A 1940s British Mark Payne composition doll, with wind-up disc playing mechanism.

Mark Payne also released a 'Queen Elizabeth' speaking/singing doll for the 1953 Coronation, using the same face and body as this example.

26in (66cm) high

£80-100   DSC

A 1940s Frank Popper pot doll, in bridal outfit and mohair wig, marked "FP210", in original box.

Pot is a material similar to composition but more chalky. British manufacturer F. Popper is best known for making 'pot' dolls.

21in (53.5cm) high

£35-45   GAZE

A German Schildkröt celluloid headed doll, with a leather body and celluloid arms, blue sleeping eyes and open mouth with teeth, marked "SiR Germany 13 1926".

1926   17.25in (43cm) high

£60-80   **WDL**

A CLOSER LOOK AT A PLASTIC DOLL

Madame Alexander dolls are renowned for their authentic clothes and well-modelled and 'made-up' faces. Jacqueline Kennedy is a highly sought-after character.

She is complete and in mint condition, even retaining her delicate stockings, card tag and her original hair style and 'make-up'.

Jacqueline, along with her daughter Caroline, was only produced from 1961-62. They are hard to find today.

This outfit is rare and perfectly matches popular styles of fashionable young women of the day.

A French celluloid baby doll.

c1920   20in (51cm) high

£100-150   **BEJ**

An American Madame Alexander Jacqueline Kennedy vinyl doll, with original clothes and in original condition, with card hand tag.

1961-62   21in (53.5cm) high

£300-400   **MEM**

A 1930s French Petitcolin celluloid boy doll.

21in (53.5cm) high

£40-50   **DSC**

A rare American Madame Alexander Caroline Kennedy doll, in mint condition, in original box.

This scarce doll is rare in mint condition, and rarer still with her original box and card tag.

£220-280   **MEM**

A late 1950s American Character Doll Co. Betsy McCall hard vinyl doll, in her original blue dress with her original hairstyle, in excellent condition.

Betsy McCall began life as a paper doll in McCall's magazine. American Character Doll released this highly popular version in 1957.

8in (20.5cm) high

£70-100   **MEM**

A CLOSER LOOK AT A REVLON DOLL

The Revlon doll was issued by the renowned Ideal Toy Corporation in 1956 and used the famous Revlon name and a lower price to compete against other fashion dolls.

She was available with an extensive range of hairstyles and in many different outfits, all named after Revlon products of the time, such as 'Queen of Diamonds'.

She is complete with all her clothes, earrings and shoes and retains her original red-painted nails and lips

The upswept hair retains its original style and is said to be scarce.

An American Character Doll Co. 'Sweet Sue' hard plastic doll, with original clothes, hair style and card hand tag.

Sweet Sue's hair is rooted in a skull cap, which was an exclusive patent owned by the American Character Doll Company.

20.5in (52cm) high

£150-200   **MEM**

An American Ideal 'Little Miss Revlon' hard vinyl doll, complete with clothing and accessories, lacks box.

If she had her box and tag in mint condition, she could fetch up to 50 per cent more.

c1958   11in (28cm) high

£80-120   **DIM**

A 1970s British Burbank Alexandra Rose vinyl doll, with soft body and legs.

22in (56cm) high

£15-25   **DSC**

A 1950s Palitoy girl doll, the plastic head with painted features and cloth body, reg. design no. 824 206 for 1937.

c1938   19in (48.5cm) high

£8-12   **GAZE**

A 1950s 'Girl' hard plastic 'walker' doll, by Palitoy.

Her cheek colouring is not worn and her mohair wig is still curled. She is a 'walker' doll meaning she turns her head as she walks. Palitoy released her in conjunction with 'Girl' comic, published by Hulton Press which is why she has the logo on her belt, dress and hair ribbon. Hard plastic dolls by Palitoy typically have lilac eyes.

14in (35.5cm) high

£80-120   **DSC**

A 1970s Tri-ang Pedigree 'Mam'selle' vinyl doll, in mint condition with original box.

19.5in (49.5cm) high

£20-30   **GAZE**

A 1950s Pedigree Delite hard plastic baby doll.

14in (35.5cm) high

£50-60   **DSC**

A Sasha doll, with blonde hair, dressed in blue cord dress, tights and shoes.

c1985   *16in (40.5cm) high*

£80-120   **GAZE**

A CLOSER LOOK AT A PLASTIC DOLL

Her body and limbs are made from a form of thin rubber or latex, stuffed with kapok, to emulate real skin.

Her head is made from hard plastic and is very clean.

The latex tended to split over time, making complete, undamaged dolls rare today – this example has only one split on her hand.

Pedigree dolls have been collectable for years, but are becoming increasingly desirable in finer condition.

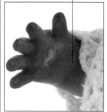

A rare 1950s Pedigree 'Beauty Skin Delite' doll, in replaced clothes.

18in (45.5cm) high

£70-100   **DSC**

An American Terri Lee ballet dancer doll, in original condition with her original pink dress.

The presence of the original dress is rare as they were often lost and replaced.

10.25in (26cm) high

£60-80   **MEM**

A 1960s American vinyl 'Go-Go' doll, with original clothing, shoes and sunglasses.

19.75in (50cm) high

£15-25   **NOR**

An Elizabeth Taylor plastic fashion doll, in mint condition in original box, with MGM licensing wording, in mint condition with original box.

These dolls, made after her role as a prostitute in the 1960 film 'Butterfield 8', are very rare as Taylor is said to have disallowed dolls to be made of her until a deal with Mattel in 2000.

Box 14in (35.5cm) high

£180-220   **DIM**

A 1930s Princess Elizabeth paper doll, with 11 outfits.

12in (30.5cm) high

£150-200   **BEJ**

A 1930s 'Princess Margaret Rose' paper doll with 11 outfits.

Doll 12in (30.5cm) high

£100-150   **BEJ**

A CLOSER LOOK AT A HALF DOLL

This large doll is complexly modelled – the arms would have been separately moulded and attached.

Half dolls were attached to fabric 'dresses' at their waists, which were used as pin cushions or to cover powder boxes or other objects.

Her face is charming and full of character, and the flowers and extra detail are painstakingly modelled, attached and painted.

Most half dolls were made in Germany from the late 19thC to the 1930s – this example is attributed to the prestigious Capodimonte factory.

A 1930s porcelain half-lady or pin doll wearing a red bonnet.

4.5in (11.5cm) height

£40-50 CSO

An Italian large half doll, in the form of a lady, attributed to Capo Di Monte.

6in (15cm) high

£450-550 JDJ

An American Bliss two-storey printed paper-on-wood doll's house, some bubbling to paper, but overall bright, lacks front steps and a piece of railing paper possibly replaced.

Bliss are a sought-after name in doll's houses, and are known for their attention to detail and use of traditional American domestic architectural features.

16.50in (42cm) high

£450-550 JDJ

An early 20thC homemade, scratch-built model of 'Rose Cottage', with detailed decoration including lean-to and pig sty, with penny-operated lighting mechanism.

13.75in (35cm) high

£250-350 ROS

A group of ebonised wooden doll's house furniture, displayed in a wooden room setting; together with additional mahogany finished doll's house furniture.

The label shows that this was made in 1912 by a craftsman, probably at home, to display at an exhibition of furniture at London store Maples.

Setting 11.5in (29cm) high

£180-220 F

An unusual leather and painted metal doll's watch, with moveable metal hands.

c1910 Face 0.5in (1.5cm) diam

£70-100 BEJ

COLLECTORS' NOTES

■ The popularity of vintage eyewear has risen dramatically over the past five years, as people looking for an individual, often 'retro', personal look have begun to compete against collectors. As such, prices have risen and even contemporary designers look to the styles of past decades for inspiration amid a flurry of coverage in fashion magazines.

■ The value of much vintage eyewear lies in the style or look of the frames, the name of the maker or designer, the material and the condition. Always aim to buy frames that are most representative of the period they were produced in. The 1950s and '60s are currently the most popular decades, with highly stylized cat's-eye and bug-eyed, or cupped shapes, being the most desirable.

■ Fashions change regularly, but currently, large lensed frames such as the ever-popular 'Jackie O' style and certain 1960s and '80s designs are also in vogue. Colourful or complex plastics, and those with appealing or period printed or carved designs, are also popular.

■ Condition is important. Values are not usually affected too seriously by missing or scratched lenses, as many wearers and collectors will prefer to fit lenses of their own. However, if the original lens were unusual, such as having a graduated tone, value will be affected as these can be hard to replace.

■ Split, cracked, brittle or glued frames should be avoided, as these are very difficult, if not impossible to repair, especially invisibly. Those that have bent over time can be reshaped by professionals using heat. However, this can only be done providing the curving is not too great. Look for 'dead' unused shop stock, which is unworn.

■ Look out for famous names, not just those such as Alain Mikli and Emmanuelle Khahn in the world of eyewear, but also in the world of fashion, including Christian Dior, Emilio Pucci and Pierre Cardin. As well as all the above, look out for frames that have that extra 'something', which is perhaps best summed up as 'specs appeal'.

A pair of 1950s-60s American plain black gent's frames, marked "US Optical MADE IN USA".

5in (12.5cm) wide

£18-22   **BB**

A pair of French grey and silver striated plastic frames, with "CA" monogram, marked "Frame France YVAN".

5.25in (13.5cm) wide

£20-30   **BB**

A pair of 1950s silver and white grey pearlescent plastic frames, the corners inset with two small metal stars.

5in (12.5cm) wide

£18-22   **BB**

A pair of 1950s American Raybert 'Baccara' triple-laminated brown, white and clear plastic frames, hand-cut down on brows in a flame-like pattern.

The three colours of plastics are shown to dramatic effect in the typically 1950s carved areas.

5.75in (14.5cm) wide

£120-180   **VE**

A pair of American white plastic sunglasses, with pink lenses, marked with "Suntimer AA" motif.

5.5in (14cm) wide

£80-120   **VE**

A pair of French Alain Mikli black plastic and gilt metal frames, with moulded textured pattern, marked "Hand Made in France".

5in (13cm) wide

£150-200   **VE**

A pair of 1960s yellow opalescent plastic hexagonal frames, with 'O-O' motif.

5in (13cm) wide

£22-28   **BB**

A pair of 1960s French 'blonde tortoiseshell' plastic sunglasses, with blue lenses.

6in (15.5cm) wide

£100-150 VE

A pair of 1960s French large oval 'blonde tortoiseshell' plastic sunglasses.

This over-sized, almost 'bug-eyed' look has become popular once again after the style was reintroduced by Dior and Blinds and popularised by Madonna and U2's Bono.

5.75in (14.5cm) wide

£100-150 VE

A pair of American white and pale brown laminated 'bug-eyed' sunglasses, with graduated lenses and matching side lenses, marked "Mod Twist".

The side lenses have no real purpose apart from extending the 'Op Art' look of these shades. The colour of the lenses cleverly mirrors the colour of the brown base plastic, under the white lamination.

£200-250 VE

A CLOSER LOOK AT A PAIR OF CARDIN GLASSES

The frames are by Pierre Cardin, who was a major international designer during the 1960s and was responsible for many key fashion movements of the period.

While the round frames are typical of the 1960s, the shape, straight-style of the arms and use of tortoiseshell plastic strongly resemble early 19thC frames.

Unusually, they fold down into a small and strong structure, making them ideal for carrying around safely. The folded arms also protect the lenses.

A pair of 1960s French Pierre Cardin 'tortoiseshell' plastic folding frames.

6in (15cm) wide

£150-200 VE

A pair of Emilio Pucci 'Portofino' printed black plastic sunglasses.

Fashion designer Emilio Pucci was known for his brightly, often psychedelically, coloured geometric and swirling printed patterns. Here fabric has been laminated under plastic. Interestingly, Pucci has a famous branch of its boutiques in Portofino.

6.5in (16.5cm) wide

£180-220 GAZE

A pair of 1960s American laminated red white and blue plastic sunglasses, stamped "MAY USA" with "BGN SPORTS STRIPE" sticker.

This fashionable style of frame is often known as 'Jackie O' after Jackie Onassis Kennedy, who regularly seen sporting this look. The colouring of this pair makes them highly patriotic. May & Co. are a collectable name.

5.25in (13.5cm) wide

£150-200 VE

A pair of 1960s blue striated and clear plastic frames, unmarked.

5.25in (13.5cm) wide

£150-200 VE

A pair of 1960s French red plastic frames, with integral grid 'lenses', marked "Made in France".

The 1960s saw a wide variety of highly unusual shapes and decorative treatments, many inspired by the 'future' and outer space, including thin slits and such 'grids'.

6in (15cm) wide

£70-100   **VE**

A pair of 1960s French white square sunglasses, with original lenses, marked "Made in France".

These frames were inspired by the shapes of TV screens, as televisions became regular and much-loved features in most homes around the world.

6in (15cm) wide

£100-150   **VE**

A pair of late 1950s-early 1960s pearlised 'champagne' plastic laminated on black plastic sunglasses, the top rim carved by hand with lines, marked "Made in France".

These highly stylized retro specs have the colour and shape of the 1950s but have been affected by the slightly eccentric style of the coming 1960s.

6.25in (16cm) wide

£80-120   **VE**

A pair of 1960s French laminated white, pearlised grey plastic and black plastic diamond-shaped sunglasses, marked "Made in France".

The geometric form and contrasting colours of the frames were inspired by the growing 'Op Art' movement of the 1960s, championed by artists such as Bridget Riley and Viktor Vasarely.

6in (15.5cm) wide

£200-250   **VE**

A pair of 1960s large green plastic sunglasses, with light blue lenses, marked "135 852 506".

The wide top edge of the frame both covered and imitated eyebrows.

2.75in (7cm) high

£80-120   **VE**

A pair of 1960s French Pierre Cardin 'Renée' large hexagonal 'light tortoiseshell' plastic frames, marked "Hand Made in France Renee".

The famous designer name, popular in his day, increases the value of these visually striking frames.

6.25in (16cm) wide

£150-200   **VE**

A pair of 1970s Ted Lapidus gold polka-dot on black and metal 'bamboo' sunglasses, marked "TL 07 48".

6in (15cm) wide

£150-200   **VE**

A pair of American graduated green and yellow plastic large unisex frames, unmarked.

5.75in (14.5cm) wide

£18-22   **BB**

A pair of Christian Dior sunglasses, with curving metal frames and Optyl graduated lenses, marked "Made in Austria".

Optyl is a lightweight plastic.

5.25in (13.5cm) wide

£120-180   **VE**

A CLOSER LOOK AT A PAIR OF MAKE-UP GLASSES

A pair of 1950s American Victory black 'cat's-eye' sunglasses, with new lenses and inset metal V-shapes, the arms marked "USA".

5.5in (14cm) wide

£22-28 **BB**

Frames made for special uses are scarcer than standard frames, but appeal mainly to eyewear collectors.

The shape of the frame is typically 1950s, being similar to the popular and fashionable 'cat's-eye' styles. The straight arms are unusual, allowing them to be put on and taken off easily.

The heavy look, often using bold, single colours was popular at the time.

The lens holders are hinged allowing them to be flipped down to help with the application of make-up and flipped up for distance viewing.

They are well-made, using fine quality materials and are in mint condition with no wear and strong and intact brass hinges.

A pair of 1950s French 'fantasy' rhinestone-inset frames, the top edge with moulded curves, the arm marked "France".

These fabulous hand-cut one piece 'fantasy' styles are hotly sought-after, particularly if completely carved and embellished with rhinestones.

4.5In (11.5cm) wide

£180-220 **VE**

A pair of 1950s black plastic 'cat's-eye' hinged make-up frames, marked "FRAME FRANCE".

5in (13cm) wide

£30-50 **BB**

£30-50 **BB**

A pair of 1960s French striped 'tortoiseshell' Lucite laminated on black Lucite 'bug-eyed' frames.

6.5in (16.5cm) wide

£30-50 **BB**

A pair of 1980s Swatch sunglasses, with two interchangeable fronts, laminated grey pearl plastic backs, the arms moulded "Swatch".

Typically 1980s in terms of colour, different 'fronts' could be clipped onto the standard frames. The bottom shot shows the inside of the frames with a front clipped on.

5.5in (14cm) wide

£70-100 **VF**

A pair of 1960s Italian Samco wire frames, with a set of interchangeable coloured circular lenses in a folding plastic case, the case marked "Samco Italy".

Depending on your mood you could look at the world through rose, blue or even grey tinted spectacles.

Case 12.25in (31cm) high

£30-40 **BB**

FIND OUT MORE...

Specs Appeal – Extravagant 1950s & 60 Eyewear, by Leslie Pina and Donald-Brian Johnson, published by Schiffer Books, 2002.

Eyeglass Retrospective – Where Fashion & Science Meet, by Nancy Schiffer, published by Schiffer Books, 2000.

COLLECTORS' NOTES

■ The 1950s saw a rejuvenation of design after emerging from the restrictions and privations of WWII.

■ New materials, developed in part because of the war, meant that man-made products such as vinyl, formica, Draylon and nylon were very much the vogue. Colours were bright, but often in pastel cheerful tones, black and white were a common combination, and decoration was stylish and whimsical.

■ These new materials also meant that items could be mass-produced like never before and saw the emergency of the 'throw away' culture. This means that pieces were often produced in large numbers, for example Ridgway's Homemaker dinnerware, making them affordable and easy to find. Examples by known designers are more likely to hold and rise in value as are those in the best condition.

■ The emergence of the teenager meant much was aimed at this youthful audience with frivolous designs to the fore. Glamour was also in after the drab war years, and popular motifs include pin-up girls, poodles, scenes of Paris and elegant, elongated women. With the continuing rise of celebrity movie stars and singers such as Marilyn Monroe and Elvis Presley, items or endorsed by or featuring famous people are also desirable.

A 1950s Beswick 'Circus' pattern toast rack, decorated with underglaze colour transfer.

6.25in (16cm) long

£35-45   **BAD**

A 1950s Beswick 'Circus' pattern sugar bowl, decorated with underglaze colour transfer.

4.75in (12cm) wide

£25-35   **BAD**

A 1950s Beswick 'Ballet' pattern mustard pot, decorated with underglaze colour transfer.

This pattern was later renamed Pavlova'. The ballet and the circus were both popular themes during the 1950s.

2.75in (7cm) high

£10-15   **MA**

A 1950s Burleigh ware 'Viscount' transfer-printed pattern sauce boat.

8in (20cm) long

£18-22   **BAD**

A 1950s Foley China 'The Gay Nineties' fancy dish, designed by Maureen Tanner.

c1956   5in (13cm) high

£10-15   **GROB**

A 1950s 'Teenage Caper' cup, with gilt trim, marked "Made in England" to the base.

This cup sums up the 1950s in many ways with the arrival of the teenager and rock 'n' roll. The reverse shows a Gaggia espresso machine, which helps to date this piece to c1957 when coffee bars began appearing in London.

c1957   3.25in (8.5cm) diam

£20-25   **MA**

A Ridgway Potteries Ltd 'Homemaker' pattern part coffee service, the pattern designed by Enid Seeney in 1956-57, comprising a coffee pot and cover, six coffee cups and saucers and a two-handled soup dish and plate, high, printed marks.

Homemaker plates are commonly found as they were produced and sold in the thousands. Coffee pots are much harder to find as people only tended to buy one. They also display the pattern well, making them more valuable.

1957-70   Coffee pot 7.5in (19cm) high

£150-200   **DN**

A 1950s Swedish JIE, Gaꞑiopla ceramic biscuit barrel, designed by Anita Nylund, with wooden lid, labelled "Gogay tableware", impressed "J I E - SWEDEN 22-3".

6.25in (16cm) high

£35-45   **TCM**

A CLOSER LOOK AT A LADY HEAD VASE

She retains her original eyelashes, earrings and necklace, adding to her value.

Lady head vases were initially sold in florists as gifts containing flowers and were often thrown away once the flowers had died.

Named examples are not necessarily more desirable; the quality of the design and moulding, and the elegance of the form and facial expression are more important.

The protruding bow and tail of her scarf could be easily damaged, but in this case are complete.

A 1950s NAPCO lady head vase, with necklace and eyelashes, marked "NAPCO 1956 C2633C" printed mark and National Potteries Co. Cleveland "MADE IN JAPAN" silver foil label.

5.25in (13.5cm) high

£60-70   **TSIS**

A 1950s Arthur Wood cylindrical hand-painted storage jar.

6.5in (16.5cm) high

£10-15   **MTS**

A set of five late 1950s/early 1960s Cortendorf 'boomerang' shaped dishes, marked "Made in West Germany".

Boomerang or kidney shapes, such as seen on these dishes, are typical of 1950s design.

5.25in (13.5cm) wide

£10-15 (each)   **GROB**

A 1950s German Goebels poodle salt and pepper set in shaped dish, marked "foreign", with bee in V mark.

Poodles call to mind elegant Parisian ladies and feature in many 1950s designs.

Tray 4.75in (12cm) wide

£70-90   **BAD**

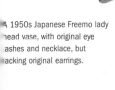

A 1950s Japanese Freemo lady head vase, with original eye lashes and necklace, but lacking original earrings.

5.5in (14cm) high

£60-80   **MAC**

A 1950s Japanese Napco lady head vase, her green bonnet decorated with flowers, transfer mark "NAPCO C3812C 1959".

5.5in (14cm) high

£70-100   **MAC**

A CLOSER LOOK AT A FREDERICK WEINBERG SCULPTURE

American sculptor Frederick Weinberg was active from the 1950s onwards and is known for his abstract figural designs. ⎯⎯⎯

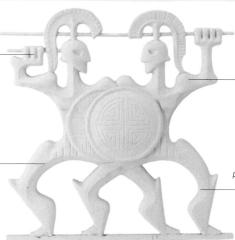

Weinberg was also influenced by Africa and tribal art, as can be seen in his other works on this page.

From the mid-1940s and through the 1950s designs became for organic, rejecting the stark angular lines of early Modernism. ⎯⎯⎯

As well as sculpture, he also produced lighting and pieces for shop window displays.

A Frederick Weinberg wall relief, reinforced fibreglass casting, depicting stylized Trojan warriors, signed "F. Weinberg" on the back.

34in (85cm) high

£600-800   **SDR**

A Frederick Weinberg salmon-coloured molded plaster abstract figural sconce, with some chips.

36in (90cm) high

£350-450   **SDR**

A Frederick Weinberg spray-painted cast iron figural sculpture.

9in (23cm) high

£100-150   **MG**

A Frederick Weinberg cast iron giraffe figural sculpture, painted orange later.

11.5in (29.5cm) high

£220-280   **MG**

A Frederick Weinberg spray-painted cast iron horse figural sculpture, stamped "©F.W."

7.75in (19.5cm) high

£100-150   **MG**

A 1950s '****ocraft' teak headrest or stool, with triangular Design Centre sticker.

This small piece of furniture is based on an African headrest that meets Mid-Century Modern in terms of material and line.

14.25in (36cm) high

£10-20   **GAZ**

FIFTIES

An American Alamo Savings & Loan Association 'The Satellite Bank' plated metal rocket-shaped money bank, marked "Duro Mold & Mfg. Inc. Detroit 34 Mich".

A set of six transfer-printed tall glasses, each decorated with a different scene of an ethnic couple dancing and playing instruments, with gilt rims.

These were produced by the same manufacturer as the following set.

5in (12.5cm) high

£50-60   **MA**

A set of six 'Hawaiian Melody' tall glasses, with transfer-printed scenes, each glass different, and gilt rims.

5in (12.5cm) high

£50-60   **MA**

The 'Space Race' between the US and the Soviet Union began around the launch of Russia's Sputnik 1 satellite on October 4th, 1957. It was to have a huge influence on design with motifs such as rockets, spaceman helmets, flying saucers and shooting stars appearing on all manner of objects.

10in (25cm) high

£80-120   **CVS**

A 1950s Celebrity 110-volt Coffee Clutch instant tea and coffee kit for home, travel and office, containing two melamine cups, two melamine milk or water containers, a heating element and a melamine spoon, contained in a printed bag.

8in (20.5cm) wide

£70-100   **MTS**

Four 1950s music-themed paper bags, for holding 45rpm singles.

8in (20cm) wide

50p-£1 (each)   **MA**

A Marx Toy battery-operated red Dalek, in excellent condition and in original box marked "©BBC 1974".

c1974

£100-150 SAS

A Marx Toys battery-operated yellow Dalek, in excellent condition and in original box marked "©BBC 1974".

c1974

£100-150 SAS

A Denys Fisher Doctor Who Tardis, in excellent condition and in original box.

The two buttons on the top of Tardis worked a mechanism that could make an action figure seem to disappear inside the toy. This toy did not sell particularly well at the time, perhaps due to the two additional and distracting buttons, and can be hard to find today.

c1977

£100-150 SAS

A CLOSER LOOK AT TWO DOCTOR WHO ACTION FIGURES

This was the only one of Denys Fisher's Doctor Who range to be issued by Italian company Harbert.

The Doctor also retains his sonic screwdriver and extra-long scarf.

The Giant Robot only appeared in one storyline but resulted in an extremely accurately modelled action figure. He retains his shoulder shields, which is unusual.

Denys Fisher's Doctor Who figures were manufactured by US firm Mego whose film, TV and music related figures are collectable in their own right.

Two Denys Fisher Doctor Who action figures, comprising the Doctor in a Harbert Italian language box and the 'Giant Robot', both complete and in excellent condition and in original boxes.

c1976

£220-280 SAS

A Codeg 'Mechanical Dalek' silver and blue plastic clockwork figure, 117-22, in excellent condition, with original box marked "©BBCTV 1965".

Dalek toys were also made by Palitoy and Marx, which can also be seen on this page. The Codeg versions are usually the most valuable.

c1965

£450-550 SAS

A Palitoy Doctor Who battery-operated Talking K-9 toy, 73009, in excellent condition and in original box.

Following the success of their Talking Dalek toys, Palitoy released the Talking K-9 soon after. The audio is supplied by a crude miniature record player inside.

c1978

£150-200 SAS

A Palitoy Talking Dalek battery-operated figure, in original box marked "©1975 British Broadcasting Corporation".

c1975 7in (18cm) high

£120-180 GAZE

"Doctor Who: The Missing Adventures - The Ghosts of N-Space", by Barry Letts, published by Virgin Publishing.

1995

£6-8   TP

"Doctor Who: The Missing Adventures - Downtime", by Marc Platt, published by Virgin Publishing.

1996

£6-8   TP

"Doctor Who - The Handbook: The First Doctor", by Howe, Stammers and Walker, published by Virgin Publishing.

1994

£7-10   TP

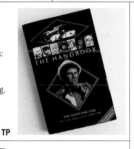

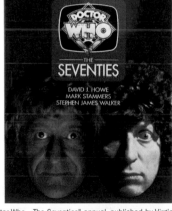

"Doctor Who - The Handbook: The Sixth Doctor", by Howe, Stammers and Walker, published by Virgin Publishing.

1993

£7-10   TP

'Doctor Who Annual 1982', published by BBC TV and distributed by World Distributors.

1981

£7-9   MTS

A "Doctor Who - The Seventies" annual, published by Virgin Publishing.

1994   *12in (30.5cm) high*

£20-30   TP

Doctor Who Annual 1984', published by BBC TV and distributed by World Distributors.

1983   *10.5in (27cm) high*

£12-18   MTS

A Doctor Who 'Get Well Soon' greeting card, the inside with "What the Doctor ordered", the back marked "A Dennis A. Ian print licensed the BBC Enterprises Ltd.", in original plastic wrapper.

7.25in (18.5cm) high

£2-3   MTS

A Doctor Who greeting card, the inside with "Always happy days", the back marked "A Dennis A. Ian print licensed the BBC Enterprises Ltd.", in original plastic wrapper.

7.25in (18.5cm) high

£2-3   MTS

A Walt Disney's Black Hole 'V.I.N.Cent' plastic action figure, by Mego, lacks white plastic arms to front.

This film was not a great success for Disney at the time. The Mego toys were equally unpopular making them hard to find today. VI.I.N.Cent was part of the first wave of figures released in 1979. The second series, released in 1980 is much scarcer. This example is incomplete and is lacking its 'arms'. Boxed examples could be worth up to £50.

1979   2.25in (6cm) high

£5-7   **KNK**

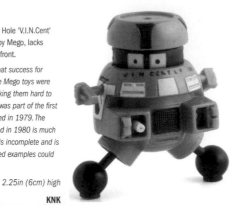

'Blow Up', soundtrack stereo LP, MGM E/SE-4447.

1966

£25-35   **GAZE**

A 'The Blues Brothers' pin.

Although John Belushi and Dan Aykroyd performed, in character, as a real band, the Blues Brothers started in a sketch on a tv show.

1.5in (3.5cm) diam

£10-15   **LDE**

A 1960s A.C. Gilbert for Sears James Bond figure.

3.5in (9cm) high

£6-8   **KNK**

A 1960s A.C. Gilbert for Sears James Bond's Auric Goldfinger figure.

One of a set of 10 Bond figures including Dr. No, Miss Moneypenny, M and Bond in three different poses.

3.25in (8.5cm) high

£6-8   **KNK**

An MB 'James Bond Thunderball' 007 Jigsaw puzzle, complete with 1,000 pieces.

c1965   Box 14.25in (36cm) wide

£15-25   **NOR**

A 'The Real James Dean Story' magazine.

11.25in (28.5cm) high

£35-45   **NOR**

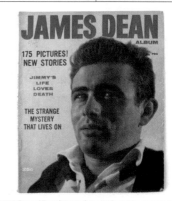

A 'James Dean Album' magazine, produced to commemorate the life of the actor, with black and white images.

c1956   11in (28cm) high

£80-120   **NOR**

A 1960s 'I Like Richard - Dr Kildare' pin.

The character of Dr James Kildare first appeared on the silver screen in 1937 played by Joel McCrea. When the TV series was created in 1961, the character was taken over by Richard Chamberlain who became a teen idol. The series ended in 1965.

2.25in (5.5cm) diam

£35-45 LDE

A 'The Loves of Hercules' advertising laminated pocket calendar, with full-length portrait of Jayne Mansfield.

1964 4.25in (10.5cm) high

£15-20 LDE

A 'Jerry Lewis in The Nutty Professor' pin.

c1963 3.25in (8cm) high

£15-25 LDE

A 'Saturday Night Fever' pin, the back marked "Paramount Pictures".

c1977 1.5in (4cm) diam

£60-70 LDE

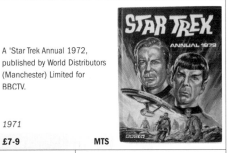

A late 1970s Starsearcher bubblebath/shampoo and sponge bath set, by K.L. Harris Ltd. England, boxed in Star Wars imitation packaging.

8in (20cm) high

£18-22 MTS

A 'Star Trek Annual 1972, published by World Distributors (Manchester) Limited for BBCTV.

1971

£7-9 MTS

A Kenner Terminator 2 'Secret Weapon' Terminator carded action figure.

1991 11.75in (30cm) high

£2-3 KNK

'The Thomas Crown Affair', original soundtrack LP SULP 1218, released by United Artists.

1968

£6-8 GAZE

A Mae West signed Grauman's Chinese Theatre program.

Grauman's Chinese Theatre is probably Hollywood's best known movie theatre and is home to a famous collection of Hollywood star footprints.

9.5in (24cm) high

£30-40 LDE

COLLECTORS' NOTES

■ Machine-made pressed glass was produced from the early 19thC. It was perfected by the 1880s when developments allowed for complex moulds and sophisticated machinery, that were often fully automated. Due to this, and the nature of the material itself, identical pieces could be mass-produced inexpensively, opening glass up to the masses.

■ Imitation cut glass was a popular, early style. The glass in this section was made from the 1920s-'30s, between the World Wars, and was largely inspired by the work of Lalique. Due to this comparatively short period of manufacture, certain pieces can be hard to find today.

■ Jobling and Bagley in Britain were two notable manufacturers, although many Czechoslovakian factories also produced similar pressed glass, often in strongly Art Deco styles. Both Jobling and Bagley began producing this type in the early 1930s, with Jobling, who had moulds made by continental factory Franckhauser, ceasing at the outbreak of WWII.

■ Colours affect value, with opalescent glass being the most desirable. The stronger the opalescence, the more valuable it will usually be. British companies generally used green, pink, blue, amber and clear 'flint', while Czechoslovakian companies had a wider range of colours and tones, such as turquoise. German examples, such as those by Walther & Sohn, are usually stronger in tone.

■ There are many different shapes, with most being both decorative and functional. Centrepieces are a mainstay and were highly popular at the time, particularly as wedding gifts amongst the middle classes. Vases were the next most popular object.

■ Condition is important. Scratches, scuffs, chips and cracks will reduce value considerably. All values given here reflect items in mint condition with no damage unless stated, in which case the price reflects the damage. Surprisingly, mould lines, internal bubbles and even internal ash (workers were allowed to smoke while working) do not affect value. However, a collector will always prefer a perfect piece.

■ Modern reproductions do exist but are of little interest. They are generally lighter and smaller, and sometimes in different colours. Frosted areas can also be rougher as they are sandblasted rather than acid-etched.

A 1930s 'Seated Lady Holding Torch' pink pressed glass comport, by an unknown maker, with registered number 755635 for 16th June 1930.

Although the design was registered by M. & J. Guggenheim Ltd, the maker is not known. This is the sister piece to the blue 'Four Cherubs' also on this page.

10.5in (26.5cm) high

£100-150 AAB

A 1930s pink pressed glass two-piece compote, of a dancing girl holding her dress aloft.

From the shade of pink used, this is likely to be Czechoslovakian.

10.25in (26cm) high

£180-220 AAB

A 1930s two-piece pressed glass comport, possibly by Brockwitz, with moulded floral arcs and floral garland decoration to bowl.

10.75in (27.5cm) high

£180-220 AAB

A 1930s German Walther 'Nymphen' green pressed glass two-piece comport.

As the bowl was often damaged or lost, the base is often sold as a candlestick due to the recess that would hold the bowl fitment.

12.5in (30.5cm) high

£120-180 AAB

A 1930s light blue pressed glass 'Four Cherubs Comport', by an unknown maker, with registered number for 15th July 1930.

This is comparatively common. The version with roses on the bowl is worth around 25 per cent more.

7.5in (19cm) high

£100-150 AAB

A German Walther 'Luttich' pink pressed glass four-piece centrepiece, with black glass base.

This is also known as 'Hollander' or 'Undine' depending on the style of the bowl the figure comes in

8.5in (22cm) high

£70-100 AAB

A 1930s Sowerby 'Flora' Rosalin pink pressed glass three-piece centrepiece, with moulded pattern of roses on the dish.

This is a comparatively common centrepiece.

8.5in (22cm) high

£40-60 AAB

A 1930s German Walther 'Schwalben' pink pressed glass three-piece centrepiece.

9in (23cm) high

£80-120 AAB

A 1930s German Walther 'Pelicans' pink pressed glass two-piece centrepiece.

The bowl is highly susceptible to damage, this example is intact.

11.5in (29.5cm) diam

£70-100 AAB

A CLOSER LOOK AT A CENTREPIECE

The figurine is more desirable than the bowl, and can be more desirable than the complete piece.

The figurine is worth nearly the same value on her own as the complete piece.

A 1930s amber pressed glass 'Windy Wendy' three-piece centrepiece, by an unknown maker, with moulded hobnail bowl.

Guggenheim figurines also fit this bowl, perhaps indicating it was made by that factory.

9.75in (25cm) high

£120-160 AAB

A 1930s Jobling 'Dancing Girl & Block' yellow pressed glass three-piece centrepiece.

From the catalogue number of 11900, it appears that this would have been designed in the summer of 1934. It is rare to find matching coloured bases, rather than black, as fewer were made.

9.5in (24cm) high

£100-150 AAB

This is the tallest of the lady figurines made, with her visual impact making her desirable.

Examples seen in the US often have opaque figurines and clear bowls.

A 1930s American Cambridge Glass Co. 'Draped Lady' centrepiece, the Depression glass-type bowl moulded with a grape pattern.

Bowl 12.5in (31.5cm) diam

£180-220 AAB

A very rare 1930s American Fenton jade green pressed glass three-piece 'September Morn' centrepiece, with repaired figurine in a waterlily bowl.

Introduced in 1928, the figurine was based on the lady in Paul Chabas' 1912 painting 'September Morn', which became famous after US anti-vice crusader Anthony Comstock tried to have the 'dirty picture' suppressed.

Bowl 6in (15.5cm) diam

£80-120 | **AAB**

A CLOSER LOOK AT A JOBLING CENTREPIECE

This is design number 2541, based on an original design by Etienne Franckhauser, who created many of the moulds for Lalique and Sabino.

Earlier examples have roses entwined in her hair near the base, these are rarer.

Jobling jade green glass is more brittle than others and the components are often found damaged – this is in perfect condition.

The bowl is in the common 'Fir Cones' design, which was the first decorative glass design Jobling registered on 29th September 1932. For a more common amber bowl please see p278.

A 1930s Jobling jade green pressed glass three-piece 'Statue & Block' centrepiece.

12.5in (32cm) high

£100-150 | **AAB**

A 1930s German Walther green pressed glass four-piece 'Lucretia' centrepiece.

This bowl also appears with a turned-over lip, showing that the form of bowls could be modified.

9in (23cm) high

£80-120 | **AAB**

A 1930s Sowerby green pressed glass two-piece centre piece, with figurine of draped nude.

Sowerby ladies are generally not as well detailed as those by other companies.

8.5in (22cm) diam

£40-60 | **AAB**

A Czechoslovakian 'Uranium' green pressed glass two-piece centrepiece, with hobnail bowl.

This was produced in 12 colours, with this and black being the rarest. Standard colours can be worth up to £70.

Bowl 10.25in (26cm) diam

£80-120 | **AAB**

A 1930s Bagley blue pressed glass free standing 'Andromeda' figure, with flower bloom ring.

The 8.5in (22cm) version is very rare. In satin green, this set can be worth up to £120.

Figurine 6.75in (17cm) high

£40-60 | **AAB**

A 1930s German Walther blue pressed glass three-piece 'Shamrock' centrepiece, commonly known as 'Parasol Lady', in four leaf clover bowl.

13.25in (33.5cm) diam

£200-250 | **AAB**

A 1930s Art Deco style turquoise pressed glass two-piece centrepiece, the figurine modelled after Isadora Duncan.

The set is found in other colours. The feet are susceptible to damage.

Bowl 12in (30.5cm) diam

£150-250 | **AAB**

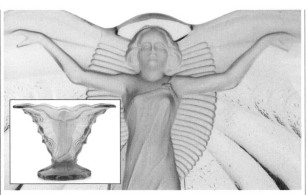

A 1930s German Walther 'Schmetterling' pink pressed glass vase, with frosted, acid-etched areas.

Schmetterling is German for butterfly.

8.5in (22cm) high

£150-250   AAB

A 1930s German Walther & Sohn 'Windsor' vase.

This came in two sizes, with this being the larger of the two. It can be found in pink, green, blue and clear 'flint'.

8in (20.5cm) high

£100-150   AAB

A 1930s Bagley Art Deco pink pressed glass 'Diamond Vase'.

This is shown without the black base or flower 'frog' insert. It can be worth up to £45 if complete.

4.25in (11cm) high

£25-35   AAB

A late 1930s Jobling pink pressed glass 'Celery' vase, cat. no. 11800, with registered design no. for 6th Sept 1934.

During WWII decorative pieces could not be made, so wartime examples were marked 'Celery' to add an air of functionality.

8in (20cm) high

£70-100   AAB

A late 1930s Art Deco Jobling amber pressed glass 'Celery' type vase, catalogue number 11700 with registered design number 795462 for 8th August 1934.

7.75in (19.5cm) high

£70-100   AAB

A 1930s Czechoslovakian amber pressed glass mermaid vase, with machine-cut base.

Each mermaid around the vase is different.

9.25in (23.5cm) high

£80-120   AAB

A 1930s Art Deco Jobling blue pressed glass 'Open Footed Vase', catalogue number +11600, with moulded registered design number '796181' for 6th Sept 1934.

Prior to the shape being registered, pieces were marked 'Pat Applied For'.

10.5in (27cm) high

£80-120   AAB

A late 1930s Art Deco Jobling 12-sided opalescent blue 'Ribbon Fish Vase', catalogue number 12000 and with registered design number 800439 for 19th Feb 1935.

8.5in (22cm) high

£250-350   AAB

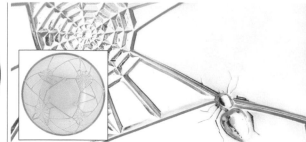

A 1930s Jobling amber pressed glass 'Fir Cone' bowl, catalogue no. 5000, registered design no. 777133 for 29th Sept 1932.

This was the first decorative (rather than functional) glass design Jobling registered.

8.5in (22cm) high

£25-35   **AAB**

A 1930s Jobling 'Uranium' green pressed glass 'Spider Web Bowl', with the spiders forming the three low feet, catalogue number 2567, registered design number 792167 for 21st April 1934.

Uranium green is generally more desirable than other colours, which are worth up to £100.

8.25in (21cm) diam

£80-120   **AAB**

A 1930s Jobling opalescent pressed glass 'Bird Design Bowl', catalogue number 7000 with registration number 780717 for 17th February 1933.

This design and colour strongly resembles French designs, however the opalescence on this example is very weak.

7.45in (19cm) diam

£120-180   **AAB**

A 1930s Sowerby 'Ladye Pot' lime green pressed glass powder puff pot.

Pale blue is usually worth less, at up to £100.

6.75in (17cm) high

£100-150   **AAB**

A 1930s German Walther 'Lydia' blue and clear pressed glass powder puff jar, shape no.41228.

This is also available in Cloud glass, but it is very rare. See the DK Collectables Price Guide 2006 by Judith Miller and Mark Hill for examples of Cloud glass.

5.5in (14cm) high

£100-150   **AAB**

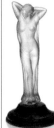

A 1930s Art Deco frosted, clear pressed glass figurine of a draped nude, possibly French, by an unknown maker, mounted on a wooden base.

This is a large, well-moulded and appealing figurine, with a naturalistic pose and good proportions.

9.25in (23.5cm) high

£100-150   **AAB**

A 1930s Czechoslovakian Art Deco green pressed glass figurine of a draped nude, mounted on a matching pedestal.

There is also a long-haired version of this figurine, which is of roughly the same value.

9.5in (24cm) high

£50-80   **AAB**

A 1930s Czechoslovakian Hoffman frosted clear pressed glass seated boy figurine, with butterfly mark.

This is usually found with a flat base and no protrusion. The butterfly mark on pressed glass indicates Hoffman as the manufacturer, not Baccarat as some books have erroneously indicated.

3.75in (9.5cm) high

£80-120   **AAB**

A 1930s Bagley blue pressed glass 'Tulip Lamp', no. 3025.

This shape is also found as a vase, the only difference being there is no hole for the wire.

8.25in (21cm) high

£120-160 **AAB**

A 1930s French Art Deco Sabino 'Danse de la Lumiere' pink pressed glass lamp, with moulded wording and "Pat Appld".

A 1930s Bagley green pressed glass star-shaped lamp, no. 934.

The condition is very important on these lamps, as the corners are easily chipped or cracked.

15in (38cm) high

£200-300 **AAB**

11.5in (29cm) high

£1,200-1,800 **AAB**

A 1930s Czechoslovakian Art Deco clear frosted pressed glass mantel clock.

Egyptian forms influenced the Art Deco movement. This design also appears on a similar dressing table set.

6.5in (16.5cm) high

£200-300 **AAB**

A 1930s German Walther & Sohn blue pressed glass 'Windsor' clock and 'Rheingold' vases garniture.

The clock is the rarest and most desirable component and is worth around £100 alone.

Vases 6in (15cm) high

£100-150 **AAB**

An American 'Bottom's Up' jade green pressed glass stirrup cup, moulded "Patent 77725", mounted on a black glass base.

This is more common in clear 'flint', being worth up to £100, and rarest in opalescent jade green, being worth up to £200.

Cup 3.5in (9cm) high

£120-180 **AAB**

A late 1930s Bohemian Carlshutte pink pressed glass two-piece sailing boat flower display, registered number 812656 for 3rd June 1936.

10.75in (27.5cm) long

£70-100 **AAB**

A 1930s Czechoslovakian clear and frosted pressed glass 'polar bear on ice' ashtray, for the French market, marked "Tchecoslovaquie" on the base.

c1933 9.25in (23.5cm) long

£100-150 **AAB**

A 1930s Stuart amber cut glass decanter, with cut banded decoration and faceted neck.

11in (28cm) high

£80-100   **GC**

A Stuart cut glass goblet, cut with stylized fern leaves, the stem with diagonal cuts, acid-etched on the base "Stuart".

6.75in (17cm) high

£15-20   **GC**

A late 1930s Stuart lens and square-cut glass footed bowl, the foot with star-cut base.

The designer of this bowl is uncertain. The legendary Ludwig Kny was succeeded by Reginald Pierce in 1937 who stayed at Stuart until 1939, with John Luxton joining later, in 1948.

9.5in (24cm) diam

£300-400   **MHT**

A 1950s Webb Corbett cut glass vase, designed by Irene Stevens, unmarked.

11in (27.5cm) high

£300-500   **WW**

A 1930s Stevens & Williams Sea Green cut glass vase, designed by Keith Murray, with heavy facets and hatching.

British cut glass underwent a large stylistic change in the 1930s and '50s, bringing it into line with modern design ethics of the day. Although Murray produced over 1,000 designs for Stevens & Williams (Royal Brierley) from 1932-39, many were only made in very small quantities due to the lack of interest in the market at the time. The monumental size and design of this vase makes it rare.

12in (30.5cm) high

£800-1,200   **GC**

An early 1960s Webb's Crystal for Coventry Cathedral vase, designed by David Hammond, with engraved cross and Webb's Crystal blue foil label, the base with acid-etched "WEBB'S" name.

6.5in (16.5cm) high

£180-220   **MHT**

A Webb Corbett 'Wheatsheaf' small vase, designed by Irene Stevens.

4.75in (12cm) high

£20-30   **MHT**

A 1930s Royal Brierley 'Streamline' cut glass vase, designed by Keith Murray, rounded hexagonal section, cut with deep bands, unmarked.

10.25in (25.5cm) high

£300-400   **WW**

A Whitefriars cut glass vase, designed by Geoffrey Baxter, with spiralling cut and wheat pattern and star-cut base.

4.25in (11cm) high

£30-50   **MHT**

A Sowerby amber cloud glass vase.

This is probably the only known example of Sowerby amber cloud glass. This shape was usually produced in clear 'flint' glass.

7.5in (19cm) high

£80-100 STE

A CLOSER LOOK AT A CLOUD GLASS FLOWER SET

This shape of flower bowl was produced from 1922 into the early 1960s.

All components of flower sets are usually in a matching colour – this example has black components as no matching clear blue examples have yet been found.

It is differentiated from the more common pattern no. 21 as it has no recess to hold the flower holder or, as on later examples, four short protrusions to do that job.

This is in the very rare clear blue colour – blue streaks in matte clear 'flint' glass – produced in the early 1960s only. Davidson's standard blue, made from 1925-34, had purple streaks on blue glass.

A Davidson clear blue cloud glass three-piece flower set, pattern no. 20.

Davidson cloud glass can be dated to a period from the shape and the colour.

c1962 *10.5in (27cm) diam*

£450-550 STE

A Davidson briar cloud glass 'Ripple' vase.

Cloud glass was introduced by George Davidson & Co. in 1923 and was largely discontinued after WWII, going completely out of production in the early 1960s. It is made by adding trails of a darker glass to a lighter base and then pressing the piece, causing random, abstract swirls to be created. Each piece is uniquely patterned. It was also produced by Brockwitz, S. Reich & Co. and Walther in Europe, and Sowerby and Jobling in Britain.

1957-61 *7in (18cm) high*

£60-80 STE

A Davidson tortoiseshell cloud glass vase, pattern no. 293.

Not commonly seen, tortoiseshell is actually amber cloud glass with both sides polished – most cloud glass has one matte side.

1931-36 *6.5in (16.5cm) high*

£25-35 STE

A Davidson 'Good Companion' amber cloud glass lamp, pattern no. 804, design number 804952 for 31st July 1935.

Davidson made two electric lamps, this model being named after J.B. Priestley's book. Green and purple versions are rare. The design number relates to the pattern on the shade, rather than the base.

1935-57

£300-400 STE

A Davidson amber cloud glass barleytwist candlestick, pattern no. 283.

c1912-30 *3in (7.5cm) high*

£30-40 STE

GLASS

A Davidson briar cloud glass vase, pattern no. 1907TD.

The 'T' in the shape number stands for 'Tiny'. 'D' was used for 'Downturned rim'.

1957-60   4.75in (12cm) wide

£15-20   STE

A Davidson green cloud glass 'Everest' ashtray, registered May 1938, made for T.H. Lawley & Company Ltd.

1938-41 5in (12.5cm) wide

£60-80   STE

A Walther 'Malachit' cloud glass 'Rotterdam' pattern plate.

1935-39   8.75in (22cm) diam

£80-120   STE

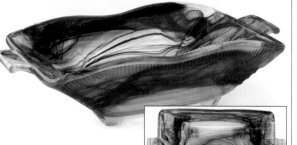

A Walther 'Malachit' cloud glass 'Perseus' dish.

1935-39   12.25in (31cm) diam

£80-120   STE

An S. Reich & Co. pink cloud glass chamberstick.

1925-30   4in (10cm) wide

£80-100   STE

An S. Reich & Co. light green cloud glass chamberstick.

1925-30   4in (10cm) wide

£80-100   STE

FIND OUT MORE...

www.cloudglass.com

Davidson Glass – A History by Chris & Val Stewart, 2005, ISBN 0955036305.

A rare S. Reich & Co. cobalt blue cloud glass 'Viktoria' trinket set.

The 'Viktoria' is the only trinket set known to have been produced in cloud glass by Reich. A water jug, tumblers, sugar and cream were also made in this pattern.

1925-30   11in (28cm) wide

£500-600   STE

COLLECTORS' NOTES

- Modern glass design, produced in the former Communist country of Czechoslovakia from c1945-c1989, has becoming increasingly popular and sought-after over the past five years. Previously, very little was known about developments as the country was behind the 'iron curtain' or was restructuring after the 'velvet revolution' of 1989. Information is now emerging and cooperation is growing, enabling researchers and collectors to learn more.
- Leading names include Stanislav Libensky, Frantisek Vízner, Pavel Hlava, René Roubícek and Jirí Harcuba. Although some problems existed, the Communist regime generally allowed them to work freely, enabling them to experiment and produce innovative, modern designs, which are only just being widely understood. Many also trained the next generation of designers, who continue to push the boundaries of glass design and technique today.
- As well as the unique, studio-type or architectural pieces produced by these designers, mass-produced, often hand-pressed, glass was also made in the many factories that made up the historic Bohemian glass industry. The largest included Crystalex and the Sklo Union, the latter a conglomerate of existing glass factories that was created in 1965. They produced very high quality hand-pressed glass in quintessentially modern designs by leading, specially trained, glass designers of the time such as Frantisek Peceny and Adolf Matura.
- Most of the designs were produced for long periods, from the 1950s-80s, and in large numbers, with much being exported. Many designs date from the early 1960s, but some pieces were made from existing pre-WWII moulds. Always aim to buy pieces in the best condition possible as comparatively large numbers of examples survive and prices are also comparatively affordable.
- Many designs have been identified, but work is still being undertaken to identify all the designs, makers and designers. Look out for a shiny shallow depression on the base with a flat machine-cut rim and good quality moulding. Although this is not a truly reliable hallmark, it is a good indication that the piece is certainly Central European in origin.

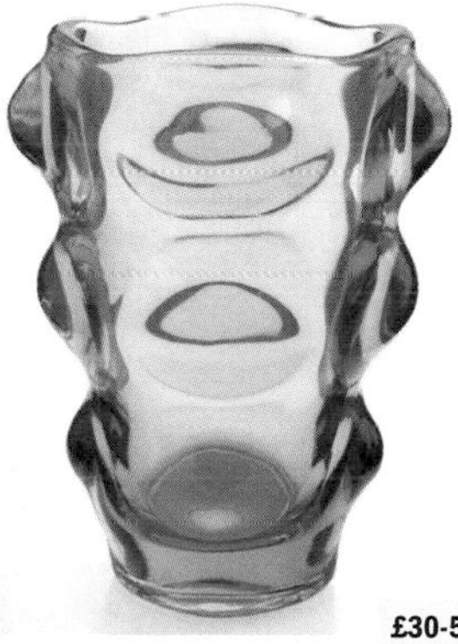

A Sklo Union light blue 'egg' vase, pattern number 20047, designed by Frantisek Vízner in 1962 for the Hermanova Glassworks.

7.75in (19.5cm) high

£30-50 **GROB**

A Sklo Union small brown lobe rimmed vase.

This design is similar to those of James Hogan for Whitefriars, and pressed glass from some French factories. The base, however, clearly identifies it as being from the Sklo Union factories. From known drawings of a similar vase, it is probably an early design by Frantisek Vízner.

5.75in (14.5cm) high

£20-30 **GC**

A Sklo Union vase, pattern number 13162, with curved rim and bark textured exterior, designed by Frantisek Vizner for the Hermanova Glassworks in 1962.

5.5in (13.5cm) high

£30-50 **MHC**

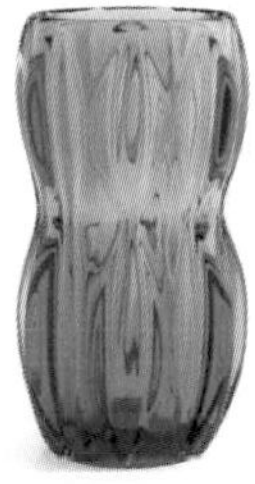

A Sklo Union green lobed and waisted vase.

This is also found in other colours such as yellow and blue.

6in (15cm) high

£15-20 **GC**

A grey glass vase, possibly by Sklo Union or a Scandinavian factory, with moulded concentric squares.

9.75in (24.5cm) high

£30-40 **GC**

A Sklo Union vase, with protruding bands with concave 'lenses', designed by Frantisek Peceny in 1961.

This was still available from distributors into the early 1970s, and came in three sizes.

8in (20cm) high

£20-30 **MHC**

A CLOSER LOOK AT A SKLO UNION VASE

A Sklo Union wide clear hobnail jardinière, pattern number 13236, designed by Rudolf Jurnikl in 1964.

This pattern is also found in tall vases, low vases and ashtrays in various different colours including a strong purple.

8.5in (21.5cm) long

£20-25 GC

The moulded pattern is cleverly designed to be read two ways – as a face looking at the viewer or as two profiles kissing one another.

It was also available as a lower, wider footed vase, which is worth around the same value.

A Sklo Union 'Head' series vase, pattern number 3484/145, designed by Adolf Matura for the Libochovice Glassworks in 1972.

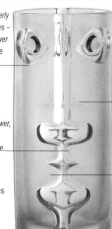

Press moulding was not the only technique used here. After being moulded, it has been fire-polished to give a shiny, reflective finish and then parts have been treated with acid to produce a matte, frosted appearance.

Adolf Matura is considered an important modern Czech glass designer and is known for his functional tableware such as the 'Praha' range designed in 1971.

9in (23cm) high

£50-70 MHC

A Sklo Union amethyst glass ashtray, pattern number 983/17, with moulded cigarette rests, designed by Adolf Matura for the Libochovice Glassworks in 1962.

6in (15.5cm) diam

£10-15 GC

A Jurnikl amethyst glass ashtray, pattern number 1045/17, with undulating rim, designed by Rudolf Jurnikl for the Rosice Glassworks in 1962.

6.75in (17cm) diam

£20-30 GROB

A Harrachov Glassworks (Borske Sklo) 'Harrtil' glass bowl, with internal webbing of woven glass fibres.

These ashtrays are often mistaken for Murano. The development of this technique of casing glass fibres in glass by Milos Pulpitel and Milan Metalek was revolutionary. Organic forms and pulled rims are typical.

1955-60 5.25in (8cm) wide

£20-30 AG

A Cesky Kristal mould blown glass vase, designed by Pavel Hlava in 1959, with internal conical forms and graduated red to yellow colouring, and with engraved signature to base.

This questions the distinction between a sculptural object and a practical vase.

Tallest 14.25in (36cm) high

£200-300 WW

A Novy Bor (Crystalex) mould-blown lidded jar, with green body, pink lid and blue knop, designed by Eric Hoglund, signed and dated "E. Hoglund-92 Novy Bor".

Hoglund is better known for his 1960s-70s designs for Swedish factory Boda.

£35-45 GAZE

A CLOSER LOOK AT AN ENGRAVED VASE

Jiří Harcuba (b.1928) is one of the most respected and experienced glass engravers in the world, and has both studied and taught at numerous prestigious institutions.

The geometric pattern of lines and shapes of different widths and depths is typical of Harcuba's spontaneous approach to engraving, where he almost 'draws' onto the surface.

This piece is dated 1965, the year Harcuba won first prize at the national Czechoslovakian glass exhibition and, unusually for the time, taught at the Royal Academy, London.

The back has a polished concave 'lens' which magnifies the designs when it is viewed through it.

A Jiří Harcuba hand-cut glass pillow-shaped vase, with a deeply cut cross-hatched pattern in the form of an abstract tree, the reverse with concave cut polished 'lens' to view main panel, signed "J. Harcuba 1965".

1965   8.25in (21cm) high

£2,000-3,000   **PC**

A 1930s Moser of Karlsbad waisted and facet-cut vase, with thick applied gilt rim.

5.25in (13.5cm) high

£60-80   **MHT**

A set of six Moser of Karlsbad hand-engraved amber shot glasses, each with a similar tree, kingfisher and rushes design, in an "Bohemia Moser Praha" card box.

As they are hand-engraved, each glass has a slightly different design.

2.25in (6cm) high

£60-80   **MHT**

A Novy Bor vase, with internal dark and light blue spiralling vertical veins and horizontal white lines.

8in (20cm) high

£80-120   **MHT**

A Palme König green spiralling ribbed glass vase, with slight fumed iridescence.

This colour and form with its frilled rim are typical of the company's designs, which were similar to Loetz designs.

c1905   6.5in (16.5cm) diam

£60-80   **MHT**

A Skrdlovice Glassworks purple heart-shaped vase, with random internal bubbles, designed by Vladimir Jelínek.

c1960   5.75in (14.5cm) high

£300-400   **MHT**

A Jiří Harcuba hand-cut glass pillow-shaped vase, with a deeply cut abstract rounded oak leaf type pattern, signed "J. Harcuba 1965".

1965   8.25in (21cm) high

£2,000-3,000   **PC**

FIND OUT MORE...

Czech Glass 1945-1980: Design In An Age Of Adversity, by Helmut Ricke, published by Arnoldsche, 2005.

COLLECTORS' NOTES

■ Dartington Glass was founded as part of the charitable Dartington Hall Trust, with production beginning in June 1967. The chief designer was Frank Thrower, who worked closely with Swedish glass blower Eskil Vilhelmsson, who had been employed from Bjorkshult in Sweden. Forms and colours were heavily inspired by the Scandinavian designs popular at the time. Thrower had worked at Wuidart, who imported Scandinavian glass, from 1953-60.

■ Compared to other British glass designers such as Ronald Stennett-Willson at King's Lynn and Wedgwood, and Geoffrey Baxter at Whitefriars, Thrower's designs have been largely ignored. He was responsible for some 500 designs, mainly for tableware, that made up around 95 per cent of the company's output. As such, examples are not too hard to find today and tend to be less expensive than these other factories' designs. Avoid examples with liming from water, scratches or chips as this detracts from the clarity and value of the glass.

■ Size, form and colour are the main indicators to value of Dartington pieces. Late 1960s and '70s decorative wares such as vases, with typical mould blown patterns such as stylized flowers and the 'Greek Key' pattern tend to be the most desirable. 'Midnight' grey and clear tablewares, produced into the 1980s and beyond are currently less valuable. Wedgwood acquired a controlling 50 per cent stake in Dartington in 1982, and the company still continues to produce many of Thrower's designs today.

A Dartington rectangular 'Daisy' vase, designed by Frank Thrower, with leaves, flower and stalk motifs.

6.25in (16cm) high

£30-40   **GC**

A Dartington cobalt blue large 'Daisy' vase, designed by Frank Thrower.

7.25in (18.5cm) high

£50-70   **GC**

A Dartington petrol blue vase, designed by Frank Thrower, with moulded stylised flowers.

14in (35.5cm) high

£50-70   **FD**

A Dartington Midnight grey square vase, designed by Frank Thrower, with tulip-type top vase.

6in (15cm) high

£30-40   **GC**

A Dartington Kingfisher blue vase, designed by Frank Thrower, with hammered finish flared rim and moulded diamonds and stylised flower patterns on alternating panels.

6in (15cm) high

£20-30   **GC**

A Dartington clear bark-effect textured square vase, designed by Frank Thrower, with flared rim.

3.5in (9cm) high

£7-10   **TCM**

A Dartington square-section vase, designed by Frank Thrower, with cylindrical neck and moulded hobnails and stars on alternating panels.

3.25in (8.5cm) high

£20-30   **GC**

A Dartington kingfisher blue hexagonal vase, designed by Frank Thrower, with moulded rectangular and boss decoration.

4in (10cm) high

£35-45   **GC**

A CLOSER LOOK AT A DARTINGTON VASE

This colour is known as 'flame' red and was only produced for a few years, at the start of the company's production.

This is a comparatively large size and is one of Thrower's most recognisable patterns and forms, with its trumpet-flared neck.

Examples are very rare and highly sought after today.

The colour is not a simple red – holding it to light shows the varied colours of the cased orange and red glass.

An early, rare Dartington 'flame' red Greek Key pattern vase, designed by Frank Thrower.

c1969   5in (13cm) high

£150-200   **GC**

A Dartington midnight grey ship's decanter, designed by Frank Thrower, with flat stopper and heavy base.

As with all 'ship's decanters', the wide, heavy base was designed to prevent the decanter falling over on choppy seas.

9in (23cm) high

£25-35   **GC**

A Dartington midnight grey bulbous decanter, designed by Frank Thrower, with heavy base.

8.25in (21cm) high

£25-35   **GC**

A scarce Dartington midnight grey vase, designed by Frank Thrower, with flat rim.

Note the similarity of form to Ronald Stennett-Willson's 'Top Hat' vases for King's Lynn and Wedgwood Glass.

7.5in (19cm) high

£50-70   **GC**

A Dartington display goblet, designed by Frank Thrower, with heavy foot.

The bowl has internal spiralling textures, while the foot and stem have external spiralling textures.

5.75in (14.5cm) high

£10-15   **GC**

A Dartington tall ice cream bowl, designed by Frank Thrower, with bark effect textured finish.

These are very much in the style of Scandinavian glass factory, Iittala.

7in (18cm) high

£15-20   **NPC**

An American Hazel Atlas Glass Co. 'Royal Lace' pattern green dessert dish.

2.75 (7cm) high

£7-10 GROB

An American Hazel Atlas Glass Co. 'Royal Lace' pattern green Depression glass trio set.

Plate 5.75in (14.5cm) diam

£10-15 GROB

An American Hazel Atlas Glass Co. 'Royal Lace' pattern green Depression glass pitcher.

Depression glass was mass-produced inexpensively during the 1920s and '30s using a mechanical pressing technique. Its bright colours and low prices made it attractive in difficult times. Today, most collect by patterns, which cross natural, geometric and historical themes. Always aim to buy in the best condition possible as large quantities were made.

6.75in (17.5cm)

£15-25 GROB

An American Hazel Atlas Glass Co. 'Royal Lace' pattern cobalt blue Depression glass twin-handled cup.

Royal Lace was made from 1934-41.

4.25in (10.5cm) high

£8-12 GROB

An American Hazel Atlas Glass Co. 'Royal Lace' pattern pink Depression glass plate.

6in (15cm) diam

£4-5 GROB

An American Jeanette Glass Co. 'Cherry Blossom' pattern pink Depression glass twin-handled cup.

3.25in (8.25cm) high

£10-15 GROB

An American Jeanette Glass Co. 'Cherry Blossom' pattern pink Depression glass cup and saucer.

Cherry Blossom was produced from 1930-39. Crystal, Jadeite and red are the rarest colours.

5.5in (14cm) diam

£20-25 GROB

An American Jeanette Glass Co. 'Cherry Blossom' pattern pink Depression glass milk jug.

3.25in (8.5cm) high

£10-15 GROB

An American Hazel Atlas Glass Co. 'Moderntone' pattern colbalt blue Depression glass trio set.

Moderntone was made from 1934-42 and again in the late 1940s and '50s.

Plate 6in (15cm) diam

£25-30 GROB

COLLECTORS' NOTES

■ Langham Glass was founded in Langham, Norfolk in 1979 as a direct descendent of Wedgwood Glass in King's Lynn. The founders included Paul Miller, the master glassmaker at Wedgwood, and Ronald Stennett-Willson, who had founded and designed the ranges for King's Lynn Glass, which became Wedgwood Glass in 1969.

■ Thus the company started with the ideal combination of an experienced blower and an experienced and notable designer. Miller was responsible for designing and developing many of the animals made at Wedgwood, and he continued this range at Langham, where it is still a core range today.

■ Ronald Stennett-Willson initially designed the main ranges for Langham, which included clear crystal tableware, such as tumblers and goblets, and the brightly coloured, swirling 'Vortex' range. Look for examples with clearly demarcated swirls in bright colours and appealing shapes that work well with the design.

■ As Stennett-Willson's designs for King's Lynn and Wedgwood have been recently reappraised in terms of modern glass design, examples have risen in value and desirability enormously. This interest is sure to spread to his later work as the quality of his designs becomes further appreciated. As such, prices for even his later pieces that are now out of production are likely to rise.

An early and heavy Langham Glass green and white cylinder vase, designed by Ronald Stennett-Willson, signed "Langham" on the rounded base.

9in (23cm) high

£40-60　　　　GC

A Langham Glass pink and deep burgundy swirl 'Vortex' cylinder vase, designed by Ronald Stennett-Willson, with flared rim.

7in (18cm) high

£30-40　　　　GC

A Langham Glass green and blue swirl 'Vortex' cylinder vase, designed by Ronald Stennett-Willson, with flared rim.

7in (18cm) high

£35-45　　　　GC

A Langham Glass blue and white swirl 'Vortex' waisted footed bowl, designed by Ronald Stennett-Willson, with clear foot.

5.75in (14.5cm) high

£20-30　　　　GC

A Langham Glass 'Vortex' waisted footed bowl, designed by Ronald Stennett-Willson, with clear foot.

When held to the light, the deep red glows a rich ruby.

5.75in (14.5cm) high

£25-35　　　　GC

A Langham Glass brown swirled 'Vortex' bowl, designed by Ronald Stennett-Willson, with applied rim and paper label.

4.25in (11cm) high

£20-30　　　　GC

A Langham Glass brown speckled and white swirl 'Vortex' vase, designed by Ronald Stennett-Willson.

5.75in (14.5cm) high

£20-30　　　　GC

COLLECTORS' NOTES

■ Mdina was founded on Malta in 1968 by ex-Royal College of Art tutor Michael Harris (1933-94). Studio glass techniques has just arrived in the UK from the US and Harris quickly adapted them to function on a commercial basis. Colours are typically in the greens, blues and sand of the Mediterranean landscape and examples are chunky, being rendered in thick glass. Shapes include vases, bowls, dishes and paperweights.

■ Characteristic shapes, such as the 'Fish' vase, are the most desirable, as are large pieces. Production was aimed at the tourist market, as well as export, and tended to be focused on smaller, portable pieces. Harris did not approve of signing pieces with his name, making those that are signed in this way rare. Most other pieces are simply signed with the studio name. Harris left in 1972 and pieces produced after this date currently slightly less desirable, although all Mdina glass has become increasingly sought-after in recent years.

■ After leaving Malta, Harris founded his second studio on the Isle of Wight in the same year. Ranges from the 1970s tend to be executed with broad swirls of colour, in deep blues, ochres, browns and pink. The turning point in the studio's history came in 1978, when Harris and RCA student William Walker devised the 'Azurene' range, where surfaces are decorated with silver and 22ct gold leaf. This became one of most popular and collected ranges produced and is still sought-after today.

■ Other popular, best selling ranges include 'Meadow Garden' and 'Golden Peacock' However, as the market is still growing, look out for rarities produced for short periods of time, as these can be valuable. The level of experimentation begun by Harris has been continued by his widow Elizabeth and son Timothy, and many innovative and colourful ranges have been produced. As with Mdina, both values and the number of collectors are increasing, making this a vibrant collecting area.

A 1970s Mdina vase, in amethyst-tinted glass with applied blue-green trails.

7.25in (18.5cm) high

£30-50 GAZE

A Mdina 'Tricorn' vase, with turned-over rim and polished base.

The slightly off-centre and bulbous nature of this vase reinforces the handmade nature of Mdina glass. This is a large and uncommon Tricorn form.

c1970 7in (18cm) high

£150-200 ART

A Mdina deep purple 'Fish' vase, the purple core cased in clear and then purple glass.

These smaller Fish vases are early and were likely to have been made by Harris himself. Purple is a rare, early colour – in more standard colours they can be worth up to £100.

1968-69 6in (15cm) high

£150-200 MHC

A large Mdina glass 'Sculpture', designed, made and signed on the base by Michael Harris.

In a spectacle for the audience, Harris trailed molten glass onto a surface to create these visually impactful sculptures. The size and his signature make this even more valuable.

c1970 12.25in (31cm) high

£300-500 CHEF

A scarce Mdina glass large 'Tricorn' dish, with swirling green/beige pattern and polished base.

It is difficult to control the glass to form this tricorn shape. This shape was only produced towards the end of Harris' time at Mdina, and in very small numbers. The green swirls turn a sandy brown when light passes through them.

c1971 14.5in (37cm) widest

£180-220 PC

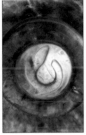

A 1970s Isle of Wight Studio Glass 'Lollipop' vase, with internal green and blue swirls cased in clear glass.

6.5in (16.5cm) high

£70-100 **GAZE**

A CLOSER LOOK AT AN ISLE OF WIGHT GLASS CHARGER

Pink & Blue Swirls is a comparatively scarce range as it did not prove as popular as other ranges, such as 'Aurene' and particularly 'Tortoiseshell'.

This example is signed by Michael Harris on the base, which adds further to its rarity and value.

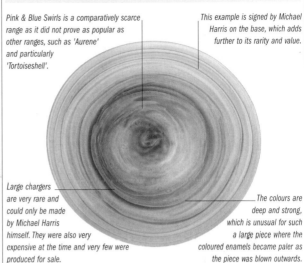

Large chargers are very rare and could only be made by Michael Harris himself. They were also very expensive at the time and very few were produced for sale.

The colours are deep and strong, which is unusual for such a large piece where the coloured enamels became paler as the piece was blown outwards.

An Isle of Wight Studio Glass 'Pink & Blue Swirls' charger, made by Michael Harris, with polished base, signed "Michael Harris Isle of Wight".

c1974-76 19in (48.5cm) diam

£550-650 **GAZE**

An Isle of Wight Studio Glass 'Aurene' cylinder vase, the base with impressed 'flame' pontil mark.

This is much more typical of the rich and bold colouring of this range. The iridescent streak is left when salts escape from the join near the pontil rod and is not a sign of fumed iridescence.

c1975-c1982 8in (20cm) high

£70-100 **ART**

An unusual Isle of Wight Studio Glass 'Aurene' globe vase, with impressed 'flame' pontil mark to base.

This example is unusual as it is primarily in clear glass. The light coating of enamels at the top and base gives a delicate feel to the piece.

c1975-c1982 5in (12.5cm) high

£40-60 **TGM**

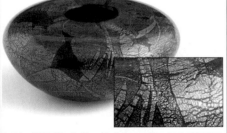

An Isle of Wight Studio Glass black 'Azurene' low bowl, with silver and gold leaf and flat polished base.

This example is from the studio's archive room and was used as a 'model' piece for other glassmakers to copy due to its superb Azurene finish. This shape is sometimes known as the 'Doughnut'.

c1979 4.75in (12cm) diam

£60-80 **ART**

An early Isle of Wight Studio Glass pre-Minimal range Azurene dove, with silver and gold leaf and triangular label to base.

1981-82 1.5in (4cm) high

£25-35 **ART**

An Isle of Wight Studio Glass 'Blue Azurene' Lollipop vase, with flat polished base.

1979-88   *9in (23cm) high*

£70-100   **TGM**

A CLOSER LOOK AT AN ISLE OF WIGHT STUDIO GLASS VASE

Jazz was designed by Timothy Harris, Michael Harris' older son, who continues to design and produce award-winning glass at the Isle of Wight studio.

The range was arguably ahead of its time and did not sell well, making it very rare today.

Coloured powdered enamels were laid on a surface and a finger drawn through them to give the pattern – the hot glass body was then rolled over them to coat the surface.

A colour variation called 'Rhythm & Blues' using blue and grey tones on white was also produced – this is even rarer than 'Jazz'.

An Isle of Wight Studio Glass 'Jazz' vase, designed and made by Timothy Harris, with opaque white glass background and pulled, curling rim.

1992-93   *6in (15cm) high*

£180-220   **PC**

An Isle of Wight Studio Glass 'Golden Peacock Royale' perfume bottle, with gold foil and trailed iridescent swirls.

The trailed stopper is a hallmark of this range, which was one of the most popular at the time, selling in large numbers.

1987-98   *4in (10cm) high*

£50-80   **PC**

An Isle of Wight Studio Glass 'Nightscape' glass paperweight, with triangular black sticker.

c1990   *3in (7.5cm) high*

£50-80   **GAZE**

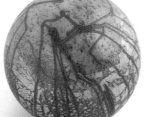

An extremely rare Isle of Wight Studio Glass 'Pink Fizz' paperweight.

This is a variation of 'Golden Rain' designed by Timothy Harris. The surface is slightly fumed to give a gentle iridescence bringing the gold foil and mottled pink to life.

1987   *2.25in (5.5cm) high*

£80-120   **MHC**

An Isle of Wight Studio Glass Meadow Garden 'Poppy' globe vase, with flat polished base.

Globe vases in this size from this range were produced for one year only

1988   *4in (10cm) high*

£50-70   **PC**

FIND OUT MORE...

Michael Harris: Mdina Glass & Isle of Wight Studio Glass, *by Mark Hill, published by Mark Hill Publishing, www.markhillpublishing.com, ISBN 978-0-9552865-1-3.*

www.isleofwightstudioglass.co.uk

COLLECTORS' NOTES

■ Glass has been made on the Venetian island of Murano since the 13thC. During the 1950s, designs underwent a radical transformation, breaking away from the traditional forms and patterns made for centuries. Old techniques were not abandoned, but were used in innovative ways. Colours became brighter, more exuberant, and almost painterly. Forms and patterns grew ever more abstract, often being sculptural.

■ At the forefront of this design renaissance were historic, leading factories such as Venini, Seguso, Salviati and A.V.e.M. (Arte Vetreria Muranese). They employed new designers such as Dino Martens, Fulvio Bianconi and Flavio Poli to breathe new 'modern' life into their hand-blown glass. Today, pieces by these factories and designers tend to fetch the largest values, particularly landmark designs such as the 'fazzoletto' or 'Oriente' vases.

■ Many of these designs were copied in subsequent decades by the vast number of smaller factories producing glass for the tourist market. Along with novelty forms such as clowns and fish, these tend to be less valuable but make an accessible and visually rewarding entry to the market. Examine pieces carefully as chips, scratches and errors such as internal bubbles (unless intended as part of the pattern) devalue a piece. Look out for wildly colourful and exuberant forms and read reference books to help you spot hidden but notable designer treasures.

An A.V.e.M clear cased vase, in the shape of a seated llama, designed by Manfredo Brosi and Ferdinando Toso, with stripes of opaque yellow, purplish-black and white glass.

c1954   7.6in (19cm) high

£80-120   **VZ**

An A.V.e.M vase, designed by Giulio Radi, with an opaque white body cased in amber and purple-black glass, the exterior with gold foil inclusions.

c1950   8.5in (21.5cm) high

£800-1,200   **VZ**

A Michele Burato hand-blown sculptural glass 'Pietra Focaia' vessel, of elliptical form with marbelized red and chartreuse pattern on black ground, with aventurine accents, signed, dated and titled on base.

2002   20in (51cm) high

£1,000-1,500   **SDR**

A Cenedese 'D' vase, designed by Antonio da Ros, the dark turquoise core heavily cased in flashed yellow glass, with, manufacturer's label to base .

c1962 10.6in (26.5cm)

£800-1,200   **VZ**

A Salviati incalmo vase, with a bottle green base and a wide clear glass lip with white spirals.

1960   10in (25.5cm) high

£500-600   **JN**

A Seguso Vetri D'Arte sommerso glass vase, the amethyst bowl cased in red and cased again in clear glass, possibly designed by Flavio Poli.

1960   7in (18cm) high

£400-500   **JN**

A Seguso Vetri D'Arte tapering red glass vase, with aventurine inclusions, the base acid etched "Seguso, Murano".

15in (37.5cm) high

£200-300   **WW**

GLASS

A Venini amber 'Corroso' glass amphora vase, with acid-etched stamp to base.

The lightly textured, almost matte 'corroso' effect is obtained by treating the surface of the glass with acid.

10.25in (26cm) high

£100-150 GC

A CLOSER LOOK AT A MURANO GLASS VASE

This form is also known as a 'fazzoletto', the Italian word for 'handkerchief'.

This example is marked with the Venini acid stamp – the form was widely copied and if you want to collect Venini examples always look for this mark.

The witty form was designed by Paolo Venini and Fulvio Bianconi around 1949-50 and was meant to represent a dropped handkerchief 'frozen' in time and space.

As well as being executed in an unusual bold red-cased white, typical of the 1960s and '70s, it is very large, hence its high value.

A 1960s Venini large red cased opaque white handkerchief vase, the base with "Venini Murano" acid stamp and Venini round gold foil label.

10.25in (26cm) high

£1,000-1,500 MG

A Venini brown bottle vase, designed by Tony Zuccheri.

1966-70 *9in (23cm) high*

£350-450 JN

A Venini glass 'Spicchi' bottle vase, designed by Fulvio Bianconi, with purple glass bands, with acid mark "venini murano ITALIA" to base.

Here, coloured glass panels have been melted onto the body to add colour. This technique was widely copied by other makers.

1950 *9.25in (23cm) diam*

£1,500-2,000 HERR

A Venini amber glass pitcher, with pulled lip and acid etched mark to base.

7.75in (20cm) high

£80-120 TCM

A Venini red and blue glass 'Clessidre' hourglass sculpture, designed by Paolo Venini in 1955, unmarked.

5in (12.5cm) high

£350-450 SDR

A Zanetti Vetreria Artistica glass pelican sculpture, designed by Licio or Oscar Zanetti, with applied purple glass beak and feet, the base signed " Zanetti" in vibropen.

Zanetti was founded on Murano in 1959 by glassmaker Oscar Zanetti and his son Licio. Sculptural forms such as birds and other motifs from nature are typical of the company's production.

9.25in (23.5cm) high

£450-550 MG

A Murano sommerso glass vase, with blue/green and green glass layers heavily cased in clear glass, and pulled rim.

Such asymmetric, curving and almost organic forms were typical of the 1950s and '60s and were inspired by Flavio Poli's work with the sommerso technique during the 1940s and '50s at Seguso Vetri D'Arte.

6.25in (16cm) high

£150-250   **HLM**

A Murano small purple, blue and clear cased asymmetric teardrop-shaped glass vase, with pulled rim.

6.25in (16cm) high

£100-200   **HLM**

A Murano sommerso glass vase, the ovoid red body heavily cased in yellow and with two pulled wings.

10.25in (26cm) high

£40-60   **HLM**

A Murano sommerso large blue, amber and clear cased glass vase.

Note how the many cut facets add an optical element to the sommerso design. This style can also be found on ashtrays, which tend to be less popular and valuable than vases.

9.75in (24.5cm) high

£70-100   **GAZE**

A Murano glass vase, with applied red and blue stripes and gold inclusions.

Compare this to the 'Spicchi' vase on the previous page, as it is made in a similar manner.

3.25in (8cm) high

£20-30   **GC**

A 1950s Murano glass ashtray, with pulled, curled rim and controlled internal bubbles.

8.5in (21.5cm) wide

£30-50   **GC**

A Murano glass cobalt blue tricorn-shaped ashtray, with internal controlled bubbles.

5.5in (14cm) wide

£15-25   **GROB**

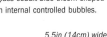

A Murano glass large glass clown-shaped decanter, with applied bow tie, 'buttons', shoes, hands and facial features.

16.5in (42cm) high

£180-220   **MG**

A Murano yellow and green glass bird sculpture, with elongated 'S' shaped neck and green striped body.

12.5in (32cm) high

£60-80   **MG**

FIND OUT MORE...

DK Collectors Series: 20th Century Glass, by Judith Miller, published by DK, 2004.

A Danish Kastrup blue vase, designed by Jacob Bang.

c1960 9.75in (24.5cm) high

£80-100 GC

A Danish Kastrup antique green vase, designed by Jacob Bang.

c1960 5.75in (14.5cm) high

£35-45 GC

A CLOSER LOOK AT A SCANDINAVIAN VASE

The 'Naebvase' or 'Beak Vase' was designed by Lütken in 1951 and can be found in different forms and sizes, this being the most commonly seen.

The name comes from the shape of the rim, which is created by pulling the molten glass with tongs and then swinging the piece, with gravity elegantly elongating the pulled areas.

The asymmetric, organic form is typical of both 1950s Scandinavian glass design and Lütken's designs during this period – it is also typically found in this colour or clear, colourless glass.

Beware of unmarked examples, and those marked "H2" as they often bear faults, which disturb the design. Until 1962 pieces were dated around the monogram.

A 1960s-70s Danish Holmegaard aqua 'Beak' vase, designed by Per Lütken, the base engraved with artist's monogram and factory production number "15272".

6.5in (16.5cm) high

£30-50 FD

A Danish Kastrup smoke grey conical vase, designed by Jacob Bang.

c1960 10in (25.5cm) high

£30-35 GC

A Danish Kastrup small green conical vase, designed by Jacob Bang.

8in (20.5cm) high

£20-25 GC

A Danish Kastrup capri blue angular vase, designed by Jacob Bang, with original label.

Jacob Bang (1899-1965) joined Holmegaard as Chief Designer in 1927. He left the glass industry in 1941 but rejoined Kastrup in 1957. He is known for his clean-lined, ultra-modern forms with no surface decoration.

c1960 8.25in (21cm) high

£45-55 GC

A Danish Holmegaard smoke grey 'Aristocrat' decanter, designed by Per Lütken, with six 'Scanada' glasses.

Designed in 1956, this was produced until 1990. The decanter alone can be worth up to £100.

15in (38cm) high

£100-150 FD

A Finnish Iittala 'Kalvolan Kanto' vase, designed by Tapio Wirkkala, the base signed "_3241 Tapio Wirkkala".

'Kalvolan Kanto' means 'tree stump', demonstrating the influence the Scandinavian landscape had on Wirkkala's designs. It is an early modern Scandinavian glass design, dating from 1947, and was part of a range that caused great sensation at the Milan Triennale in 1951.

4.5in (11.5cm) high

£180-220   **MHT**

A Finnish Iittala 'Pinus' vase, designed by Tapio Wirkkala, the base signed "TW".

8.75in (22.5cm) high

£120-180   **MHT**

A 1970s Finnish Iittala 'Ultima Thule' textured glass beaker, designed by Tapio Wirkkala.

Ultima Thule was designed for Finnair to commemorate their first trans Atlantic flights in 1967. A smaller tumbler was the first piece designed.

5in (12.5cm) high

£10-15   **MHT**

A Finnish Iittala large ribbed, bark-textured vase, designed by Timo Sarpaneva, the base engraved "TS".

14.75in (37.5cm) high

£120-180   **MHT**

A Finnish Iittala flanged glass vase, from the 'i-glass' range, designed by Timo Sarpaneva, etched "T.SARPANEVA 2318".

The i-glass range was launched in response to criticism that Iittala was moving away from functional tableware. All pieces were mould-blown in different colours, promoting colourful combinations.

c1958   *9.5in (24cm) high*

£120-150   **MHT**

A Finnish Iittala blue-cased vase, designed by Erkki Versanto, the base signed "Erkki Versanto 3654".

Versanto (1915-90) worked as an in-house designer from 1936-80 and was responsible for many tableware designs.

c1960   *6in (15cm) high*

£50-70   **MHT**

A Finnish Karhula green vase, designed by Goran Hongell, with engraved Gothic 'MV' monogram.

Hongell was a designer for Karhula from 1932-57. His designs are more angular than the work of his contemporary Alvar Aalto. Cut rims and thick walls are also typical. Hongell won a Milan Triennale gold medal in 1954. Karshula had been part of the same company as Iittala since 1917.

A Finnish Iittala clear dish, designed by Tapio Wirkkala, engraved with lines and "Tapio Wirkkala Iittala 3336".

5in (13cm) wide

£120-180   **MHT**

c1937

£180-220   **MHT**

GLASS

A Kosta smoke grey glass vase, designed by Vicke Lindstrand, engraved on the base "KOSTA A3141".

6in (15cm) high

£40-60 **MHT**

A Kosta vase, designed by Vicke Lindstrand, with thin and slightly thicker vertical cut lines, engraved "LG 198" on the side.

5.25in (13.5cm) high

£70-90 **MHT**

A Kosta 'Sunflower' bottle, designed by Goran Warff, engraved "KOSTA 477190 Warff" on the base.

4.75in (12cm) high

£40-60 **MHT**

A CLOSER LOOK AT A KOSTA VASE

Lindstrand joined Kosta in 1950, after leaving Orrefors, and revived the fortunes of the company with his designs, which generally incorporated engraving.

The presence of a letter 'G' in the mark indicates a more prestigious hand-cut design. This work effectively makes each piece unique.

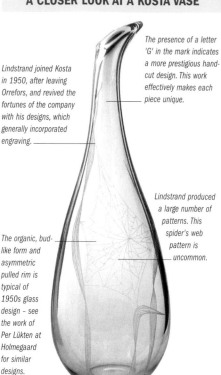

Lindstrand produced a large number of patterns. This spider's web pattern is uncommon.

The organic, bud-like form and asymmetric pulled rim is typical of 1950s glass design - see the work of Per Lükten at Holmegaard for similar designs.

A 1950s Kosta vase, designed by Vicke Lindstrand, engraved with a spider's web hanging between reeds, signed to the base "KOSTA LG 2384".

15.75in (40cm) high

£250-350 **MHT**

A Kosta rectangular section vase, designed by Goran Warff, with two bands of cut diamonds.

8in (20.5cm) high

£60-80 **MHT**

A Kosta blue/grey glass dish, heavily walled, signed "KOSTA WH 5596" on the base.

10.5in (26.5cm) diam

£120-160 **MHT**

A 1980s Kosta Boda multi-coloured cast, cut and polished glass sculpture, designed by Kjell Engman and engraved "K. Engman" on the base.

Engman joined Boda in 1978, two years after the merged Boda, Afors and Kosta companies were renamed Kosta Boda AB.

5.25in (13.5cm) high

£100-150 **GAZE**

A Riihimaën Lasi Oy yellow 'Pompadour' candlestick, designed by Nanny Still in 1966.

Nanny Still (b.1926) joined the company in 1949. 'Pompadour' can be found in a number of shape and colour variants.

9in (23cm) high

£40-60 NPC

A 1970s Riihimaën Lasi Oy straw yellow vase, the design attributed to Tamara Aladin.

Tamara Aladin (b.1932) joined the company in 1959 and is known for her strongly geometric, flanged forms.

11in (28cm) high

£40-60 FD

A Riihimaën Lasi Oy large honey coloured vase, designed by Tamara Aladin.

During the 1930s and '50s a group of talented designers were taken on as freelance designers by Riihimaën Lasi Oy and dominated design into the 1970s. Pieces were modern in appearance and were generally mould-blown using spinning moulds to ensure an even distribution of glass. Colours were strong and jewel-like and forms were typically geometric with clean surfaces. Due to a drop in quality and the closure of certain glass manufacturers, many retailers, such as Britain's Boots the Chemists, ordered glass from Riihimäki during the 1970s. These designs do not appear in Riihimäki's catalogues, possibly as they were made solely for export. As such, these designs can currently only be attributed to designers based on their style.

11in (28cm) high

£50-80 FD

A Riihimaën Lasi Oy yellow vase, the design attributed to Tamara Aladin.

7in (18cm) high

£30-40 NPC

A Riihimaën Lasi Oy yellow vase, the design attributed to Tamara Aladin, pattern no. 1939.

9.75in (25cm) high

£25-35 NPC

A Riihimaën Lasi Oy yellow 'Stromboli' range vase, designed by Aimo Okkolin in 1963, with factory label.

Aimo Okkolin (1917-82) trained as an engraver and cutter and worked for Riihimäki from 1937. He was related to the company's owners.

8.75in (22cm) high

£30-40 NPC

A Riihimaën Lasi Oy deep blue vase, the design attributed to Tamara Aladin, pattern no. 1939.

9.75in (25cm) high

£25-35 NPC

A Riihimaën Lasi Oy blue vase, the design attributed to Nanny Still.

25in (63.5cm) high

£20-30 NPC

A 1970s Riihimaën Lasi Oy flanged vase, the design attributed to Helena Tynell, in an unusual light blue glass.

Examine pieces carefully as chips, scratches and liming reduce desirability, as they detract from the purity and strength of the colour. Some colours are more desirable and scarcer than other, with striking, stronger examples often being more sought-after. Some shapes are rarely found in certain colours.

11in (28cm) high

£40-60   **FD**

A 1970s Riihimaën Lasi Oy mould-blown blue 'Ahkeraliisa' vase, designed by Helena Tynell in 1968, with factory label to rim.

Tynell joined the company in 1946, three years before the Scandinavia-wide competition was held in 1949. This is one of her most sought-after designs and was available in a number of colours. Ahkeraliisa the Finnish name for the 'Busy Lizzie' flower.

8.5in (21.5cm) high

£60-90   **GAZE**

A 1970s Riihimaën Lasi Oy 'Grapponia' bottle, designed by Nanny Still in 1968.

Although often used today decoratively as a 'solifleur', this bottle was intended to be functional tableware.

c1970   7.5in (19cm) high

£50-80   **FD**

A Riihimaën Lasi Oy green 'Tuuliki' vase, the design attributed to Tamara Aladin.

8in (20cm) high

£30-40   **NPC**

A Riihimaën Lasi Oy tapered green 'Stromboli' range vase, designed by Aimo Okkolin.

7in (18cm) high

£20-30   **NPC**

A 1960s-70s Riihimaën Lasi Oy red waisted vase, by an unidentified designer.

7in (18cm) high

£25-35   **NPC**

A Riihimaën Lasi Oy amethyst bullet-shaped vase, the design attributed to Aimo Okkolin.

9.5in (24cm) high

£35-45   **NPC**

A 1970s Riihimaën Lasi Oy 'Quadrifolio' glass vase, designed by Nanny Still in 1967.

This is often attributed to Tapio Wirkkala for Iittala, due to its texture. However, the shape and knobbly effect is different to his work.

7.75in (19.5cm) high

£50-80   **FD**

COLLECTORS' NOTES

■ As Scandinavian glass is renowned for the clarity and purity of its transparent colour, cased glass tends to be largely under-rated and ignored. Its importance was noted by the important Czech glass artist Stanislav Libensky as early as 1972, who admired both the visual effect and the fact that it could be mass-produced cost effectively, which he felt could not be done as efficiently in Czechoslovakia at the time.

■ Holmegaard of Denmark is the most notable factory that produced such cased glass, with the 'Carnaby' range designed by Per Lütken in 1968 and produced from 1969-76, being currently the most desirable and valuable. Michael Bang's similar 'Palet' range designed in 1970 is also sought-after. In 1965, the Holmegaard, Kastrup and Odense factories were amalgamated under the Holmegaard name.

■ In all examples shown here, opaque white glass was overlaid with coloured transparent glass to give a bright and appealing visual effect, with the colour sometimes varying due to the thickness of the coloured overlay. Pieces were blown into moulds and spun at high speed to ensure an even distribution of glass around the mould. Shapes were clean-lined and modern, and colours bright, reacting against 1950s forms that were inspired by nature and placing them firmly in the 1970s aesthetic.

■ A number of other Scandinavian factories including Alsterfors also produced cased glass and the origin of many pieces is yet to be identified. Look for clean-lined modern forms that exemplify the movement, large sizes and brighter 'Pop' colours.

A Danish Holmegaard 'Carnaby' yellow cased vase, designed by Per Lütken, with original factory sticker

1969-76   9in (23cm) high

£80-120   **FD**

A Danish Holmegaard 'Carnaby' light blue cased vase, with bulbous neck.

Note the rounded rim on Holmegaard pieces, which is not machine-cut and flat.

1969-76   9in (23cm) high

£100-150   **GC**

A Danish Holmegaard 'Carnaby' light blue cased carafe or pitcher, designed by Per Lütken.

1969-76   8in (20.5cm) high

£60-80   **GC**

A CLOSER LOOK AT A CASED GLASS VASE

This vase is part of a range of glass designed in 1968 and named after the most popular street in 'Swinging London' that set the trend for many fashions of the 1960s and '70s.

The strong red colour fits with the prevalent 'Pop' fashion of the period and would have complimented period room interiors.

The 'Carnaby' range is often confused with the 'Palet' range, which was designed by Jacob Bang's son Michael in 1970. The shape identifies which range a piece is from.

Although made from glass, the shiny opaque appearance and curving form recalls plastic, which was a popular material of the period, being used particularly for furniture.

A 1970s Danish Holmegaard white and yellow cased hanging lampshade, possibly designed by Michael Bang.

17in (43cm) high

£30-40   **FD**

A Danish Holmegaard 'Carnaby' red and white cased vase, designed by Per Lütken, with original factory sticker.

c1969-76   8.75in (22cm) high

£120-180   **FD**

A Danish Kastrup purple and white cased torpedo-shaped vase, designed by Jacob Bang.

13in (33cm) high

£80-120   **GC**

A Swedish Alsterfors green cased 'UFO' shaped vase, possibly designed by Per-Olaf Strom.

The 1960s styled 'space-aged' form and bright colour makes this a desirable piece. Note the subtle variation in the colour from the base to the 'UFO', created by the differing thickness of the green glass. Also note the rim is machine-cut flat, unlike Holmegaard pieces.

8in (20cm) high

£50-60   **GC**

A Danish Kastrup purple tear drop-shaped cased white vase, designed by Jacob Bang.

The austere cased glass forms designed by Jacob Bang echo his earlier designs from the 1930-50s. For other examples, please see p 296 of this book.

16.5in (42cm) high

£80-120   **GC**

A 1970s Swedish Alsterfors blue and white cased vase, designed by Per-Olaf Strom, etched on the base "PO Strom 70".

Strom's designs are characterised by highly modern geometric and angular forms.

9.75in (25cm) high

£35-45   **GC**

A 1970s Swedish green cased ribbed and flared vase, by an unidentified factory.

11in (28cm) high

£20-30   **GC**

A 1970s Swedish green-blue cased, flared and stepped vase, possibly by Alsterfors.

7.5in (19cm) high

£25-35   **GC**

A 1970s Swedish red cased vase, possibly by Alsterfors, with large hollow base.

6in (15cm) high

£25-35   **GC**

A 1970s Swedish deep blue cased stepped/ribbed vase, possibly by Alsterfors.

7in (17.5cm) high

£40-60   **GC**

A pair of 1970s Scandinavian yellow cased candlesticks or vases, with plated metal rims.

These are probably Danish and possibly made by Kastrup's sister factory at Odense.

6.5in (16.5cm) high

£30-50   **GC**

A Swedish Afors Glasbruk bottle, with moulded band of vertical lines, designed by Bertil Vallien.

Vallien joined Afors in 1963, the year before it merged with Kosta. He has since become one of Sweden's most avant garde and revolutionary glass designers, known particularly for his sculptural works.

7.25in (18.5cm) high

£40-60　　　　　　MHT

A Swedish Afors Glasbruk deep blue vase, designed by Bertil Vallien, with moulded band of vertical ribs.

c1965　　7in (17.5cm) high

£40-60　　　　　　MHT

A Swedish Alsterfors opaque blue glass geometric vase, designed by Per-Olof Ström, the base with etched signature and date.

1968　　9.5in (24cm) high

£60-80　　　　　　FD

A Swedish Alsterfors abstract moulded and textured glass vase, designed by Per-Olof Strom, the base with etched signature and date.

1968　　　　　　10in (25.5cm) high

£50-70　　　　　　FD

A Swedish Alsterfors goblet, designed by Per-Olof Strom.

7.25in (18.5cm) high

£15-20　　　　　　GC

A Swedish Aseda clear glass vase, with white spiralling internal threading, designed by Bo Borgstrom.

This design is usually found in red.

9.5in (24cm) high

£20-30　　　　　　MHT

A Swedish Aseda knobbly vase.

11in (28cm) high

£20-30　　　　　　NPC

A 1970s Dansk Design Ltd. clear glass decanter, with teak stopper, designed by Gunnar Cyren, the base marked "DENMARK".

12in (30cm) high

£50-70　　　　　　MHT

A Swedish Flygsfors 'Coquille' vase, designed by Paul Kedelv.

The Coquille range, named after the French word for 'shell', is usually found in low bowl forms, rather than tall vases, making this piece comparatively rare.

c1960   11.75in (30cm) high

£70-90   **GC**

A Johanfors etched teardrop-shaped goblet vase, designed by Bengt Orup, etched with a stylized skyscraper design, the base hand-inscribed "Johanfors Orup" and with Johanfors label.

11.5in (29cm) high

£120-140   **GC**

A CLOSER LOOK AT A JOHANFORS GOBLET

Bengt Orup (1916-96) worked as the leading artist for Johanfors from 1951 until 1972, when the factory was sold to Orrefors.

It is very finely blown and of a large size, and is meant for display rather than a specific usage.

The acid-etched design is very modern – Orup's experience as an engraver and graphic designer no doubt came into play with this design.

Orup ran his own studio where he worked as a painter, engraver and sculptor.

A Johanfors goblet-shaped vase, designed by Bengt Orup, acid-etched and sandblasted with a design of stylized people.

11.5in (29cm) high

£100-150   **GC**

A Norwegian Hadeland heavily cased purple bowl, designed by Willy Johansson, with internal green blob in foot, and signed "WJ 54 HADELAND".

Willy Johansson joined Hadeland in 1936 as an apprentice under his glassblower father Wilhelm. In 1947, he became a designer, remaining there until 1988. He was interested in colour contrasts, as shown in this design.

c1956   3.5in (9cm) high

£40-50   **MH**

A Norwegian Hadeland grey bowl, probably designed by Willy Johannsson, with applied white enamelled rim.

These bowls are often thought to be made by Whitefriars, due to the clean lines and colour. However, the glass on these bowls is much thicker, the colour is different and the applied opaque rim is a feature of many of Johansson's designs.

11in (28cm) diam

£100-150   **MHT**

A Swedish Gullaskruf goblet, designed by Arthur Percy.

Percy (1886-1976) worked for Gullaskruf from 1951-70. Many of his designs are thinly blown and elongated. This goblet is blown in one hollow piece down to the separate solid, cylindrical stem.

9.5in (24cm) high

£50-60   **MHT**

A Swedish A.B. Kalmar Glasbruk lobed vase, with amethyst internal banding and original label.

4.75in (12cm) high

£20-30   **MHT**

A Finnish Nuutajärvi Nöstjo yellow vase, designed by Kaj Franck, with dimpled base and machine-cut rim and signed "KF Nuutajärvi Nöstjo 64".

Franck (1911-89) brought about a design revolution at Nuutajärvi when he became art director in 1950. He was responsible for the company's first modern designs and remained pre-eminent until his departure in 1976. From 1965-68 his designs were not marked at his request, with his name appearing on most of his designs after this date.

c1964   10.25in (26cm) high

£180-220   MHT

A Finnish Nuutajärvi Nöstjo yellow vase, designed by Kaj Franck, with dimpled base and machine-cut rim and signed "KF Nuutajärvi Nöstjo 64".

c1964 10in (25.5cm) high

£180-220   MHT

A Norwegian Magnor graduated electric blue and clear vase, with original label.

5in (12.5cm) high

£15-20   MHT

A Finnish Nuutajärvi Nöstjo blue moulded vase, designed by Kaj Franck, with flared rim and foot.

c1966   5in (12.5cm) high

£70-90   MHT

A Finnish Nuutajärvi Nöstjo clear 'Pikku-Majakka' vase, designed by Oiva Toikka.

Although very similar to Nanny Still's 'Pomapdour' range, the use of clear glass and a wider, shorter rim shows this to be different. The name means 'little lighthouse'.

c1965   9in (23cm) high

£70-90   NPC

A Swedish Pukeberg pink bowl, designed by Staffan Gellerstedt, with label.

As with most factories, Pukeberg designers came to prominence during the 1950s. The Pukeberg logo of a gather of glass on a rod was designed in the 1960s by Ann Warff, wife of Goran, who also worked for Kosta.

c1976   6in (15cm) diam

£30-40   NPC

A Norwegian Randsfjord brown, black and cream swirling clear-cased vase, designed by T. Torgersen, with blue paper label to base.

5.75in (14.5cm) high

£80-100   GC

A Swedish F.M. Ronneby lampbase, with continental light fittings.

Due to the colouring, this glass is often confused with Mdina glass. Ronneby was founded independently in Sweden in 1961 by Josef and Benito Marcolin. Mats Jonasson produced some signed paperweights at the factory before its closure in 1990.

10.25in (26cm) high

£50-70   MHT

A Swedish 1960s Skrufs Glasbruk AB textured clear glass vase, with bark-like finish.

This is similar to some of Tapio Wirkkala's designs for littala, but has thicker glass and a flat, machine-cut rim and base. Textured glass was very fashionable from the late 1960s-70s, with designs inspired by the rugged Scandinavian landscape.

7.5in (19cm) high

£35-45   **MHT**

A CLOSER LOOK AT A STROMBERG VASE

The use of strong colour is unusual for this factory – more typical designs are in cool coloured or clear glass.

This piece is likely to have been designed by Gunnar Nylund (1904-89) who designed for the factory from 1952-75 and introduced more typical 1950s forms.

The asymmetric, bud-like form is typically 1950s, but is again unusual for Stromberg, whose designs are usually more like the oval bowl also on this page.

These heavily cased forms are scarcer, more technically complex and more visually appealing than more typical designs, and have probably not yet reached their peak in value and desirability.

A Strombergshyttan curved heavily cased yellow glass vase, engraved "Stromberg 973".
c1959   *4.25in (10.5cm) high*

£80-100   **MHT**

A Swedish Skrufs Glasbruk AB clear knopped, textured bottle, designed by Bengt Edenfalk, with polished pontil.

7.75in (19.5cm) high

£60-80   **MHT**

A Swedish Skrufs Glasbruk AB vase, designed by Bengt Edenfalk.

Edenfalk joined Skrufs as their first full-time chief designer in 1953.

£40-70   **NPC**

A Smalandshyttan grey cased bowl.

Just as 'Lasi Oy' means 'glass company', 'hyttan' means hut, implying a factory. This factory was based in Smaland, Sweden, in the same area as Strombergshyttan, Kosta and many other glass factories.

3.75in (9.5cm) high

£20-30   **MHT**

A Strombergshyttan spherical heavily cased brown-grey vase, engraved "Stromberg 0937" on the base.

3.5in (9cm) high

£100-150   **MHT**

A Strombergshyttan ice blue oval dish, with curving machine-cut rim and heavy walls.

The austere form and colour, thick walls and cut, polished rim are more typical Stromberg features. The majority were designed by Gerda Stromberg, the wife of the founder Edward, who worked as a designer from 1933-46. However, similar (but often more flowing) work was also designed by H.J. Dunne-Cooke, who was British importer Elfverson & Co.'s buyer and designer.

9.75in (25cm) wide

£60-80   **MHT**

GLASS

COLLECTORS' NOTES

■ Schott was founded in 1884 in Thuringia, Germany by Otto Schott and began by making optical glass. The renowned Carl Zeiss was an early partner until his death in 1888. Bauhaus designer Wilhelm Wagenfeld was an early designer, who worked from 1931-35, with a clear glass teapot being among his notable designs.

■ One of his assistants was Heinrich Loffelhardt (1901-79), who was employed as a freelance designer from 1954. Many of his designs were for tableware, which was made at the Vereinigte Farbenglaswerke plant in Zweisel, Bavaria. The plant had been acquired by Schott in 1927 and used for optical glass manufacture.

■ In the 1970s, Loffelhardt and his colleague Wilhelm Kuchler augmented their growing and successful range of tableware with a range of art glass also made at Zweisel. The growth in popularity of studio glass from the late 1960s onwards undoubtedly influenced them in this decision. The majority are heavily cased in clear glass, with strong, vibrant colours including blue and green.

■ One popular range had streams of randomly sized internal bubbles trapped under the outer layer. Apart from distinctive colours, heavy casing and bubble patterning, Schott Zweisel pieces can be recognised by the large polished concave pontil mark on the base. Pieces were marketed under the Zweisel and 'Cristallerie Zweisel' brands. Large, bubbled designs in the characteristic blue are currently the most desirable and valuable.

A 1970s Schott Zweisel heavily cased tall vase, with pulled curving rim.	A 1970s Schott Zweisel blue-cased bulbous vase, with lobed rim.	A 1970s Schott Zweisel green glass vase, with applied clear glass flower.	A 1970s Schott Zweisel green waisted vase, with heavily cased base.
9.75in (24.5cm) high	7in (17.5cm) high	7.75in (19.5cm) high	9.25in (23.5cm) high
£50-60 GC	**£15-25** GC	**£45-55** GC	**£40-60** GC

A 1970s Schott Zweisel amber vase, with large internal bubbles.

975in (24.5cm) high

£50-60 GC

A 1970s Schott Zweisel tall vase, with large internal bubbles.

9.75in (24.5cm) high

£50-60 GC

A 1970s Schott Zweisel vase, designed by Heinrich Loffelhardt, with densely packed random internal bubbles.

This is one of the more commonly found shapes from this factory, but also one of the more desirable shapes, particularly in larger sizes.

6in (15cm) high

£50-70 GC

A 1970s Schott Zweisel spherical candleholder, designed by Heinrich Loffelhardt, with internal bubbles.

The inside is hollow, with access gained from the machine-cut base.

4in (10cm) high

£40-60 GC

COLLECTORS' NOTES

- The contemporary glass movement of spheres and orbs developed in the 1980s onwards from the creation of art glass marbles and paperweights by contemporary studio glass artists, who mainly work in the US. From such simple toys has sprung a new, exciting and dynamic art glass movement. Spheres tend to be larger than marbles, with the tag 'orb' being reserved for the largest examples.

- The designs are not painted on the interior or exterior of the sphere, but are contained within the sphere, being carefully hand-worked in hot, coloured glass and most often in more than one layer. The glass designs are then encased in a top layer of clear 'crystal' or 'borosilicate' glass.

- Spheres really need to be handled and viewed in person to best appreciate the intricate detail within, and myriad reflections and magnifications caused by the curving surface. The skill involved in their creation show how far the studio glass movement has progressed since the late 1960s.

- Names to look out for include Paul Stankard, Jesse Taj, David Salazar, Dinah Hulet, Rolf Wald and James Alloway. New artists come to the field every year, each bringing their own style and skill, making this a vibrant and ever-changing market. Prices are currently comparatively affordable for such detailed, unique works.

- Watch out for new young makers, examining their work and comparing it to established names. Many artists make their own murrines, which are also known as 'milli', 'millefiori' or 'murrini'. Some artists such as Jesse Taj and David Strobel sell their murrines for others to incorporate into their own designs.

- As well as established marble collectors, a new younger audience has been attracted to the market. Images from cartoons and sub-cultures are often included, making this art form highly relevant to today. Spheres are intricate, easy to display and offer great variety. Values should increase as the market grows.

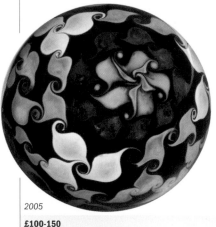

A Nick Bartlett translucent burgundy and beige rake pull sphere, signed "NB05".

When held to the light, the interior reveals a crescent shaped 'veil', which is a characteristic feature of Bartlett's larger designs.

2005   2.75in (7cm) diam

£100-150   **BGL**

A Shane Caswell 'Sea Floral' sphere, signed with a signature cane.

The colour is 'pulled' into the sphere with a vacuum process.

2005   1.5in (4cm) diam

£30-45   **BGL**

A Teri Conklin double-faced sphere, with dichroic fume and pulled stringers and a rake pull torsade.

2005   1.75in (4.5cm) diam

£35-45   **BGL**

A Drew Fritts banded swirl sphere, with dichroic and multicoloured strands, signed and dated "AF 2005 7".

2005   1.75in (4.5cm) diam

£60-80   **BGL**

A Steve Hitt double-layered 'Cedars' sphere, with butterfly and floral murrines, signed "SH03".

The decoration is applied in separate layers, giving depth and perspective to the design.

1.75in (4.5cm) diam

£80-120   **BGL**

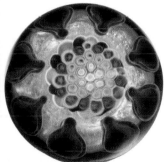

A Josh Howard hollow marble or sphere, the surface with applied glass 'stringer' designs.

This piece is actually hollow, so is very light in weight.

2004   1.5in (4cm) diam

£35-45   **BGL**

A CLOSER LOOK AT A SPHERE

Dustin Morell is well known for his Vortex spheres, which are extremely well executed in bright colours.

They are complex to make and give the impression that the centre of the concave vortex is deeper than the corresponding outside surface of the sphere.

Vortex spheres started off being very, very small marbles, and only grew in size as glass artists became more skilled – larger examples such as this are sought-after.

The back is executed very carefully as the hot glass used to decorate it can burn through the thin, opaque background layer into the vortex when dripped onto the surface.

A Dustin Morell orange 'Vortex' sphere, with honeycomb back, signed "DKM 2004".

2004   2.25in (6cm) diam

£70-100   **BGL**

A Jerry Kelly 'Millfiori' sphere, with self-made murrines and pulled 'stringers', signed "JK05".

2005   2in (5cm) diam

£60-80   **BGL**

A Shawn Messenger gathered millefiori 'Flora' marble.

Each of the millefiori is made from a sliced glass cane and is placed in position by hand.

2005   2in (5cm) diam

£60-80   **BGL**

A Kris Parke rake pull swirl sphere, in black, red, purple and orange on a white base.

2005   1.5in (4cm) diam

£30-50   **BGL**

A Tony Parker marble or sphere, with internal twisted ribbon and dichroic band, with applied heart murrines.

1990   2in (5cm) diam

£50-70   **BGL**

A Tony Parker 'Marilyn Monroe' sphere.

Marilyn's face is composed of black frit, which is trailed onto the white surface and then melted into it.

1990   1.5in (4cm) diam

£50-70   **BGL**

GLASS

A Jim Hart torchworked sphere, with dichroic base under curving patterns applied to the surface, and a signature heart-shaped cane.

1.5in (4cm) diam

£45-55 BGL

A CLOSER LOOK AT A SPHERE

Cathy Richardson (b.1949) is a noted glass artist who has studied at the respected Pilchuck and Corning glass schools.

She assembles many lampworked glass elements before encasing them in clear glass with a complicated and difficult vacuum process.

Richardson's love of nature is clear – she holds a doctorate in geology, which shows in her detailed seabeds, and she grew up in Virginia where she gained her love of the seaside.

This is a comparatively large sphere and has two layers of designs, which add depth and perspective. Three layer spheres are even more valuable.

A Cathy Richardson double layered 'Coral Reef' orb, signed "C. RICHARDSON 2004".

2004 *2.75in (7cm) diam*

£100-150 BGL

A Josh Sable 'Reticello' sphere, with rake pull base and sides, and stained glass window-like reticello double vortex, signed "SABLE 2003".

2003 *2in (5cm) diam*

£70-100 BGL

A David Salazar experimental paperweight-style sphere, with 'painted' glass butterflies, flora and fauna on a surface.

Salazar is one of the best known proponents of the Californian style of 'painting' with glass and has over 25 years of experience of glassmaking.

1.5in (4cm) diam

£70-100 BGL

A Jesse Taj 'Flora' sphere, with self-made murrines of a butterfly, sun, dragonfly and lion's head within a torsade, signed "TAJ 03 3/03 Wilkinson".

Jesse Taj is well known for his wide variety of finely made murrines.

2003 *1.5in (4cm) diam*

£80-120 BGL

A Beth Tomasello paperweight style sphere, with lampwork flora and berries on a ground glass base.

2004 *1.5in (4cm) diam*

£60-80 BGL

FIND OUT MORE...

Contemporary Marbles & Related Art Glass, *by Mark Block, published by Schiffer Books, 2001.*

The Encyclopaedia of Modern Marbles, Spheres & Orbs, *by Mark Block, published by Schiffer Books, 2005.*

COLLECTORS' NOTES

- The studio glass movement developed in the US during the 1960s after glassmakers Harvey Littleton and Dominick Labino found ways to free glass making from the confines of the factory in 1962. This allowed artists to make glass themselves, although many still choose to work in teams.

- The movement spread to the UK and Europe in the late 1960s and '70s, and as artists and makers practiced techniques, the level of skills developed and pieces became more appealing and more finely made. The breadth of techniques mastered also developed and glass became increasingly seen as an art form rather than a craft during the 1980s.

- Originators such as Dale Chihuly, William Morris, Marvin Lipofsky and Dan Dailey have become legendary and their works are valuable. However, works by successive 'generations' can be affordable. Date is not always an indicator of value, and some early examples are crudely formed although they do reflect this important development in glass history.

- Buy a reference book and look out for names that have strong collecting bases behind them, or who have works featured in public collections. The secondary market at auctions and dealers is still developing and bargains can be had. Recent graduates can make an interesting contemporary gamble, but one that will always pay off if you buy because you like the piece.

- Today the market is extremely diverse and vibrant, and crosses Europe, the UK and the US. Boundaries are constantly being pushed, resulting in a myriad of different designs in a rainbow of colours across many price ranges. The increasing solid interest in the area that developed during the 1990s is sure to continue and studio and contemporary glass should become a hot collecting area.

- Only a single price is given for some pieces as this reflects the retail price of that individual contemporary piece.

'Alfred's Mirror', by Keith Cummings, kiln-formed opaque glass inlaid and decorated with copper wire, copper bands and glass faux pearls.

This piece was inspired by the 9thC 'Alfred's Jewel' in the Ashmolean Museum, Oxford, which was made for King Alfred.

2003 14.5in (37cm) long

£2,000-2,500 CG

'Aesculus', by Kate Jones and Stephen Gillies, from cased, sandblasted and cut glass, signed on the base "Gillies Jones Aesculus 2004/08 Rosedale".

This is formed from glass coated with a layer of coloured glass, which is then masked off and sandblasted to create the pattern.

2004 11.5in (29.5cm) diam

£1,890 CG

A Sam Herman vase, with swirled inclusions of mauve, ochre and blue, the base with incised marks.

American Sam Herman is one of the founding fathers of studio glass and was the first to bring the ideas to the UK. His work is typified by a painterly approach to colour and pattern, and is rising in value and desirability today.

1980 6in (15.5cm) high

£70-90 CHEF

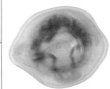

A large Sam Herman glass bowl, of irregular, freeblown form, streaked with green glass, the base with etched signature.

1971 18in (46cm) wide

£180-220 WW

A Glasform iridescent vase, designed and made by John Ditchfield, with waterlily leaves pattern, the base signed "Glasform1=8/L".

4.25in (11cm) high

£70-100 GAZE

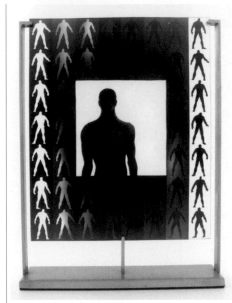

'Eclipse', by Alison Kinnaird, engraved, sandblasted and cased glass panel, with figural designs, mounted on a metal stand.

Kinnaird is an important glass engraver internationally and was awarded an MBE in 1997. Her work is in many museums and galleries including the Victoria & Albert Museum, London.

2001   *Panel 11.5in (29.5cm) high*

£3,600   **CG**

A unique Skyline 'pebble' form, designed by Peter Layton.

Although the form is more typical of Layton's designs, the colour and pattern was from a new and experimental range. The delicate and varied colouration is particularly appealing.

2004   11.5in (29cm) wide

£1,500   **PL**

A Paradiso disc, by Peter Layton.

The Paradiso range was inspired by painters such as Howard Hodgkin, emulating their colour and abstract 'brushed on' patterns.

2004   11.5in (29cm) diam

£2,400   **PL**

A large Mirage 'stone form', designed by Peter Layton.

Mirage was inspired by the landscape seen by Layton on a visit to the ancient city of Petra in Jordan. Layton is one of Britain's most respected glass artists, with a varied and long experience. Today he runs the London Glass Blowing studio with a team of glass makers and designers.

2004   13.5in (34cm) wide

£3,000   **PL**

A rare Peter Layton dropper bottle, made at the London Glassblowing Workshop.

This is an extremely unusual shape for this range and may have been an experimental piece. The clear 'bubbles' are arranged in a spiral pattern, but appear to be banded. The skill of the glassmaker has meant that as this piece was blown out the internal pink lines in each bubble shape have not been widened.

c1989   20cm (8in) high

£70-100   **PC**

An Annette Meech goblet, with clear stem and spotted green and blue on a white background bowl, signed "Annette Meech 1978" to the base.

1978   7in (17.5cm) high

£80-120   **MHT**

A Simon Moore vase, the flared and waved green body bordered and decorated with clear swirls, on a black glass pedestal, engraved "Simon Moore 88" to rim.

1988   9in (23cm) high

£50-80   **ROS**

A 'Stream Bowl' by Keïko Mukaïdé, in kiln cast blue glass with enamelled powder surface.

This was possibly cast in a sand mould as grains of sand are bonded to the outside.

2003   12.5in (31.5cm) widest

£1,100   **CG**

An American Michael Nourot glass perfume bottle, with a central band of gold foil on a black ground.

2004   5in (13cm) high

£80-120   **AGW**

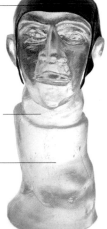

An Okra perfume bottle and stopper, designed and made by Richard Golding, with iridescent and trailed design with floral detail, the base engraved "Okra 87 WS LSB No. 9".

1987   6.5in (16.5cm) high

£60-80   **GAZE**

'Europe – The Past Is Not Enough' by Ronald Pennell, green overcased glass vase made by Karl Nordbruch, then engraved on a diamond wheel by Ronald Pennell, signed with an "RP" monogram.

Pennell is one of Britian's most important glass engravers, whose designs are based on stories and are engraved onto the bodies without preparatory drawings.

2003   8.25in (21cm) high

£3,600   **CG**

'Dog Days A Sun Fetish' by Ronald Pennell, amethyst glass cased vessel made by Karl Nordbruch and engraved by Ronald Pennell, signed with an "RP" monogram.

Of this work, Pennell says 'There are many ways to connect with past civilisations and cultures. In this work a man and his dog are confronted by three strange figures including one who is holding a symbolic sunburst'.

2003   8in (20.5cm) high

£3,800   **CG**

A CLOSER LOOK AT A DAVID REEKIE HEAD

David Reekie (b.1947) is an internationally renowned glass artist known for his cast glass works of the human form, which often convey emotions or highlight the human predicament.

This was part of a series of four similar heads sold to a London gallery, with this being the only example looking upwards.

Even though pieces are cast in moulds, each piece is unique and is not repeated.

The simple head form is related to Reekie's early landmark work 'Construction with Guarding Figures' from 1977.

A large blown 'Seascape' bowl, designed and made by Anthony Stern.

These reveal a landscape effect as the bowl is turned and light passes through it.

2003   8.75in (22cm) high

£1,500-2,000   **ASG**

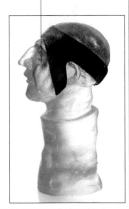

A David Reekie cast soda/barium glass head, with hand-made lead head cap, the base hand inscribed "D.REEKIE 1986".

As well as in key private collections, Reekie's work can be found in the Victoria & Albert Museum, London, and museums in the US, Denmark and France.

1986   6.5in (16.5cm) high

£500-700   **PC**

A large 'African Vase', by Anthony Stern, made from lightly iridised light blue glass blown into a cone made from woven reclaimed African telephone wire woven in Kwazululand and accented with cowrie shells by Stern.

The glass is blown into the wire cone, while still molten.

2004   11.75in (30cm) high

£1,200-1,800   **ASG**

An American cameo and engraved glass lamp base, designed and made by Valerie Surjan, the black glass with engraved and cameo floral design.

2004   12in (30.5cm) high

£1,200-1,800   **AGW**

A tapering blue glass vase, designed and made by David Traub, signed "Traub 93".

1993   7.75in (19.5cm) high

£20-30   **GAZE**

'Jug & Cup', by Koichiro Yamamoto, of cast and polished glass, signed on base "Koichiro C Jug & Cup 2001".

A Rachael Woodman cased vase, with hot-worked striated deep grey exterior and yellow interior.

c1990   8in (20cm) high

£600-800   **JH**

Convex surfaces such as this cannot be machine-polished, so must be polished by hand. In the largest piece, the handles are cavities running through the piece, giving an optical illusion. Yamamoto was shortlisted for the Jerwood Prize.

2001   6in (15.5cm) high

£1,600   **CG**

An American Zelique Studio heart-shaped 'Hanging Wisteria' perfume bottle, designed and made by Joseph Morel, with 'painted flamework', signed "J.M. 2001 WHK8".

The internal pattern is made by 'torchwork' where a small blowtorch is used to partially melt the glass, allowing it to be bent, joined and formed before being cased in clear glass.

4.25in (11cm) high

£120-180   **BGL**

A small 20thC blown studio glass bottle, with surface enamel decoration and applied coloured bands, with impressed maker's pontil mark.

5in (13cm) high

£20-30   **PC**

FIND OUT MORE...

Collectors Guide: 20th Century Glass, by Judith Miller, published by DK, 2004.

Artists in Glass, by Dan Klein, published by Mitchell Beazley, 2001.

GLASS

COLLECTORS' NOTES

■ Ronald Stennett-Willson (b.1915) has entered the lexicon of iconic 20thC glass designers. He began working for importers Rydbeck and Norstrom in 1935, and moved to J. Wuidart in 1951, where he was exposed to the innovative designs and popularity of Scandinavian glass. His first designs during the 1950s, for companies such as Lemington Glass, show strong Scandinavian influences.

■ He became Reader in glass at the Royal College of Art in 1961 and taught there, helping to establish the groundwork for hot glass working, until 1966 when he left to found King's Lynn Glass in Norfolk. There, he introduced many of his most sought-after ranges, including the 'Sheringham' and 'Brancaster' candlesticks

■ Lines are typically clean and modern, with strong, or otherwise cool colours that captured the aesthetics of the period and continued the Scandinavian influence. King's Lynn Glass was so successful that it was acquired by Wedgwood in 1969. Wedgwood Glass itself was acquired by Caithness in 1988 and the King's Lynn factory closed in 1992. Today his designs are highly desirable and rising in value.

A Wedgwood pink-red 'Top Hat' vase, designed by Ronald Stennett-Willson, shape RSW21/1.

This vibrant colour is rare and uses colloidal gold to give its strength of colour. This was also used to produce Amberina, developed by Joseph Locke of New England, USA. When reheated, the golden yellow becomes a deep, fiery red.

4in (10cm) high

£70-90   GC

A Wedgwood orange 'Angular' vase, designed by Ronald Stennett-Willson, model no. RSW10.

Although the form is not too hard to find, this particular colour is extremely rare.

6.25in (16cm) high

£80-120   GC

A Wedgwood Glass experimental blue speckled vase, designed by Ronald Stennett-Willson, with flared rim and tapered base.

7in (18cm) high

£250-300   GC

A Lemington Glass tall blue vase, designed by Ronald Stennett-Willson.

This early piece shows the influence of Scandinavian glass on many of Stennett-Willson's designs and is a rare shape.

c1960   11in (28cm) high

£120-180   GC

A Wedgwood cased white and orange speckled squat glass vase, designed by Ronald Stennett-Willson.

4.25in (11cm) high

£60-80   GC

A 1970s Wedgwood 'dome' paperweight, model no. RSW12, designed by Ronald Stennett-Willson.

4in (10cm) high

£25-30   MHT

A Wedgwood purple textured mould-blown glass cylinder vase, designed by Ronald Stennett-Willson, model RSW25.

10in (25.5cm) high

£70-90   GC

COLLECTORS' NOTES

■ The 'Blown Soda' range was introduced by Whitefriars at the 1962 annual Blackpool trade fair. It was designed by Geoffrey Baxter, who had joined as assistant designer in 1954. Their jewel-like colours and simple, often geometric, forms show Baxter's modern design ethics, as well as the prevailing influence of Scandinavian glass designs at that time.

■ The soda glass used is typically thin, meaning pieces are light in weight, and were blown into a mould to give a uniform shape. Some shapes were adapted from moulds made for lighting. They were originally launched in midnight blue, shadow green and amethyst, then ruby, golden amber, twilight, and finally pewter.

■ The range was very popular and can be easily found today, although smaller examples are more common than larger examples. Certain shapes, such as the decanter and glass are rare, and some shapes are rare in certain colours. The range was long-lived and its modern design still has great appeal today, and is largely more affordable than Baxter's later 'Textured' range.

A Whitefriars midnight blue 'Blown Soda' range bulbous vase, pattern no. 9597 designed by Geoffrey Baxter, with tall, slightly flared neck.

c1963   *5in (14cm) high*

£40-50   **GC**

A Whitefriars amethyst 'Blown Soda' range vase, designed by Geoffrey Baxter, with cylindrical neck.

                              7in (18cm) high

£60-90   **GC**

A Whitefriars ruby 'Blown Soda' range medium bulbous vase, pattern no. 9599, designed by Geoffrey Baxter.

Note the different shapes and neck lengths on these similar looking vases.

c1963   *7in (17.5cm) high*

£30-40   **GC**

A Whitefriars midnight blue 'Blown Soda' range vase, pattern no. 9602, designed by Geoffrey Baxter.

c1963   *6.75in (17cm) high*

£80-100   **GC**

A Whitefriars amethyst 'Blown Soda' bulbous vase, designed by Geoffrey Baxter.

c1962-64   *4in (10cm) high*

£40-60   **MHT**

A Whitefriars pewter 'Blown Soda' range waisted vase, pattern no. 9638, designed by Geoffrey Baxter.

Note the applied white enamel rim. This is a rare feature as the enamel rarely bonded to the soda glass successfully. These vases can also be found in shadow green.

c1963   *7.5in (19cm) high*

£60-80   **TCS**

A Whitefriars ruby 'Blown Soda' waisted vase, pattern no. 9594, designed by Geoffrey Baxter, with later label.

c1963   *8in (20.5cm) high*

£15-25   **GC**

GLASS

A Whitefriars midnight blue 'Blown Soda' range 'bow tie' vase, pattern no. 9591, designed by Geoffrey Baxter.

c1963 5.5in (14cm) high

£30-40 GC

A Whitefriars amethyst 'Blown Soda' range vase, pattern no. 9474.

This shape, similar to a hyacinth vase, was introduced during the 1950s in golden amber, sea green, twilight and ruby.

c1963 7.75in (19.5cm) high

£50-70 GC

A Whitefriars amethyst 'Blown Soda' range 'stem cup', pattern no. 9593, the design attributed to Geoffrey Baxter.

c1963 6in (15.5cm) high

£80-100 GC

A Whitefriars ruby 'Blown Soda' range vase, pattern no. 9596, designed by Geoffrey Baxter.

It is easy to imagine that this form was derived from a lampshade design.

c1963 9.5in (24cm) high

£30-50 GC

A Whitefriars amethyst 'Blown Soda' range vase, pattern no. 9553, designed by Geoffrey Baxter.

This is the early label. In 1962 Whitefriars changed their label, making it more stylized.

1962 4.75n (12cm) high

£10-15 GC

A Whitefriars ruby 'Blown Soda' range large 'pinched' or 'dented' vase, pattern no. 9362, designed by Geoffrey Baxter.

These were introduced in the 1966 catalogue.

c1967 10.5in (27cm) high

£60-80 MHT

A Whitefriars midnight blue 'Blown Soda' range mushroom vase, pattern no. 9639, designed by Geoffrey Baxter, with white enamelled rim.

c1963 7in (18cm) high

£120-180 TCS

A scarce Whitefriars shadow green decanter and glass, pattern no. M122, with later label.

The glass fits over the neck to form a cover, but is often missing leading many to assume these decanters are rare vases.

6.75in (17cm) high

£40-60 GC

COLLECTORS' NOTES

■ Whitefriars was founded in London in the 1600s and was acquired by James Powell in 1834 when it became known as 'Powell & Sons'. In 1926, the factory moved to Wealdstone, Middlesex. It became known as Whitefriars once again in 1962. Most collectors, however, refer to much of the 20thC glass as 'Whitefriars'.

■ 19thC and early 20thC pieces by designers such as Harry Powell, William Wilson and James Hogan are sought-after. But it is the post war designs, mainly designed by Geoffrey Baxter that have increased the most. He remained with the company until its demise due to financial problems in the harsh economic climate of 1980.

■ Baxter's quintessentially modern designs reflected the influences of the times they were made in, but were also innovative, with a unique British direction. During the 1950s, they took on a modern Scandinavian influence in terms of form and clarity of colour, with clean lines, casing, strong or cool colours

and lack of surface decoration. Scandinavian glass was popular at the time and many other British factories also followed these principles.

■ 1967 saw the unveiling of Baxter's 'Textured' range that was to become the pinnacle of his achievements and the most sought-after range today. Moulds with internal textures were used to create glass with strong surface textures and in bright colours that matched the interiors of the time. The 'Studio' range, designed by Peter Wheeler and Baxter, and inspired by the growing studio glass movement of the late 1960s, is also highly collectable, with each piece being unique.

■ Always consider the form, size and colour of a piece as these affect value considerably. New colours were introduced in 1969. Key designs such as the 'Banjo' and 'Drunken Bricklayer' have become iconic. Smaller pieces from the 'Late Textured' range of the 1970s are not as desirable as they lack the visual impact, large sizes and 'freshness' of the late 1960s designs.

A Whitefriars large footed vase, designed by James Hogan.

c1948   7.75in (20cm) high

£40-60   **TCM**

A Powell & Sons bulbous clear 'Flint' glass decanter, probably designed by Harry Powell.

Cut glass examples are more valuable and can fetch up to £250.

c1880-90   13in (33cm) high

£80-90   **GC**

A Whitefriars ocean blue glass vase, designed by Geoffrey Baxter in 1957, with square base and four side ribs.

9.5in (24cm) high

£40-60   **GC**

A Whitefriars golden amber glass vase, designed by William Wilson in 1935, with square cut base.

1935-c1938   8in (20cm) high

£70-90   **GC**

A Whitefriars kingfisher blue cased vase bud vase, designed by Geoffrey Baxter.

8.5in (21.5cm) high

£20-30   **MHT**

A Whitefriars dusk grey tapering glass vase, designed by Geoffrey Baxter.

7.5in (19cm) high

£18-22   **NPC**

GLASS

A Whitefriars arctic blue tall 'Beak' vase, designed by Geoffrey Baxter in 1957, pattern number 9437, with organic, pulled rim.

The cool colour and organic bud-like form show the influence of contemporary Scandinavian designs, particularly Per Lütken's 'Naebvase' or 'beak' vase of 1952.

22in (56cm) high

£250-300   GC

A CLOSER LOOK AT A WHITEFRIARS BOTTLE

The white enamel streaks did not adhere to the blue surface easily, causing technical problems.

The range was also made in ruby red, with the same problems.

The manufacturing problems meant the range was only made for a very short period of time in 1961. As a result, very few pieces were made.

The range was due for launch at the important 1962 Blackpool sales fair. Its failure led to the development of the much ignored Blown Soda range.

A very rare Whitefriars blue cylindrical bottle, designed by Geoffrey Baxter, with white striations.

1961   11.25in (28.5cm) high

£250-350   GC

A very rare Whitefriars lichen heavily clear-cased vase, designed by Geoffrey Baxter.

This colour combination of green-streaked pewter is very rare. A number of Baxter's designs were influenced by nature.

c1970   5in (12.5cm) high

£200-250   GC

A Whitefriars full lead crystal 'Cirrus' small baluster vase, with complex aqua internal streaks and heavily gold coloured cased foot.

Although this appears similar to Baxter's early 1970s 'Streaky' range, it was a later range, appearing in the 1980 catalogue.

c1980   4.75in (12cm) high

£80-100   GC

A Whitefriars orange-streaked Studio range bulbous vase, designed by Geoffrey Baxter, pattern number 9803, with 'iridescent' silver chloride streaks.

1972-80   7in (18cm) high

£200-300   GC

An experimental Whitefriars Studio range charger, designed by Peter Wheeler and Geoffrey Baxter, with white enamel back and grey and green marbled front.

c1968-69   10.5in (27cm) diam

£320-380   TCS

A Whitefriars ruby red dish, designed by Geoffrey Baxter, with inverted lip and asymmetric opening.

5.5in (14cm) diam

£20-30   NPC

GLASS

A Whitefriars kingfisher blue 'Banjo' textured vase, designed by Geoffrey Baxter in 1966, pattern number 9681.

Kingfisher and tangerine were launched later, in 1969.

1969-c1973   13in (33cm) high

£700-900   **GHOU**

A Whitefriars tangerine orange 'Banjo' textured vase designed by Geoffrey Baxter in 1966, pattern number 9681.

1969-c1973   13in (33cm) high

£600-800   **GC**

A Whitefriars willow grey 'Banjo' textured vase, designed by Geoffrey Baxter in 1966, pattern number 9681.

1967-c1973   *12.5in (32cm) high*

£800-1,200   **BIG**

A Whitefriars tangerine orange 'Bamboo' textured vase, designed by Geoffrey Baxter in 1966, pattern number 9669.

1969-c1970   8in (20cm) high

£120-180   **CHEF**

A Whitefriars cinnamon brown 'Bamboo' textured vase, designed by Geoffrey Baxter in 1966, pattern number 9669, with label.

1967-c1970   *8.25in (21cm) high*

£150-200   **GAZE**

A Whitefriars aubergine tall 'Greek Key' textured vase, designed by Geoffrey Baxter, pattern number 9810.

1972-74   *8in (20cm) high*

£80-120   **GC**

A Whitefriars sage green tall 'Greek Key' textured vase, designed by Geoffrey Baxter, pattern number 9810.

1972-74   *7.75in (19.5cm) high*

£80-120   **GAZE**

A Whitefriars ruby red 'Chess' textured glass vase, designed by Geoffrey Baxter, pattern number 9817.

1972-74   *5.75in (14.5cm) high*

£60-80   **GAZE**

A Whitefriars aubergine small 'Drunken Bricklayer' textured vase, designed by Geoffrey Baxter in 1966, pattern number 9673.

Although this popular shape, inspired by a pile of bricks, was available from 1967-c1977, it was only shown in aubergine in the 1972 catalogue, the year it was introduced. Baxter was said to have disliked this colour.

1972   *8in (20.5cm) high*

£250-300   **GC**

A Whitefriars aubergine 'Aztec' textured vase, designed by Geoffrey Baxter, pattern number 9816.

1972-74   7in (18cm) high

£50-80   GAZE

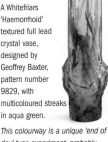

A Whitefriars 'Haemorrhoid' textured full lead crystal vase, designed by Geoffrey Baxter, pattern number 9829, with multicoloured streaks in aqua green.

This colourway is a unique 'end of day' type experiment, probably made by a glass blower in his spare time. It was available as part of the standard range in sage, kingfisher and lilac colours.

c1974   12.5in (30.5cm) high

£300-400   GC

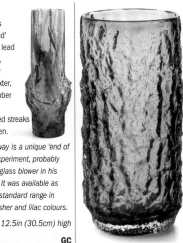

A Whitefriars pewter grey 'Bark' textured vase with tapered foot, designed by Geoffrey Baxter, pattern number 9734.

These are the largest of the bark textured cylindrical 'Log' vases, and are distinguished by the tapered foot. They were not popular at the time and were only produced in pewter, tangerine, ruby and kingfisher for a couple of months in 1969, making them rare today.

10.5in (26.5cm) high

£200-250   GC

A very rare Whitefriars kingfisher blue 'Teardrop' textured vase, designed by Geoffrey Baxter, pattern number 9848.

c1974   11in (28cm) high

£300-500   GC

A very rare Whitefriars kingfisher blue 'Poppy' or 'Rugby Ball' textured vase, designed by Geoffrey Baxter, pattern number 9827.

These rare and heavy vases were produced in two sizes, this being the larger, and in kingfisher, lilac and sage colours.

c1974   11in (28cm) high

£300-400   GC

A Whitefriars indigo 'Fish Scale' or 'Union' textured vase, designed by Geoffrey Baxter, pattern number 9758.

This texture was made using overlapping large headed tin tacks nailed into wood.

1971-74   5in (12.5cm) high

£40-60   GC

A Whitefriars sage green 'Pot Belly' textured vase, designed by Geoffrey Baxter, pattern number 9832.

1974-80   5in (12.5cm) high

£30-50   GC

A Whitefriars ruby red flared textured vase, designed by Geoffrey Baxter, pattern number 9831.

c1974   8in (20cm) high

£50-70   GC

A Whitefriars kingfisher blue 'Hourglass' textured vase, designed by Geoffrey Baxter, pattern number 9836.

c1974   6in (15cm) high

£40-60   GAZE

FIND OUT MORE...

Whitefriars Glass, by Lesley Jackson, published by Richard Dennis, 1996.

GLASS

A Caithness Glass small clear cased Moss green vase, shape number 4019/115, designed by Domhnall O'Broin and retailed by Heal's.

c1965   *5.25in (13cm) high*

£15-20   **GAZE**

A Caithness Glass Heather purple 'Morwen' decanter, shape number 4025/D, designed by Domnhall O'Broin.

Caithness was founded in 1961 with Domnhall O'Broin as main designer until 1966. Many designs were produced into the 1970s and '80s.

c1965   *9.75in (25cm) high*

£30-40   **GAZE**

A CLOSER LOOK AT A DAUM VASE

This vase was designed in 1987 by famous French furniture, object and interiors designer Philippe Starck (b.1949) whose designs are collected internationally.

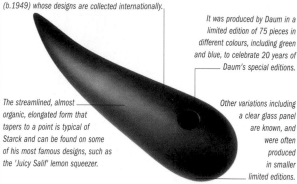

It was produced by Daum in a limited edition of 75 pieces in different colours, including green and blue, to celebrate 20 years of Daum's special editions.

The streamlined, almost organic, elongated form that tapers to a point is typical of Starck and can be found on some of his most famous designs, such as the 'Juicy Salif' lemon squeezer.

Other variations including a clear glass panel are known, and were often produced in smaller limited editions.

A French Daum L'Etrangete tear-shaped sculptural vase, designed by Philippe Starck, with small round opening, of deep purple glass with stain finish, etched "Daum/Starck" and numbered "14/75".

c1987   *22.5in (57cm) long*

£1,000-1,500   **SDR**

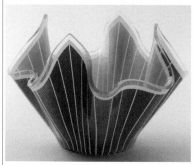

A 1960s Chance beige striped screen-printed handkerchief vase.

Always look at the bases of such heavily screen-printed examples as wear to the exterior screen-printing devalues a piece.

4in (10cm) high

£35-45   **MHT**

A Gozo Glass vase, from the 'Gozo Gold Red' collection, with orange and purple applied straps and gold foil, polished base.

Gozo Glass was set up by Michael Harris in 1989 and is still in operation today. Many designs and forms are similar to those created by Harris for Isle of Wight Studio Glass (see pages 290-292), such as the use of 22ct gold foil on this example.

£15-25   **ART**

A 1930s Hartley Wood multicoloured streaked vase, with broken pontil mark.

Charmingly wonky forms are typical. The company specialised in stained glass windows, hence the bold colours.

7.25in (18.5cm) high

£70-90   **GC**

A Hartley Wood blue and yellow streaked commemorative glass vase, with stamped pontil mark "HW 1892 1992".

This was produced to commemorate the company's centenary and resembles the decorative pieces produced during the 1930s.

1992   *8.25in (21cm) high*

£40-60   **GC**

A CLOSER LOOK AT AN ART DECO GLASS VASE

Mazoyer was based in Moulins, France from c1910-45 and worked with glass and porcelain as well as producing enamelled decoration.

The decoration is typical of Art Deco designs in its use of black and white and near geometric and strongly linear stylization.

Designs such as this were often taken or adapted from patterns books of the period, which also inspired ceramics and textile designers.

An Albert Mazoyer enamelled glass vase, richly painted in blues and black with flowerheads and branches, black painted mark.
c1930

£300-400

Mazoyer pieces are sought-after for their decorative appeal and are not common, this example has also been signed.

13.5in (34cm) high

ROS

A Nazeing blue and white 'cloud' bowl, with wide flared rim.

5.5in (14cm) diam

£20-30　　　　　　　　　　NPC

A boxed set of six Ravenhead 'Chunkies' glasses, with blue stylised leaf design, designed by Alexander Hardie Williamson.

Box 11.2in (28.5cm) wide

£18-22　　　　　　　　　　MTS

One of a pair of German Ritzenhoff limited edition screen-printed glasses, from an edition of 2,000, designed by Ettore Sottsass in 1995, boxed.
1995　　　　　　6in (15cm) high

£100-150　　　　　　　　　GM

A Rosenthal Studio Linie opaque white cased glass vase, designed by Bjørn Wiinblad, with transfer decoration.

10.25in (26.5cm) high

£50-70　　　　　　　　　GAZE

A Stuart Strathearn large 'Ebony & Gold' cylinder glass vase, with applied gold foil.

This range was designed by Iestyn Davies, who had worked at Michael Harris' Isle of Wight studio. The design is similar to Harris's 1978 'Azurene' range. 'Ebony & Gold' was only produced for a short period due to its expense, and other reasons. Large pieces are scarce.
1986-87　　　　9.25in (23.5cm) high

£60-90　　　　　　　　　GC

GLASS

A 20thC mould blown glass vase, of goblet form, with a ribbed stem, the base unmarked.

12.5in (30cm) high

£50-80   GAZE

A conical glass studio vase, with applied trailed clear glass decoration, the base engraved "Gail D. Gill".

7in (18cm) high

£12-18   GAZE

A red glass and vaseline glass vase, with frilled rim and moulded prunts.

6in (15cm) high

£12-18   GAZE

A 1970s knobbly clear cased brown cylinder vase, with moulded textured exterior.

Textured glass was fashionable during the 1960s and '70s, with designs by Whitefriars and the numerous Scandinavian factories proving extremely desirable.

7in (18cm) high

£12-18   NPC

A 1960s dark amber glass vase, the sides with pulled areas, the base unmarked.

11.5in (29cm) high

£10-15   GAZE

A large flower mould-blown rectangular vase, with machine-cut rim, moulded and stylised floral or snow flake decoration.

The maker has not been confirmed, although it is very similar to designs by Dartington and W.S. Jones.

12in (30.5cm) high

£30-50   GC

An amethyst coloured mould-blown glass decanter and stopper, the base unmarked.

8.5in (21.5cm) wide

£12-18   GAZE

An Art Deco engraved and etched glass plaque, with stylized design depicting a nude and a dolphin.

9.5in (24cm) diam

£80-120   GORL

An Italian-style free-blown glass fish ornament.

12.5in (30cm) long

£8-12   GAZE

A CLOSER LOOK AT A PLAYBOY MAGAZINE

Vintage Playboy magazines are a popular collecting area, the value depending on a number of factors.

The popularity of the featured playmate adds desirability – in this case Marilyn Waltz, in her second of three appearances. She was one of only four woman to be Playmate of the month more than once.

The quality of the short stories and features is also important. This issue features Ray Bradbury's Fahrenheit 451, other popular authors include Arthur C. Clarke.

Other factors include the appearance of controversial celebrities and important interviews. Early issues are also desirable – this is the first anniversary issue, which adds to the value.

"Playboy", May 1954, with Joanne Arnold as Playmate of the month, feature on 'Fahrenheit 451' (part 3) by Ray Bradbury; 'Kill the Umpire' by Jack Strausberg; 'How to Apply for a Job' by Shepherd Mead, his first article.

11in (28cm) high

£220-280 **NOR**

"Playboy", April 1954, with Marilyn Waltz as Playmate of the month, features including Ray Bradbury's Fahrenheit 451 (part 2) and Jaaz: The Metronome All Stars featuring photos and story on Benny Goodman, Count Basie, Jack Teagarden, Harry James, Bob Haggert, Gene Krupa and others; 'Advice on the Choice of a Mistress' by Benjamin Franklin and 'Pleasures of the Oyster' by Thomas Mario.

11in (28cm) high

£400-500 **NOR**

"Playboy", January 1955, with short stories including 'The Concrete Mixer' by Ray Bradbury, 'The Ears of Johnny Bear' by John Steinbeck.

This issue's Playmate of the month was model Bettie Page (b.1923). She is best known for her ground-breaking fetish and bondage modelling for Irving Klaw and Bunny Yeager. Interest in her revived in the 1980s and she inspired a number of models including Dita von Teese. A biographical film titled 'The Notorious Betty Page' was released in 2006, which should introduce her to a wider audience.

11in (28cm) high

£200-300 **NOR**

"Playboy", May 1955, with Marguerite Empey as Playmate of the month, and featuring pictorials showing Bunny Yeager taken by herself, Terry Shaw and Bettie Page.

Bunny Yeager was a pin-up model who went on to become a famous pin-up photographer herself, working with famous models including Bettie Page. She won 'Photographer of the Year' in 1959 and was nominated as one of the top 10 photographers in the US. She is still working today.

11in (28cm) high

£180-220 **NOR**

"He", March 1956, articles including 'Hollywood's Lush set, are Women masochists?'.

5.75in (14.5cm) high

£40-50 **NOR**

"Risk", March 1957, featuring 'Nights of Sin & Gin' and a Bunny Yaeger cover photo.

5.75in (14.5cm) high

£10-15 **NOR**

MAGAZINES

LIFE', Feb 21st 1964, the cover apparently showing Lee Harvey Oswald holding a copy of Communist paper 'Daily Worker' and the Mannlicher Carcano rifle later used to assassinate President John F. Kennedy.

This photograph is considered by some to be fake and Oswald himself claimed his head had been superimposed over someone else's body. Conspiracy theorists point to the fact that the shadow cast by the body is in the 11 o'clock position, while the shadow under the nose would result from the sun being overhead. Also that the rifle is too long in comparison for Oswald's height and that there appears to be a splice line under his lip. Despite these claims, photograph experts and the House Select Committee on Assassinations in the 1970s maintained the photograph is genuine.

13.75in (35cm) high

£15-25   NOR

"Newsweek", Nov 13 1967, with Jane Fonda as Barbarella on the cover.

10.75in (27.5cm) high

£15-20   NOR

"Photoplay", October 1958, with Elvis Presley and Jerry Lewis on the cover.

The appearance of big name stars like Elvis on the cover will increase the value of a vintage magazine.

10.75in (27.5cm) high

£50-70   NOR

"TV Guide", vol. 1, no. 26, Sept 1953, featuring George Reeves as Superman, in near mint condition.

TV Guides are a popular collecting area. This example is one of the most collectable.

8.25in (21cm) high

£300-400   NOR

"Vanity Fair", October 1927, cover art by 'Benito', original price 35 cents a copy.

It is the Art Deco style of the art work as well as the title that makes this magazine valuable.

12.75in (32.5cm) high

£40-70   DD

"Vogue", June 1946.

The uncluttered cover of this issue, with its minimal use of text and simple image are typical of earlier covers.

11.5in (29cm) high

£30-40   VM

"Vogue", September 15, 1965.

12.75in (32.5cm) high

£20-30   VM

"Vogue", June 1998, with Kate Moss cover.

Covers featuring supermodels and famous faces are more likely to retain, or increase their value.

11.25in (28.5cm) high

£30-40   VM

COLLECTORS' NOTES

■ Handmade marbles can be identified by the presence of a rough 'pontil' mark where the marble was removed from the glass rod during its manufacture. The earliest made marbles are traditionally the most desirable and valuable, but due to the scarcity of fine examples and rising prices, later machine-made and contemporary marbles from the 1920s onwards are eclipsing them. Notable manufacturers to look for include Peltier, Akro Agate and particularly The Christensen Agate Company.

■ The 1950s-60s saw Far Eastern and South American glass marbles take over. Of poorer quality and produced in large numbers, very few are sought-after today. From the 1990s, a market in contemporary glass marbles has developed and continues to grow

strongly. Other materials such as china, earthenware and stones usually date from the mid-late 19thC.

■ The type of marble affects value considerably. Look at the pattern and colour as well as the size. Minute differences can re-categorise a marble and affect value. Symmetry in design and unusual or bright colours are important considerations, along with 'eye-appeal', which can vary from collector to collector.

■ Condition is important, particularly on machine-made marbles. Chips, scuffs and play wear that affects the pattern will reduce value. Marbles in truly mint condition can sell for up to double the value of a used marble. Packaging can also have a value of its own, as so much was thrown away. Marbles shown here are in near-mint to mint condition.

A German handmade oxblood 'Opaque' marble.

Other colours such as black and white (often used for voting in a ballot box) are more common.

c1860-c1920   0.5in (1.5cm) diam

£30-40   **AB**

A German handmade end-of-day 'Submarine' marble.

Submarine marbles are rare, and have alternating multilayer sub-surface and surface panels over or under ribbons and on a transparent base. Those with mica chips are even rarer.

c1860-c1920   0.75in (2cm) diam

£40-50   **AB**

A German handmade 'Striped Transparent' marble.

c1860-c1920   1in (2.5cm) diam

£5-6   **AB**

A German handmade 'Slag' marble.

Here the pontil mark is clearly visible on the right-hand side. The number of and the appealing colours make this desirable.

c1860-c1920   0.5in (1.5cm) diam

£20-30   **AB**

A German handmade end-of-day 'Cloud' marble.

Cloud marbles have splodges of colour, that have not been stretched into bands, on a transparent base.

c1860-c1920   0.75in (2cm) diam

£60-80   **AB**

A German handmade green 'Mica' marble.

c1860-c1920 0.75in (2cm) diam

£10-14   **AB**

A handmade German 'Cane End' marble and a handmade 'Swirl Ribbon' core marble.

The marble on the right comes from the end of a glass cane, part of which is still attached. The marble on the left comes from within a cane as the swirl appears through the entire marble.

c1860-c1920   1in (2.5cm) diam

£15-25   **AB**

MARBLES

A Christensen Agate Company 'Peach Slag' machine-made marble.

Although slags were produced by all marble companies, this very scarce peach colour is unique to the Christensen Agate Company.

1927-29   0.5in (1.5cm) diam

£180-220   **AB**

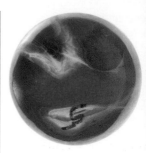

A Champion Agate Company 'New Old-Fashioned' machine-made marble.

This style of marble was produced from the company's founding in 1938 until the 1970s and was reintroduced in the 1980s.

c1984   0.5in (1.5cm) diam

£6-8   **AB**

A Christensen Agate Company 'American Agate' machine-made marble.

'American Agates' can be distinguished from 'Swirls' by the bright 'electric' colours, which range from red to orange, on an opaque or opalescent base.

1927-29   0.75in (2cm) diam

£60-80   **AB**

A 1930s-40s Peltier Glass Company 'Experimental Rainbo' machine-made marble.

Colours tend to be less vibrant on Peltier's 'Rainbos', with colours lying in the surface only.

1in (2.5cm) diam

£40-60   **AB**

An Akro Agate Company 'Carnelian' machine-made marble.

Carnelian and 'ade' marbles are fluorescent under UV lighting due to the presence of uranium in the base glass.

0.75in (2cm) diam

£12-18   **AB**

An Akro Agate Company 'Lemonade Oxblood' machine-made marble.

Lemonade refers to the translucent yellowy white colour. A combination with oxblood is one of the more common variations of a Lemonade swirl.

0.75in (2cm) diam

£60-80   **AB**

A Christensen Agate Company 'Swirl' machine-made marble.

0.75in (2cm) diam

£8-12   **AB**

A 1920s-30s Peltier Glass Company 'National Line Rainbo Ketchup & Mustard' machine-made marble.

Vibrant 'National Line Rainbo' marbles are among the most popular produced by Peltier, with collectors giving them names based around their colours.

0.75in (2cm) diam

£100-150   **AB**

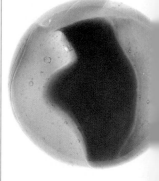

A Peltier Glass Company 'Clear Rainbo' machine-made marble.

0.5in (1.5cm) diam

£15-25   **AB**

A CLOSER LOOK AT A MARBLE

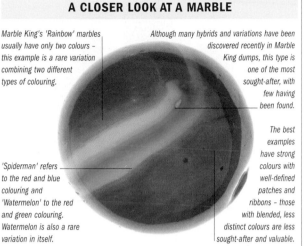

Marble King's 'Rainbow' marbles usually have only two colours – this example is a rare variation combining two different types of colouring.

Although many hybrids and variations have been discovered recently in Marble King dumps, this type is one of the most sought-after, with few having been found.

'Spiderman' refers to the red and blue colouring and 'Watermelon' to the red and green colouring. Watermelon is also a rare variation in itself.

The best examples have strong colours with well-defined patches and ribbons – those with blended, less distinct colours are less sought-after and valuable.

A 1950s Marble King Inc. 'Watermelon/Spiderman Hybrid Rainbow' machine-made marble.

0.5in (1.5cm) diam

£300-400 **AB**

A rare M.F. Christensen & Son Company 'Persian Turquoise Opaque' machine-made marble.

c1910   0.5in (1.5cm) diam

£50-70 **AB**

A Champion Agate Company 'Swirl' machine-made marble.

0.75in (2cm) diam

£10-15 **AB**

An American 'Metallic Swirl' machine-made marble, by an unknown West Virginia maker.

0.5in (1.5cm) diam

£7-10 **AB**

A Peltier Glass Company 'National Line Rainbo Blue Galaxy' marble.

This is an extremely rare and desirable marble with superb ribbons and colouring. The black and yellow ribbons contain aventurine (minute copper flakes), making them sparkle.

0.75in (2cm) diam

£750-850 **AB**

An American 'Aventurine Swirl' marble, by an unknown West Virginia maker.

0.5in (1.5cm) diam

£6-8 **AB**

An Akro Agate Company 'Silver Oxblood' marble.

0.5in (1.5cm) diam

£15-20 **AB**

A Vitro Agate Company 'Parrot' marble.

With four or more bright colours, 'Parrots' are the most popular Vitro Agate Company marbles. Look out for the colours forming a 'V' shape, which adds value. Large sizes such as this are typical.

1 in (2.5cm) diam

£40-50 **AB**

MARBLES

A Ravenswood Novelty
Company 'Swirl' marble.

*c1931-c1955   0.75in (2cm)
diam*

£10-15   **AB**

A Christensen Agate Company
'Chocolate Pistachio Swirl' marble.

0.75in (2cm) diam

£30-40   **AB**

A rare Akro Agate Company box of 'Swirl' marbles.

*This early card box with sliding window lid contains a metal insert,
which is extremely rare. The marbles within it are worth around £12,
the rest of the value being for the box in this condition.*

c1925

£50-80   **AB**

An Alley Agate Company 'Swirl'
marble.

0.75in (2cm) diam

£8-12   **AB**

A 'Pinwheel' hand-painted china
marble, with rough pink band and
a flower motif.

*China marbles, made from
porcelain typically have white
bodies. Look out for landscape
scenes, which are very rare. Brown
and lavender are scarce colours.*

0.75in (2cm) diam

£40-60   **AB**

A rare larger hand-painted
china marble, with bands and a
flower motif.

£220-280   **AB**

A large hand-painted china
marble, with blue flower motifs.

*The flowers are comparatively well-
painted and more numerous on this
marble, as well as being in better
condition, meaning a higher value.*

1.5in (4cm) diam

£300-500   **AB**

A 'Doughnut Bullseye'
hand-painted china
marble.

*Bullseye motifs are
slightly more commonly
found than flowers,
but the thick 'doughnut'
motifs indicate early
production.*

*1840s-1870s
0.75in (2cm) diam*

£30-40   **AB**

An extremely rare and large gutta percha marble.

*Most non-glass marbles are made from clays, china or stone. Gutta
percha, made from a tree gum, was developed in 1843 by Dr William
Montgomerie and is considered the first true plastic of importance.
Golf balls are commonly found in this material and are known as
'gutties'. Marbles are scarcely found and it is also the large size,
colour, condition and patterning that make this example so valuable.*

c1850   *1.5cm (4in) diam*

£200-300   **AB**

FIND OUT MORE...

www.marblecollecting.com

Marbles: Identification & Price Guide, *by Robert Block, published by
Schiffer Publishing, 2002.*

COLLECTORS' NOTES

■ Mechanical music devices take a number of forms; a musical box with a revolving metal cylinder, boxes containing a flat metal disc, the phonograph and the gramophone. The majority were produced from the mid-19thC to the early 20thC, and were clockwork-driven by winding springs.

■ Musical boxes are among the earliest, dating generally from the mid-19thC to the 1900s. They contain cylinders with protruding pins that strike metal teeth of different lengths on a metal comb to produce the sound. The decorative quality of the case, the complexity of the movement, the number of tunes, its size and maker affect value considerably.

■ Thomas Edison's 'phonograph' uses a needle, 'soundbox' and horn to make sounds picked up from fine grooves in a wax-like cylinder. The same system was used with flat discs by Emile Berliner, who developed the 'gramophone' in 1887. By the turn of the century, the gramophone had overtaken the phonograph in terms of popularity.

■ Again, the decorative appeal of the case, the size and the maker count towards general value. The model is also worth considering. The horn also adds to desirability and value, particularly if decorated and original. Beware of the many reproductions on the market, which tend to use tropical woods and have bright yellowy brass horns.

■ Children's gramophones, most often made from tinplate, can be sought-after. Look for charming scenes in bright colours and notable makers, such as Bing. In all instances, condition is important. Replaced or broken teeth on a comb reduce value. Beware of winding seized mechanisms as this can cause serious and expensive damage.

An American 'Graphophone Champion' horn gramophone, in an oak case with four turned corner columns, the funnel hand-painted with floral designs.

Horn 19.25in (48cm) diam

£400-600 ATK

An American Durable Toy and Novelty Corp. of New York toy projector, with 'Durotone' gramophone, the tin plate body printed to simulate wood, hand crank-operated but with electric projecting light.

£350-450 ATK

A German Bing child's clockwork gramophone, in a yellow 'crocodile skin' lithographed tin case formed as a suitcase.

c1925

£80-120 ATK

A late 1940s-to-early 1950s American Lindstrom Corporation, of Bridgeport Conn., printed metal child's electric gramophone.

13.5in (34cm) long

£60-80 NOR

An American Edison 'Model D' phonograph, with 'H' reproducer for four-minute cylinders, housed in an oak case with lid and horn.

1909-14

£300-400 ATK

An American Edison 'Model D' phonograph, with 'H' reproducer for four-minute cylinders, housed in an oak case with lid and horn.

1902

£350-450 ATK

An American Edison 'Gem Model A', with 'C' reproducer and black horn, contained in an oak case, with three cylinders.

The popular and affordable Gem was produced by Edison from 1899 to 1914 in various models.

A German Symphonion Musikwerke disc musical box, for 5.25in discs, with 76-teeth in duplex comb, with one disc.

c1900

£300-500 ATK

A German Polyphon Musikwerke 'Euphonion' disc music box, for 8.5in discs, 42 teeth in music comb, contained in a walnut case with lithographed picture in lid.

Symphonium or Polyphon cases with serpentine fronts, inlaid wood and original prints set into the lid are more valuable.

10.5in (26cm) wide

£400-600 ATK

A CLOSER LOOK AT A MUSICAL BOX

Symphonium are renowned for their large floor standing or wall-mounted disc musical boxes that produced complex and wonderful, resonant sounds.

The carved walnut case is typically highly ornate and is in excellent condition, with the original gilt transfer lettering on the glass door.

A clockwork mechanism revolves a large metal disc pierced with holes. The pierced and bent parts strike metal 'teeth' of different widths on 'combs' to produce the sound.

They were originally made to be played in stores or at events and are operated by putting a penny in the slot - the larger the discs and the more ornate the case, the rarer it is likely to be.

A German Symphonion Model No. 33 'Lyra' upright disc musical box, with 84 teeth on two music combs, complete with winding key and one disc.

c1900

34in (85cm) high

£2,000-3,000 ATK

A Swiss B.A. Brémond cased brass cylinder musical box, with eight melodies and hidden bells, the comb with 98 teeth, eight teeth to operate the bells, the front and lid inset with inlays.

25.25in (63cm) wide

£220-280 ATK

A Swiss Mermod Frères brass cylinder musical box, with four airs, steel comb with 102 teeth, with original tune sheet.

c1875 15.25in (38cm) wide

£400-600 ATK

An American musical photograph album, with brass clasp and celluloid cover depicting a U.S. warship, probably the U.S.S. Olympia, playing 'The Liberty Bell' and 'Manhattan Beach' marches, on felt-covered base with folding stand with 1895 patent date, tune card and instruction sheet.

c1900 12.5in (31.5cm) wide

£100-150 EG

A mechanical singing bird cage, probably French, both birds with heads and beaks moving as the sound plays, unmarked.

10.5in (26cm) high

£250-350 ATK

A rare German felt-covered pig music box, wind the tail and he plays music, with painted wooden trotters.

c1910 6.75in (17cm) long

£150-250 SOTT

A well-made copy of a Bowie knife, with white metal crosspiece, quillons pierced and engraved, white metal gripstrap and mother-of-pearl grips, in silver-mounted sheath with American eagle frog stud, good condition, well-aged for effect.

£700-900   **W&W**

A silver-mounted Skean dhu for the Argyll & Sutherland Highlanders, by Marshall & Aitken, with carved bog oak hilt and glass pommel, in silver-mounted sheath, blade stained, hallmark for Edinburgh. *1918*

£250-300   **W&W**

A well-made copy of an American presentation bowie knife, stamped "Broomhead & Thomas Celebrated American Hunting Knife", white metal crosspiece, with mother of pearl grips, in white metal sheath applied with silver escutcheon, aged for effect.

£350-450   **W&W**

A well-made copy of a hunting knife for the American market, stamped "Manson Sheffield", white metal crosspiece, hallmarked silver cutlery pommel, ivory grip with silver escutcheon, in white metal sheath, aged for effect.

£700-800   **W&W**

A early 20thC nielloed silver-mounted kindjal, with twin fullers etched with scrolls, silver hilt and sheath with silver wire filigree work and nielloed bands to front, ornamental handing band and button finial, plain silver back nielloed with Arabic cartouche an vegetable decoration, top of pommel slightly crushed with small crack.

£350-450   **W&W**

An 18thC Indian katar, the slender fullered blade with thickened point, the hilt gold damascened overall with flowers and foliage, five slender grip bars good condition, some age wear, some moderate rust to hilt, damascene worn.

£150-250   **W&W**

A rare Polish horseman's fighting axe, the mahogany shaft complete with pommel pierced for a thong, "XII" smiths' mark.

c1700   *28in (71cm) long*

£350-450   **MUR**

A rare 19thC heavy military camp axe, deeply stamped "H Macneal Gordon Highlanders", on its original wooden shaft, in good condition.

£280-320   **W&W**

A Malayan bronze swivel cannon lantaka, moulded muzzle and breech with tubular socket for an aiming stick, twin dolphin loops, raised sights and small crocodile in relief, on its bronze rowlock, cracked around breech.

£350-450   **W&W**

A Y-shaped Enfield combination tool, comprising nipple key, oil bottle, turnscrew and pricker, stamped "T & CG", good condition, worm missing.

£80-120   W&W

A nickel silver percussion cap dispenser, blued spring, cover plate stamped "M-Sykes, in good condition.

£120-180   W&W

An Argyll & Sutherland Highlanders officers gilt and silver-plated waist belt plate, together with a small brass dish with turnover rim, stamped with regimental badge; two rank crowns, good condition.

Plate 6in (15cm) diam

£80-120   W&W

A Continental brass-mounted powder horn, hinged charger, graduated nozzle, shaped retaining spring, brass border and four hanging rings, good condition, some age wear overall.

c1800

£100-150   W&W

A limited edition Ashmor 'A Member of Royal Air Force Ground Crew 'The Faithful Erk'' porcelain figure, of an RAF Battle of Britain Corporal from an edition of 500, very good condition.

£150-250   W&W

A limited edition Ashmor 'Royal Air Force Bomber Aircrew 1941-1944' porcelain figure, from an edition of 250, very good condition.

£200-300   W&W

A limited edition Ashmor 'A Woman Pilot of the Air Transport Auxiliary September 1939-1945' porcelain figure, from an edition of 250, very good condition.

£200-300   W&W

A limited edition Ashmor 'A Member of the Womens' Auxiliary Air Force 1939-45 'The WAAFS'' porcelain figure, from an edition of 350, very good condition.

£150-250   W&W

COLLECTORS' NOTES

- Examples of items documenting our planet's natural history and prehistory have been collected for centuries and reached an apex during the Georgian and Victorian periods. The 'wunderkammer' or 'cabinet of curiosities' often contained interesting fossils and minerals, sometimes collected on travels, that were seen as signs of education and distinction.

- Although the area is a highly specialised one, attracting keen collectors interested in geological phenomena and the exploration of prehistoric life, a market based around the decorative appeal of specimens is often highly active. As a result, values today are based as much around the visual impact and eye-appeal of specimens as other criteria.

- Collectors or those wishing to add an unusual piece to an eclectic interior should also consider the type of mineral or fossil, as some are rarer than others, and the size as large examples are nearly always worth more than smaller ones. Fakes are known, including those cast from moulds or comprised of many parts of fossils assembled on a rock 'matrix' base. Always buy from reputable dealers or auction houses.

- The preparation is also important, particularly with fossils. Fossils that have been sandblasted or acid-etched, to remove excess rock will usually have less detail or damaged specimens. Some are still covered with rock particles, which can obscure the fossil or interrupt its visual appearance. Smaller pieces are very affordable and can be found easily, making the market accessible, but larger and finer examples as seen here are much rarer and fetch high prices.

A Triassic period fossilised Kiechousaur specimen, from China, 230 million years ago.

This is a well-positioned specimen, and has a further specimen disarticulated next to it.

11.5in (29cm) high

£800-1,000   **BLO**

An American Eocene period fossilised fresh water ray, collected from Green River, Wyoming, 55 million years old.

22.5in (57cm) high

£1,000-1,500   **BLO**

An American Eocene period 'mass mortality' fossilised fishplate, containing Knightae and Diplomystus species, collected from Green River, Wyoming, 55 million years old.

27.5in (70cm) high

£1,000-1,500   **BLO**

Two Permian period fossilised mesosaurs in their own matrix, collected in Brazil, 260 million years old.

To find two complete specimens on the same matrix is rare.

28.25in (72cm) wide

£2,000-3,000   **BLO**

An Eocene period fossilised Harpactocacinus species crab on its own matrix, 55 million years old.

7in (18cm) wide

£250-350   **BLO**

A Carboniferous period fossilised Scaphocrinites species crinoid (sea lily), collected in Morocco, 360 million years old.

47.25in (120cm) wide

£5,000-6,000   **BLO**

A rare Triassic period fossilised Traumatacrinus species crinoid (sea lily), collected in Hunan, China, 230 million years old.

This large specimen features exquisite preparation work and shows very fine detail, hence its high value.

25.5in (65cm) high

£6,000-,7000   **BLO**

A CLOSER LOOK AT A FOSSIL

Mass mortality refers to the fact that a number of creatures died at the same time and are contained in the same 'matrix' rock closely together.

This example has been very well prepared and exhibits fine detailing. It has also not been abrasively cleaned or over-painted, and is in original condition.

It is very rare due to its extremely large size and the large number of densely packed and intact fossils it contains.

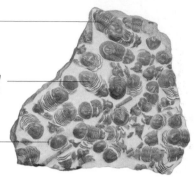

Trilobites are one of our planet's first complex life forms and became extinct before the dinosaurs - they attract many keen collectors today.

A rare Middle Ordovician period 'mass mortality' Xenasaphus species trilobite specimen, collected in Volhov, St Petersburg, Russia, 470 million years old.

Beware of fakes made up from a number of different species, or overly reconstructed trilobites, particularly from Morocco.

25.5in (65cm) wide

£9,000-10,000   BLO

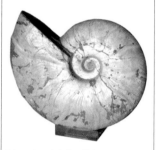

A Jurassic period silver iridescent Cleoniteras species ammonite, collected in Madagascar, 160 million years old.

7in (18cm) wide

£400-500   BLO

A Carboniferus period large polished Goniatite specimen on its own matrix, collected in Morocco, 360 million years old.

21.5in (55cm) high

£800-1,000   BLO

A fossilised Arietites species Ammonite, collected in Schoppenstedt, Braunschweig, Germany.

17in (43cm) high

£1,500-2,000   BLO

A Miocene period fossilised Charcharadon Megalodon species shark's tooth, collected in Atacama, Chile, 12 million years old.

4.75in (12cm) high

£550-650   BLO

An Oligocene period Oreodont skull, collected in Badlands, South Dakota, United States of America, 35 million years old.

This skull is very well prepared.

8in (20cm) wide

£550-650   BLO

A fossilised dinosaur's egg, mounted on a Chinese wooden stand, collected in outer Mongolia, 60-70 million years old.

6in (15cm) high

£220-280   OG

A smokey quartz cluster, from Madagascar.

13.5in (34cm) high

£350-450   BLO

An interesting quartz point specimen, with mica and gem-grade aquamarine, from Pakistan.

This quartz crystal displays a beautiful Tourmaline crystal inclusion. This is a very rare combination.

7.5in (19cm) high

£450-550   BLO

A pair of Bolivian amethysts.

These are far less common than their Brazilian counterparts and of a far better quality in terms of size, colour and structure.

Largest 6.75in (17cm) high

£180-220   BLO

An amethyst 'cathedral', from Brazil.

Cathedral is the term used to describe these tall, arching geodes. The value of this lies in its large size, shape and the fact that it is not broken.

27.25in (69cm) high

£1,800-2,200   BLO

A polished orbicular jasper freeform, Madagascar.

The unusual colouring include pinks, yellows and greens adds to the value of this piece.

6.75in (17cm) high

£350-450   BLO

A fine polished amber specimen, from Chiapas, Mexico.

2.25in (6cm) long

£150-250   BLO

A large malachite freeform, from the Democratic Republic of Congo.

14.25in (36cm) high

£1,700-2,000   BLO

A nickle-iron meteorite, from Campo Del Cielo, Argentina.

Meteorites are usually composed of iron as stone usually breaks up upon entry. Composition, size, weight and form affect value.

3.25in (8cm) wide

£500-600   BLO

A Jurassic period septarian concretion mudstone, one face polished and cut with a flat base, from Madagascar. (160 million years ago).

Septarian concretions or nodules are hard masses of sedimentary rock containing angular cavities that typically contain crystals, usually Calcite. They are typically broken open to reveal their contents, and are often polished flat.

10.75in (27cm) high

£200-300   BLO

COLLECTORS' NOTES

■ Sought-after brands including Waterman, Parker, Montblanc and Dunhill Namiki still lead the market, particularly large examples, and those with precious metal overlays. The best of Dunhill's 1930s maki-e lacquer models occupy the very high end of the market, but prices have dropped recently so now is a good time to buy.

■ In the past, collectors tended to concentrate on pens produced in their own country. As the market matures and prices rise, collectors are looking further afield and formerly less appreciated brands are becoming

sought-after. For example, England's brightly coloured and highly useable Conway Stewarts are now proving popular on both sides of the Atlantic.

■ As many collectors use their pens, condition and completeness is very important. Replaceable parts such as nibs and clips should be original, and cracked or damaged examples should be avoided.

■ As modern limited editions are often bought for investment, many are kept in pristine condition – values for used examples are therefore unlikely to rise.

An American Parker model 25 eyedropper-filling pen, smooth black hard rubber with Parker Fountain Pen 5 nib with triangular vent hole, polished and one nib tine lacks iridium, but in very good condition.
c1905

£80-120 **BLO**

An American Parker model 16 eyedropper-filling pen, the gold-filled filigree overlay signed on the barrel overlay, with Parker Lucky Curve 'lazy S' nib, overlay slipped, in fair to good condition.
c1905-15

£180-220 **BLO**

A rare American Parker model 16 Jack-Knife Safety baby eyedropper-filling pen, with gold-filled filigree over smooth black hard rubber, 'turban cap' and Parker Lucky Curve Pen 3 keyhole nib, in very good condition.

The name 'turban cap' comes from the shape of the top of the cap, which is found on some early Parker pens.
1912-16

£350-450 **BLO**

A Canadian Parker Lucky Curve Duofold Special button-filling pen, jade green Permanite with Duofold 'P' medium nib, even but not unattractive darkening, otherwise in very good condition.

The Parker Duofold came in a wide range of colours and a number of sizes. Early examples, larger sizes and rare colours such as 'Mandarin yellow' are the most sought-after.
1927

£80-120 **BLO**

A Canadian Parker oversize Vacumatic filling pen, emerald pearl hooped celluloid with Parker Vacumatic two-color arrow medium nib, in very good condition, but barrel threads lengthened.

Much like the earlier Duofold, the Vacumatic was made in a wide range of variations, which differ greatly in value. This oversized model is popular with collectors, while smaller models are generally worth under £40.
1935

£150-200 **BLO**

A 1930s Canadian Parker Premiere button-filling pen, marbled blue and black, Canadian 14K medium nib, in very good to excellent condition.

£70-90 **BLO**

An English Parker Duofold Senior button-filling pen, light and dark burgundy pearl marble celluloid, with Parker Duofold 'N' medium nib, slight fading, otherwise in very good condition.
c1945

£100-150 **BLO**

A new-old-stock American Parker Blue-Diamond Major Vacumatic filling pen, silver pearl celluloid with gold Parker Arrow USA 6 nib, in mint condition, with two stickers, nib possibly inked.
1946

£70-90 **BLO**

An American Parker 51 Blue-Diamond Vacumatic-filling pen, Buckskin with gold-filled Custom cap, double jewels and medium nib, otherwise generally very good condition.

This is the earlier version of the 51 with a Vacumatic filling system. This is indicated by the screw-off section at the end of the barrel which covers the filling plunger. It was replaced by the Aerometric system in 1948.

1945

£200-300 BLO

A new-old-stock 1950s American Parker 51 Custom pen, burgundy Aerometric-filler, with gold-filled Insignia design cap and fine nib, in mint condition.

Probably Parker's best known and most popular pen, this version of the 51 was produced in vast numbers from 1948 until 1968. The majority of surviving examples were made in the 1950s and '60s and, in standard colours and well-loved condition, are worth under £30.

£80-120 BLO

A new-old-stock mid/late-1960s American Parker 61 cartridge-filling pen, turquoise with chrome trim, Lustaloy cap and medium nib, in mint condition with 61 cartridge barrel chalk marks, and 61 convertible $12.50 swinger tag with nib grade, rare in this condition.

£70-100 BLO

A English Parker 61 'Cumulus' pen set, gold-plated 'Cloud' design (plain clouds on heavy wavy-line background) with medium nib, and matching push-cap ballpoint, in Parker hard duo box, in near mint condition, pen excellent.

1976-80

£180-220 BLO

A late 1960s American Parker 75 vermeil 'Crosshatch Grid' pattern pen, marked "Sterling & 14K GF" and "Made in U.S.A.", with flat tassies, section ring with '0' reference and Parker 14K Point USA code 69 fine stub nib, in excellent condition.

£100-150 BLO

A French Parker 75 Laqué duo pen set, Jasper Red Quartz lacquer with Parker .585 France fine nib, matching push-cap ballpoint, in mint condition, with tag on pen.

1979

£120-180 BLO

An American Parker Falcon 50 stainless steel pen, brushed steel with medium nib, in mint condition with swinger tag.

c1980

£40-50 BLO

A CLOSER LOOK AT A PROTOTYPE PARKER PEN

This brass prototype was produced by Devlin to show the finish and final design of the pen, which was produced in 18ct gold.

It is believed that Parker intended an edition limited to only 1,000 pieces but as only one gold example has been seen, it is probable that the line never went into full production.

Although the shape of the pen was based on the existing budget 'Arrow' range, the textured finish is the typical of the work of contemporary goldsmith Stuart Devlin.

Devlin was born in Australia in 1931 and awarded a scholarship to the Royal College of Art, London in 1958. He was responsible for designing the new Australian decimal coinage in 1963.

A prototype Parker 'Limited Prestige Range' pen, designed and made by Stuart Devlin, the brass body with textured, sculptured finish, guide for positioning of hallmarks, and Parker Arrow medium nib, in mint condition.

1982

5in (13cm) long

£200-300 BLO

An extremely rare American Waterman's 'second model' No. 5 straight-holder eyedropper filling pen, smooth black hard rubber with two line imprint with "Feb 12" and "Nov 4 1884" patent dates, three-fissure feed and Waterman's Ideal New York 5 nib with arrow-head vent and second breather hole, in excellent/near mint condition.

This is an extremely rare large-size early Waterman in superb condition with an unusual nib.

1884-89

£550-650 BLO

A rare American Waterman's 222 'Barleycorn with Nameplate' pattern eyedropper-filling pen, with white-metal half-overlay with nameplate space, taper cap, three fissure feed, and (later) Waterman's 2 nib, in excellent condition with a crisp overlay, boxed.

The Barleycorn pattern is a surprisingly difficult overlay to find on a Waterman's pen, possibly because the company chose to promote more flamboyant styles.

1899

£350-450 BLO

A scarce American Waterman's 18 eyedropper-filling pen, chased black hard rubber with Waterman's 8 nib, some mild oxidation.

Despite this small image, the model 18 was the largest standard production Waterman at the time.

1900-07

£200-300 BLO

An American Waterman's 414 'Filigree' pattern eyedropper-filling pen, three-leaf filigree overlay signed "Sterling" on the barrel, with Clip-Cap and Waterman's 4 nib, in Waterman's hard eyedropper box, in very good condition.

1908-15

£200-250 BLO

A new-old-stock American Waterman's 45 safety filling pen, chased black hard rubber with Waterman's 5 fine nib, possibly with pre-owned nib.

Although early, standard plain black pens, such as this, are not generally valuable, the fact it is in unused condition makes it desirable.

c1910

£70-100 BLO

An American Waterman's 5-size 'Sheraton' pattern gold-filled rotary pencil, with black hard rubber nozzle, ball of clip brassed.

These pencils are hard to find in this size

c1917

£50-70 BLO

An American Waterman's 05521/2 L.E.C. 'Pansy Panel' pattern lever-filling pen, gold-filled, fully covered overlay, with 'Clip-Cap' and Waterman's medium flexible 2 nib, light wear on post.

1925-27

£100-150 BLO

A rare large-size American Waterman's 456 'Basketweave' pattern lever-filling pen, marked "Sterling" on cap, barrel and clip, with Waterman's 6 medium nib, some oxidation and wear from use on hard rubber, otherwise in very good condition.

Large size pens are generally harder to find and more valuable. It is likely that less were made as the large size was not as comfortable to use for most people and they would have been more expensive to buy at the time.

1924-27

£1,000-1,500 BLO

An American Waterman's 4521/2 L.E.C. 'Basketweave' pattern lever-filling pen, marked "Sterling" on clip, cap, barrel, and lever, with Waterman's Reg US 2 nib, in very good condition.

1928-30

£120-180 BLO

An American Waterman's 4521/2 LEC 'Hand-Engraved Vine' pattern lever-filling pen, marked "Sterling" with Waterman's 2 nib, some wear from use, generally in very good/excellent condition.

L.E.C stands for Lower End Covered and indicates a fully overlaid pen.

1928-30

£180-220 BLO

A 1920s American Waterman's 56 Cardinal lever-filling pen and pencil, Cardinal red hard rubber with Clip-Cap and Waterman's 6 medium nib, with similar rotary pencil, boxed, both in excellent condition, clips differ slightly.

£300-400   **BLO**

An extremely rare American Waterman's 51V Ripple lever-filling pen, red and black hard rubber with Waterman's Ideal Reg US 1 medium-broad nib, minor oxidation, otherwise in excellent condition.

1928-30

£70-100   **BLO**

A Canadian Waterman's 92 'Silver Lizard' lever-filling pen, silver pearl 'lizardskin' celluloid with Waterman's Canada 2 oblique medium nib, in excellent condition.

1931-34

£200-300   **BLO**

A Canadian Waterman's Lady Patricia lever-filling pen, Nacre (pearl and black) celluloid with Waterman's 2 'ballpoint' nib, in excellent condition, a rare colour to find in the Lady Patricia.

A rigid 'ballpoint' nib has a smooth, round ball of iridium on the tip of the nib, which would have made it suitable for making carbon copies.

1932-33

£70-100   **BLO**

A Canadian Waterman's 94 'Steel Quartz' (red-flecked grey marble) lever-filling pen, with chrome trim and Waterman's 4 medium nib, engraved name and light surface marks, generally in good/very good condition.

1934-39

£40-60   **BLO**

A Canadian Waterman's 3V lever-filling pen, burgundy pearl marble celluloid with Waterman's Canada 2 broad nib, with box and papers, in near mint condition, a great example.

1935-38

£100-150   **BLO**

A Canadian Waterman's 3 lever-filling pen, red-flecked dark blue-grey pearl marble celluloid, with Waterman's Ideal 2 medium-stub nib, in excellent condition.

1935-39

£40-60   **BLO**

An American Waterman's Hundred Year lever-filling pen, smooth red transparent lever-filler with triple cap band, with medium Hundred Year Pen nib, cap lip shortened.

The thin lip of the cap on this model is often cracked or has been shortened, as in this example. An undamaged example would command a premium.

c1941

£70-100   **BLO**

A 1970s French Waterman CF silver 'Barleycorn' pattern cartridge-filling pen and ballpoint, marked "Argent Massif" and with French control marks, 18ct fine nib, with box, leaflet and tags and card sleeve, in inked mint to mint condition.

Often mistakenly thought of as Waterman's first cartridge-filling (CF) pen, it was actually preceded by a 1936 model that used refillable glass cartridges and ink pellets that were mixed with water.

An American Waterman's oversize Emblem lever-filling pen, black with replaced standard-size Emblem medium nib.

c1942

£70-90   **BLO**

£80-120   **BLO**

A rare American A.A. Waterman 291M-3+ eyedropper filling pen, chased black hard rubber with "Not Connected With..." barrel imprint, A.A. 14k No.2 medium flexible nib, in very good condition.

Arthur A. Waterman, unrelated to Lewis Edson Waterman, started his pen company prior to 1900. In 1907, L.E. Waterman sued the company for trademark infringement and won, resulting in all further A.A. Waterman pens being imprinted with "Not Connected with the L. E. Waterman Company".

c1915

£25-35 BLO

A rare American Chilton 77S pneumatic-filling pen, pearl and black celluloid with Greek-key design cap band and Chilton Pen 14K nib, with only minor yellowing to the celluloid.

c1930

£100-120 BLO

An American Conklin 5 NL crescent-filling pen, wave-chased black hard rubber with Conklin 4 Toledo nib, in very good condition.

1910-18

£50-80 BLO

An American Conklin 5000-word Nozac piston-filling pen and pencil set, facetted green herringbone Pyrolin, with word gauge and Conklin Toledo medium nib, with matching pencil, pen professionally overhauled, pencil cap slips and needs attention.

1934-38

£200-300 BLO

An American Dunn 8-size Camel pump-filling pen, smooth black hard rubber, red Casein pump handle, plain clip, Dunn Pen Camel medium-fine nib, in very good condition, a rare and large pen.

c1921-24

£180-220 BLO

A 1920s Canadian Eclipse 'Mandarin Yellow' flat top, oversize Lucky Curve Senior-style pen in yellow celluloid with green ends and Warranted 14K medium nib, in very good to excellent condition.

This is very similar to Parker's Lucky Curve Duofold Senior, which was much copied at the time. A Mandarin yellow Parker Duofold, one of the rarest colours in that range, in a similar size and condition could be worth up to £600.

£100-150 BLO

A late 1920s American John Holland 4-size Jewel lever-filling pen, pearl and black celluloid lever-filling pen, with 'Bell' clip and Jewel John Holland 'Cin O' nib, lacks iridium, but rare and in decent condition.

'Pearl and black' marbled plastic was used by a number of pen manufacturers. The 'pearl' sections often become discoloured to a muddy brown/green, which reduces the value, but this example has a nice, clean colour.

£100-150 BLO

A late 1920s American Le Boeuf Unbreakable 65 lever-filling pen, grey-white swirl celluloid with Le Boeuf Springfield Mass 6 fine nib, in excellent condition.

Although a relatively small company, in existence for little more than 10 years, Le Boeuf pens are highly sought-after. Frank Le Boeuf developed a new manufacturing process in 1918, which meant pens could be produced in coloured and patterned plastics found on no other pens.

£250-350 BLO

An American Wahl-Eversharp Coronet lever-filling pen set, the lined gold-filled body with jet Pyralin inlay, Eversharp Manifold fine nib with ink shut-off valve, matching repeater pencil, in unmarked hard duo presentation box, in very good condition, light ring of wear on pen from cap.

1936-38

£400-500 BLO

A very rare English Burnham rolled gold button-filler, marked rolled gold around the clip screw, with rectangular chequer and plain line design and Burnham nib, ding in blind cap, otherwise in excellent condition.

Metal-covered Burhams are rare, they are also more commonly found as lever-fillers.

c1935

£180-220   BLO

A rare 1920s English Conway Stewart Dinkie No. 540, striated light blue and turquoise ('toothpaste') Casein with Conway Stewart medium nib, discolouration by cap band and barrel threads, in excellent condition.

Small ringtop pens, such as this, were designed for ladies to wear on a ribbon around their necks or on a chatelaine. They are usually more affordable than larger examples making them ideal for collecting on a budget.

£60-80   BLO

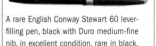

A rare English Conway Stewart 60 lever-filling pen, black with Duro medium-fine nib, in excellent condition, rare in black.

1958-63

£50-70   BLO

A 1950s English Conway Stewart 58 'Cracked Ice' lever-filling set, silver pearl-veined black marble celluloid with Duro Conway Stewart medium nib, and The Conway No 33 pencil, in Conway Stewart duo-box, mild brassing on pen clip, otherwise in excellent condition.

The scarce 'Cracked Ice' finish, named by collectors, is one of the most popular with Conway Stewart enthusiasts.

A rare 1920s Scottish De La Rue rolled gold Onoto, fully covered fine barley design, with metal section and De La Rue 3 medium nib, professionally restored overlay on cap crown and plunger cover, otherwise in very good condition.

£60-80   BLO

£250-350   BLO

A Scottish De La Rue Onoto [5235-93] plunger-filling pen, light and dark burgundy pearl marble celluloid, with De La Rue Onoto 5 two colour medium nib, in very good condition.

c1948

£60-80   BLO

An early 1930s English Esterbrook 'Relief' No 22-L midsize lever-filling pen, light and dark blue pearl marble celluloid with red band and Esterbrook Relief 14ct 2 medium-oblique nib, in very good condition.

£50-80   BLO

A 1920s English Mabie, Todd & Co 'Blackbird' safety filling pen, chased black hard rubber with later Blackbird nib, "made by the 'Swan' Pen People", in very good condition, a few teeth marks.

£70-100   BLO

A rare 1920s English Mabie, Todd & Co Swan Eternal 444B/61 lever-filling pen, mottled red and black hard rubber with Swan Eternal 4 medium nib, in very good condition.

£150-200   BLO

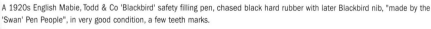

An English Mabie, Todd & Co. Blackbird Self-Filler BB2/46 lever-filling pen, 'Oriental Blue' (blue and light blue with bronze marble), Blackbird 14 ct medium nib, in excellent condition.

1934-37

£180-220   BLO

A German Montblanc 1-M safety filling pen, smooth black hard rubber with Simplo 1 fine nib, in excellent condition.

Montblanc were known as the Simplo Filler Company from their founding in 1908 until after WWII when the brand name Montblanc was phased in.

1920-25

£200-250   **BLO**

A German Montblanc L25 Meisterstück push-knob filling pen, luxury pearl and black marble celluloid, with later Montblanc 14ct broad-oblique nib, in mint condition.

Coloured Montblanc pens are very rare. This luxury example is in mint condition and also has a scarce broad oblique nib making it more desirable.

1931-34

£600-800   **BLO**

A German Montblanc 224 'PL' push-knob filling pen, platinum pearl striated celluloid with Montblanc 4 nib, in slightly later Montblanc kidney-shaped card box, scratch on blind cap and mild oxidation, otherwise in near mint condition.

1935-37

£550-650   **BLO**

A Danish Montblanc 2 button-filling pen, coral red with 14ct M fine nib, in very good condition, slight wear and brassing.

1937-46

£120-180   **BLO**

A German Montblanc 3341/2 M piston-filling pen, black with broad steel 41/2 Montblanc nib, the cap with Stöffhaus cap imprint, in excellent condition.

Stöffhaus was a German retailer.

1937-38

£150-200   **BLO**

A CLOSER LOOK AT A MONTBLANC PEN

It is in near mint condition. As pens are intended for use, dings and dents are common on metal overlaid pens.

Initially, Montblanc did not make their own metal overlays so they commissioned German silversmith Sarastro to produce them. They can be identified by the 'S' mark.

Metal overlaid Montblancs are exceedingly rare.

Overlays made or commissioned by the manufacturer are the most desirable, followed by contemporary overlays produced for importers or individuals. Modern overlays are also added to old pens, some with the intention to deceive.

A very rare German Montblanc 14ct gold octagonal 132 piston-filling pen, with eight-sided engine-turned and polished overlay, two-colour 4810 P nib, in black leather Stöffhaas case with mother-of-pearl button, in near mint condition, one pinhead ding; signed "S 585 (Sarastro)".

c1938

£1,500-2,000   **BLO**

A rare Danish Montblanc 25 push-knob filling pen, green marble celluloid, 12-sided with 4810 medium-fine nib, in very good condition with light wear, although clip screw possibly glued on.

Faceted Montblancs are rare.

1939-43

£350-450   **BLO**

A German Montblanc 242-B 'PL' piston-filling pen, platinum pearl striated celluloid with Montblanc broad nib, in near mint condition.

1950-54

£200-250   **BLO**

A CLOSER LOOK AT A NAMIKI PEN

Maki-e lacquer decorated pens are some of the most valuable and desirable every produced. Those made by Namiki are particularly finely made.

Value of maki-e pens depends on size, condition, subject matter and the quality, type and level of lacquer decoration.

The quality of the hand-painted decoration is exceptional. It would have taken many months of painstaking work to complete.

Tsuba are an unusual subject matter and adds greatly to the value. Flora, fish and birds are much more typical.

A mid-1920s Japanese Namiki maki-e lacquer lever-filling pen, medium-large 6-size, the unusual red raden ground inlaid with iridescent aogai (mother-of-pearl) shell and decorated with sakura (plum) blossom, five different tsuba (sword guards) in high relief using a variety of maki-e and lacquer techniques, a red seal kao hidden amongst the decoration of the fifth, with Namiki 6 14K nib, in superb condition.

£10,000-15,000 **BLO**

A late 1920s Japanese Namiki maki-e lacquer ringtop lever-filling pen, decorated with a temple amongst trees in a mountain landscape and inlaid with aogai, with (replaced) warranted nib, cap ring and posting wear.

£400-500 **BLO**

A 1930s Japanese Platinum maki-e lacquer balance lever-filling pen, decorated in gold and red with uguisu (nightingale) in a flowering plum tree, with silver clip and similar lever, with 14K Highclass nib, in very good/excellent condition.

£450-550 **BLO**

A fine 1950s Japanese Pilot maki-e R-type piston-filling pen, decorated with a dragon emerging through storm-clouds and lightning, in gold, silver and red iroe-hiramaki-e and togidashi-maki-e; the dragon writhing as it moves through the rolling storm clouds, clutching the tama (sacred pearl) whilst ascending from the sea to the heavens, with gold-filled clip and Pilot 14K 4 fine nib, signed Keizo above a red seal kao, with Kokko-kai to the right of the signature, in near mint condition.

Dragons featured on a small series of 1950s Pilot pens made by a group of freelance maki-e masters. It is a bold and evocative subject matter, its sinuous shape ideally suited to the medium.

£3,000-4,000 **BLO**

A Japanese Pilot maki-e deluxe cartridge/convertor-filling pen, decorated with gold bamboo stems pruned to encourage new growth and with purple-bronze leaves in togidashi-hiramaki-e and nashiji and mura nashiji background, signed Ei with red seal kao and kokko-kai, with 14K 585 Pilot M 190 nib, in near mint/mint condition.

Bamboo is a common decorative theme on maki-e and is symbolic of fidelity, constancy, and long life in Japanese culture.

1978-1980s

£500-800 **BLO**

A CLOSER LOOK AT A LIMITED EDITION FOUNTAIN PEN

The Lorenzo de Medici was the first from Montblanc's limited edition 'Patrons of the Arts series and is the most sought-after.

The design and decoration is based on a c1920 Montblanc safety-filling fountain pen.

It is part of the annual 'Patron of Art' series, all of which are limted to 4,810 pieces.

This example is still sealed in the factory's plastic sleeve and retains all of its paperwork, boxes and card outers. Any other state would reduce the value considerably.

A German limited edtion Montblanc 'Lorenzo de Medici' piston-filling pen, from an edition of 4,810, with hand-engraved silver octagonal overlay, two-colour 4810 18K M nib, in box with paperwork, pen sealed mint; some wear to box card outers. *1992*

£3,500-4,000 — BLO

A German limited edition Montblanc 'Hemingway' ballpoint, from an edition of 30,000, orange-red and brown, in mint condition, with box, papers, fountain pen outer box.

The first release from Montblanc's Writers edition, the fountain pen and ballpoint were produced in relatively large numbers compared to the Patron of Art edition.

1992

£350-450 — BLO

A German limited edition Montblanc 'Oscar Wilde' 0.9mm propelling pencil, from an edition of 12,000, pearl and black resin with vermeil clip marked "925", with box and papers, in near mint condition.

Limited edition pencils and ballpoints are a more affordable way to collect modern editions and are usually made in smaller numbers.

1994

£120-180 — BLO

A German limited edition Montblanc 'F.M. Dostoevsky' piston-filling pen, from an edition of 17,000, decorated black resin barrel, polished black cap with decorated trim and blue cabochon stone set in clip, dated and decorated 4810 M nib, in box with paperwork, in 'inked mint' condition.

1997

£300-400 — BLO

A German limited edition Montblanc 'F. Scott Fitzgerald' piston-filling pen, from an edition of 18,500, white pearl barrel with contrasting silver-banded black cap and barrel end, silver 'Art Deco' clip, dated two-colour 4810 M nib, in box with paperwork, in 'inked mint' condition.

2002

£280-320 — BLO

A German limited edition Montblanc 'Jules Verne' piston-filling pen, from an edition of 18,500, blue guilloché lacquer cap and barrel, decorated 4810 M nib, in box with leaflet, no outer box or slipcase, in mint condition.

2003

£280-320 — BLO

A German limited edition Pelikan 'Spirit of Gaudi' piston-filling pen, from an edition of 1,000, black resin with Gaudi-inspired silver overlay, 18C-750 white gold M nib, in box with paperwork, in mint condition.

2002

£450-550 — BLO

A German limited edition Pelikan 'Xuan Wu' Asia 851/888, "Ag 925" mark, 18ct M nib, in box with paperwork, in mint condition.

2001

£600-700 — BLO

A rare American limited edition Bexley Deluxe II model 2006 cartridge/convertor filling pen, from an edition of 250, Mandarin Yellow acrylic with faux button-filler, marked "Bexley" on wide cap band and "10k" on cap band and clip, numbered decal on blind cap, two-colour Bexley 14k medium nib, in near mint condition.

This is inspired by Parker's iconic Lucky Curve Duofold, produced in the 1920s and '30s.

c2000

£120-180 BLO

An English limited edition Conway Stewart 'Churchill' lever-filling pen, from an edition of 500, red and black ripple hard rubber with 18ct gold band, Conway Stewart 18ct Gold medium nib, in mint condition with box, cigar, ink bottle, papers and card outer.

2000

£200-300 BLO

A French limited edition Waterman Edson Signé Boucheron cartridge/convertor-filling pen, from an edition of 3,741, sapphire blue Edson with 18ct-gold latticed overlay by Boucheron, 18k 750 M nib, in presentation box with paperwork, in near mint condition.

c1996

£500-800 BLO

An Italian limited edition Ancora 'Cielo' vacumatic-style filler demonstrator pen, from an edition of 204, transparent sky blue acrylic, with vermeil trim and 18ct 1919 fine nib, in mint condition with box and papers.

1998

£300-400 BLO

An Italian numbered edition Montegrappa 'Oriental Zodiac - The Dragon' pen set, with silver barrel overlay of a dragon, two-colour medium nib and matching screw-cap rollerball, each with cloth, tray, papers, casket, card outer box and sleeves, in mint condition.

While not from a limited edition, pens are individually numbered.

1998

£650-750 BLO

An Italian limited edition OMAS 'Galileo Galilei' piston-filling pen, from an edition of 4,692, pearl-veined black marble acrylic, with broad two-colour arrow nib, in near mint condition with silver-grey box, circular booklet and card outer.

1993

£220-280 BLO

An Italian limited edition Visconti 'Uffizi' pen, from an edition of 500, silver filigree over teal granite celluloid, with Visconti 18K white gold nib, box and outer, in 'inked mint' condition.

1993

£280-320 BLO

An Italian limited edition Visconti 'D'Essai Platinum' pen, from an edition of 100, silver-pearl hooped laminated celluloid, with Visconti 18k .750 medium nib, very rare, inked, with certificate.

The four pens in the D'Essai series were Visconti's first limited editions and were made from a small cache of 1940s vintage celluloid.

1994

£180-220 BLO

A Japanese limited edition Namiki Emperor Collection 'Steppes Flowers' pen, signed Kyusai, decorated in togidashi maki-e with two quails in front of flowers and tall grasses and signed Kyusai and Kokko Kai with red seal kao and 18 Karat Namiki 50 fine nib, in leather pouch, with box, card cover and papers, inked.

c2000

£1,500-2,000 BLO

A Japanese Namiki 'The Panda' pen, from an edition of 700, maki-e lacquer, signed Kyusai with red seal kao and Kokokai broad 18k gold nib, in mint condition with papers and casket.

£500-600 BLO

An 1870s American ornate cast iron patent inkstand with thermometer, the square base decorated with a palmette frieze and similar feet, the shaped front with Sphinx figurine, cast patented "July 4 1876" on the base, with fitted glass inkwell.

£150-200   **BLO**

A CLOSER LOOK AT AN INKWELL

The 'Isobath' was an expensive inkwell made by Doulton in Lambeth for the notable printing company, and later fountain pen maker, De La Rue.

The hemisphere and lid are often lost or broken, but here they are complete and intact. There are only a couple of small chips to the frilled edge.

The main body contains the ink and a hard rubber, swinging hemisphere which forces the ink into the small side receptacle to keep it at a constant full level.

They are found in many different decorative designs and come with or without trays. This example has the more desirable frilled tray and fine decoration all over the body.

A very rare Doulton stoneware 'Chiné-ware' De La Rue Isobath inkwell, with decorators' marks including Fanny Sayers, Rosetta Hazeldine and Edith Herapath or E.Hibberd.

1888-1890   *6.25in (16cm) high*

£180-220   **BLO**

A rare English Perry & Co. patent Perryian gravitating inkstand, the shaped brass holder with an octagonal glass inkwell on swivel-mounts, on scallop-shaped base with sprung grip and penrest.

c1850   *2.25in (5.5cm) high*

£80-120   **BLO**

An Elkington Art Manufacturers Association inkwell, the central glass inkwell set in a copper surround modelled as a naturalistic tree-trunk, with three shield-shaped panels of leaves and berries and three different bearded faces with scroll support.

c1897

£50-80   **BLO**

A rare Morton's patent glass inkwell, with nickel-plated iris diaphragm, stamped "Morton's Patent" on the rotating cover.

1870s-1900   *2.25in (6cm) wide*

£80-120   **BLO**

A German patent automatic 'Constant Level' inkwell, moulded glass with screw-in bulb-shaped reservoir and shaped well, with metal cover.

This design was protected under patent no. 4699, which was granted to Heinrich Gerhardt of Nuremberg on 17th August 1878.

1878-91   *3.75in (9.5cm) high*

£100-150   **BLO**

A mid-19thC William Mitchell ceramic 'Syphon' inkwell, the cylindrical white glazed stoneware well with spout and integral plinth base, with black stencilled "William Mitchell/London" within an ellipse on the base, and two incised characters or numerals, in very good condition.

£40-60   **BLO**

A novelty elephant inkwell, probably French, dark patinated spelter modelled as a lively elephant, hinged cover on the back over a glass liner, in very good condition, although probably originally gilded.

1860s-70s   *3in (7.5cm) high*

£70-100   **BLO**

A CLOSER LOOK AT A DESK BASE

The design is not applied with paint, but by the time-consuming maki-e lacquer process, which would have taken weeks to complete. Compare it to the pen on p345.

Kosan is a comparatively unknown artist, but the design of a bird eating fruit in a basket is charming. It also appears in a 1931 Dunhill advertisement, on a Unique pocket lighter.

It was produced under the partnership of luxury goods retailer Dunhill and Japanese company Namiki, who specialised in maki-e lacquerwork. The partnership began in 1926 and lasted into the 1930s.

This example combines two different types of lacquerwork – maki-e, where the pigment is sprinkled onto the lacquer before it dries and hardens, and the scarcer urushi, where the coloured lacquer is applied with a brush.

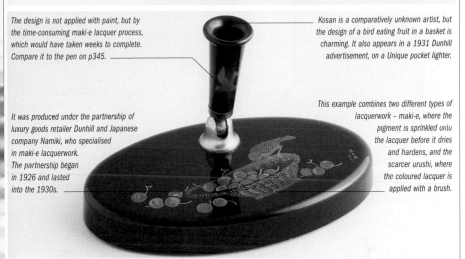

A 1930s Dunhill Namiki maki-e and urushi lacquer desk base, signed by Kosan and executed in takamaki-e and urushi on a roiro-nuri background.

6in (15cm) high

£300-400　　　　　　　　　　　　　　　　　　　　　　　**PC**

An American Parker Duofold bronzed metal desk set, with tulip and jade Permanite Duofold Junior pen with taper and additional cap.

c1930

£70-100　　　　　　　**BLO**

An unusual 1950s American Parker 51 Magnetix gold anodised aluminium desk set, with four pen rests, 'Magic Wand' tulip and black 51 Aerometric desk pen.

£80-120　　　　　　　**BLO**

A 1930s American Wahl-Eversharp Doric green marble double desk base, with two brass columns supporting an octagonal Elgin 8-day clock and two lined green Doric tulips and matching Gold Seal Doric lever-filling desk pens.

£300-400　　　　　　　**BLO**

A 19thC cold cast metal 'Wild Boar' shaped penwipe, probably German, painted in white and black, with painted brown and black eyes and pink snout.

£80-120　　　　　　　**BLO**

A late 19thC English silver-plated baby's bootee penwipe, with eyelets for the laces and black bristles.

4in (10cm) wide

£60-90　　　　　　　**BLO**

A English chrome-plated 'Boot Wipe' penwipe, set with white and black bristles.

1890s-c1910　　　　3.5in (9cm) wide

£70-90　　　　　　　**BLO**

PENS & WRITING EQUIPMENT

A late 1950s/60s Parker 51 or 61 14-pen case, with dark red cloth cover, cream plush-lined tray and gold-coloured Parker logo on the white satin lid lining.

8.5in (22cm) wide

£150-200   **BLO**

An early 1950s Parker 51 freestanding wooden shop display stand, with six grooves and three inset discs with card prices, stamped "The Parker Pen Company" and "Made in England" on the back.

£200-250   **BLO**

A Persian brass writing utensil box, with lid for writing utensils and a small ink pot, decorated with floral and fairy tale-like animals and figures.

Often known as a 'qualandan' and dating from the 18thC, examples of this type of portable penholder are generally much later, dating from even as late as the late 20thC.

10.5in (26cm) long

£10-20   **WDL**

A set of early 20thC brass postal scales, with calibrated pan and cantilever section on an oak base, with four loose weights.

£40-60   **BIG**

A late 1880s cast-iron folding pen rack, with two sprung sides and arms to hold six pens, marked "Pat'd. apl'13.1880 Jan 12. 1886 pat'd. in Europe".

3.5in (9cm) wide

£80-120   **BLO**

A 1960s Olivetti Synthesis 45 plastic letter rack, designed by Ettore Sottsass in 1973.

This was part of a range of stationery objects, designed by this notable Postmodern architect and designer. They could be mixed and matched in different colours.

7.25in (18cm) wide

£25-35   **GM**

A 1980s English Sheaffer brown glazed ceramic ashtray, made by Wade for the Arabic market, with gold lettering.

£50-60   **BLO**

An early 20thC MacNiven & Cameron Waverley white and brown enamelled and embossed pen nib advertising sign, with some chips.

£180-220   **BLO**

A 1940s American Parker 'V-Mail' package, comprising a display card for Parker "Micro-Film Black" 'V-mail Quink', two boxed bottles of 'V-mail Quink', and a box of 'Wolf Envelope Co. V-mail' combined letters and envelopes.

'V-mail' was developed in the last years of WWII and replaced the slow process of sending bulky non-critical personal letters to troops by sea or air. Letters were microfilmed and then reproduced near the recipient's base, meaning 2lbs of microfilm replaced 100lbs of mail. To support this, Parker promoted their special 'Microfilm Black Quink', enabling letters to be reduced and enlarged by V-mail without losing definition.

9.75in (25cm) high

£60-90   **BLO**

COLLECTORS' NOTES

■ Before the development of specially designed commercial bottles for individual perfumes, stylish ladies would buy perfume and decant it into a perfume bottle for use at their dressing tables. The vessel used to transport the perfume was plain and functional. These decorative bottles were popular during the late 19thC, and began to tail off during the 1910s and '20s as custom-designed perfume bottles began to proliferate.

■ The majority were produced in France and Czechoslovakia, with some French bottles being designed by notable makers such as Lefébure, Depinoix, Viard and Lalique. Most of these are made from pressed glass, sometimes stained with colour to highlight the moulded design. Czechoslovakian examples can be in pressed or cut glass and often have large and extravagant stoppers etched or cut with figures or complex stylised floral motifs.

■ Companies in Italy and Germany also made examples that are collectable today. Materials include precious metals and ceramics, but the majority found are in glass. Large examples and those in the prevailing styles of the day, such as Art Nouveau and Art Deco, tend to be the most desirable, particularly if by a notable designer.

■ Look out for chips and damage, especially around the rim and on the stopper. Feel edges and designs with your finger, checking for chips or repaired polished areas, which will appear flat. Compare the stopper to the bottle as these can be replaced. Do not scrub stained areas as this may remove the applied stain.

An Art Deco Czechoslovakian cut-glass perfume bottle, the stopper etched with a nude female figure.

c1930   Bottle 10in (25.5cm) high

£100-150   **LB**

An Art Deco clear glass perfume bottle, the stopper decorated with dancing female figures.

c1920s   9.25in (23.5cm) high

£220-280   **TRIO**

A Czechoslovakian large cut-glass perfume bottle, with cut-out and star cut stopper.

c1930s   Bottle 10.5in (26.5cm) high

£100-150   **LB**

A 1930s Art Deco amber-coloured glass perfume bottle, the smoky clear glass stopper featuring two herons, signed and marked "Czechoslovakia".

The mark in English shows that this was intended for export.

c1930   8.25in (21cm) high

£220-280   **TRIO**

A French Art Deco pressed glass atomiser, by Viard, with green stain, metal fittings and puffer.

Bottles by sculptor and glassmaker Julien Viard are similar in style to those of his contemporary, René Lalique. Viard also designed bottles for perfumier Dubarry.

c1930   6in (15cm) high

£150-200   **TDG**

An unmarked perfume bottle, in frosted pressed glass with stain and painted details.

The design of this bottle is also very similar to Lalique and is both floral and feminine, suiting the contents.

c1920s   5in (12.5cm) high

£700-900   **RDL**

A late 1920s Art Deco clear glass perfume bottle, with black puffer.

6.75in (17cm) high

£180-220   TRIO

An Art Deco clear glass perfume bottle and stopper, with black decoration.

c1920s   4.5in (11.5cm) high

£150-200   TRIO

A late 1920s Art Deco clear glass perfume bottle, with black decoration and puffer.

4.75in (12cm) wide

£120-180   TRIO

£80-120   LB

A 1930s Czechoslovakian Art Deco cut-glass atomiser, the pyramid-shaped bottle with stepped sides and carved and painted decoration.

3.5in (9cm) high

An Art Deco clear glass bottle and stopper, with overlaid floral decoration.

3.5in (9cm) wide

£220-280   TRIO

A 1920s clear glass perfume bottle, possibly by Viard, with blue glass decoration and atomiser, with replaced tassel.

6.5in (16.5cm) high

£150-200   LB

A CLOSER LOOK AT A PERFUME BOTTLE

Although it looks like glass, the bottle is actually made from a type of colourless plastic called Lucite that was popular from the 1930s. _____

The form is _____ architecturally inspired and brings to mind the skyscrapers that were being built at the time.

The geometric, stepped form is typically Art Deco.

The squared sides of the cylindrical blue Lucite bottle reflect the colour and give an interesting optical effect.

A 1930s Art Deco Lucite scent bottle, with asymmetrical faceted Lucite stopper.

6.75in (17cm) high

£220-280   TDG

A French perfume bottle, by Lefébure & Cie glassworks, in frosted glass with sepia stain.

c1910   5.75in (14cm) high

£1,000-1,500   RDL

A 1920s/30s Czechoslovakian Art Deco perfume bottle, with gilt detailing, metal fittings and puffer.

3.75in (9.5cm) wide

£200-250 TRIO

An early 20thC German elliptical glass perfume bottle, of opaque milk glass with blue, yellow and orange trails, brass mounting and spherical stopper.

3.25in (8cm) high

£20-30 KAU

A French perfume bottle, silver-cased clear glass with blue, green and orange bands, elliptical shape with brass mounting and spherical stopper.

c1930 *2.5in (6.5cm) high*

£25-35 KAU

An Italian perfume bottle, clear glass with blue and white zanfirico spiral threads, and with an engraved, hinged stopper.

c1930 *2in (5cm) high*

£20-30 KAU

An early 20thC English zanfirico-style clear and white perfume bottle, with a glass stopper.

c1910 *2in (5cm) long*

£60-90 TRIO

An Art Deco green glass ovoid perfume bottle, with silver hinged lid and glass stopper.

c1920s *4.25in (11cm) high*

£180-220 TRIO

A pair of 1930s hand-carved cast phenolic perfume holders, with ivory stems.

These tribal sculpture-inspired bottles are rare, especially with their ivory stems. The style is typical of the exotic influences on the Art Deco movement.

4.75in (12cm) high

£300-400 MG

A 1930s Czechoslovakian novelty gold-plated atomiser, the metal fitment in the form of a small 'urinating' boy or cherub.

4.75in (12cm) high

£80-120 LB

A French Art Deco silver perfume bottle, embossed with a serpent around the neck and a spider on the stopper.

c1928 *3in (7.5cm) high*

£80-120 TDG

COLLECTORS' NOTES

■ Pez peppermint flavoured sweets were invented by Viennese confectioner Eduard Haas III in 1927. Originally sold in tins, Oskar Uxa designed a new dispenser shaped like a cigarette lighter in 1948. These are known as 'regulars' today.

■ Pez was introduced to the US in 1952. To appeal to children, new fruit flavours were introduced and dispensers were enhanced with character heads.

■ Early characters included Santa Claus, Space Trooper, and Popeye. The range was soon expanded with cartoon and film characters and holiday themes. Companies such as eBay and Nivea have also commissioned promotional dispensers.

■ Many characters have been redesigned over the years and collectors often try to collect all the variations of their favourite dispensers. Pre-1987 dispensers lack feet and are generally more desirable. Plain 1950s 'regulars' and early figural designs are among the most sought-after types.

■ Look for rare variations such as unusual colours. Pez now produce a range of dispensers and other merchandise aimed directly at collectors.

A 1960s 'Nurse' Pez dispenser, made in Austria, no hat, patent number 2 620 061.

The 'Nurse' pez dispenser with the hat can be worth up to £50-80

4.25in (11cm) high

£40-60   **SOTT**

An early 1970s 'Sheik' Pez dispenser, from the Pez Pals series, with red band around the burnoose and without feet.

Versions with a black headband are worth around 10% more.

4.5in (11.5cm) high

£30-50   **DMI**

An early 1970s Walt Disney's 'Mickey Mouse' Pez dispenser, first non-die-cut version, with removable nose, without feet.

4in (10cm) high

£8-12   **DMI**

A late 1970s Walt Disney's 'Scrooge McDuck' Pez dispenser, original version with feet.

This original version used the same mould as a Donald Duck dispenser, and includes applied glasses, sideburns and hat. These pieces were often lost, making complete examples relatively scarce.

4.5in (11.5cm) high

£8-12   **DMI**

An early 1970s 'Indian Chief' Pez dispenser, with a white headdress and without feet.

These dispensers came in a huge range of multicoloured headdresses, but white is the most common.

4.5in (11.5cm) high

£45-55   **DMI**

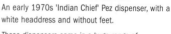

A late 1970s Walt Disney's 'Dumbo' Pez dispenser, without feet.

4.25in (11cm) high

£20-30   **DMI**

A 'Bunny' Pez dispenser, made in Yugoslavia, with no feet and fat ears, patent number "3 942 683".

The patent number places the date of manufacture between 1976 and 1990.

4.25in (11cm) high

£8-12   **SOTT**

An MGM's 'Barney Bear' Pez dispenser, complete in original packaging.

Commissioned by the US toy store FAO Schwartz.

1999 9.5in (24cm) high

£2-4   **DMI**

A 1980s Looney Tunes' 'Bugs Bunny' Pez dispenser, with first version head and with feet.

5in (12.5cm) high

£2-4   **DMI**

A 1980s Looney Tunes' 'Sylvester the Cat' Pez dispenser, non-US version with whiskers and with feet.

4in (10cm) high

£3-5   **DMI**

An 1980s Looney Tunes' 'Tom' Pez dispenser, with multi-piece face and with feet.

4in (10cm) high

£5-8   **DMI**

An 1980s Looney Tunes' 'Roadrunner' Pez dispenser, with stencil eyes and with feet.

4.75in (12cm) high

£5-8   **DMI**

A Looney Tunes' 'Daffy Duck' Pez dispenser, with first head design and feet.

4.5in (11.5cm) high

£3-5   **DMI**

A late 1970s Looney Tunes' 'Speedy Gonzales' Pez dispenser, first version of head, with feet.

4.5in (11.5cm) high

£5-8   **DMI**

An early 1990s Looney Tunes' 'Tuffy' Pez dispenser, with multi-piece face and with feet.

4in (10cm) high

£5-8   **DMI**

An early 1980s Warner Bros' 'Merlin Mouse' Pez dispenser, with feet.

4.75in (12cm) high

£5-8   **DMI**

An early 1990s 'Garfield with Teeth' Pez dispenser, from the first series.	A mid-1990s 'Donatello' Pez dispenser, from the Teenage Mutant Hero Turtles series, with angry face.	A 'Luke Skywalker' Pez dispenser, from the second Star Wars series.	A late 1990s 'Darth Vader' Pez dispenser, from the first Star Wars series.	An 'Incredible Hulk' Pez dispenser, with original packaging and candy.
4.25in (11cm) high	4.25in (11cm) high	1999 4in (10cm) high	4.5in (11.5cm) high	
£1-2 DMI	£1-2 DMI	£1-2 DMI	£1-2 DMI	£4-5 SOTT

A 'Pilot' Pez dispenser, from the Pez Pals series, with glow-in-the-dark face.	A 'Bubbleman' Pez dispenser, with translucent crystal head.	A late 1990s 'Blinky Bill' Pez dispenser, from the Kooky Zoo series.	A late 1990s 'Elephant' Pez dispenser, from the Kooky Zoo Crystal series, with translucent crystal plastic head.
c1990 4.5in (11.5cm) high	c1999 4.5in (11.5cm) high	4.25in (11cm) high	4in (10cm) high
£3-5 DMI	£2-4 DMI	£1-2 DMI	£2-4 DMI

An early 1970s 'Mr Ugly' Pez dispenser, with olive green face and without feet.

There are variations with differently coloured heads, of these the chartreuse green face is the most valuable, usually fetching up to £40-60. However, models with feet fetch considerably less.

4in (10cm) high

£20-30   **DMI**

A 1970s three-piece 'Witch' Pez dispenser, without feet

This is a common colour combination.

4.25in (11cm) high

£8-12   **DMI**

A 1990s 'Misfit Snowman' Pez dispenser, manufactured for a mail-in offer.

Misfits are standard characters produced in limited numbers in unusual colours.

4.5in (11.5cm) high

£2-3   **DMI**

A 'Jack-in-the-Box' promotional Pez dispenser, marked on the back of the head "Mfg for Jack in the Box restaurants".

Commissioned by the Jack-in-the-Box fast food chain in the US.

c1999 4.75in (12cm) high

£2-4   **DMI**

A 'Honey-Nut Cheerios' short-stem Pez dispenser.

Commissioned as a special offer with Honey-Nut Cheerios breakfast cereal.

2001 2.75in (7cm) high

£6-10   **DMI**

A Pez dispenser, commissioned for the FX Show collectors fair, "The Coolest Show On Earth".

2005 4.25in (11cm) high

£6-8   **DMI**

A 'USA Hearts' Pez dispenser, manufactured after the terrorist attacks on 11th September 2001.

2002 4.5in (11.5cm) high

£1-2   **DMI**

An early 1990s 'Truck' Pez dispenser, from the 'D' series, with glow-in-the-dark trailer.

4in (10cm) long

£5-7   **DMI**

A late 1990s 'Psychedelic Flower' Pez dispenser, collector's edition remake.

3.75in (9.5cm) high

£6-8   **DMI**

FIND OUT MORE...

Collectors' Guide to Pez, by Shawn Peterson, published by Krause Publications, 2nd Edition, 2003.

The Museum Pez Memorabilia, 214 California Drive, Burlingame, California, 94010, USA.

www.pezcentral.com

www.pezcollectors.com

COLLECTORS' NOTES

■ The development of plastic has been of undoubted key importance to the 20thC – our world would be very different if it had not been developed. The first 'plastic' materials, such as celluloid, were used in the late 19thC but Bakelite, developed in 1907 by Belgian chemist Dr Leo Baekeland, is considered the first true synthetic plastic.

■ Dubbed the 'material of 1,000 uses', it is found primarily in darker colours such as brown and black, and occasionally in red, green and blue. Its development generated a boom in the plastics industry and led to a vast number of different plastics being made. Thus, not all plastics are true 'Bakelite' although the term 'bakelite' is commonly applied to many early plastics.

■ The 'golden age' lasted from c1910 to the 1950s, when cheaper injection moulded plastics took over. The adaptability of the material in terms of colour and form saw it being used for cost-effective mass production of many different objects from electrical insulators to kitchenware to jewellery.

■ Two key indicators to value are colour and form. Plastic allowed domestic pieces to break away from the dominance of dull woods and plain metals, so brighter colours are more desirable, particularly in strong tones such as cherry red. 'Catalin' was a phenolic resin made by the Catalin Corporation in the US, and is known particularly for its vibrant colours. Blue, red and green Bakelite is generally rare.

■ The Art Deco style was dominant during this period and it is this that collectors seek out. Look for quintessential Deco designs, such as clean lines, stepped designs, streamlining and geometric forms. Condition is also all-important, with chips, cracks and repairs affecting value considerably, particularly for more common pieces, which should be avoided. Some colours have faded, darkened or changed over time, but this often does not affect value as seriously.

A 1930s butterscotch cast phenolic cylindrical cigarette box, the lid unscrewing to act as an ashtray.

3in (8cm) high

£100-150   **MG**

A 1930s slightly marbled cherry red Catalin cigarette box, with carved yellow Catalin cigarette shaped handle .

4in (10cm) high

£300-500   **MG**

A 1930s Art Deco amber and yellow marbled powder box, with moulded vertical ribbing , the lid with triangular finial.

3.25in (8cm) high

£50-70   **MI**

A late 1930s-1940s mottled green cast phenolic round powder box, with elliptical, domed lid, some darkening.

5in (12.5cm) diam

£250-350   **MG**

A very rare reverse carved 'Apple Juice' bakelite powder box, with carved lines and flowers on the lid.

This form of Lucite is known as 'Apple Juice' due to the colour. The flower has been carved into the lid from the underside, a technique used frequently with costume jewellery in this material. The resulting cavities can be filled with coloured paste, the remains of which can be seen in the detail.

4.25in (11cm) diam

£300-400

MG

A 1930s Art Deco amber and yellow marbled cast phenolic cigarette box, the lid and handle made from a single piece of phenolic

4in (10cm) long

£250-400   **MG**

A 1950s Lucite and bakelite cigarette box, the Lucite finial reverse carved and injected with colour to form a rose surrounded by leaves.

5.25in (13.5cm) long

£300-400   **MG**

A 1930s cream urea-formaldehyde jewellery box, moulded with stylised acanthus leaves.

6in (15cm) long

£20-30   **JBC**

A CLOSER LOOK AT A PLASTIC BOX

This dressing table box was designed by famous and skilled glass designer Rene Lalique, who also designed perfume bottles and jewellery.

It is the only example of Lalique using plastics - liquid plastic acts very much like molten glass and Lalique was skilled at producing moulded glass.

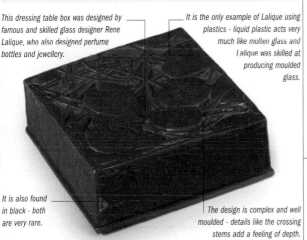

It is also found in black - both are very rare.

The design is complex and well moulded - details like the crossing stems add a feeling of depth.

A Lalique red celluloid "Cerises" powder box, moulded "R. Lalique".
c1923

2in (5.5cm) diam

£600-800   **DRA**

A 1930s American Art Deco moulded red and black cigarette box, with stepped handle, the base moulded "Made in USA".

8in (20cm) long

£400-500   **MG**

A 1930s clear and black Lucite cigarette holder and dispenser, with carved rope twist border.

Cigarettes lie horizontally in the box, and are viewed from the central vertical 'window'. To take a cigarette, the rope twist border is pulled up, moving the stack upwards, until a cigarette falls onto the concave ridges on either side.

5.25in (13.5cm) high

£80-120   **MG**

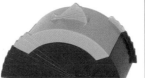

A 1930s Art Deco green and black cigarette box, with metal globe finials, the base with moulded "GE" mark, for General Electric.

5in (12.5cm) long

£300-400   **MG**

A 1930s Art Deco design 'Cleopatra' phenolic resin box, with green lid and black base.

This sums up Art Deco very well in its choice of colours, geometric, fan decoration and curving form.

5.75in (14.5cm) long

£80-120   **MI**

PLASTICS & BAKELITE

A 1930s orange Catalin mantle clock pencil sharpener, with transfer-on-paper inset dial with metal retaining ring.

1in (3cm) high

£50-70   MG

A 1930s green Catalin mantle clock pencil sharpener, with transfer-on-paper inset dial with metal retaining ring.

2in (5cm) high

£50-70   MG

An early 1940s American carved marbled brown Catalin American tank pencil sharpener, with transfer decoration and black inserted Catalin tank barrel.

1.75in (4.5cm) long

£50-70   MG

An early 1940s American red and black carved WWII plane pencil sharpener, with transfer decoration.

2.25in (6cm) long

£50-70   MG

A CLOSER LOOK AT A DESK BASE

This was made by British company J.Dickinson, under the name 'Carvacraft' - pieces are marked with a stamp underneath.

The curving shape and stepped edges are typical of late Art Deco, when streamlining became a key style, particularly in the US.

It is part of a set of desk accessories including a stamp wipe, an ink stand, a small clip board, a rocker blotter and a rare picture frame and letter rack.

These are found in three colours; amber, yellow and the very rare green.

An amber Carvacraft double pen holder, with double pen tray to front.
c1948   *6.5in (16.5cm) wide*

£60-80   MHC

A late 1930s American orange carved Catalin 'Charlie McCarthy' pencil sharpener, with intact transfer decoration.

McCarthy was the brainchild of ventriloquist Edgar Bergen. Their radio debut was in 1936 and they became instantly popular, with McCarthy receiving an honourary degree from Northwestern University in 'Innuendo and Snappy Comebacks' in 1938. 1939 saw a popular film 'Charlie McCarthy, Detective'.

1.75in (4.5cm) high

£60-80   MG

An American Chase yellow cast and carved Catalin and chrome blotter.

The Chase Metalware company made domestic items in their characteristic chrome and brass finish during the 1930s - today they are highly sought-after.

5.25in (13.5cm) long

£30-40   MG

A 1930s red and clear Lucite tiered desk ornament, with applied gold plastic horsehead motifs.

2.5in (6.5cm) high

£60-80   MG

An Art Deco Brookes & Adams red and green marbled 'Bandalasta' ware teaset, with moulded marks to base.

Bandalasta ware was made from moulded urea thiourea formaldehyde by Streetly Manufacturing. Such colourful pieces were found primarily in picnic sets. Made in a variety of different colours, the red marbled example is the rarest and most desirable.

1927-32   *Teapot 6.75in (17cm) wide*

£600-800   **JES**

Two differently marbled Brookes & Adams 'Bandalasta' picnic 'horns' or beakers.

1927-32   *5in (12.5cm) high*

£12-18 (each)   **JBC**

A rare 1930s American cast clear and amber swirled Catalin cruet set on a tray, each piece overlaid with thin tiles of chromed metal to give a chequerboard effect.

Tray 3.5in (9cm) high

£150-200   **MG**

A pair of 1930s cast and carved orange Catalin salt and pepper shakers, with yellow Catalin inserts.

2.5in (6cm) high

£30-50   **MHC**

A 1930s Art Deco brown mottled Bakelite toast rack, with shaped handle and sprung metal holders.

5.5in (14cm) wide

£15-20   **MHC**

A 1920s-30s American unmarked green mottled urea formaldehyde revolving toothpick holder and dispenser.

This was probably made for use in restaurants.

4.75in (12cm) high

£5-7   **BH**

A 1950s Thermos Model no. 931 blue and cream ice bucket, with Thermos interior and plastic basket.

Found in a variety of colours, these are frequently missing their plastic basket or have damaged Thermos linings.

6in (15.5cm) high

£25-35   **GROB**

A late 1920s Bakelite Corporation mottled brown Bakelite dish, with moulded V pattern to the outside, with moulded mark to base.

Items with this mark are original products of Baekeland's 'Bakelite Corporation', with the infinity symbol intending to indicate the many uses of his plastic. This version, with a tri-lobed border, dates from after 1926, but before 1956 when the infinity symbol became larger.

5in (13cm) diam

£40-50   **MG**

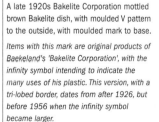

A 1930s-40s Smiths brown mottled Bakelite key wound mantel clock, with hour striking.

Smiths, based in England, made a vast range of clocks in a great variety of coloured plastics into the 1950s.

8in (20cm) high

£30-50 — **MHC**

A French 1930s Art Deco Blangy brown mottled Bakelite key wound mantel clock.

The strong and distinctive Art Deco styling of this clock, and the detailing of ships at sea on the face, make it highly desirable.

5.25in (13cm) high

£150-200 — **PC**

A CLOSER LOOK AT A CLOCK

The design exemplifies Art Deco, with its geometric shapes, clean lines and stepped 'skyscraper' appearance - it is also very similar to the famous 'Air King' radio design by Harold van Doren.

It was rumoured to have been designed by notable Deco designer Paul Frankl, although no factory records directly link him with this design although they do very clearly with the chrome-plated, enamelled metal and glass No.431 'Modernique' of c1928.

It was available in a walnut effect, white or green 'Vinylite' plastic - the marbled green is extremely rare.

As well as for its iconic design, it is celebrated as being the first Telechron alarm clock and the first self-starting electric alarm clock made.

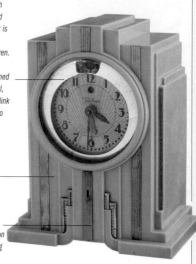

An Art Deco Warren Telechron Co, of Ashland Massachusets, Telechron '700 Electroalarm' 'Vinylite' electric mantel clock with alarm and light bulb.

7.75in (19.5cm) high

£350-450 — **CAT**

An American Art Deco Taylor yellow and green mottled and carved Catalin desk thermometer and hydrometer, the card face with company advertising for Steel Heddle Mfg Co.

4in (10cm) high

£100-150 — **MG**

A Wurlitzer Wireless bakelite speaker, of circular form on disk feet, moulded "W" mark.

6.75in (17cm) high

£70-100 — **WW**

A 1950s brown Bakelite and metal 45rpm holder, with lyre-shaped handle.

Brown Bakelite was used for domestic items as late as the 1950s. The lyre-shaped handle alludes to the musical contents of the case.

11.75in (30cm) long

£400-550 — **MG**

A late 1940s white urea-formaldehyde 'Rototherm' desk thermometer.

These can be found in a variety of different colours and as a matching barometer. The 'industrial' design is inspired by aircraft and car dashboard dials.

6.75 in (9cm) high

£20-30 — **MHC**

A Bakelite desk lamp with magnifier, on a teardrop-shaped wood base with bent metal arm with a bakelite framed glass magnifier.

c1930   13.5in (34.5cm) high

£200-300   **SK**

A CLOSER LOOK AT A BAKELITE LAMP

This lamp was designed in 1945 and is typical of the streamlined styles of the 'Machine Age' period.

It was made by the French company Jumo, who are noted for their innovative lamp designs and it uses popular materials of the period such as chrome, brass and plastic.

It folds down to form a sleek, streamlined shell-like form that resembles the front of trains of the period - the pivoting shade can be angled and the arm bent low or pulled tall and straight.

It was available in black, green and cream versions - black is the most commonly found with cream, and particularly green, being much rarer.

A late 1940s 'Jumo' 'streamlined' late Art Deco phenolic desk lamp for Brevette, the black/brown bakelite case with internal extendible arm, factory stamp to the base, France.

17.75in (45cm) high extended

£700-1,000   **ROS**

A 1930s Art Deco pink and black urea formaldehyde plastic ashtray, made for the 'Queen Mary' cruise liner, marked "British Buttner Product".

4.5in (11.5cm) high

£100-150   **JES**

A 1930s German brown Bakelite CB Rotor Auto 1001 friction powered car, with chips, complete with original box.

4.75in (12cm) high

£60-80   **LAN**

An Art Deco Roanoid Ltd thiourea-formaldehyde and bakelite ashtray.

These were made for Dunlop in five different colours. The three cigarette rest arms fold inwards, tightly locking the ash in, and a weighted base also means the ashtray never falls over.

3.25in (8cm) high

£50-80   **SWO**

A 1930s small carved yellow Catalin desk sculpture, with applied carved birds.

Novelties like these are often unique, large and complex examples can fetch high prices.

2.25in (6cm) high

£40-60   **MG**

A 1930s circular cast marbled amber Catalin Catholic wall plaque, with inset diamante and Catholic 'IHS' motif.

5.25in (13.5cm) diam

£60-80   **MG**

A pair of 1930s cast butterscotch Catalin novelty dice, with black painted dots.

2in (5cm) wide

£220-280   **MG**

COLLECTORS' NOTES

■ Posters have become increasingly desirable to general buyers, as well as collectors, due to their visual impact, snapshot of social history and reflection of period design. Most buyers choose to collect or buy in one particular area, such as travel or product advertising posters. It is possible to concentrate on specific themes within these areas, for example the Art Deco style, airline posters or posters advertising food and drink.

■ The 'golden age' of the poster was arguably the period from the turn of the 20thC, when graphics began to be used by mainly French designers, until other media such as television took over in the 1950s. Styles such as Art Nouveau, Art Deco and Modernism are strongly represented and prove a draw today.

■ There are a number of factors to consider, including the brand depicted, the overall design and artwork and the artist. Eye appeal is also an important consideration, particularly for those who wish to buy posters to display. Posters for notable brands with a strong following or by famous artists, such as Adolphe Mouron (Cassandre), will be desirable and usually very valuable.

■ Also consider the condition as posters were made to be displayed and most often were used. Tears, especially to the image, will affect the value seriously. Folds and creases can be repaired, providing the surface of the image is not rubbed and removed. Backing posters on linen is a good idea for storage and display, but this should only be done by a professional.

■ With travel posters, consider the brand, mode of transport and the imagery. Bold colours, period stylized designs and major names in travel such as White Star, BOAC, Air France and Canadian Pacific will be a draw to many buyers. A notable artist will further enhance the value, as will popular destinations such as ski resorts or famous holiday locations.

■ Beware of reproductions, which are commonplace. Inspect originals at reputable dealers and auction houses carefully to learn how to distinguish between modern prints and originals. Thicker, glossy paper and the presence of pixels are an indication of a reproduction.

'London, Trafalgar Square', designed by Donald Blake and printed for RE(ER) by Jordison & Co.

British railway posters came in two sizes and formats, to fit standard advertising hoardings.

50in (127cm) wide

£1,500-2,000 ON

'London, St Pauls', designed by J. Bateman and published by the LNER.

The bottom strip with the text has been cut off and reattached, devaluing this poster.

40in (102cm) high

£450-550 ON

'Visit London, Travel by Train', designed by Gordon Nicol and printed for BR(WR) by Waterlow & Sons Ltd.

40in (102cm) high

£180-220 ON

'Cheltenham for Health and Pleasure', designed by Claude Buckle and printed for GWR and LMS by Lowe & Brydone, folds.

40in (102cm) high

£500-700 ON

'Essex, Travel by Rail', designed by Terence Cuneo and printed for the LNER by the Baynard Press.

1945 40in (102cm) high

£350-450 ON

'Old World Market-Places Boston', designed by Austin Cooper and printed for the LNER by Adams Bros., mounted on linen.

40in (102cm) high

£180-220   ON

'Bournemouth Go By Train', anonymous designer, published for the BR(SR).

c1970   40in (102cm) high

£70-100   ON

'Deal For Your Holidays' designed by P. Shine and printed for Deal Town Council and Belgian State Railways by David Allen & Sons Ltd., mounted on linen.

1924   40in (102cm) high

£350-450   ON

'Enjoy A Holiday In Northern Ireland', designed by Costelloe and printed for the Ulster Transport Authority by Stafford, mounted on linen.

40in (102cm) high

£300-400   ON

'Ulster, Northern Ireland', designed by Greene and printed for the BR(LMR) by Waterlow & Sons Ltd.

40in (102cm) high

£350-450   ON

'Isle of Man', designed by Peter Collins and printed for the BR(LMR) by Waterlow & Sons Ltd., folds.

50in (127cm) wide

£120-180   ON

'Hints for Holidays', designed by Ronald Brett and printed for the Southern Railway by Sanders Phillips & Co. Ltd., restored and mounted on linen.

This type of colourful, bold and highly suggestive imagery is sought-after.

'Littlehampton, Go by Train', designed by Studio Seven and printed for SR(BR) by Gilbert Whitehead & Co Ltd.

40in (102cm) high

£80-120   ON

1933   40in (102cm) high

£400-600   ON

A CLOSER LOOK AT A RAILWAY POSTER

This poster was designed by Terence Cuneo (1907-96), who is often considered the best railway painter in the world.

Cuneo was skilled at catching a moment in time and showing the grandeur of locomotives. This image depicts two powerful engines at rest with men working on them.

His realistic and dramatic style is loved and sought-after by collectors, and the streamlined A4 Pacific is perhaps the most loved LNER locomotive type.

GIANTS REFRESHED

"PACIFICS" IN THE LNER LOCOMOTIVE WORKS, DONCASTER

He often included a mouse 'hidden' in his images as a trademark; here a cat sits inquisitively in front of the blue locomotive.

'Giants Refreshed' designed by Terence Cuneo and printed for the L.N.E.R. by Waterlow & Sons Ltd. "Pacifics" in the LNER Locomotive Works Doncaster.

c1945   50in (127cm) high

£2,200-2,800   ON

'West Riding Limited, The First Streamline Train', designed by Shep and printed for the LNER by the Baynard Press, folds.

Shep was the name used by Charles Shepherd (b.1892), who was head of the studio at the Baynard Press. He designed posters for London Transport as well as the LNER and SR. The style of the train and the feeling of movement make this especially desirable.

30in (76cm) high

£1,200-1,800   ON

'Hampton Court by Tram', designed by Herrick and printed for the London Underground by the Baynard Press.

40in (102cm) high

£100-150   ON

'At Your Service', designed by Leo Dowd and printed for London Transport by the Baynard Press.

40in (102cm) high

£120-180   ON

'Kew Gardens', designed by George Sheringham and printed for the London Underground by Vincent Day Brooks.

1924   40in (102cm) high

£80-120   ON

'Staggered Travelling Saves Busy Workers' Time', designed by Pat Keeley and printed for London Transport by Waterlow & Sons Ltd., mounted on linen.

An interesting and early example of promotion of flexi-time at work.

1945   40in (102cm) high

£120-180   ON

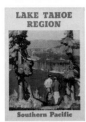

'Lake Tahoe Region, Southern Pacific', designed by Maurice Logan for the Southern Pacific railroad.

23.25in (59cm) high

£350-450   **ON**

'Shasta Route, Southern Pacific', designed by Maurice Logan for the Southern Pacific railroad.

Maurice Logan (1886-1977) was one of San Francisco's most influential artists and poster designers.

23.25in (59cm) high

£350-450   **ON**

'New Orleans, Southern Pacific' designed by Maurice Logan for the Southern Pacific railroad.

23.25in (59cm) high

£80-120   **ON**

'Martha's Vineyard, The New Haven Railroad', designed by Ben Nason for the New Haven Railroad.

After WWII, the railroad launched a publicity campaign to attract holidaymakers to the island. After arriving at Wood Hole, they were taken by ferry to the island. The masthead shown here represents local whaling history.

c1945   42in (106.5cm) high

£600-800   **SWA**

'The Royal York', by an anonymous designer for the Canadian Pacific Railway.

Built for the Toronto railway in 1929, the hotel was the largest in the British Commonwealth.

c1930   40in (102cm) high

£1,200-1,800   **SWA**

'Demain Matin Cote d'Azur', designed by Roland Hugon and printed for the SNCF by Paul Martial.

1938   39in (99cm) high

£350-450   **ON**

'Balaton', designed by Bereny Bortnyik, advertising a two-for-one travel deal.

Balaton, in Hungary, is the largest lake in Central Europe and is a popular tourist destination. The surreal Modernist collage style is desirable.

37.5in (95cm) high

£350-450   **SWA**

'Holland Bulbtime', designed by E.G. and printed for Netherlands Railways by L.Van Leer & Co, linen-backed.

39in (99cm) high

£50-70   **ON**

'Japan' designed by P. Irwin Brown for the Japanese Government Railways.

Brown also designed posters for British railway companies. The 'flat' design with broad areas of colour recalls the style of Japanese prints.

1934   37.25in (94.5cm) high

£300-500   **SWA**

'Aberdeen & Commonwealth Line, England to Australia', designed by Longmate and printed by Gibbs & Gibbs Ltd.

The Aberdeen & Commonwealth Line was formed in 1932 when Shaw, Savill & Albion acquired the Aberdeen Line (founded 1825) and Australia's Commonwealth Line fleet from the bankrupt White Star Line. In 1936 Furness, Withy & Co. acquired Shaw, Savill & Albion and in 1938, the 'Aberdeen' name was dropped.

1930s   40.5in (103cm) high

£650-750   **ON**

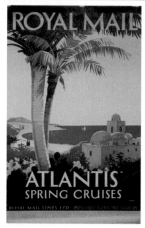

'Royal Mail Atlantis Spring Cruises', designed by Daphne Padden and printed for Royal Mail Lines Ltd. by Baynard Press.

Royal Mail Lines Ltd. was founded out of the crisis caused when the Kylsant Shipping Empire, which owned White Star and other lines, went bankrupt in 1932. It took on the Royal Mail Steam Packet Company's routes and survived as a name until the early 1970s. These 1930s posters are desirable due to the bright, colourful and idealised artwork that drew tourists to book tickets to these idyllic lands.

40in (102cm) high

£350-450   **ON**

'Aberdeen & Commonwealth Line, Australia via Malta, Port Said & Colombo', designed by P.H. Yorke and printed by Howard Jones Roberts Leete Ltd.

The presence of a Scottie dog makes this poster also appeal to other types of collector.

40.5in (103cm) high

£500-700   **ON**

'Shaw Savill Line New Zealand via Panama Canal', designed by E. Waters and printed by Gibbs & Gibbs Ltd.

40.5in (103cm) high

£550-650   **ON**

'Royal Mail Atlantis Summer Cruises', designed by Daphne Padden and printed for Royal Mail Lines Ltd. by Baynard Press, small tears.

40in (102cm) high

£350-450   **ON**

'Aberdeen & Commonwealth Line England-Australia Malta', designed by E.J. Waters and printed by Gibbs & Gibbs Ltd.

40.5in (103cm) high

£250-350   **ON**

'Shaw Savill & Albion Line New Zealand Direct' designed by E. Waters.

This uses two New Zealand related icons, Mt. Taranaki, Egmont, and Captain Cook.

39.75in (101cm) high

£250-350   **ON**

'Royal Mail Atlantis Cruises', designed by Daphne Padden and printed for Royal Mail Lines Ltd. by Baynard Press, small tears.

40in (102cm) high

£350-450   **ON**

A CLOSER LOOK AT A SHIPPING POSTER

This poster shows the famous Art Deco masterpiece the Normandie, which was once the fastest, largest and most luxurious cruise liner in the world.

Montague Black painted many famous White Star liners, including the Olympic and the ill-fated Titanic. His images are sought-after.

She first arrived in New York in 1935 and then completed 138 transatlantic voyages. Original period images are highly desirable today.

The scale of the ship is shown in a dramatic way and setting, hallmarks of Black's style.

'Adriatica, Toute La Méditerranée Orientale, by an anonymous designer, with a ship on the horizon and its course across the globe.

The design is very similar to Cassandre in its choice of colours, lines and sense of movement.

c1938   39in (99cm) high

£300-400   **SWA**

'French Line C.G.T., An Express Luxury Service France-England-U.S.A. S.S. Ile de France E.S. Normandie', designed by Montague B. Black and printed in England.

The Normandie met a sad fate in 1942, while being converted into a troop carrier in New York, when she was accidentally set on fire and sunk. She was broken up in 1947.

40in (102cm) high

£3,000-4,000   **ON**

'Cruise on the Great Lakes Canadian Pacific', designed by Peter Ewart.

Ewart designed many posters for the vast Canadian Pacific company.

35in (89cm) high

£400-600   **SWA**

'Cunard White Star To Europe Via North America', designed by Tom Curr, showing the RMS Queen Mary leaving New York.

39.75in (101cm) high

£1,200-1,800   **SWA**

'French Line G.C.T. Paris, Paris All The Way To New York', designed by K. Herkomer and printed by Hill Siffken & Co.

1934   40in (102cm) high

£1,800-2,200   **ON**

'Hamburg Amerika Linie, Mediterranean Cruises', designed by Albert Fuss and printed by Muhlmeister & Johler.

39.75in (101cm) high

£250-350   **ON**

'Lloyd Triestino, Australia', designed by Gino Boccasile and printed by Pizzi & Pizio, Milan.

Lloyd Triestino was an Italian shipping line founded in 1937. This poster depicts the Romolo, which was scuttled in 1940 to avoid enemy capture.

c1938   37.5in (95.5cm) high

£400-600   **SWA**

'AOA to USA', designed by Jan Hewitt & George Him and printed by W.R. Royle & Son Ltd for American Overseas Airlines.

1948   40in (102cm) high

£150-250   ON

'AOA – USA Par Le Stratocruiser Deux Ponts', by an anonymous designer, printed by W.R. Royle & Son Ltd.

40in (102cm) high

£150-250   ON

'BOAC – Time is Money, Save it by Flying BOAC', possibly designed by Abram Games and printed in Great Britain, mounted on linen.

Notable designer Abram Games (1914-96) is known to have designed posters for BOAC, and this is very much in his style. He often takes an object related to the theme or subject of the service or item and gives it an almost surreal, stylized appearance on a graduated background.

30in (76cm) high

£280-320   ON

'Ship TWA Air Cargo' by an anonymous designer.

Air Cargo was formed in 1941 to carry freight from the four largest US airlines comprising United, American, Eastern and TWA. After WWII, most airlines set up independent freight services.

38.5in (98cm) high

£300-500   SWA

'TWA', by an anonymous designer, showing a woman gazing longingly at a cactus with a cowboy watching on.

37.75in (96cm) high

£1,200-1,800   SWA

'Mexico Tomorrow Via Pan American', by an anonymous designer, showing a DC-3 and a Mexican woman in traditional dress.

c1940   41in (104cm) high

£400-600   SWA

'PAN AM, Rio' by an anonymous designer, showing Oba-Oba dancers from Oswaldo Sargentelli's famous night-club in Rio de Janeiro.

c1970   36.5in (92.5cm) high

£1,000-1,500   SWA

'Swissair, Lisboa-Nova Iorque Sem Escala Con DC-7C', showing the Chrysler Building, New York.

SwissAir went bankrupt in 2001 and are now known as 'Swiss'.

1960s   40in (102cm) high

£120-180   ON

'Lenzerheide, Switzerland', designed by Heinze & Pedreff and printed by Anstalt C. J. Bucher, small tears.

40in (102cm) high

£120-180 ON

A CLOSER LOOK AT A TOURISM POSTER

Swiss designer and architect Daniele Buzzi is known for his poster designs produced to attract people to his home region of Ticino.

The image is of the Madonna del Sasso Sanctuary and the surrounding sub-tropical vegetation. It brings to mind more obviously popular tourist destinations such as the Mediterranean and South America.

The image is eye-catching, being bright, bold and colourful with stylized forms, which are typical hallmarks of Buzzi's work.

This poster dates from the 1920s. His post-WWII work is less desirable as it became less colourful and appealing.

'Locarno, Golf, Casino, Tennis', designed by Daniele Buzzi.

1926 *39.5in (100.5cm) long*

£300-500 SWA

'Montana Vermala, Valais Suisse Alt 1500m', by an anonymous designer and printed by A. Marsens.

Although advertising Swiss resorts known for their skiing, as indicated by the snowy mountains in the background, these do not usually appeal to skiing poster collectors, due to the lack of skiing imagery.

40in (102cm) high

£120-180 ON

'Kandersteg Switzerland', designed by 'CM' and printed by Orell Fussli.

39.5in (100cm) high

£100-150 ON

'Thun Plage Switzerland', designed by Clare and printed by Casserini-Aebi, small tears and loss.

40in (102cm) high

£220-280 ON

'Nassau in the Bahamas', colour lithograph photographic image poster published by the Development Board Nassau.

1938 *41in (104cm) high*

£350-450 ON

'Join The Smart Set in Nassau and The Bahamas', by an anonymous designer.

c1960 *42.5in (108cm) high*

£300-400 SWA

'Carnaval 1937, Panama', by an anonymous designer, printed by Senefelder, Ecuador.

'Australia, The Tallest Trees in the British Empire', designed by Trompf and published by the Australian National Travel Association.

'Melbourne', designed by Max Forbes, published by the Australian National Travel Assoc.

Although not an official Olympics poster, the games are mentioned at the base and the boy holding sports equipment has a ticket to the games in his pocket.

'Leningrad', Russian-produced tourism poster for the city.

The 'Liberty Monument' to victims of the revolution can be seen in the centre of the park as the exaggerated statue of Lenin looks over Russians and tourists visiting the park.

1937   26.25in (66.5cm) high

£300-400   **SWA**

40in (102cm) high

£450-550   **ON**

c1956   39in (99cm) high

£350-450   **SWA**

c1935   38.5in (98cm) high

£450-550   **SWA**

'Annecy La Plage', designed by Robert Falcucci and printed for PLM by Gds Ets de l'Imp Generale.

1935   39in (100cm) high

£600-700   **ON**

'USSR Health Resorts', Russian-produced poster for the Black Sea coast 'Russian Riviera' known for its vegetation, spas and resorts.

39.25in (99.5cm) high

£800-1,200   **SWA**

'Norway, The Land of the Midnight Sun', designed by Ivar Gull and printed by Norsk Lithografsk.

39.5in (100cm) high

£220-280   **ON**

'Spain Glorious Spring', by an anonymous designer and printed by Union Grafica SL Tolosa, mounted on linen.

39.5in (100cm) high

£280-320   **ON**

'Vecoux Winter Sports in France', printed for the SNCF by Paul Martial.

39.5in (100cm) high

£300-400　　　　　　ON

'8 Jours de Neige Blanche – Une Année de Joues Roses', designed by Roland Hugon and printed for the SNCF by Paul Martial.

1938　　　39in (99cm) high

£200-300　　　　　　ON

'Join the Sun on a Ski-run in France', designed by Dubois and printed for French Tourist Office by S. A. Courbet, mounted on linen.

39.5in (100cm) high

£250-350　　　　　　ON

'Norway, The Home of Ski-ing', designed by J.E. and showing a stylized image of two skiers relaxing on the mountainside.

c1936　　　39.5in (100cm) high

£850-950　　　　　　SWA

'The New Constam Lift at Strawberry Lodge', showing a man and woman in blue snowsuits walking towards a lodge and watching a lift taking skiers up the mountain.

The constantly circulating Constam ski lift was developed by ardent skier Ernst Constam in 1934 and resulted in him being elected to the US National Ski Hall of Fame. Popular with skiers and poster collectors, ski posters are now highly sought-after. Consider the colours, imagery, general 'eye appeal' and location shown. Those with bold, dramatic figurative images for famous resorts from the golden age of the 1930s tend to fetch higher prices.

41in (104cm) high

£700-1,000　　　　　　SWA

'Sunapee, New Hampshire', published by the State of New Hampshire Recreation Division.

25in (63.5cm) high

£700-1,000　　　SWA

'Wintersport, Schwarzwald', designed by Arthur Hauptmann and printed for German Railways by Druck, mounted on linen.

27.5in (70cm) high

£350-450　　　　　　ON

'Lenzerheide 1500m Graubunden 4900ft Grisons Switzerland', Swiss skiing advertising poster designed by Heinze.

40.25in (102cm) high

£250-350　　　　　　ON

'Buy Delicious South African Oranges, The Empire Summer Orange' designed by Edward Cole, folds.

19.75in (50cm) high

£100-150 **ON**

'Buy Delicious South African Oranges', designed by Edward Cole, folds.

By 1921, scientists had agreed that vitamins were necessary for good health. In 1928 vitamin C was isolated, and in 1932 it was proven to prevent scurvy. With the Great Depression affecting the US and Europe during the 1930s, and WWII and the previous Spanish 'flu epidemic having further affected the world around 1918, the intake of vitamins became national obsessions. Oranges, apples and onions were rich, natural sources of vitamin C and were promoted heavily through poster campaigns and recipe books devised by government health authorities and importers. Promotion of these fruits also encouraged world trade, adding a further commercial benefit to the British Empire and other nations. Today, these posters form a fascinating and highly decorative snapshot of social history during the 1920s-40s, particularly those with people in period style poses.

30in (76cm) high

£180-220 **ON**

'Three Ring Oranges, Seedless Grapefruit, South Africa's Best', by an anonymous designer.

19.75in (50cm) high

£15-20 **ON**

'You Can Always Tell A Jaffa By Its Juice', designed by Edward Cole, folds.

19.75in (50cm) high

£80-120 **ON**

'Who's Afraid of the Big Bad Wolf!' Eat more Oranges and keep away 'Flu', designed by W. Hicks, folds.

With its wording 'Apologies to Walt Disney', this poster plays on the popular Walt Disney animated short film 'The Three Little Pigs', released in 1933 and a follow-up 'The Big Bad Wolf' released in 1934, with 'flu being represented by the 'wolf at the door'.

c1934 *20in (51cm) high*

£120-180 **ON**

'Eat More Oranges And Keep Away Flu', designed by Muriel Harris, folds.

30in (76cm) high

£100-150 **ON**

'Blue Goose, Every morn I bring you Sunshine and the World's Best Grapefruit', by an anonymous designer, folds.

30in (76cm) high

£22-28 **ON**

'A South African Orange Grove', by an anonymous designer, folds.

30in (76cm) wide

£80-120 **ON**

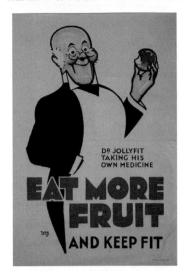

'New Zealand Apples, The Empire's Star Turn', designed by Edward Cole, folds.

19.75in (50cm) high

£100-150 ON

'Buy New Zealand Apples, They're Great', designed by F. Kenwood Giles, folds.

30in (76cm) high

£80-120 ON

'Dr Jollyfit taking his own medicine, Eat More Fruit And Keep Fit', designed by Alfred Leete, folds.

Illustrator Alfred Leete (1882-1933) is best known for his 1915 design of the 'Your Country Needs You' wartime recruitment poster featuring a pointing Lord Kitchener.

30in (76cm) high

£40-50 ON

'Fyffes' Bananas', by an anonymous designer and printed by Johnson Riddle & Co Ltd for Fyffes.

29.5in (75cm) wide

£60-80 ON

'Eat More Fruit And Be More Beautiful', designed by Septimus Edwin Scott, folds.

Septimus Edwin Scott (1879-1965) exhibited at the Royal Academy and the Royal Watercolour Society, and became one of the highest paid and most respected of all British poster artists. Later in life, when his style had gone out of fashion, he worked on comic books.

30in (76cm) high

£300-400 ON

'There's A World Of Goodness In An Onion – They Will Keep You Fit!, by an anonymous designer.

19.75in (50cm) high

£60-80 ON

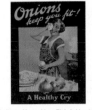

'Onions Keep You Fit! A Healthy Cry', designed by J. Gough.

19.75in (50cm) high

£60-80 ON

'Don't Get That Bottled Up Feeling – Onions Will Keep You Fit', designed by an anonymous designer.

19.75in (50cm) high

£50-80 ON

'Le Thon Amieux-Frères', French tuna fish advertising poster by an anonymous designer and printed by Draeger, restored and mounted on linen.

47.5in (120.5cm) high

£350-450   ON

'Celle Que Je Bois Top Bronnen', designed by Jean d'Ylen and printed by Vercasson, mounted on linen.

D'Ylen (1866-1938) studied under famous poster designer Leonetto Cappiello and his influence can be seen in d'Ylen's use of colour, dark backgrounds and humour.

23in (58.5cm) high

£350-450   ON

A CLOSER LOOK AT A POSTER

Little is known about Leon Dupin (b. c1900), but his Modernist and Art Deco style posters are well designed and sought-after.

Stylized forms and bold colours are typical of his designs.

Most of Dupin's work was done between 1929 and 1936, for the French Joseph Charles printworks, the company that printed this poster.

The poster advertises a French charcuterie from Alsace. The figure pierces the red logo with his fork, as one would pierce a slice of sausage.

'Charcuterie – Conserves, Roess, Siége, Andsolheim, Haut-Rhin', designed by Leon Dupin and printed by Joseph Charles, Paris.

1944   47in (117.5cm) high

£800-1,000   SWA

'Escargots Ménetrel', French advertising poster for snails, designed by Rudd and printed by Gaillard, mounted on linen.

61in (155cm) high

£250-350   ON

'Pedro Presents – New Season's Brazil Nuts, Delicious – So crisp & so milky, British poster, by an anonymous designer.

30in (76cm) high

£20-30   ON

'More Potatoes – Please, Potatoes pay for careful cooking', designed by Edward Cole and issued by the Potato Marketing Board.

19.75in (50cm) high

£40-60   ON

'English Tomatoes Refresh-Invigorate-Sustain', 1940s photomontage poster published by Glass House Marketing Association, folds.

15in (38cm) high

£50-70   ON

'Peugeot' advertising poster, designed by Andre Girard.

Andre Girard is best known for his work for Columbia Records. The sense of speed as a car zooms around a corner, as well as the bold colours and fame of the brand, make this a valuable poster.

c1929   63.75in (162cm) high

£1,500-2,000   **SWA**

'NSU' racing motorcycle advertising poster, designed by H. Weiss.

1953   33.75in (86cm) high

£45-55   **ON**

'The Quick-Starting Pair, Shell Oil and Petrol', poster no. 132, designed by Jean d'Ylen and issued by Shell-Mex Ltd., restored and mounted on linen.

1926   44.5in (113cm) wide

£1,200-1,800   **ON**

'These Men Use Shell, You Can Be Sure of Shell', poster no. 506, designed by Derek Sayer and printed by Waterlow, small tears.

1937   45in (114cm) wide

£180-220   **ON**

'The New Michelin Tyre, Durable, Non-Skid', by an anonymous designer and printed by L. Serre & Cie, mounted on linen.

This poster can be dated from the pattern of the tread as it is not shown in the Michelin poster reference work. Items showing the Michelin man are desirable.

c1927   78.75in (200cm) high

£600-800   **ON**

'Longines', designed by Jean d'Ylen and printed by Vercasson, mounted on linen, restored.

21.5in (54.5cm) high

£550-650   **ON**

'La Rapidisima Hispano-Olivetti', printed by Llauger SA, Barcelona.

A rather odd contrast of a typewriter and steam train, the message is presumably that you'll be typing out work faster than a speeding steam train if you use an Olivetti.

52.5in (133.5cm) high

£1,200-1,800   **SWA**

'Zenith', designed by Jean d'Ylen and printed by Vercasson, mounted on linen.

1928   35.5in (90cm) high

£1,200-1,800   **ON**

A CLOSER LOOK AT AN ADVERTISING POSTER

This poster was designed by eccentric illustrator Louis Wain (1860-1939), known for his drawings and paintings of cats, which are now highly sought-after by collectors.

Wain is better known for his book illustrations and drawings, he created comparatively few advertising pieces.

This is typical of his style, with mad-eyed, personified cats engaging in human activities - here listening to an early Marconi radio set with headphones at a garden party.

Typical of his erratic style, it is amusing to note that none of the cats are wearing the hats or boots the poster is advertising.

'Jacksons' World Famous Hats & Boots For Ladies and Gents', colour lithograph poster, printed by Tom G. Porter Printer, Leeds, folds.

30.5in (77.5cm) wide

£7,000-8,000   **ON**

'Need A Light? Get The Name Right', 1970s Brymay matches advertising poster, by an anonymous designer, folds.

59.5in (151cm) high

£60-80   **ON**

A 1980s Marlboro cigarettes advertising poster.

The rugged Marlboro man promotes the fact that 'real men' smoke. As smoking becomes increasingly unfashionable worldwide, ephemera related to it may rise in value, especially if typical.

22in (56cm) wide

£15-25   **CLG**

'Arrow Collars and Shirts', designed by J.C. Leyendecker.

This is typical of Leydendecker's elegant 1920s-30s style and is perhaps the forerunner of today's 'preppie' styled Abercrombie & Fitch advertising.

27.5in (70cm) high

£1,000-1,500   **SWA**

'Raviba, Pour Teindre Et Raviver Les Bas', French sock advertising poster designed by Jean d'Ylen and printed by Vercasson, with stains and damage.

17in (43cm) high

£180-220   **ON**

'La Maison Du Porte Plume', on a beige background, designed by Jean d'Ylen and printed by Publicite E. V. Ferdi, mounted on linen.

Showing 'unbranded' pens by Swan, Waterman and Parker, this will also appeal to writing equipment collectors. It is also available on a white background.

c1930   61in (155cm) high

£1,200-1,800   **ON**

'Robys Premier Fils', French alcohol advertising poster, printed by Affiches Stentor Paris, mounted on linen.

1936   76.5in (194cm) wide

£650-750   **ON**

'Come Along, Boys! Enlist To-Day, No.122, by an anonymous designer for the Parliamentary Recruiting Committee.

The Parliamentary Recruitment Committee released a large number of posters, each with its own number. Images showing smart uniforms, camaraderie and appealing to a sense of duty or protection of our sceptred isle and naturally did not portray the horrors of trench warfare waiting for recruits.

c1916   *30in (76cm) high*

£150-200   **ON**

A CLOSER LOOK AT A WAR RECRUITMENT POSTER

Savile Lumley (d.1950) was a popular book illustrator and poster designer. He also provided the drawings for several magazines and comics including The Boy's Own Paper and The Champion Annual.

Britain had no conscription policy at this time, so psychological persuasion was used, aiming to shame men into volunteering by suggesting their sense of family duty, masculinity and honour was at stake.

This is perhaps his most famous design and motto, and both have become iconic.

The message is reinforced by the girl on her father's knee with a book waiting for a story and the boy playing with toy soldiers and a cannon.

'Daddy, What did YOU do in the Great War', no. 79, WWI recruitment poster, designed by Savile Lumley for the Parliamentary Recruiting Committee.

1915   *30in (76cm) high*

£350-450   **ON**

'Follow me! Your Country Needs You', no. 41, designed by E.V.Keeley for the Parliamentary Recruiting Committee.

c1916   *30in (76cm) high*

£22-28   **ON**

'Be Ready!, Join Now', no. 81, by an anonymous designer for the Parliamentary Recruiting Committee, mounted on linen.

c1916   *39in (99cm) high*

£60-80   **ON**

'Halt! Who Goes There?', no. 60, by an anonymous designer for the Parliamentary Recruiting Committee.

1915   *39in (99cm) high*

£22-28   **ON**

'There's Room For You, Enlist To-Day, no. 122, designed by W.A. Fry for the Parliamentary Recruiting Committee.

c1916   *30in (76cm) high*

£22-28   **ON**

'Your Country's Call, Isn't this worth fighting for? Enlist Now', no. 87, by an anonymous designer for the Parliamentary Recruiting Committee.

c1916   *30in (76cm) high*

£40-60   **ON**

'Women Of Britain Say – "GO!"', no. 75, designed by E.V. Keeley for the Parliamentary Recruiting Committee.

1915	30in (76cm) high
£280-320	**ON**

A CLOSER LOOK AT A RECRUITMENT POSTER

Illustrator Flagg (1877-1960) was a child prodigy, working on the staff of LIFE by the age of 15 and becoming one of the US' most famous artists by 1900.

He designed 46 posters for the US government during WWI, this is the most famous and over 4million were printed and displayed from 1917-18.

The iconic image first appeared on a July 1916 issue of Leslie's magazine, titled 'What Are You Doing for Preparedness?'. Flagg was then asked by the US government to adapt it into a poster.

The origin of the model is an enigma – some say it was a soldier on a train, other that it was Flagg himself so that he did not have to pay for a model to pose.

'I Want YOU for U.S. Army', designed by James Montgomery Flagg, some damage and restoration.

The dramatic image of a man pointing had been used successfully for wartime recruitment in Britain by Alfred Leete, whose pointing Lord Kitchener appeared in September 1914.

1917	40in (100cm) high
£1,500-2,000	**FRE**

'Don't stand looking at this Go and Help!', no. 73', by an anonymous designer for the Parliamentary Recruiting Committee.

c1915	50in (127cm) wide
£150-200	**ON**

'Boys! Come Along You're Wanted, no. 80, designed by an anonymous designer for the Parliamentary Recruitment Committee.

c1915	30in (76cm) wide
£50-80	**ON**

'Step Into Your Place', no. 104, by an anonymous designer for the Parliamentary Recruitment Committee.

c1916	30in (76cm) wide
£30-50	**ON**

'He did his duty, Will You do Yours?', no. 20, by an anonymous designer for the Parliamentary Recruiting Committee.

c1915	30in (76cm) high
£18-22	**ON**

'A.T.S.', designed by Abram Games and printed by Multi Machine Plates for HMSO.

This example is signed in pencil by the artist and dated 1942.

1942	15in (38cm) high
£180-220	**ON**

'Men of London, Each Recruit Means Quicker Peace, Join To-Day', published by the Central Recruiting Office.

17in (43cm) high

£22-28   ON

'Remember Belgium, Buy Bonds, Fourth Liberty Loan', designed by Ellsworth Young, mounted on linen.

This dramatic image showing a German soldier hauling a Belgian girl along as her village burns shocked many at the time.

30in (76cm) high

£350-450   ON

'Buy Victory Bonds, For Industrial Expansion', designed by Arthur Keelor, mounted on linen.

36.25in (92cm) high

£180-220   ON

'Tittle Tattle Lost The Battle', designed by G. Lacoste, American WWII propaganda poster, framed.

The style of the hidden Hitler listening in to conversations was devised by Kenneth Bird under the name 'Fougasse' and made famous in his 'Careless Talk Costs Lives' campaign during WWII.

21.25in (54cm) high

£180-220   ON

'War Loan, Back the Empire with your Savings, Invest Now', no. 21, by an anonymous designer, mounted on linen.

30in (76cm)

£60-80   ON

'It May Cost Life, Think Before You Write', designed by Noke and printed for HMSO by C&P.

19.75in (50cm) high

£45-55   ON

'El 11 Març Sortirà Companya Revista de La Dona', designed by I.G. Viladot.

This 1930s Spanish Civil War poster is very much in the style of artist Georges Braque.

39in (100cm) high

£500-700   CL

'In War And Peace We Serve', designed by Reginald Mayes and printed for GWR/LMS/LNER/SR by Jas. Truscott & Son Ltd.

This poster was meant to show how Britain's railways served the country equally well in war and in peacetime. Look out for Helen McKie's interiors of Waterloo station that have a similar message as these can fetch over £2,000.

40.25in (102cm) high

£200-300   ON

'Marionetten-Theater, Münchener Künftler', designed by Lucian Bernhard and printed by Hollerbaum & Schmidt, Berlin.

Designed to look like a stage, the poster is typical of Bernhard's (1883-1972) Modernism, with flat tones and no outlining.

'Minnie Dupree "A Rose O' Plymouth-town"', American poster for the Broadway production.

1902	80in (203cm) high	1910	36.75in (92cm) wide	c1910	39in (99cm) high
£550-650	**CL**	**£400-500**	**SWA**	**£200-300**	**CL**

'Original American Barés', advertisement for the singer, dancer, equilibrist and musical imitator.

'A Gentleman from Mississippi', American theatrical or film advertising poster.

'Count the First – Living Proof of The Darwin Theory', American animal show poster.

c1910	41in (104cm) wide	c1914	41in (104cm) high
£400-500	**CL**	**£250-350**	**CL**

'D'Oyly Carte Opera Company', designed by Dudley Hardy and printed by David Allen & Sons, mounted on linen.

30in (76cm) high	
£60-80	**ON**

'Zu Ehren Pablo Casals', designed by B. Olonetzki, advertising a benefit concert to honour cellist Pablo Casals's 75th birthday.

'Josephine Baker Ziratron', by an unknown designer.

This rare and highly appealing poster advertises Baker's Israeli performances.

1951	50in (125cm) high	1954	28in (70cm) high
£500-600	**SWA**	**£800-1,200**	**SWA**

'Dzieje Grzechu' (Story of a Sin), designed by Jerzy Flisak, Polish film poster for the Waleriana Borowczyka film.

1975   *33in (84cm) high*

£80-120   **CLG**

'Malzonkowie Roku II' (The Scarlet Buccaneer), designed by Andrzej Krajewski, Polish film poster for the Jean-Paul Rappeneau film.

1972   *33in (80cm) high*

£70-100   **CLG**

'Trema' (Stagefright), designed by Marek Freudenreich, Polish Film poster for the Alfred Hitchcock film.

1966   *33in (84cm) high*

£220-280   **CL**

'Morderca Samotnych Kobiet', designed by Andrzej Bertrandt, Polish film poster for the Helmut Nitzschke film.

1972   *33in (84cm) high*

£70-100   **CLG**

'Tango', designed by Maria Ihnatowicz, Polish film poster for the Stanislav Barabas film.

5,900 of these posters were printed.

1967   *33in (84cm) high*

£120-180   **CLG**

'Sanjuro Samuraj Znikad', (Sanjuro), 1960s Polish poster for the Akira Kurosawa film, designed by Andrzej Krajewski.

Printed in an edition of 4,200 copies for the 1962 film, this poster is rare today.

1968   *33in (84cm) high*

£150-200   **CLG**

'Zmoklá Nedele', designed by Richard Fremund, Czech film poster for the Marton Keleti film.

Fremund was one of the noted artists who gave birth to the avant garde Czech poster design movement.

1962   *33in (84cm) high*

£120-180   **CLG**

'Fortel a Jak ho Ziskat' (The Knack ... and How To Get It), Czech poster for a Richard Lester film.

1965   *33in (84cm) high*

£100-150   **CLG**

POTLIDS

COLLECTORS' NOTES

- Coloured printed pot-lids appeared in the mid-1840s, and are one of the earliest types of visually appealing packaging. Products include bear's grease (its many uses included rifle-cleaning and hair styling), and meat or fish paste. Major pot-lid makers were F.R. Pratt, T.J. & J. Mayer and Brown-Westhead & Moore.

- It is not usually possible to date pot-lids precisely as so many were produced over long periods, with no records remaining. Form, events depicted and certain makers' marks can help to date some to within a date range. Over 350 different images are known, many taken from watercolours by artist Jesse Austin.

- Earlier lids, from before 1860, are usually flat and light in weight, with fine quality prints, and often have a screw thread. Lids from 1860 to 1875 are heavier and have a convex top. Later lids are heavier still, are often flat, and the printing tends to be of a lower quality. Run your finger over a lid and if you can feel the transfer, it is likely to be a later reproduction.

- Rare variations and designs and attractive, strongly coloured examples fetch the highest prices. Chips to the flange and rim do not affect value seriously. Chips to the image, or restoration, can lower values by 50-75 per cent. Complex borders usually add value.

- Numbers given here relate to reference no. in K.V. Mortimer's book 'Pot-Lids and other Colour Printed Staffordshire Wares', published by the Antique Collectors' Club, 2003.

A Pratt 'The Listener' domed pot-lid, no. 130, with black marbled border, restored.

This is a later version – earlier examples have a yellow striped apron. Look out for the exhibition example with a wide gold band, as this can fetch over £800.

4.25in (10.5cm) diam

£55-65 SAS

A Pratt 'Lady, Boy and Goats' pot-lid, no. 276, with hairline crack.

This image was based on Sir Edwin Landseer's watercolour 'Harvest time in the Scottish Highlands'.

3in (7.5cm) diam

£25-35 SAS

A Cauldon 'Charity' pot-lid, no. 133.

This version with a line border is the most common and this example had considerable restoration, hence its low value. Had it not been so damaged it may have fetched around £50.

5in (12.5cm) diam

£30-40 SAS

A Pratt 'The Swing' pot-lid, no. 327.

4.25in (11cm) diam

£80-120 SAS

A Pratt 'The Wolf And The Lamb' pot-lid, no. 343.

This is a comparatively common lid.

4.25in (10.5cm) diam

£25-35 SAS

A Pratt 'On Guard' pot-lid, no. 334.

Two variations, both of the same value, are known. One has a bucket under the seat, the other a dog. It was produced for a long period after around 1860.

4.25in (10.5cm) diam

£45-55 SAS

A late 19thC 'Negro and Pitcher' pot-lid, no. 311.

4.75in (12cm) diam

£120-180 **SAS**

A CLOSER LOOK AT A POT-LID

This is an early lid and has some under-glaze hand painting. It is also from an unknown factory.

It can be found in a number of variations, with a green or red coat and with a gold band (as here), a marbled flange or vignetted. All are very rare.

The image is taken from 'Pleasures of Life' by famous Georgian satirical caricaturist Thomas Rowlandson (1756-1827).

This example is from the Abe Ball collection. Ball was a pioneering and notable pot-lid collector and researcher.

A 'How I Love to Laugh' pot-lid, no. 367, with black mottled flange and tall matching base.

3in (7.5cm) diam

£1,800-2,200 **SAS**

A 'Tam-o-Shanter' pot-lid, no. 199, with shallow flange.

4.25in (11cm) diam

£100-150 **SAS**

A Bates, Brown-Westhead & Moore (Cauldon) 'Tam-o-Shanter and Souter Johnny' (346) pot-lid, no.198, with shallow flange and hairline crack.

4.25in (10.5cm) diam

£40-60 **SAS**

A Pratt 'Lady Brushing Hair' pot-lid, no. 111.

Look out for examples with a bared breast or a gold band as they can be worth more than twice this value.

2.75in (7cm) diam

£220-280 **SAS**

A Bates, Elliot & Co. 'Summer' pot-lid, no. 335.

The presence of a registration mark underneath indicates an earlier and more valuable example.

4.5in (11cm) diam

£35-45 **SAS**

A 'The Matador' pot-lid, no. 78.

This may have been produced by Mayer and is a very rare lid.

3.5in (8.5cm) diam

£700-800 **SAS**

A late 19thC Pratt 'Thames Embankment' pot-lid, no. 245.

4.25in (10.5cm) diam

£40-50 **SAS**

A later issue of Mayer's 'New Houses of Parliament, Westminster' pot-lid.

5.25in (13cm) diam

£120-180 **SAS**

A late 19thC Pratt 'The New Blackfriars Bridge' pot-lid, no. 244.

4.5in (11cm) diam

£20-30 **SAS**

A Mayer 'Buckingham Palace' pot-lid, no. 174.

Beware of reproductions that are flat and heavier than the slightly domed originals.

5.25in (13cm) diam

£220-280 **SAS**

A late 19thC Pratt 'Albert Memorial' pot-lid, with coaches.

The version without coaches can be worth slightly more.

4.25in (10.5cm) diam

£70-90 **SAS**

A 'Windsor Castle and St. George's Chapel' pot-lid, no. 175, probably by Cauldon, chipped.

An undamaged example with rare advertising wording for S. Graftey may fetch up to £500.

3.5in (9.5cm) diam

£50-70 **SAS**

A Mayer 'Osborne House' pot-lid, no. 179.

This version with a white border and crown is the most valuable.

5in (12.5cm) diam

£70-90 **SAS**

A Mayer 'Great Exhibition 1851' pot-lid, no. 142, restored.

c1851 *4.25in (10.5cm) diam*

£40-60 **SAS**

A Mayer 'The Interior of the Grand International Building of 1851' pot-lid, no. 143.

Look out for examples with the band but no wording and a different roof, which can fetch up to £800.

c1852   5.25in (13cm) diam

£250 350   **SAS**

A Pratt 'Interior View of Crystal Palace' pot-lid, no. 145.

4.5in (11.5cm) diam

£350-450   **SAS**

A Pratt 'Philadelphia Exhibition 1876' circular pot-lid, no. 155.

A rare rectangular version of this lid, which does not show the coach and horses, can be worth over twice the value of this lid.

4.5in (11cm) diam

£45-55   **SAS**

A late 19thC Pratt 'Paris Exhibition 1878' pot-lid, no. 153, with hairline crack.

4.5in (11cm) diam

£45-55   **SAS**

A Mayer 'New York Exhibition 1853' pot-lid, no. 154, with minor hairline crack to rim.

This example with an oak-leaf band is one of the most valuable versions.

5.25in (13cm) diam

£550-650   **SAS**

A Pratt 'L'Exhibition Universelle de 1867' pot-lid, no. 152.

4.75in (12.5cm) diam

£70-90   **SAS**

A 'The Administration Building World's Fair, Chicago 1893' pot-lid, possibly by Pratt.

Grey is the most common colour, buff or yellow prints are extremely rare – other colours are only rumoured to exist.

4.25in (10.5cm) diam

£350-450   **SAS**

A 'Gothic Archway' pot-lid, no. 309.

This is a very rare lid and a number of variations are known. It was produced by an unidentified maker for medical supplies maker and retailer S. Maw & Sons of London.

3.25in (8cm) diam

£2,000-2,500   **SAS**

A Pratt 'Deer Drinking' pot-lid, no. 277, with hairline crack.

4.25in (10.5cm) diam

£45-55 **SAS**

A Pratt 'Country Quarters' pot-lid, no. 273.

4.75in (12cm) diam

£80-120 **SAS**

A late 19thC 'The Swallow' pot-lid, no. 287, restored.

3.75in (9.5cm) diam

£120-180 **SAS**

A CLOSER LOOK AT A POT-LID

An example with a window behind the inkwell and quill is the least valuable, usually fetching up to £50.

This lid is paired with 'A Pretty Kettle of Fish' showing four dogs fighting over a cauldron of fish soup.

Along with many pot-lid patterns, this image is also found on other wares, in this instance, tea plates.

This version with a fancy border and title is the most valuable version.

A Pratt 'Lobster Sauce' pot-lid, no.57, first issue with title.

4.25in (10.5cm) diam

£180-220 **SAS**

A 'The Snow-drift' (276) pot-lid, no. 267.

This image is based on Sir Edwin Landseer's 'Highland Shepherd's Dog In The Snow'. Usually values are the same whether the wording is present or not.

4.25in (10.5cm) diam

£30-40 **SAS**

An early and very rare 'Bear in a Ravine' advertising pot-lid, no. 14, with restored flange.

2.5in (6.5cm) diam

£1,500-2,000 **SAS**

A Mayer 'The Kingfisher' pot-lid, no. 286, gold line border, restored.

This very rare and beautiful example, from the Abe Ball collection, has a gold border. It is an early lid, later issues have greenish tinges.

5.25in (13cm) diam

£650-750 **SAS**

A Mayer 'Pegwell Bay, Ramsgate, Still Life Game' pot-lid, no. 43, with a hairline crack.

4.25in (10.5cm) diam

£40-60 SAS

A 'Shells' pot-lid, no. 75.

Shell pot-lids were made either by Pratt or Mayer. The number and type of shells shown helps identify these visually similar lids.

4.5in (11cm) diam

£60-80 SAS

A 'Shells' pot-lid, no.73, restored.

3.25in (8cm) diam

£55-65 SAS

A 'Shells' pot-lid, no. 72, framed.

This is the most common of the shell pattern pot-lids.

5in (12.5cm) diam

£22-28 SAS

A Pratt 'Rose & Convolvulus' pot-lid, no. 401, with gold line.

4in (10cm) diam

£180-220 SAS

A very rare Mayer 'Balaklava, Inkerman, Alma' pot-lid, no. 204.

This Crimean war commemorative lid shows (clockwise) the Earl of Cardigan, the Duke of Cambridge, Lord Raglan and General Simpson. It would have fetched more if it had not been damaged and restored. Beware of later examples that have weaker colours as these are generally worth about a quarter of this value.

5in (12.5cm) diam

£250-300 SAS

A very rare Mayer 'Alma' Crimean war commemorative pot-lid, no. 203.

This example, from the notable Cashmore collection, has a fancy border highlighted in gold. It is the rarest and most valuable variation.

5.25in (13cm) diam

£1,200-1,800 SAS

A 'Royal Coat of Arms' pot-lid, no. 173, without name, restored.

4.25in (11cm) diam

£500-600 SAS

COLLECTORS' NOTES

■ Loose powder compacts first became popular in the 1920s when it became more acceptable for women to apply makeup in public. After World War II, the rise of the working woman meant more disposable income to spend on beauty products, such as face powder and lipstick, portable enough to be carried in handbags. Silver screen stars set the trend for powder compacts and increased their popularity.

■ During the early years face powder was imported from France but many compacts were supplied by American makers. Most examples were made of sterling silver, silver plate, chrome plate, or gold plate. Other fashionable materials were also used such as Bakelite and tortoiseshell. Look out for examples that reflect the style of an era – Art Deco is hugely popular.

■ Compacts came in many shapes, sizes and price brackets. Some had mechanisms that played music and others, such as a Schuco soft toy range, concealed a powder container inside novelty casing.

■ When buying, look out for examples in excellent condition. Check that mirrors are intact and that exteriors have not been damaged through use. As many compacts were stored in purses and pockets and so were subject to wear, examples in good condition are hard to finder and thus are sought after.

■ Desirable names include Stratton and Kigu in the UK and Elgin in the US. Stratton was particularly innovative, introducing a self-opening lid to prevent broken fingernails. Equally appealing is the Salvador Dali 'Bird-in-Hand' compact, designed for Elgin.

An Art Deco blue and green guilloché enamel and silver powder compact, Birmingham hallmark.

1937   *2.75in (7cm) diam*

£80-120   **SH**

A 1930s American La Mode yellow guilloché enamel compact, with flower embossed sides.

                       2.75in (7cm) diam

£100-150   **MGT**

A 1930s Coty white metal compact, decorated with an image of a sailing ship, from their Paris range.

                       2.5in (6.5cm) diam

£20-30   **MGT**

A Japanese tri-colour inlaid gold and silver powder compact.

c1920   *2in (5cm) diam*

£200-250   **SH**

A 1950s Kigu black enamel compact, with cut-out ivorine insert of two dancers, marked "Made in England. Patented".

                       3.5in (9cm) diam

£40-60   **MGT**

A 1920s Vinolia Aralys satyr powder compact, with registered design mark "732540" for 1927.

                       2in (5cm) diam

£80-100   **SH**

A 1930s Atkinson's Art Deco white metal compact, for pressed powder.

£80-120   **MGT**

A 1930s Gwenda butterfly wing compact.

Butterfly wings have been used in jewellery and small decorative objects since the 1920s, initially in Europe. Use peaked in the 1950s, but they are still used in some places today. The material is often used to simulate the sky or sea with a reverse-painted design placed over the top. Older pieces are usually more desirable, as are examples with good quality decoration.

3.25in (8.5cm) diam

£50-70   **MGT**

A 1930s Coty butterfly wing powder compact, with unusual use of different types of wing.

2in (5cm) diam

£50-70   **MGT**

A 1930s Dubarry Baby-Jack compact, with foil design of a fairy, with Dubarry logo.

2.25in (5.5cm) diam

£80-100   **MGT**

A 1930s Gwenda powder compact, with foil-backed design of a courting couple, with original puff and sifter.

The addition of the original puff and sifter makes this example more desirable. The foil-backed sky effect can be mistaken for butterfly wings, so check pieces carefully.

2.25in (5.5cm) diam

£40-60   **SH**

A 1950s English Melissa gilt metal powder compact, with lucite swan insert.

2.75in (7cm) diam

£30-50   **MGT**

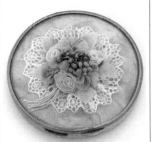

A 1930s/40s French powder compact, with silk flowers under a plastic dome.

2.75in (7cm) diam

£30-40   **SH**

A 1930s French plastic transfer printed compact, depicting romantic couple, enhanced with gilding and with brass frame.

£40-60   **MGT**

A Stratton R.M.S. Queen Mary liner powder compact.

This is likely to have been bought from an onboard shop.

c1960   2.5in (6.5cm) diam

£70-100   **MGT**

A 1960s 'The Beatles' gilt powder compact, no maker's mark.

This desirable compact appeals to collectors of Beatles memorabilia as well as compact collectors.

3in (7.5cm) diam

£100-150   **MGT**

A 1930s Japanese Princess Deco enamelled clam shell-design powder compact, no maker's mark.

3.25in (8.5cm) high

£80-100 **MGT**

A 1950s Russian enamelled silver shell powder compact, with gilt-washed interior, Russian hallmark.

3.25in (8.5cm) high

£120-180 **MGT**

A 1930s American Elgin Ford V8 advertising compact, with separate rouge and powder compartments.

3.5in (9cm) high

£40-60 **MGT**

A 1930s American Elgin oval guilloché enamel powder compact, with separate rouge and powder compartments.

3.25in (8.5cm) high

£80-120 **MGT**

A 1930s La Mode padlock powder compact, with tri-coloured goldtones original puff and label.

3in (7.5cm) high

£100-120 **SH**

A La Mode heart guilloché enamelled powder compact.

c1937   2.5in (6.5cm) high

£80-120 **SH**

A 1940s American Elgin tri-colour teardrop powder compact, with original advertising booklet inside.

3.75in (9.5cm) high

£40-60 **MGT**

A French Jonteel white metal deep hexagon powder compact, with embossed ibis on the cover.

c1921   1.5in (4cm) wide

£40-60 **SH**

A 1930s hexagonal blue guilloche-on-brass tango powder compact, possibly Austrian, with rotating sieve mechanism, no maker's mark.

The appealing colour, unusual form and great condition make this desirable.

2.25in (5.5cm) wide

£150-200 **MGT**

A 1910s/20s French girl-on-a-swing powder compact, decorated with stove-baked enamel signed "Gamel".

3in (7.5cm) wide

£100-150　SH

A late 1940s Stratton Pontoon-shape power compact, decorated with enamelled bluebirds, marked "Pro PAT".

3in (7.5cm) wide

£30-40　MGT

A 1940s/50s Schildkraut square mother-of-pearl compact, with petite-point insert.

2in (5cm) wide

£40-60　MGT

A 1950/60s amber-coloured powder compact, with glass jewelled top.

2.25in (5.5cm) wide

£25-35　SH

An Austrian Framus red enamel on gilt and red carved bakelite powder compact, with unusual spring action opening.

3.25in (8.5cm) wide

£100-150　MGT

A 1940s Zeigfeld Glorified Girl striped plastic compact.

4.5in (11.5cm) wide

£60-80　MGT

A 1930s Art Deco green enamelled powder compact, with unusual clip fastening, no maker's mark.

3in (7.5cm) wide

£60-80　MGT

A 1930s silver and enamel scenic tango powder compact.

2.25in (5.5cm) wide

£120-180　SH

A 1920s Art Deco silver-plated tango powder compact, decorated with a silhouette lady and with tassel and separate coin compartments.

2.5in (6.5cm) high

£80-120　SH

A CLOSER LOOK AT A POWDER COMPACT

This is an early example of a compact intended for use outside of the house.

The additional powder compartment and lipstick holder add appeal and the compact retains its original puffs and lipstick, increasing the value.

These compacts could be heavily used, resulting in wear. This example is in good condition and the decoration is well-executed

Guilloché enamelled powder compacts are sought-after and the shape of this example is particularly attractive.

A 1920s blue guilloché enamel bag-shaped powder compact, with separate blush and lipstick, original puffs and lipstick.

3.25in (8.5cm) wide

£200-250 **SH**

A 1950s German Zast black plastic and goldtone metal handbag-shaped powder compact, marked "UO NR 7780".

3in (7.5cm) wide

£30-40 **SH**

A late 1930s/early 1940s Henriette black and gilt metal dragon design fan compact.

5in (12.5cm) wide

£70-90 **MGT**

A 1940s Volupte figural hand powder compact, known as the 'Gay Nineties Mitt', decorated with a printed black 'lace' mitten and floral bracelet.

4.5in (11.5cm) wide

£350-450 **MGT**

A Pygmalion Sonata gilt metal piano powder compact, with folding legs.

c1954 2.75in (7cm) wide

£120-150 **MGT**

A 1940s plastic army officer's cap powder compact, unmarked but probably by Henriette.

3in (7.5cm) wide

£60-80 **MGT**

An unusual 1920s French bottle-shaped powder compact, with powder in lid and mirror on base.

2in (5cm) high

£30-45 **SH**

A 1940s/50s American Derneys 'Three Secrets' powder box and perfume, with original outer box.

6in (14.5cm) wide

£35-45   SH

A 1920s Art Nouveau L.T. Piver Poudre Pompia powder box.

This example is empty, a sealed box with its original contents could be worth around £100.

3.75in (9.5cm) high

£40-50   SH

A 1940s Richard Hudnut Lady Dubarry large oval powder box, opened but with outer box.

4in (10cm) high

£20-30   SH

A 1930/40s French Lenthérique Bal Masqué powder box, with theatrical mask decoration, sealed with outer box.

3in (7.5cm) diam

£30-45   SH

A 1920s French Jonteel Ibis Cold Cream powder box, empty.

3in (7.5cm) diam

£10-20   SH

A 1940s French Bourjois Soir de Paris powder box, open with contents.

3in (7.5cm) diam

£8-15   SH

An American Heather 'Geranium' rouge tin, by Heather Co. NJ USA, with original puff.

c1925   *1.75in (4.5cm) diam*

£18-25   SH

A 1930/40 Tangee 'Gay Red' dry rouge compact tin, by George Luft Co, with original puff.

1.5in (4cm) diam

£10-15   SH

A rare 1920s French Coty Falling Puffs design powder box, designed by Lalique.

3.25in (8.5cm) diam

£10-15   SH

FIND OUT MORE...

Collector's Encyclopedia of Compacts, *Carryalls and Face Powder Boxes Vols. I & II*, by Laura Mueller, published by Collector Books, 1993 & 1997.

Vintage and Vogue Ladies' Compacts, by Roselyn Gerson, published by Collector Books, 2001.

British Compact Collectors' Club, PO Box 131, Woking, Surrey, GU24 9YR.

Compact Collectors, P.O. Box 40, Lynbrook, NY 11563, USA.

COLLECTORS' NOTES

■ Railwayana continues to be a popular collecting area, although, as with many areas, more common items, such as carriage prints, are much less sought-after by collectors at present.

■ Signs are still one of the major collecting areas. Examples taken from trains, including nameplates and shedplates are among the most popular, however cab-side number-plates are currently in a slight decline.

■ The market for station signs, particularly totems is still strong, however collectors are being selective and pay a premium for examples in original condition and that are fresh to the market.

■ Provenance or a connection to a named locomotive, station or line can add value. Many items from the 'big four' groups: the London, Midland & Scottish (LMS);

London & North Eastern Railways (LNER); the Southern Railway (SR); and the Great Western Railway (GWR) also tend to attract a premium. Memorabilia from smaller, and often short-lived lines, can also be valuable, as production would have been limited.

■ The period between the 1920s and the advent of nationalisation in 1948 is the most popular period, followed by the period from 1948 until The Beeching Report of 1963, which lead to the closure of a number of stations and lines. This can also mean that pieces from this period are also more expensive, so more recent examples, including those from diesel and electric locomotives can provide more affordable alternatives.

■ Signs in particular are being reproduced, probably accounting for the premium paid for examples in original condition. So examine pieces carefully and only buy from a reputable dealer or auction house.

A British Railways (Southern) dark green 'Bognor Regis' station totem sign.

£350-450   **GWRA**

A British Railways (Southern) light green 'Clapham Junction' station totem sign, with white flange, excellent condition.

Arguably the most popular of all Southern totem signs, Clapham Junction claims to be the busiest station on the world.

£650-750   **GWRA**

A British Railways (Southern) dark green 'Coulsdon South' station totem sign, with white flange, few face chips and edge chipping.

£220-280   **GWRA**

A British Railways (Southern) light green 'Guildford' station totem sign, excellent condition.

Ex LSWR station between Woking and Godalming.

£450-550   **GWRA**

A British Railways (Scotland) blue 'Cupar' station totem sign, in extremely good condition.

£500-600   **GWRA**

A British Railways (Scotland) light blue 'Grantown-on-Spey West' station totem sign.

£1,000-1,500   **GWRA**

A British Railways (Scotland) blue 'Slateford' station totem sign.

Ex Caledonian Railway station between Carstairs and Edinburgh. It is both a desirable station and a desirable line as indicated by the value.

£2,200-2,800   **GWRA**

A CLOSER LOOK AT A TOTEM SIGN

Melksham is situated between Chippenham and Trowbridge, and was a Great Western Railway station. GWR is perhaps the most collectable of the 'big four' railways.

This sign is in excellent, original condition. Totem collectors prefer signs in original condition.

MELKSHAM

When this sign was sold at auction in 2003, it was the first time it had appeared on the market, making it sought after with collectors.

The station closed in April 1966 and vintage totems from closed stations are usually more desirable.

A British Railways (Western) 'Melksham' station totem sign, with brilliant colour and deep shine, minor blemishes.

£3,500-4,500   **GWRA**

BLACKPOOL SOUTH

A British Railways (Midlands) 'Blackpool South' station totem sign.

Ex Preston & Wyre Railway station, which at one time was between Central Station and Kirkham. As with all totems from this location, it has faded considerably because of the environment, but is still intact.

£550-650   **GWRA**

A large and rare British Railways (Midlands) 'British Railways' totem sign, some chipping and edge damage.

£120-180   **GWRA**

DANE ROAD

A British Railways (Midlands) 'Dane Road' station totem sign, some chipping around and into 'Road' and some overall mottling.

Ex Manchester South Junction & Altrincham Railway station between Sale and Stretford.

£400-500   **GWRA**

GARSTON

A scarce British Railways (Midlands) 'Garston' station totem sign.

Ex LNWR station between Liverpool and Widnes.

£1,200-1,800   **GWRA**

OXFORD ROAD

A British Railways (Midlands) 'Oxford Road' station totem sign.

Ex Manchester South Junction & Altrincham Railway station between Timperley and London Road, Manchester. This sign was sold in the 1960s on the platform at Altrincham station during the celebrations for the arrival of the Electric Services.

£1,000-1,500   **GWRA**

TAMWORTH

A British Railways (Midlands) 'Tamworth' station totem sign.

Ex-LNWR station on the West Coast main line (Low Level) between Rugby and Stafford, or, could equally been from the ex-MR station (High Level), between Birmingham and Derby.

£600-700   **GWRA**

WINDSOR & ETON
CENTRAL

A British Railways (Western) 'Windsor & Eton Central' station totem sign, extremely good condition.

Ex GWR terminus on the branch from Slough.

£1,000-1,500   **GWRA**

KENNINGTON

A London Transport Northern Line 'Edgware/Kennington' enamel destination indicator, with brass ends.

£20-30   GWRA

PADDINGTON

A British Railways 'Paddington/Didcot' wooden carriage board, maroon background with cream lettering, excellent condition.

32in (80cm) wide

£200-300   GWRA

An LMS Midland Railway style 'Redditch South' signalbox nameboard, wood with screwed-on cast iron letters.

73in (182.5cm) wide

£550-650   GWRA

HERTFORD NORTH

A British Railways (Eastern) 'Hertford North' enamel running-in-board.

84in (210cm) wide

£60-80   GWRA

NORTH BERWICK

A British Railways (Scotland) 'North Berwick' enamel running-in-board, in two parts, good light blue colour.

North Berwick is an ex-North British Railway station on the branch from Drem.

130in (330cm) long

£100-150   GWRA

A British Railways (Scotland) 'Drem' enamel double-sided running-in-board, one side blank, somewhat faded.

Ex North British Railway station between Edinburgh and Dunbar.

72in (180cm) wide

£150-200   GWRA

RAMSGATE

A Southern Railway 'Ramsgate' enamel target sign, very good condition.

Ex SECR coastal location between Canterbury and Margate.

£500-600   GWRA

ELTHAM PARK

A Southern Railway 'Eltham Park' enamel target sign.

Ex SECR station between Blackheath and Bexley Heath.

£100-150   GWRA

RAILWAYANA

A rare Monmouth Railway cast-iron trespass sign, 'Caution, Trespassers On Any Part Of The Railway Are Liable To A Penalty Of Two Pounds', bottom right corner missing, not affecting the lettering.

£180-220   GWRA

A CLOSER LOOK AT A STATION SIGN

This wording is very unusual and had not been seen on the market before at the time of sale.

Flangless signs such as this are much weaker than flanged examples. They are much harder to find in good condition.

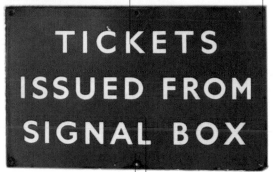

TICKETS ISSUED FROM SIGNAL BOX

Tickets would normally be issued from the ticket office, but in this instance it would appear that the station was not sufficiently busy to require a separate building.

It was taken from Waddon Marsh Halt, which was an ex-LBSCR station between Croydon and Mitcham Junction. It was demolished in 1997.

A rare British Railways (Southern) 'Tickets Issued From Signal Box' flangeless enamel sign.

21in (53.5cm) wide

£500-600   GWRA

WAITING AND LADIES ROOM

A British Railways (Southern) 'Waiting and Ladies Room' dark green enamel doorplate, in mint condition.

18in (45.5cm) wide

£350-450   GWRA

A British Railways (Midlands) 'Camden Road Junction' enamel signal box sign, very good condition.

52in (130cm) wide

£400-500   GWRA

7 FROM MILITARY SIDING SHUNT 6

An unusual '7 from Military Siding Shunt 6' enamel signal box lever plate, white lettering on red background.

£30-40   GWRA

LOCK UP

An LNER 'Lock Up' cast-iron doorplate, face only repainted.

£120-180   GWRA

SHAKESPEARE

A British Railways (Southern) 'Shakespeare' enamel signal box board, very good condition.

72in (180cm) wide

£250-350   GWRA

PRIVATE

A rare British Railways (North Eastern) 'Private' doorplate, black-edged flangeless style, overall in excellent condition.

The tangerine colour indicates that this sign was from a North Eastern region station. This was a small region, meaning fewer examples would have been made. The black-edged lettering is also rare.

£200-300   GWRA

A CLOSER LOOK AT A LOCOMOTIVE NAMEPLATE

The Hall class of locomotive is actually one of the least popular classes to collect.

At the time of the sale, this name had not appeared at auction before, making it desirable.

The Acton Hall was a Great Western Railway locomotive, one of the most sought-after regions to collect.

It is in original condition, which adds greatly to its saleability.

An 'Acton Hall' Hall Class 4-6-0 locomotive nameplate, no. 4982, in original condition.

This locomotive was built in January 1931 and was first allocated to a Weymouth shed. Its last shed allocation was Plymouth Laira. It was withdrawn from service in May 1962 and was scrapped at Swindon Works.

£6,000-8,000   **GWRA**

An 'Abertnant' industrial locomotive nameplate, face restored.

This 0-6-0ST locomotive was built by Manning Wardle & Co. Ltd in 1921 and was numbered 2015.

41in (102.5cm) wide

£800-1,200   **GWRA**

A 'Cowburn' industrial locomotive nameplate, together with a matching worksplate, top of plate stamped "R", original patina on back.

This locomotive belonged to the National Coal Board at Pooley Hall Colliery, Polesworth near Tamworth and was scrapped in the mid-1960s at Birds, Long Marston, from where this plate was obtained. Named after the tunnel on the Hope Valley Line between Manchester and Sheffield.

30in (75cm) wide

£4,500-5,500   **GWRA**

A 'Kapai' industrial locomotive brass nameplate, together with a matching worksplate, restored.

The locomotive no. 1532 was made at Peckett's in Bristol in 1920 and went to the National Coal Board Pooley Hall Colliery, Polesworth nr. Tamworth, Staffs. It was scrapped at Birds Commercial Motors, Long Marston where this nameplate was obtained at the time. Kapai is a municipality in the Philippines, but it was more likely named for the Maori "It is good".

19in (47.5cm) long

£1,500-2,000   **GWRA**

A 20thC 'Kent' cast brass locomotive-type nameplate, possibly from a colliery engine, having raised high relief letters and squared fixing holes.

19.75in (50cm) wide

£450-550   **BIG**

A '9D' oval shed plate.

Buxton 1948-63 and Newton Heath 1963-73.

£150-200　　　　　　　　　　　GWRA

A '54A' oval shed plate, from Sunderland 1948-58.

This desirable shedplate is from a depot that closed early, as many stayed open into the 1960s. It is also in original condition, as it would have come from the locomotive, a desirable feature with collectors.

A '52K' oval shed plate, from Consett until 1965.

£180-220　　　　　　　　　　GWRA

£350-450　　　　　　　　　　GWRA

A '81A' oval alloy shed plate, face may have been restored but lots of old paint on back and around edge remains, four hole variety as fitted to Hymeks and others.

Old Oak Common until 1973.

£100-150　　　　　　　　　　GWRA

An 'LMS Built 1894 St Rollox' oval brass worksplate.

A large 'Andrew Barclay Sons & Co, Kilmarnock, Caledonia Works, No. 1807.1923' oval brass worksplate "Andrew Barclay No 1807 1923".

Andrew Barclay worksplates are particularly sought-after. They are also larger and more decorative than most other name plates.

16in (40cm) wide

£280-320　　　　　　　　　　GWRA

£500-600　　　　　　　　　　GWRA

A 'Built Derby 1953' oval worksplate, face repainted.

£60-80　　　　　　　　　　GWRA

An unusual 'Built 1962 Darlington' worksplate, with chunky lettering.

£70-90　　　　　　　　　　GWRA

An 'LMS Built Derby' worksplate, reputedly from a 2-6-4T ex Willesden scrap line, face restored.

£80-120　　　　　　　　　　GWRA

A CLOSER LOOK AT A NUMBERPLATE

A '73094' smoke box numberplate.

Ex-British Railways Standard Class, built Derby December 1955 and allocated to Shrewsbury. It was later moved to Patricroft and finally Gloucester Barnwood where this was rescued from the locomotive on the 9th June 1963.

£650-750   GWRA

Numberplates from named locomotives are more desirable as it usually indicates a commercial locomotive from a major region.

As it is a named locomotive, the owner may well try to reunite the numberplate with the name plate.

A '73 111' yellow livery, flame-cut cabside numberplate.

Ex BR/English Electric Electro Diesel Class 73 Locomotive built January 1966 and originally numbered E6017.

24in (60cm) wide

£50-70   GWRA

The Kingstone Grange is a popular locomotive and items relating to it are desirable.

Its connection to the GWR also adds to it value.

A '6820' brass cabside numberplate.

From an ex GWR 'Grange' Class 4-6-0 locomotive 'Kingstone Grange', built Swindon in January 1937, first allocation Newport Ebbw Junction. It was a well-travelled locomotive, and was also allocated to Pontypool Road, Exeter, Worcester, Newport and Cardiff. Finally stored at Swansea East Dock and scrapped at Birds, Morriston in October 1965.

£2,800-3,200   GWRA

A Southern Railway 'S.R. 230 Ashford' large oval wagon plate, with S[E]R kite-mark between, face only restored, back lightly washed.

£50-80   GWRA

A large 'S 1952 273 Lancing' oval wagon plate, face only restored, back lightly washed.

£150-200   GWRA

An 'LMS No. 4189 1930' tenderplate.

Ex 2-6-0 'Crab' locomotive originally numbered 13154, later 42854.

1930

£70-100   GWRA

A 'G.W.R. Cylinder Oil' cast iron plate, unrestored.

6in (15cm) wide

£70-100   GWRA

A Cheshire Lines Railway bridgeplate number 35.

£60-80   GWRA

A Great Northern Railway lorry or cart lamp, with brass-rimmed front cowl and bevelled glass side aperture, stamped "GNR" on chimney, missing bullseye lens.

£350-450   **GWRA**

A CLOSER LOOK AT A KEY TOKEN

Key tokens were given to drivers to operate the blocks on single track lines and helped to ensure that two trains did not try to appoach the same section of single track at the same time.

Key tokens have the name of the section of track they correspond to engraved or etched on them, another popular feature with collectors.

As much railway memorabilia tends to be bulky and therefore difficult to display, small items such as key tokens are popular with collectors.

This token is from a GWR section between Torquay and Kingswear, in Devon.

A 'Goodrington - Churston' alloy key token, alloy construction with traces of blue paint, original condition.

£250-300   **GWRA**

This lamp is from a small line, making it rare, it is also stamped with a specific place name: Shoreham Permanent Way, a popular feature with collectors. If the lamp had not been painted yellow by the previous owner, and was in original condition, it could have fetched approximately £100 more.

£600-700   **GWRA**

A London, Brighton & South Coast Railway three-aspect handlamp, marked "SHOREHAM PER. WAY", complete with an S.B.R. reservoir and SR burner, bears large, brass, fully titled plate on the side and also a brass 'B' plate on the reducing cone, on the collar is the original location plate "P. WAY DIV. HORSHAM", painted yellow.

An LNER Great Northern triple piecrust pattern three-aspect handlamp, brass-plated, markcd "London & North Eastern Railway C.Vicar, K X Goods", complete with LNER reservoir, LNER burner and both red and blue aspect glasses, painted in silver to indicate the authority of C. Vicar who was the Head Shunter at Kings Cross Goods Depot.

£40-60   **GWRA**

A scarce Somerset & Dorset three-aspect hand lamp, embossed "LMS, Midland Pattern" and with "S & D" properly stamped on the reducing cone, unrestored and complete with reservoir and unmarked burner.

£120-180   **GWRA**

A 'Coity Jcn - Tondu' alloy key token, with traces of yellow paint, excellent, original condition.

£100-150   **GWRA**

A G.W.R. 'Taunton No. 2' metal first aid cabinet, with hand-painted lettering and numbered "204", no contents.

£80-120   **GWRA**

A British Railways (Western) chain-driven, fusée movement time recorder clock, by The Gledhill – Brook Time Recorders Ltd., Huddersfield, Halifax, London & Birmingham, complete with mechanism, ribbon and keys, ivorine plate beneath dial reads "BR-W 5713".

£800-1,200   GWRA

A LNWR Fletchers solid cast iron train describer, nine segments on the face, six of which have a description, brass front rim, on original mahogany base, in superb condition throughout.

£550-650   GWRA

A Midland Railway mahogany cased, signal box block instrument, stamped with "MR Co" on roof, bears two ivorine plates "Down Line" and "North Walsall Junction".

£100-150   GWRA

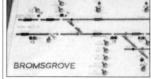

An LNWR block instrument, plated Oxford Port Meadow, up and down lines indicated, complete with under slung bell.

£200-300   GWRA

A GWR signal box block instrument, 'Up Line' - 'Down Line' with bell above.

£220-280   GWRA

A British Railways 'Bromsgrove' illuminated signal box diagram, in mahogany box with lift-up lid, the brass hinges marked "BR".

£150-200   GWRA

A British Railways Western Region Paignton South signal box diagram, dated 1963, in original GWR frame.

£400-500   GWRA

A British Railways (SR) Lancing signal box diagram, illuminated type with cut-outs for TC indicator lamps.

c1980   *45in (114.5cm) wide*

£80-120   GWRA

A GWR Hotels solid copper saucepan, stamped on the side with company initials.

8in (20cm) diam

£100-150   **GWRA**

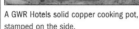

A GWR Hotels solid copper cooking pot, stamped on the side.

12in (20cm) diam

£120-180   **GWRA**

A Southern Railway brass ashtray, 'sunshine' lettering around the rim with the SR Shipping House Flag in one rim segment.

4in (10cm) diam

£50-60   **GWRA**

A Great Western Railway Hotels dinner plate, by Bridgwood, England.

7in (17.5cm) diam

£35-45   **GWRA**

A North Eastern Railway Hotels Department china cup, by Crown, Staffordshire, large colour crest on side and blue, gold trimmed rim.

2in (5cm) diam

£35-45   **GWRA**

J.E. Wigston, 'The Flying Scotsman at Speed', oil on canvas, signed and dated.

1975   *30.5in (76.5cm) wide*

£220-280   **L&T**

A GWR 'Locomotives Old and New' jigsaw, book type box containing 'Literature of Locomotion, Aug 1933' pamphlet and a single sheet 'Holiday Haunts' pamphlet.

£150-200   **GWRA**

A 'Popular Game of Railway Race', presumably by Glevum, including a three-fold board with colour lithographic printing, three painted lead locomotive gaming pieces and a die.

c1911   *11.75in (30cm) wide*

£35-45   **BLO**

A mid-20thC black rail guards hat, with shiny leather binding, size 6 7/8.

£22-28   **BIG**

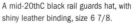

COLLECTORS' NOTES

■ Rock and Pop memorabilia continues to make the headlines with million pound items coming up for sale around the world. Despite this is there is something for every pocket, ranging from records, merchandise, autographs and even items owned by the stars themselves.

■ It is this latter category that tend to garner the highest prices. Instruments or clothing used by an artist are always sought-after and a connection to a significant event lends a greater cachet. This area can mean high prices so check for a cast-iron provenance.

■ Stars such as the Beatles and Elvis had their image attached to a mind-boggling array of merchandise, which is open to a wider market. Look for examples in mint condition or retaining original packaging.

■ The punk movement is a hot collecting area, as the music and the fashions of the period are back in vogue. The outrageous Sex Pistols were only together for a few years, so tickets and posters from their concerts are desirable as are items connected to Sid Vicious who died in 1979 at the young age of 21.

■ Autographs are another popular area, but always ensure they are genuine. The huge demand for autographs from people like Elvis, the Beatles and the Rolling Stones meant that band members would often sign for each other, as would assistants or fan club staff.

A very rare 'Mersey Beat' music paper, volume I #4 August 17th 1961, featuring early Beatles content.

The 'Mersey Beat' had a close association with the Beatles, it was founded by one of Lennon's fellow students from the Liverpool Art College, Bill Harry. Brian Epstein, who went on to manage the band wrote a column for the paper.

1961

£50-70 GAZE

The Beatles, 'Love Me Do', UK single 45-R 4949, released by Parlophone, with red label.

The red label denotes the first pressing, later pressings have a black label and are worth slightly more. The red label version was re-released in 1982, but can be distinguished by the word 'mono' on the label.

1962

£40-60 GAZE

An American 'The Beatles Sound Best on KRLA' pin.

Californian radio station KRLA have the distinction of being the first first southland station to air the band.

2.25in (5.5cm) diam

£35-45 LDE

A 1964 The Beatles 'Beat Monthly' calendar.

11in (28cm) high

£70-100 GAZE

A Beatles lithographed tin tray, by Worcesterware.

c1964   13in (33cm) wide

£25-35 GAZE

The Beatles with Tony Sheridan and Guests, 'My Bonnie', rare US LP SE4215, released by MGM, with inner.

1964

£50-70 GAZE

The Beatles Quiz Book, printed by William Collins Sons and Company Limited.

1964   11in (28cm) wide

£15-25 GAZE

A Foyles Luncheons guest list and table plan, for a lunch to mark the publication of John Lennon's 'In His Own Write', 23rd April 1964, bearing signatures of John Lennon, Lionel Bart and Alma Cogan.

£300-400 GAZE

A 1960s The Beatles pendant necklace, with small black and white press photograph of the group.

1in (2.5cm) wide

£28-32 GAZE

A 1965 Beatles pocket diary.

4.25in (11cm) high

£60-80 GAZE

The Beatles, 'Les Beatles dans Leurs 14 Plus Grands Succès', French LP OSX231, released by Odeon.
1965

£350-450 GAZE

A Saunders Enterprises card cut-out George Harrison coat hanger.
c1965 *15.25in (38.5cm) high*

£70-100 GAZE

A Paul McCartney guitar-shaped 'jewellery brooch', produced by Invicta Plastics, on the original card.
c1965

£25-35 GAZE

The Beatles, 'Beatles For Sale', Australian LP PMCO1240, released by Parlophone.
1965

£18-22 GAZE

A pair of 1960s Dutch Beatles stockings, patterned with rows of the Beatles heads and printed design to the top band.

£22-28 GAZE

A collection of Beatles memorabilia, comprising a Beatles fan club membership booklet bearing signatures, a 'Magical Mystery Tour' UK double EP MMT 1-2, released by Parlophone, 'Introducing the Beatles', US LP VJLP 1062, released by Vee-Jay, 'All My Loving', UK EP GEP 8891, released by Parlophone, and a Cavern Club membership card.

£800-1,000 ROS

The Beatles, 'Magical Mystery Tour' UK mono double EP MMT-1, released by Parlophone, in excellent condition.

1967

£40-60 GAZE

The Beatles, 'Penny Lane/Strawberry Fields' UK double A-side single R5570, released by Parlophone, with original picture sleeve.

250,000 copies of this single were released in the picture sleeve.

1967

£25-35 GAZE

A John Lennon and Yoko Ono pin.

This image was used as the controversial cover of the 'Unfinished Music No.1: Two Virgins' album released by John and Yoko in 1968. Outraged distributors sold the album in a brown paper wrapper and a number of copies were impounded for obscenity.

c1968 2.25in (5.5cm) diam

£40-50 LDE

The Beatles, 'Strawberry Fields', Dutch record club-issue LP DS018, released by Parlophone.

1968

£80-120 GAZE

The Beatles, 'Love Me Do', red vinyl 'For Juke Boxes Only!' single S7-56785, issued by Capitol.

The first of a series of juke box singles reissued by Capitol, this was intended to be in black vinyl only but the pressing machine still had red vinyl in it from a previous pressing and a number were printed by mistake. The exact number of red copies made is uncertain, but it is probably somewhere between 300 and 1,200.

1992

£10-15 GAZE

Four large Beatles plastic key rings, with press photography.

c1968 5in (12.5cm) high

£25-35 GAZE

The Beatles, 'Please Please Me', Japanese issue LP AP 8675, released by Apple, with different cover and colour inserts.

c1969

£22-28 GAZE

ROCK & POP

A 'Best Wishes, Elvis Presley' badge, the back marked "Elvis Presley Enterprises 1956".

3in (7.5cm) diam

£60-70   LDE

Elvis Presley, 'Rock n' roll', first UK LP CLP 1093, released by HMV.

1956

£150-250   GAZE

An 'Elvis' badge.

3.75in (9.5cm) diam

£60-70   LDE

Elvis Presley, 'Got a Lot o' Livin' To Do!', Malaysian issue LP PR-101, by Pirate Records.

1976

£30-40   GAZE

An 'Elvis Monthly Special' book, published by Albert Hand, distributed by World Distributors (Manchester) Ltd.

1977

£5-7   MTS

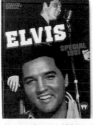

A pack of Elvis Collectors Series bubble gum cards, by Boxcar Enterprises Inc.

1978   4in (10cm) wide

£8-12   MTS

An 'Elvis Monthly Special 1981' book, published by Albert Hand, distributed by World Distributors (Manchester) Ltd.

1981

£5-7   MTS

An packet of promotional Elvis Presley 'Tickle Me' feathers, sealed.

Released to promote Presley's western comedy-musical 'Tickle Me'.

1965   11.5in (29cm) high

£60-70   LDE

A 'Bay City Rollers' badge.

2.25in (5.5cm) diam

£15-20 LDE

The Beach Boys, 'LA Light', UK picture disc LP CRB 11-86081, released by Caribou Records.

1979

£7-10 GAZE

Jeff Beck, 'Boston Tea-Party', Japan acetate LP.

1969

£35-45 GAZE

A 'San Francisco likes Tony Bennett' badge, with ribbon.

3.25in (8.5cm) diam

£22-28 LDE

Marc Bolan, 'The Wizard', UK demo 45 single F 12288, released by Decca.

1965

£220-280 GAZE

David Bowie, 'Ragazzo Solo, Ragazza Sola', rare UK single, BW 704 208, released by Philips, second edition.

1969

£40-60 GAZE

David Bowie, 'El Rey Del Gay Power', Spanish issue double compilation LP DCS 15044, released by Deram, with gatefold cover.

1973

£70-90 GAZE

A 'Maxine Brown Fan Club' badge.

2in (5cm) diam

£30-40 LDE

An early Kate Bush colour photo, signed with dedication, with certificate of authenticity.

£60-80 GAZE

Johnny Cash, 'The Fabulous Johnny Cash', US LP BPG 62042, released by CBS, bearing signature on reverse.

Cash's death in 2003 re-ignited interest in his work and in memorabilia connected to him. The success of the Oscar-winning biopic 'Walk the Line' has also contributed to this.

1961

£35-45   **GAZE**

Dead or Alive, uncut picture disc featuring Pete Burns.

Burn's appearance on Celebrity Big Brother in 2005 has renewed interest in his band. It remains to be seen how long this interest will last.

£15-20   **GAZE**

Lonnie Donegan, 'Lonnie', 10in UK LP Nixa NPT 19027, released by Pye.

Lonnie Donegan, known as 'The King of Skiffle' was a huge influence on many 1960s UK bands including John Lennon and Paul McCartney.

1957

£7-9   **GAZE**

Donovan, 'A Gift From a Flower to a Garden', UK double LP boxed set NPL 20000, with navy blue box, released by Pye.

This was also produced with a black box, which is worth the same amount.

1968

£22-28   **GAZE**

The Doors, 'LA Woman', UK single K 42090, released by Elektra, the cover with rounded corners and die-cut PVC window.

1971

£12-18   **GAZE**

Eagles, 'One of These Nights', 12in LP, released by Asylum, bearing signatures of members of the band.

1975

£80-120   **GAZE**

Georgie Fame, 'Yeh Yeh', US LP LP 8292, released by Imperial, with white label promo.

1964

£8-12   **GAZE**

A 1950s 'Go Man Go! – Crazy Man Crazy!' Eddie Fisher badge.

1.75in (4.5cm) diam

£10-20   **LDE**

A late 1970s 'The Four Tops at The Sands', Atlantic City pin.

3in (7.5cm) diam

£20-30   **LDE**

Jimi Hendrix, 'Isle of Wight', Japanese LP MP2217, released by Polydor, with original cover and obi.

1971

£70-90   GAZE

Jimi Hendrix Experience, 'Band of Gypsys', LP released by Polydor.

1973

£10-15   GAZE

Jimi Hendrix Experience, 'Axis Bold as Love', French LP 0820167, first edition released by Barclay with unique cover.

1968

£120-180   GAZE

A 'Herman's Hermits' badge.

3.5in (9cm) diam

£20-30   LDE

A 'High Hopes – Emerald Room, Wildwood, NJ' card badge, with ribbon, marked "Aura Badge Co. Tommy Tatler Booking Management".

3.25in (8.5cm) diam

£40-50   LDE

INXS, 'Shabooh Shoobah', UK LP PRICE 94, released in Mercury, signed by all the group including Michael Hutchence, with certificate of authenticity.

1984

£70-100   GAZE

Joy Division, 'An Ideal For Living', rare picture disc album.

1978

£15-25   GAZE

A 1970s 'The Combined Led Zeppelin I & II', songbook, Kinney Music Ltd.

c1973

£18-22   GAZE

Led Zeppelin, 'The Song Remains the Same', Japanese double LP WPCR11619, released by Atlantic, with booklet and obi.

1976

£10-15   GAZE

Joni Mitchell, 'Court and Spark', UK LP SYLA 8756, released by Asylum, Half Speed Master album.

1974

£6-8   **GAZE**

The Modern, 'Industry', green vinyl single 9877069, released by Mercury, signed by the band in the sleeve.

Emerging band The Modern had this, their second single, banned from the UK charts due to fans and friends buying multiple copies in order to raise the band's position – the first time such action had been taken. It will be interesting to see how this effects the value of the single in the secondary market.

2006

£3-5   **MHC**

A 'The Monkees' pin, by Raybert Productions Inc 1966.

3.5in (9cm) diam

£25-35   **LDE**

Mott the Hoople, 'Live with David Bowie', rare German LP LTD 1073.

1973

£15-25   **GAZE**

Patti Smith Group, 'You Light Up My Life', LP PSG 44, live in Santa Monica.

1978

£10-20   **GAZE**

Pink Floyd, 'Psychedelic Games for May', limited edition picture disc, SNAP - 01.

£22-28   **GAZE**

A Pink Floyd Saville Theatre Programme, for October 1967, one of the earliest Floyd programmes in existence.

£180-220   **GAZE**

A Pink Floyd 'See Emily Play' original sheet music book.

1967

£80-120   **GAZE**

Pink Floyd, 'A Saucerful Of Secrets/The Piper At The Gates Of Dawn', limited edition German set of the bands first two LPs 1C 062-04 190/1C 062-04 292, released by EMI/Columbia.

1973

£150-250   **GAZE**

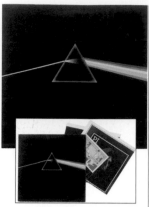

Pink Floyd, 'The Dark Side of The Moon', UK LP SHVL 804, released by Harvest with two sticker and two posters.

1973

£10-20   GAZE

A CLOSER LOOK AT A QUEEN SINGLE

To celebrate this award, EMI decided to release a special limited edition single and chose Queen for the honour.

In 1978 EMI were awarded the prestigious Queen's Award To Industry For Export Achievement. This was in part due to the success of Queen and their hit Bohemian Rhapsody.

The record was supposed to be purple, the band's signature colour and was to match the sleeve. Due to a production error they were printed in blue and it was decided to keep the blue colour.

This single was recently listed No. 5 on Record Collectors all time rarest 100 singles.

Queen, 'Bohemian Rhapsody', limited edition UK blue vinyl single PS EMI 2375, released by EMI in an edition of of 200, special EMI In House "Queens Award For Export".

Although the edition was limited to only 200, un-numbered test pressings and end-of-run copies are on the market but lack the sleeve and the special illustrated label. They are usually worth around £500.

1978

£2,400-2,800   GAZE

Queen, 'The Best of ...", rare 1980s Korean LP, with unique cover, long since deleted.

£35-45   GAZE

Queen, 'I Want It All', UK single QUEEN 10, released by Parlophone, the picture sleeve bearing signatures of the group, obtained from an official fan club member.

1989

£200-300   GAZE

Queen, 'Queen's First E.P.', very rare UK demo EMI 2623, released by EMI.

1976

£15-25   GAZE

Roxy Music, 'Manifesto', UK picture disc LP, EGPD 001, released by Polydor/E.G.

1979

£10-20   GAZE

Sex Pistols, 'No One Is Innocent/My Way ', Japanese single PC 1978, YK-109-AX, released by Virgin with lyric insert.

1978

£35-45   GAZE

Siouxsie and the Banshees, 'Cities in Dust', live in Brussels double LP, released by Wonderland.

1986

£30-40 GAZE

The Soft Machine, 'The Soft Machine', French issue LP, released by Barclay with unique cover.

1969

£30-40 GAZE

Soft Machine, 'Soft Space UK Harvest', 'A' demo, HAR 5155, released by Harvest.

1978

£10-20 GAZE

Bruce Springsteen, 'As Requested Around the World' LP, very rare US DJ only LP, Columbia AS 97.

1981

£30-40 GAZE

Tyrannosaurus Rex, 'Unicorn/Beard of Stars', re-issued double album TOOFA 9, released by Cube/Pye.

1978

£15-20 GAZE

A 'The Supremes Fan Club' badge.

2.5in (6.5cm) diam

£60-70 LDE

Roger Waters, 'Music From the Body', rare Italy issue LP 3C 064-04615, released by Harvest with unique Italy-only cover.

1974

£50-70 GAZE

The Who, 'Tommy', UK double LP 2657 002, released by Track with original booklet.

1973

£20-30 GAZE

The Yardbirds, 'The Yardbirds', rare Swedish LP SSX 1018, released by Columbia.

This LP was released first with this 'Studio Cover' and then with a second pressing 'Street Cover'. This cover was shot by photographer Dezo Hoffman, famous for shooting bands including The Beatles and cementing their carefully crafted image.

1965

£35-45 GAZE

COLLECTORS' NOTES

■ The development of transfer-printing in the late 18thC, along with improved manufacturing and distribution methods in the 19thC, allowed royal commemorative ceramics to become more widely available. Many items were produced from the reign of Queen Victoria onwards.

■ As there is a huge variety of items available, many collectors choose to limit their collection to a particular personality, subject area or time period.

■ The quality of an item is a key indicator to value, with those by well-known makers, made from high quality materials and with fine decoration usually being the most valuable. Designers to look for include Eric Ravilious, Charlotte Rhead and Richard Guyatt.

■ Condition is also vital as so many pieces were produced in large numbers. Always buy pieces in the best condition possible, as this will help to maintain or increase values.

■ As well as ceramics, many other different items have been produced for royal events such as coronations, jubilees, births and deaths. Trinkets and 'ephemeral' card and paper items can be found regularly at affordable prices and can make a satisfying collection.

■ With modern wares, look for limited editions and 'deluxe' versions made in low numbers. Some collectors tend to prize items with photographic images while others prefer those with just coats of arms or ciphers.

A Queen Victoria and Prince Albert Royal Wedding plate, unmarked.

1840   6.25in (16cm) diam

£350-450   **RCC**

A Staffordshire Queen Victoria Coronation six-sided plate, in excellent condition and bright colours.

Despite the ready availability of Queen Victoria Jubilee pieces, earlier coronation commemoratives are much harder to find.

1837   7.5in (19cm) wide

£500-600   **RCC**

A Prince Albert Victor, Duke of Clarence commemorative white parian bust, by Robinson & Leadbeater.

7.5in (19cm) high

£220-280   **RCC**

A silk of Prince Albert, the Prince Consort.

9in (23cm) high

£40-50   **RCC**

A Queen Victoria and Prince Albert commemorative plate, decorated in pink lustre, printed in pink and enamelled in colours with portraits entitled "Victoria and Albert".

c1851   8.75in (22cm) diam

£50-70   **SAS**

A Queen Victoria and Prince Albert commemorative cup and saucer, printed in pink and enamelled in colours with portraits entitled "The Royal Family".

c1851

£60-80   **SAS**

A Prince Albert In Memoriam tall jug, with moulded decoration and decorative handle, registered design mark.

1861   8in (20cm) high

£140-160   **RCC**

A Queen Victoria commemorative plate, featuring an unusual full-length portrait, possibly German.

10.5in (26.5cm) diam

£80-120 RCC

A CLOSER LOOK AT A COPELAND TYG

The plainer standard edition has no lip and is less desirable. It can be worth up to £1,400.

The portraits include Queen Victoria, Field Marshall Lord Roberts and the Most Honorable Marquis of Salisbury.

The Transvaal was incorporated into the British Empire in 1900, following the second Boer War.

This deluxe version was limited to only 100 pieces. The small edition means this tyg will always be sought-after.

A Copeland Edition De Luxe 'Transvaal Tyg', from an edition of 100, Thomas Goode subscribers copy.

c1900 6in (15cm) high

£2,000-2,200 RCC

A Doulton Burslem Queen Victoria Diamond Jubilee beaker.

c1897 3.75in (9.5cm) high

£120-130 RCC

A Doulton Lambeth Queen Victoria Diamond Jubilee stoneware mug, printed in brown with young and old portraits.

£40-60 SAS

A German Queen Victoria Diamond Jubilee beaker, with portraits of the Royal Family.

c1897

£80-100 RCC

A Copeland Queen Victoria Diamond Jubilee moulded teapot, with green and gilt decoration.

c1897 9in (23cm) wide

£220-280 RCC

A Chown limited edition 'Royal Dynastic Plate', commissioned by Paul Wyton and Joe Spiteri to commemorate the centenary of Queen Victoria's Diamond Jubilee, from an edition of 50.

1997 10.5in (26.5cm) diam

£100-140 RCC

A Coalport King Edward VII Coronation plate, with wavy rim.

1902   10in (25.5cm) diam

£100-120   **RCC**

A Winton King Edward VII In Memoriam plate.

1910

£60-80   **RCC**

A Copeland King Edward VII In Memoriam two-handled vase, from an edition of 100, Thomas Goode subscribers copy.

1910   7in (18cm) high

£1,000-1,400   **RCC**

An English King George V & Queen Mary Coronation egg cup, with gilt rim.

1911   2.75in (7cm) high

£15-20   **RCC**

A Shelley late Foley King George V & Queen Mary Coronation teapot, with gilt trim.

1911

£100-150   **RCC**

A Wilkinson Ltd. 'HM King George V – Pro Patria' character jug, designed by Francis Carruthers Gould, issued by Soane & Smith Ltd during WWI, decorated in underglaze colours, enamelled and gilded, the underside with printed manufacturer's and retailer's mark and facsimile signature of Carruthers Gould.

12.25in (30.5cm) high

£900-1,000   **SAS**

A Princess Mary, Princess Royal and Henry, Viscount Lascelles Royal Wedding beaker.

1922   4in (10cm) high

£150-180   **RCC**

A King George V & Queen Mary Silver Jubilee mug, with flag-shaped handle.

1935   7in (18cm) high

£30-40   **RCC**

A Crown Staffordshire King George V & Queen Mary Silver Jubilee lidded pot, in the form of a crown.

1935

£80-90   **RCC**

A Ridgway Prince Edward, Prince of Wales Investiture plate.

1911 *9in (23cm) diam*

£70-90 **RCC**

A Shelley cup and saucer set, commemorating Prince Edward, Prince of Wales' visit to South Africa, with gilt rims.

1925

£40-60 **SAS**

A Prince Edward, Prince of Wales tapering pottery beaker, with named naval portrait.

c1925

£40-60 **SAS**

A Melba China King Edward VIII globe, decorated in colours on an inscribed base.

1937 *3.5in (9cm) high*

£80-120 **SAS**

A Bovey Pottery 'The Three Reigns of 1936' three-handled mug, with portraits of George V, Edward VIII and George VI.

c1936 *3.5in (9cm) high*

£80-120 **RCC**

A Hammersley King Edward VIII Coronation mug, with the abdication date added.

Without the abdication the value would be £40-50.

c1936 *3.5in (9cm) high*

£120-150 **RCC**

A Shelley Edward VIII Coronation plate.

c1936 *9in (23cm) diam*

£40-50 **RCC**

A J. & J. May Wallis Simpson In Memoriam mug.

1986 *3.5in (9cm) high*

£45-55 **RCC**

A Lady Grace China limited edition 'The King's Dilemma' character jug, by Peggy Davies Ceramics, commemorating the 60th Anniversary of Edward VIII's abdication, from an edition of 350.

1997 *9.5in (24cm) high*

£150-200 **RCC**

A King George VI & Queen Mary plate, commemorating their visit to the Delhi Dunbar, India.

1911   *5.5in (14cm) diam*

£25-35   **RCC**

A Paragon King George VI & Queen Elizabeth Coronation preserve pot.

4in (10cm) high

£50-60   **RCC**

An Aynsley King George VI & Queen Elizabeth Coronation plate, with raised laurel wreaths to the centre.

1937   *10.5in (26.5cm) diam*

£80-120   **RCC**

A Royal Albert Crown China King George VI & Queen Elizabeth Coronation mug, with photographic portrait of the Royal Family by Marcus Adams.

1937   *4in (10cm) high*

£20-30   **RCC**

A Royal Doulton King George VI & Queen Elizabeth Coronation mug, with 'G' shaped handle.

1937   *3.5in (9cm) high*

£120-150   **RCC**

A Compton & Woodhouse Queen Elizabeth the Queen Mother commemorative plate.

8in (20cm) diam

£30-60   **RCC**

A Chown limited edition Queen Elizabeth the Queen Mother 101st birthday mug, commissioned by Paul Wyton & Joe Spiteri, from an edition of 70, with two portraits on a pink ground.

2001   *3.75in (9.5cm) high*

£25-35   **RCC**

A Chown limited edition Queen Elizabeth the Queen Mother In Memoriam plate, commissioned by Paul Wyton & Joe Spiteri, from an edition of 25.

2002   *8in (20cm) diam*

£50-70   **RCC**

A Creampetal Grindley Princesses Elizabeth and Margaret commemorative plate.

c1936   *10.5in (26.5cm) wide*

£60-90   **RCC**

A Paragon bowl commemorating the birth of Princess Elizabeth, printed in brown with named and dated portrait after Marcus Adams, lined in red and gilt.

1926   5.5in (14cm) diam

£35-45   SAS

A Crown Derby Queen Elizabeth II Coronation musical tankard, playing 'The National Anthem'.

1953   5.5in (13.5cm) high

£50-70   SAS

A Wedgwood Queen Elizabeth II Coronation mug, designed by Richard Gyatt.

1953   4in (10cm) high

£70-90   RCC

A Queen Elizabeth II Coronation mug, with E-shaped handle.

1953   3.5in (9cm) high

£20-30   RCC

A Paragon Queen Elizabeth II Coronation loving cup.

1953   6in (15cm) wide

£60-80   RCC

A Wedgwood 'Embossed Queen's Ware' Queen Elizabeth II Coronation milk jug.

1953   6in (15cm) wide

£20-30   RCC

A Mercian China Queen Elizabeth II Silver Jubilee plate, designed by A. Kitson Towler, DFA, from an edition of 60 commissioned by the Commemorative Collectors' Society.

This is from a series of 12 different plates.

1978   10.5in (26.5cm) diam

£45-55   RCC

A Mercian China Prince Philip, Duke of Edinburgh Silver Jubilee plate, designed by A. Kitson Towler, DFA, from an edition of 60 commissioned by the Commemorative Collectors' Society.

10.5in (26.5cm) diam

£45-55   RCC

A tankard commemorating the restoration of Windsor Castle, from The Royal Collection.

1997   3in (7.5cm) high

£25-35   RCC

A Royal Stafford Queen Elizabeth II Golden Jubilee teapot.

2002 *11in (28cm) wide*

£40-50 RCC

A Paragon Princess Margaret plate, commemorating her birth.

1930 *9.5in (24cm) diam*

£80-120 RCC

A limited edition Princess Margaret 60th Birthday commemorative plate, commissioned by Peter Jones China, from an edition of 5,000.

1990 *8.5in (21.5cm) diam*

£35-45 RCC

A Halcyon Days Queen Elizabeth II Gold Wedding beaker.

1997 *4in (10cm) high*

£120-130 RCC

A Coronet Pottery 'The Ladies of August' commemorative plate, with portraits of Queen Elizabeth the Queen Mother, Princess Margaret and Princess Anne.

These three members of the Royal family have birthdays in August.

1990 *10.5in (26.5cm) diam*

£45-55 RCC

A Panorama Studios Ceragraphics Princess Anne and Captain Mark Phillips Royal Wedding mug.

1973 *4.25in (11cm) high*

£20-30 RCC

A Coalport Princess Anne 'Save the Children' commemorative plate, from an edition of 10,000.

The Princess Royal has been president of Save the Children since 1981.

9in (23cm) diam

£30-40 RCC

An Aynsley limited edition Princess Anne and Commander Timothy Laurence Royal Wedding mug, commissioned by Peter Jones China, from an edition of 2,000.

1992 *3.75in (9.5cm) high*

£50-60 RCC

A Wedgwood Prince Andrew and Sarah Ferguson Royal Wedding mug.

1986 *3in (7.5cm) high*

£30-40 RCC

A Crown Derby limited edition Prince Charles' Investiture as Prince of Wales dragon figurine, from an edition of 250, with original box.

The delicate extremities are easily damaged, so undamaged examples are sought-after. The addition of the original box adds to the value.

1969   5.25in (13.5cm) high

£600-800   RCC

A Paragon Prince Charles Souvenir mug.

This would have been released to coincide with his mother's coronation.

c1953   3in (7.5cm) high

£45-55   RCC

A Carlton Ware Prince Charles and Lady Diana Spencer Royal Wedding cup, with double-heart handle.

1981   4.5in (11.5cm) high

£30-50   RCC

A Coronet Pottery Prince William plate, commemorating his birth.

1982   10.5in (26.5cm) diam

£50-70   RCC

A Wedgwood mug commemorating the birth of Prince William, designed by Richard Guyatt.

1982   3in (7.5cm) high

£35-45   RCC

A Royal Doulton limited edition 'The Princess of Wales' commemorative plate, from an edition of 10,000, painted by John Merton.

1991   10.5in (26.5cm) diam

£80-120   RCC

A Chown limited edition Diana, Princess of Wales In Memoriam loving cup, commissioned by Paul Wyton & Joe Spiteri, from an edition of 400.

1997   3in (9.5cm) high

£70-90   RCC

A Crummles limited edition Prince William 21st birthday pill box, commissioned by Paul Wyton & Joe Spiteri, from an edition of 30.

2003

£70-90   RCC

A Chown Prince Charles and Camilla Parker-Bowles Royal Wedding mug, commissioned by Paul Wyton & Joe Spiteri.

The date of this wedding was postponed by one day so that Prince Charles could attend the funeral of Pope John Paul II.

2005   3.75in (9.5cm) high

£25-35   RCC

A Victorian scrap of a Dutch boy holding a small cane and string.

3.25in (8cm) high

£3-4　　　　　　　**AOY**

A Victorian scrap of a Dutch boy holding a goose.

3.25in (8cm) high

£3-5　　　　　　　**AOY**

A Victorian scrap of a lady holding a fan.

3.5in (9cm) high

£6-7　　　　　　　**AOY**

A small Victorian scrap of an elegant lady.

Scraps were produced from the early 19thC until the 1930s, with the 'golden age' being 1860s-1900s. They were collected and stored in albums, or used to decorate greetings cards, boxes or large room screens. Note the protruding tabs of white paper on this example. These were used to hold scraps together on a printed sheet, the blank areas of the sheet having been mechanically stamped out. Each scrap would be torn gently away from the sheet for use. The lady on this scrap also shows Victorian ideals of beauty with her gentle eyes, small nose, rosebud lips, porcelain-like skin and flower encrusted dress.

2.25in (5.5cm) high

£5-7　　　　　　　**AOY**

A Victorian or Edwardian scrap of cricketers.

3.25in (8cm) wide

£5-7　　　　　　　**AOY**

A Victorian scrap of Santa Claus in a black suit.

It is unusual to find Santa Claus in a black suit, revealing its early date. Haddon Sundblom's 1930s advertising campaign for Coca-Cola lays claim to popularising a red-suited Santa.

2.75in (7cm) high

£4-5　　　　　　　**AOY**

A Victorian scrap of Santa Claus and child bearing gifts.

2in (5cm) high

£3-4　　　　　　　**AOY**

A large Victorian scrap of a parrot or macaw.

4in (10cm) high

£3-4　　　　　　　**AOY**

COLLECTORS' NOTES

■ Look out for 1960s & '70s memorabilia which makes a bold visual statement in terms of form, colour and pattern. The work of leading companies and notable designers may fetch higher prices, but even un-named designs can be desirable if they capture 'the look'. Items which inspire fond memories or, for younger buyers, a sense of fascination for this colourful and exciting time, are the most sought after.

■ Bright, acid and often clashing colours dominate - look for hot pinks, oranges and yellows. Designs explode in psychedelic or 'flower power' patterns, and the sinuous Art Nouveau style of the 1900s was given a lurid makeover. Pop, and Op, art inspired designs are also popular.

■ Other recurring themes include youth, love and peace. Items relating to 'Swinging' London, where images of Union jacks, marching bands and old military iconography were repackaged in an anti-establishment manner, are also prized. Most were aimed at, and were popular with, tourists.

■ Continuing from the 1950s, the development of plastics and laminates was closely related to themes of the future, but also convenience. The new informality saw fun and functional ceramics. being used – mugs replaced cups and saucers and functional, and often fun, oven-to-tableware became fashionable.

■ Condition is important as most pieces were used and worn – truly mint examples will be more desirable.

An English Ironstone Tableware flower power plate, by Washington Potteries, Staffordshire, England.	An English Ironstone Tableware flower power plate, by Washington Potteries, Staffordshire, England.	An American Deka Plastics Inc. printed plastic tray, by Deka, Elizabeth, NJ.	A small square plate, by Surrey Ceramics, with abstract floral design, impressed marks.
7.25in (18cm) diam	7.25in (18cm) diam	13in (32.5cm) diam	4in (10cm) wide
£5-7 **MTS**	£5-7 **MTS**	£30-40 **MTS**	£10-15 **TCM**

An English Ironstone Tableware flower power teacup and saucer, by Washington Potteries, Staffordshire England.

This is typical of many 1960s ceramic designs, which exploded in a riot of colourful flowers.

3.25in (8cm) high

£7-10 **MTS**

A set of four 1960s Staffordshire Potteries stacking mugs, transfer-printed with caricatures of fashionable people.

Three Hornsea 'Zoodiac' mugs, designed by John Clappison.

The name of the range is a pun on the design, which combines animals and signs of the zodiac. Hornsea are well known for their novelty mugs.

1974   3.5in (9cm) high

£15-20 each **FD**

3.5in (9cm) high

£30-40 **MTS**

A Midwinter 'Tango' milk jug, designed by Eve Midwinter.

1969-76   *5.25in (13cm) long*

£7-9   **MTS**

A 1960s Price Bros. coffee pot, printed and impressed marks "Price Made in England".

The cylinder was a commonly used shape for tableware during the 1960s, as it was modern, easy to manufacture and displays a pattern extremely well. Portmeirion are perhaps the best known maker of cylindrical tableware during this period, with designs by Susan Williams-Ellis.

9.5in (24cm) high

£25-35   **TCM**

A 1960s Arthur Wood & Sons 'flower power' moulded and hand-painted floral string holder.

These string holders are more commonly seen with pigs as decoration. Arthur Wood & Son acquired Carlton Ware in 1967, and continued to produce under that tradename.

5.75in (14.5cm) diam

£20-30   **MTS**

A CLOSER LOOK AT A HORNSEA POTTERY VASE

Hornsea Pottery was one of the most prolific producers of home and table ware from the 1950s through the 1980s, and are probably most famous for their brown and green 'Heirloom' range.

'Rainbow' was designed by John Clappison, Hornsea Pottery's most prolific and talented designer. He designed for the factory from 1955-72 and 1976-84, devising most of its major ranges.

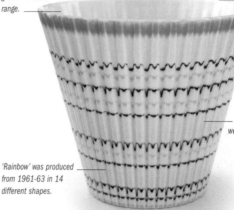

'Rainbow' was produced from 1961-63 in 14 different shapes.

The coloured bands were applied by a fine spray gun – earlier examples have blue banding, with grey bands indicating a later example.

A Hornsea Pottery 'Rainbow' moulded small plant pot holder, the base with mould number "563".

1961-63   *4.75in (12.5cm) high*

£20-25   **AGR**

A 1970s transfer-printed chintz tea storage jar, marked "Portugal" on the base.

5.5in (14cm) high

£10-15   **MTS**

A large unmarked hand-thrown ovoid vase, decorated with a modernist pattern of sgraffito triangles and hand-painted yellow circles.

£40-60   **PSI**

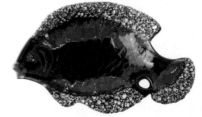

A French 'Vallauris' orange and brown glazed fish dish, with "VALLAURIS" stamp to base.

£15-20   **GAZE**

A CLOSER LOOK AT A CARLTON WARE MONEY BOX

This is part of a series of six money boxes, including a pirate, a clown, a Beefeater and a Scotsman.

This is one of the rarest from the series, probably as it did not have as much appeal to the children of the day as more exciting characters, such as a pirate.

The series was designed by Vivienne Brennan, who is also known for her bug-eyed frog and snail money box designs.

Money boxes are frequently damaged, particularly from use. This example is in excellent condition with no damage.

A Carlton Ware pirate money bank.

8in (15cm) high

£40-50   **MTS**

A 1960s Carlton Ware 'gentleman' ceramic money box.

6.5in (16cm) high

£50-60   **MTS**

A pair of 1960s/70s Carlton Ware salt and pepper shakers, with transfer-printed design of cooks in aprons.

4in (10cm) high

£30-40   **MTS**

A pair of 1960s/70s Carlton Ware salt and pepper shakers, of an Arabian king and queen.

each 3.5in (8.5cm) high

£40-60   **MTS**

A 1970s Italian ceramic money box, in the form of a stylised owl, with painted mark and serial number.

6.75in (17cm) high

£40-60   **TCM**

A 1970s orange ceramic elephant money bank, marked "Italian".

7.5in (19cm) high

£18-22   **MTS**

A 1960s Arthur Wood & Sons hand-painted piggy bank.

These are more commonly found with floral patterns.

6in (15cm) long

£20-30   **MTS**

A pair of 1960s 'I was Lord Kitchener's Valet ' salt and pepper shakers, with 'I was In Carnaby Street' wording to reverse.

5.75in (14.5cm) high

£40-50 MTS

A 1960s 'I was Lord Kitchener's Valet' mug, titled 'I Was In Carnaby Street'.

Ceramics bearing the Union Jack and Carnaby Street slogans were popular souvenirs for foreign tourists during the 1960s when Swinging London was at its peak. 'I Was Lord Kitchener's Valet' was a shop specialising in selling vintage clothes and regimental uniforms, which had become part of 'street fashion'. Owned by Ian Fisk, it also sold new souvenirs bearing the Union Jack and Lord Kitchener and enjoyed patronage from celebrities such as Jimi Hendrix.

3.5in (8.5cm) high

£40-50 MTS

A 1960s 'I was Lord Kitchener's Valet' printed tin tray, titled 'I was In Carnaby Street', with a little rust.

12.5in (31cm) wide

£40-60 MTS

A 1960s 'I was Lord Kitchener's Valet ashtray, titled 'I was In Carnaby Street'.

c1969   4.5in (11.5cm) high

£30-50 MTS

A 1960s Bilton's Ironstone 'I was Lord Kitchener's Valet' plate, titled 'British Dish'.

6.75in (17cm) high

£30-40 MTS

A 'Lady Jane of Carnaby Street Production Cheers' ashtray.

Lady Jane, owned by Harry Fox, was a fashionable women's clothing shop on Carnaby St. Objects marked with the shop's name are far rarer than clothes. 'Lady Jane' was also the title of a Rolling Stones song released in 1966.

5.75in (14.5cm) diam

£50-60 MTS

A 1960s 'Gear of Carnaby Street London' ceramic piggy bank.

The Union Jack was the global symbol of 'Swinging London' during the 1960s.

4.75in (12cm) long

£40-50 MTS

A 1960s Crown Ducal London 'Carnaby St. W1' road sign ashtray, for 'I was Lord Kitchener's Valet'.

4.5in (11cm) diam

£20-30 MTS

An Associated Biscuits Ltd 'Swinging London' biscuit tin, with images of tourist destinations and popular Carnaby Street shops such as 'I Was Lord Kitchener's Valet' and 'Lord John'.

c1966   8.75in (22cm) wide

£30-40 MTS

A rare 'Cool Britannia' tin tray, with a psychedelic Britannia holding a knitting needle with an arc of thread behind her.

14in (35cm) wide

£100-150 MTS

A Polypops printed tray showing Queen Victoria.

The style of the design recalls Pop artist Peter Blake, whose images were very popular during the 1960s. In line with the fashion for vintage, military and dandy like clothing, many historic icons such as Lord Kitchener and Queen Victoria were given a camp '60s makeover.

20.25in (50.5cm) high

£80-120 MTS

A 1960s JRM Design 'Harriet' pattern printed metal tray, designed by Ian Logan.

14in (35cm) wide

£25-35 MTS

A 1960s JRM Design 'Lollipop' pattern printed metal tray, designed by Ian Logan.

Ian Logan is a notable British designer who manages to capture the zeitgeist of an age appealingly. He has worked with a number of high profile clients and continues to design today, with a shop near the Barbican, London.

22.5in (56cm) wide

£50-70 MTS

An American psychedelic printed tin tray.

14.25in (35.5cm) diam

£30-40 MTS

A set of six laminated plastic and cork drinks coasters, designed by Ian Logan.

3.5in (9cm) diam

£25-30 MTS

A set of six 1960s Baret Ware 'Mauve Flower Time' printed metal drinks coasters.

3.25in (8cm) diam

£10-15 MTS

A Marks & Spencer St Michael flower power biscuit tin.

5.5in (14cm) high

£8-12 MTS

A 1960s American Ohio Art psychedelic printed tin recipe card box.

3.75in (9.5cm) high

£20-30 MTS

A 1970s yellow plastic desk tidy, probably Italian, with white plastic drawers.

4.5in (11.5cm) high

£10-12 DTC

A group of six early 1970s Pentagram stacking and interlocking moulded plastic ashtrays, with registered number 954.589 for 1971.

Plastic was a popular material during the 1960s, with space age connotations. New advances in plastics and injection moulding allowed it to be used durably for furniture and small, inexpensive pieces in ultra-modern forms and fashionably bright colours. Designers such as Finland's Eero Aarnio and Denmark's Verner Panton revelled in the freedom it gave them. The oil and energy crisis of the early 1970s slowed development temporarily, but it soon recovered.

each 1.75in (4.5cm) high

£10-15 (each) MTS

A 1970s Pentagram plastic interlocking 'clam' trinket box, designed by Alan Fletcher.

6.25in (15.5cm) diam

£30-40 MTS

An early 1970s white moulded plastic interlocking 'clam' table lighter.

3.5in (9cm) diam

£20-30 MTS

A 1970s black plastic table lighter.

4.75in (12cm) high

£7-10 DTC

A 1970s Ronson black plastic table lighter.

3.75in (9.5cm) high

£8-12 DTC

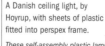

A 1960s lamp, with a flexible plastic neck, ceramic base and sheet metal hood.

7in (18cm) high

£40-60 FD

A Danish ceiling light, by Hoyrup, with sheets of plastic fitted into perspex frame.

These self-assembly plastic lamp shades were popular during the 1960s, with many being designed and made in Denmark. They would arrive in flatpacks to be assembled at home.

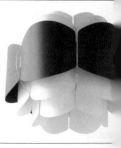

£30-50 GAZE

A CLOSER LOOK AT AN 8-TRACK PLAYER

The 8-track cartridge format, released in September 1965, was designed by William Lear who was also responsible for designing the Lear Executive jet. It was initially designed for Ford cars.

This was one of the most popular 8-track portables made, summing up the format for many people. It continues to be sought-after today

Contemporary advertising read 'Dynamite 8', playing on the fact that this set looked like an explosives detonator, whereas pushing the plunger actually changed the track.

It was available in five different colours – tomato red is the most typical of the 1970s.

A Panasonic red plastic cased 'Dynamite 8' 8-track player, model RQ-830S.

c1972

9in (23cm) high

£30-40 NOR

A 1960s American printed vinyl musical photo album, by Annabel, in mint condition, boxed.

13.5in (33.5cm) high

£60-90 MTS

A 1960s American General Electrics plastic clock radio, model C3300A.

7.5in (18.5cm) wide

£80-120 MTS

A 1960s American plastic Ray-O-Vac flower printed 'New Boutique Lite' torch, boxed.

10in (25.5cm) high

£10-15 MTS

A 1970s plastic '7Up' padded cushion, designed for use at an outdoor pop concert.

13.75in (35cm) wide

£30-40 MTS

An American printed plastic double flask-holder, with zip lock and handle.

8in (20cm) high

£30-40 MTS

A box of moulded plastic 'Style Sexy Drinking Straws', in the form of canoodling naked couples, made in Hong Kong, boxed.

box 16in (40cm) high

£25-35 MTS

A 1960s/70s American for the German market 'Harlekin Multi-set', made by Phoenix Glass, with nine glass beakers in multi-coloured plastic holders, with original box.

Without the box, the value of the full set is more than halved.

Box 14.5in (37cm) diam

£50-70 MA

A CLOSER LOOK AT A 1960S CANDLEHOLDER

This sculptural form is comprised of a number of modular sections, each holding three candles, that fit together into many differently shaped structures.

The design is similar to leading British metal designer Robert Welch's three-stemmed candelabrum, released in 1958 and inspired by a visit to a Jackson Pollock art exhibition.

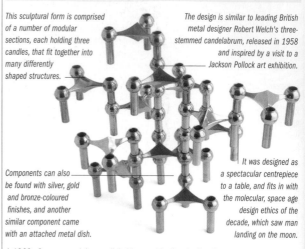

Components can also be found with silver, gold and bronze-coloured finishes, and another similar component came with an attached metal dish.

It was designed as a spectacular centrepiece to a table, and fits in with the molecular, space age design ethics of the decade, which saw man landing on the moon.

A 1960s German modular candleholder combination, by Nagel.

Each module 4in (10cm) wide

£150-200 (set) FD

An early 1960s home-made cushion, with hand-woven designs of people dancing and musical notes.

c1964 *13.5in (34cm) wide*

£30-50 MTS

A 1960s wire, felt and plastic children's coat hook, in the form of a cheery elf or Little Red Riding Hood.

11.5in (29cm) high

£10-15 MTS

A 1960s miniature home houseplant plastic gardening set, on a flower shaped stand.

Houseplants had come into fashion with the new, young home makers of the 1950s.

9in (23cm) high

£12-18 MTS

A 1960s/70s 'flower power' vinyl sewing kit and holder.

5.25in (13cm) wide

£6-8 MTS

A 1960s orange and pink 'string art' picture of a butterfly, on a black felt background.

14.75in (37.5cm) wide

£15-20 NOR

A 1960s French printed card 'Papiers' card folding rubbish bin.

The use of music hall imagery is typically 1960s.

12.75in (32cm) high

£30-40 MTS

An American Russ Berrie & Co. Inc cast hard plastic figurine, with 'I Know What You Want For Your Birthday But I Don't Know How To Wrap It' imprinted wording and manufacturer's stamp to back.

Of such plastic figurines, ones like this with erotic messages are the most sought-after and valuable.

1976   5.75in (14.5cm) high

£6-8   **NOR**

A 1970s American Russ Berrie & Co. Inc sand-filled cast hard resin bust, with 'I Miss Your Touch' imprinted wording and manufacturer's stamp to back.

1971   6in (15.5cm) high

£5-6   **NOR**

A 1960s home-made and hand-painted moulded plaster-of-Paris 'Hippie', with 'Rock & Roll' and 'Vote for Love' messages, signed on the base "Anna Love Melanie".

8.75in (22cm) high

£10-15   **NOR**

A 1960s German vinyl nodding head witch troll, the base marked "HEICO".

Heico are known for their highly collectable trolls, but Thomas Dam is the name to look out for.

7in (18cm) high

£25-35   **NOR**

A 1960s plastic 'Peace on Barrel' urinating toy, lacks spootaoloo, but with original box.

To use this rather anti-establishment Hippie-inspired amusement, fill the barrel with water, push the button at the back and the man 'urinates'.

6.25in (16cm) high

£12-18   **NOR**

A 1960s painted composition money box, in the form of a telephone box, with teenagers and Scottie dog.

7in (17.5cm) high

£10-15   **NOR**

A 1960s/70s small ceramic cat, with hand-painted detailing, possibly Japanese.

2.25in (6cm) high

£7-10   **TCM**

A 1960s moulded papiér mâche model of lion, hand-painted in bright psychedelic colours and wearing a crown.

6.75in (17cm) high

£20-25   **MTS**

A 1960s cast resin sculpture, with inset thermometer and deep sea themed internal decoration, including a real seahorse.

4.75in (12cm) high

£7-9   **MTS**

A 1960s/70s psychedelic printed orange and pink 'Gay Day' giraffe, made in South Africa.

18.5in (46.5cm) high

£15-25   MTS

A 1960s/70s psychedelic printed fabric dog.

20.5in (51cm) long

£10-15   MTS

A Wupper Design (UK) Ltd plastic 'Mr Wupper' ceiling mounted moulded plastic spring mobile, mint and boxed.

6.5in (16cm) high

£50-70   MTS

An American Springbok Editions 'Psychedelic Mother Goose Puzzle', designed by Larry Bowser, complete and boxed.

c1970   *4.25in (10.5cm) diam*

£15-20   MTS

An American Springbok Editions 'Zany Zodian Puzzle', designed by Donni Giambone, complete and boxed.

Springbok Editions were founded in Missouri in the early 1960s by Katie & Robert Lewin. They were so successful that Hallmark acquired the company in 1967. Today their colourful, often circular, puzzles are sought-after by both puzzle collectors and enthusiasts.

c1970   *4.25in (10.5cm) diam*

£15-20   MTS

A Cliff Richards 'Slottizoo' printed card cat, complete and unused, with card envelope.

This does not appear to be related to the pop and musical singer Cliff Richard.

14.25in (35.5cm) high

£25-35   MTS

An American Hasbro 'The Game of Love', complete and boxed.

Typical of the 1960s in terms of design and theme, this game is very similar to MB's popular 'Twister' released in 1966.

1969   *box 19.5in (48.5cm) wide*

£40-60   MTS

A 1960s printed card balloon pump, with image of band player.

7.5in (18.5cm) high

£4-5   MTS

COLLECTORS' NOTES

■ Peter Max was born in Berlin, Germany in 1937, and spent his formative years in Shanghai. He and his family settled in the US in 1953. He went on to study at the Arts Student League in Manhattan.

■ By combining stylized comic strip graphics with undulating lines and psychedelic colours, underpinned by his formal training, Max produced some of the most striking and influential art of the era. His 'cosmic' style, typified by chunky line drawings filled with blocks of colour, was a huge

commercial success, appearing on everything from pencil cases to movie posters and telephone directories.

■ The imagery of skyscapes, sunbursts and clouds, inspired by his childhood in China, trips to India, Africa and Israel, and his love of astronomy appealed to a generation that was open to experimenting with mystical cultures and mind-altering drugs.

■ Peter Max has subsequently designed postage stamps for the United Nations and painted commissioned work for five US Presidents.

An American Peter Max printed paper school book cover.

13.25in (33cm) high

£30-40   **MTS**

An American Peter Max printed paper school book cover.

13.25in (33cm) high

£30-40   **MTS**

An American Peter Max Paper Airplane Book, A Pyramid Book, New York, complete.

1971   7in (17.5cm) high

£30-40   **MTS**

An American Peter Max 'Hello' inflatable plastic cushion.

11.5in (29cm) high

£50-70   **MTS**

A Peter Max screen printed tin tray.

13.25in (33cm) diam

£40-50   **MTS**

A 1960s American plastic printed coathanger, with mirror lenses.

13.5in (34cm) high

£80-120 | **MTS**

A 1960s American plastic printed coathanger, with mirror lenses.

13.5in (34cm) high

£80-120 | **MTS**

An Italian 'CIR' printed fabric sticker, printed "CIR TORINO MADE IN ITALY", depicting a man in a hat.

5in (12.5cm) high

£20-30 | **MTS**

An Italian 'CIR' printed fabric sticker, printed "CIR TORINO MADE IN ITALY".

5.75in (14.5cm) high

£20-30 | **MTS**

A 1960s Disco Light pair of sunglasses, with wipers and lights, mint and carded.

card 8.75in (22cm) high

£25-35 | **MTS**

A 1960s printed vinyl handbag/travel bag.

13.5in (34.5cm) wide

£20-25 | **MTS**

A 1970s flower power vinyl purse.

8in (20cm) wide

£10-15 | **MTS**

A flower power vinyl travelling wash bag.

7in (18cm) wide

£7-10 | **MTS**

A 1970s flower power sun hat.

15in (38cm) wide

£10-15 | **MTS**

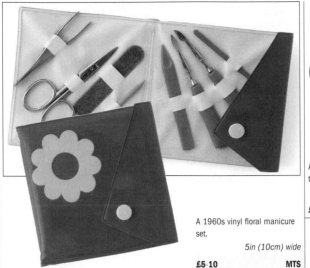

A 1960s moulded plastic flower dressing table mirror, moulded "MADE IN ENGLAND".

7.75in (19.5cm) diam

£15-20 MTS

A 1960s vinyl floral manicure set.

5in (10cm) wide

£5-10 MTS

A 1960s Daisy plastic bead child's purse, with lining and label reading "Designed by Miss Ellen Made in British Hong Kong".

6in (15.5cm) wide

£10-15 NOR

A Mushroom mirror, made in Japan by Seymour Mann Inc., the dome shaped mirror swivelling on its base, with original box.

9in (23cm) high

£20-25 MTS

A 1960s Mary Quant vinyl travelling toiletry set, missing some contents.

8in (20cm) wide

£20-30 MTS

A 1970s necklace made out of cutlery.

Jewellery made out of cutlery was very popular during the 1970s.

10.25in (26cm) high

£20-25 NOR

A 1960s Wristo by Aitron Solid State wristwatch radio.

10.5in (26cm) high

£35-45 MTS

SIXTIES & SEVENTIES

COLLECTORS' NOTES

■ Of the many companies that designed and produced items celebrating 'Swinging' London during the 1960s, and '70s, DODO Designs Ltd was one of the most prolific and best remembered.

■ It specialised in metal wares printed with brightly coloured designs that usually poked gentle fun at the Establishment, British history and the British character. Quality was very fine and the variety was vast, particularly as regards enamelled plaques.

■ .Following the Pop Art movement of the period it also took artwork or logos for well-known British brands, and used them decoratively. The Union Jack and Lord Kitchener were regularly used and items were sold in popular tourist destinations as well as Carnaby Street.

■ Enamelled plaques tend to be the most collectable items today, along with printed tins. Pieces with no address or a Westbourne Grove address, printed on the reverse are earlier in date. Look for bright colours and designs typical of the period. Damage such as chipping to the enamel reduces value considerably as pieces are still largely readily available.

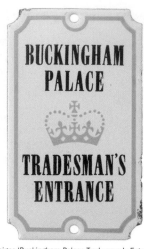

A Dodo Designs 'Buckingham Palace Tradesman's Entrance' enamelled plaque, with two line Westbourne Grove printed mark.

4.5in (11.5cm) high

£10-15   **MTS**

An early Dodo Designs 'Throne Room, enamelled plaque, the reverse stamped 'MADE IN ENGLAND DODO DESIGNS' on two lines.

4.5in (11.5cm) high

£10-15   **MTS**

A Dodo Designs 'No Camping Piccadilly Circus' enamelled plaque, with Westbourne Grove printed mark.

4.5in (11.5cm) high

£8-12   **MTS**

A Dodo Designs 'Bed & Breakfast French Lessons Given' enamelled plaque, with Westbourne Grove printed mark.

4.5in (11.5cm) high

£8-12   **MTS**

A later Dodo Designs 'Bank of England', enamelled plaque, the reverse with circular Tunbridge Wells printed logo.

4.5in (11.5cm) high

£10-15   **MTS**

A Dodo Designs 'No.10 Downing St' enamelled plaque, the reverse printed 'DODO DESIGNED 185 WESTBOURNE GROVE LONDON W11 ENGLAND FINEST PORCELAIN ENAMEL MADE IN ENGLAND'.

4.5in (11.5cm) high

£8-12   **MTS**

A Dodo Designs 'UK RULES OK' Union Jack enamel plaque, with later circular Tunbridge Wells logo printed on reverse.

4.5in (11.5cm) wide

£15-20   **MTS**

A Dodo Designs 'Players are requested...', enamelled plaque, with Tunbridge Wells address printed on reverse.

4.5in (11.5cm) high

£8-12   MTS

A Dodo Designs 'The Royal Mint' enamelled plaque, with circular Tunbridge Wells printing. to reverse.

4.5in (11.5cm) high

£8-12   MTS

A Dodo Designs 'Camp Coffee' Tunbridge Wells enamelled plaque, with circular Tunbridge Wells printing. to reverse.

14.5in (36cm) high

£20-30   MTS

A Dodo Designs 'Colman's Mustard' enamelled sign.

Like other such signs, this was not official company advertising.

11in (27.5cm) high

£30-50   MTS

A Dodo Designs 'Sunlight Soap' enamelled metal sign, by permission of Lever Bros, with Tunbridge Wells printing.

8.5in (21.5cm) high

£25-35   MTS

A 1960s Dodo Designs 'Lord Kitchener' printed tin, with a hinged lid and a Union Jack background.

6in (15cm) wide

£30-40   MTS

A Dodo Designs plastic-coated printed cotton Golden Shred tote bag.

Advertising related pieces tend to be most desirable and valuable.

23.5in (59cm) high

£25-35   MTS

An extremely rare 1960s Dodo Designs painted fibreglass shop display mannequin, with hole for mouth that used to 'smoke' cigarettes, from the original Dodo Designs shop.

20.75in (52cm) high

£250-350   MTS

COLLECTORS' NOTES

■ As smoking becomes increasingly less accepted and less fashionable, so the market for vintage smoking accessories grows. Collectors appreciate the fine quality workmanship of pieces produced from around 1900 to the 1950s. During the 1920s and '30s smoking was highly fashionable, with wealthy people demanding fine accessories and it is these items that are particularly sought-after today.

■ As well as the fine materials and decoration, practicality plays a part in value. Many Victorian pieces are finely made and appealing but are impractical as they were aimed at pipe smokers who are far less numerous than cigar or cigarette smokers today. Many older humidors are no longer airtight, meaning they cannot be used without conversion. As such, practical items related to cigar or cigarette smoking tend to be more desirable.

■ Lighters are one of the most collectable examples of smoking memorabilia and names such as Dunhill, Thorens and Ronson are amongst the most popular. Dunhill in particular is noted for its fine lighters and smoking accessories, which are only a small part of its range of gentlemen's accoutrements. Look out for unusual features, such as built-in compacts or watches.

■ Eye-appeal, subject matter and humour are three further features that are worth considering as they can add value. This is particularly true for pieces produced from the 1950s onwards, which can be of lower intrinsic quality. Links to a famous personality or brand, or a sought-after theme such as erotic imagery, can make a later piece desirable and an earlier piece yet more desirable.

A Dunhill 'Miniature' Aquarium petrol table lighter, with intaglio underwater scene of a tropical fish among waterweeds, the reverse with two tropical fish against a bright blue/green background, cast marks.

The complexity, colouring and 'eye appeal' of the design affects value, with this being a good example.

c1950   2.75in (7cm) high

£2,000-3,000   **WW**

A Dunhill 'Miniature' Aquarium petrol table lighter, with intaglio underwater scene of fish among plants against a vivid blue/green ground, the reverse with a single fish, stamped marks.

This lighter is worth more, not only as it is a slightly scarcer 'Miniature', but also because it is in such fine condition with its vivid colours and lack of scratches, wear to the gold plating, or flaking to the internal paint.

c1950   2.75in (7cm) high

£2,500-3,500   **WW**

A Dunhill 'Miniature' Aquarium petrol table lighter, with intaglio underwater scene of two Angel fish among waterweeds, the reverse with two tropical fish, on a silvery blue background, cast marks.

c1950   2.75in (7cm) high

£800-1,000   **WW**

A Dunhill 'Miniature' Aquarium petrol table lighter, with intaglio underwater scene of a tropical fish among waterweeds, the reverse with two tropical fish, on a silver blue and yellow background, cast marks.

c1950   2.75in (7cm) high

£1,000-1,500   **WW**

A CLOSER LOOK AT A DUNHILL AVIARY LIGHTER

Dunhill introduced the 'Aquarium' lighter in 1949 and they were sold from the 1950s into the 1960s in 'Standard', 'Half Giant' and 'Miniature' sizes.

The gold-plated body was covered with six rounded Lucite (Perspex) panels, which were reverse-carved by hand and then hand-painted and decorated. Flakes to the paint or foil and surface scratches reduce value.

A Dunhill 'Half Giant' Aquarium petrol table lighter, with intaglio underwater scene of a tropical fish, the reverse with an angel fish, on a bright blue ground, cast marks.

The bright blue background is unusual as backgrounds are usually predominately green or green with beige.

c1950   3.5in (8.5cm) high

£1,800-2,200   **WW**

A Dunhill 'Half Giant' Aquarium petrol table lighter, with intaglio underwater scene of a tropical fish among waterweeds, the reverse with three tropical fish, on a pale green background, cast marks.

c1950   3.5in (8.5cm) high

£1,200-1,800   **WW**

This is the 'Miniature', which is slightly scarcer than the horizontal format 'Half Giant' size, but not as rare as the taller 'Standard'.

Aquarium lighters with fish are more common – bird designs, known as 'Aviary' lighters, are rare; with horses, ships and other scenes being scarcer still.

A Dunhill 'Miniature' Aviary petrol table lighter, with river scene of a duck wading, the reverse with a swimming duck on a bright blue ground, cast marks to base.

c1950   2.75in (cm) high

£2,000-3,000   **WW**

A Dunhill 'Half Giant' Aquarium petrol table lighter, with intaglio underwater scene of two swordtail fish, the reverse with a tropical fish, on a silver-blue background, cast marks.

c1950   3.5in (8.5cm) high

£1,500-2,500   **WW**

A Dunhill 'Half Giant' Aquarium petrol table lighter, with cast marks to base.

4in (10cm) wide

£1,000-1,500   **FRE**

A 1950s Dunhill 'Joseph Lucas' perspex and chrome table lighter, with lion decorated side panels and ribbed surround, inscribed on the base "Plastic and Styling by Joseph Lucas Ltd, Birmingham, England".

This lighter was produced by Dunhill for Joseph Lucas, a leading manufacturer of plastics, lighting and car accessories. Despite its shape, it is different from other Aquarium lighters as it has moulded, not carved, decoration. Lucas may also have supplied Dunhill with the perspex used on Aquarium lighters.

4in (10cm) wide

£350-450 **BIG**

A CLOSER LOOK AT A DUNHILL WATCH LIGHTER

First made by Swiss company 'La Nationale', Dunhill watch lighters were introduced in 1926 at the request of a wealthy South American client, Santiago Soulas.

Examples in solid gold are extremely rare, particularly in this condition, as they were a highly expensive, luxury item in their day.

It is marked with Wise & Greenwood's original 1920 Unique lighter patent and "264" on all separately made parts, showing that they are original.

The octagonal interior watch compartment behind the flip-down front, the lack of a secondary striking wheel and shape of the dial, as well as the import mark, show this to be a very early design.

A Swiss Dunhill 'Unique A' 18ct gold pocket watch lighter, with Art Deco flip-down watch panel around an inset watch with Arabic numeral dial and jewelled lever movement signed "Dunhill", the case with Swiss control marks, London import mark for 1926 and signed "Dunhill Switzerland".

1926 *1.75in (4.5cm) high*

£3,000-4,000 **HAMG**

A 1950s Dunhill 'Giant' silver-plated table lighter, stamped marks.

An oversize, table variation of the 'Unique' pocket lighter, this was first offered in 1929. Earlier examples have an external bent piece of metal acting as a snuffer arm 'spring'.

4.25in (10.5cm) high

£120-180 **WW**

A very rare Japanese Dunhill-Namiki Savory maki-e lacquer and silver-plated lighter, decorated with gold and silver hira maki-e showing a bird in flight over grass, signed "Shobi" with red seal kao and "Namiki-kan" on one edge, wear from use including rubbed grass and signature.

Shobi Makizawa was born in 1880 and studied under Shosai Shiroyama before joining the staff of Iwate Prefectural Technical High School in 1905. He became an independent artist in 1907, and was recruited to Namiki by the maki-e master Gonroku Matsuda becoming one of the six founding committee members of the Kokkokai artist group in August 1931. His signature is sometimes translated as Shoei and Shohmi. Maki-e lacquer decoration can take many weeks to complete, depending on its complexity.

c1937

£400-500 **BLO**

A 1980s French Cartier gold and enamel pocket lighter, with foliate engraved arabesque decoration and blue and turquoise enamel designs, in excellent condition.

£500-700 **BLO**

An American 'Koopman's Magic Pocket Lamp' chrome-plated brass gasoline pocket lighter, by Magic Introduction Co. of New York, with exploding cap dies and striker.

The patent for this very early mechanical pocket lighter was granted in 1889.

c1890

£80-120 **ATK**

An American Art Metal Wares Inc of Newark, NJ cast-iron dog-shaped table lighter.

Art Metal Wares was owned by Louis V. Aronson and later became the famous Ronson company.

c1916   4in (10cm) high

£100-150   **ATK**

A rare Austrian 'Bully' standing bulldog cast metal semi-automatic table lighter.

When the dog's tail is pushed down, the head pops open lighting the wick.

1914   8in (20cm) long

£180-220   **ATK**

A German 'Sophisticated Monkey' cast metal petrol table lighter.

c1914   6.25in (16cm) high

£80-120   **ATK**

A 1950s Belgian 'Le Mannequin Pis' cast iron petrol table lighter, a striking wheel on the boy's rear shoots a spark forward lighting a wick covered by his hand.

3.25in (8cm) high

£35-45   **ATK**

An English Art Deco brass nude dancer table petrol striker lighter.

8.25in (22cm) high

£200-250   **ATK**

A 1950s chromed metal 'jet plane' table lighter, on an adjustable base with bakelite platform.

£70-100   **ROS**

A late 1950s Japanese Evanus 'cat and lamp' ceramic, chrome-plated brass and enamel novelty table lighter.

This lighter was patented by Hikojiro Sugimoto in 1956.

5.5in (14cm) high

£100-150   **CVS**

A reproduction German 'Döbereiner' clear glass table lighter, the lid with igniting mechanism.

This was one of the first lighters in the world and was invented by Johann Wolfgang Döbereiner in 1822, under the name 'Gasopyrion'. The principle is similar to a 'Molotov Cocktail' where hydrogen is mixed with oxygen on a platinum sponge to produce the flame. However, like 'Molotov Cocktails' themselves, the results were sometimes highly explosive.

c1970

£180-220   **ATK**

A late 19thC or early 20thC Continental ceramic tobacco jar, in the form of a Scotsman's head, the base inscribed "8959 59".

5.75in (14.5cm) high

£60-80   **PWE**

A late 19thC or early 20thC Continental ceramic tobacco jar, in the form of a caricatured Irish man with a cheroot, green hat and feather, the base stamped "9675 09" and painted "77".

6.25in (16cm) high

£50-70   **PWE**

A late 19thC or early 20thC Continental large ceramic tobacco jar, of a man in a purple bobble hat, possibly a jockey, the base inscribed "3606 20".

9in (23cm) high

£60-80   **PWE**

A late 19thC or early 20thC Continental ceramic tobacco jar, of a smart, moustachioed man smoking a cheroot and wearing a brown hat with a green feather.

6.75in (17cm) high

£50-70   **PWE**

A late 19thC or early 20thC Continental ceramic tobacco jar, of an exotic lady in a head dress, the base stamped "3578 24".

The hand-painted detailing and moulding is much finer on this example, leading to its higher price. The exotic female subject matter is also more appealing.

6in (15cm) high

£70-100   **PWE**

A 1920s English printed tin humidor, designed by George W. Horner & Co.

6.75in (17cm) high

£30-40   **PKA**

A turned dark wood tobacco jar, with lid, the base engraved "CJD Petzer AC Petzer St Helena 1900".

St Helena is famous as being the island to which Napoleon was exiled in 1815 until his death in 1821. In 1900, it was again used to hold Boer War prisoners.

6in (15cm) diam

£35-45   **W&W**

A late 19thC or early 20thC Continental ceramic tobacco jar, in the form of an unripened nut or bean, smoking a cigarette, base stamped "JM5 3528".

Tobacco jars were made on the Continent around the turn of the 20thC, before pre-rolled cigarettes had become widely popular. Most are made in ceramic, although wood or metal examples are known. Bernard Bloch at Bohemia's Eichwald factory was a prolific maker, as was Germany's notable Conte & Boehme factory. Most are in the form of heads, which allowed for characters and expressions – amusing or animal forms and famous personalities are among the most popular. Value is determined by the subject matter, the quality of the moulding, painting and the overall condition. Examine rims carefully for cracks or chips.

c1900   6.25in (16cm) high

£350-450   **PWE**

A CLOSER LOOK AT AN ASHTRAY

A German 'Dog with Basket' cast brass match stand.

c1890   2in (5cm) high

£25-35   **ATK**

A German porcelain match holder, in the form of a seated Chinese man, sticking out his articulated tongue.

c1850   3.25in (8cm) high

£40-60   **ATK**

These novelty bird smoker's companions were retailed by Dunhill but made under the YZ trademark by Henry Howell & Co. of London during the 1920s-30s.

This is unusual as all parts are in cast phenolic plastic. Most are made from hardwoods also used in cane production, with only the beak being cast phenolic.

Λ Dunhill briar wood 'nutbird' striker and ashtray, with match holder.

3in (8cm) high

£40-60   **MG**

A French Art Deco moulded amethyst glass spherical ashtray, inlaid with sterling silver.

3.5in (9cm) high

£50-70   **NOR**

There are many different forms, with shagreen (sharkskin) match striking panels, holes in the body to store matches, and even attached dinner gongs.

Howell was founded in 1832 and manufactured walking canes and umbrellas. A change in fashion and a series of dry winters lead to the company closing in 1936.

An English YZ for Dunhill burgundy and black cast phenolic ashtray, the base stamped "YZ Trademark Made in England".

These novelty pieces are also known as 'nutbirds' by collectors.

3.5in (9cm) high

£200-300   **MG**

A souvenir ceramic ashtray, of a man's head with a bee on his nose and an open mouth, with transfer for Conneaut Lake Amusement Park, PA to base.

It's the amusing expression, the characterful moulding and the survival of the bee that makes this desirable.

3.5in (9cm) high

£15-25   **TOA**

Λ Japaneoe ceramic novelty dog ashtray, with gaping mouth.

3.5in (8.5cm) high

£30-40   **RH**

A 1930s wooden cigarette box, topped with a chrome-plated figure of Bonzo and ashtray.

8.75in (22cm) wide

£20-30   **GAZE**

A late 19thC walnut table top smoker's companion, the central two-handled jar with domed cover, apertures for 10 pipes with match holder, striker and ashtray, on a circular base.

9.5in (24cm) high

£120-180   **CLV**

A 1950s Italian clockwork cigarette dispenser, with transfer-printed exotic bird pattern, metal devil's head-shaped feet and an angel finial, with Swiss clockwork mechanism rotating the central panels to reveal cigarettes stored inside.

13.5in (34cm) high

£220-280   **V**

A 1950s Cartier 18ct gold cigarette case, engraved "AEG", the button with five square-cut inset sapphires, marked "Cartier", in original Cartier red leatherette case, good condition.

£1,000-1,500   **BLO**

A late 19thC German silver cigarette box, with enamel decoration of a naked lady on a bed, stamped "935A".

The style and lady are typical of the 'Naughty Nineties' of late 19thC Belle Epoque Europe. Erotic subjects are highly sought-after, particularly in as good condition and as finely painted as this example.

3.5in (9cm) high

£350-550   **MG**

Two 19thC Asian 'Chuck Muck' lighters, in leather, brass, copper and iron, one ornamentation missing, the second one with coral.

Often mistaken for small purses, the pocket stored a piece of flint and some wool or dry flammable material. The flint would be struck against the iron base near the wool to create sparks, which would set the wool on fire. Later examples are often found.

5.25in (13cm) high

£100-150   **ATK**

A Victorian silver-mounted crocodile cigar case, Birmingham 1899.

£80-120   **GORW**

A Swiss Thorens chrome-plated brass gasoline counter or bar refill can, with pump, both side engraved.

c1940   *5.5in (14cm) high*

£80-120   **ATK**

FIND OUT MORE...

The Dunhill Petrol Lighter – A Unique Story, by Luciano Bottoni & Davide Blei, published by Unique Srl, 2004 *ISBN: 88-901596-0-X.*

Lighters – Accendini, by Stefano Bisconcini, published by Edizioni San Gottardo, 1984.

COLLECTORS' NOTES

■ Smurfs first appeared under the name 'stroumpf' in the 1950s and were supporting characters in a Belgian comic strip starring two boy adventurers called Johan & Peewit. The artist was the Belgian cartoonist Pierre Culliford (b.1928) who is also known as Peyo. They became instantly popular and soon had a cartoon devoted solely to them.

■ The first figurines were introduced in 1965, and the increasing popularity of the comic strip was backed up by Father Abraham's 1977 'Smurf Song' and a series of TV cartoons by Hanna Barbera. In addition to a vast range of collectables, over 400 different Smurf figurines have been designed and millions of examples produced, covering all manner of activities from music to emotions to sports.

■ Look on the base of a Smurf to find out more. A number related to the mould used is stamped on the base and is used by Smurf collectors to correctly identify their figure. The maker's mark, which can vary from 'Schleich' to 'Bully' to 'W.Berrie & Co.', can help to give a clue as to the period when that Smurf was made. The presence of a 'CE' marking indicates a more modern, or even contemporary, model.

■ The date is not the date that a particular model was made, but is either the date that the shape was released, or the date that a worn out mould was replaced with a new one. Shapes can be made for many years, and even reintroduced later. Dates given here indicate the production period for that shape. Coloured dots indicate where the Smurf was painted, for example yellow for Portugal and red for Sri Lanka.

■ As millions of Smurfs have been made, most are of a low value, but highly accessible to the budget collector looking for a fun and relevant character collectable. Look out for variations, as these can be worth more. Consider size, form, colour and the material used. Shapes produced for short periods of time, such as a Cheerleader Smurfette can also fetch higher prices.

■ Avoid buying examples that are overly dirty or scuffed and look for truly mint examples with their original surface 'sheen'. Where an item is boxed, it is best that the box is in similarly mint condition. Memorabilia connected to the Smurfs can be more varied than the figures themselves and offers great (often useable) variety to a collection.

A 'Gift and Flower' Smurf figure, no.20040, licensed by Schleich Peyo.	A 'Jester' Smurf figure, with gold painted stars on his hat, licensed by Schleich Peyo. *Look out for hats with green stars as these can be worth up to double the value of the example with gold stars.*	A 'Beer' Smurf figure, no.20078, licensed by Schleich Peyo, with Bully stamp.	A 'Soccer' Smurf figure, no. 20035, licensed by Schleich Peyo. *The variation with a yellow top is said to be rarer than this example with a red top.*
Intro 1978 2.25in (5.5cm) high	*1976-91 2in (5cm) high*	*1974-92 2in (5cm) high*	*1978-90 2.25in (5.5cm) high*
£2-3 NOR	**£2-3** NOR	**£2-3** NOR	**£2-3** NOR

A 'Fiddler' Smurf figure, with a brown hat, no.20159, licensed by Schleich Peyo.	A 'CB Operator' Smurf figure, no.20143, with short antenna, licensed by Schleich Peyo. *Look out for a rarer variation with a longer aerial, which can be twice as much as this example.*	An 'Astro Smurf' figure, no.20003, with finger up and no red stripe. *This is one of the most popular Smurfs, and was incorrectly rumoured to be worth large sums of money some years ago.*
1983-89 2in (5cm) high	*1982-96 2.25in (5.5cm) h.*	*1969-86 2in (5cm) high*
£2-3 NOR	**£4-5** NOR	**£4-6** F

A 'Brainy' Smurf figure, with black glasses, no.20006, licensed by Schleich Peyo.

Variations with yellow or red glasses exist and can be worth slightly more.

1969-84   1980 2in (5cm) high

£1-2   NOR

A CLOSER LOOK AT A SMURF

Some claim that this model is much rarer than most think, as it had to be withdrawn shortly after it was introduced, as the use of the 'S' motif on his chest was not licensed from DC Comics.

Interestingly, 'Superman' Smurf was also released in 1981, just after the release of the first two Superman films starring Christopher Reeve.

This is often confused with 'Superman' Smurf, no.20127, which shows a Smurf with a black eye mask and no 'S' chest motif flying over a comet or rocky moonscape.

There is a colour variation of this figurine with a white base and red shoes, but this does not affect the value considerably. However, be aware that prices in general for this figurine vary dramatically.

A 'Smurferman' figure, no.20119, with "Bully, W.Germany" mark.

1981 to 2000 (?)   2.5in (6cm) high

£50-80   NOR

A 'Valentine Smurfette' Smurf figure, no. 20156, licensed by Schleich Peyo.

The arrow is missing on this example. Variations with longer arrows over 3cm long are worth up to double the value of those with shorter arrows.

2.25in (5.5cm) high

50P-£1   NOR

A 'Graduate Smurfette' Smurf figure, no. 20151, licensed by Schleich Peyo.

Some collectors deem these to be rare, as they were only issued in 1989.

1989   2.25in (5.5cm) high

£3-5   NOR

A 'Santa Smurfette' Smurf figure, no.20153, licensed by Schleich Peyo.

Although different shades of green can be found on the gift, values are roughly the same.

1983-90   2in (5cm) high

£6-8   NOR

An 'Aero Smurf' metal diecast plane, by Ertl, licensed by Schleich Peyo.

1982   3.25in (8cm) long

£2-3   NOR

An Irwin 'Mushroom Umbrella' Smurf figure, no.20118, licensed by Schleich Peyo, in mint condition and carded.

This model was first released in 1981, but this example is a later version.

1995 -2002   7.75in
                        (19.5cm) high

£6-8   NOR

A Galoob Smurf wind-up walker figure, licensed by Schleich Peyo.

3.25in (8cm) high

£10-15   NOR

A Wallace Berrie Christmas Smurf ceramic figurine, licensed by Schleich Peyo.

Ceramic Smurf figurines are sought-after by many collectors.

1982   *3.25in (8cm) high*

£15-20   NOR

A Helm collapsible Smurf toy, licensed by Schleich Peyo.

Push the bottom of the base in and he 'collapses' before springing upright again when released.

3.75in (9.5cm) high

£10-15   NOR

A Wallace Berrie 'Papa Smurf' Smurf pencil sharpener, licensed by Schleich Peyo.

1983   *6in (15.5cm) high*

£10-15   NOR

A 'Papa Smurf' Smurf pencil top, licensed by Schleich Peyo.

2in (5cm) high

£6-8   NOR

A 'Golf' Smurf keyring, licensed by Schleich Peyo.

1980-93   *2.25in (5.5cm) high*

£3-4   NOR

A Smurf 'Is It Break Time Yet? mug, licensed by Schleich Peyo.

3.5in (9cm) high

£4-6   NOR

A 'Small Green' Smurf house, no. 40012, with removeable lid, licensed by Schleich Peyo.

Houses tend to be desirable, particularly large playsets, as less were sold. This house can also be found with a red or blue roof. In violet, it is Smurfette's house.

1978   *4in (10cm) high*

£10-15   NOR

A Smurf plastic bathroom or bedroom dressing gown hook, licensed by Schleich Peyo.

5in (13cm) high

£4-6   NOR

FIND OUT MORE...

Der Schlumpf Katalog 4, by Frank Oswald, published by Oswald Gaschers, 2003.

Unauthorised Guide To Smurfs Around The World, by Terry & Joyce Losonsky, published by Schiffer Publishing, 1999.

COLLECTORS' NOTES

■ Soft toys are as loved by collectors today as they were by their original owners. The manufacture of soft toys also pre-dates teddy bears, with Marguerite Steiff making pin-cushions during the 1890s. Major manufacturers include Steiff in Germany and Merrythought, Farnell and Chad Valley in the UK.

■ Most collectors collect specific animals, and cats and dogs are popular. Steiff made a range of insects and creatures and, although they are an acquired taste, these and similar examples by other companies also have their devoted fans. Look out for comic book or cartoon characters as these can often be worth more due to increased demand and nostalgic longing.

■ Like teddy bears, many were dearly loved by their original and subsequent owners, so are often found dirty, damaged, faded or repaired. This reduces value considerably as they can be hard to clean. Like teddy bears, never put a soft toy in a washing machine as this can cause damage to the stuffing at the very least.

■ In addition to makers, sizes and characters, also look out for quirky or cute appearances as 'eye appeal' is a considerable factor to desirability and thus to value. As soft toys are not yet as popular as teddy bears, they usually make comparatively less expensive purchases and will form a satisfying and fun collection.

A early Steiff velvet pull-along dachshund soft toy, on a metal frame with wheels.

This is an extremely early and rare Steiff animal, dating from before the ear button was introduced in 1904. The wheel bar going through the feet, rather than the feet resting on top of the bar indicates an early example as well.

c1900   8in (20cm) long

£800-1,200   **LHT**

A 1920s-30s Steiff 'Molly' seated white mohair dog soft toy, with ear button and metal framed tag.

c1928-30   5.5in (14cm) high

£300-400   **SOTT**

A 1950s-60s Steiff 'Molly' mohair dog soft toy, with card tag, bell and ribbon.

4.25in (11cm) high

£70-100   **HGS**

A 1960s Steiff recumbent 'Collie' mohair dog soft toy, number 4250/25, with card tag, ear button and fabric tag.

12.5in (32cm) long

£80-120   **TCT**

A 1950s-60s Steiff 'Arco' mohair German Shepherd dog soft toy, with card tag, button and collar.

4.25in (11cm) high

£80-120   **HGS**

A 1920s/30s Steiff mohair and felt Pomeranian dog soft toy, with ribbon and bells, lacks button.

5.25in (13cm) high

£400-500   **SOTT**

A CLOSER LOOK AT A SOFT TOY

Steiff pull-along animals are early and popular toys, and included bears, a lion and an elephant.

The saddlecloth is often missing, and the back worn through use - this example is in excellent, complete condition.

Larger examples such as this could also be ridden by small children.

The original camel is rare, but was re-released as a limited edition of 1,000 by Steiff in 2000.

A Steiff mohair pull-along camel on wheels, with button in ear and original fabric saddlecloth.

c1908   19.75in (50cm) high

£700-900   **HGS**

A 1950s/60s Steiff fabric 'Tom Cat' soft toy, with tags and ribbon.

Black cats were often intended for the export to the UK and the US, where they were considered symbols of luck. This is an unusual form, and is hard to find today, possibly as he was largely unappealing.

6in (15cm) high

£100-150   **HGS**

A 1950s Steiff 'Snurry' mohair snoozing cat soft toy, in original condition.

This shape is also quite hard to find.

6in (15cm) wide

£80-120   **SOTT**

A Steiff 'Liege' mohair goat soft toy.

1934-43   7.75in (19.5cm) high

£200-300   **SOTT**

A 1930s Steiff fox soft toy, with button in ear.

11in (28cm) long

£250-350   **LHT**

A 1950s/60s Steiff mohair ladybird child's stool, with metal legs.

The seat pad is often worn through use and affects value considerably. The ladybird was also made as a stuffed toy.

20in (51cm) long

£180-220   **LHT**

A Steiff velvet and felt 'Kalle Stropp' grasshopper soft toy, with bendable limbs, in excellent condition.

With his friend Grodan Boll the toad, Kalle Stropp was a character from a Danish fairy tale by Thomas Funck. He was only made in 1956 and is very rare.

8.5in (21.5cm) high

£800-1,000   **LHT**

A 1930s Steiff wool 'pompom' chick, with metal legs and red tag and button on leg.

2.75in (7cm) high

£200-300   **LHT**

A Steiff wool 'pompom' chick, with wire feet and felt beak.

c1930-59   *1.5in (4cm) high*

£30-40   **HGS**

A 1930s Steiff wool 'pompom' owl, with metal feet and felt beak.

Steiff's 'pompom' animals, also known as 'Woolies', were made from the 1930s-50s and were intended to be affordable with pocket money. Post war examples generally have less detailing, such as felt or wire beaks, and often have plastic legs. Birds tend to be the most common animal found, although this owl is rarer. Small accompanying aviaries and trees were also sold, but these are rare.

2.75in (7cm) high

£250-350   **LHT**

A 1950s Steiff wool 'pompom' sparrow, with straw in felt mouth and button and tag on plastic legs.

It is rare to find the straw still present.

2.5in (6.5cm) high

£40-50   **HGS**

A 1930s Steiff wool 'pompom' raven, with red padded felt beak, glass eyes, and button and tag on metal legs.

2.5in (7cm) high

£30-40   **HGS**

A 1920s/30s Steiff wool 'pompom' cat, with glass eyes and original fabric bow.

A Steiff wool 'pompom' cat, stock no. 3505, with button and tag in ear.

A Steiff wool 'pompom' mouse, stock no. 7354-04, with glass eyes, whiskers and rubber tail, in mint condition.

A 1930s Steiff wool 'pompom' squirrel, with bushy tail and whiskers and button in ear.

2.5in (7cm) high	*1954-58* *2.25in (6cm) high*	*1968-84* *1.5in (4cm) high*	*2.75in (7cm) high*
£200-300 **LHT**	**£30-40** **HGS**	**£30-40** **HGS**	**£150-200** **LHT**

A 1950s American Agnes Brush 'Peter Rabbit' brushed cotton soft toy, in original condition.

Note the obvious whiskers. This was to differentiate him from the similar Piglet toy, that the company also made as part of their Winnie The Pooh series.

9in (23cm) high

£150-200 HGS

A CLOSER LOOK AT A SOFT TOY

Eugene Jeep is a friendly dog-like character from Popeye, and was introduced to the cartoon by E.C. Segar in 1936.

He is in very good and bright condition with his original paw printing, the velveteen usually becomes worn and dirty with play.

Dean's Rag Book, founded in 1903 is a notable English company who also made teddy bears, other soft toys and printed fabric children's books.

He was produced in small numbers only as a licensed product, making him very rare today.

A 1930s Dean's Rag Book 'Lucky Jeep' velveteen soft toy.

Jeep, ruler of Jeep Island, can only say 'Jeep', eats only orchids and can foretell the future.

12in (30.5cm) high

£600-800 LHT

A 1930s French Blanchette golden mohair soft toy, with original stitched nose and glass eyes.

3.5in (9cm) high

£60-80 LHT

A 1930s Chad Valley velvet 'Bonzo' soft toy, with printed face.

Condition is critical to value as the fabric is dirtied easily. The face can also rub off and the red tongue lost though play.

5.25in (13.5cm) high

£300-350 TCT

A 1930s Chad Valley velvet happy bull soft toy, with glass eyes and button in tail.

8in (20cm) long

£80-120 LHT

A 1950s Chiltern Toys pink bunny soft toy, in near mint condition, with original card sample and retail tags.

8.5in (21.5cm) high

£100-150 LHT

A Dean's Rag Books mohair chimpanzee soft toy, with moulded rubber face and hands, with original tag.

c1960 *17in (43cm) high*

£35-45 RBC

A 1920s Farnell 'Pip' mohair dog soft toy, from the Mascot range.

Pip, Squeak (a penguin) and Wilfred (a rabbit) appeared in a popular 1920s Daily Mirror cartoon by Bertram Lamb and Austin Payne, which was introduced in 1919. They are also the names given to a series of three British and Empire commemorative medals from WWI that were issued in 1919.

A 1930s Farnell 'Alpha Toys' mohair girl elephant soft toy, in original condition with original tag and clothing.

A boy version was also sold. Alpha Toys was Farnell's premium brand.

12in (30.5cm) high

£200-300   **LHT**

4in (10cm) high

£100-150   **LHT**

A Schuco felt and fabric rooster soft toy, with poseable limbs.

c1957   12in (30.5cm) high

£180-220   **TCT**

A 1920s Schuco felt, flocked and printed metal and mohair tumbling monkey, with rigid revolving arms.

Although the dressed monkey is a recognisable and iconic animal for Schuco, tumbling teddies are worth much more.

8.5in (21.5cm) high

£250-350   **LHT**

A Schuco black mohair 'YesNo' 'Felix' toy, in excellent condition.

Moving his tail makes him nod or shake his head. This mechanism is typical of Schuco. He will be popular to both Felix and Schuco, and soft toy collectors, hence his high value. Felix is also rarer than the more common monkey or bear.

c1930   5in (12.5cm) high

£700-900   **LHT**

A 1930s British William J. Terry blond and brown mohair and pink felt stuffed teddy dog, slightly worn.

This is very rare and unusually large. W.J. Terry was founded around WWI, when German imports were banned.

19in (48.5cm) high

£400-600   **LHT**

A 1960s Native American warrior and horse felt soft toy, unmarked.

9.5in (24cm) long

£15-20   **RBC**

A late 19thC American Arnold Print Works 'Tabby's Kitten' printed fabric cat soft toy, printed "PAT.JULY 5.92 AND OCT 4.92".

These were supplied on fabric squares to be cut out, sewn together and stuffed at home.

6.5in (16.5cm) high

£8-12   **HGS**

COLLECTORS' NOTES

■ Vintage fishing equipment and memorabilia has only recently come to the fore of sporting memorabilia collecting and is a growing niche market.

■ Rare rods and reels occupy the top of the price range, with examples by famous makers such as Hardy Bros., Allcock and Farlow among the most collected. Unmarked versions are usually more affordable.

■ Technical developments to reels during the late 19th to mid-20thC resulted in a number of interesting variations that attract collectors today. Look for

models such as 'multiplying', 'half crank', 'cage', and 'freespool clutch'.

■ As fishing equipment was produced for use, and was often exposed to harsh weather, condition affects value greatly. Avoid damaged, incomplete or heavily restored examples and those that have incorrect, replaced parts.

■ Familiarise yourself with the array of component parts for reels and other equipment to aid with informed buying. Old retailers catalogues are useful for this.

A Hardy Bros 3.25in Perfect fly reel Dupl. Mark II.

£180-220   CLV

A Hardy Bros 3.5in Uniqua fly reel.

£100-150   CLV

A Hardy 'Perfect' 3in fly reel, with ivory handle.
c1900

£250-350   MAI

A Hardy Brothers 'Triumph' 3in alloy fly reel.

£200-300   MAI

A Hardy brass Birmingham plate wind reel.
2.25in (5.5cm) diam

£150-200   TEN

A brass reel, with Hardy stamp.
2.5in (6.5cm)

£200-250   TEN

A Hardy brass platewind reel, with rod in hand trademark.
4in (10cm) diam

£60-90   TEN

A Hardy all-brass casting reel, with 2in drum and carved crank arm, stamped "Hardy MKIV".

£50-60   GORL

A Hardy 'Perfect' alloy trout fly reel.

3.5in (9cm) diam

£250-350 TEN

A 1950s Hardy 'Perfect' alloy salmon fly reel.

4.25in (11cm) diam

£220-280 TEN

A Hardy 'Perfect' alloy reel.

4in (10cm) diam

£200-300 TEN

A Hardy 'Sunbeam' 7/8 reel, cased.

3.5in (9cm) diam

£40-60 TEN

A Hardy 'Marquis' 9/10/11 disc reel, cased.

4in (10cm) diam

£70-100 TEN

A Hardy 'Marquis' no.2 salmon reel, with two spare spools.

4in (10cm) diam

£70-100 TEN

A Hardy 'Marquis' 9/10/11 reel, cased.

4in (10cm) diam

£50-70 TEN

A Hardy 'Silex' no. 2 reel.

4.5in (11.5cm) diam

£100-150 TEN

A Hardy 'The Eddystone' alloy and brass sea fishing reel.

6in (15cm) diam

£40-60 TEN

An early 20thC Allcocks & Co Ltd 4in wood and brass spineback reel.

£30-40   MAI

An A. Carter & Co. of South Moulton Street 3.5in Dingley alloy fly reel, with cut-away rim.

£70-100   MAI

An Allcocks patent six-spoke alloy centrepin aerial reel with brass foot.

The aerial design was supposedly inspired by a spoked bicycle wheel that was introduced at the same time, c1896. It is a popular variation with collectors.

4in (10cm) diam

£400-500   TEN

An S.E. Cooke 'Long Cast' alloy reel.

£30-40   MAI

A Milwards 3in wood and brass starback reel.

£25-30   MAI

A James Ogden of Cheltenham brass and bakelite 2.75in plate wind fly reel.

£80-100   MAI

A Pflueger 'Summit no. 1995' multiplier reel, in pigskin case.

£35-45   MAI

A Nottingham-type 4.5in wood and brass spine back reel.

£22-28   MAI

A late Victorian brass 4in salmon reel, inscribed and dated 1897.

£60-80   MAI

A rare oak folding line-winder, with brass fittings and horn handle and a trout fly reel, both by Hardy Bros Ltd Alnwick.

£450-550   MSA

A CLOSER LOOK AT A HARDY ROD

This is one of Hardy's most sought-after models of fishing rod.

The Casting Club de France rod was made from 1911 to 1961, and in both 7ft and 8ft lengths, this is the 8ft version.

It is in complete and perfect condition, and was probably never used.

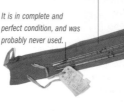

All Hardy rods were given an individual serial number, this example can be dated to 1954.

A Hardy 'Casting Club de France' Palakona three-piece split bamboo cane fly rod, with extra tip, original guarantee and care labels and green canvas sleeve.

£450-550   MAI

An early eel gleave, with five tines and original handle.

These gruesome looking items were used for spearing eels, the arrow-shaped points were to prevent the wriggling creature from getting free.

£50-60   MUR

A 19thC six-tine fish spear, in very good condition.

7.5in (19cm) long

£40-60   MUR

A Solingen 'Overland Fisherman's Friend' multiple tool, in leather scabbard.

£22-28   MAI

A vintage japanned tin fly box, containing assorted wet and dry flies.

£30-40   MAI

A vintage japanned tin fly box, containing assorted salmon flies.

£35-45   MAI

A pike fly.

£35-45   MAI

COLLECTORS' NOTES

■ As the nation's favourite sport, football memorabilia continues to be one of the most sought-after types of sporting collectables. Values tend to be driven by popular teams, key players and important matches. Although early programmes and tickets can be very desirable, age does not necessarily equal value.

■ Memorabilia connected to modern superstar players such as David Beckham will continue to attract a premium, as will that of his predecessors such as Stanley Matthews, Bobby Charlton, George Best and Pelé. Manchester United are the most widely collected British team due to their long history of characterful players, success on the pitch and tragedy off.

■ Programmes connected to significant matches, such as FA Cup finals, international games and early, pre-war games are desirable, although annotated examples are less desirable than those in mint condition. More recent programmes are much more affordable, mainly as fans tend to keep them in good condition and clubs print them in bulk. Although they are unlikely to rise in value significantly in the near future, they make an appealing collecting area for a smaller pocket.

■ Signed shirts, boots and other equipment tend to occupy the higher end of the market, but be sure to check the provenance carefully before buying.

An Arsenal v Sheffield 1936 FA Cup Final tie ticket.

Arsenal won the match 1-0. This is an early, pre-WWII ticket from an important game and features Arsenal, a collectable team.

1936   3in (7.5cm) high

£150-200   **MM**

A 1966 World Cup First Day cover, signed by Sir Alf Ramsey and the 10 surviving England finalists.

Perhaps the highlight of English football to date, items connected to the 1966 World Cup are highly sought-after.

1966

£220-280   **GBA**

A Bolton Wanderers v West Ham United 1923 F.A. Cup final tie ticket stub.

This ticket is even earlier than the previous ticket making it significantly more desirable.

1923

£1,200-1,800   **GBA**

A copy of 'The Story of Jesus', signed in pencil by the Busby Babes and Sir Matt Busby.

Manchester United's Busby Babes were considered one of the greatest squads to ever play together. Eight members of the team died in the 1958 Munich air disaster.

£700-1,000   **GBA**

An 'Evening Chronicle United Souvenir' 32-page Manchester United commemorative publication, entitled 'Munich to Wembley 1958', dated April 23rd.

1958   23.5in (59.5cm) high

£35-45   **MM**

A Manchester City Football fixtures list for the 1896-97 season, with cloth covers, the interior with printed first and second team fixtures, ink results and fixture changes.

This is an early example with the team only adopting the name in 1894.

1896

£400-500   **GBA**

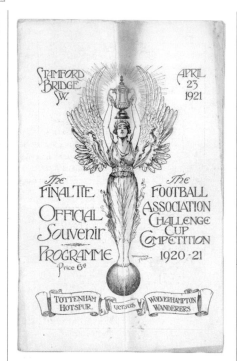

A Tottenham Hotspur v Wolverhampton Wanderers 1921 F.A. Cup Final tie programme.

Programmes from before WWII are generally of value, and the earlier the better.

£1,800-2,200 GBA

A Bolton Wanderers v West Ham United 1923 F.A. Cup Final tie programme, 28th April.

1923

£1,200-1,800 GBA

An England v Scotland 1936 international match programme, played 4th April at Empire Stadium, Wembley.

1936

£120-180 GBA

A Portsmouth v Brentford 1942 London War Cup Final programme.

Due to paper rationing, programmes and other ephemera from the war years are scarce.

1942

£180-220 GBA

A World Cup 1966 final tie programme, with details neatly completed in ink.

Despite its historic importance, programmes from the 1966 World Cup final are not hard to find as so many were kept in good condition to commemorate the great event.

1966 9in (23cm) high

£60-80 MM

An Inter Milan v Celtic 1967 European Cup Final programme.

1967

£180-220 GBA

A scarce Ajax v Juventus 1973 European Cup final programme, played in Belgrade, 30th May.

1973

£2,500-3,500 GBA

An official match programme for the Pelé tribute game, featuring Cosmos v Santos at the Giants Stadium in New Jersey, played Oct. 1st 1997.

11in (28cm) high

£70-100 MM

A signed David Beckham England v Greece No. 7 international long-sleeved jersey, the spare shirt signed in black marker pen to upper chest.

As well as being possibly the most famous footballer currently playing the game, this shirt is from a key game where Beckham's dramatic last minute goal from a trademark free kick secured England's qualification for the 2002 World Cup finals at the expense of Germany.

2001-02

£1,000-1,500 GBA

A signed David Seaman England goalkeeping jersey, worn in his final England international match v Macedonia, 16th October 2002, long-sleeved, signed in black marker pen "SAFE HANDS", "DAVID SEAMAN', with mud and turf stains.

Do not be tempted to wash signed shirts, the stains add to the provenance and although the signatures may be in indelible ink, they may still fade in the wash.

£800-1,000 GBA

A signed Kenny Dalglish Liverpool No.7 jersey, short-sleeved, signed in black marker pen by Dalglish on the No.7, and additionally to the reverse by Bob Paisley, Phil Neal, Alan Hansen, Ronnie Whelan, Mark Lawrenson, Graeme Souness & Alan Kennedy.

£600-800 GBA

A signed Michael Owen Liverpool No.18 jersey, worn during his fifth League appearance against Blackburn Rovers.

£800-1,000 GBA

A CLOSER LOOK AT A SIGNED FOOTBALL SHIRT

Jaap Stam is considered one of the best defenders in football.

In winning the Champions League final, Manchester United secured 'the treble' of the F.A. Premier League, the F.A. Cup and the Champions League, being the first English club and only the fourth club in Europe ever to do so.

Manchester United are supported and collected internationally.

This was a key match in the club's history. The shirt belonged to a high profile player and was worn at the match.

A signed Jaap Stam Manchester United 1999 Champions League final match-worn No.6 jersey, signed in black marker pen, turf marks.

1999

£4,500-5,500 GBA

A 'Zico' Brazil No.10 1986 World Cup jersey, worn in the match versus Poland.

Brazil beat Poland 4-0 in the second round match played on 16th June. Brazil is the most successful international football team and is supported around the world.

1986

£700-1,000 GBA

A signed England World Cup squad football, signatures include Kevin Keegan, Ray Clements and Phil Neale.

c1974

£60-80   **MAI**

A signed Adidas match ball from the Bayer Leverkusen v Real Madrid 2002 Champions League final, played at Hampden Park, signed by seven members of the Leverkusen team including Michael Ballack.

Obtained by a steward on duty at the match, the ball was signed in the Leverkusen dressing room.

2002

£180-220   **GBA**

A signed Liverpool 1977 European Cup final squad football, extensively signed in black marker pen and including Bob Paisley, Terry McDermott, Emlyn Hughes, Phil Neal, Rob Jones, David Fairclough, Jimmy Case, Peter Thompson, Joe Fagan, Ray Clemence, Kevin Keegan, Steve Heighway.

c1977

£220-280   **GBA**

A signed photograph of Garrincha, showing celebrations after Botafogo won the 1963 Brazilian Cup final, signed in biro, mounted above a title plaque, framed and glazed.

14.5in (37cm) wide

£80-120   **GBA**

A colour print of the 1953 F.A. Cup final, signed by Stanley Matthews, also signed by the artist.

1953   *25.5in (65cm) wide*

£70-100   **GBA**

A Pelé autograph, mounted with a photograph of the footballer, signed in black marker pen and with a title plaque, framed and glazed.

21in (53.5cm) high

£100-200   **GBA**

A silver and enamelled football medal, for the "Evening Dispatch Nignog Football League Intermediate B Champions 1938-1939", hallmark for Chester 1938.

1938

£25-35   **MAI**

A George Best lamp and original shade, with plastic base, carved wood football and printed paper shade, with facsimile signature.

15.25in (38cm) high

£70-90   **MTS**

COLLECTORS' NOTES

◼ Golfing's long heritage and continued popularity as a sport helps to make related memorabilia one of the most popular sport collecting areas.

◼ While very early pieces, from the birth of the game in the 15thC until the 19thC are rare and expensive, the late 19thC and early 20thC can offer more affordable pieces. Early clubs and balls tend to occupy the high-end of the market, but just about anything with a golfing theme can be of interest.

◼ The Victorians' passion for the game spilled over into ceramics, glass, silverware and books. Well-known manufacturers such as Royal Doulton and Spode produced themed wares, collected by both golfing enthusiasts and aficionados of the pottery, making them doubly desirable.

◼ Prints, paintings and photographs of old courses and famous players through the ages form an important historical record and are always sought-after. Depictions of women golfers are much scarcer and will usually fetch a premium

◼ As golfing equipment was generally play-used, condition has a great effect on value. Specialist auctions are now fairly commonplace, often taking place around the time of the Open Championship in July and offer a great opportunity to view a wide range of items.

A CLOSER LOOK AT A GOLF CLUB

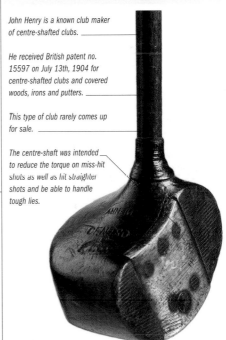

John Henry is a known club maker of centre-shafted clubs.

He received British patent no. 15597 on July 13th, 1904 for centre-shafted clubs and covered woods, irons and putters.

This type of club rarely comes up for sale.

The centre-shaft was intended to reduce the torque on miss-hit shots as well as hit straighter shots and be able to handle tough lies.

An R. Forgan, St Andrews transitional brassie, the scared head stamped with "R. Forgan" and Prince of Wales feathers, the sole with horn insert above the brass plate, leather insert to face, lead counterweight, hickory shaft, with wrapped soft leather grip.

£400-600   **L&T**

A W. Park, Musselburgh transitional brassie, the scared head with horn insert above the brass plate, leather insert to face, lead counterweight, hickory shaft, wrapped soft leather grip.

£250-350   **L&T**

A James Hutchison, North Berwick transitional play club, the scared head stamped "Hutchison", ebony insert to sole, leather insert to face, lead counterweight, fruitwood shaft, wrapped soft leather grip, defective.

£350-450   **L&T**

An R. Simpson of Carnoustie longnose playclub, the scared beech head with horn insert to sole, lead counterweight, later hickory shaft.

£600-800   **L&T**

A rare John Henry 'Centro' centre-shafted driver, horn insert to face, lead counterweight, hickory shaft.
c1890

£4,000-6,000   **L&T**

A D.M. Patrick Special longnose spoon, hickory-shafted, the beech head with ebony sole and lead counterweight.

£650-750   **L&T**

A Reginald Brougham metalwood, the alloy head with wooden insert to the face, stamped trademark incorporating clubs design, hickory shaft, wrapped leather grip.

£300-500   **L&T**

An R. Forgan, St Andrews smooth-faced mid-iron, with maker's shaft stamp and original full-length hide grip and underlisting.

c1895   *41in (104cm) high*

£40-60   **WW**

A W. Park, Musselburgh, smooth-faced lofting iron, long hosel, hickory shaft, wrapped soft leather grip.

£250-350   **L&T**

A W. Park of Musselburgh smooth-faced general iron, with a 4.5in (11.5cm) hosel complete with period grip and underlisting, stamp mark faded.

c1895

£60-90   **WW**

An R.L. Urquhart Patent adjustable head iron, almost smooth face, the adjuster release button unusually set at the front of the hosel, the hickory shaft stamped, "R. Sayers, selected", wrapped leather grip.

Club design was not regulated until 1909 and prior to then a number of ingenious designs, such as this example were patented. This adjustable club, patented c1895 meant that the angle of the head could be altered to suit the shot meaning less clubs needed to be carried.

An R. Simpson 'Premier' putter, the iron head with mesh patterned face, the hickory shaft stamped maker's name, wrapped leather grip.

£400-600   **L&T**

A rare Simpson Carnoustie Pat lump back iron, stamped "The Perfect Balance", with hand-cut diamond pattern face markings and full-length leather grip.

£80-120   **WW**

£400-600   **L&T**

A smooth-faced rut niblick, by Gibson, with a 4.5in (11.5cm) hosel and fitted with a full-length hide grip.

£60-90   **WW**

A 'Baxpin' concave face mashie niblick, by Gibson and Gadd.

£30-50   **WW**

A Tom Stewart, St. Andrews left-handed smooth-faced rut niblick, stamped cleek mark, long hosel, hickory shaft, wrapped leather grip.

£250-350   **L&T**

A F. H. Ayres Harry Vardon Autograph niblick, stamped "Harry Vardon Totteridge by F.H. Ayres", with the Maltese cross mark, shaft stamped below rubberised grip.

37in (94cm) high

£25-35   **WW**

A J.&A. Simpson, Edinburgh smooth-faced cleek, hickory shaft, wrapped smooth leather grip.

£80-120   **L&T**

A Standard Mill Co. smooth-faced cleek, early "S.M." and crescent stamped mark, hickory shaft, part wrapped leather grip.

£200-300   **L&T**

A Robert White, St. Andrews smooth-faced cleek, long crimped hosel, hickory shaft, wrapped smooth leather grip.

£120-180   **L&T**

A smooth faced cleek, with long crimped hosel, hickory shaft, wrapped leather grip.

£60-100   **L&T**

A Ben Sayers smooth-faced driving mashie, showing the maker's North Berwick oval stamp mark and an early Stewart pipe mark, with full length hide grip and underlisting.
c1898

£30-40   **WW**

A heavy ribbed-face mashie, stamped "Accurate" with a superb full-length original hide grip with underlisting.

£50-70   **WW**

A Jack Nickolas Ping Anser putter, made by Karston Co. for Slazenger, patent no. D2C7227, brass head, steel-shafted.

£350-450   **L&T**

A Tom Stewart, St. Andrews 'Tom Morris' wry necked putter, stamped cleek and Tom Morris portrait marks, hickory shaft, wrapped leather grip.

£150-250   **L&T**

A Fred Saunders, Highgaten 'Straight Line' aluminium putter, hickory shaft stamped.

£350-450   **L&T**

A Winkworth Scott patent putter, with square section, steel shaft, wrapped leather over wood, square section grip.

£300-500   **L&T**

A ebonized fruitwood putter, scared head, indistinctly stamped, horn insert to sole, hickory shaft.

£120-180   **L&T**

A un-named cone-shaped wooden head putter, with hatched face, hickory shaft stamped "A.L. Johnston".

£2,000-2,500   **L&T**

An Ernest Jones swing trainer practice club, with weighted square mesh pattern ball head, spring hosel and hickory shaft.

£400-600   **L&T**

A CLOSER LOOK AT A GOLF CLUB

This double-faced, hence Duplex, is a rare hammer-headed club.

The Scottish Dalrymple family have a long association with golf, David Dalrymple, Lord Hailes (1726-92) was captain of the Honourable Company of Edinburgh Golfers at Leith Links.

The shaped design is intended to give the wooden head greater strength and durability.

Sir Walter laid out a nine-hole golf course near Berwick in 1894, and also supported the formation of the Ladies Golf Club in 1888.

A rare Sir Walter Hamilton-Dalrymple 'Duplex' club, with brass sole plate, with hickory centre shaft.

£3,000-5,000   **L&T**

A Sunday club, with ivory insert to the face, ebony and lead insert to the sole, lead counterweight, the head stamped I.S., pine shaft mounted with a plated band, inscribed, "A Relic of the Tay Bridge Disaster, 28th December 1879, I. Simpson".

On the evening of December 28th, 1879, during a violent storm, the Tay Rail Bridge collapsed with a train on it killing over 70 people including the son-in-law of the designer Sir Thomas Bouch.

£350-450   **L&T**

A CLOSER LOOK AT A GUTTY BALL

The gutty ball was invented by the Rev. Dr. Robert Adams in 1848 and utilized gutta percha and natural inelastic latex.

The condition of this example, which retains most of its original paint and may never have been used, adds greatly to its value.

They completely replaced feathery balls within a few years, as they were much cheaper to produce and could be manufactured with a textured surface resulted in improved aerodynamics.

The McEwan family began its association with golf in c1770, when James McEwan setup business in Leith, Edinburgh.

A rare 'P. McEwan' mesh pattern gutty ball.

£3,000-5,000   L&T

A Capon Heaton & Co. Ltd 'Green Ring' dimple golf ball, with green ring to both poles, stamped.
c1912

£200-300   L&T

An 'Eclipse' patent mesh gutty golf ball.
c1905

£350-450   L&T

A rare 'Joyce Indented' gutty ball, with impressed shamrocks all over the ball, retaining most of the original paint, looks unused.

The impressed shamrock design is unusual, as is the unused condition, both adding to the value.

£5,000-8,000   L&T

An autographed Maxfli golf ball, signed in felt pen by Arnold Palmer.

£100-150   WW

The 'Victor' bramble pattern rubber core ball, painted red for winter usage.

£280-320   L&T

A No. 5 Dunlop 'Lattice' wrapper rubber core ball.

£150-200   **L&T**

A No. 2 Warwick Dunlop wrapped rubber core ball.

£150-200   **L&T**

A No. 3 Penfold wrapper rubber core ball.

£150-200   **L&T**

An unused Silver King Red Dot square mesh ball, in original box.

£220-280   **L&T**

A No. 1 Silver King HV wrapped rubber core ball.

£150-200   **L&T**

A Slazenger Silver King wrapped rubber core ball.

£180-220   **L&T**

A Spalding 'Needled' Top-Flite wrapped dimple ball.

£150-200   **L&T**

A 'The Colonel' wrapped rubber core ball, No. 31, by the St. Mungo Mfg. Co., of America.

£150-200   **L&T**

A 'Cadet' wrapped rubber core ball, by the St. Mungo Mtg. Co. of America, in original wrappers.

£180-220   **L&T**

A.B., " Told at the 19th Hole: Humorous St. Andrews Golf Stories", published by J. & G. Innes, St. Andrews, pictorial wrappers.

c1930s

£250-350 L&T

W. & R. Chambers, "Golfing: A Handbook...", first edition, published by W. & R. Chambers, Edinburgh, illustrated by Ranald M. Alexander.

1887

£200-300 L&T

Glenna Collett, "Ladies in the Rough", first edition, published by Knopf, New York, assisted by James M. Neville, foreword by Bobby Jones.

1928

£150-250 L&T

W. Dalrymple, "Handbook to Golf", first edition, with diagrams and positions and instructions from Amateur and Professional Champions, engraved illustrations, advertisements, original red pictorial cloth boards, Edinburgh.

1895

£250-350 L&T

Robert Hunter, "The Links", first edition, published by Scribner's, New York, illustrated from photographs; plus golf course drawings; decorative endpapers with Dr. MacKenzie's St. Andrews golf course illustration present.

1926

£350-450 L&T

Bobby Jones, "Rights and Wrongs of Golf", first edition, published by A.G. Spalding & Bros., New York, photograph frontispiece of Jones, rebound in green leather flexible cover, gilt lettering to cover, original wrappers missing.

1935

£220-280 L&T

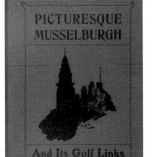

H.B. Martin, "St. Andrew's Golf Club, 1888-1963", first edition, published by St. Andrew's Golf Club, New York, limited to 500 copies privately printed, illus., portrait frontispiece of John Reid, foreword by Alexander B. Halliday.

1938

£250-350 L&T

William Charles Maughan, "Picturesque Musselburgh and its Golf Links", first edition, published by Alexander Gardner, Paisley, illustrated by R. Gemmel Hutchison.

1906

£400-600 L&T

Gene Sarazen, Denny Shute, Ralph Guldahl, & Johnny Revolta, "From Tee to Cup by the Four Masters", first edition, published by Wilson Sporting Goods, signed on title page by Ralph Guldahl.

1937

£80-120 L&T

A ROUND OF THE LINKS

VIEWS OF THE

GOLF GREENS OF SCOTLAND

ETCHED BY GEORGE AIKMAN, A.R.S.A

FROM WATER COLOUR DRAWINGS BY

JOHN SMART. R.S.A.

John Smartt, "A Round of the Links: Views of the Golf Greens of Scotland", facsimile edition of the original of 1893, published by Heritage Press, Aberdeenshire, illustrated from etchings by George Aikman from watercolours by Smart.

1980

£120-180 L&T

J. H. Taylor, "Taylor on Golf: Impressions, Comments and Hints", second edition, published by Hutchinson & Co., London, illustrated with 48 illustrations.

1902

£250-350 L&T

"The Funny side of Golf - From the Pages of Punch', in original pictorial boards, new leather green and gilt spine, foxing.

c1909 11.25in (28.5cm) high

£80-120 WW

Anonymous, "The Seeding and Care of Golf Courses", first edition, published by O.M. Scott & Sons, Marysville, Ohio, illustrated with vignette drawings.

1922

£400-500 L&T

An Open Golf Championship at Muirfield Official programme, for Wednesday, 8th May 1929, cream paper wrappers.

£300-400 L&T

A Open Golf Championship Official programme, Friday 2nd July 1948, autographed in pencil on the back cover by James Braid, R.A. Whitcombe and two others.

£350-450 L&T

An official souvenir programme from the 16th Ryder Cup Golf Matches, Royal Birkdale Golf Club, 7th, 8th & 9th October.

1965

£120-180 L&T

A 1975 Ryder Cup Victory Dinner menu card, signed by numerous players and officials.

£500-700 L&T

A Ryder Cup dinner menu, dated 20th September 1969, signed by the United States and Great Britain teams.

1969

£280-320 SWO

A George IV One Pound bank note, issued by Andover Old Bank in Andover on 5th October 1825 for Joseph Wakeford, William Wakeford and Robert Wakeford, serial number 12174.

8in (20.5cm) wide

£180-220 WW

A Foley china puzzle jug, printed and painted with a scene of two golfers and caddie; and with another golfer and caddie to the reverse, gilt rim.

See other puzzle jugs on page 180.

5.25in (15cm) high

£250-350   **L&T**

An Arthur Wood 'Golf' mug, with golf bag handle and printed in colours with golfing figures.

c1950   5.25in (13cm) high

£18-22   **SAS**

A 19thC Copeland late Spode golfing jug, relief decorated with golfers and caddies, surmounted by an ornamental border on a two-tone blue ground, printed and impressed marks to the underside.

7in (17.5cm) high

£350-450   **L&T**

A white jasperware cream jug, decorated in relief with golfers.

4in (10cm) high

£120-180   **WW**

A Foley China ribbed beaker, with printed scene of golfers and caddy, and crossed club motif to reverse with motto reading "Far and Sure".

3.75in (9.5cm) high

£140-180   **MSA**

A Taylor-Tunnicliffe pottery match holder, hand-painted with a scene of Old Tom Morris and caddie.

c1890   2.25in (6cm) high

£200-300   **L&T**

An early 20thC Weller 'Dickensware' pottery vase, or tall tapering cylindrical form, with bulbous base, decorated with a lady golfer amongst trees, printed marks to the underside.

Depictions of female golfers are much scarcer than male players as they only started actively playing in the early 20thC.

9.75in (24.5cm) high

£650-750   **L&T**

A Royal Doulton transfer printed seriesware cereal bowl, depicting Crombie golfing figures and the caption "Every dog has his day and every man his hour", marked.

c1911   7.75in (19.5cm) diam

£150-200   **WW**

A Rudolstadt porcelain golfing plate, transfer-printed and painted with a scene of lady golfers and caddy, the border with a continuous landscape design, printed mark to the reverse.

9.75in (24.5cm) diam

£300-400   **L&T**

CENTRE: A silver-plated golfing comport stand, formed as three upright, longnose clubs, conjoined by a naturalistic circular platform surmounted by a figure of a golfer, the whole supporting an etched glass circular dish.

11in (27.5cm) high overall

£600-800 **L&T**

LEFT & RIGHT: A pair of silver-plated golfing candlesticks, each formed as three upright, longnose clubs supporting a mesh pattern ball nozzle, and on a circular base surmounted by a mesh pattern ball.

10in (25.5cm) high

£400-600 **L&T**

A Lytham & St Annes silver golfing trophy, of two-handled circular form, applied in relief with the club badge and inscribed "Aggregate Prize, Spring Meeting 1931, Won by...", on an ebonized circular plinth, Birmingham hallmark for 1926.

£150-250 **L&T**

A silver golfing trophy, the plain shaped bowl supported by four golfing irons on a circular ebonised base, hallmarked for Birmingham 1918.

£60-80 **MAI**

A North Manchester Golf Club silver medal, the obverse decorated in relief, with a golfer at the top of his swing and a caddie behind, the reverse inscribed, 'Monthly competition, won by H.B. Wood, 23rd November, 1895' apparently unmarked.

The North Manchester golf course was designed by the famous designer and player James Braid. It was first opened in 1894 making it one of the oldest courses in the region.

1.25in (3cm) diam

£1,200-1,800 **L&T**

An Oxford University Golf Club silver medal, the obverse decorated in relief with the college emblem and motto and "Oxford University Golf Club" to the outer rim, reverse relief cast with a laurel wreath, engraved "Inter Collegiate Cup, 1914, Trinity, W.F.C. McClure", apparently unmarked.

2in (5cm) diam

£120-180 **L&T**

A Reg Horne's Ryder Cup British Players sterling silver badge, relief decorated centrally to the obverse with the Ryder Cup, 1947, and inscribed in the border Reg Horne, British Player, clasp to the reverse, Robert A. Hudson, Portland, Oregon.

1947 *1.5in (4cm) diam*

£400-600 **L&T**

An 'Aircraft Depot Golf Club, B.F.I.' silver medal, relief decorated in the round with a laurel wreath, inscribed centrally "Winner, 1st Div. Handicap, Easter 1935".

1.5in (4cm) diam

£40-60 **L&T**

A silver-plated golfing ink well set, featuring a Victorian golfer mounted on a circular naturalistic base complete with matching glass ink wells with plated tops, together with a plated quill pen and another pen.

12in (30.5cm) wide

£350-450 **MM**

A pewter cigarette box mounted with a golf ball and club, inscribed "Dak Ladies International Golf Tournament Wentworth 1958" and "Foursomes Winner".

4.75in (12cm) wide

£80-120 **SWO**

An Art Deco silver golfing trophy, of two-handled, tapering circular form, inscribed "Purfleet and Erith Golf Challenge Trophy", on ebonite circular plinth, Birmingham hallmark for 1961; and a small Oldham & District Silver two-handled golf trophy, on ebonite circular plinth, Sheffield hallmark for 1960.

£150-250 **L&T**

A pair of bronze golfing bookends, by the Bradley & Hubbard Mfg. Co., relief-cast respectively with a gentleman and lady golfer in a landscape.

5in (13cm) high

£280-320   **L&T**

A pair of patinated bronze golfing bookends, by Frankhart Inc., each as a golfer in the follow-through, on a shaped base.

9in (23cm) high

£200-300   **L&T**

A 'Dunlop-Man' nickel-plated car mascot, the caricature golfing figure standing on a Dunlop 31 golf ball with later ebonised plinth.

5in (13cm) high

£70-100   **L&T**

A 'Dunlop-Man' brass table bell, the caricature golfing figure standing on a Dunlop 31 golf ball.

£60-80   **L&T**

A Douglass sand tee gun, marked "patent applied for".

£350-450   **L&T**

A collection of Peter Oosterhuis medals, badges and memorabilia, including a 1977 Ryder Cup cloth badge; a 1975 Ryder Cup cloth badge; a Walker Cup cloth badge and two lapel pins; a 1968 World Amateur Golf Council badge; a 1982 US Open Golf Championship badge; and a 1992 PGA Tour money clip.

English golfer Oosterhuis (b.1948) represented England in the 1967 Walker Cup and 1968 Eisenhower Trophy. He then turned professional, winning the 1981 British PGA Championship. Since retiring from playing he has been a commentator for CBS Sports and the Golf Channel among others.

£400-600   **L&T**

A Swiss Dom Watch & Cie 'Domatic Score' golf scorer, in the form of a wristwatch, with original strap, instruction pamphlet and box.

£30-50   **MSA**

An American golfing fan, with wooden handle and unusual image of a lady golfer, copyrighted 1904.

13.75in (35cm) high

£80-120   **VSC**

An un-named Automaton-type caddie, badly damaged.

£120-180   **L&T**

COLLECTORS' NOTES

- There is a wide choice of items available to collectors of horse racing memorabilia ranging from race equipment and uniforms, to ceramics and glass, painting and prints to bronzes and silverware.

- Unique or limited edition bronzes and paintings tend to form the top tier of memorabilia with ceramics and printed material being more affordable. Horse racing became a professional sport during the reign of Queen Anne (1702-14) meaning that many different collectables have been produced over the years.

- Look for memorabilia commemorating famous horses, such as Brown Jack, Arkle, Red Rum and Shergar, or related to famous jockeys such Fred Archer, Lester Piggott, Harry Wragg and Frankie Dettori. Pieces from well known races such as the Grand National, Ascot and the St Ledger Stakes will also be desirable.

After John Frederick Herring Sr, 'The Flying Dutchman, engraved by J. Harris, aquatint from the Fores's Celebrated Winners series.

The Flying Dutchman won The Derby and The St Leger in 1849.

Image 27.25in (69cm) wide

£1,500-2,000   **GBA**

A W.W. Rouch & Co. platinum process black and white photograph of Lemberg, the 1910 Derby winner.

£50-60   **GBA**

An 'in memorium' colour lithograph of Fred Archer (1857-86), with printed signature, framed by a black cloth-draped horse shoe.

c1886   *18in (46cm) wide*

£220-280   **GBA**

A Brown Jack commemorative silk square, featuring a photographic print of Brown Jack with Steve Donoghue, and printed details of the gelding's pedigree and race record, framed and glazed.

23in (58.5cm) wide

£250-350   **GBA**

A Crepello commemorative Derby-winner silk scarf.

1957

£150-200   **GBA**

A Trigo commemorative Derby-winner silk scarf.

1929

£150-200   **GBA**

A Blenheim commemorative Derby-winner silk scarf.

1930

£150-250   **GBA**

A 19thC bronze of a standing thoroughbred, unsigned.

9.25in (23.5cm) high

£1,000-1,500 GBA

A 19th-20thC 'After the Race' bronze, signed "G* Ferrari", mid-brown patina height.

13in (33cm) high

£3,500-4,000 GBA

The 1987 Chester Vase won by Dick Hollingsworth's 'Dry Dock', in the form of a silver cup and cover, hallmarked Sheffield, 1923, on an onyx base set with a plaque inscribed "Chester Vase 1987".

'Dry Dock' was by 'High Line', out of 'Boathouse'. The Chester Vase winner was also placed in the St Leger.

1923 9in (23cm) high

£180-220 GBA

A Fred Archer commemorative earthenware jug.

Flat race jockey Fred Archer was the most successful jockey of the Victorian period. Due to his unusual height of 5ft 10in, Archer was forced to diet to meet the correct weight. The effect on his health, coupled with depression following his wife's death, lead him to commit suicide at the age of 29.

c1886

£350-450 GBA

An early 20thC French milliner's conformiteur, with metal label of "Allie Maillard".

These were used by milliners for measuring jockey's heads.

£150-200 MAI

A large carved and painted wood saddler's advertising figure, probably modelled on Fred Archer in the colours of Mr Manton, with whalebone whip.

52in (132cm) high

£1,200-1,800 GBA

A set of autographed racing silks, the crossbelts signed by 17 flat jockeys including Lester Piggott, Willy Carson, Pat Eddery, Frankie Dettori, Walter Swinburn, Ray Cochrane, George Duffield, Alan Munro, Michael and Richard Hills.

£280-320 GBA

A set of King George V's royal racing silks, with gold braid, velvet cap, the purple now faded towards a blue tone.

These silks were kept at the Hon. Aubrey Hastings's racing stables at Wroughton where the King had a horse, St Sylvestre, in training in 1928.

c1928

£3,500-4,000 GBA

A vintage bookmaker's chrome-plated display board, by Reddish of London, with a lion mask detail, below a change tray, pole fitting for a separate tripod base, complete with bookmaker's satchel, a brass money box and a small quantity of betting tickets.

£1,500-2,000 GBA

FIND OUT MORE...

The National Horseracing Museum. *99 High Street, Newmarket, Suffolk CB8 8JL Tel: 01638 667 333 www.nhrm.co.uk*

COLLECTORS' NOTES

- The first official piece of Olympic memorabilia released was a set of stamps for the 1896 games, issued by the organising committee to balance the event's budget. Olympic coins followed much later in 1951.

- Lapel badges have been produced since the games restarted. They are an affordable way to start a collection and are usually easy to obtain, with participation medals forming the next step up the ladder. These medals were given to all the participants, officials and members of the International Olympic Committee, so numbers produced can be quite large.

- Memorabilia from the earliest games tends to be scarce, and so the most valuable, making more recent games a good place to start for collectors on a budget.

- Look for pieces connected to countries that no longer 'exist', such as the German Democratic Republic or the Soviet Union, as historical interest can add to their value and desirability.

A rare 1920s Olympic Trials Amateur Athletics Union of Canada bronze badge, by Stock & Bickle.

£80-120   **BLO**

A 1932 Los Angeles Olympics cycling event ticket.

1932   *3.25in (8cm) diam*

£15-25   **LDE**

A 1932 Los Angeles Olympics Closing Ceremony ticket.

1932   *4.25in (11cm) long*

£50-70   **LDE**

A 1932 Los Angeles Olympics swimming event ticket.

1932   *4.25in (11cm) wide*

£40-50   **LDE**

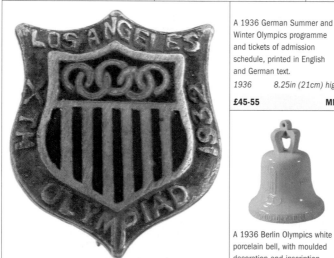

A 1932 Los Angeles Olympics participant's pin.

1932   *0.5in (1cm) high*

£15-25   **LDE**

A 1936 German Summer and Winter Olympics programme and tickets of admission schedule, printed in English and German text.

1936   *8.25in (21cm) high*

£45-55   **MM**

A 1936 Berlin Olympics white porcelain bell, with moulded decoration and inscription, small chip.

1936   *5in (12.5cm) high*

£40-50   **SAS**

A 1936 German Olympics woven ribbon.

1936   *4.25in (10.5cm) high*

£70-90   **LDE**

A 1936 German Winter Olympics 'Garmisch Partenkirchen' enamelled metal badge.

1936   *2in (5cm) high*

£70-100   **LDE**

An extremely rare 1954 Badminton Olympics Horse Trials silvered Judge or Official's plaque, with crowned portcullis, motto around horseshoe, suspension bar at rear, slight wear to plating.

1954   *5.25in (13cm) high*

£180-220   **BLO**

A 1960 Rome Olympics blue enamel on brass pin.

1960   *0.75in (2cm) wide*

£25-35   **LDE**

A 1964 Tokyo Olympics commemorative gilt metal tray, hammered with Olympic rings above the title and inscribed with the winners of the individual and team fencing events to each side, decorated with a foliate border, in original fitted case.

This tray was produced after the games, but its exact provenance is unknown.

18.5in (47cm) wide

£150-250   **MM**

A 1964 Innsbruck Winter Olympics enamel-on-brass pin.

1964   *2in (5cm) wide*

£30-40   **LDE**

A 1980 Moscow Olympics commemorative teapot, marked "Made in Russia".

1980   *5.5in (14cm) high*

£40-60   **RCC**

A 1984 Los Angeles Olympics baseball cap, by Adidas, with 'Sam' the Eagle mascot on the front.

£4-5   **BR**

A set of ten 1988 Calgary Winter Olympics silver coins, each depicting a different sport in the Olympic games, issued by the Canadian mint, in a fitted presentation case.

1988   *14.75in (37.5cm) wide*

£120-180   **MM**

A US Postal Service Olympics pin.

0.75in (2cm) high

£1-2   **BH**

FIND OUT MORE...

www.collectors.olympics.org, *The Olympics Collectors Commission, official collectors' website.*

A rare American flat-top tennis racket, with string detailing at the top, and hand-etched and dated 1876.

Flat-top rackets were popular during the 1880s, By the 1890s the top of the racket began to curve, gradually becoming more oval and more in line with today's equipment.

27.25in (69cm) high

£250-350   **VSC**

A very rare pair of small 19thC wooden tennis rackets, with green velvet-covered handles.

9in (23cm) high

£200-300   **MSA**

A tennis player oak and brass hanging paper clip.

c1900   8.25in (15cm) long

£220-260   **MSA**

A Wm. Sykes Ltd. "Lawn Tennis Racket Gut Preservative" card box, containing a bottle of preservative and brushes.

Box 4.25in (11cm) wide

£60-80   **MSA**

A brass-cased lawn tennis measure, with label to surface including the measurements for the court.

£20-30   **MAI**

A spelter figure of a tennis player, mounted on a pink marble base.

10.75in (27cm) high

£350-450   **MSA**

An official Jubilee souvenir from the All England Lawn Tennis Club by A. Wallis Myers, entitled 'Fifty Years of Wimbledon - The Story of the Lawn Tennis Championships 1877-1926'.

10.75in (27.5cm) high

£80-120   **MM**

A Muller of 147 Strand, London racket catalogue, complete with prices, also covering tennis access and cricket bats, cover price 23p.

c1934   7.75in (19.5cm) high

£15-25   **MM**

A humourous French colour sketch, signed by Chenet, depicting a tennis match with a dog in the foreground and the caption "This time she will not call it out".

15.75in (40cm) wide

£35-45   **MM**

A Slazenger cricket bat, with the signatures of the 1976 England Cricket team on the face and the Surrey and Kent teams verso.

1976

£70-90   **ROS**

A full-size Duncan Fearnley cricket bat, signed by both the England and South Africa teams who played at Lords, June 1998.

£30-40   **MAI**

A 'Cricket' nursery plate, printed in black with a named cricket scene, fine hairline crack.

c1860   *7.25in (18cm) diam*

£80-120   **SAS**

A Sid Barnes cricketing jug, 'The English Team in Australia'.

Sidney George Barnes (1916-73) played for Australia and his native New South Wales. Despite his outstanding records as a player, at least one of which still stands, he is perhaps better known for his bizarre behaviour.

1908   *5.5in (14cm) high*

£70-80   **RCC**

A lemonade set, screenprinted with hunting scenes, comprising a jug and four tumblers, plus four other similar tumblers.

Following the ban on hunting with dogs, it is possible that there will be a rise in the value of hunting-themed memorabilia.

£60-80   **MAI**

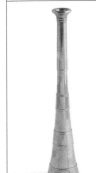

A Henry Keats silver-plated hunting horn, of typical form, inscribed "Henry Keats, Sutton Scotney".

£150-200   **MAI**

A Staffordshire Pottery milk jug, decorated with fox hunting scenes.

£10-20   **MAI**

A small octagonal nursery 'Kite Flying' plate, printed in black, hairline crack.

Kiting memorabilia is not as widely collected as many sporting themes and there are far fewer examples. Although the market is fairly small, items can fetch high prices among specialists.

c1830   *4.5in (11.5cm) diam*

£100-150   **SAS**

A Copeland 'Rugby' pottery jug, moulded with two rugby scenes, the neck decorated with grass, brown printed mark, minor star crack to base.

c1900   *6in (15cm) high*

£100-150   **SAS**

COLLECTORS' NOTES

■ Visitors to the J. & J. Wiggin stand at the 'Ideal Home Exhibition' in London in 1934 witnessed the first use of stainless steel on functional, domestic items such as teapots, toast racks and milk jugs. Stainless steel had been 'accidentally' discovered in 1913, but it was not considered for commercial use until 1928 when William Wiggin's wife asked her husband to make a toast rack from the 'new' material that was strong, resilient and did not need constant polishing.

■ The range was marketed under the brand 'Olde Hall', named after the factory's location in an old Salvation Army hall, and became instantly successful. Some pre-WWII designs were by Harold Stabler, but it was not until the arrival of Robert Welch as consultant designer in 1955 that the company's modern designs really took off. During the 1960s and '70s, it became a

mainstay of kitchens the world over, often being given as wedding presents.

■ The shape and range is an important indicator to value, with the iconic 'Campden' (1957) and 'Alveston' (1964) teapots and accessories, being among the most desirable. Pieces marked 'Olde Hall' were made from 1928-59 and those marked 'Old Hall' from 1959-84, when the company closed due to competition from cheaper Far Eastern imports.

■ Old Hall leads collectable stainless steel and was, and still is, an affordable way of bringing functional period metalware design into the home. Pieces can still be found in charity shops and online auctions inexpensively. Condition is very important and those with dents, dings or excessive scratches should be avoided, particularly if a very common shape.

An Old Hall stainless steel 'Avon' teapot, designed by Robert Welch in 1967, stamped with registered design number 928252.

5.75in (14.5cm) high

£65-75   **GC**

An Old Hall stainless steel 'Avon' milk jug, designed by Robert Welch in 1967.

4in (10cm) high

£15-25   **GC**

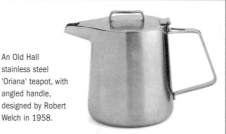

An Old Hall stainless steel 'Avon' coffee pot, designed by Robert Welch in 1967.

The fine quality of this range can be seen in the perfect fit of the lid, which leaves only a thin seam.

7in (17.5cm) high

£65-75   **GC**

An Old Hall stainless steel 'Oriana' teapot, with angled handle, designed by Robert Welch in 1958.

5.75in (14.5cm) high

£50-60   **GC**

An Old Hall stainless steel 'Oriana' milk jug, designed by Robert Welch in 1958.

3.5in (9cm) high

£15-20   **GC**

An Old Hall stainless steel tall two-pint 'Connaught' coffee pot, designed by Leslie Wiggin in 1959.

7in (17.5cm) high

£15-25   **GC**

A CLOSER LOOK AT AN OLD HALL TEAPOT

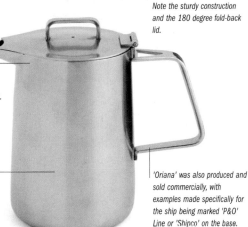

Note the sturdy construction and the 180 degree fold-back lid.

The range was designed by Old Hall's consultant designer and noted modern metal designer Robert Welch. He was also responsible for the company's famous Alveston tea set, among many other items.

The Oriana range was designed for the P&O cruise liner 'Oriana' in 1958, with J. & J. Wiggin winning the contract to supply all of the stainless steel hollow ware.

'Oriana' was also produced and sold commercially, with examples made specifically for the ship being marked 'P&O' Line or 'Shipco' on the base.

An Old Hall stainless steel 'Oriana' coffee pot or hot water jug, designed by Robert Welch in 1958.

5.75in (14.5cm) high

£50-60   **GC**

An Old Hall stainless steel large vase, from the Alveston range designed by Robert Welch.

This large size is very rare.

9.75in (25cm) high

£75-85   **GC**

A rare Old Hall stainless steel stemless bud vase, from the Alveston range, designed by Robert Welch.

6in (15.5cm) high

£10-20   **GC**

An Old Hall stainless steel cake basket, designed by Robert Welch, with swivel handle.

10in (25.5cm) diam

£15-20   **GAZE**

An Old Hall stainless steel small bud vase, from the Alveston range, designed by Robert Welch.

7.25in (18.5cm) high

£10-20   **GC**

An Old Hall stainless steel candlestick, from the Alveston range, designed by Robert Welch.

11.75in (30cm) high

£50-60   **GC**

A pair of Old Hall stainless steel triple candlesticks, from the Campden range, with teak foot pads, designed by Robert Welch.

This is one of Welch's most celebrated and desirable designs for Old Hall. Examples lacking the wooden feet are generally worth under 50 per cent of the value quoted here.

9in (23cm) high

£60-75 (each)   **GC**

STAINLESS STEEL

COLLECTORS' NOTES

■ Although Old Hall leads the way, consider other fine quality manufacturers who employed leading designers or silver or goldsmiths of the day. A good example is Viners of Sheffield who, for a brief time in the late 1960s, employed Stuart Devlin to design a collection. Devlin went on to be appointed the Queen's goldsmith in 1984, amongst many other achievements.

■ The resulting 'Devlin Collection' displays Devlin's hallmark design features, rich gilt textured areas contrasting against plain, highly polished silver areas. Texture was popular amongst many metalworkers of the period and as such it represents late 20thC metalware design very well. There were nine designs in all, including wine goblets, dishes and a cylindrical posy vase.

■ The range was short-lived as the adhesive that bonded the parts together (they are not screwed together) was not robust and over time pieces broke apart when dropped or knocked. However, many pieces still exist at affordable prices, although this may change as collectors reassess the importance of the range. Always buy pieces in the best condition you can and look out for the black cylindrical card boxes.

■ Other notable names include Gerald Benney, a similarly important contemporary of Welch and Devlin, and Keith Tyson. All studied at the important Royal College of Art, London under Professor Robert Goodden. Arne Jacobsen's designs for Stelton are also highly notable, although prices are considerably higher due to his wider fame.

A late 1960s Viners 'Devlin Collection' stainless steel small wine or water goblet, with textured gold-plated stem, designed by Stuart Devlin, the foot with inset plastic base.

5.25in (13.5cm) high

£15-25   **GC**

A late 1960s Viners 'Devlin Collection' stainless steel champagne goblet, with textured gold-plated stem, designed by Stuart Devlin, the foot with inset plastic base.

4.5in (11.5cm) high

£15-25   **GC**

A late 1960s Viners 'Devlin Collection' stainless steel candleholder, with textured gold-plated stem, designed by Stuart Devlin, the foot with inset plastic base.

A late 1960s Viners 'Devlin Collection' tall stainless steel goblet, with textured gold-plated stem, designed by Stuart Devlin, the foot with inset plastic base.

7in (18cm) high

£15-25   **GC**

6in (15.5cm) high

£15-25   **GC**

A pair of late 1960s Viners 'Devlin Collection' stainless steel nutdishes or candleholders, with textured gold-plated bases, designed by Stuart Devlin.

5in (13cm) diam

£40-60   **GC**

A late 1960s Viners 'Devlin Collection' stainless steel 'Violet Bowl', with pull-off, friction fit gold-plated textured domed top.

3.25in (8cm) high

£40-50   **GC**

A set of six settings of Viners stainless steel 'Design 70' fish knives and forks, designed by Gerald Benney RCA, boxed.

Box 7.75in (19.5cm) wide

£70-90 **GC**

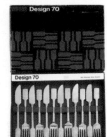

A set of six Viners 'Studio' grapefruit spoons, mint and boxed with original packaging.

These sets are worth considerably less without their boxes, packaging and in used condition.

5in (13cm) long

£50-60 **GC**

A set of six Spear & Jackson stainless steel 'Champagne' grapefruit spoons, boxed.

Each 6.25in (16cm) long

£25-35 **GC**

A pair of 1970s Sapphire Nova stainless steel grapefruit spoons, designed by Keith Tyson RCA, boxed with leaflet.

7.75in (19.5cm) wide

£35-40 **GC**

A 1970s Danish Stelton 'Cylinda Line' coffee pot, the base stamped "Lauffor Stainless Stelton Denmark".

This popular range was designed by Danish architect and furniture designer Arne Jacobsen in 1967. Despite its visual simplicity, it is challenging to manufacture. Legend has it that the first designs were drawn on a napkin.

8in (20cm) high

£90-100 **GC**

A 'Chichester' stainless steel gravy boat and matching dish with angled handle.

8.5in (21.5cm) long

£15-25 **GC**

A pair of stainless steel filled tubular curving candleholders, marked "Dansk".

6in (15cm) wide

£70-90 **GC**

FIND OUT MORE...

The Old Hall Club, www.oldhallclub.co.uk

A Catalogue for the Collector, by Michael Bennett, published by The Old Hall Club, available from the website above.

A used Victoria half-penny Jubilee series stamp.

The 'Jubilee' series replaced the 'lilac and greens' in 1887, to commemorate 50 years of Victoria's rule. The vibrant and colourful designs were a stark contrast to anything that had come before.

c1890   1in (2.5cm) high

£1-1.50   **SD**

A used Victoria three-penny Jubilee series stamp.

c1890   1in (2.5cm) high

£5-10   **SD**

A used George V Indian 10 rupee stamp, with a cancellation mark for 13th November 1924.

1.5in (3.5cm) high

£6-10   **SD**

A set of four unused George VI Gold Coast (present day Ghana) five shilling stamps.

Stamps with a higher value are generally rarer and so more desirable.

c1940   2.75in (7cm) wide

£30-40   **SD**

An unused set of four George VI Jamaican 2 1/2d stamps.

Sets of unused stamps are more valuable than the same number of loose stamps.

c1940   3.75in (8.5cm) high

£4-6   **SD**

An unused George VI 2 cent Malayan stamp.

This stamp was originally issued for the Straits Settlements and has been marked "BMA Malaya" (British Military Administration) following the liberation of the Malayan peninsula from the Japanese in 1945.

c1945   1in (2.5cm) high

30-50P   **SD**

An unused George VI half-crown Festival of Britain stamp.

c1951   1.75in (4.5cm) wide

£1-3   **SD**

An American 'Victory' issue stamp.

This example is clean, unhinged and perfectly centred, centring being important to stamp collectors. This stamp was produced to commemorate the victory of WWI in March 1919.

1919   1in (2.5cm) wide

£5-7   **RSB**

An American $3 Definitive stamp, showing the Space Shuttle Challenger STS-7 in orbit.

Look out for themed stamps. Like birds, space is a popular theme.

1995   1.5in (4cm) wide

£4-5   **RSB**

FIND OUT MORE

www.stanleygibbons.com - *comprehensive catalogues and other information and services from their website.*

Stamp Collecting for Dummies, *by Richard L. Sine, published by Hungry Minds Inc 2001.*

Gibbons Stamp Monthly, *a magazine published by Stanley Gibbons with news and features about philately.*

National Philatelic Society Library, *British Philatelic Centre, 107 Charterhouse Street, London, EC1M 6PT, tel: 020 7336 0882 for opening times.*

COLLECTORS' NOTES

■ For the last 50 or more years taxidermy has been seen by many as extremely unfashionable, slightly distasteful and probably cruel. However, the past few years have seen a resurgence of interest in vintage examples from collectors, interior decorators and people looking for unusual examples to add to eclectic interiors or collections.

■ Stuffed animals were popular decorative effects during the mid-to late Victorian, and Edwardian eras. They began to go out of fashion during the 1930s, and most commercial outlets closed by the 1970s. Most towns had at least one practitioner. Animals were usually mounted in naturalistic settings in glazed cases or contained under glass domes to protect them from dust and other damage.

■ Birds are one of the most commonly found animals, along with various head 'masks' mounted on shields or plaques. Fish have retained more consistent popularity, mainly due to interest from anglers, and prices can be high. Other popular animals are those that are genetic or biological anomalies, such as albinos or those with clear physical abnormalities. Exotic animals such as giraffes and tiger are also highly valued, mainly as they are rarer.

■ The type of animal, size, quality of mounting, condition and eye appeal of the whole piece are important factors to consider. The maker is also important with names such as Rowland Ward, Peter Spicer, James Gardner and John Cooper being among those who are sought-after. Some maker's labels survive, but the quality can often be discerned from the setting and the way the animal is preserved.

■ Always consider condition, as it is very hard to repair damaged or faded examples, although cases can be repaired more easily. It is important to note that it is only vintage pieces that are increasing in interest. We do not condone or wish to promote the creation of modern examples. The sale and movement of stuffed animals is closely controlled by the government and collectors should acquaint themselves with the relevant laws.

A stuffed and mounted green woodpecker, in naturalistic setting and three-sided glazed display case.

This example is more appealing than the example on the right, due to the finer condition and colouring, the better case with glazed sides and blue background, and a better arranged setting.

14in (35.5cm) high

£50-70   **MAI**

A stuffed and mounted green woodpecker, in naturalistic setting and simple glazed display case.

14in (35.5cm) high

£25-35   **MAI**

A stuffed and mounted jay sitting on a branch in a naturalistic setting, contained in a glazed wooden display case.

15in (38cm) high

£20-30   **MAI**

A stuffed and mounted French partridge in a naturalistic setting contained in a glazed wooden case, bearing a label for "G.White Salisbury".

15in (38cm) high

£20-30   **MAI**

A stuffed and mounted English grey partridge and snipe, in a glazed display case, bearing maker's label verso, reading "Wm Drew Ornithologist, – begs leave to inform the curious that he has on sale a number of rare and valuable British birds stuffed with or without cases – rare foreign and domestic birds bought dead or alive – birds stuffed after the most approved method and on reasonable terms".

15in (38cm) wide

£60-80   **MAI**

A stuffed and mounted kestrel with starling prey, in naturalistic setting and glazed display case.

13in (33cm) high

£60-80　　　　　　　　　**MAI**

A stuffed and mounted long-eared owl, in naturalistic setting and three-sided glazed display case, bears label verso inscribed "B White, 10 Norwood Terrace, Bath Road, Cheltenham" and dated "August 8 1908".

1908

£100-150　　　　　　　　**MAI**

A stuffed and mounted parakeet sitting on a branch in a naturalistic setting, contained in a three-sided glazed wooden display case

12.5in (31cm) high

£30-50　　　　　　　　　**MAI**

A stuffed and mounted canary, in naturalistic setting and glass fronted display case.

8in (20cm) high

£25-35　　　　　　　　　**MAI**

A pair of stuffed and mounted bramble finches in a naturalistic setting, one in flight, one grounded, under a glass dome.

It is worth considering that glass domes themselves are expensive to replace, so always aim to buy undamaged examples.

14in (35.5cm) high

£50-70　　　　　　　　　**MAI**

A collection of stuffed and mounted exotic birds, including a lance-tailed manakin, a broad bill, finches, a bee eater and a Baltimore oriole, mounted on a naturalistic branch setting under a glass dome.

This is a large and complex display with great visual impact. The type of bird also affects the value, with rarely seen examples identified by experienced ornithologists often fetching high prices.

25.5in (65cm) high

£220-280　　　　　　　　**MAI**

A stuffed and mounted sparrow hawk, in a naturalistic setting on a mossy stump, under a glass dome.

20.5in (52cm) high

£150-200　　　　　　　　**MAI**

A CLOSER LOOK AT A STUFFED FISH

Cased fish by renowned maker John Cooper & Sons of Radnor Street, London (founded c1830), are amongst the most sought-after on the market.

The use of a bow-fronted case with a gold linear trim and gilt lettering is typical of the company.

Changes to the design of cases allow rough dating. This is an example of an earlier design with a blue background and many reeds and ground details, mid-20thC examples are green and sparsely furnished.

Age is not usually a major indicator of value – eye appeal, condition, the complexity of the mounting and the size of the fish for its species are more important.

A stuffed and mounted Chubb in naturalistic setting and and three sided bow fronted glazed display case, inscribed "Chubb - taken by B J Woodhall, River Severn above Bewdley, Dec. 1927 Wgt 3lbs 7 ozs and label inscribed "Preserved by J Cooper & Sons...".

Malloch of Perth and Homer in London are two other popular makers to look for.

1927

£500-600   **MAI**

A stuffed and mounted brown trout in naturalistic setting and three-sided bow fronted glazed display case, bears label inscribed "River Severn Holt Fleet, 20th July 1949" and "Preserved and mounted by John Betteridge & Son...".

Betteridge & Son was founded in 1872 in Birmingham and was active until 1958, specialising in display work for museums.

1949

£250-300   **MAI**

A stuffed and mounted brown trout in naturalistic setting and three sided bow fronted glazed display case, inscribed "Caught at Holden Wood Reservoir with rod and line, Sept 3rd 1901" and bears label inscribed "Preserved by J Cooper & Sons, 28 Radnor Street, St Luke, London EC..."

1901

£350-450   **MAI**

A stuffed and mounted brown trout in naturalistic setting and glazed display case, bears label inscribed "E.C. Saunders, Naturalist and Taxidermist, Church Plain, Great Yarmouth.....".

£120-180   **MAI**

A stuffed and mounted pike in naturalistic setting and and three-sided bow fronted glazed display case, bears labels inscribed "Caught by M. Ross, River Trent, 26th October 1949 on a Devon Minnow, 18lbs 7 ozs", and "From Schumach & Son".

1949

£300-500   **MAI**

A pair of stuffed and mounted graylings in naturalistic setting and three-sided glazed display case, bears label inscribed "Two Grayling caught by T H W Price at the River Lug, 14 Mar. 1958....".

1958

£220-280   **MAI**

A stuffed and mounted eel in a naturalistic setting, contained in a three-sided bow fronted glazed display case bearing a label inscribed "Eel, Edgbaston Res. 22nd Aug 1949 6lbs 1oz" and "Specimen fish preserved and mounted John Betteridge & Sons ....".

1949

£280-320   **MAI**

A stuffed grey squirrel, in an inquisitive pose, and mounted on an oak plinth.

6in (15cm) high

£15-20   **MAI**

A stuffed and mounted grey squirrel playing a piano.

This whimsical style is popular with many collectors and was typical of the notable Potter Collection. However, this is a comparatively simple example, hence its lower value.

12in (30.5cm) wide

£60-80   **MAI**

A CLOSER LOOK AT TWO FOX HEADS

Peter Spicer & Sons of Royal Leamington Spa, operated from c1798-1960 and are considered one of the best taxidermists, being known for their engaging and realistic, high quality work.

Spicer's produced a great many fox head 'masks' and became famous for them, and these are in very fine, bright condition, with no damage to the ears or snout as is commonly seen.

The heads are heavy as they are mounted on specially cast plaster manikins.

After the recent ban on fox hunting in Britain, these have become even more sought-after as representing part of British countryside social history, particularly in lively styles and fine condition.

Two stuffed, mounted and posed fox heads, on wooden shield-shaped plaques, the reverses stamped "P. Spicer & Sons Taxidermists Leamington".

11in (28cm) high

£150-200   **MSA**

A red squirrel posed on its hind legs in a naturalistic setting, under a glass dome.

A license is required to import or export this piece as the red squirrel is an endangered species.

13in (33cm) high

£25-35   **MAI**

A Rowland Ward mounted long-horned goat head, on an ebonised shield and label "Astor 1922".

Rowland Ward (1835-1912) was said to be the best taxidermist in the world. His company was founded in London c1872 and ran until 1977. His father Henry worked under, and provided taxidermy for, John James Audubon, naturalist and creator of the famous 'The Birds of America'.

41.75in (106cm) high

£600-800   **SWO**

A stuffed and mounted mole, posed as emerging from a burrow, under a glass dome.

8in (20cm) high

£50-70   **MAI**

A small stuffed terrapin.

Small pieces like this have become popular again as quirky desk accessories. However, buyers should be aware that many unmounted pieces were originally components of larger assemblages.

6.75in (17cm) long

£20-25   **PC**

FIND OUT MORE...

A Record of Spicer's: 1798-1960, by Robert Chinnery, privately published, 2001.

A Guide to Restoring Old Cases of Taxidermy, by Christopher Frost, privately published, 1997.

COLLECTORS' NOTES

■ Technology is updated and changed on an almost daily basis and has become vital to the way we live our lives. This revolution began in the 1970s with less expensive electronic pocket calculators, digital watches, and computers that did more than play games.

■ Most collectors choose to focus on one area, with calculators, mobile phones and pocket TVs being among the most popular. Although early computers are gaining ground, their size makes storing a collection hard.

■ There are a number of factors to consider as regards value. Look for landmark models or those that were considered the first of their type, or forerunners of key movements. Models that captured the public eye are also important, particularly to nostalgics who hark back to items that were long desired and maybe once owned.

■ Design is a further important feature. Many, such as the early Sinclair calculators and the first Apple iMac, have gone on to become design classics. Manufacturer's names and models are also important as a 'look-alike' design by a less well-regarded name will generally be worth less, while popular ranges such as 'Game & Watch' will usually fetch higher sums.

■ Always aim to buy in the best condition possible, and preferably in working condition. Check for battery compartment covers, damage to screens, cracked cases and wear to finishes. Original boxes and instructions will add value as most were thrown away.

A Casio TV-21 black and white liquid crystal pocket television.

This example could have a backlight fitted, which resulted in a thicker lid. An earphone was needed for audio and as an antenna.

1985   4.75in (12cm) wide

£10-20   **PTC**

A Casio TV-21 black and white liquid crystal pocket television, with red case and original box.

Red is a scarcer colour than black and the value is further bolstered by the box.

1985   4.75in (12cm) wide

£20-30   **PTC**

A Casio TV-300 colour liquid crystal pocket television.

This was one of the first and smallest colour TVs ever made.

c1988   4.5in (11.5cm) wide

£20-30   **PTC**

A Citizen 06TA LCD pocket television.

This was the first pocket television with an LCD screen, and is commonly found today. A backlight could be purchased for night-time viewing and low power consumption meant battery life was better than other models.

1986   4.5in (11.5cm) wide

£10-15   **PTC**

A Realistic 'Pocket Vision 3' black and white liquid crystal portable pocket television.

£12-18   **PTC**

A Sony FD-210 'Watchman' black and white pocket television.

This was the first Watchman model and used a pre-LCD, CTR screen.

1982   6in (15cm) high

£30-50   **PTC**

A German Adler 80C calculator.

1975   *3in (7.5cm) high*

£8-12   **PTC**

A Casio JL-810 LCD electronic calculator.

c1982

£5-8   **PTC**

A Casio fx-31 scientific calculator.

1978   *5.75in (14.5cm) high*

£7-10   **PTC**

A Commodore Business Machines model 786D electronic calculator.

1975   *5.25in (13.5cm) high*

£8-15   **PTC**

A Commodore Business Machines model 899A LED electronic calculator.

c1975   *5.75in (14.5cm) high*

£12-15   **PTC**

A Japanese Decimo 'VatMan Extra M' electronic calculator.

This calculator comes from an enormous range of models, some of which included a key which dealt with VAT with one key press.

1975   *5.25in (13cm) high*

£8-12   **PTC**

A Prinztronic C44 mains-powered calculator.

Prinztronic was the trade name used by UK electronics retailer Dixons.

c1972   *9.5in (24cm) high*

£8-10   **PTC**

A Sharp EL-120 electronic calculator.

Although can it calculate up to nine digits at a time, only three digits were shown on the tiny screen in a power-saving measure.

6.75in (17cm) wide

£15-30   **PTC**

An American Texas Instruments TI-30 LCD electronic calculator.

An earlier model had a red LED screen.

6in (15cm) high

£5-10   **PTC**

A CLOSER LOOK AT A COMPUTER GAME

A Mattel Electronics Model 9879 'Auto Race' hand-held game.

This was the earliest, entirely electronic, hand-held game sold to the public and had no moving parts.

1976   3in (7.5cm) wide

£40-60   HLJ

The company was founded by Masaya Nakamura in 1955 and became known as Namco in 1971. It was sold to Bandai in 1993.

PacLand had a side-scrolling landscape environment, rather than the typical flat maze structure of Pac-Man, and is considered the first of its kind as it arrived before Super Mario Bros.

Namco released its first video game 'Gee Bee' in 1978 and released its best-selling game 'PacMan' two years later. Both, like PacLand, were designed by Toru Iwatani.

This example is in full working condition and retains its battery cover and box.

A Namco Systema 'PacLand' hand-held arcade-style computer game, with original box.

PacLand was also released for other computer formats including Commodore and Atari.

1984

£10-15   PTC

A Grandstand Astro Wars tabletop game.

This 'shoot'em up' game was extremely popular at the time and can be found comparatively easily in varying conditions.

1981   5.75in (14.5cm) wide

£20-35   PTC

A TomyTronic Model 7621 'Shark Attack' 3D hand-held game.

Note the shape of the case, which mimics the head of a shark, even to the point of having eyes on the side. This was released to capitalise on the popular film 'Jaws' released in 1975.

1983

£10-25   PTC

A Nintendo Model PB-59 'Pinball' multi-screen LCD Game & Watch hand-held computer game.

Nintendo's numerous 'Game & Watch' consoles have become increasingly collectable over the past few years, particularly if they retain their boxes. A Panorama Donkey Kong can fetch over £300.

1983   4.25in (11cm) wide

£20-40   PTC

A Nintendo Model BJ-60 'Black Jack' multi-screen LCD Game & Watch hand-held computer game.

1985   4.25in (11cm) wide

£15-30   PTC

A Sega Game Gear hand-held console.

Sega's Game Gear was effectively a portable version of the earlier Master System and was a competitor to the smaller Game Boy. However, its poor battery life and larger size meant it was not as successful. Check that the sound works on vintage models.

1992

£20-40   PTC

An Amstrad 'PenPad' PDA 600, with writing stylus, box and manuals.

Along with the more expensive, contemporaneous Apple Newton, the PenPad was one of the first PDAs to offer handwriting recognition.

1993   6.25in (16cm) high

£5-10   **PTC**

A CLOSER LOOK AT A RABBIT TELEPHONE

The Rabbit marks an important crossing point between the home phone and the development of the mobile phone.

The service allowed subscribers to take their home phone handset out and about with them and use it to make calls and pick up messages near a Rabbit basestation, very much like wireless internet HotSpots today.

The service was launched in 1992 and gained 10,000 subscribers, however cheaper mobile phones call costs and the ability of mobiles to also receive calls wherever the owner was, led to its closure in December 1993.

Most Rabbit handsets and accessories were discarded in favour of mobile phones, particularly when the system was switched off, making examples rare today.

A Rabbit CT2 telephone handset and base station.

Rabbit was founded in 1989 by Hutchison Whampoa, the leading telecommunications and industrial conglomerate behind the Orange network, and now '3'. The company is said to have lost around £170 million in the failed venture.

1992-93

£5-10   **PTC**

A Psion Series 3a personal organiser, with 2MB of RAM memory.

The clamshell Series 3 followed the popular CM and LZ models, which had sliding covers. It was based on the very rare MC series of laptops, but proved more successful. Although not fetching large sums now, mint and boxed examples are probably worth hanging on to.

1991-93   6.5in (16.5cm) wide

£15-25   **PTC**

A Cybiko combined hand-held electronic organiser, email composer/reader, games machine, and walkie-talkie.

This is the original model of the Cybiko, released in 2000. It was aimed at teenagers and had over 400 games and could act as a walkie talkie within 300 metres of another unit. After releasing the Cybiko Xtreme a few years later, the company discontinued hardware to focus on games. Is this a collectable of the future?

c2001   5.75in (14.cm) high

£10-15   **PTC**

A Voice Organiser pocket recording device and manual, by Voice Powered Technology.

c1993

£10-20   **PTC**

A Grundig Stenorette 2070 portable dictation machine.

1989   6in (15cm) high

£8-12   **PTC**

An Acorn A3010 professional computer and monitor.

There is a rare German version of this computer, which lacks the green coloured keys and has a German language keyboard.

c1992   18.5in (47cm) wide

£15-20   **PC**

FIND OUT MORE...

Collectable Technology, by Pepe Tozzo, published by Carlton Books, 2005.

COLLECTORS' NOTES

■ Teddy bears derived from US President Theodore Roosevelt's refusal to shoot a bear on a hunting trip in 1902. Entrepreneur Morris Michtom produced a toy bear to commemorate the event to sell in his Brooklyn store and started a craze that is still with us today. Although the US produced the first bears, it was Germany that produced the most and, arguably, the best.

■ Germany's Steiff (founded 1886) is considered the finest maker, and bears made from 1902 to the 1930s are highly desirable, often fetching large sums. Bing, Hermann and Schuco (1921-1970s) are other notable German names. In the UK, Farnell (1908-1960s), Chad Valley (1915-1978), Merrythought (1920-today) and Chiltern (1915-1970s) are amongst the most collectable names. Date ranges given refer only to bear production.

■ Early American bears are scarce and can be hard to identify. For all bears, learn how to recognise forms as this often gives the best indication to the maker and the period, particularly if a bear is not marked.

For those looking to seek out bargains in a crowded market, learn how to recognise bears by smaller makers that others may not know.

■ Earlier, pre-WWII bears tend to have humped backs, long arms with upturned paws and pronounced snouts. Filling tends to be harder than modern bears and mohair is commonly used. Bears from the 1950s onwards tend to be plumper, with rounder faces and bodies and shorter limbs. As sources for desirable early bears dry up and they become more expensive, later bears from the 1950s onwards, and those by less famous makers, are becoming more desirable.

■ As well as the maker, date and form, the size, colour and condition are important. Large bears or those in unusual colours will usually fetch more, as will those in better condition with intact fur. Beware of official replica bears, which look like older bears, and also the increasing number of fakes. If in doubt, smell a bear, as the smell of age cannot yet be replicated. Another factor is eye appeal – the cute look of a bear can lead collectors to pay a higher price.

A Steiff small brown mohair teddy bear, lacks button in his ear.

c1907   10in (25.5cm) high

£450-650   **TCT**

A Steiff blonde mohair teddy bear, with brown woven nose and boot button eyes.

This bear comes with his original gift certificate, dated 1908, which adds to the desirability and value.

c1908   14in (35.5cm) high

£1,800-2,200   **HGS**

A Steiff cinnamon mohair teddy bear, with blank metal button in his ear.

The blank ear button was used on early bears from c1905 only. This bear is very light in weight, another indication of an early bear, in addition to the form.

c1905   16in (40.5cm) high

£2,000-2,500   **TCT**

A Steiff blonde mohair teddy bear, lacks button in his ear.

c1907-10 9.75in (25cm) high

£1,000-1,500   **HGS**

A Steiff blonde mohair teddy bear, with typical early form, felt pads, woven nose and black boot button eyes.

c1910   17in (43cm) high

£2,000-3,000   **LHT**

A rare Steiff white mohair teddy bear, with original felt pads, boot button eyes and light brown woven nose.

This fine teddy is rare on two counts – he has a very early blank button and he is white, which is an uncommon colour. He is also in excellent conditon with his original light brown stitched nose.

c1905   12.5in (32cm) high

£1,800-2,200   **HGS**

A CLOSER LOOK AT A STEIFF BEAR

'Centre seam' teddies are so-called due to the sewn seam running down the centre of their heads, which gives them appealing faces.

He displays many characteristics of desirable early bears such as long, curved limbs, a humped back, a pronounced muzzle, and large out-turned paws with original felt pads.

This seam only appeared on every seventh bear and allowed for economical use of fabric – centre seams are thus six times rarer than other bears of the period.

As well as being comparatively large, this teddy is in excellent condition with long plush – on more worn bears, the seam is more visible.

A Steiff brown mohair 'centre seam' teddy bear, with original felt pads, black boot button eyes and woven nose.

c1907   20in (51cm) high

£4,500-6,500   **TCT**

A Steiff blonde mohair teddy bear, with original pads, black boot button eyes and woven nose, in overall extremely clean condition.

c1908   13in (33cm) high

£800-1,200   **HGS**

A Steiff blonde mohair teddy bear, with original pads, glass eyes and woven nose, dressed in a sailor's uniform.

Dressing bears in uniform was popular during the 1920s, the period this suit dates from. This colour and style of button was used from c1920 to the 1950s.

c1919   12in (30.5cm) high

£750-950   **TCT**

A Steiff blonde mohair teddy bear, with original clothing, felt pads, woven nose and boot button eyes, lacks button in ear.

This bear is not in as fine condition as others, and some of his stuffing has degraded, but he is comparatively early.

c1910   13in (33cm) high

£700-1,000   **TCT**

A 1920s Steiff blonde mohair teddy bear, with early face, original pads, woven nose and black boot button eyes.

17in (43cm) high

£1,200-£1,800   **LHT**

A 1950s Steiff blonde mohair teddy bear, with original pads, woven nose and black boot button eyes.

Note the rounder, plumper and 'stumpier' limbed form of later bears, compared to the earlier examples shown here.

20in (51cm) high

£300-500   **LHT**

A 1950s Steiff brown 'Teddy Baby', with red collar and bell.

Teddy Babies typically have flat feet so they can stand, and open mouths.

9in (23cm) high

£150-250   HGS

A 1950s Steiff white mohair miniature 'Teddy Baby', with velour face and feet.

The 'Teddy Baby' was introduced in 1930 and was modelled on a bear cub. White is the most desirable colour.

3.5in (9cm) high

£350-450   TCT

A 1950s Steiff 'TeddyLi' with poseable plastic arms, legs and feet, and original clothes and tag.

He is hard to find complete and in excellent condition.

4.75in (12cm) high

£300-400   TCT

A 1950s Steiff small 'Zotty' bear, with original tag and ribbon.

The name 'Zotty' derives from the German word 'zottig' for 'shaggy', which is descriptive of the mohair.

6in (15cm) high

£70-100   HGS

A Steiff white mohair and velour 'Zooby' teddy bear.

'Zooby' is based on a Russian circus bear, and like Zotties, it typically has an open mouth.

1954-60 10.5in (26.5cm) high

£200-250   LHT

A 1950s-60s Steiff small blonde mohair teddy bear, with original woven nose and black eyes.

6in (15cm) high

£30-50   TCT

A Steiff small white mohair 'Strong Museum' replica bear, with original ear tag and button.

These bears were made for the famous Margaret Woodbury Strong Museum of Juvenalia and Toys in Rochester, New York.

c1983   15in (38cm) high

£150-200   TCT

A Steiff large brown mohair 'Margaret Woodbury Strong Museum' teddy bear, with original tags.

The secondary market for replica bears is not yet strong, so keep them in mint condition with all paperwork and boxes.

c1983   23.25in (59cm) high

£250-350   TCT

A 1920s Farnell white mohair teddy bear, with original pads, brown woven nose and glass eyes.

White is a rare colour. Early Farnell bears typically have long plump arms, long snouts, woven claws and feet pads inset with cardboard.

19in (48.5cm) high

£1,500-2,000 **LHT**

A CLOSER LOOK AT A FARNELL BEAR

Founded in 1908, Farnell is known as the 'English Steiff' for its fine quality, highly desirable and valuable teddies.

Only limited numbers were made, making this example rare. Black was neither a standard or a popular colour for teddies.

Black bears were made as mourning bears to commemorate the tragedy of the Titanic – as such they appeal to many collectors today.

Steiff also made black Titanic mourning bears. One, from only 500 made, sold for over £80,000 in 2000.

A very rare Farnell black mohair mourning bear, with original eyes, nose stitching and pads.

1912-14

14in (35.5cm) high

£2,000-3,000 **LHT**

A Farnell blonde mohair 'Alpha' bear with original paw pads, black boot button eyes and stitched nose, slightly worn.

This is an unusual size. The Alpha bears are typical of Farnell and it is their best known range. Farnell's factory was known as the Alpha Works and the Alpha trademark itself was registered in 1925. The character of Winnie the Pooh was based on the Alpha bear bought for the real-life Christopher Robin in 1921.

9in (23cm) high

£600-800 **LHT**

A Farnell blonde mohair 'Alpha' teddy bear, with original paw pads, stitched nose and glass eyes.

c1914 14in (35.5cm) high

£800-1,200 **LHT**

A 1920s Farnell golden mohair teddy bear, with black boot button eyes, re-stitched black nose and mouth and replaced felt foot pads, worn.

18.5in (47cm) high

£150-200 **SAS**

A Farnell blue mohair 'Mascot' range miniature bear, in a knitted wool dress.

c1914 5in (12.5cm) high

£200-300 **LHT**

A Farnell red mohair 'Mascot' range miniature bear, in a knitted wool dress.

These patriotically red, white or blue coloured bears were made to be sold and given to soldiers going to fight in WWI. Colours such as this are more valuable than blonde or golden mohair.

c1914 5in (12.5cm) high

£200-300 **LHT**

A 1920s Farnell blonde mohair teddy bear hand puppet, with original glass eyes and stitched nose.

9in (23cm) high

£200-300 **LHT**

A 1930s/40s Chiltern golden mohair 'Hugmee' teddy bear, with original foot pads, woven nose, glass eyes and original tag.

Original tags are rarely found, without one, he would be worth £150-250.

13in (33cm) high

£400-500   LHT

A 1930s/40s Chiltern golden mohair teddy bear, with original foot pads, woven nose, glass eyes.

Note the style of the nose with two extended stitches on top – this is a typical feature of 1930s Chiltern bears.

20in (51cm) high

£280-320   LHT

A CLOSER LOOK AT A CHILTERN BEAR

The 'Master Teddy' is Chiltern's earliest bear, and was first produced in 1915.

He retains his rare collar and bow tie and original, early 'googly' eyes and red felt tongue.

He is typically dressed and only the visible mohair parts are made from mohair, the rest is made from cloth.

All examples of the 'Master' bear are rare, particularly very early examples like this.

A Chiltern blonde mohair 'Master Teddy' with original clothing, stitched nose and tongue, in good condition.

1915   12.5in (32cm) high

£800-1,200   LHT

A 1940s Chiltern golden mohair 'Hugmee' teddy bear, with orange and black glass eyes, original brown painted cloth pads and label on right foot, worn.

14.5in (37cm) high

£100-150   SAS

A Chiltern powder blue mohair teddy bear, with feltpads, woven nose and replaced glass eyes.

Powder blue is extremely rare.

c1930   14.5in (37cm) high

£280-320   LHT

A 1950s Chiltern golden mohair 'Hugmee' teddy bear, with internal musical bellows and original tag.

Without the tag and in less than immaculate condition, his value would fall to less than £400.

16in (40.5cm) high

£600-800   LHT

A 1950s Chiltern blonde mohair 'Ting-a-Ling' teddy bear, with original glass eyes, black stitched nose, mouth and claws, rexine paw pads pads and Internal bell In body, worn.

11.75in (30cm) high

£100-150   SAS

A 1950s Chiltern golden mohair 'Ting A Ling Druin' teddy bear, in original condition with card inset feet allowing him to stand.

11in (28cm) high

£220-280   LHT

An early Chad Valley blonde mohair teddy bear.

Chad Valley produced its first bears in 1915 and continued to produce them until the 1970s when they suffered a decline in sales. The company was sold to Palitoy in 1978.

c1919   10in (25.5cm) high

£400-600   LHT

A Chad Valley golden mohair teddy bear, in original condition with cork-filled limbs and celluloid covered button.

The cork-filled limbs, general form and style of button denote an early date.

1918   13in (33cm) high

£500-700   LHT

A late 1940s Chad Valley art silk musical teddy bear, with internal wind-up Thorens musical mechanism.

Swiss company Thorens are well-known for their excellent musical boxes.

     14in (35.5cm) high

£400-500   LHT

A Chad Valley golden mohair 'Aerolite' teddy bear, with glass eye, black stitched nose, mouth and claws and Aerolite metal rimmed button in ear, worn with losses, some repair.

c1925   20.5in (52cm) high

£100-150   SAS

A 1930s Chad Valley golden mohair 'Magna' teddy bear, with glass eyes, typical black stitched horizontal nose, mouth and claws and cloth label on left foot, general wear.

     14.5in (37cm) high

£100-150   SAS

A 1950s Chad Valley golden mohair teddy bear, with glass eyes, black stitched muzzle and claws and brown velvet pads.

     14.25in (36cm) high

£80-120   SAS

A late 1950s Chad Valley dark brown wool-mix teddy bear, with felt pads, stitched nose, glass eyes and post-1953 label to right foot.

     16in (40.5cm) high

£100-150   LHT

A late 1960s Chad Valley Chiltern golden mohair teddy bear, with card tag, lacks foot label.

Chiltern was taken over by Chad Valley in 1967 and for a few years labels bore both names.

     11in (28cm) high

£120-180   LHT

A CLOSER LOOK AT A SCHUCO MINIATURE

German company Schreyer & Co (Schuco) is well-known for its 'gadget' bears and soft toys produced between 1920 and 1970.

The bear's head pulls off to reveal a perfume bottle. Other examples contain concealed compacts or lipsticks.

The clip shows that he was also meant to be worn.

The peachy orange is a rarer colour than golden or blonde, and adds value and desirability.

A 1930s Schuco peach-coloured mohair perfume bottle bear, with pin back.

3.5in (9cm) high

£600-800   **LHT**

A 1950s Schuco blonde mohair 'Tricky' 'YesNo' teddy bear, with plastic tag.

The soft filled body and limbs indicate this rare example was made for a baby or a very small child. The Schuco Tricky was introduced in 1953.

3.5in (9cm) high

£220-280   **HGS**

A 1950s Schuco blonde mohair 'Tricky' musical 'YesNo' teddy bear, with plastic tag.

Introduced in 1921, the 'YesNo' movement made teddy nod or shake his head, depending on how the tail was moved.

21in (53.5cm) high

£700-900   **LHT**

A Schuco blonde mohair 'YesNo' teddy bear, with brown and black glass eyes, black stitched nose and mouth, some wear.

5in (12.5cm) high

£70-100   **SAS**

A 1950s Schuco gold plush miniature bear, in excellent condition.

3.5in (9cm) high

£70-100   **HGS**

A 1950s Schuco brown mohair 'Berlin' miniature teddy bear, with crown, sash and original pin.

It is hard to find these bears, first produced in the 1950s and based on the city's logo, with the crown and sash intact.

2.5in (6.5cm) high

£60-90   **SAS**

An early Schuco blonde mohair clockwork tumbling miniature bear, with key.

Schuco are also very well-known for their tinplate toys with wind-up mechanisms. These were also employed in their famous tumbling bears.

4.75in (12cm) high

£250-350   **SF**

A Steiff black and white mohair panda, with open mouth and card inset feet allowing him to stand, with tag reading "made in the US Zone Germany".

Pandas became popular alternatives to teddy bears after the first real-life panda was introduced into Chicago Zoo in 1937 and into London Zoo in 1938.

1947-53   *11in (28cm) high*

£350-400   **LHT**

A 1950s Steiff black and white mohair panda, with open mouth and card inset feet allowing him to stand.

8.5in (21.5cm) high

£200-250   **HGS**

A 1940s British black and white wool plush panda nightdress or pyjama case, with clear and black glass eyes and zip-up back.

17.25in (44cm) high

£60-80   **SAS**

A 1940s British black and white mohair panda, possibly by Tara Toys, with clear and black glass eyes and rexine pads, some general wear.

22in (56cm) high

£80-120   **SAS**

A Farnell 'Mascot' range panda, in excellent, original condition.

c1939-40   *4.5in (11.5cm) high*

£100-150   **LHT**

A Steiff black and white mohair panda, on all fours, with original tag and bell.

5.5in (14cm) long

£80-120   **SOTT**

A Steiff white mohair polar bear, with original paw pads, stitched nose and mouth and collar.

17.5in (44.5cm) high

£1,000-1,500   **LHT**

A Chad Valley white mohair polar bear, in excellent original condition.

Polar bears became popular after the celebrated birth of Brumas to Ivy. Brumas was the first polar bear born in captivity.

c1950   *15in (38cm) high*

£600-800   **LHT**

A 1950s Steiff small white mohair polar bear, on all fours, with original paw pads, stitched nose and mouth and boot button eyes, with tag and bell.

6.25in (16cm) long

£70-100   **HGS**

A CLOSER LOOK AT A HECLA BEAR

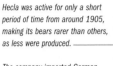

Hecla was active for only a short period of time from around 1905, making its bears rarer than others, as less were produced.

The company imported German materials and used immigrant German toy makers to make its high quality bears - as such they can look very much like Steiff or other German bears.

Typical features that distinguish Hecla from Steiff include wide-set ears and a rounder shaped head, set back into the body.

The closely set eyes and light red/brown nose and claw stitching are also other typical Hecla features.

An American Hecla blonde mohair teddy bear, with original glass eyes, stitched nose and mouth and paw pads.

c1907-10   12in (30.5cm) high

£800-1,200   **TCT**

An American Hecla blonde mohair teddy bear, with original pads, eyes and stitched nose and mouth.

c1907   15in (38cm) high

£800-1,200   **TCT**

An early American blonde mohair teddy bear, by an unknown maker, with original paw pads, glass eyes and stitched nose.

c1908   11.5in (29cm) high

£300-350   **TCT**

A 1940s Knickerbocker cinnamon bear, with original glass eyes, stitched nose and velveteen paw pads.

Knickerbocker was founded in 1869 and produced bears from c1920 to the 1980s. The one-piece rounded face with a thin, short snout indicates an early bear, and the round, low set ears are a hallmark of Knickerbocker designs.

c1935   16.25in (41cm) high

£150-200   **SOTT**

An American Woolnough golden mohair 'Winne The Pooh' teddy bear, in original condition, with foot stamp.

c1930   14in (35.5cm) high

£2,000-2,500   **TCT**

An early American blonde mohair teddy bear, with original paw pads, black stitched nose and mouth, boot button eyes.

When teddy bears became fashionable after 1902, a great number of American factories sprang up to produce them, many in New York. The majority of these bears bore no markings or tags and companies came and went. Typical American features include short, pointed feet and round ears set low on the head.

c1908   10in (25.5cm) high

£400-500   **HGS**

A 1920s American light golden mohair teddy bear, with triangular-shaped head, rounded low set ears, orange and black glass eyes, black stitched nose, mouth and claws, worn and pads replaced.

19in (48cm) high

£150-200   **SAS**

A 1950s-60s German Anker Drolly plush teddy bear, with velveteen pads and original tag.

7.25in (18.5cm) high

£80-120   **LHT**

A 1960s British Blue Ribbon Playthings gold mohair teddy bear, with tag, in excellent condition.

Without the tag he would be worth £60-80.

14in (35.5cm) high

£150-200   **LHT**

A 1950s German Diem grey mohair teddy bear, with internal growler.

This teddy is very similar to Steiff's Zotty bear and is unusual in grey.

16.5in (42cm) high

£100-150   **LHT**

A 1950s German Diem gold mohair teddy bear, in excellent condition.

15.5in (39.5cm) high

£80-120   **LHT**

A very rare German Rudolf Haas brown-tipped beige mohair 'Nickle Nackle' teddy bear, in excellent condition.

'Nickle Nackle' bears turn their heads from left to right when the right arm is moved and nod when the left arm is moved. This mechanism was patented by Rudolf Haas in 1928.

c1930   *21in (53.5cm) high*

£800-1,200   **LHT**

A German Jopi blonde mohair teddy bear, the body with internal musical bellows.

Jopi was registered as a trademark in 1922 and the name is formed from the first two letters of the founder's name, Josef Pitrmann.

c1922   *13.5in (34cm) high*

£400-600   **HGS**

A Merrythought golden mohair 'Cheeky' bear, with orange plastic eyes, orange velvet muzzle, brown felt and cotton pads, black stitched nose, mouth and claws and bell inside.

12.5in (32cm) high

£80-120   **SAS**

A 1930s-40s Merrythought golden mohair teddy bear, with original paw pads, label, ear button, black boot button eyes and stitched nose and mouth.

These bears are often mistaken for Chiltern Hugmee's due to their shape and nose stitching.

23in (58.5cm) high

£300-400   **LHT**

A 1920s British Omega blonde mohair teddy bear, with original paw pads, the feet with inset card, nose stitching and eyes.

Note the similarity to Farnell's Alpha bears.

c1920   14.5in (367cm) high

£700-900   **LHT**

A 1950s German Petz cinnamon mohair teddy bear, with original glass eyes, black stitched nose, mouth and claws, felt pads and white plastic button on chest.

21.25in (54cm) high

£120-180   **SAS**

A 1940s British Pixie Toys blonde mohair small teddy bear, in original condition with ear tag.

Pixie Toys was founded in 1930 by the wives of two glassmakers in Stourbridge. Many of its bears, produced until its closure in 1962, are similar to Merrythought bears due to the employment of an ex-Merrythought designer.

8.5in (21.5cm) high

£150-200   **LHT**

A 1920s British Omega golden mohair teddy bear, in original condition.

This is a very rare, large size for Omega. Note the early form, which takes in so many typical features.

24in (61cm) high

£1,000-1,500   **LHT**

A German Strünz blonde mohair tumbling teddy bear, with metal framed arms, in original condition.

Strünz made bears from 1904 and was in direct competition to Steiff. Strünz even used a similar ear button until 1908. In excellent, working condition this bear could be worth between £1,200-1,800.

c1912   10in (25.5cm) high

£400-500   **LHT**

A late 1950s Irish Tara Toys brown mohair teddy bear, in original but worn condition.

Tara Toys was founded by the Irish government under the name Erris Toys in 1938. It became Tara Toys in 1953 and Soltoys in 1969, before closing in 1979.

36in (91.5cm) high

£180-220   **LHT**

A 1940s-50s Belgian Unica pink art silk teddy bear, in original condition.

10in (25.5cm) high

£200-300   **LHT**

A 1930s/40s German Weiersmüller blonde mohair teddy bear, with card inset foot pads allowing him to stand.

7.75in (19.75cm) high

£200-300   **LHT**

A CLOSER LOOK AT A TEDDY BEAR

Tumbling bears, with their metal-framed arms and clockwork mechanism that lifts the body over the arms, are unusual and scarcer than standard teddies.

It is hard to identify the country of origin, but it is likely to be Germany as German companies such as Schuco and Steiff produced acrobatic tumbling bears.

A blonde mohair clockwork tumbling teddy bear, with accompanying photograph of a small girl holding the bear.

The cute face makes this bear all the more appealing.

c1914-20

£200-300

The photograph of the original owner holding this bear adds not only a charming provenance but also a great amount to the value and desirability.

She obviously looked after him very well as he is still in excellent condition, with his original fur, eyes and intact stitching.

8in (20cm) high

LHT

A 1920s British golden mohair teddy bear, with original orange and black glass eyes, clipped muzzle, black stitched nose and mouth, and replaced pads, worn.

24in (61cm) high

£40-60   **SAS**

A 1920s British golden mohair teddy bear, with original orange and black glass eyes, black stitched nose, mouth and claws, felt pads and hump, general wear and thinning.

13.5in (34cm) high

£100-150   **SAS**

A 1960s large golden brown mohair teddy bear, with original plastic eyes, paw pads, black stitched nose, mouth and claws, with general wear.

40in (101.5cm) high

£120-180   **SAS**

A 1960s British small gold plush teddy bear, with black and orange glass eyes, and stitched nose and mouth.

6in (15cm) high

£12-18   **SAS**

A 1950s Irish golden mohair teddy bear, with original glass eyes, black stitched nose and mouth opening mechanism (altered and inoperative), some wear.

20.5in (52cm) high

£70-100   **SAS**

A 1950s-60s Polish golden mohair teddy bear.

This bear is more valuable than most of its type as it looks a little like Sooty and is in great condition.

9in (23cm) high

£40-60   **LHT**

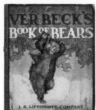

'Mother Goose's Teddy Bears', by Frederick L. Cavally Jr, in poor condition with tears, fading and water damage.	'Verbeck's Book of Bears', by Hanna Rion, Hayden Carruth, Frank VerBeck and 'The Bear Himself', published by J.Lippincott Company of Philadelphia.	'The Travelling Bears at Play', by Seymour Eaton, illustrated by Francis P. Wightman and William K. Sweeny, published by Edward Stern & Co Inc, Philadelphia. *This is one from a series of books.*	'Teddy-B & Teddy-G The Bear Detectives', by Seymour Eaton, illustrations by Francis P. Wightman and William K. Sweeny, published by Edward Stern & Co Inc, Philadelphia 1909.
1907 11.25in (28.5cm) high	*1906 10.5in (26.5cm) high*	*1907 11.25in (28.5cm) high*	*11.25in (28.5cm) high*
£60-80 HGS	**£70-100** HGS	**£50-70** HGS	**£50-70** HGS

An American CUB shoe polish teddy bear advertising badge, with advertising motto to reverse.

From c1903 to the 1920s, popular and eyecatching teddy bears were used to advertise many different products.

1.5in (4cm) diam

£20-30   HGS

An American 'The Big Store' teddy bear badge.

Ephemera, such as books and advertising, with a teddy bear image is also sought-after by dedicated teddy bear collectors, particularly if charming or connected to the industry or a well-known brand. This badge promoted the fact that the popular teddy bears were sold in this store.

c1910   *1in (3cm) diam*

£150-200   LDE

An American Baby Bear Bread 'Nip Tuck & Tige' advertising button, by Whitehead Hoag for Baby Bear Products Inc.

1933   1in (2.5cm) diam

£20-30   HGS

A pair of American Majestic Refrigerator die-cut polar bear advertising standees, printed by Amagamated Lithographers.

14.5in (37cm) wide

£200-250   SOTT

An American badge for the "Seventh Annual Reunion Baer Family" in "Kutztown Park Aug. 4th 06".

1906   2.25in (5.5cm) diam

£20-30   HGS

FIND OUT MORE...

Bears, by Sue Pearson, published by De Agostini, 1995.

Teddy Bear Encyclopedia, by Pauline Cockrill, published by DK, 2001.

COLLECTORS' NOTES

■ The commercial production of tools started c1700. Before this time workers made their own tools as and when they were needed. However, during the Industrial Revolution demand for ready-made tools grew rapidly and remained high until the 1930s-40s.

■ Planes are one of the most popular types of tools to collect, with famous makes such at Stanley and Norris being particularly collectable. These makers numbered each of their models, and collectors aim to amass as many of the models made by a manufacturer as possible.

■ The Stanley market is dominated by the US and the benchmark currency is in dollars, so currency fluctuations can affect values. The Norris market, dominated by the UK, can be similarly affected.

■ Recent years have seen a surge of interest in collecting saws, so these can probably be expected to fetch higher sums than they have in the past.

■ Specialist tools used for specific or rarely practiced tasks are usually valuable, for example tools used by musical instrument makers or coach-makers. This is due to their comparative rarity and usually fine craftsmanship.

■ The condition of the tool will affect its value. An unused tool in its original packaging is generally more desirable than a well-worn or damaged tool.

A very scarce Millers gunmetal smoothing plane, steel-soled, ebony infill, in fine condition.

£450-550 **MUR**

A Millers no. 41 plane, with fillister bed, in very good condition.

£700-900 **MUR**

An iron smoothing plane, by The Birmingham Tool Co., with original blade, in very good condition.

This is the smallest plane produced by this company. Smaller-sized tools are generally more desirable and valuable.

6in (15cm) long

£1,200-1,800 **MUR**

An unusual Stanley rebate plane, marked "Stanley 190" with Stanley rule and level blade, a few tiny blowholes to the casting, possibly a prototype.

£300-500 **MUR**

A very rare Spiers adjustable 'Plane o' Ayr' smoothing plane, in very good condition.

£650-750 **MUR**

A Scottish iron smoothing plane, cove front, unusual elm infill, and moulded front bun, in fine condition.

£450-550 **MUR**

A CLOSER LOOK AT A PLANE

This is a pre-war Norris plane, these are of better quality and are generally of more value than those made post war.

The rosewood infill, a sign of a high quality plane, is in very good condition.

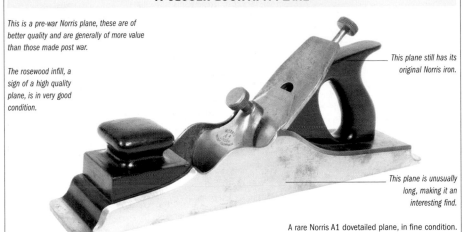

This plane still has its original Norris iron.

This plane is unusually long, making it an interesting find.

A rare Norris A1 dovetailed plane, in fine condition.
16.5in (42cm) long

£1,500-2,000   **MUR**

A unusual dovetailed panel plane, inlaid with boxwood, in very good condition.

£350-450   **MUR**

A Frost, Norwich iron panel plane, in good condition.

Metal planes marked "Frost" are very rare.

13.25in (33.5cm) high

£350-450   **MUR**

A Spiers dovetailed panel plane, with rosewood infill and rare embossed lever cap, in very good condition.

£300-500   **MUR**

A reproduction Stanley no. 1 smoothing plane, in fine condition.

In the early 1960s and '70s there were about six different varieties of reproduction Stanley no. 1's produced. Ironically, they are rarer than the originals and collectable in their own right.

£220-280   **MUR**

A scarce Preston 1340 smoothing plane, with rosewood handles, in very good condition.

£220-280   **MUR**

An unusual Scottish transitional cast iron smoothing plane, in very good condition.

£180-220   **MUR**

A Chaplin's patent fore plane.

£80-120   **MUR**

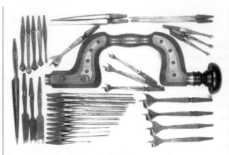

A very rare Ultimatum brace, by William Marples, with boxwood infill, in fine condition.

This model of brace was normally filled with ebony. Models infilled with boxwood are rarer and therefore more collectable.

£2,000-3,000　　　　　　　　　　　　**MUR**

A rare 1880s Marples beech plated brace, complete with set of bits and original finish, in fine condition.

It is most unusual to find a working tool of this age unused and complete with all of its original bits.

£350-400　　　　　　　　　　　　**MUR**

A rare early long sweep horn 'Ultimatum' brace, by William Marples, with early chuck, estucheon engraved "67 Spring Lane", crack to centre of handle.

£450-550　　　　　**MUR**

An ebony and brass-framed brace, by Thomas Turner, Sheffield, in very good condition.

£180-220　　　　　**MUR**

A rare Joseph Cooper patented beech brace, cracks to ivory ring.

£250-350　　　　　**MUR**

A rare 18thC brace, stamped "1 Sym" at the top of the web, in very good condition.

£100-200　　　　　**MUR**

A beech coopers' brace, by W. Caskin, Burton on Trent, in very good condition.

£70-100　　　　　**MUR**

A very rare brass-plated beech brace, by H.D., London, with ebony head, in fine condition.

£120-180　　　　　**MUR**

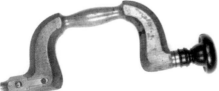

A beech brace, in very good to fine condition.

£50-80　　　　　**MUR**

A very early 18thC iron two-bar cagehead brace, in good condition.

£50-80　　　　　**MUR**

A CLOSER LOOK AT A HORSE MEASURE

Only a few of this type of tool have been discovered, so this is a very rare find. Special tools for niche tasks are generally rare.

It is marked with a maker's name and patent, adding interest and value.

It is well made using fine materials and retains it original case.

Equestrian tools are highly desirable to collectors.

A rare brass and boxwood pocket horse measure, by Cooper W. Jones & Co., patent no. 13266, in fine condition.

£280-320   **MUR**

A very fine early 19thC brass station finder, in good condition.

£100-150   **MUR**

A straight edge/rule, in brass relief and taken from an ivory rule, remounted on a mahogany and rosewood straight edge, in very good condition.

£280-320   **MUR**

A rare Coggeshall two-fold boxwood rule, marked "Morris Fecit", with various scales and a boxwood slide for timber calculations.

This was almost certainly made by William Morris II, working as a rule maker 1801-33.

24in (61cm) long

£150-200   **MUR**

An unusual mid-18thC boxwood rule, with thick section, heavy square brass joint and tips scaled on the four flats.

48in (123cm) long

£200-250   **MUR**

A boxwood, brass and ivory shoe rule, by F.B. Cox, in very good condition.

£25-35   **MUR**

A rare brass-heading rosewood mortise gauge, with brass calibrated rule in stock, in very good condition.

£70-100   **MUR**

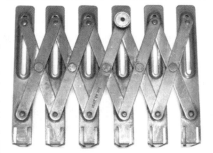

A scarce patented brass dovetail gauge, in very good condition.

£50-80   **MUR**

A late 19thC carved mahogany and boxwood marking gauge, in fine condition.

£40-70   **MUR**

A rare Panther saw, by Woodrough & McParkin, Cincinnati, Ohio, with applewood handle and additional carving around the cheeks, in fine condition.

Interest in collecting saws has increased in the last few years, as a result, items such as this are increasing in value.

£800-1,200 MUR

An unused Atkins 400, in original box and greaseproof paper, in fine condition.

£700-1,000 MUR

A brass back tenon saw, by Disston, Philadelphia, with applewood handle, in fine condition.

£60-90 MUR

A brass back tenon saw, by Frost, Norwich, in fine condition.
18in (45.5cm) long

£50-80 MUR

A brass back tenon saw, by Spear & Jackson, in fine condition.
c1900 *16in (40.5cm) long*

£60-90 MUR

A copper salt saw, engraved with the Tyzack logo and "Salt Saw" in script, in very good condition.

£40-60 MUR

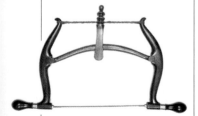

A beech and rosewood bowsaw, with German silver handles, and fruitwood winder, in very good condition.
Blade 8in (20.5cm) long

£250-300 MUR

A rare 18thC miniature bowsaw, made of fruitwood and ebony, in very good condition.
6in (15cm) wide

£180-220 MUR

A mahogany and ash bowsaw, with octagonal boxwood handles.
Blade 13.5in (34.5cm) long

£40-60 MUR

A late 17thC/early 18thC musical instrument maker's plane, with iron sole, moulded iron bridge with front protrusion, the side lightly engraved "L.E. Schott' and "1791" and "1681", and other indecipherable engravings.

This is a rare item as not only is it for a specific task and of an early date, but dated European metal planes are rare.

6.5in (16.5cm) long

£5,000-6,000   **MUR**

A flat-soled brass violin maker's plane, by Preston, slightly corroded toothing iron, otherwise in very good condition.

2in (5cm) high

£150-250   **MUR**

An ivory and ebony barristers' seal hammer, in fine condition.

£450-550   **MUR**

An unusual handled hatters' brimming plane, in very good condition.

£70-100   **MUR**

A small filemakers' hammer, with correct replacement boxwood handle and three chisels, in very good condition.

8in (20.5cm) high

£180-220   **MUR**

An 18thC tiny surgeons' iron brace, with blackwood head, in good condition.

£300-500   **MUR**

A rare undertaker's brace, by I.C. Tell, with turn screw bit, in very good condition.

£280-320   **MUR**

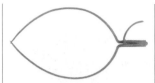

A pair of 18thC coachmakers' or wheelwrights' iron calipers, in good condition.

28in (71cm) long

£100-150   **MUR**

A pair of beech and steel coachmakers' left and right tailed rebates, compassed steel sole, in fine condition.

7.5in (19cm) long

£150-200   **MUR**

A pair of miniature coachmakers' pistol routers, one with ivory handles, in very good condition.

7in (18cm) long

£120-180   **MUR**

A rare coachmakers' compassed reed, in beech with full boxing and adjustable reversible boxwood fence, in very good condition.

This tool is a shave, which applies a moulding. It is a rare tool, especially as its purpose is so specific.

9.5in (24cm) long

£120-180   **MUR**

A rare and unusual coachmakers' beech plough, by Budd, with snicker iron and wedge, in very good condition.

This tiny plough was probably made by the factory as a one-off.

4.25in (11cm) long

£120-180   **MUR**

A divers' knife, with brass sheath and lignum handle, in very good condition.

14in (35.5cm) long

£150-200   **MUR**

A 19thC brass and steel hand-lathe, on a later mahogany stand.

£300-400   **GHOU**

FIND OUT MORE...

The Ultimate Brace – A Unique Product of Victorian Sheffield, by Reg Eaton, published by Erica Jane Publishing, 1989.

Dictionary of Woodworking Tools, by R.A. Salaman, published by Astragal Press, 1997.

COLLECTORS' NOTES

■ Introduced by Mettoy Limited in 1956, Corgi Toys still produce limited editions today.

■ The company developed innovative, ingenious and attractive features for their toys that helped them compete against rivals Dinky. Corgi was the first to add plastic windows, and opening doors and boots to their cars, and in 1959 it was the first toy manufacturer to use real spring suspension.

■ Corgi are also well-known for their film and TV related toys, which include various James Bond, Batman and The Man from U.N.C.L.E. vehicles. These can be among the most popular today.

■ Look out for rare colour variations and other versions sought-after by collectors.

■ The original boxes and instructions will add greatly to the value, but like the toys, they must be complete and in good condition to fetch the highest prices.

A Corgi No. 259 Citröen 'Le Dandy' coupé, metallic dark red with yellow interior, in original box with instructions.

£150-200   **W&W**

A Corgi No. 245 Buick Riviera, metallic gold body, complete with original box.

1964-68

£35-45   **GAZE**

A Corgi No. 440 Ford Consul Cortina Super Estate Car, with golfer, caddie and clubs on trolley, in original box.

1966-69

£150-200   **W&W**

A Corgi No. 205 Riley Pathfinder Saloon, red body, boxed.

1956-62

£80-120   **W&W**

A Corgi No. 1110 Bedford S-type Articulated Tanker, finished in red with 'Mobilgas' logos to sides and rear and silver spun hubs.

The later, Dutch version with 'Shell Benzeen' logos can be worth up to 10 times as much.

1959-64

£100-150   **W&W**

A Corgi No. 1101 S-type Carrimore Car Transporter, complete with original box.

1957-62

£20-30   **GAZE**

A Corgi No. 354 Commer Military Ambulance, green, dark tinted glass and roof light, in mint condition, in blue and yellow carded box in good, although grubby, condition.

1964-66

£90-100   **VEC**

A Corgi No. 438 Land Rover 190 WB, spun hubs, mint condition, with box.

The LEPRA livery version can be worth up to four times as much.

1963-77

£120-180   **VEC**

A Corgi No. 107 Batman Batboat and Trailer, in very good condition, box in good to very good condition, two small holes.

This version is more desirable than the later version made 1975-81, which has no suspension on the trailer and Whizzwheels. It is usually worth about 50 per cent less with box.

1967-70

£100-150   **SAS**

A Corgi No. 261 James Bond Aston Martin DB5, metallic gold, boxed with display insert.

1965-69

£120-180   **W&W**

A Corgi No. 336 James Bond Toyota 2000 GT, as seen in 'You Only Live Twice', complete with original box and sealed instructions.

This Corgi toy has rocket launchers, despite the fact that they weren't featured in the film.

1967-69

£150-200   **GAZE**

A Corgi No. 266 Chitty-Chitty-Bang-Bang, with four figures, excellent condition, lacks box.

1968-72

£60-80   **SAS**

A Corgi No. 290 Kojak Buick, in original box, in excellent to mint condition, box in excellent condition.

1976-77

£80-120   **SAS**

A Corgi No. H859 Magic Roundabout 'Mr McHenry's Trike and Zebedee', in excellent condition, box in very good condition.

1972-74

£120-180   **SAS**

A Corgi No. 277 'Monkees' Monkeemobile, red body with red roof.

1968-72

£30-40   **GAZE**

A CLOSER LOOK AT A CORGI JUNIORS TOY

Corgi Juniors toys were only produced in blister packs.

Examples still sealed in their original packs are usually the most valuable.

These smaller scale models were originally released in 1965 as Husky and were exclusively sold through Woolworths. The name changed to Juniors in 1970.

A larger scale version of this model was also produced as No. 802 from 1969-72 and is worth about twice as much as this version.

A Corgi Juniors No. 1008 Popeye Paddle Wagon, with Whizz Wheels, in original card packaging, in excellent condition, unopened card in very good condition.

1971-72

£150-200   **SAS**

A Corgi No. 258 The "Saint" Volvo P1800, in original box, in very good condition, box in good condition.

Look for the extremely rare version with the Saint logo in blue. All other versions are worth about the same as this one.

1968 70

£150-200   **SAS**

A Corgi No. 292 Starsky and Hutch Ford Torino, in excellent to mint condition, the pictorial window box in very good condition.

1977-82

£120-180   **SAS**

A Corgi Gift Set No. 24 Commer Constructor set, with two three-quarter ton chassis with interchangeable bodies comprising a milk float, pick-up, van and ambulance, original unopened box.

1963-68

£150-200   **W&W**

A Corgi Gift Set No. 33 Tractor and Beast Carrier, comprising a Fordson Power Major tractor with beast carrier and animals, boxed with display insert.

In 1968 the Power Major tractor (No. 55) was replaced with the Super Major tractor (No. 67). This later version is worth about 25 per cent less.

1965-68

£180-220   **W&W**

A Corgi Gift Set No. 2 Land Rover and Rice's Pony Trailer, complete with original box.

Complete gift sets are very desirable as many were broken up.

1958-1968

£120-180   **GAZE**

A Corgi Gift Set No. 32 Tractor, Shovel & Trailer Set, with a Massey Ferguson 65 tractor, driver and tipping trailer, boxed with display insert.

1965-68

£250-350   **W&W**

A Corgi Gift Set No. 10 Rambler Marlin Set, with a Marlin rambler sports fastback with Ottersport Kayak and camping trailer, boxed with display insert, missing figure and kayak.

This is usually a relatively sought-after Gift Set, but the missing figure and kayak reduce the value.

1968-69

£70-100   **W&W**

COLLECTORS' NOTES

■ Originally introduced as 'Modelled Miniatures' in 1931 by the makers of the Mecanno construction sets, the first Dinky vehicles were designed as accessories for Hornby trains. The first car produced after the company changed the name of the range to 'Dinky' was the 23a sports car.

■ By 1935 there were over 200 models to choose from. Road vehicles made up the majority of the output, but planes, ships and other models were also produced.

■ Output slowed during the war, but in 1947 the popular 'Supertoys' range of slightly smaller scale vehicles was introduced.

■ Design and model numbers help to date Dinky toys. Pre-war examples are harder to come by and can fetch a premium. Early post-war reissues, with their wider wheels and black base plates, can also be valuable. Models from the 1950s and 60s, particularly vans with advertising transfers, are rapidly growing in popularity and 1970s models of vehicles from cult film and TV shows are also desirable.

■ To fetch the highest values, toys must be undamaged and in as near to shop-sold condition as possible. Boxes are very important and can double the value.

■ Variations in colour or detailing can increase value. Look out for models made in France, or for specific markets such as South Africa. Gift sets complete with their packaging are currently very popular.

A Dinky 38 Series late export issue Armstrong Siddeley coupé.

This particular model is a later export issue of a previously available model and was renumbered 104.

1950-55

£100-150 W&W

A Dinky 38 Series late export issue Sunbeam Talbot sports car, no. 38b.

This particular model was renumbered 101.

1950-55

£120-180 W&W

A Dinky no. 108 MG Midget sports car, with competition finish in red and tan, complete with racing driver, boxed, some wear.

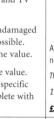

1955-59   3.25in (8.5cm) long

£100-150 W&W

A Dinky no. 157 Jaguar XK 120 coupé, in red, boxed.

1959-62

£80-120 W&W

A Dinky no. 157 Jaguar XK 120 coupé, in grey and yellow, boxed.

The two-tone paintwork is one of the most valuable variations for this model.

1957-59

£120-180 W&W

A Dinky no. 148 Ford Fairlane, in light green, complete with original box, repairs to one flap.

Look out for the rare blue variations, produced for export to South Africa, which can be worth up to eight times more.

1962-65

£30-40 GAZE

A Dinky no. 191 Dodge Royal sedan, in light green with black flash, with box, repairs to one flap.

The cream-bodied variation with a blue flash is the most valuable version of this model.

1959-64

£25-35 GAZE

A Dinky no. 130 Ford Corsair, in metallic red, boxed, repairs to one flap.

1964-66

£20-30 GAZE

A Dinky no. 344 (Plymouth) Estate Car, with box, repairs to one flap.

1954-61

£30-40 GAZE

A Dinky no. 154 Hillman Minx saloon, boxed, rear lights added.

1955

£100-150 W&W

A Dinky no. 449 Chevrolet El Camino pick-up truck, in turquoise and cream, with box, repairs to one flap.

Different shades of turquoise are known but this does not affect the value.

1961-69

£22-28 GAZE

A Dinky no. 257 Canadian Nash Rambler Fire Chief's car, with box, repairs to one flap.

1960-69

£25-35 GAZE

A Dinky no. 264 R.C.M.P. Ford Fairlane, damaged, with box, repairs to one flap.

The RCMP are the Royal Canadian Mounted Police. The model could be bought with two Mounties as accessories.

1962-65

£22-28 GAZE

A Dinky no. 281 Pathé News Fiat 2300 camera car, with box and instructions.

1968-70

£12-18 GAZE

A Dinky no. 450 Trojan van, in red with matt black roof, marked with "Esso" logo, with box.

1954-57   *3.25in (8.5cm) long*

£100-150   **W&W**

A Dinky no. 451 Trojan 'Dunlop' van, boxed.

1954-57

£120-180   **W&W**

A Dinky no. 480 Bedford 10 CWT 'Kodak Van', paintwork with small scratches, but with original box.

1954-56

£120-180   **ATK**

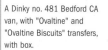

A Dinky no. 481 Bedford CA van, with "Ovaltine" and "Ovaltine Biscuits" transfers, with box.

1955-60   3.25in (8.5cm) long

£100-150   **W&W**

A Dinky no. 482 Bedford 10 CWT 'Dinky Toys' van, in excellent condition in excellent condition box.

1956-60

£200-250   **W&W**

A Dinky no. 34b Royal Mail Van, red, black, black ridged wheels, in good condition.

Open rear windows can add up to 50% to the value.

1948-51

£50-80   **VEC**

A Dinky no. 504 Supertoys Foden 14-ton tanker, in very good condition, boxed.

1948-52

£180-220   **W&W**

A Dinky no. 504 Supertoys Foden 14 ton tanker, with first-type dark blue cab with light blue flash.

A Dinky no. 918 Supertoys Guy 'Ever Ready' van, in excellent condition, in excellent condition box.

1955-58

£200-250   **W&W**

Although this is a desirable model, the wear to the paintwork, seen by the spotting on the tank, and lack of box has reduced the value considerably.

£50-60   **GAZE**

A Dinky no. 25d 'Petrol' Tanker, type three black chassis, plated radiator, black ridged wheels, excellent condition.

The orange body with this transfer, or the grey body with a 'POOL' transfer, are the most valuable variations.

1946-47

£120-180 VEC

A Dinky no. 522 Big Bedford lorry, with maroon cab.

The variation with a blue cab and yellow back can be worth up to twice as much.

1952-54

£30-40 GAZE

A Dinky no. 958 Supertoys Guy Warrior snowplough, with moveable plough blade, complete with original box.

If the box shows a silver-coloured plough blade, and it is found on the model too, the value can double.

1961-66 7.75in (19.5cm) long

£40-50 W&W

A Dinky no. 25f Market Gardener's Lorry, type three black chassis, black ridged wheels, in near mint condition.

1945-47

£150-200 VEC

A Dinky no. 261 Morris 'Post Office Telephones' Service Van, very good condition.

1955-61

£25-35 SAS

A Dinky no. 968 BBC TV Roving Eye Vehicle.

This is a high price for this toy, but both the toy and its box are in excellent condition and the piece is totally complete, with its original internal packing piece, and fitted aerial and cameraman.

1959-64

£180-220 SAS

A Dinky no. 988 ABC TV Transmitter Van, pale grey, pale blue, red side flash, pale grey Supertoy wheels, excellent condition, in good condition box.

1962-69

£180-220 VEC

A French Dinky no. 32E Fire Engine Berliet Premier Secours, dark red and silver with white tyres, boxed, minor wear, minor chips to ladder.

£150-200 W&W

A Dinky no. 949 Wayne School Bus, deep yellow, red side flash, red interior and plastic hubs, excellent condition, missing decal to rear, in good condition blue and white striped box.

£60-90 VEC

A Dinky no. 949 Wayne School Bus, red interior, red plastic hubs, good condition, in good condition box.

This model is a lighter yellow than the standard version shown to the right, which makes it considerably scarcer and more valuable.

£200-300 VEC

A Dinky no. 961 Swiss Postal Bus, yellow, cream roof, dark blue interior, excellent condition, in good condition Swiss box.

1973-77

£100-150 VEC

A Dinky no. 952 Vega Major Luxury Coach, white, metallic purple side stripe, blue interior, excellent condition, including box.
1964-71

£70-100 VEC

A Dinky no. 889 Autobus Parisien, dark green, pale blue centre, brown interior, dark green hubs, excellent condition, in fair condition box.

£150-200 VEC

A French Dinky no. 889 Autobus Parisien, grey interior, red hubs, excellent condition, including box, complete with leaflet.

£250-300 VEC

A Dinky no. 953 Continental Touring Coach, red plastic hubs, excellent condition, in good condition box.
1963-65

£250-350 VEC

A Dinky no. 281 Luxury Coach, in cream with orange flashes and cream hub, boxed.

The mid-blue body is the most valuable, at up to twice the value of this version.

1954-59

4.5in (11.5cm) long

£120-180 W&W

A CLOSER LOOK AT A DINKY AIRCRAFT GIFT SET

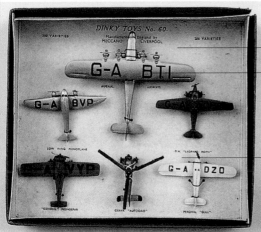

This is a complete, very early set and comprises a no. 60c Percival Gull, a no. 60f Autogiro, a no. 60a Imperial Airways Liner, a no. 60d Low-Wing Monoplane and no. 60e General Monospar.

All models are in excellent condition, with only the Imperial Airways Liner fuselage showing the metal fatigue commonly associated with Dinky's airplanes.

The registration markings on the wings show this is the second issue of this set – the first issue, without marks, was the first Dinky aeroplane gift set produced (1934-5) and can be worth around 20 per cent more.

The box artwork is appealing, but the cellotaped corners, reduce its value slightly.

Λ Dinky No. 60 British Aeroplane gift set.

1936-41

£1,000-1,500   VEC

A Dinky no. 60r 'Caledonia' Empire Flying Boat, very good, box fair to good condition.

1937-40

£150-200   SAS

A Dinky no. 62p Armstrong Whitworth Airliner "Ensign", silver, red propellers, G-A DSR, gliding pin and hole, good condition, fatigued throughout, in good condition box, slightly sun-faded.

1945-49

£180-220   VEC

A Dinky no. 63 Mayo composite Aircraft and Seaplane, silver, red propellers, red plastic roller, good condition, Mayo plane showing signs of fatigue, in good condition box.

1939-41

£350-450   VEC

A Dinky no. 62r De Haviland 'Albatross' Mail Liner, with original box, dated May 1940.

1939-41   *Box 4.5in (11.5cm) wide*

£70-80   GORL

A Dinky no. 60s 'Medium Bomber' gift set, comprising two no. 62n Fairey 'Battle' bombers in camouflage, both in excellent condition with no visible signs of fatigue, in excellent condition box.

1938-41

£350-400   VEC

Λ Dinky no. 61 RAF Airplane gift set, comprising a no. 60h Singapore Flying Boat, two no. 60n Fairey Battle Bombers and two no. 60p Gloster Gladiators, all in good condition but fatigued with damage to wings, in good condition but faded box.

1937-41

£300-400   VEC

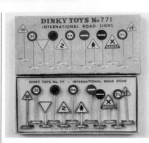

A set of 12 Dinky No. 771 International Road Signs, near mint condition, in good condition box.

1953-65

£60-90 **VEC**

A set of 24 Dinky no. 772 British Road Signs, near mint condition, one road sign broken at base, in good condition box.

1959-63

£150-200 **VEC**

A Dinky no. 4 boxed set of 0-gauge model railway Engineering Staff figures.

1954-56 *5.5in (14cm) wide*

£80-120 **F**

A Dinky no. 6 Shepherd Gift Set, box good, near mint.

1954-56

£150-200 **CHEF**

A CLOSER LOOK AT A DINKY TOYS BOX

Empty boxes appeal to collectors who buy them to fill them, increasing the value of a loose set.

Export-market boxes with their different designs are rarer still.

The design shows that this example was produced for the US market – sometimes red labels are found bearing the name of the US distributor H. Hudson Dobson.

Their survival is comparatively rare as many were thrown away.

An empty Dinky green and blue speckled pattern no. 6 Commercial Vehicles Set box for the US export market, fair condition with some taping.

1948

£150-200 **SAS**

A Dinky no. 47 road signs set, with closed triangles, box repaired.

1935-41 *Box 7in (18cm) wide*

£100-150 **GAZE**

A Dinky no. 964 Elevator Loader, in very good condition, with fair condition box.

1954-68

£25-35 **GAZE**

A Dinky pre-war no.45 Garage with gloss doors, very good to excellent condition.

£200-250 **SAS**

A Tri-ang Spot-On No. 154 Austin A40 Farina Saloon, pink, black roof, red interior, in excellent condition, in slightly grubby box.

1961

£80-120 VEC

A Tri-ang Spot-On No. 184 Austin A60 Cambridge, light blue, with skis, white interior, grey roof rack, skis and poles, in excellent condition, decals applied to front and rear, in fair condition box.

1963

£40-60 VEC

A Tri-ang Spot-On No. 118 BMW Isetta Bubble Car, red, cream interior, in excellent condition, in fair condition box.

1960

£70-100 VEC

A Tri-ang Spot-On No. 120 Fiat Multipla Estate, bright blue, cream interior, in very good condition, in good condition box.

1960

£60-80 VEC

A Tri-ang Spot-On No. 115 Bristol 406 Saloon, metallic green, red interior, in excellent condition, in excellent condition box, a tiny amount of graffiti to one side.

1960

£150-200 VEC

A Tri-ang Spot-On No. 100 Ford Zodiac, light blue lower body, grey upper, red interior, near mint condition, in fair condition box, one inner end flap missing.

The 'sl' version with battery-operated lights is slightly more desirable.

1959

£80-120 VEC

A Tri-ang Spot-On No. 309 'Z Cars' Ford Zephyr, boxed with paperwork.

1965

£100-150 W&W

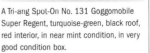

A Tri-ang Spot-On No. 131 Goggomobile Super Regent, turquoise-green, black roof, red interior, in near mint condition, in very good condition box.

1960

£80-120 VEC

A Tri-ang Spot-On No. 183 Humber Super Snipe Estate Car, pale blue, white interior, two figures, roof rack and load, in excellent condition, in poor condition box.

1963

£100-150 VEC

A Tri-ang Spot-On No. 217 Jaguar 'E' type, beige, white interior, excellent condition, a couple of minor chips to bonnet, in good condition box complete with leaflet.

The mid-blue and light grey colourways are the most desirable and can be worth double this and other colours.

1963

£100-150 VEC

A Tri-ang Spot-On No. 193 NSU Prinz 4, beige, cream interior, driver, in excellent condition, in very good condition box.

1963

£70-100 VEC

A Tri-ang Spot-On No. 166 Renault Floride Convertible, pink, cream interior, near mint condition, in slightly grubby box with leaflet.

1962

£150-200 VEC

A Tri-ang Spot-On No. 157sl Rover 3-litre, with lights, pale blue, red interior, good condition, some damage to front and rear bumpers, in poor condition box.

1963

£40-60 VEC

A Tri-ang Spot-On No. 165/1 Vauxhall Cresta, pale blue, white interior, in excellent condition, in fair condition box.

1961

£100-150 VEC

A Tri-ang Spot-On No. 216 Volvo 122s, red, cream interior, sunroof, in excellent condition, in fair condition box.

1963

£100-150 VEC

A scarce Tri-ang Minic clockwork police Traffic Control Car, No. 29m, with detachable loud speaker, boxed.

£100-150 W&W

A scarce Tri-ang Minic clockwork delivery van, No. 81m, in dark blue LNER livery, boxed.

£70-100 W&W

A CLOSER LOOK AT A MATCHBOX TOY CAR

A Matchbox Series No. 75a Ford Thunderbird, in cream with peach side panels, boxed.

Lesney, established 1948, is best known for its Matchbox and Models of Yesterday ranges. In 1996 the company became part of Mattel Inc. who continue to use the Matchbox name today.

1960

£70-100　　　　　**W&W**

A Matchbox Series No. 22b Vauxhall Cresta, in light metallic brown with blue/green side panels, boxed.

The version with a pale pink body, blue/green side panels and grey plastic wheels can be worth ten times this colourway.

1958

£120-180　　　　**W&W**

This cream coloured Cougar is significantly more valuable than the metallic lime green version or any of the later versions from the Superfast series.

It is one of the most sought-after from the Matchbox '1-75' series.

It is in excellent condition; as with all die-cast toys, the condition has a huge effect on value.

It retains its original box, which is in good condition. Boxes are desirable as so many were thrown away when they were first bought.

A rare Matchbox 62c Mercury Cougar, cream with white interior and chrome hubs, in excellent condition, in good condition box.

1968

£1,800-2,200　　　　**SAS**

A limited edition Matchbox 'Models of Yesteryear Club' Y5/42 Leyland Titan double-decker bus, from an edition of 5,000 for the Matchbox International Collectors' Association.

1992

£5-8　　　　**GAZE**

A Matchbox No. 7 Major Pack Thames Trader Cattle Truck, excellent condition, boxed.

1960

£70-100　　　　**SAS**

A Matchbox Series MG1 Service Station & Showroom, in red and yellow livery, with original box, together with a No. 1 Accessory Pack box containing a freestanding Esso sign and boxed petrol pumps, minor wear.

8.5in (21.5cm) wide

£60-80　　　　**W&W**

c1948

£300-500　　　　**SAS**

A Lesney Moko Milk Cart, with six crates, horse and driver, in very good condition, boxed.

This is one of the first die-cast toys issued by Lesney in 1948. It is also complete with its six crates and driver, and original box. The version with the blue driver is worth approximately 20 per cent more.

A Tekno No. 814 U.N. Jeep, in white with brown seats and driver, U.N. decals to bonnet and sides, in excellent condition, in good condition box, missing one inner end flap.

Tekno starting making tinplate toys in Denmark in 1920 and by the 1960s they were producing their popular 1:43 scale die-cast vehicles. In 1974 they were taken over by their Dutch importer Van Min and production moved to Holland. Today they specialise in truck models. Look out for their model of the Mercedes-Benz 230SL and commercial vehicles with unusual liveries.

£80-120   **VEC**

A Tekno pale green and dark green Volkswagen Micro-Bus, in very good condition with faint corrosion to hubs.

£50-70   **SAS**

A Tekno 'Eddie Stobart Ltd' Scania articulated truck.

14.25in (36cm) long

£60-80   **W&W**

A Tekno 'Atchison Topeka Ltd' Scania articulated tanker.

11.75in (30cm) long

£60-80   **W&W**

A Tekno 'Kosangas' Mercedes Benz LP322 truck, complete with gas bottle load and sack barrow, finished in orange and blue, in near mint condition, in poor condition box.

£150-200   **VEC**

A Tekno 'Scandinavian Airlines' Caravelle SE210, in excellent condition.

£70-100   **VEC**

A Tekno 'Sabena' Douglas DC7C, in silver, white and blue, with four propellers, in excellent condition.

£180-220   **VEC**

A Tekno 'Scandinavian Airline Services' Douglas DC76, in white, lilac and silver, with four propellers, in excellent condition.

£70-100   **VEC**

A Tekno No. 488x Transport plane, in silver, fuselage painted blue, red propellers, in excellent condition, in good condition early box.

£150-200   **VEC**

A Japanese Aeromini Super VC10, in white, blue and silver, in excellent condition, in good condition box.

£70-100   **VEC**

A Benbros Euclid rear dump truck, in good condition, some heavy chips to top, in good condition box, slight puncture mark to one side and slightly crushed.

Dating Benbros toys is very difficult as few contemporary adverts or catalogues exist today.

£70-100   **VEC**

A Benbros motor cycle rally rider, with rubber tyres, with detachable rider, in original box with period illustration.

3.25in (8.5cm) long

£40-50   **W&W**

A Britains 1400 Bluebird Land Speed Record Car, with detachable chassis, in very good condition, box in good condition.

1936

£150-200   **SAS**

A Chad Valley Fordson Major E27N clockwork tractor, unboxed, in worn condition.

1952

£150-200   **CHEF**

A Chad Valley Fordson Major E27N tractor, in very good condition, box damaged.

Toy manufacturers Chad Valley started producing metal toys during the 1940s. Their Wee-Kin range of die-cast toys were made for the Rootes Group who made the Sunbeam car. Chad Valley are probably best known for their precise tractor models such as this example and, of course, their teddy bears.

1952

£450-550   **CHEF**

A Chad Valley Wee-Kin Series No. 238 grey Sunbeam Talbot, in excellent condition.

1949-53

£180-220   **SAS**

A rare Charbens model steamroller, with dark green matt body and red spoked wheels and roller, some damage.

4.5in (11.5cm) long

£200-300   **W&W**

A rare French C.I.J. No. 210 'Air Maroc' Caravelle, in silver, red, green and white, in excellent condition, and in excellent condition box, slight tear mark, complete with inner packing.

C.I.J. (Compagnie Industrielle du Jouet) only made model aircraft from 1959-61 and released only 11 different models. They are all sought-after.

c1960

£350-450   VEC

A rare Creak's 'Yesteryear Code 3' Crossley model 48 police vehicle, with City of London Police black livery, boxed with certificate.

£50-70   W&W

A rare Creak's 'Yesteryear Code 3' model T Ford police vehicle, model AC90, boxed with certificate.

'Yesteryear Code 3' models are produced by Lesney or Matchbox, but have had their livery or decoration changed by another company without the permission of the manufacturer. Therefore, they are not deemed official Models of Yesteryear toys by collectors.

£40-60   W&W

A rare Creak's 'Yesteryear Code 3' 1945 MG 'TC' police vehicle, in black Liverpool Police livery, model 974, boxed with certificate.

£50-70   W&W

A Crescent NN 691 HMS Eagle aircraft carrier, with six miniature aircraft and cardboard inserts, boxed.

7.75in (19.5cm) long

£30-40   GAZE

An Eligor Scania 'William Nicol Ltd' articulated tanker, number 112749.

14.25in (36cm) long

£60-100   W&W

A Franklin Mint 1965 Seagrove ladder fire escape engine, precision die-cast model in 1:32 scale, hand-finished with many detailed parts, mounted on a wooden plinth.

£45-55   W&W

A Johnny Lighting Custom Jaguar XKE, by Topper.

£20-30   SOTT

TOYS & GAMES

A Lone Star RAC series land rover, with aerial, boxed.

£120-180   **W&W**

A Mettoy No. 810 large-scale red limousine, with clockwork mechanism and registration MTY 810, fair condition.

Mettoy, taken from METal TOY and founded by Phillip Ullmann in 1933, are best known for their Corgi range, launched in 1948, see pages 512-514 for our Corgi section.

1948-58

£25-35   **SAS**

A Morestone No. 3 14-ton flat lorry with chains, green cab and chassis, cream back, silver chains, green wheels, excellent condition, in good condition but incorrect box.

1955-56

£150-200   **VEC**

A Morestone No. 2 Foden long-distance diesel wagon, light beige cab and chassis, red back, beige wheels, near mint condition, in good condition box.

Despite the box flaps being correct, the image on the front of the box is different. The box design is similar to those of Dinky's SuperToys Foden models, which were popular at the time and Morestone were presumably trying to cash in on that success.

1955-56

£120-180   **VEC**

A Morestone No. 4 14-ton express delivery diesel wagon, orange cab and chassis, grey back, orange wheels, excellent condition, in excellent condition box.

1955-56

£60-90   **VEC**

A 1970s Nicky Toys Sea Vixen naval jet fighter, silver, black nose cone, RAF roundels, excellent condition, in good condition box.

In 1968 Atamco Private Ltd, Calcutta, purchased a number of obsolete dies from Dinky and produced them under the trade name Nicky Toys.

£120-180   **VEC**

A PMI, South Africa, Karrier Bantam and trailer, green cab, brown back, plastic push-along model, excellent condition, some distortion to trailer back, in box.

12in (30cm) long

£180-220   **VEC**

A Shackleton 'Foden FG 6-wheel Tipper Lorry', in red and yellow livery, box worn.

Shackleton was started in 1939 and made wooden lorries and doll's houses prior to WWII. Production of die-cast lorries, based on the Foden FG began in 1948 with all the individual parts, including the clockwork motors being made in-house. The range was expanded in 1952, but the company closed the same year. Shackleton models are sought-after today.

1950-52

£500-600   **ROS**

A limited edition Solido 'James Bond – Goldfinger's Rolls Royce', from an edition of 100, in yellow and black, complete with Goldfinger and Oddjob figures, in mint condition including gold tube.

French toy manufacturer Solido began in 1932 and made die-cast toys from the start. Its post WWII models are popular and include military vehicles and an accurately modelled London bus. The James Bond theme makes this example desirable to Solido collectors as well as James Bond enthusiasts. The edition number is also very small.

£400-500 **VEC**

A Shackleton clockwork 'Foden FG 6-Wheel Platform Lorry', in first version box.
1948-52 *12.75in (32.5cm) long*

£280-320 **ROS**

A Solido Age d'Or Bugatti Royal, in dark blue, complete with original box and accessories.

£5-10 **GAZE**

A Solido 219 USA M41 tank, with unused rockets on sprue, excellent condition, in very good condition box.

£60-70 **SAS**

A Solido TWA Super Constellation, silver blue, white, four propellers, in good condition, in excellent condition box, complete with leaflet.

£120-180 **VEC**

A Tonka No.2200 Jeep dispatcher, boxed with booklet.

Box 10in (25.5cm) wide

£20-30 **GAZE**

A Wells Brimtoy Pocketoy 9/510 long wheelbase truck, with open tinplate body, red plastic cab and chassis and clockwork mechanism, complete with original box and key.

5in (12.5cm) long

£40-60 **W&W**

A Wells Brimtoy Pocketoy 9/520 articulated six-wheel covered lorry, with "Transport London Birmingham Glasgow" decals to sides, opening top, hinged rear door, red plastic cab and chassis and clockwork mechanism, complete with original box and key.

6in (15cm) long

£80-120 **W&W**

A CLOSER LOOK AT A TRAIN

Jerome Secor founded Secor in 1872 in Connecticut and became known for his clockwork and mechanical toys.

The form, decoration and material indicates an early date - early American toys of this period are scarce and desirable .

This example is made from cast iron, not tinplate, which is relatively unusual.

Secor was later sold to Ives, one of the most noted American model train manufacturers.

An American hand-painted cast iron Secor clockwork train.

c1882 9in (23cm) long

£800-1,200

AMJ

A German lithographed tinplate 'penny toy' locomotive '345', with one carriage, possibly by Distler, marked "Made in Germany".

8.5in (21cm) long

£45-55　　**WDL**

A scarce and large early tinplate clockwork steam twin dome Continental locomotive.

7in (18cm) wide

£60-80　　**W&W**

A Chad Valley LMS lithographed tinplate clockwork locomotive.

10in (25.5cm) long

£25-35　　**GAZE**

An 'O' gauge 4-4-0 clockwork locomotive.

11in (28cm) long

£300-400　　**GAZE**

A late 1920s Hornby O-gauge No. 2 tender clockwork locomotive, 4-4-0 and six wheel tender in black, RN 2711, two fixed front buffer beam lights.

£150-200　　**W&W**

A Bassett Lowke 0-6-0 clockwork locomotive.

9.75in (25cm) long

£250-350　　**GAZE**

A CLOSER LOOK AT A TRAIN

Grey is rarer than black, which is a much more common colour.

Pre-war trains are harder to find as less examples were made and survive today.

It has a large six-wheel tender, which is unusual as most are around half the size and have four wheels.

This example is in very good condition for a pre-war toy, with only light scratches to the paintwork – this makes it desirable to a collector.

A late 1930s American Lionel Standard gauge locomotive and tender, the tender stamped "392W".

c1937

Locomotive 15.5in (39.5cm) long

£600-700   **BOM**

A Bassett Lowke LMS electric compound 4-4-0 locomotive and tender.

15.5in (39.5cm) long

£100-200   **GAZE**

A Bassett Lowke O-gauge 4-4-0 A3 Pacific locomotive, with 12-volt centre scape pick-up and tender.

20in (51cm) long

£650-750   **GAZE**

A 4-6-2 12-volt electric locomotive and tender, restored.

22in (56cm) long

£180-220   **GAZE**

A Hornby Dublo 'Caledonian' passenger train set, boxed. Box

20.5in (51.5cm) wide

£80-120   **GAZE**

A Tri-ang R3.A electric model railway, with assorted accessories.

Box 19in (48.5cm) wide

£60-80   **GAZE**

A German Trix 1200 'Der Adler' Set, in excellent condition, in very good condition lidded box.

£70-100   **SAS**

COLLECTORS' NOTES

■ The 'golden age' of the tin sand pail was from the 1930s until around 1960, when the less expensive and more resilient plastic began to take over. Reminiscent of sunny days on Blackpool or Brighton beaches, they are popular with nostalgic adults who collect to recall their childhood.

■ All tin pails have lithographed rather than hand-painted designs, colours are typically bright and cheerful and interiors are often plainly decorated in contrasting colours. Prolific makers included the 'Ohio Art Metal', 'US Metal Toys' and T. Cohn as well as notable tinplate toy maker J. Chein.

■ The design and condition are two major indicators for value. Most designs contain children or animals,

often in a beach setting. Look out for patriotic themes or characters, which can add cross-market appeal, leading values to rise. Disney characters and Rosie O'Neil's 'Kewpie' are particularly popular. Other themes such as outer space and circus scenes are also sought-after.

■ As they were made to be used, and most often were, it is very hard to find pails in truly mint condition. Most have dents, dings, or designs that were scratched through contact with sand and days of play. Avoid those that have rusted areas or too much damage, especially if it obscures the design. Mint condition boxed sets including sifters, spades and molds can fetch high sums, sometimes up to £500.

A 1950s American lithographed tin sand pail, by Ohio Art Co., artwork by Dan Dean.

5in (12.5cm) high

£20-30   **SOTT**

A 1950s American lithographed tin sand pail, by Ohio Art Company.

7.75in (19.5cm) high

£25-35   **SOTT**

A 1950s American lithographed tin sand pail, by US Metal Toys.

7.5in (19cm) high

£70-100   **SOTT**

A 1950s American lithographed tin sand pail, by T. Cohn.

3.75in (9.5cm) high

£20-30   **SOTT**

An Acme Toys lithographed tin sand pail.

c1960   *5in (12.5cm) high*

£20-30   **DH**

A 1950s American lithographed tin sand pail, by US Metal Toys.

4.75in (12cm) high

£35-45   **SOTT**

A Lilo Product lithographed tin pail.

c1960   *4in (10cm) high*

£25-35   **DH**

TOYS & GAMES

A 1950s American lithographed tin sand pail, by US Metal Toys.

7.5in (19cm) high

£45-55 SOTT

A 1950s American lithographed tin sand pail, by J. Chein.

5.5in (14cm) high

£40-50 SOTT

A 1950s American lithographed tin sand pail, by J. Chein.

Chein, of New York and New Jersey, produced toys from c1903 to 1979. Their tinplate toys are always lithographed and are generally of good quality.

7.25in (18.5cm) high

£40-60 SOTT

A 1940s Happynak Series sand pail.

3.5in (9cm) high

£25-35 DH

A 1950s lithographed tin sand pail, decorated with a flying saucer over a beach.

The theme of space was immensely popular during the 1950s and sand pails with such motifs have cross market appeal and are sought-after, despite the rather incongruous combination of subjects seen here.

5.75in (14.5cm) high

£70-90 DH

A French embossed lithographed tin sand pail, showing two children on a country road.

This is both an early pail and extremely well decorated. It is also in excellent condition for its age, hence its rarity and corresponding high value.

c1900 5.75in (14.5cm) high

£150-250 DH

A 1950s American lithographed tin sand pail, by US Metal Toys.

4.25in (11cm) high

£50-70 SOTT

An American miniature tin sand pail, with striped decoration.

This pail can be dated to the early 20thC by the plain decoration and the simple metal handle. If the pattern were more complex and appealing and it were larger, it would attract a higher value.

c1900-15 2.75in (7cm) high

£12-18 SOTT

FIND OUT MORE...

Sand Pail Encyclopedia: A Complete Value Guide for Tin-litho Sand Toys, by Karen Horman, Polly Minic, published by Hobby House Press, 2002.

TOYS & GAMES

COLLECTORS' NOTES

■ Being less costly, more versatile and enabling the inclusion of finer details, tinplate had overtaken wood and other materials as material for toys by the mid-19thC. Germany grew to be the centre of production, spawning notable names such as Marklin (founded 1856), Gerbruder Bing (1863-1933), Schreyer & Co, known as 'Schuco', (1912-78) and Lehmann (founded 1881). The US also grew to be important with prolific makers including Louis Marx (1896-1912).

■ Tinplate made in the 19thC tends to be hand-painted, before the introduction of more cost effective colour transfer-printed 'lithography'. This tends to be the most desirable, particularly large models of cars and boats by notable makers. The surface tends to be slightly uneven and brush marks can often be seen. Lithographed surfaces tend to be uniformly flat and shinier.

■ After WWII, the centre of production moved to the Far East, particularly Japan. Toys became more novelty in format and often included interesting multiple 'mystery actions', including sound. With the introduction of battery power, lights could also be included. Robots are particularly collectable. In the West, developments in injection-moulded plastic had taken over in the post war period.

■ In all instances, aim to buy examples in as fine condition as possible, particularly post war items which are more numerous and generally less expensive. Additional boxes add value. With items like 'penny toys', small toys sold on late 19thC and early 20thC street corners for one penny, condition is extremely important and a truly mint example will command a considerable premium. Transport toys, particularly elegant cars, planes and zeppelins, tend to be the most desirable forms although novelty figures have an appealing charm that makes them similarly desirable.

An early German tinplate penny toy, in the style of a chauffer driven limousine.

4.5in (11.5cm) wide

£70-100   **W&W**

An early German Georg Fischer tinplate penny toy, in the style of a two draw town sedan, picture of driver to window.

£60-80   **W&W**

An early German tinplate penny toy, in the style of a truck, with driver.

£60-80   **W&W**

An early German tinplate penny toy, in the style of an open limousine, lacks driver.

4.5in (11.5cm) wide

£50-70   **W&W**

A scarce tinplate clockwork military lorry, with driver, canvas rear tilt and simple steering system.

The form and style is very similar to Wells Mettoy.

9.75in (25cm) wide

£150-200   **W&W**

A 1930s German Schuco Examino 4001 clockwork tinplate car.

These forms were also produced after the war.

5.5in (14cm) long

£60-80   **GAZE**

A British GTP lithographed tinplate automatic garage, with three cars and poor condition box.

6in (15cm) wide

£25-35   **GAZE**

A German Schuco lithographed silver tinplate and plastic BMW racing car, signed "BMW Formel 2 260 PS 280 km/h" and model number "1072".

c1969   *10in (25cm) long*

£50-80   **KAU**

A 1960s Japanese Bandai Cadillac lithographed red tinplate gear shift car, with forward, reverse and neutral gears and 'hi' and 'low' speed action, simple steering mechanism and working front lights, boxed.

10.5in (26.5cm) long

£100-150   **W&W**

A Japanese Masudaya TM Modern Toys tinplate and plastic Boeing 727 aircraft, with battery-operated mechanism.

19in (48.5cm) long

£40-60   **GAZE**

A painted tinplate twin-engine transport aircraft, restored.

20in (51cm) wide

£30-40   **GAZE**

A Lehmann EPL 651 silver-gold and red Airship EPL-1, lacks both stabilising flaps, in fair to good condition.

£100-150   **SAS**

A Japanese Haji lithographed tinplate Pan Am Boeing Vertol 707 battery-operated helicopter, with plastic propellers.

Japanese makers often invented or combined elements of design and logos. Surprisingly however, Pan Am did operate shuttle Vertol helicopters.

13in (33cm) long

£70-90   **RBC**

A German tinplate penny toy of a boat, in the style of an early 20th battleship with naval guns and twin funnels, mounted on three wheels.

3.25in (8.5cm) long

£40-60   **W&W**

An early German tinplate penny toy, in the style of an ocean liner, mounted on three wheels.

4.5in (11.5cm) wide

£70-100   **W&W**

A Sutcliffe Nautilus clockwork lithographed tinplate submarine, marked "Nautilus Copyright Walt Disney Productions", complete with key.

This was produced after Walt Disney's '20,000 Leagues Under the Sea' starring James Mason and Kirk Douglas, and was sold into the 1970s. The body was very similar to Sutcliffe's 'Unda Wunda' submarine toy, but was a different colour.

c1954

£35-45   **GAZE**

TOYS & GAMES

An American Marx lithographed tinplate clockwork 'Main St', in superb, bright and shiny condition.

Winding up the toy makes the buses and cars go up and down the street, in and out of the garages. Japanese companies produced similar toys, but they are usually smaller and much less detailed.

1927   24in (61cm) long

£700-900   **TRA**

A late 1920s American Marx 'Busy Bridge' lithographed tinplate clockwork toy.

24in (61cm) long

£300-400   **TRA**

A German Arnold clockwork lithographed tinplate car game 549/1, with a rocket car and looping course, slight damage to original box.

£120-180   **LAN**

An early American Fallows wind up hand-painted tinplate toy, of two horses, cart and cart rider, lacks string reins.

Fallows was founded in Philadelphia the 1880s and took on the Fallow name in 1894. Their toys were hand-painted and of very fine quality - as such as they are much sought-after today. The company closed when lithographed tin toys were introduced during the late 1880s.

c1885   6.25in (16cm) long

£1,000-1,500   **AMJ**

A German Günthermann clock-work handpainted tinplate woman, with an umbrella and basket, partly overpainted and umbrella replaced.

Gunthermann are known for their high quality tinplate toys, often in whimsical forms.

7.25in (18cm) high

£300-500   **LAN**

A German Schuco clockwork police man, marked "Flic 4520, Made in US-Zone Germany'.

c1947   5in (12.5cm) high

£70-100   **GAZE**

A German tinplate clockwork rifleman, in prone position with sparking gun.

4.25in (11cm) long

£100-150   **GAZE**

A 1950s/60s West German Dux Astroman battery-operated plastic robot, lacks antenna and booklet, box with graphics by Arlat.

14in (35.5cm) high

£350-450   **GAZE**

A 1950s Japanese Nomura 'Charley Weaver' lithographed tinplate and rubber bartender.

Nomura, otherwise known as TN, were one of the biggest and most prolific post war Japanese tinplate and plastic toy producers.

12in (30.5cm) high

£15-25 GAZE

A West German lithographed tinplate ice cream vendor and tricycle, with composition and tinplate vendor, marked "Made in US-Zone Germany".

c1950 *4.25in (11cm) high*

£25-35 GAZE

A 1920s German Lehmann lithographed tinplate 'Climbing Monkey', with original box.

The box has a US patent date of 1903. The monkey moves up and down the string. Note that reproductions exist, but generally have brighter colours and checked trousers.

£150-250 GAZE

A CLOSER LOOK AT A TINPLATE TOY

This is the hardest to find of the 'telephone' series' of tinplate toys.

It is in excellent, working condition and has its even rarer original card box.

The lithography is unique and is not found on any other toy from the series.

It is an appealing subject with good multiple actions - the telephone rings and lights up and the teddy speaks.

A scarce 1950s-60s 'Teddy the Manager' battery powered tinplate toy, retailed by Cragston (S&E), boxed.

£200-300 W&W

A 1950s Japanese TPS lithographed tinplate clockwork dog, marked "NGS Made in Japan".

When wound up, this cute puppy's tail spins and his head rocks and ears flap.

5in (12.5cm) high

£50-70 TRA

A 1960s Japanese Masudaya TM Modern Toys battery-operated 'Walking Bear' toy, with original box.

11in (28cm) high

£10-15 GAZE

A 1950s American Wolverine embossed and lithographed tin watering can, with a merry-go-round scene.

10in (25.5cm) high

£18-22 SOTT

COLLECTORS' NOTES

■ Lead figure-making began in Germany in 1777 with Johann Hilpert's commemorative figure of Frederick the Great on horseback. Early figures – Zinnfiguren – were flat. Among the first companies to make three-dimensional figures were Paris-based Lucotte and Germany company Heyde and Haffner.

■ In 1893, William Britain Junior patented a hollow casting process which halved the cost of producing figures. This allowed for the economic manufacture of large numbers of figures and Britains became the largest manufacturer of lead soldiers in the world. The company were responsible for setting the standard figure height as 2in (54mm).

■ The fine detailing and authenticity of their uniforms make Britains soldiers very popular today.

■ After the horrors of the First World War lead soldiers became less appealing to buyers. Companies began to focus on the production of civilian characters such as the farm series.

■ Watch out for customisation, whereby a figure is amended by replacing its head or making other changes. Re-painted areas and a lumpy surface can be signs. Oxidation, a relatively common problem, can destroy fine details and ruin painted finishes, affecting the price of the figure. Look for sets that were not popular at the time of release as these may be scarce and desirable today. Boxes also add to value.

■ When the use of lead in children's toys was banned due to its toxicity in 1966, some manufacturers switched to producing plastic figures.

A Britains Life Guards set 1, comprising five mounted cantering horses, an officer and four troopers, in full dress uniform, with swords drawn.

c1953

£70-100　　　　　　　　　　**W&W**

A Britains Royal Scots Greys set 32, comprising five mounted troopers, in scarlet dress uniform, in original box tied to stringing card.

c1953

£70-100　　　　　　　　　　**W&W**

A Britains Golden Highlanders firing set 157, comprising four standing, three kneeling and three lying figures, in full dress with white helmets.

c1908

£100-150　　　　　　　　　　**W&W**

A Britains 11th Hussars dismounted set 182, comprising four standing horses, three soldiers and an officer with swords drawn.

c1946

£70-100　　　　　　　　　　**W&W**

A Britains British Infantry in Active Service set 195, comprising seven soldiers and an office with a knobbed stick, all with sand-coloured shrapnel helmets, in original box with Whisstock label.

c1916

£70-100　　　　　　　　　　**W&W**

A Britains Grenadier Guards set 312, comprising seven soldiers with rifles shouldered and one officer with a drawn sword, all marching in greatcoats, in original Whisstock labelled box.

c1948

£70-100　　　　　　　　　　**W&W**

A Britains set 1913 Scottish Rifles Cameronians, boxed.

The Cameronians are one of the most sought-after from the Scottish regiments.

£250-350　　　　　　　　　　**W&W**

A Britains French Cuirassiers set 138, comprising four mounted men and an officer with swords, in original box, with post war painting.

£80-120   **W&W**

A Britains Royal Horse Artillery gun team at the gallop set 39, third version, comprising an 18-pounder gun, limber, plain wire tracer, horses with light harness, four galloping outriders and officer.

1924-32

£250-350   **W&W**

A late 1940s Britains West African Togoland Warriors set 202, with seven figures, in original box.

£70-100   **W&W**

A Britains German infantry set 432, marching in grey field dress, in original box, minor damage.

£100-150   **W&W**

A Britains Belgian Grenadiers set 2009, comprising of seven soldiers with rifles shouldered and an officer with sword drawn, all in greatcoats, in original 'Regiments of All Nations' box.

c1948

£250-350   **W&W**

A Britains Swedish Life Guards set 2035, comprising eight marching figures, seven soldiers with rifles shouldered and an officer with his sword sheathed, all in ceremonial dress, in original box tied onto packing card.

c1949

£60-80   **W&W**

A Britains British Army covered tender no. 1433, of half-track rear axle type, with a long bonnet, rubber-tyred front wheels, opening cab doors, drop tailgate and canvas tilt load bed cover on wire frames, with original maroon paper covered box and blue picture lid.

£120-180   **W&W**

A rare Britains 4.5in Anti-Aircraft Gun no. 1522, with elevating, rotating and firing mechanism, with a small searchlight and a Bren Gun Carrier No. 1876.

£250-350   **W&W**

A scarce post-WWII Britains Centurion diecast tank no. 2150, in military olive green, with a rotating turret and elevating gun, solid tracks with four small running wheels.

The version with Desert Warfare finish, issued as no. 2156, is slightly more desirable.

£150-200   **W&W**

Six Britains Salvation Army Figures, second version with shorter skirts, comprising three female Salvationists with 'War Cry', one with tambourine, two empty-handed, very good condition.

£650-750 VEC

Five Britains 'Eastern Peoples', comprising a shepherd, a boy, a man and two women, very good condition, with only minor paint chips.

£150-200 VEC

A Britains 'Wolverhampton Wanderers' Famous Football Teams, comprising ten footballers, goalkeeper, referee, two linesmen, corner flags and goalpost, very good condition, two figures with losses, box with illustrated label, tears and marks.

£700-800 VEC

A rare Britains Railway Station Set 158, 1925 version, 25 pieces comprising 13 passengers and staff, together with trolleys and various pieces of luggage, excellent condition, in very good condition green box with illustrated lid, two edges slightly torn.

£1,000-1,500 VEC

A Britains Rodeo Set 2043, comprising three mounted cowboys, two on foot, steer and wild horse, bench and four seated cowboys, metal fence bases and wooden poles, very good condition, in very good condition box with illustrated label, insert card slightly distorted and with old marks, lid slightly creased.

£700-1,000 VEC

Two rare Britains Tournament knights, together with a mounted marshall, herald and two squires with standards.

£60-100 W&W

A Britains Knight of Agincourt No.1663 mounted knight on rearing horse with lance, minor paint loss to shield, very good condition in very good condition 'stone' type box, no insert.

£80-120 VEC

A Britains Hunt Series, comprising two mounted huntswomen astride, one huntswoman at the gallop side saddle, one huntswoman mounted halted side saddle, one mounted huntsman, two male and two female huntspersons on foot, 14 hounds, mainly good condition, some paint loss overall, one horse's hoof broken.

£250-300 VEC

A Britains Racing Colours of Famous Owners 'The Duke of Norfolk', excellent condition, in very good condition box.

£300-400 VEC

A Britains 'Man with Garden Roller' no. 715, 'Man with Swing Water Barrow' no. 564, 'Man with Wheelbarrow' no. 547 and a lawnmower no. 051, no man, all very good condition.

£70-100 VEC

A Britains 'Boy on Swing' no. 619 and a 'Boy and Girl on See-Saw' no. 618, both in very good condition.

£150-200 VEC

A Britains 'Farm Series' No. 5F green farm wagon, green shafts, red wheels, pair of brown horses and a carter with whips, generally very good condition, paint loss to wagon floor.

£70-100 VEC

A Britains new model 'Tree-trunk' set 58F, with sectional branches, in good condition, together with a 'Horse Rake' set 8F, green with red wheels, brown horse, in good condition.

£50-70 VEC

A Britains 'Model Farm Series' farm display set 120F, comprising four cows, five sheep, two lambs and two hens, together with a set 121F containing three horses, nine sheep, two lambs and two hens, very good condition, in very good condition green boxes, some marks and stains, two lid corners torn.

£150-200 VEC

A collection of 12 Britains Cococubs figures, comprising Mrs Pie Porker, Tiny Tusks, Mr Pie Porker, Squire Rooster, Peter Pum Poodle, and seven further smaller figures, mainly good condition.

£120-180 VEC

A Britains 'Zoological Series' set 32, comprising a lion, a lioness, a camel, a zebra, a gorilla, a kangaroo, two pelicans, two monkeys, two penguins, a polar bear, one coconut palm tree, two date palm trees, very good condition, in a fair white box with illustrated label, corners torn, partially crushed box base ends.

£180-220 VEC

A Britains 'Petrol Pumps' set 101V, comprising National Benzole, BP and Shell petrol pumps mounted onto a grey metal base transfers, complete, very good condition, in very good condition box with illustrated lid.

£150-200 VEC

A scarce 1940s Britains 'Zoo' set 3Z, with two palm trees and assorted animals, in original box.

£220-280 W&W

A John Hill 'Drover' with red flag and stick, together with a tramp with stick and bundle over shoulder, both in excellent condition.

£45-55   VEC

A John Hill 'King Neptune' figure, complete with quadrant, together with a very rare 'Greyhound Race Starter', both in excellent condition.

£70-100   VEC

A collection of 15 John Hill 'Station' figures, comprising a guard with flag and whistle, porter with suitcase, porter with trolley, five pieces of luggage, engine driver with oil on, stoker with shovel, two schoolboys, girl with basket, together with a rare grey punt, all very good condition.

£80-120   VEC

A collection of 18 John Hill 'Station' figures, comprising a station master, two porters with sack barrows, two porters with suitcase, guard with flag and whistle, stoker, two men with straw hats, two gentlemen with bowler hats, lady with parasol, old gentleman with bowler hat, miller and two men carrying sacks, in mainly good condition.

£150-200   VEC

A scarce John Hill three-dimensional scenic play pack no. 2, with a turreted castle background and four mounted guardsmen.

£100-150   W&W

A John Hill 'Miniature Hunting' series, comprising of huntsman standing beside horse, mounted huntsman, mounted huntswoman, huntswoman standing with hound, group of three hounds, together with a (possibly) Heyde small scale mounted huntswoman and Man.

£150-200   VEC

A collection of 26 John Hill 'Cowboys and Indians', two cowboys on bucking broncos, cowboy firing rifle behind lying horse, cowboy firing pistol fixed arm, Indian on horseback rifle broken, mounted cowboy holding rifle, spare horse, eight Indians with tomahawks, four further Indians, one Indian chief, two walking cowboys, two small scale cowboys firing, a cowboy firing rifle, and rare cowgirl with whip, all very good.

£150-200   VEC

An interesting collection of 21 John Hill animals, including horses and foals, four cows, three calves and two bulls, all very good to excellent condition.

£80-120   VEC

A collection of Timpo 'Civilian' figures, comprising four policemen and one policewoman, zoo keeper with broom and two farm girls feeding poultry, some paint loss to one policeman.

£25-35   **VEC**

A collection 11 Timpo 'Railway' figures, comprising station master, guard with flag and whistle, guard with whistle, engineer with lamps, porter carrying luggage, a rare US 'Red Cap' black porter carrying luggage, a mechanic, three policemen and policewoman, all very good condition.

£150-200   **VEC**

A collection of 15 Timpo 'Wild West' figures, comprising a Sheriff, two seated cowboys with guitars, one with accordion, camp fire, one other, three crawling Indians, two with drums, two with bows and arrows, squaw etc, all very good.

£100-150   **VEC**

A collection of 11 Timpo 'Wild West' figures, comprising six seated cowboys with guitars, two with accordions, seated Indian chief, one with drum, squaw with baby, all very good condition.

£90-100   **VEC**

A collection of Timpo mounted cowboys, including Buffalo Bill, two Annie Oakleys, cowboys with lassos, ten horses, all very good condition, some lassos replaced.

£70-100   **VEC**

A collection 21 Timpo 'Farm' figures, comprising farmer, shepherd, drover, two women with pitchforks, woman feeding poultry, carrying pail, milkmaid seated, four men with pitchforks, colour variations, two benches, two bushes, man with hand plough, a very rare water cart, no horse, two ladders.

£150-200   **VEC**

A collection of 24 Timpo 'Farm Animals', four cows, one bull, two calves, one bullock, three horses, a mule, two foals, a pig with piglets, two geese, a duck, four cockerels, a peacock and a dog, all very good condition.

£100-150   **VEC**

A collection of 16 Timpo 'Zoo Animals', a rearing elephant, a baby elephant, a water buffalo, a camel, a lion, a tiger, an eagle, a kangaroo, a monkey on tree, a chimpanzee, a turtle, a penguin, a pelican, a stork, a zoo keeper with broom and rare zoo inspector, all very good condition.

£150-200   **VEC**

A Timpo's 'Arctic' series collection, comprising of a sledge, dog team, 'Eskimo' with whip, shooting rifle and walking, igloo, two penguins, polar bear and two seals, all very good condition, slight dent to igloo.

£70-100   **VEC**

A pre-WWII Charbens 'The Coal Cart', comprising a black coal wagon, brown horse, coalman carrying sack, seven coal sacks, some paint loss to horse, with box and illustrated label, old marks, small edge torn.

£250-300 VEC

A Charbens No. 500 'Gypsy Caravan', comprising of green caravan, red wheels and shafts, cream roof, brown horse, mainly good, some re-touching, replacement front axle, in fair original box with illustrated label.

£200-250 VEC

A Charbens No.817 Tip Cart, yellow cart, red wheels and shafts, brown horse, in excellent condition in very good box.

£70-100 VEC

A post WWII Charbens model 'Tree Wagon', comprising of yellow pole wagon, red wheels, log load, two horse team and driver, minor fatigue to axles and contained in a very good condition box with illustrated label, box base partially split.

£70-100 VEC

A rare 1950s Cherilea 'Journey into Space' set 1001, comprising rocket, six spacemen, three robots, two space animals, in original illustrated box, one helmet missing.

The Journey into Space series is one of Cherilea's most sought-after.

£650-750 VEC

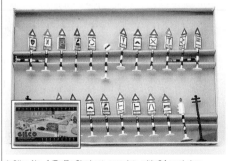

A Gilco No. 4 'Traffic Sign' set, complete with 24 road signs, traffic lights, telegraph poles and two extra Belisha beacons, overall condition good to excellent in good box.

£70-100 VEC

A F.G. Taylor 'Keep Left' road lamp, a cottage with water wheel, a dovecote, a fireplace with kerb, a water pump from a water cart, a deck chair and a vacuum cleaner.

£120-180 VEC

Two F.G. Taylor Roman Chariots, both pulled by two white horses, ten large hedge sections, two small of the same, six straight railing sections, together with two dovecotes, water pump, well and garden seat by unconfirmed makers, Dinky Esso pump station, motorcycle, three station signs.

£120-180 VEC

Five Reynolds pirate figures, by H.R. Products, comprising Cutty Carver, Captain Hook, Black Jack, no sword, Long John Silver and Wall-eye Jim, no pistol, in very good condition.

H.R. Products, also known as Reynolds, was only active for a few years early in the 1950s. Its high-quality figures, many of which were modelled by Norman Tooth who also worked for Timpo, are sought-after today.

c1951

£150-200 VEC

Five Reynolds 'Viking' figures, by H.R. Products, with axe over head, drawing sword, with axe at side, with dagger, dagger broken, and rare chief in light blue cloak, winged helmet and raised sword, all very good condition.

£150-200 VEC

A Little Legion Scots Greys Trooper 1, BW/1, Somerset Light Infantry, 12th Light Dragoons, Officer, Mounted British Infantry, Boer War.

£180-220 VEC

A Roydon Blacksmith's Set, comprising forge, anvil and two blacksmiths, no tools, in very good condition.

£45-55 VEC

A Salco 'Milk Cart', with Pluto and Donald Duck, mainly good condition.

£150-200 VEC

A Taylor & Barrett cat, basket and four kittens, together with a dog, kennel and four puppies, rabbit warren, two rabbits eating carrots, one running, four baby rabbits, all very good condition.

£150-200 VEC

A collection of 13 Taylor & Barrett civilian figures, including zoo visitors, woman and child, twins holding hands, seated man from 'Visitors Tea Set', postman, farmer, cowman, woman feeding lamb, Owl, Dog, seated old woman, two children, in good condition.

£120-180 VEC

A set of six rare diecast space figures, including a Crescent Dan Dare 'Treen' alien and 'Sir Hubert Guest' figure, two Charbens spacemen and two Hill/Cherilea figures.

£100-150 W&W

A Star Wars – The Power of the Force 'Anakin Skywalker' action figure, by Palitoy.

The older version figure of Anakin Skywalker was only produced for a short period of time. In the US it was only available as a loose figure via a mail-in offer. All carded figures were released outside of the US on either a Power of the Force or tri-logo card.

1985   4in (10cm) high

£15-25   **KNK**

A Star Wars – The Empire Strikes Back 'Bossk' action figure.

This rare variation has an unpainted arm, a standard loose example would be worth under £10.

c1980   4in (10cm) high

£100-150   **KNK**

A rare Star Wars – Return of the Jedi 'Lumat' action figure, with bow and unpainted face.

On this rare variation, the face is unpainted. Standard complete figures are worth around £10.

c1984   2.75in (7cm) high

£100-150   **KNK**

A rare Star Wars – Power of the Force 'Amanaman' action figure, lacks skull staff.

First released on a Power of the Force card and then on a tri-logo card, this figure is desirable in any condition, particularly in the US where it is harder to find.

c1985   4.25in (10.5cm) high

£30-50   **KNK**

A Micromachines Star Wars 'Rebel Blockade Runner', by Galoob.

These were only sold in boxed sets and were not available individually.

c1995   2.25in (6cm) long

£1-2   **KNK**

A Micromachines Star Wars – Return of the Jedi 'Speeder Bike with Rebel Pilot'.

c1996   1.75in (4.5cm) long

£1-2   **KNK**

A Star Wars 'Heroes' Super Sonic Power van, gyro-powered with 'Blazin' Action'.

A similarly incongruous Darth Vadar themed van, worth the same, was also produced.

1978   7.25in (18.5cm) long

£30-40   **NOR**

A Star Wars – The Power Of The Force (II) 'Greedo' carded action figure.

This is the first version released under the Power of the Force (II) banner, and the most desirable.

9in (22.5cm) high

£6-8   **KNK**

A Star Wars – The Power of The Force (II) 'TIE Fighter Pilot' carded action figure.

This figure was first issued with the 'small parts' warning on a sticker. Later versions have the warning printed directly onto the card. The first version, shown above, is worth about twice as much as the second version.

1995   9in (22.5cm) high

£6-8   **KNK**

A 19thC English small bone playing chess set, one side stained red, the other side left natural, in a wooden box with a sliding lid.

the king 2.25in (5.5cm) high

£60-100   **BLO**

A unusual 19thC boxwood and ebony old English pattern chess set, the kings with interesting finials, in a mahogany box with a sliding lid.

the king 3in (7.5cm) high

£150-200   **BLO**

A unusual 19thC Jaques Staunton 'coloured' ivory chess set, one side stained yellow, the other side stained green, the yellow king stamped "Jaques London" on the underside of the base, in a mahogany box with a green label.

This is an extremely unusual colour for an ivory set by Jaques. There appears to be no trace of any previous staining, so it can be assumed that the set was dyed at its time of manufacture. One possibility is that this set was used as a prototype to discover the effect of other dye colours apart from the more usual cochineal red then in use.

the king 2.75in (7cm) high

£1,200-1,800   **BLO**

An Irish boxwood and ebony chess set, possibly Dublin, kings with baluster knops and elongated tops with concave finials, queens with large ball finials, bishops with tulip shaped tops, knights as carved horse's heads, rooks as castles with ramparts and reeded decoration, pawns with baluster knops and ball finials, in a mahogany box with a sliding lid.

c1850   the king 3in (7.5cm) high

£300-400   **BLO**

A cast pewter chess set, one side in polished pewter, the other side with an oxidised finish, king topped with crowns and crosses and with multi-knopped columns, queens similar, but of smaller size, bishops with ball finials, knights as horses' heads, rooks as turrets, pawns with baluster knops and ball finials, in a wooden box.

c1930   the king 4in (10cm) high

£300-400   **BLO**

A cast lead 'Rose' chess set, painted red and black, some flaking to paintwork, the design based on the popular Staunton set and patented by Mildred Rose.

1942   the king 2in (5cm) high

£35-45   **BLO**

An English ceramic chess set, one side with a brown glaze, the other side a creamy brown colour, the pieces signed "JU", together with a mahogany and satin-birch chess board.

c1970   the king 3.5in (9cm) high

£150-200   **BLO**

A late 19thC German 'Régence' style boxwood and ebonised chess set, in a wooden box with a sliding lid, the pieces wrapped in original light pink waxed paper.

the king 3in (7.5cm) high

£180-220 **BLO**

A CLOSER LOOK AT A CHESS SET

Max Esser (1885-1943) was born in Pomerania, and studied at the Berlin Academy under August Gaul, before joining Meissen as a designer.

Despite being in delicate porcelain, it is undamaged. Each piece is skillfully hand-painted and gilded, with fine details typical of Meissen.

This famous set was designed in 1923, and would have been expensive to buy.

This set appeals to collectors of Meissen figures as well as chess sets.

A 20thC Meissen porcelain 'Sea Life' chess set, designed by Max Esser, one side a coral colour, the other side grey and white, kings and queens as sea anemones, bishops as lobsters, knights as sea horses, rooks as octopi, pawns as starfish, with Meissen underglaze crossed swords mark in blue.

the king 3.25in (8cm) high

£8,000-12,000 **BLO**

A late 19thC unusual hardwood chess set, possibly German, one side a chesnut brown, the other side dark brown or black, the set of an unusual pattern and design.

Note the Germanic picklehaube 'helmeted' knights and the almost Islamic type pawns.

the king 3.75in (9.5cm) high

£600-800 **BLO**

A 19thC Swiss pearwood 'Bear of Berne' chess set with a nice patination, contained in a 19thC wooden box.

The many different and charming poses, finely carved fruit wood and small details such as crowns make this set sought after.

the king 3.25in (8.5cm) high

£1,800-2,200 **BLO**

A 20thC Portuguese Vista Alegre handpainted porcelain figural chess set, modelled as Medieval Christians versus Moors.

Such religious or political historical themes are typical during the 20thC

the king 4.25in (11cm) high

£1,500-2,000 **BLO**

A scarce Czech Republic silver and silvergilt 'Selenus' pattern chess set, marks for Prague, duty mark for 1810-1824.

This pattern was first seen in "Chess or the King's game" published in 1616 under the assumed name of 'Gustavus Selenus'.

c1815 *the king 2.25in (6cm) high*

£3,500-4,000 **BLO**

A 20thC Italian silver metal heraldic bust chess set, one side with darker, oxidised bases, each piece decorated with coats of arms and stamped '900' and with 'S P' maker's mark.

the king 3in (7cm) high

£1,000–1,500 **BLO**

A mid-20thC Italian olive wood chess set, probably from Sorrento, one side lacquered black, together with a Sorrento inlaid wooden chess board of a later date.

king 2.25in (5.5cm) high

£300-400 **BLO**

A early/mid-19thC Cantonese Chinese export ivory 'puzzleball' chess set, modelled as the Chinese versus the Mongols, all raised on puzzleball bases.

the king 5in (13cm) high

£220-280 **BLO**

A fine Cantonese Chinese export ivory 'King George' chess set, the kings as King George III, queens as Queen Charlotte, bishops as clergy, knights as rearing horses, rooks as elephants bearing towers, pawns as footsoldiers with shields and raised spears.

Green staining on Cantonese chess sets is unusual, the more common colour usually being red. Another rare feature of this set is that there are two European monarch kings and two consort queens. The style of carving on both sides is identical, so we can be sure that this is a complete set from one workshop. This is thus a desirable and valuable example.

c1800 *the king 5in (12.5cm) high*

£2,500-3,000 **BLO**

A fine Cantonese Chinese export ivory figural 'King George' chess set, modelled as the Chinese versus the Europeans, white king and queen as George III and Queen Charlotte, bishops as Christian bishops, knights as archer horsemen, rooks as elephants, pawns as footsoldiers, all raised on oval gadrooned bases.

c1810 *the king 5.5in (14cm) high*

£1,800-2,200 **BLO**

A Cantonese Chinese export 'Burmese' style chess set, the kings and queens with with foliate carved, pierced finials.

Although this set shows some similarities to Indian sets and the so-called 'Burmese' patterns, it is more likely to have been produced in Canton.

c1820 *the king 3.25in (8.5cm) high*

£250-350 **BLO**

A early 19thC Chinese export painted ivory 'King George' chess set, modelled as the Europeans versus the Chinese, the European king and queen as George III and Queen Charlotte and the bishops as mandarins.

the king 4.5in (11.5cm) high

£700-1,000 **BLO**

An early 19thC Cantonese 'Burmese' pattern chess set of large size with extensive finely carved foliate decoration, one red pawn replaced, loss to white queen's filigree top, in a mahogany box.

the king 5.5in (14cm) high

£1,000-1,500 **BLO**

A 20thC Chinese hardwood 'puzzleball' chess set, from Hong Kong, one side in boxwood, the other side in coromandel, all the chessmen with puzzleball knops, in a chip-carved wooden box with a hinged lid.

the king 6in (15.5cm) high

£70-100 **BLO**

A 19thC Cantonese export Staunton-pattern ivory chess set.

the king 4in (10cm) high

£700-1,000 **BLO**

A 20thC Japanese rock crystal and obsidian chess set, with bishops as mitres, knights as horses' heads and rooks as turrets.

king 2.25in (6cm) high

£120-180 **BLO**

A 19thC Anglo-Indian Staunton-pattern ivory chess set, one side stained red, the other side left natural, in a mahogany box with a sliding lid.

the king 2.75in (7cm) high

£350-450   **BLO**

An Indian-export ivory chess set, from Vizagapatnam, each piece with extensive carved foliate and floral decoration, the brown king missing the upper half.

c1810   *the king 5.25in (13.5cm) high*

£700-1,000   **BLO**

An Indian ivory chess set, from Vizagapatnam, the pieces with elaborate and extensive carved decoration, kings with ruff collars and elongated spires, queens similar, but with shorter finials, bishops as mitres with crosses, knights as horses' heads over elaborately decorated circular bases, rooks as raised turrets with flags, pawns with spires, in a mahogany box with a sliding lid.

the king 5.5in (14cm) high

£800-1,200   **BLO**

A 19thC Indian export ivory chess set, the kings with pierced tops and spray finials over nautical crown collars, queens with bud finials, bishops with feathered mitres, knights as horses' heads, rooks as rusticated turrets with spire finials, pawns with baluster knops, in a mahogany, ivory and boxwood inlaid box.

the king 3in (7.5cm) high

£300-400   **BLO**

An Indian ivory 'Elephant' chess set, from Rajhasthan, one side with black stained bases, the other side left natural, kings as elephants with covered howdahs, queens as elephants with a prince in the howdah, bishops as camels, knights as horse, rooks as elephants, pawns as footsoldiers, in a blue presentation case.

c1950   *the king 2.75in (7cm) high*

£150-250   **BLO**

An Anglo-Indian monobloc ivory chess set, the kings with baluster knops and reeded urn-shaped finials, queens with baluster knops and ball finials, bishops with elegant split mitres, knights as horses' heads, rooks as turrets with battlements, pawns with ball finials.

c1820   *the king 3.25in (8.5cm) high*

£700-900   **BLO**

A 20thC Indian carved stone chess set, the kings with pierced crowns, queens similar, bishops with further pierced decoration and elongated finials, knights as horses' heads, rooks as turrets, pawns with domes, together with a wooden box .

the king 2.75in (7cm) high

£40-60   **BLO**

A Northern Indian so called 'Muslim' ivory chess set, one side with green stained rings to the base, the other red.

Research suggests strongly that these 'Muslim' sets were in fact, as much an ancient Hindu pattern used in North India.

c1930   *the king 2.25in (5.5cm) high*

£150-200   **BLO**

An unusual Swiss fully articulated ball-jointed steel plate and aluminium-bodied male figure, with composition head and cigarette.

8in (20cm) high

£40-60   **W&W**

An A.C. Gilbert James Bond 007 action figure, 16101, with instructions, pistol, pistol adaptor, goggles, snorkel and flippers, fair condition, vest torn, in fair condition box, with small paper tear.

c1965

£150-200   **SAS**

A Luntoy (London Toy Company) painted diecast metal articulated 'Mr. Turnip Head' puppet, lacks strings and metal controller.

Along with his friends Sarah Swede and Colonel Beetroot, Mr Turnip Head appeared on 'Whirligig', one of the first children's TV programmes with a variety of characters, that began in 1950. "Lawky Lawky Lum!"

c1953

£40-60   **SAS**

A Pelham Puppets SL21 'Wolf' puppet, with original yellow box.

Founded by Robert Pelham in 1947 as 'Wonkey Toys', the company was Britain's foremost producer of stringed puppets until its closure in 1997. 'Wolf' has a moulded head and can be found in a variety of different clothes.

c1963

£60-70   **ROS**

A Pelham Puppets composition 'Muffin the Mule' puppet.

6.75in (17cm) long

£50-80   **ROS**

A rare 1950s Tri-ang Minic Elephant and Howdah, with clockwork walking action, boxed and with packaging, faded.

Box 8in (20cm) wide

£100-150   **W&W**

A Japanese KT Trademark Cheeky Scotch celluloid dog and tinplate wind-up boot toy, with rare original box.

Celluloid is thin and very easily damaged, this example is in mint condition. Wind him up and the dog spins around the boot.

8.25in (21cm) long

£100-150   **TRA**

A Mettoy for Coral Plastics T17 London Transport Routemaster Bus, with registration number MTY 875, excellent condition, in good condition box.

£40-60   **SAS**

A CLOSER LOOK AT A NOAH'S ARK

Noah's Arks were popular toys in the 19thC, and were deemed special items to be brought out for educational play on Sundays.

The finer the carved and painted detailing and the more complete and numerous the animals are, the more valuable an example is likely to be.

Many of the craftsmen had never actually seen the animals they were carving and used engravings and prints as inspiration. As a result many animals can look very unusual.

A 19thC continental wooden Noah's Ark, with painted exterior decoration, hinged lid and prow door, containing approximately 140 carved wooden animals and eight human figures, some damage and restoration.

Larger examples are worth more. These objects appeal to collectors of folk art as well as to toy collectors.

21.25in (54cm) long

£600-800   **ROS**

An Oscar board game, by Henry Hirst & Son, England, complete.

Board 25.5in (65cm) wide

£25-35   **GAZE**

A Waddingtons 'Bonanza Michigan Rummy Game', produced with permission from NBC.

1964   14.5in (36.5cm) wide

£20-30   **MTS**

An 'Aviation...The Aerial Tactics Game of Attack and Defence' game, by H. P. Gibson & Sons, including a two-fold board, box, rulebook, 42 blue tokens, and 42 red tokens.

An airforce variation of L' Attaque, representing the Royal Air Force just before the Battle of Britain. The naval version was Dover Patrol. Note the anachronistic use of airships.

c1938   Board 15in (38cm) wide

£50-80   **BLO**

A mid-19thC French gold two-piece puzzle or gimmal ring, one part inscribed inside 'Alexandrine', the other 'Rome 12 Mars 1858'.

Puzzle or 'gimmal' rings are actually tokens of betrothal or friendship and derived their names from the Italian 'gemelli' meaning 'twins'.

£180-220   **DN**

A Japanese Zippy Zither, with sheet music, "FMT" trade mark, boxed.

Box 17in (43.5CM) wide

£15-20   **GAZE**

A 1960s Piko Spielwaren child's toy washing machine, with applied "Made in GDR" label, with sterling price sticker.

Box 10.25in (26cm) high

£8-12   **GAZE**

COLLECTORS' NOTES

■ Tribal art is the term used to describe the cultural, ritual and functional production of the indigenous peoples of Africa, Oceania, South East Asia and the Americas. As such, it was primarily made for actual use, rather than for purely aesthetic appreciation.

■ Pieces are collected not only for their deep historical and ethnographic significance, but also for their immense visual impact when displayed in today's eclectic interiors. Many items deal with core human themes such as life and death, fertility and spiritual beliefs. Not all tribes made the same items, and many collectors choose to focus on one notable subject, such as West African masks, Navajo weavings or Southwestern American pottery.

■ Key indicators to value are age and provenance. Older pieces with a verifiable history are generally the most valuable, particularly if they were collected from the

area they originated in before the early 20thC. Wear and use adds patination, which is another good sign to look for, but handle as many original pieces from reputable dealers or auction houses as possible, as this patina can be faked.

■ Most pieces found on the market today date from the late 19thC or 20thC onwards. The fact that pieces were used regularly, combined with the extreme climates of many countries, mean that many older pieces have decayed or been destroyed.

■ Interest in the market has risen greatly in the past decade with the upper end of the market being highly priced and the preserve of experienced and wealthy collectors. However, as so many pieces were produced, particularly in the 20thC, and for the tourist market rather than for use, a great many more people can gain access to this exciting and developing field.

A Navajo 'Teec Nos Pos' woven tapestry, in 14 different colours.

c1980   27in (68.5cm) high

£150-200   **ALL**

A Navajo rug from the Ganado area, in diamond step pattern with crosses.

Geometric patterns are typical of most Navajo weavings and were one of the earliest designs used. Early blankets were made to be worn.

c1980   33in (84cm) wide

£80-120   **ALL**

A Navajo natural coloured hand-spun wool weaving, from the Two Gray Hills area.

c1970   32in (34.5cm) wide

£120-180   **ALL**

A 20thC Southwest Navajo pictorial weaving, in natural and commercially dyed homespun wool, with central cornstalk with various coloured birds and feathers, bordered on length with serrated triangles.

Navajo pictorial rugs tend to date from the 20thC, and were designed to appeal to tourists and the commercial market. Motifs include elements important to the Navajo lifestyle such as corn, livestock and birds.

53in (132.5cm) long

£1,200-1,800   **SK**

A 20thC Southwest Navajo pictorial weaving, with natural and commercially dyed homespun yarns, depicting seven multicoloured Yei figures on a white ground with two-colour border.

A Yei is a Navajo spiritual or holy figure.

59in (147.5cm) wide

£800-1,000   **SK**

A Navajo tapestry, by Gladys Tsosie from Kayenta, Arizona.

c1980   27in (68.5cm) wide

£35-45   **ALL**

A CLOSER LOOK AT A BASKET

A Southwest coiled basketry bowl, the flared form with braided rim, a bold eight-point star at the base, and radiating stepped devices.

c1900　　　　　15.5in (37.5cm) diam

£1,000-1,500　　　　　　　**SK**

Star, flower or concentric patterns are typical motifs of the Havasupai and other Southwestern groups.

The black areas are created using cane made from the long seed pods of the 'Black Devil's Claw'. The seeds from this annual flowering plant are highly nutritious.

Havasupai geometric designs are similar to Western Apache examples, but are generally less complex.

This example came from the Wistariahurst Museum, Massachusetts, so has an identified provenance.

An early 20thC Southwest Havasupai coiled basketry shallow bowl, with bold black geometric designs.

The Havasupai tribe are based in the Havasupai Reservation, Arizona.

11.5in (29cm) diam

£650-750　　　　　　　**SK**

A Native American river cane square-section double trinket basket, from the Chitimacha tribe.

Both the form and patterns of this example are typical of the tribe's work.

c1910　　　　　5in (12.5cm) wide

£550-650　　　　　　　**D&G**

A Southwest pottery olla, with concave base and black and red geometric and abstract floral devices, cream-coloured background.

This olla is from the San Ildefonso village, birthplace of renowned Southwest potter Maria Martinez.

c1900　　　　　11in (27.5cm) diam

£1,200-1,800　　　　　　　**SK**

A Southwest pottery olla, from San Ildefonso, with concave base with black and red geometric and abstract floral devices on a cream-coloured ground.

c1900　　　　　12in (30cm) diam

£1,400-1,600　　　　　　　**SK**

A Native American Pueblo pottery bowl, depicting 'Thunderbird', from the Jeddito tribe.

'Thunderbird' is a powerful bird spirit associated with natural forces such as wind, thunder and lightning. The 'spirit line' on the interior of this bowl is broken so as to allow the spirit of the bird to escape.

8.25in (21cm) diam

£800-1,200　　　　　　　**D&G**

A late 19thC Central Plains Lakota tribe quilled pictorial cloth and hide vest, partially quilled with multicoloured floral and American flag devices on the front, the back with two horses, flags, and abstract floral devices, further decorated with multicoloured ribbons and metallic sequins.

22in (55cm) long

£1,200-1,800　　　　　　　**SK**

A late 19thC Central Plains Lakota tribe beaded boy's vest, of buffalo hide with some cloth trim, fully beaded with multicoloured geometric devices on a white ground.

From the Wistariahurst Museum, MS.

19in (47.5cm) long

£1,200-1,800 SK

A mid-19thC Great Lakes crescent-shaped feathered cape, with two long tabs down the front, feather tufts on the inside, the outside with various domesticated bird feathers sewn on in a bold geometric pattern.

Feathered clothing is fragile and highly susceptible to discolouration, damage and wear.

26in (65cm) wide

£1,200-1,800 SK

An early 20thC Plains painted wood and hide drum, both sides painted with red 'sunburst' variations, together with a drum beater.

18in (45cm) diam

£400-500 SK

An Inuit carved wood mask, with high cheekbones and pierced at the mouth, nostrils, and eyes.

Inuit is the generally accepted modern description for the Alaska, Canada, Greenland, and Eastern Russia-based peoples formerly known as Eskimoes. However, not all groups refer to themselves as 'Inuit' and pieces produced up to the mid-20thC, before the term Inuit was in general use, are often still referred to as 'Eskimo'. The term Inuit will be used here throughout for consistency.

10.5in (26cm) high

£800-1,000 SK

A 20thC Inuit carved wood mask, the hollow stylized form with pierced mouth and protruding upper lip, large cheeks, and brow with small pierced eyes and large pierced nostrils.

As there were few or no trees, wooden masks, often representing influential ancestral figures or spirits, were often made from driftwood.

10in (25cm) high

£800-1,000 SK

An early 20thC Inuit polychrome carved wood mask, pierced at the mouth, nostrils, and eyes, with traces of red pigment at the mouth, overall white pigment, label on the back reads "Eskimo, St. Michaels, Kuskokwim Alaska."

The terrifying or malevolent appearance of many Inuit masks is due to the fact that Inuit saw many spirits as a constant menace in their perilous world.

8in (20cm) high

£1,800-2,200 SK

An early 20thC Inuit polychrome carved wood mask, in the form of a walrus, with pierced mouth, nostrils, and eyes, wood whisker inserts, painted with brick red pigment, black and white kaolin details, collection label on the back reads "Nonivagmiut Eskimo, Nunivak Island, Alaska".

9in (22.5cm) high

£1,200-1,800 SK

A late 20thC North West Coast hand-carved Tlingit-style revival carving of a fighting figure, with dagger.

18in (46cm) high

£35-45 ALL

An early 20thC Inuit hand-carved driftwood fetish, of a figure with flipper arms and whale fluke nose.

8in (20cm) high

£150-200 ALL

An unusual 20thC African hand-carved hardwood figure of a shaman, with an effigy staff and other adornments.

20in (51cm) high

£80-120 ALL

An African Songye carved wood house charm, holding a figure in its arms, embellished with strips of metal, shells and nails and wearing a lizard skin loin cloth, the hollow antelope horn on its head containing 'magical' substances and with a separate figure tied to each shoulder.

Such fetishistic magical materials are known as 'Bishimba'. This figure would have been used to protect a village from death and disease.

67in (170cm) high

£700-800 RTC

Five African Yoruba carved wood Ibeji dolls, comprising three male and two female images, three with trade bead attachments.

Ibeji dolls are the best known Yoruba figures and represent deceased twins. They are treated almost like living children and are honoured with prayers and libations.

11in (28cm) high

£180-220 SK

A mid-20thC African Yoruba Ifa tapper instrument.

Ifa is the divination system used by the Yoruba tribe. The tapper is used at the start of the ritual where a bowl is tapped rhythmically to invoke the presence of past diviners and of Ifa, the god of divination, to help with the subsequent predictions.

8in (20cm) high

£60-80 OHA

Two African carved wood staffs, one with small breasts, brass tacked eyes, and elaborate coiffure, the other with stylized facial features and elongated head, dark patinas, both with stands.

30in (75cm) high

£180-220 SK

An unusual African Zulu War-period knobkerry, with flared hardwood shaft, egg shaped head and a good patina.

27in (68.5cm) long

£280-320 W&W

An African Dan carved wood 'Gaegon' mask, with large protruding beak, the articulated lower jaw with animal hair covering, pierced slit eyes, with dark patina from use.

Gaegon masks are used for singing and dancing during village festivals which, today, are performed for tourists.

9in (22.5cm) high

£600-800 SK

An African Yoruba carved wood helmet mask, the hollow form with pronounced facial features, pierced eyes and elaborate coiffure.

14in (35cm) high

£500-600 SK

A 19thC African carved gourd container.

Although it looks like a dropper bottle, this is actually used for inserting laxative enemas made from berries!

5in (12.5cm) high

£350-450 WJT

An early 20thC headhunter's rattan hat, with bird's beak and additional embellishments, from the Bontoc/Igorot people of the North Phillipines.

10in (25.5cm) high

£1,200-1,800 WJT

An early 20thC headhunter's rattan hat, decorated with a bird's beak and head, from the Highlands of Burma, India.

9in (23cm) long

£350-450 WJT

A 19thC human tooth trophy necklace, from the Kiribati (previously known as Gilbert Islands), South Pacific.

31in (78.5cm) long

£1,200-1,800 WJT

A mid-20thC New Guinea polychrome carved wood headdress, the conical form in the shape of a face with stylized painted features, the rattan headband with feather remnants.

16in (40cm) high

£80-120 SK

A late 19thC Maori carved hardwood 'Taiaha', one end in the form of a stylized effigy head with protruding tongue and abalone inlaid eyes.

The Taiaha club, with its paddle-shaped, tapering blade, was one of the main Maori weapons. Due to its shape it is often mistaken for a spear, with an ornately carved end.

38in (95cm) long

£800-1,000 SK

An early/mid-20thC wooden spear with metal tip, decorated with animal skin, from the Naga Tribe, in the Highlands of Burma and India.

65in (165cm) long

£220-280 WJT

A pair of Vietnamese tribal beaded woven-fibre trousers and a bag, with elaborated beaded and embroidered cuffs, the bag with elaborate finger-woven multicoloured geometric beadwork and brass bell attachments.

Pants 20in (50cm) long

£650-750 SK

An Indonesian Pua woven textile.

Pua textiles are woven primarily by the Iban tribe of Sarawak, Boreo. There are a number of different types including the pua sungit, pua kumbo and pua karab.

£150-200 SK

An early 20thC Asian hand-carved and painted monkey mask, of ironwood or similar hard wood.

8.5in (21.5cm) high

£25-35 ALL

COLLECTORS' NOTES

■ The past two years has seen a popular revival in wristwatches, partly led by fashion magazines and TV programmes promoting a smarter look for men. This has prompted many to invest in a fine quality vintage watch. As well as being inherited or received as gifts, vintage watches are also found at dealers' shops, auctions, shows and flea markets.

■ The style of a watch can help you to date it, although vintage styles are popular with today's makers. Small, round 'pocket watch' like shapes with wire lugs are usually early 20thC. Rectangular watches, or simple circular watches with clean-lined designs are usually from the 1930s. From the late 1940s onwards, watches became highly stylized and more innovative in shape, often taking on the styles of contemporary jewellery.

■ Simple, classic styles, particularly from the 1930s and '50s are popular today. Fine quality watches by names such as Rolex or Longines can often be found at lower prices than contemporary examples, sometimes even in precious metals. 1960s and '70s watches are particularly in vogue with many of today's watchmakers copying these styles. Cases tend to be large and heavy, with futuristic designs and use of stainless steel, colour and plastic.

■ The brand, movement, materials and functions of a watch will help indicate its value. Leading brands, such as Patek Philippe, are highly sought-after and within a brand certain 'iconic' models will be more desirable, such as Cartier's 'Tank'. The quality of the movement is important and should be correct for that particular watch. The more complex the watch is, the more valuable it is likely to be. Most prices given here are taken from the 'World Wide Traders Mark Room Floor'.

A WWI Rolex military silver wristwatch, with 15 jewel movement.

The shape of this watch clearly shows how early wristwatches were derived from pocket watches. Watches of this period often have narrow straps.

1.5in (3.5cm) diam

£350-450　　**GHOU**

An early 1920s Rolex gold-plated ladies' wristwatch, the white porcelain dial with painted red "12".

Although neither the movement nor the dial are signed, the case is usual for Rolex watches of this time.

£450-550　　**ML**

A 1930s Art Deco Rolex elongated rectangular gent's wristwatch, with 17-jewel movement, seconds dial and platinum curved case.

1.75in (4.5cm) long

£4,500-5,500　　**ML**

A 1930s Rolex Precision 14ct rose gold-cased wristwatch, with 17-jewel movement, in mint condition.

£500-700　　**ML**

A Rolex 'Oyster Perpetual Explorer' gentleman's stainless steel bracelet watch.

1.25in (3.5cm) diam

£1,500-2,000　　**GHOU**

A 1950s Tudor Oyster shockproof wristwatch, with dated presentation engraving to back

Tudor has been a sub-brand of Rolex since 1945. Although Tudor movements have fewer jewels than Rolex watches, the same Oyster case is used.

1959

£250-350　　**BLO**

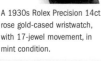

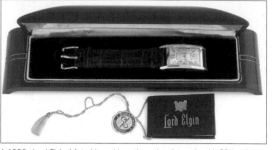

A 1930s Lord Elgin 14ct white gold gentleman's wristwatch, with 23-jewel movement, diamond-set dial, complete with original Art Deco Bakelite box and swingtags.

Lord Elgin denotes higher end watches by Elgin, with 23-jewel movements. This is indicated by the precious metal case and diamond-set dial on this watch.

£450-650   **ML**

A 1930s Elgin wristwatch, with 17-jewel movement, 14ct solid green gold cambered case and radium hands and numbers.

It is more unusual for watches to be made of gold in colours other than yellow, such as green or pink.

£150-250   **ML**

A 1950s Lady Elgin cocktail wristwatch, with 14ct white gold case and unusual conical top winding knob.

£150-200   **ML**

An early transitional Elgin wristwatch, with stainless steel case, the dial set at 90 degrees.

This watch is unusual due to the unusually set dial. It is also transitional, meaning both pendant wound and key wound.

c1920

£70-100   **ML**

A 1950s Lord Elgin 'Dunbar' asymmetric gold-filled cased wristwatch, with 23-jewel movement.

£120-200   **ML**

A 1950s Elgin 19 wristwatch, with 19-jewel movement, gold-filled case, angled lugs and second dial.

The case style with angled lugs here is known as 'horned'

£100-150   **ML**

A Lord Elgin gold-filled wristwatch, with block lugs.

The 'sword' shaped hour and minutes hands are typically 1950s in style.

£140-200   **ML**

A 1950s Lord Elgin Shockmaster 14ct gold-filled wristwatch, with 23-jewel movement, seconds dial, arrow head and dot markers and shaped case.

1.5in (3.5cm) high

£100-150   **ML**

Λ 1930s Longines 14ct yellow gold 'Diamond Dial' wristwatch, with diamond-set gold markers at '12', '3' and '9' and hooded lugs, the 17-jewel movement signed Longines, in original box.

Hooded lug were popular during 1930s, but disappeared afterwards.

£200-250 ML

A 1950s Swiss Longines 'Admiral' gold-filled automatic gentleman's wristwatch, with textured and plain gold 'mystery' face, and case.

A 'mystery' dial has hands or indicators that appear to float with no visible means of movement, but actually move with the central dial.

£150-250 RSS

A mid-1930s Swiss Longines wristwatch, with 'exploding' number dial sterling silver case and raised, curved crystal.

A 1950s Longines stainless steel wristwatch.

A 1970s Longines 'Ultronic' stainless steel diver's watch.

£200-300 ML | **£120-180** RSS | **£150-200** RSS

A 1970s Longines 'Record' automatic sports watch.

A 1930s Hamilton 14ct white gold-cased rectangular wristwatch, with Hamilton 980 17-jewel movement, and sterling silver, diamond-set dial.

A very rare 1930s Hamilton 'Brock' 14ct white gold wristwatch.

These watches are much more common in yellow gold. A similar yellow gold version of this watch would be worth up to £150.

£150-200 RSS | **£500-700** ML | **£500-700** ML

A 1930s Art Deco platinum rectangular wristwatch, with Hamilton 982 19-jewel movement, black diamond-set dial and hooded lugs.

A Hamilton 'Tonnneau Plain' square white gold-filled wristwatch, with 17-jewel movement and oversize numbers.

A 1970s Hamilton gold-plated LED multi-function digital watch.

As with many early digital watches, push the side button to turn the red LEDs on momentarily.

£800-1,200   **ML** | **£120-180**   **ML** | **£250-300**   **PC**

A CLOSER LOOK AT A PAIR OF BULOVA WATCHES

The watches are sometimes known as drivers watches and are designed to fit the wrist, with the case also tapering from top to bottom.

The Art Deco stepped sides are an appealing and period stylistic feature that adds to the value.

A rare 1950s Christmas packaged Bulova pink gold-filled wristwatch, with 17-jewel Bulova movement.

It is rare to find the complete original packaging. The watch on its own can be worth up to £100.

7in (18cm) high

£150-200   **ML**

A 1960s Bulova stainless steel wristwatch, with two-tone blue enamelled face.

1.75in (4.5cm) high

A 1930s Bulova Art Deco ladies' cocktail wristwatch, with 14ct gold case and strap, set with diamonds and rubies.

It is very rare to find a matching set of a ladies' and a gentleman's watch of this type.

These examples are in excellent condition. Due to the many protruding edges the gold-plating can wear off easily over time.

A matching pair of 1930s Bulova 'Right Angle' 10ct rolled gold-cased wristwatches.

£70-100   **ML** | **£150-200**   **ML** | **Left: £100-150 Right: £150-200**   **ML**

A 1970s Baume & Mercier 18ct gold gentleman's wristwatch, with 17-jewel movement.

£300-400   **BLO**

A 1970s Longines 'Record' automatic sports watch.

£150-200   **RSS**

A 1970s French Pierre Cardin asymmetric 'fashion' stainless wristwatch.

Cardin produced unisex watches, many of which have large, shaped cases in a futuristic style that matched his clothing designs.

1.5in (4cm) widest

£120-180   **ML**

A 1970s French Pierre Cardin stainless steel circular 'fashion' wristwatch, with silvered dial and simple markers and hands.

Early Cardin watches like this used high quality Jaeger Le Coultre watch movements.

£120-200   **ML**

A 1950s Le Coultre gentleman's wristwatch, with 14ct gold case, 17-jewel movement and unusual scalloped lugs.

£250-350   **ML**

A CLOSER LOOK AT A JAEGER LE COULTRE WATCH

These early Jaeger Le Coultre alarm watches are becoming increasingly collectable. The alarm was one of Le Coultre's best features of the period, along with the Powermatic model.

The alarm, developed by 1952, is operated by turning the winder to move the central dial so that the arrow points to the time for the alarm.

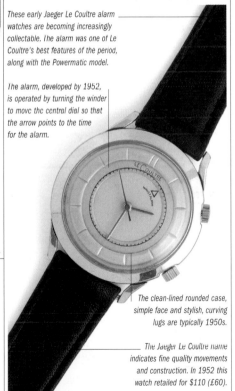

The clean-lined rounded case, simple face and stylish, curving lugs are typically 1950s.

The Jaeger Le Coultre name indicates fine quality movements and construction. In 1952 this watch retailed for $110 (£60).

A 1950s Jaeger Le Coultre 'Wrist Alarm' gold-filled gentleman's wristwatch, with 17-jewel movement and internal bell alarm.

£200-300   **ML**

A 1960s Dunhill gentleman's silver wristwatch.

Vintage Dunhill pieces are highly sought-after for their high quality and comparative rarity.

£800-1,200   **BLO**

A 1930s Gruen Curvex 'Precision' wristwatch, with 14ct white gold strap and case, faceted magnifying crystal, and inset diamonds at '12', '3' and '9'.

Gruen's Precision range was guaranteed to meet US railroad standards for accuracy.

£400-550 ML

A CLOSER LOOK AT A GRUEN WATCH

Curved, rectangular watches were highly fashionable during the mid-1930s. Gruen developed a special standard-sized curved 'Curvex' movement in 1935 that allowed cases to become truly curved.

Despite being launched with great fanfare, and being aimed at young people through selected advertising, they were not commercially successful and had disappeared by 1940, only reappearing briefly in 1950 and in the 1990s.

'Ristside' driver's watches developed from these and are amongst the most sought-after Gruen watches today. The highly curved case ensured the watch stayed on the side of the wrist only, making it easily visible when driving.

The case style with parallel lines identify this model as the 'Lord', one of the first Ristside driver's watches, available from 1937.

A Gruen Precision Curvex Ristside 'Lord' driving wristwatch, with 17-jewel Curvex '330' movement, gold-filled case, silver dial with second dial and gold hands and numbers.
c1937 1.5in (4cm) high

£400-650 ML

A 1930s American Illinois white gold-filled wristwatch, with 19-jewel movement and fancy 'Marquis' engraved case.

£150-200 ML

An American Illinois wristwatch, with 17-jewel movement, and 'Special' nickel-plated case.
1929

£150-250 ML

A 1930s Movado 'Non Magnetic' 14ct pink gold wristwatch, with Zenith 17-jewel movement.

To prevent watches stopping when they became magnetised, Tissot developed a non-magnetic hair spring in 1930. It was soon adopted by other manufacturers.

£120-180 ML

A Swiss Louvic gold-filled 'coin' watch, with 17-jewel movement, the sprung hinge lid embossed with the reverse of a coin.
1.5in (3.5cm) diam

£120-180 ML

A late 1960s Swiss Nileg chrome-plated wristwatch, with 17-jewel movement, the black dial marked "17 RUBIS Incabloc".

Incabloc relates to a branded shock absorber for a watch's movement.

1.5in (4cm) high

£70-100   **ML**

A 1930s Omega wristwatch, with 15-jewel movement, and unusual hands.

£120-180   **ML**

An Omega 18ct white gold ladies' cocktail bracelet wristwatch, with diamond-set lugs, cal. 484 17-jewel movement, triple signed.

0.75in (1.5cm) diam

£450-550   **GHOU**

An Omega military issue wristwatch, once belonging to Lieut. E.G. Maund, D.F.M, R.N.V.R, pattern H.S.8, in original box with provenance.

Provenance can add to the value of a watch, particularly if the owner was notable or famous.

£180-220   **ROS**

An American Pierce gold-filled dress wristwatch, with 17-jewel movement, inset diamanté and curving curled applications, steel back.

£40-50   **ML**

A French Alain Silberstein quartz wristwatch.

Silberstein is a French architect who owns his own watch company producing 'designer' watches that became popular in the 1990s.

£300-350   **RSS**

A Swiss Tressa Lux 'Space Man' chrome-plated steel wristwatch, with original Corfam plastic strap.

This watch was designed by Andre Le Marquand in 1972 and was based on the helmets worn during the 1969 moon landing. He was also responsible for the famous Spaceman Audacieuse.

£350-400   **RSS**

A 1960s Waltham Self Winding wristwatch, with 17-jewel Incablock movement.

1.5in (4cm) high

£100-150   **ML**

A 1960s/70s Swiss Wittnauer dual timezone wristwatch, with oval gold-filled case.

1.5in (3.5cm) diam

£100-150   **ML**

FIND OUT MORE...

Wristwatch Annual 2006: The Catalog of Producers, Models & Specifications, *published by Abbeville Press, 2006.*

Wristwatches: A Connoisseur's Guide, *by Frank Edwards, published by Firefly, 1997.*

COLLECTORS' NOTES

■ Launched in 1983, the first Swatch range of twelve watches was plain in comparison to today's brightly coloured, heavily designed models. Since then, the company has released two new collections every year.

■ Conceived as fun, disposable 'second watches', hence the contraction 'Swatch', they were inexpensively produced, consisting of only 51 components in a plastic case. They were marketed at an affordable price, and proved extremely popular. By 1984 over one million units had been produced.

■ Many well-known designers and artists worked with Swatch including Keith Haring, Kiki Picasso, Vivienne Westwood and Christian Lacroix. Today their models are some of the most sought-after by collectors.

■ Swatch collecting reached a peak in the early 1990s. While the market is not as strong as it once was, there is a smaller but stable marketplace for discontinued and limited edition models and a number of dedicated websites and internet auctions. Some models can fetch high prices: an original 1984 'Jelly Fish' can be worth several hundred pounds.

■ Look for watches in mint, unworn condition, with the original packaging and paperwork. These are the most desirable and will hold their value better.

■ Check that the strap is original and correct for the model – a replaced strap can reduce the value of a Swatch by half. Buckle marks also reduce the value, but there are methods for flattening bent straps.

A Swatch '12 Flags' wristwatch, GS 101, from the Skipper series, with black strap.

A '4 Flag' variation was also available.

1984

£150-200 ML

A Swatch 'Yamaha Racer' wristwatch, GJ 700, from the Coral Reef series, with black strap.

1985

£120-180 ML

A Swatch first series wristwatch, GB 701, with black plastic strap, stamped "C84".

1983

£180-220 ML

A Swatch 'Nicholson' wristwatch, GA 705, from the Plaza series, with date function and black strap.

1985

£80-120 ML

A Swatch 'Black Magic' ladies' wristwatch, LB 106, from the Carlton series, with shiny gold hands and black strap.

The 1988 version of this watch (LB 119) has matte gold hands and is usually worth half the value of this.

1985

£70-100 ML

A Swatch 'Sir Swatch' wristwatch, GB111, from the Coat of Arms series, with replaced black strap.

This model was available as a Maxi at approximately half the value. Look for the rare special gift set, which can have a value of £150-200.

1986

£30-40 ML

A Swatch 'Ping Pong White' wristwatch, GW105, from the Calypso Beach series, with white strap.

1986

£40-50 ML

A Swatch 'Ruffled Feathers' wristwatch, GF 100, from the Kiva series, with brown strap.

1986

£25-35 ML

A Swatch 'Commander' wristwatch, GB 115, from the Nakiska series, with black ridged strap.

1987

£50-70 ML

A Swatch 'Newport Two' ladies' wristwatch, LW108, from the Indigo Blues series, with blue strap.

1987

£50-80 ML

A Swatch 'Pulsometer' wristwatch, GA 106, from the Connaught series, with black ribbed strap.

1987

£15-20 ML

A Swatch 'X-Rated' wristwatch, GB 406, from the Neo Geo series, with black ribbed strap.

1987

£120-180 ML

A Swatch 'Calafatti' wristwatch, GK 105, from the Vienna Deco series, with clear and black striped strap.

As with other clear plastic straps, this one has faded to yellow over time.

1987

£40-50 ML

A Swatch 'Blue Bay' ladies' wristwatch, LK 106, from the Color Tech series, with ribbed grey band.

1987

£20-30 ML

A Swatch 'Hearstone' wristwatch, GX 100, from the Heavy Metal series, with brushed chrome-plated case and ribbed black strap.

1988

£40-60 ML

A Swatch 'Rosehip' wristwatch, GP 100, from the Alfresco series, with textured clear strap.

The strap and the case tend to discolour over time to green.

1989

£60-80 ML

A Swatch 'Glowing Arrow' wristwatch, GX 109, from the M.O.C.A series, with metallic grey strap.

This model was also made with a 'twist-o-flex' band, GX 110/111, which can be worth double.

1989

£35-45 ML

A Swatch 'Greenroom' wristwatch, GN 103, from the Bondi Beach series, with transparent fuchsia strap.
1989
£40-60   ML

A Swatch 'Gilda's Love' wristwatch, GB 133, from the Desert Flowers series, with stamped burgundy leather strap.
1990
£25-35   ML

A Swatch 'Hice-Speed' ladies' wristwatch, LL 110, from the Cold Fever series, with decorated white strap.
1991
£10-20   ML

A Swatch 'Rave' wristwatch, GK 134, from the D.J. Ten-Strikes series, with decorated clear strap.
1991
£10-20   ML

A Swatch 'In Our Hands' automatic wristwatch, released for the first Earth Summit, in Rio de Janeiro, boxed and with original receipt for £47.50 from Croydon's department store.
1991   Box 9.75in (25cm) long
£15-25   GAZE

A Swatch 'Time & Stripes' Automatic wristwatch, SAN 105, with skeleton back, window face and striped strap, with original packaging.
1993
£18-22   ML

A Swatch 'Tisane' wristwatch, GK 162, from the Tranquille series, with patterned blue strap.
1993
£12-18   ML

A late 1980s Swatch Guard Too watch guard, mint and boxed.
£2-3   ML

A Swatch red replacement watch strap.
The packaging helps date the strap.
1985-6   6.75in (17.5cm high)
£7-9   ML

FIND OUT MORE...

www.swatch.com - Official company website.

www.etswatch.com - Collectors' website with a comprehensive list of models.

W. B. S. Collector's Guide for Swatch Watches, by Wolfgang Schneider, published by W B S Marketing, October 1992.

Almost Everything You Need to Know About Dealing & Collecting Swatch Watches, by Roy Ehrhardt, Larry Ehrhardt, published by Heart of America Press, October 1996.

WINE & DRINKING

COLLECTORS' NOTES

■ Perhaps the most collectable item in this area is the corkscrew, with many collectors choosing this focus due to the enormous range in types and prices. The first recorded mention of a screw being used to draw a cork was in 1681, but it was the 19thC, the 'age of invention', that saw many thousands of patents being issued for different designs.

■ Corkscrews can be classified into two types; 'straight pull', where the strength of the user is used to draw the cork out, and 'mechanical', where a mechanism helps to draw out the cork. It is usually the latter category that is the most interesting, desirable and valuable. The former category can, however, provide key examples of vintage pieces at more affordable prices.

■ Look for examples with ingenious mechanisms, or those made from precious materials or with maker's

names. Such names can often help to identify the date of the patent, although many corkscrew designs were copied by other makers at a later date. Damage to the end of the screw (or worm) and missing or replaced parts will also devalue a corkscrew.

■ Cocktail shakers risen in value immensely over the past decade and are a collecting area of their own. Some are very rare, particularly those that would have been expensive in their day, often being made from precious materials, or those that display fine Art Deco design features of the period.

■ Names such as Revere and Asprey are highly valuable and desirable, as are those in novelty shapes from the 1930s. Items from the 1950s are becoming increasingly sought-after, although many tend to be less well-made. In general, always look for good design, fine quality or else for a sense of fun and novelty!

A straight-pull corkscrew, with naturally formed and coloured Scottish stag antler handle, turned steel stem and plain helical worm.

c1890   4.75in (12cm) long

£10-15   **CSA**

A late19thC/early 20thC nickel-cased pocket corkscrew.

The handles of these corskscrews unscrew and detach from the middle, with the worm folding in, to be stored within the tube for easy portability.

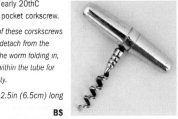

c1900   2.5in (6.5cm) long

£40-60   **BS**

An early 20thC American Clough-type advertising corkscrew, the wooden handle with wire fitting for hanging.

Clough-types were made from one piece of wire formed into a corkscrew by machine. The process was invented by W. Rockwell Clough in 1875 and most examples are inexpensive advertising corkscrews such as this.

£25-35   **CA**

An early 19thC Henshall-type straight-pull corkscrew, with wooden handle with brush and 'button'.

The metal disc, or 'button', gripped the top of the cork, helping to unstick it from the sides of the bottle. The wooden handle was used for brushing cork or dust remains from the lip.

3.5in (9cm) wide

£50-60   **MUR**

A cast brass two-finger figural ship corkscrew.

c1930   7in (17.5cm) long

£12-14   **CSA**

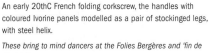

An early 20thC French folding corkscrew, the handles with coloured Ivorine panels modelled as a pair of stockinged legs, with steel helix.

These bring to mind dancers at the Folies Bergères and 'fin de siecle' Europe.

2.25in (6cm)

£250-350   **ROS**

An early 1930s American Demley chrome-plated novelty folding corkscrew, of a gentleman in a top hat, inscribed "Old Snifter".

This was based on Senator Volstead, the Prohibitionist, and the reactions of noted US cartoonist Rollin Kirby's cartoons about Prohibition.

6.5in (16.5cm) high

£35-45 **GORL**

An early 19thC German or French brass mechanical corkscrew, with button and wire helix.

£55-65 **MUR**

A German sprung stem miniature open frame corkscrew, with Archimedean screw and turned ivory grip.

c1890   3.5in (9cm) long

£50-70 **CSA**

A 1950s English 'Valenzina' butterfly double-action metal corkscrew, with registered design number 857383 for 1949.

c1950   9.5in (24cm) long

£12-18 **CSA**

An early to mid-19thC Dowler Patent corkscrew, with turned wooden handle and brass barrel with applied 'Ne Ultra Plus' heraldic shield.

This is a variation of the Thomason-type, where the second (larger) handle is turned to move the screw worm upwards into the barrel on two vertical tracks inside the barrel. The smaller, upper handle twists the screw worm into the cork.

7.75in (20cm) long

£600-800 **SWO**

A Lund-patent two-piece corkscrew, in good condition.

This 'scissor' design was first registered by Edmund Burke in 1854, with London retailer Lund's version, with its separate worm, being registered in 1855. It can be hard to find the two separate parts together.

c1880   8in (20cm) wide

£70-100 **MUR**

A CLOSER LOOK AT A CORKSCREW

The 'Thomason' type uses a specially designed internal double helix enabling the screw worm to be forced into the cork and the cork extracted with continuous turning.

The mechanism and design were patented in 1802 by Sir Edward Thomason, but were made during the 19thC by other companies including Dowler, Wilmot and Roberts after the patent had expired 14 years later.

This example is particularly notable due to its decorated barrel, most have plain barrels with turned bands and an applied heraldic shield and usually are worth around £200-400.

This example lacks its handle brush for removing detritus from the bottle lip - surprisingly, this does not affect the value considerably, but if the handle was replaced or damaged, the value would be affected.

A James Heeley and Sons, 'A1 Patent Double Lever' steel corkscrew.

c1890

6.75in (17cm) high

£50-70 **ROS**

A mid-19thC Thomason type double-action corkscrew, with turned ivory handle and steel helix within a brass barrel with low relief fruiting vine decoration.

7.5in (19cm) high

£750-850 **ROS**

A 1920s French double-pronged Mumford-type cork extractor, with case.

This was designed by Lucian Mumford of San Francisco in 1879, and uses the two 'blades' to grip the cork inside the bottle neck and then gently pull it out as it is twisted. The cork can also be re-inserted using the same device after a half drunk bottle has been topped up, leading this to become a sneaky drinker's favourite!

3.75in (9.5cm) long

£10-15   CSA

A good 1920s champagne tap, with turned wooden handle.

Champagne taps are screwed into the cork, which is not removed. The bottle is tipped up, the valve opened and small amounts of champagne can be poured through the hollow screw and tube at will without losing the fizz.

6in (15cm) long

£80-120   BS

A Victorian champagne tap, with detachable spike.

4.5in (11.5cm) long

£10-12   CSA

A champagne tap, marked "A.N. & Co.", with case.

c1890   5.25in (13.5cm) long

£30-50   CSA

A CLOSER LOOK AT A COCKTAIL SHAKER

The Revere Copper & Brass Co. are known for their fine quality metalwares, usually in Art Deco styles.

This shaker was designed in 1938 by their Director of Design, William Archibald Welden, who was also responsible for the less glamorous, but very popular, copper bottomed stainless steel cookware.

Its curving handle, clean-lined design and architectural appearance, that bring skyscrapers to mind, are essentially Art Deco.

The use of undecorated polished chrome surfaces, that are undented and unscratched on this example, and bright plastic elements are again typical of the period.

An American Revere 'Empire' chrome-plated brass cocktail shaker, with yellow Catalin trim on the spout lid and spire finial.

12.5in (32cm) high

£1,500-2,000   MI

An American Art Deco Manning Bowman chrome-plated metal 'Connoisseur' cocktail shaker, with stepped chrome and yellow bakelite lid.

12in (30.5cm) high

£120-180   MI

A 1970s plastic cocktail shaker, with metal lid and printed design of period advertisements.

9.75in (24.5cm) high

£10-15   MTS

A Swedish Art Deco Guldsmeds Aktie Bolaget of Stockholm silver-plated nickel cocktail shaker, with black Bakelite lid, engraved with lines enhancing the curvilinear form, designed by Folke Arstrom.

1935   8.5in (20cm) high

£1,000-1,500   MI

A 1950s Canadian chrome-plated cocktail set, marked "GH", with red cast phenolic plastic handles.

The superb condition, appealing Art Deco-style design and usefulness of this piece make it desirable and valuable.

£150-200   **GROB**

A 1950s Canadian chrome-plated cocktail set on a revolving stand, with red cast phenolic handles.

It is hard to find sets such as this together in complete, undamaged condition.

13.75in (35cm) high

£180-220   **GROB**

A 1950s enamelled metal 'Rolls Royce' decanter and glass set, with moulded glass decanters and shot glasses.

These novelty pieces are becoming more sought-after, particularly in complete condition and if they attract buyers from other markets, such as automobilia.

16.5in (42cm) wide

£100-150   **DETC**

A pair of amusing glass decanters, painted to represent the Kaiser Wilhelm II and his wife, Augusta.

c1914   *8in (20.5cm) high*

£40-60   **CA**

A 1930s 'Penguin' chrome-plated ice bucket, by the West Bend Aluminum Co. of West Bend, Wisconsin, USA, with mottled brown Bakelite handles and finial.

10.25in (26cm) wide.

£15-25   **ANAA**

An Japanese battery-powered cocktail shaker, in the form of a vinyl doll, with clip holder to hold a drinking glass fitted to her waist, distributed by Poynter Products Inc. of Cincinnati Ohio.

Turn her on and her vibrating hips mix your drink!

c1969   *15.5in (38.5cm) high*

£100-150   **MTS**

A wooden folk-art model of a monkey bartender, in front of a mirrored bar with various labelled bottles of liquor.

c1935   *9in (23cm) wide*

£100-150   **DETC**

A 1950s unmarked ceramic 'cowboy' decanter and shot glasses set, with slots in his chaps to hold the barrel-shaped glasses, his head the stopper.

Cowboys were a particularly popular character in the 1950s.

10.5in (26cm) high

£25-35   **PSI**

Four 1940s American Art Deco Revere Copper & Brass Co. chrome and green Bakelite 'Empire' cocktail cups, designed by William A. Weldon.

1938   *3.25in (8.5cm) high*

£220-280   **MI**

FIND OUT MORE...

Corkscrews for Collectors, *by Bernard Watney & Homer Babbidge, published by Sotheby's Parke Bernet, 1983.*

The Ultimate Corkscrew Book, *by Donald Bull, published by Schiffer Publishing, 1999.*

A 1930s French wooden 'dumb waiter', carved and painted with a red tailcoat and blue trousers.

Despite their politically incorrect nature, these items have been rising in value steadily over the past ten years. They were made to stand next to a chair or at the side of a room and act as drink stands or ashtrays. They were popular from the late 19thC until the late 1930s, although reproductions are often seen today. The more complex and and realistic the carving and painting, or the more unusual the subject, the higher the value.

35.5in (88.5cm) high

£100-150　　　**KAU**

A late 19thC cast iron horse's head, from a fairground carousel, in good condition but with wear to the paint.

£120-180　　　**MUR**

A large late 19thC lobster claw, painted to emulate the head of Mr Punch.

18.75in (30cm) high

£500-700　　　**DN**

A late 19thC French painted canvas and carved wood ventriloquist dummy's head, with glass eyes, a lever at the nape of the neck moves the bottom lip up and down.

9in (23cm) high

£300-400　　　**ANAA**

A mid-19thC silver plated and leather dog collar, with applied silver plaque engraved 'Won by Dick at Birmingham, in a sweepstakes, 12 rats each, dogs of all weigh, Nov.10', with hallmarks for Birmingham, 1852.

1852　　　*3.75in (9.5cm) diam*

£600-800　　　**LFA**

An unusual late 19thC iron animal trap.

£40-60　　　**MUR**

A CLOSER LOOK AT A VAMPIRE PROTECTION KIT

Vampire hysteria spread through 17thC & 18thC Eastern Europe, based on legends of Russian 'Upir' demons, but there are no records of specialised anti-vampire kits from this period.

Stories of this hysteria combined with the factual historic tale of Romanian ruler 'Vlad the Impaler' influenced Bram Stoker who published novel 'Dracula' in 1897.

The publication of 'Dracula' caused a widespread sensation which led to the creation of anti-vampire items, which were meant as whimsical 'talking points' rather than practical items.

Beware of 'Vampire Killing Kits' by Professor Ernst Blomberg and bearing a gun by Nicholas Plomdeur – a British vintage firearms dealer claims to have made this kit in 1972. Copies were subsequently made by others.

A late 19thC 'Vampire Protection Kit' made by the 'Lord's Protection Company' in London, including everything mythically and culturally associated with the killing of and protection from vampires.

Such complex, well made and complete period 19thC kits are scarce. Many of the ways of killing vampires were devised by Stoker. Beware of examples made for amateur theatrical productions.

Box 22in (56cm) wide

£6,000-9,000　　　**WJT**

GLOSSARY

A

Acid etching A technique using acid to decorate glass to produce a matt or frosted appearance.

Albumen print Photographic paper is treated with egg white (albumen) to enable it to hold more light-sensitive chemicals. After being exposed to a negative, the resulting image is richer with more tonal variation.

Applied Refers to a separate part that has been attached to an object, such as a handle.

B

Baluster A curved form with a bulbous base and a slender neck.

Base metal A term describing common metals such as copper, tin and lead, or metal alloys, that were usually plated in gold or silver to imitate more expensive and luxurious metals. In the US, the term 'pot metal' is more commonly used.

Bisque A type of unglazed porcelain used for making dolls from c1860 to c1925.

Boards The hard covers of a book.

Brassing On plated items, where the plating has worn off to reveal the underlying base metal.

C

Cabochon A large, protruding, polished, but not faceted, stone.

Cameo Hardstone, coral or shell that has been carved in relief to show a design in a contrasting colour.

Cameo glass Decorative glass made from two or more layers of differently coloured glass, which are then carved or etched to reveal the colour beneath.

Cartouche A framed panel, often in the shape of a shield or paper scroll, which can be inscribed.

Cased Where a piece of glass is covered with a further layer of glass, sometimes of a contrasting colour, or clear and colourless. In some cases the casing will be further worked with cutting or etching to reveal the layer beneath.

Charger A large plate or platter, often for display, but also for serving.

Chromolithography A later development of 'lithography', where a number of printing stones are used in succession, each with a different colour, to build up a multi-coloured image.

Composition A mixture including wood pulp, plaster and glue used as a cheap alternative to bisque in the production of dolls' heads and bodies.

Compote A dish, usually on a stem or foot, to hold fruit for the dessert course.

Craze/Crazed/Crazing A network of fine cracks in the glaze caused by uneven shrinking during firing. It also describes plastic that is slowly degrading and has the same surface patterning.

Cuenca A technique used for decorating tiles where moulded ridges separate the coloured glazes, like the 'cloisonne' enamelling technique.

Cultured pearl A pearl formed when an irritant is artificially introduced to the mollusc.

D

Damascened Metal ornamented with inlaid gold or silver, often in wavy lines. Commonly found on weapons or armour.

Dichroic Glass treated with chemicals or metals that cause it to appear differently coloured depending on how it is viewed in the light.

Diecast Objects made by pouring molten metal into a closed metal die or mould.

Ding A very small dent in metal.

E

Earthenware A type of porous pottery that requires a glaze to make it waterproof.

Ebonized Wood that has been blackened with dye to resemble ebony.

E.P.N.S. Found on metal objects and standing for 'electroplated nickel silver', meaning the object is made from nickel which is then electroplated with silver.

F

Faience Earthenware that is treated with an impervious tin glaze. Popular in France from the 16th century and reaching its peak during the 18th century.

Faceted A form of decoration where a number of flat surfaces are cut into the surface of an object such as a gem or glass.

Faux A French word for 'false'. The intention is not to deceive fraudulently but to imitate a more costly material.

Finial A decorative knob at the end of a terminal, or on a lid.

Foliate Leaf and vine motifs.

G

Guilloché An engraved pattern of interlaced lines or other decorative motifs, sometimes enamelled over with translucent enamels.

H

Hallmark The series of small stamps found on gold or silver that can identify the maker, the standard of the metal and the city and year of manufacture. Hallmarks differ for each country and can consist only of a maker's or a city mark. All English silver made after 1544 was required to be fully marked.

IJKL

Incised Applied to surface decoration or a maker's mark that has been scratched into the surface of an object with a sharp instrument.

Inclusions Used to describe all types of small particles of decorative materials embedded in glass.

Iridescent A lustrous finish that subtly changes colour depending on how light hits it. Often used to describe the finish on ceramics and glass.

Lithography A printing technique developed in 1798 and employing the use of a stone upon which a pattern or picture has been drawn with a grease crayon. The ink adheres to the grease and is transferred to the paper when pressed against it.

MNO

Millefiori An Italian term meaning 'thousand flowers' and used to describe cut, multi-coloured glass canes which are arranged and cased in clear glass. When arranged with the cut side facing the exterior, each circular disc (or short cane) resembles a small flower.

Mint A term used to describe an object in unused condition with no signs of wear and derived from coinage. Truly 'mint' objects will command a premium.

Mount A metal part applied to an object made of ceramic, glass or another material, with a decorative or functional use.

Nappy A shallow dish or bowl with a handle used for drinking.

Opalescent An opal-like, milky glass with subtle gradations of colour between thinner more translucent areas and thicker, more opaque areas.

P

Paisley A stylized design based on pinecones and foliage, often with added intricate decoration. It originated in India and is most often found on fabrics, such as shawls.

Paste (jewellery) A hard, bright glass cut the same way as a diamond and made and set to resemble them.

Patera An oval or circular decorative motif often with a fluted or floral centre. The plural is 'paterae'.

Piqué A decorative technique where small strips or studs of gold are inlaid onto ivory or tortoiseshell on a pattern and secured in place by heating.

Pontil A metal rod to which a glass vessel is attached when it is being worked. When it is removed it leaves a raised disc-shaped 'pontil mark'.

Pot metal Please see 'Base metal'.

Pounce pot A small pot made of wood (treen), silver or ceramic. Found on inkwells or designed to stand alone, it held a gum dust that was sprinkled over parchment to prevent ink from spreading. Used until the late 18th century.

Pressed (Press moulded) Ceramics formed by pressing clay into a mould. Pressed glass is made by pouring molten glass into a mould and pressing it with a plunger.

R

Reeded A type of decoration with thin raised, convex vertical lines. Derived from the decoration of classical columns.

Relief A form of moulded, pressed or carved decoration that protrudes above the surface of an object. Usually in the form of figures of foliate and foliage designs, it ranges in height from 'low' to 'high'.

Repoussé A French term for the raised, 'embossed' decoration on metals such as silver. The metal is forced into a form from one side causing it to bulge.

S

Sgraffito An Italian word for 'little scratch' and used to describe a decorative technique where the outer surface of an object, usually in glazed or coloured ceramic, is scratched away in a pattern to reveal the contrasting coloured underlying surface.

Sommerso Technique developed in Murano in the 1930s. Translates as 'submerged' and involves casing one or more layers of transparent coloured glass within a layer of thick, clear, colourless glass.

Stoneware A type of ceramic similar to earthenware and made of high-fired clay mixed with stone, such as feldspar, which makes it non-porous.

T

Tazza A shallow cup with a wide bowl, which is raised up on a single pedestal foot.

Tooled Collective description for a number of decorative techniques applied to a surface. Includes engraving, stamping, punching and incising.

V

Vermeil Gold-plated silver.

Vesta case A small case or box, usually made from silver, for carrying matches.

W

White metal Precious metal that is possibly silver, but not officially marked as such.

Y

Yellow metal Precious metal that is possibly gold, but not officially marked as such.

INDEX TO ADVERTISERS

CLIENT	PAGE NO.
Dorling Kindersley	21
KCS Ceramics	121

DMG Antiques Fairs	174
Cad van Swankster & Sparkle Moore	269

KEY TO ILLUSTRATIONS

Every collectable illustrated in the DK Collectables Price Guide 2007 by Judith Miller and Mark Hill has a letter code that identifies the dealer or auction house that sold it. The list below is a key to these codes. In the list, auction houses are shown by the letter A and dealers by the letter D. Some items may have come from a private collection, in which case the code in the list is accompanied by the letter P. Inclusion in this book in no way constitutes or implies a contract or a binding offer on the part of any of our contributors to supply or sell the goods illustrated, or similar items, at the prices stated.

AAB (D)
Ashmore & Burgess
Mob: 07702 355122
info@ashmoreandburgess.com
www.ashmoreandburgess.com

AAC (A)
Alderfer Auction Company
501 Fairground Road,
Hatfield, PA 19440 USA
Tel: 001 215 393 3000
info@alderferauction.com
www.alderferauction.com

AB (A) (D)
Auction Blocks
The Auction Blocks,
P.O. Box 2321, Shelton, CT
06484, USA
Tel: 001 203 924 2802
auctionblocks@aol.com
www.auctionblocks.com

ABIJ (D)
Aurora Bijoux
Tel: 001 215 872 7808
aurora@aurorabijoux.com
www.aurorabijoux.com

AG (D)
Antique Glass at Frank Dux Antiques
33 Belvedere
Bath BA1 5HR
Tel: 01225 312 367
m.hopkins@antique-glass.co.uk
www.antique-glass.co.uk

AGO (D)
Anona Gabriel
Otford Antiques Centre,
26-28 High Steet, Otford,
Sevenoaks,
Kent TN15 9DF
Tel: 01959 522 025
info@otfordantiques.co.uk

AGR (D)
Adrian Grater
25-26 Admiral Vernon Antiques
Arcade
141-149 Portobello Road
London W11 2DY
Tel: 020 8579 0357
Mob: 07814 286 624
adriangrater@tiscali.co.uk

AGW (D)
American Art Glass Works
No longer trading

ALL (A)
Allard Auctions
P.O. Box 1030,
419 Flathead St., 4, St Ignatius
MT 59865 USA
Tel: 001 460 745 0500
info@allardauctions.com
www.allardauctions.com

AMJ (D)
American Jazz
Box 302 Ossining
NY 10562, USA
Tel: 001 914 762 5519
amjazz@optonline.net

ANAA (D)
Anastacia's Antiques
617 Bainbridge Street,
Philadelphia, PA 19147 USA
Tel: 001 215 928 0256

AOY (D)
All Our Yesterdays
6 Park Road, Kelvinbridge,
Glasgow G4 9JG
Tel: 0141 334 7788

ART (D)
Artius Glass
Street, Somerset BA16 0AN
Tel: 01458 443694
Mob: 07860 822666
wheeler.ron@ic24.net
www.artiusglass.co.uk

ASG (D)
Anthony Stern Glass
Unit 205, Avro House,
Havelock Terrace,
London SW8 4AL
Tel: 020 7622 9463
anthony@anthonysternglass.com
www.anthonysternglass.com

ATK (A)
Auction Team Köln
Postfach 50 11 19, Bonner Str.
528-530, D-50971 Cologne,
Germany
Tel: 00 49 221 38 70 49
auction@breker.com
www.breker.com

B&H (A)
Burstow & Hewett
Lower Lake, Battle,
East Sussex, TN33 0AT
Tel: 01424 772374
auctions@burstowandhewett.co.uk
www.burstowandhewett.co.uk

B (A)
Dreweatt Neate, Tunbridge Wells
Auction Hall, The Pantiles,
Tunbridge Wells,
Kent TN2 5QL
Tel: 01892 544 500
tunbridgewells@dnfa.com
www.dnfa.com

BAD (D)
Beth Adams
Unit GO43/4, Alfies Antique
Market, 13 Church Street,
Marylebone, London NW8 8DT
Mob: 07776 136 003
www.alfiesantiques.com

BAR (A)
Dreweatt Neate (Bristol)
Baynton Road
Ashton
Bristol BS3 2EB
Tel: 0117 953 0803
bristol@dnfa.com
www.dnfa.com

BB (D)
Barbara Blau
South Street Antiques Market
615 South 6th Street,
Philadelphia,
PA 19147-2128 USA
Tel: 001 215 739 4995
Tel: 001 215 592 0256
bbjools@msn.com

BEJ (D)
Bébés et Jouets
c/o Lochend Post Office,
165 Restalrig Road,
Edinburgh EH7 6HW
Tel: 0131 332 5650
bebesjouets@tiscali.co.uk

BEL (A)
Belhorn Auction Services
PO Box 20211, Columbus,
OH 43220 USA
Tel: 001 614 921 9441
auctions@belhorn.com
www.belhorn.com

BEV (D)
Beverley
30 Church Street,
London NW8 8EP
Tel: 020 7262 1576
www.alfiesantiques.com

BGL (D)
Block Glass Ltd
blockglss@aol.com
www.blockglass.com

BIB (D)
Biblion
1-7 Davies Mews,
London W1K 5AB
Tel: 020 7629 1374
info@biblion.com
www.biblion.com

BLO (A)
Bloomsbury Auctions
Bloomsbury House,
24 Maddox St, London W1 S1PP
Tel: 020 7495 9494
info@bloomsburyauctions.com
www.bloomsburyauctions.com

BOM (D)
Bob Mauriello
toystrains@comcast.net

BONR (A)
Bonhams
101 New Bond Street,
London W1S 1SR
Tel: 020 7629 6602
info@bonhams.com
www.bonhams.com

BPAL (A) (D)
The Book Palace
Jubilee House, Bedwardine Rd,
Crystal Palace
London SE19 3AP
Tel: 020 8768 0022
orders@bookpalace.com
www.bookpalace.com

BR (D)
Beyond Retro
110-112 Cheshire Street,
London E2 6EJ
Tel: 020 7613 3636
sales@beyondretro.com
www.beyondretro.com

BRB (D)
Bauman Rare Books
535 Madison Avenue, New York,
NY10022 USA
Tel: 001 212 751 1011
brb@baumanrarebooks.com
www.baumanrarebooks.com

BS (D)
Below Stairs
103 High Street, Hungerford,
Berkshire RG17 0NB
Tel: 01488 682 317
www.belowstairs.co.uk

BWH (P)
The Big White House
www.thebigwhitehouse.com

APPENDICES

C (A)
Cottees
The Market, East Street,
Wareham, Dorset BH20 4NR
Tel: 01929 552 826
auctions@cottees.fsnet.co.uk
www.auctionsatcottees.co.uk

CA (A)
Chiswick Auctions
1 Colville Road,
London W3 8BL
Tel: 020 8992 4442
sales@chiswickauctions.co.uk
www.chiswickauctions.co.uk

CAT (D)
CatalinRadio.com
Tel: 001 419 824 2469
steve@catalinradio.com
www.catalinradio.com

CG (D)
Cowdy Gallery
31 Culver Street, Newent
Gloucestershire GL18 1DB
Tel: 01531 821 173
info@cowdygallery.co.uk
www.cowdygalleryc.o.uk

CHEF (A)
Cheffins
Clifton House, 1 & 2 Clifton
Road, Cambridge CB1 7EA
Tel: 01223 213 343
fine.art@cheffins.co.uk
www.cheffins.co.uk

CHS (D)
China Search
P.O. Box 1202, Kenilworth,
Warwickshire CV8 2WW
Tel: 01926 512 402
helen@chinasearch.co.uk
www.chinasearch.co.uk

CL/CLG (D)
Chisholm Larsson
45 8th Avenue, New York
NY 10011 USA
Tel: 001 212 741 1703
info@chisholm-poster.com
www.chisholm-poster.com

CLV (D)
Clevedon Salerooms
The Auction Centre,
Kenn Road, Kenn, Clevedon,
Bristol BS21 6TT
Tel: 01934 830 111
Fax: 01934 832 538
info@clevedonsalerooms.co.uk
www.clevedon-salerooms.com

COB (D)
Cobwebs
78 Old Northam Road,
Southampton SO14 0PB
Tel: 02380 227 458
www.cobwebs.uk.com

COLC (D)
Collectors Cameras
P.O. Box 16, Pinner,
Middlesex HA5 4HN
Tel: 020 8421 3537

CRIS (D)
Cristobal
26 Church Street,
London NW8 8EP
Tel: 020 7724 7230
steven@cristobal.co.uk
www.cristobal.co.uk

CSA (D)
Christopher Sykes Antiques
The Old Parsonage, Woburn,
Milton Keynes MK17 9QL
Tel: 01525 290 259
www.sykes-corkscrews.co.uk

CSO (D)
Charlie Solomon
Otford Antiques & Collectables
Centre, 28-28 High Street,
Otford, Kent TN15 9DF
Tel: 01959 522 025
info@otfordantiques.co.uk
www.otfordantiques.co.uk

CVS (D)
Cad Van Swankster at The Girl
Can't Help It
Alfies Antiques Market,
Stand G100 & G90 & G80,
13-25 Church Street,
Marylebone, London NW8 8DT
Tel: 020 7724 8984
cad@sparklemoore.com

D (A)
Dickens Auctioneers
The Claydon Saleroom
Calvert Road, Middle Claydon
Buckingham, Bucks MK18 2EZ
Tel: 01296 714434
info@dickinsauctioneers.com
www.dickinsauctioneers.com

D&G (D)
Domas & Gray Gallery
Tel: 001 228 467 5294
info@domasandgraygallery.com
www.domasandgraygallery.com

DAC (D)
Dynamite Antiques &
Collectibles
eb625@verizon.net

DD (D)
Decodame.com
Tel: 001 239 514 6797
info@decodame.com
www.decodame.com

DETC (D)
Deco Etc
122 West 25th Street
New York, NY 10001 USA
Tel: 001 212 675 3326
deco_etc@msn.com
www.decoetc.net

DF (D)
Dad's Follies
moreinfo@dadsfollies.com
www.dadsfollies.com

DH (D)
Huxtins
david@huxtins.com
www.huxtins.com

DIM (D)
Dimech
Stand F46-49
Alfies Antiques Market
13-25 Church Street,
London NW8 8DT
Mob: 07787 130 955

DJI (D)
Deco Jewels Inc
Tel: 001 212 253 1222
decojewels@earthlink.net

DMI (P)
David Midgley
dgmidgley@yahoo.co.uk

DN (A)
Dreweatt Neate
Donnington Priory Salerooms,
Donnington, Newbury,
Berkshire RG14 2JE
Tel: 01635 553 553
donnington@dnfa.com
www.dnfa.com/donnington

DRA (A)
David Rago Auctions
333 North Main Street,
Lambertville, NJ 08530 USA
Tel: 001 609 397 9374
info@ragoarts.com
www.ragoarts.com

DSC (P)
British Doll Showcase
squibbit@ukonline.co.uk
www.britishdollshowcase.co.uk

DTC (D)
Design20c
Tel: 0794 609 2138
enquiry@design20c.co.uk
www.design20c.co.uk

DWG (D)
Griffin & Cooper
South Street Antiques Market
615 South 6th Street,
Philadelphia,
PA 19147-2128 USA
Tel: 001 215 592 0256

EAB (D)
Anne Barrett
Otford Antiques & Collectables
Centre, 28-28 High Street,
Otford, Kent TN15 9DF
Tel: 01959 522 025
info@otfordantiques.co.uk
www.otfordantiques.co.uk

ECLEC (D)
Eclectica
2 Charlton Place, Islington,
London N1
Tel: 020 7226 5625
liz@eclectica.biz
www.eclectica.biz

EG (A)
Edison Gallery
Tel: 001 617 359 4678
glastris@edisongallery.com
www.edisongallery.com

ELI (D)
Eve Lickver
P.O. Box 1778 San Marcos
CA 92079 USA
Tel: 001 760 761 0868

F (A)
Fellows & Sons
Augusta House, 19 Augusta
Street, Hockley,
Birmingham B18 6JA
Tel: 0121 212 2131
info@fellows.co.uk
www.fellows.co.uk

FAN (D)
Fantiques
Tel: 020 8840 4761
Mob: 07956 242450
paula.raven@ntlworld.com

FD (D)
Fragile Design
14-15 The Custard Factory,
Digbeth, Birmingham B9 4AA
Tel: 0121 224 7378
info@fragiledesign.com
www.fragiledesign.com

FFM (D)
Festival
No longer trading

FM (D)
Francesca Martire
Stand F131-137,
Alfie's Antiques Market
13-25 Church Street,
London NW8 0RH
Tel: 020 7724 4802
Mob: 07990 523891
info@francescamartire.com
www.francescamartire.com

FRE (A)
Freeman's
1808 Chestnut Street,
Philadelphia, PA 19103 USA
Tel: 001 215 563 9275
info@freemansauction.com
www.freemansauction.com

GAZE (A)
Thos. Wm. Gaze & Son
Diss Auction Rooms, Roydon Rd,
Diss, Norfolk IP22 4LN
Tel: 01379 650 306
sales@dissauctionrooms.co.uk
www.twgaze.com

GBA (A)
Graham Budd Auctions
P.O. Box 47519,
London N14 6XD
Tel: 020 8366 2525
gb@grahambuddauctions.co.uk
www.grahambuddauctions.co.uk

GC (P)
Graham Cooley Collection
Mob: 07968 722 269
graham.cooley@metalysis.com

GGRT (D)
Gary Grant Choice Pieces
18 Arlington Way,
London EC1R 1UY
Tel: 020 7713 1122

GHOU (A)
Gardiner Houlgate
Bath Auction Rooms,
9 Leafield Way, Corsham,
Nr Bath SN13 9SW
Tel: 01225 812 912
auctions@gardinerhoulgate.co.uk
www.gardinerhoulgate.co.uk

GORL (A)
Gorringes, Lewes
15 North Street, Lewes, East
Sussex, BN7 2PD
Tel: 01273 472 503
clientservices@gorringes.co.uk
www.gorringes.co.uk

GORW/GOR (A)
Gorringes, Worthing
44-46 High Street, Worthing,
West Sussex BN11 1LL
Tel: 01903 238 999
clientservices@gorringes.co.uk
www.gorringes.co.uk

GM (D)
Galerie Maurer
Kurfürstenstrasse 17
D-80799 Munich, Germany
Tel: 0049 89 271 13 45
info@galerie-objekte-maurer.de
www.galerie-objekte-maurer.de

GROB (D)
Geoffrey Robinson
Stand GO77-78 & GO91-92,
Alfies Antiques Market,
13-25 Church Street,
London NW8 8DT
Tel: 020 7723 0449
www.alfiesantiques.com

GWRA (A)
Gloucestershire Worcestershire
Railway Auctions
Tel: 01684 773 487 /
01386 760 109
www.gwra.co.uk

H&G (D)
Hope and Glory
131A Kensington Church St,
London W8 7LP
Tel: 020 7727 8424

HAMG (A)
Dreweatt Neate (Godalming)
Baverstock House, 93 High St,
Godalming, Surrey GU7 1AL
Tel: 01483 423 567
godalming@dnfa.com
www.dnfa.com

HERR (A)
Auktionshaus W.G. Herr
Friesenwall 35
D-50672, Cologne, Germany
Tel: 0049 221 25 45 48
kunst@herr-auktionen.de
www.herr-auktionen.de

HGS (D)
Harper General Store
Tel: 001 717 964 3453
lauver5@comcast.net
www.harpergeneralstore.com

HH (P)
Holiday Happenings

HLJ (D)
Hugo Lee-Jones
Tel: 01227 375 375
Mob: 07941 187 2027
electroniccollectables@hotmail.com

HLM (D)
Hi & Lo Modern
161 Montclair Avenue
Montclair NJ 07042 USA
sales@hiandlomodern.com
www.hiandlomodern.com

HP (D)
Hilary Proctor
Advintage, Shop E20,
Grays Antiques Market,
1-7 Davies Mews,
London W1Y 2PL
Tel: 020 7499 7001

ING (D)
Ingram Antiques
669 Mount Pleasant Road
Toronto, Canada M4S 2N2
Tel: 001 416 484 4601
ingramantiques@bellnet.ca
www.ingramgallery.com/
antiques.htm

JBC (P)
James Bridges Collection
james@jdbridges.fsnet.co.uk

JDJ (A)
James D Julia Inc
P.O. Box 830, Fairfield,
Maine 04937 USA
Tel: 001 207 453 7125
jjulia@juliaauctions.com
www.juliaauctions.com

JEG (D)
John English Gifts
6 Princes Arcade,
London SW1Y 6DS
Tel: 020 7437 2082
brian@johnenglishgifts.com
www.johnenglishgifts.com

JES (D)
John Jesse Antiques
By appointment
Mob: 07767 497 880
jj@johnjesse.com

JF (D)
Jill Fenichell
305 East 61st Street, New York,
NY 10021 USA
Tel: 001 212 980 9346
jfenichell@yahoo.com

JH (D)
Jeanette Hayhurst Fine Glass
32A Kensington Church Street
London W8 4HA
Tel: 020 7938 1539

JJ (D)
Junkyard Jeweler
sales@junkyardjeweler.com
www.junkyardjeweler.com

JL (D)
Eastgate Antiques
Tel: 01206 822 712
Mob: 07774 206 289

JN (A)
John Nicholson Auctioneers
The Auction Rooms, 'Longfield',
Midhurst Road, Fernhurst,
Haslemere, Surrey GU27 3HA
Tel: 01428 653727
sales@johnnicholsons.com
www.johnnicholsons.com

KAU (A)
Auktionshaus Kaupp
Schloss Sulzburg, Hauptstrasse
62, 79295 Sulzburg, Germany
Fax: 00 49 7634 5038 50
auktionen@kaupp.de
www.kaupp.de

KCS (D)
KCS Ceramics
Tel: 020 8384 8981
karen@kcsceramics.co.uk
www.kcsceramics.co.uk

KNK (D)
Kitsch-N-Kaboodle
South Street Antiques Market,
615 South 6th Street,
Philadelphia,
PA 19147-2128 USA
Tel: 001 215 382 1354
kitschnkaboodle@yahoo.com

L (D)
Luna
23 George Street,
Nottingham NG1 3BH
Tel: 0115 924 3267
info@luna-online.co.uk
www.luna-online.co.uk

L&T (A)
Lyon and Turnbull Ltd.
33 Broughton Place,
Edinburgh EH1 3RR
Tel: 0131 557 8844
info@lyonandturnbull.com
www.lyonandturnbull.com

LAN (A)
Lankes
Triftfeldstrasse 1, 95182,
Döhlau Germany
Tel: +49 (0)928 69 50 50
info@lankes-auktionen.de
www.lankes-auktionen.de

LAW (A)
Lawrences Auctioneers
Norfolk House, High Street,
Bletchingley, Surrey RH1 4PA
Tel: 01883 743 323
enquiries@
lawrencesbletchingley.co.uk
www.lawrencesbletchingley.co.uk

LB (D)
Linda Bee
Stand L18-21, Grays Antique
Market, 58 Davies Street,
London W1Y 2LP
Tel: 020 7629 5921
lindabee@grays.clara.net
www.graysantiques.com

LDE (D)
Larry & Diana Elman
P.O. Box 415, Woodland Hills
California CA 91365 USA

LFA (A)
Law Fine Art
The Long Gallery
Littlecote House, Hungerford
Berkshire RG17 0SS
Tel: 01635 860 033
info@lawfineart.co.uk
www.lawfineart.co.uk

LHT (D)
Leanda Harwood
Tel: 01529 300 737
leanda.harwood@virgin.net
www.leandaharwood.co.uk

LOB (D)
Louis O'Brien
Tel: 01276 32907

LYNH (D)
Lynn & Brian Holmes
By appointment
Tel: 020 7368 6412

MA (D)
Manic Attic
Alfies Antiques Market, Stand
S48/49, 13 Church Street,
London NW8 8DT
Tel: 020 7723 6105
ianbroughton@hotmail.com

MAC (D)
Mary Ann's Collectibles
South Street Antiques Center
615 South 6th Street,
Philadelphia,
PA 19147-2128 USA
Tel: 001 215 592 0256
Tel: 001 215 923 3247

MAI (A)
Moore, Allen & Innocent
The Norcote Salerooms,
Burford Road, Norcote,
Nr Cirencester, Glos GL7 5RH
Tel: 01285 646 050
fineart@mooreallen.co.uk
www.mooreallen.co.uk

MAX (D)
Maxwells Auctioneers
133a Woodford Road
Woodford Cheshire SK7 1QD
Tel: 0161 439 5182
info@maxwells-auctioneers.co.uk
www.maxwells-auctioneers.co.uk

MBO (D)
Mori Books
Amherst Book Center
141 Route 101A, Amherst,
NH 03031 USA
Tel: 001 603 882 2665
moribook@bit-net.com
www.moribooks.com

MEM (D)
Memory Lane
45-40 Bell Blvd, Suite 109,
Bayside, NY 11361 USA
Tel: 001 718 428 8181
memlnny@aol.com
www.tias.com/stores/memlnny

MC (D)
Metropolis Collectibles, Inc.
873 Broadway, Suite 201, New
York, NY 10003, USA
Tel: 001 212 260 4147
orders@metropoliscomics.com
www.metropoliscomics.com

MG (D)
Mod Girl
South Street Antiques Market
615 South 6th Street,
Philadelphia,
PA 19147-2128 USA
Tel: 001 215 592 0256

MGL (D)
Mix Gallery
17 South Main Street,
Lambertville NJ, USA
Tel: 001 609 773 0777
mixgallery1@aol.com
www.mixgallery.com

MGT (D)
Mary & Geoff Turvil
Vintage Compacts, Small
Antiques & Collectables
Tel: 01730 260 730
mary.turvil@virgin.net

MHC (P)
Mark Hill Collection
Mob: 07798 915 474
books@markhillpublishing.com
www.markhillpublishing.com

MHT (D)
Mum Had That
info@mumhadthat.com
www.mumhadthat.com

MI (D)
Mood Indigo
181 Prince Street, New York,
NY 10012 USA
Tel: 001 212 254 1176
info@moodindigonewyork.com
www.moodindigonewyork.com

MILLB (D)
Million Dollar Babies
Tel: 001 518 885 7397

ML (D)
Mark Laino
Mark of Time
132 South 8th Street,
Philadelphia, PA 19107 USA
Tel: 001 215 922 1551
lecoultre@verizon.net

MM (A)
Mullock Madeley
The Old Shippon, Wall-under-
Heywood, Church Stretton,
Shropshire SY6 7DS
Tel: 0169 477 1771
info@mullockmadeley.co.uk
www.mullockmadeley.co.uk

MSA (D)
Manfred Schotten Antiques
109 Burford High Street,
Burford, Oxfordshire OX18 4RH
Tel: 01993 822 302
enquiries@schotten.com
www.schotten.com

MTS (D)
The Multicoloured Time Slip
eBay Store: multicoloured
timeslip
eBay ID: dave65330
Mob: 07971 410 563
dave_a_cameron@hotmail.com

MUR (A)
Tony Murland Auctions
78 High Street, Needham
Market, Suffolk IP6 8AW
Tel: 01449 722 992
tony@antiquetools.co.uk
www.antiquetools.co.uk

NAI (D)
Nick Ainge
Tel: 01832 731 063
Mob: 07745 902 343
nick@ainge1930.fsnet.co.uk

NOR (D)
Neet-O-Rama
14 Division Street, Somerville,
NJ 08876 USA
Tel: 001 908 722 4600
www.neetstuff.com

NPC (D)
No Pink Carpet
Tel: 01785 249 802
www.nopinkcarpet.com

OG (D)
Ormonde Gallery
No longer trading

OHA (D)
Owen Hargreaves &
Jasmine Dahl
By appointment:
9 Corsham St,
London N1 6DP
Tel: 020 7253 2669
owen@owenhargreaves.com
www.owenhargreaves.com

ON (A)
Onslows
The Coach House, Manor Road,
Stourpaine, Dorset DT11 8TQ
Tel: 01258 488 838
enquiries@onslows.co.uk
www.onslows.co.uk

P&I (D)
Paola & Iaia
Unit S057-58, Alfies Antiques
Market, 13-25 Church Street,
London NW8 8DT
Tel: 07751 084 135
paolaeiaialondon@hotmail.com

PA (D)
Senator Phil Arthurhulz
P.O. Box 12336
Lansing, MI 48901
Tel: 001 517 334 5000
Mob: 001 517 930 3000

PB (D)
Petersham Books
C/O Biblion
1-7 Davies Mews,
London W1K 5AB
Tel: 020 7629 1374
info@biblion.com
www.biblion.com

PC (P)
Private Collection

PCC (P)
Peter Chapman Collection
pgcbal1@supanet.com

PCOM (D)
Phil's Comics
P.O. Box 3433, Brighton
Sussex BN50 9JA
Tel: 01273 673 462
phil@phil-comics.com
www.phil-comics.com

PKA (D)
Phil & Karol Atkinson
May-Oct: 713 Sarsi Tr, Mercer,
PA 16137 USA
Tel: 001 724 475 2490
Nov-Apr: 7188 Drewry's Bluff
Road, Bradenton,
FL 34203 USA
Tel: 001 941 755 1733

PL (D)
Peter Layton
London Glassblowing
7 The Leather Market
Weston Street,
London SE1 3ER
Tel: 020 7403 2800
info@londonglassblowing.co.uk
www.londonglassblowing.com

PSA (D)
Potteries Specialist Auctions
271 Waterloo Road, Cobridge,
Stoke-on-Trent ST6 3HR
Tel: 01782 286 622
enquiries@potteriesauctions.com
www.potteriesauctions.com

PSI (D)
Paul Simons
Mob: 07733 326 574
pauliobanton@hotmail.com

PTC (D)
Pepe Tozzo Collection
info@hampshirepictures.co.uk
www.hampshirepictures.co.uk

PWE (A)
Philip Weiss Auction Galleries
1 Neil Court, Oceanside,
NY 11572 USA
Tel: 001 516 594 073
info@philipweissauctions.com
ww.philipweissauctions.com

QU (A)
Quittenbaum Kunstauktionen
Hohenstaufenstrasse 1,
D-80801 Munich, Germany
Tel: 0049 89 33 00 756
info@quittenbaum.de
www.quittenbaum.de

RA (D)
Roding Arts
Tel: 01371 859 359
rodingarts@hotmail.com
http://uk.geocities.com/rodingarts/

RBC (D)
Reasons To Be Cheerful
Mob: 07708 025 579

RCC (D)
Royal Commemorative China
Paul Wynton & Joe Spiteri
Tel: 020 8863 0625
Mob: 07930 303 358
royalcommemoratives
@hotmail.com

RDL (A)
David Rago/Nicholas Dawes
Lalique Auctions
333 North Main Street,
Lambertville, NJ 08530 USA
Tel: 001 609 397 9374
Fax: 001 609 397 9377
info@ragoarts.com
www.ragoarts.com

REL (D)
Relick
8 Golborne Road,
London W10 5NW
Tel: 020 8962 0089

RH (D)
Rick Hubbard Art Deco
Tel: 07767 267 607
rick@rickhubbard-artdeco.co.uk
www.rickhubbard-artdeco.co.uk

RITZ (D)
Ritzy
7 The Mall Antiques Arcade,
359 Upper Street,
London N1 0PD
Tel: 020 7704 0127

ROS (A)
Rosebery's
74-76 Knight's Hill, West
Norwood, London SE27 0JD
Tel: 020 8761 2522
auctions@roseberys.co.uk
www.roseberys.co.uk

RR (D)
Red Roses
Vintage Modes,
Grays Antiques Market,
1-7 Davies Mews,
London W1Y 2PL
Tel: 020 7629 7034
sallie_ead@lycos.com
www.vintagemodes.co.uk

RSB (D)
Rowan S. Baker
The Covent Garden Stamp
Shop, 28 Bedfordbury,
London WC2N 4RB
Tel: 0207 379 1448
rowanbaker@btopenworld.com
www.usa-stamps.com
www.british-stamps.com

RSS (A)
Rossini SA
7 Rue Drouot
75009 Paris, France
Tel: 00 33 1 53 34 55 00
www.rossini.fr

RTC (A)
Ritchies
288 King Street East,
Toronto, Canada M5A 1KA
Tel: 001 416 364 1864
auction@ritchies.com
www.ritchies.com

RWA (D)
Richard Wallis Antiks
Tel: 020 8529 1749
info@richardwallisantiks.co.uk
www.richardwallisantiks.com

S&T (D)
Steinberg & Tolkien
193 King's Road
London SW3 5ED
Tel: 020 7376 3660

SAS (A)
Special Auction Services
Kennetholme, Midgham,
Nr. Reading, Berkshire RG7 5UX
Tel: 0118 971 2949
mail@specialauctionservices.com
www.specialauctionservices.com

SCG (D)
Gallery 1930 Susie Cooper
18 Church Street, Marylebone,
London NW8 8EP
Tel: 020 7723 1555
gallery1930@aol.com
www.susiecooperceramics.com

SD (P)
Simon Dunlavey Collection
pennyblack@despammed.com

SDR (A)
Sollo:Rago Modern Auctions
333 North Main Street,
Lambertville, NJ 08530 USA
Tel: 001 609 397 9374
info@ragoarts.com
www.ragoarts.com

SH (D)
Sara Hughes Vintage Compacts,
Antiques & Collectables
Mob: 0775 9697 108
sara@sneak.freeserve.co.uk
http://mysite.wanadoo-
members.co.uk/sara_compacts/

SF (D)
The Silver Fund
1 Duke of York Street,
London SW1Y 6JP
Tel: 020 7839 7664
www.thesilverfund.com

SK (A)
Skinner, Inc.
The Heritage on the Garden
63 Park Plaza, Boston,
MA 02116 USA
Tel: 001 617 350 5400
also at
357 Main Street, Bolton,
MA 01740, USA
Tel: 001 978 7796 241
www.skinnerinc.com

SM (D)
Sparkle Moore at The Girl
Can't Help It
Alfies Antiques Market, Stand
G100 & G90 & G80, 13-25
Church Street, Marylebone,
London NW8 8DT
Tel: 020 7724 8984
sparkle@sparklemoore.com
www.sparklemoore.com

SOTT (D)
Sign of the Tymes
Mill Antiques Center,
12 Morris Farm Road,
Lafayette, NJ 07848 USA
Tel: 001 973 383 6028
jhap@nac.net
www.millantiques.com

STE (D)
Cloud Glass
info@cloudglass.com
www.cloudglass.com

SUM (D)
Sue Mautner Costume Jewellery
No longer trading.

SWA (A)
Swann Galleries Image Library
104 East 25th Street, New York,
NY 10010 USA
Tel: 001 212 254 4710
swann@swanngalleries.com
www.swanngalleries.com

SWO (A)
Sworders
14 Cambridge Road, Stansted
Mountfitchet, Essex CM24 8BZ
Tel: 01279 817 778
auctions@sworder.co.uk
www.sworder.co.uk

TCA (A)
Transport Car Auctions
14 The Green, Richmond,
Surrey TW9 1PX
Tel: 020 8940 2022
oliver@tc-auctions.com
www.tc-auctions.com

TCM (D)
Twentieth Century Marks
Whitegates, Rectory Road,
Little Burstead, Nr Billericay,
Essex CM12 9TR
Tel: 01268 411 000
Mob: 07831 778 992 /
07788 455 006
info@20thcenturymarks.co.uk
www.20thcenturymarks.co.uk

TCS (D)
The Country Seat
Huntercombe Manor Barn,
Nr Henley on Thames,
Oxon RG9 5RY
Tel: 01491 641349
info@whitefriarsglass.com
www.whitefriarsglass.com

TCT (D)
The Calico Teddy
Tel: 001 410 433 9202
calicteddy@aol.com
www.calicoteddy.com

TDG (D)
The Design Gallery
5 The Green, Westerham,
Kent TN16 1AS
Tel: 01959 561 234
sales@designgallery.co.uk
www.designgallery.co.uk

TEN (A)
Tennants
The Auction Centre, Leyburn,
North Yorkshire DL8 5SG
Tel: 01969 623 780
enquiry@tennants-ltd.co.uk
www.tennants.co.uk

TGM (D)
The Glass Merchant
Tel: 07775 683 961
as@titan.freeserve.co.uk

TM (D)
Tony Moran
South Street Antiques Market,
615 South 6th Street,
Philadelphia,
PA 19147-2128 USA
Tel: 001 215 592 0256

TOA (D)
The Occupied Attic
Tel: 001 518 899 5030
occupied@nycup.rr.com
seguin12@aol.com

TP (D)
Tenth Planet
Unit 37a, Vicarage Field
Shopping Centre, Ripple Road,
Barking, Essex IG11 8DQ
Tel: 020 8591 5357
sales@tenthplanet.co.uk
www.tenthplanet.co.uk

TRA (D)
Toy Road Antiques
200 Highland Street, Canal,
Winchester, OH 4310 USA
Tel: 001 614 834 1786
toyroadantiques@aol.com
www.goantiques.com/
members/toyroadantiques

TRIO (D)
Trio
Showcase V0010
Grays Antiques Market,
1-7 Davies Mews,
London W1K 5AB
Tel: 020 7493 2736
www.graysantiques.com

TSIS (D)
Three Sisters
South Street Antiques Market,
615 South 6th Street,
Philadelphia,
PA 19147-2128 USA
Tel: 001 215 592 0256

V (D)
Ventisemo – Paolo Bonino
Stand G047/48/50/51
Alfie's Antiques Market,
13-25 Church Street
London NW8 8DT
Tel: 020 7723 1513
boninouk@yahoo.co.uk

VC (D)
Victor Caplin
Stand G075-76
Alfie's Antiques Market
13-25 Church Street
London NW8 8DT
Mob: 07947 511 592
victorcaplin@aol.com
http://www.maroc-n-roll.com

VE (D)
Vintage Eyeware of New York
Tel: 001 646 319 9222
www.vintage-eyeware.com

VEC (A)
Vectis Auctions Ltd
Fleck Way, Thornaby,
Stockton on Tees TS17 9JZ
Tel: 01642 750 616
admin@vectis.co.uk
www.vectis.co.uk

VM (D)
VinMag Co.
39/43 Brewer Street,
London W1R 9UD
Tel: 020 7439 8525
sales@vinmag.com
www.vinmag.com

VSC (D)
Vintage Sports Collector
3920 Via Solano, Palos Verdes
Estates, CA 90274 USA
Tel: 001 310 375 1723

VZ (A)
Von Zezschwitz
Friedrichstrasse 1a,
80801 Munich, Germany
Tel: 00 49 89 38 98 930
www.von-zezschwitz.de

W&W (A)
Wallis & Wallis
West Steet Auction Galleries,
Lewes, East Sussex BN7 2NJ
Tel: 01273 480 208
auctions@wallisandwallis.co.uk
www.wallisandwallis.co.uk

WDL (A)
Kunst-Auktionshaus Martin
Wendl
August-Bebel-Straße 4, 07407
Rudolstadt, Germany
Tel: 011 49 3672 424 350
www.auktionshaus-wendl.de

WJT (D)
William Jamieson Tribal Art
Golden Chariot Productions
468 Wellington Street West,
Suite 201, Toronto, Ontario
Canada M5V 1E3
Tel: 001 416 596 1396
wrj@jamiesontribalart.com
www.jamiesontribalart.com

WW (A)
Woolley & Wallis
51-61 Castle Street, Salisbury,
Wiltshire SP1 3SU
Tel: 011 44 172 424 500
www.woolleyandwallis.co.uk

ZDB (D)
Zardoz Books
20 Whitecroft, Dilton Marsh,
Westbury, Somerset BA13 4DJ
Tel: 01373 865 371
www.zardozbooks.co.uk

DIRECTORY OF SPECIALISTS

If you wish to have any item valued, it is advisable to contact the dealer or specialist in advance to check that they will carry out this service and whether there is a charge. While most dealers will be happy to help you with an enquiry, do remember that they are busy people. Telephone valuations are not possible. Please mention the DK Collectables Price Guide 2006 by Judith Miller when making an enquiry.

ADVERTISING

Huxtins
david@huxtins.com
www.huxtins.com

ANIMATION ART

Animation Art Gallery
13-14 Great Castle St, London
W1W 8LS
Tel: 020 7255 1456
Fax: 0207 436 1256
gallery@animaart.com
www.animaart.com

ART DECO

Art Deco Etc
73 Gloucester Road, Brighton,
Sussex, BN1 3LQ
Tel: 01273 329 268
johnclark@artdecoetc.co.uk

AUTOGRAPHS

Lights, Camera Action
6 Western Gardens, Western
Boulevard, Aspley, Nottingham,
HG8 5GP
Tel: 0115 913 1116
Mob: 07970 342 363
nick.straw@lca-
autographs.co.uk
www.lca-autographs.co.uk

AUTOMOBILIA

C.A.R.S. of Brighton
The White Lion Garage
Clarendon Place,
Kemp Town, Brighton Sussex
Tel: 01273 622 722
Fax: 01273 622 722
whiteliongarage@fsmail.net
www.carsofbrighton.co.uk

BOOKS

Biblion
1-7 Davies Mews, London W1K
5AB
Tel: 020 7629 1374
info@biblion.com
www.biblion.com

Zardoz Books
20 Whitecroft, Dilton Marsh,
Westbury, Somerset BA13 4DJ
Tel: 01373 865 371
www.zardozbooks.co.uk

BONDS & SHARES

Intercol
43 Templar's Crescent, Finchley,
London N3 3QR
Tel: 020 8349 2207
sales@intercol.co.uk
www.intercol.co.uk

CERAMICS

Beth Adams
Unit GO43/4, Alfies Antique
Market, 13 Church Street,
Marylebone, London NW8 8DT
Mob: 07776 136 003
www.alfiesantiques.com

Nick Ainge
Tel: 01832 731 063
Mob: 07745 902 343
nick@ainge1930.fastnet.co.uk
decoseek.decoware.co.uk

Beverley
30 Church Street,
London NW8 8EP, UK
Tel: 020 7262 1576
www.alfiesantiques.com

China Search
P.O. Box 1202, Kenilworth,
Warwickshire CV8 2WW
Tel: 01926 512 402
Fax: 01926 859 311
helen@chinasearch.uk.com
www.chinasearch.uk.com

Eastgate Antiques
S007/009, Alfies Antique
Market, 13 Church St,
Marylebone, London NW8 8DT
Tel: 0207 258 0312
info@alfiesantiques.com
www.alfiesantiques.com

Feljoy Antiques
Shop 3, Angel Arcade, Camden
Passage, London N1 8EA
Tel: 020 7354 5336
Fax: 020 7831 3485
joy@feljoy-antiques.demon.co.uk
www.chintznet.com/feljoy

Adrian Grater
Georgian Village, Camden
Passage,London N1
Tel: 020 8579 0357
adriangrater@tiscali.co.uk

Susie Cooper at Gallery 1930
18 Church St, London NW88EP
Tel: 020 7723 1555
Fax: 020 7735 8309
gallery1930@aol.com
www.susiecooperceramics.com

Gary Grant Choice Pieces
18 Arlington Way, London
EC1R1UY
Tel: 020 7713 1122

Gillian Neale Antiques
P.O. Box 247, Aylesbury
HP201JZ
Tel: 01296 423754
Fax: 01296-334601
gillianneale@aol.com
www.gillannealeantiques.co.uk

Louis O'Brien
Tel: 01276 32907

Mad Hatter
Admiral Vernon Antiques
Market, Unit 83, 141-149
Portobello Rd, London W11
Tel: 020 7262 0487
madhatter.portobello@virgin.net

Rick Hubbard Art Deco
3 Tee Court, Bell St, Romsey,
Hampshire SO518GY
Tel: 01794 513133
www.rickhubbard-artdeco.co.uk

Geoffrey Robinson
Stand GO77-78 & GO91-92,
Alfies Antiques Market, 13-25
Church Street, London, NW8 8DT
Tel: 020 7723 0449
unknown@unknown.com
www.alfiesantiques.com

Rogers de Rin
76 Royal Hospital Rd, Paradise
Walk, London SW34HN
Tel: 020 7352 9007
Fax: 020 7351 9407
rogersderin@rogersderin.co.uk
www.rogersderin.co.uk

Sue Norman
Antiquarius, Stand L4, 135
King's Rd, London SW34PW
Tel: 020 7352 7217
sue@sue-norman.demon.co.uk
www.sue-norman.demon.co.uk

CIGARETTE CARDS

Carlton Antiques
43 Worcester Road, Malvern,
Worcestershire WR14 4RB
Tel: 01684 573 092
dave@carlton-antiques.com
www.carlton-antiques.com

COINS

Intercol
43 Templar's Crescent, Finchley,
London N3 3QR
Tel: 020 8349 2207
sales@intercol.co.uk
www.intercol.co.uk

COMICS

Phil's Comics
P.O. Box 3433, Brighton
Sussex BN50 9JA
Tel: 01273 673 462
phil@phil-comics.com
www.phil-comics.com

The Book Palace
Bedwardine Road, Crystal
Palace, London SE19 3AP
Tel: 020 8768 0022
Fax: 020 8768 0563
www.bookpalace.com

COMMEMORATIVE WARE

Hope & Glory
131a Kensington Church St,
London W87LP
Tel: 020 7727 8424

Recollections
5 Royal Arcade, Boscombe,
Bournemouth, Dorset BH14BT
Tel: 01202 304 441

Royal Commemorative China
Paul Wynton & Joe Spiteri
Tel: 020 8863 0625
Mob: 07930 303 358
royalcommemoratives
@hotmail.com

COSTUME & ACCESSORIES

Beyond Retro
110-112 Cheshire St,
London E2 6EJ
Tel: 020 7613 3636
sales@beyondretro.com
www.beyondretro.com

**Cad van Swankster at The Girl
Can't Help It**
Alfies Antiques Market, Stand
G100 & G90 & G80, 13-25
Church St, London NW88DT
Tel: 020 7724 8984
cad@sparklemoore.com

Cloud Cuckoo Land
6 Charlton Place, London, N1
Tel: 020 7354 3141

Decades
20 Lord St West, Blackburn
BB2 1JX
Tel: 01254 693320

Fantiques
Tel: 020 8840 4761
paula.raven@ntlworld.com

Linda Bee
Grays Antiques Market, 1-7
Davies Street, London, W1Y 2LP
Tel/Fax: 020 7629 5921
www.graysantiques.com

Old Hat
66 Fulham High St, London
SW63LQ
Tel: 020 7610 6558

**Sparkle Moore at The Girl
Can't Help It**
Alfie's Antiques Market, Shop
G100 & G90 & G80, 13-25
Church St, London NW8 8DT
Tel: 020 7724 8984
sparkle.moore@virgin.net
www.sparklemoore.com

Vintage Modes
Grays Antiques Market, 1-7
Davies Mews, London W1Y 5AB
Tel: 020 7409 0400
info@vintagemodes.co.uk
www.vintagemodes.co.uk

Vintage to Vogue
28 Milsom Street, Bath, Avon
BA1 1DG
Tel: 01225 337 323

COSTUME JEWELLERY

Cristobal
26 Church St, London NW8
8EP
Tel: 020 7724 7230
steven@cristobal.co.uk
www.cristobal.co.uk

Eclectica
2 Charlton Place, Islington,
London N1
Tel/Fax: 020 7226 5625
liz@eclectica.biz
www.eclectica.biz

Richard Gibbon
34/34a Islington Green,
London N1 8DU
Tel: 020 7354 2852
neljeweluk@aol.com

Ritzy
7 The Mall Antiques Arcade,
359 Upper Street, London N1
0PD
Tel: 020 7704 0127

William Wain at Antiquarius
Stand J6, Antiquarius, 135
King's Road, London SW3 4PW
Tel: 020 7351 4905
w.wain@btopenworld.com

DOLLS

Bébés & Jouets
c/o Lochend Post Office, 165
Restalrig Road, Edinburgh EH7
6HW, UK
Tel: 0131 332 5650
bebesjouets@tiscali.co.uk

British Doll Showcase
squibbit@ukonline.co.uk
www.britishdollshowcase.co.uk

Sandra Fellner
A18-A19 and MB026, Grays
Antique Market
Tel: 020 8946 5613
sandrafellner@blueyonder.co.uk
www.graysantiques.com

Victoriana Dolls
101 Portobello Rd, London
W112BQ
Tel: 01737 249 525
Fax: 01737 226 254
heather.bond@totalserve.co.uk

Yesterday Child
1 Angel Arcade,
118 Islington High St London
N1 8EG
Tel: 020 7354 1601

FIFTIES, SIXTIES & SEVENTIES

Twentieth Century Marks
Whitegates, Rectory Road,
Little Burstead, Nr Billericay,
Essex CM12 9TR
Tel: 01268 411 000
info@20thcenturymarks.co.uk
www.20thcenturymarks.co.uk

Design20c
Tel: 01276 512329 / 0794
609 2138
sales@design20c.co.uk
www.design20c.com

Fragile Design
8 Lakeside,
The Custard Factory, Digbeth,
Birmingham B9 4AA, UK
Tel: 0121 693 1001
info@fragiledesign.com
www.fragiledesign.com

Luna
23 George Street, Nottingham
NG1 3BH, UK
Tel: 0115 924 3267
info@luna-online.co.uk
www.luna-online.co.uk

Manic Attic
Alfie's Antiques Market, Stand
S48/49, 13-25 Church St,
London NW8 8DT
Tel: 020 7723 6105
manicattic@alfies.clara.net

The Multicoloured Timeslip
eBay Store: multicoloured
timeslip
eBay ID: dave65330
Mob: 07971 410 563
dave_a_cameron@hotmail.com

Retro Etc
13-14 Market Walk, Market
Square, Old Amersham,
Bucks HP7 ODF
Tel: 07810 482900
info@retroetc.com
www.retroetc.com

FILM & TV

The Prop Store of London
Great House Farm, Chenies,
Rickmansworth, Herts WD3 6EP
Tel: 01494 766 485
steve.lane@propstore.com
www.propstore.co.uk

GENERAL

Alfie's Antiques Market
13-25 Church St, London
NW88DT
Tel: 020 7723 6066
info@alfiesantiques.com
www.alfiesantiques.com

Bartlett St Antiques Centre
5-10 Bartlett St, Bath BA12QZ
Tel: 01225 466689
Monday to Saturday (excluding
Wednesday)

Bermondsey Market
Crossing of Long Lane &
Bermondsey St, London SE1
Tel: 020 7351 5353
Every Friday morning from 5am

Brackley Antique Cellar
Drayman's Walk, Brackley,
Northamptonshire NN13 6BE
Tel: 01280 841 841

The Ginnel Antiques Centre
Off Parliment St, Harrogate,
North Yorkshire HG1 2RB
Tel: 01423 508 857
info@theginnel.com
www.redhouseyork.co.uk

Great Grooms at Hungerford
Riverside House, Charnham St,
Hungerford,
Berkshire RG17 0EP
Tel: 01488 682 314
Fax: 01488 686677
antiques@great-grooms.co.uk
www.great-grooms.co.uk

Heanor Antiques Centre
11-3 Ilkeston Rd, Heanor,
Derbyshire
Tel: 01773 531 181
sales@heanorantiquescentre.co.uk
www.heanorantiquescentre.co.uk

Heskin Hall Antiques
Heskin Hall, Wood Lane,
Heskin, Chorley,
Lancashire PR7 5PA
Tel: 01257 452 044

**Otford Antiques and
Collectors Centre**
26-28 High St, Otford,
Kent TN15 9DF
Tel: 01959 522 025
Fax: 01959 525858
info@otfordantiques.co.uk
www.otfordantiques.co.uk

Portobello Rd Market
Portobello Rd, London W11
Every Saturday from 6am

Potteries Antique Centre
271 Waterloo Rd, Cobridge,
Stoke-on-Trent ST6 3HR
Tel: 01782 201 455
Fax: 01782 201518
www.potteriesantiquecentre.com

The Swan Antiques Centre
High Street Tetsworth, nr Thame,
Oxfordshire OX9 7AB
Tel: 01844 281777
Fax: 01844 281770
antiques@theswan.co.uk
www.theswan.co.uk

**Woburn Abbey Antiques
Centre**
Woburn Abbey, Woburn,
Bedfordshire MK179WA
Tel: 01525 290 333
www.woburnantiques.co.uk

GLASS

Andrew Lineham Fine Glass
Tel/Fax: 01243 576 241
Mob: 07767 702 722
andrew@antiquecolouredglass.com
www.antiquecolouredglass.com

**Antique Glass at Frank Dux
Antiques**
33 Belvedere, Lansdown Road,
Bath, Avon BA1 5HR
Tel/Fax: 01225 312 367
www.antique-glass.co.uk

Brackley Antique Cellar

Francesca Martire
Stand F131-137, First Floor,
13-25 Alfies Antiques Market,
13 Church St, London NW8ORH
Tel: 020 7724 4802
www.francescamartire.com

Jeanette Hayhurst Fine Glass
32A Kensington Church St.,
London W8 4HA
Tel: 020 7938 1539

Mum Had That
info@mumhadthat.com
www.mumhadthat.com

**Nigel Benson 20th Century
Glass**
Mob: 07971 859 848
nigel@20thcentury-glass.com
www.20thcentury-glass.com

No Pink Carpet
Tel: 01785 249 802
www.nopinkcarpet.com

Cloud Glass
info@cloudglass.com
www.cloudglass.com

KITCHENALIA

Appleby Antiques
Geoffrey Vans' Arcade, Stand
18, 105-107 Portobello Rd,
London W11
Tel/Fax: 01453 753 126
mike@applebyantiques.net
www.applebyantiques.net

Below Stairs of Hungerford
103 High Street, Hungerford,
Berkshire,RG17 0NB
Tel: 01488 682 317
Fax: 01488 684294
hofgartner@belowstairs.co.uk
www.belowstairs.co.uk

Ken Grant
F109-111 Alfies Antiques
Market, 13-25 Church Street,
Marylebone, London NW8 8DT
Tel: 020 7723 1370
k-grant@alfies.clara.net

Ann Lingard
18-22 Rope Walk, Rye,
Sussex TN31 7NA
Tel: 01797 233 486

MECHANICAL MUSIC

Terry & Daphne France
Tel: 01243 265 946
Fax: 01243 779 582

The Talking Machine
30 Watford Way, London
NW4 3AL
Tel: 020 8202 3473
Mob: 07774 103 139
talkingmachine@gramophones.n
direct.co.uk
www.gramophones.ndirect.co.uk

PAPERWEIGHTS

Sweetbriar Gallery Ltd
56 Watergate Street
Chester, Cheshire, CH1 2LA
Tel: 01244 329249
sales@sweetbriar.co.uk
www.sweetbriar.co.uk

PENS & WRITING

Battersea Pen Home
PO Box 6128,
Epping CM16 4CG
Tel: 01992 578 885
Fax: 01992 578 485
orders@penhome.com
www.penhome.com

Henry The Pen Man
Admiral Vernon Antiques
Market, 141-149 Portobello Rd,
London W11
Tel: 020 8530 3277
Saturdays only

PLASTICS

Paola & Iaia
Unit S057-58, Alfies Antiques
Market, 13-25 Church Street,
London NW8 8DT, UK
Tel: 0771 084 135
paolaeiaialondon@hotmail.com

POSTERS

At The Movies
info@atthemovies.co.uk
www.atthemovies.co.uk

Barclay Samson
By appointment only
Tel: 020 7731 8012
richard@barclaysamson.com
www.barclaysamson.com

DODO
Stand F073/83/84,13-25
Church Street, Marylebone,
London NW8 8DT
Tel: 020 7706 1545
www.dodoposters.com

The Reelposter Gallery
72 Westbourne Grove,
London W2 5SH
Tel: 020 7727 4488
Fax: 020 7727 4499
info@reelposter.com
www.reelposter.com

Rennies
47 The Old High Street,
Folkestone, Kent CT20 2RN
Tel: 01303 242427
info@rennart.co.uk
www.rennart.co.uk

POWDER COMPACTS

**Sara Hughes Vintage Compacts,
Antiques & Collectables**
Mob: 0775 9697 108
sara@sneak.freeserve.co.uk
http://mysite.wanadoo-
members.co.uk/sara_compacts/

Mary & Geoff Turvil
Vintage Compacts, Small
Antiques & Collectables
Tel: 01730 260 730
mary.turvil@virgin.net

RADIOS

On the Air Ltd
The Vintage Technology Centre,
Hawarden, Deeside CH5 3DN
Tel/Fax: 01244 530 300
info@vintageradio.co.uk
www.vintageradio.co.uk

ROCK & POP

Beatcity
PO Box 229, Chatham,
Kent ME5 8WA
Tel/Fax: 01634 200 444
www.beatcity.co.uk

More Than Music
PO Box 2809,
Eastbourne,
East Sussex BN21 2EA
Tel: 01323 649 778
morethnmus@aol.com
www.mtmglobal.com

Tracks
PO Box 117, Chorley,
Lancashire PR6 0UU
Tel: 01257 269 726
Fax: 01257 231340
sales@tracks.co.uk
www.tracks.co.uk

SCIENTIFIC & TECHNICAL, INCLUDING OFFICE, OPTICAL

Arthur Middleton Antiques
50 Whitehall Park, Archway,
London N19 3TN
Tel: 020 7281 8445
www.antique-globes.com

Branksome Antiques
370 Poole Rd, Branksome,
Dorset BH12 1AW
Tel: 01202 763 324

Cobwebs
78 Old Northam Rd,
Southampton SO14 0PB
Tel/Fax: 02380 227 458
www.cobwebs.uk.com

Early Technology
Monkton House, Old
Craighall,Musselburgh,
Midlothian EH21 8SF
Tel: 0131 665 5753
michael.bennett-levy@virgin.net
www.earlytech.com

Stuart Talbot
PO Box 31525,
London W11 2XY
Tel: 020 8969 7011
talbot.stuart@talk21.com

SMOKING

Richard Ball
richard@lighter.co.uk

Tagore Ltd
c/o The Silver Fund, 1 Duke of
York Street, London SW1Y 6JP
Tel: 07989 953 452
tagore@grays.clara.net

Tom Clarke
Admiral Vernon Antiques
Centre, Unit 36,
Portobello Rd, London W11
Tel: 020 8802 8936

SPORTING MEMORABILIA

Manfred Schotten
109 High Street,
Burford,
Oxfordshire OX18 4RH
Tel: 01993 822 302
Fax: 0 1993 822055
enquiries@schotten.com
www.schotten.com

Old Troon Sporting Antiques
49 Ayr St,
Troon KA10 6EB
Tel: 01292 311 822

Simon Brett
Creswyke House,
Moreton-in-Marsh GL56 0LH
Tel: 01608 650 751

Warboys Antiques
St. Ives, Cambridgeshire
Tel: 01480 463891
Mob: 07831 274774
johnlambden@sportingantiques
co.uk
www.sportingantiques.co.uk

TOYS & GAMES

Automatomania
Logie Steading, Forres, Moray
IV36 2QN, Scotland
Tel: 01309 694 828
Mob: 07790 71 90 97
www.automatomania.com

Collectors Old Toy Shop & Antiques
89 Northgate, Halifax, West
Yorkshire HX1 1XF
Tel: 01422 360 434
collectorsoldtoy@aol.com

Colin Baddiel
B24-B25, Grays Antique
Market, 1-7 Davies Mews,
London W1K 5AB
Tel: 020 7408 1239
Fax: 020 7493 9344
toychemcol@hotmail.com
www.colinsantiquetoys.com

Donay Games
Tel: 01444 416 412
info@donaygames.co.uk
www.donaygames.com

Garrick Coleman
75 Portobello Rd,
London W11
Tel: 020 7937 5524
Fax: 0207 937 5530
www.antiquechess.co.uk

Hugo Lee-Jones
Tel: 01227 375 375
Mob: 07941 187 2027
electroniccollectables@hotmail.com

Intercol
43 Templars Crescent, Finchley,
London N3 3QR
Tel: 020 8349 2207
Mob: 077 68 292 066
sales@intercol.co.uk
www.intercol.co.uk

Karl Flaherty Collectables
Tel: 02476 445 627
kfcollectables@aol.com
www.kfcollectables.com

Sue Pearson Dolls & Teddy Bear
18 Brighton Square, 'The
Lanes', Brighton, East Sussex
BN1 1HD
Tel: 01273 774851
info@suepearson.co.uk
www.suepearson.co.uk

The Vintage Toy & Train Shop
Sidmouth Antiques &
Collectors' Centre,
All Saints' Rd,
Sidmouth EX10 8ES
Tel: 01395 512 588

Wheels of Steel (Trains)
Gray's Mews Antiques Market,
B10-B11, 58 Davies St,
London W1K 5LP
Tel: 020 7629 2813
wheelsofsteel@grays.clara.net
www.graysantiques.com

Pauline Parkes
Windsor House
Tel: 01608 650 993

Polly de Courcy-Ireland
PO Box 29,
Alresford,
Hampshire SO249WP
Tel: 01962 733 131

Susan Shaw Period Pieces
Saffron Walden, Essex
Tel: 01799 599217

WATCHES

Kleanthous Antiques
144 Portobello Rd,
London W11 2D7
Tel: 020 7727 3649
antiques@kleanthous.com
www.kleanthous.com

70s Watches
graham@gettya.freeserve.co.uk
www.70s-watches.com

The Watch Gallery
1129 Fulham Road, London
SW3 6RT
Tel: 020 7581 3239

DIRECTORY OF AUCTIONEERS

This is a list of auctioneers that conduct regular sales. Auctioneers who wish to be listed in this directory for our next edition, space permitting, are requested to email info@thepriceguidecompany.com by 1st February 2005.

LONDON

Bloomsbury Auctions
Bloomsbury House, 24 Maddox Street, London W1 S1PP
Tel: 020 7495 9494
Fax: 020 7495 9499
www.bloomsbury-book-auct.com

Bonhams
101 New Bond St,
London W1S 1SR
Tel: 020 7629 6602
Fax: 020 7629 8876
www.bonhams.com

Christies (South Kensington)
85 Old Brompton Rd,
London SW7 3LD
Tel: 020 7581 7611
Fax: 020 7321 3311
info@christies.com
www.christies.com

Rosebery's
74-76 Knights Hill, West Norwood, London SE27 0JD
Tel: 020 8761 2522
Fax: 020 8761 2524

Sotheby's (Olympia)
Hammersmith Rd,
London W14 8UX
Tel: 020 7293 5555
Fax: 020 7293 6939
www.sothebys.com

BEDFORDSHIRE

W. & H. Peacock
The Auction Centre,
26 Newnham St,
Bedford MK40 3JR
Tel: 01234 266366
Fax: 01234 269082
www.peacockauction.co.uk
info@peacockauction.co.uk

BERKSHIRE

Dreweatt Neate
Donnington Priory,
Donnington, Nr. Newbury,
Berkshire RG14 2JE
Tel: 01635 553553
Fax: 01635 553599
donnington@dnfa.com
www.dnfa.com

Law Fine Art Ltd
Firs Cottage, Church Lane,
Brimpton,
Berkshire RG7 4TJ
Tel: 0118 971 0353
Fax: 0118 971 3741
info@lawfineart.co.uk
www.lawfineart.co.uk

Special Auction Services
The Coach House,
Midgham Park,
Reading,
Berkshire RG7 5UG
Tel: 01189 712 949
Fax: 01189 712 420
commemorative@aol.com

BUCKINGHAMSHIRE

Amersham Auction Rooms
125 Station Rd, Amersham,
Buckinghamshire HP7 0AH
Tel: 08700 460606
Fax: 08700 460607
info@amershamauctionrooms.co.uk
www.amershamauctionrooms.co.uk

CAMBRIDGESHIRE

Cheffins
Clifton House, 1&2 Clifton Road, Cambridge CB1 7EA
Tel: 01223 213 343
Fax: 01223 271 949
fine.art@cheffins.co.uk
www.cheffins.co.uk

CHANNEL ISLANDS

Martel Maides Ltd.
The Old Bank, 29 High Street,
Channel Islands GY1 2JX
Tel: 01481 713463
Fax: 01481 700337
sales@martelmaides.co.uk
www.martelmaides.co.uk

CHESHIRE

Bonhams (Chester)
New House, 150 Christleton Road, Chester, Cheshire CH3 5TD
Tel: 01244 313 936
Fax: 01244 340 028
www.bonhams.com

Bob Gowland International Golf Auctions
The Stables, Claim Farm,
Manley Rd Frodsham,
Cheshire WA6 6HT
Tel/Fax: 01928 740668
bob@internationalgolfauctions.com
www.internationalgolfauctions.com

CLEVELAND

Vectis Auctioneers
Fleck Way Thornaby, Stockton-on-Tees, Cleveland TS17 9JZ
Tel: 01642 750616
Fax: 01642 769478
www.vectis.co.uk

CORNWALL

W. H. Lane & Son
Jubilee House, Queen Street,
Penzance TR18 4DF
Tel: 01736 361447
Fax: 01736 350097
info@whlane.co.uk

David Lay FRICS
The Penzance Auction House
Alverton, Penzance TR18 4RE
Tel: 01736 361414
Fax: 01736 360035
david.lays@btopenworld.com

CUMBRIA

Mitchells Fine Art
Auctioneers, Station Road,
Cockermouth, Cumbria CA13 9PZ
Tel: 01900 827800
Fax: 01900 828073
info@mitchellsfineart.com
www.mitchellsfineart.com

Penrith Farmers' & Kidds
Skirsgill Saleroom, Skirsgill,
Penrith, Cumbria CA11 0DN
Tel: 01768 890781
Fax: 01768 895058
info@pfkauctions.co.uk
www.pfandk.co.uk

DERBYSHIRE

Bamfords Ltd
The Old Picture Palace,
133 Dale Road, Matlock,
Derbyshire DE4 3LT
Tel: 01629 574460
www.bamfords-auctions.co.uk

DEVON

Bearne's
St Edmund's Court,
Okehampton St, Exeter,
Devon EX4 1LX
Tel: 01392 207000
Fax: 01392 207007
enquiries@bearnes.co.uk
www.bearnes.co.uk

Bonhams
Dowell St, Honiton, Devon
EX14 1LX
Tel: 01404 41872
Fax: 01404 43137
honiton@bonhams.com
www.bonhams.com

Charterhouse
The Long Street Salerooms,
Sherborne, Dorset DT9 3BS
Tel: 01935 812277
Fax: 01935 389387
enquiry@charterhouse-auctions.co.uk
www.charterhouse-auctions.co.uk

HY Duke & Sons
Weymouth Avenue, Dorchester,
Dorset DT11QS
Tel: 01305 265080
Fax: 01305 260101
enquiries@dukes-auctions.com
www.dukes-auctions.com

Onslows
The Coach House, Manor Road,
Stourpaine DT11 8TQ
Tel/Fax: 01258 488 838
www.onslows.co.uk

Semley Auctioneers
Station Rd, Semley, Nr
Shaftesbury, Dorset SP7 9AN
Tel: 01747 855122
Fax: 01747 855222
semley.auctioneers@btinternet.com
www.semleyauctioneers.com

ESSEX

Ambrose
Ambrose House, Old Station Rd, Loughton, Essex IG10 4PE
Tel: 020 8502 3951
Fax: 020 8532 0833
info@ambroseauction.co.uk
www.ambroseauction.co.uk

Sworder & Sons
14 Cambridge Rd, Stansted Mountfitchet, Essex CM24 8DE
Tel: 01279 817778
Fax: 01279 817779
auctions@sworder.co.uk
www.sworder.co.uk

GLOUCESTERSHIRE

Bruton Knowles
The Tithe Barn, Southam,
Cheltenham,
Gloucestershire GL52 3NY
Tel: 01242 573904
Fax: 01242 224463
www.bkonline.co.uk

Dreweatt Neate (Formerly Bristol Auction Rooms)
Bristol Salerooms, St. John's
Place, Apsley Road, Clifton,
Bristol BS8 2ST
Tel: 0117 973 7201
Fax: 0117 973 5671
bristol@dnfa.com
www.dnfa.com/bristol

Cotswold Auction Co.
Chapel Walk Saleroom,
Chapel Walk, Cheltenham,
Gloucestershire GL50 3DS
Tel: 01242 256363
Fax: 01242 571734
info@cotswoldauction.co.uk
www.cotswoldauction.co.uk

Mallams Fine Art Auctioneers and Valuers
26 Grosvenor Street,
Cheltenham GL52 2SG
Tel: 01242 235712
Fax: 01242 241943
cheltenham@mallams.co.uk
www.mallams.co.uk/fineart

Moore, Allen & Innocent
The Norcote Salerooms,
Burford Road, Norcote,
Nr Cirencester, Glos GL7 5RH
Tel: 01285 646 050
fineart@mooreallen.co.uk
www.mooreallen.co.uk

HAMPSHIRE

Andrew Smith & Son
The Auction Rooms, Manor
Farm, Itchen Stoke, nr.
Winchester SO24 0QT
Tel: 01962 735988
Fax: 01962 738879
auctions@andrewsmithandson.com

Jacobs & Hunt Fine Art Auctioneers
Lavant Street,
Petersfield GU32 3EF
Tel: 01730 233 933
Fax: 01730 262 323
auctions@jacobsandhunt.com
www.jacobsandhunt.com

HEREFORDSHIRE

Brightwells
The Fine Art Saleroom,
Ryelands Rd, Leominster,
Herefordshire HR68NZ
Tel: 01568 611122
Fax: 01568 610519
fineart@brightwells.com
www.brightwells.com

HERTFORDSHIRE

Tring Market Auctions
Brook Street, Tring HP23 5EF
Tel: 01442 826 446
Fax: 01442 890 927
sales@tringmarketauctions.co.uk
www.tringmarketauctions.co.uk

ISLE OF WIGHT

Ways, The Auction House,
Garfield Rd, Ryde,
Isle of Wight PO33 2PT
Tel: 01983 562255
Fax: 01983 565108
www.waysauctionrooms
.fcbusiness.co.uk

KENT

Dreweatt Neate
Tunbridge Wells Saleroom,
The Auction Hall, The Pantiles,
Tunbridge Wells, Kent TN2 5QL
Tel: 01892 544500
Fax: 01892 515191
tunbridgewells@dnfa.com
www.dnfa.com/tunbridgewells

Gorringes
15 The Pantiles,
Tunbridge Wells TN2 5TD
Tel: 01892 619 670
Fax: 01892 619 671
auctions@gorringes.co.uk
www.gorringes.co.uk

LANCASHIRE

Capes Dunn & Co.
The Auction Galleries,
38 Charles St,
Manchester, M1 7DB
Tel: 0161 273 1911
Fax: 0161 273 3474

LEICESTERSHIRE

Gilding's
Roman Way Market,
Harborough, LE16 7PQ
Tel: 01858 410414
Fax: 01858 432956
sales@gildings.co.uk
www.gildings.co.uk

Tennants Co.
Millhouse, South Street,
Oakham, Rutland LE15 6BG
Tel: 01572 724 66
Fax: 01572 72 4422
oakham@tennants-ltd.co.uk
www.tennants.co.uk

LINCOLNSHIRE

Golding Young & Co.
Old Wharf Rd, Grantham,
Lincolnshire NG31 7AA
Tel: 01476 565118
Fax: 01476 561475
enquiries@goldingyoung.com
www.goldingyoung.com

MERSEYSIDE

Cato, Crane & Co
6 Stanhope St,
Liverpool L8 5RE
Tel: 0151 709 5559
Fax: 0151 707 2454
www.cato-crane.co.uk

NORFOLK

Gaze and Son
Diss Auction Rooms, Roydon
Road, Diss IP22 4LN
Tel: 01379 650306
Fax: 01379 644313
sales@dissauctionrooms.co.uk
www.twgaze.com

Keys Auctioneers & Valuers
Aylsham Salerooms, Palmers
Lane, Aylsham, Norfolk NR11
6JA
Tel: 01263 733195
www.keysauctions.co.uk

Knights Sporting Auctions
The Thatched Gallery,
The Green, Aldborough,
Norwich, Norfolk NR11 7AA
Tel: 01263 768488
Fax: 01263 768788
www.knights.co.uk

NOTTINGHAMSHIRE

Mellors & Kirk Fine Art Auctioneers
Gregory Street, Nottingham,
Nottinghamshire NG7 2NL
Tel: 0115 9790000
Fax: 0115 9781111
enquiries@mellors-kirk.com
www.mellors-kirk.co.uk

Dreweatt Neate
The Nottingham Salerooms,
192 Mansfield Road,
Nottingham NG1 3HU
Tel: 0115 962 4141
Fax: 0115 969 3450
nottingham@dnfa.com
www.dnfa.com/neales

T Vennett-Smith Auctioneers and Valuers
11 Nottingham Road, Gotham,
Nottingham NG11 0HE
Tel: 0115 9830541
Fax: 0115 9830114
info@vennett-smith.com
www.vennett-smith.com

OXFORDSHIRE

Mallams
Pevensey House, 27 Sheep St,
Bicester, Oxfordshire OX6 7JF
Tel: 01869 252901
Fax: 01869 320283
bicester@mallams.co.uk
www.mallams.co.uk

Mallams (Oxford)
Bocardo House, 24a St.
Michaels Street, Oxford,
OX1 2EB
Tel: 01865 241358
Fax: 01865 725483
oxford@mallams.co.uk
www.mallams.co.uk

Soames Country Auctions
Pinnocks Farm Estate,
Northmoor, Witney OX8 1AY
Tel: 01865 300626
soame@email.msn.com
www.soamesauctioneers.co.uk

SHROPSHIRE

Halls Fine Art
Welsh Bridge,
Shrewsbury SY3 8LA
Tel: 01743 231 212
Fax: 01743 271 014
FineArt@halls.to
www.hallsgb.com

Walker Barnett & Hill
Cosford Auction Rooms,
Long Lane, Cosford,
Shropshire TF11 8PJ
Tel: 01902 375555
Fax: 01902375566
www.walker-barnett-hill.co.uk

Mullock Madeley
The Old Shippon,
Wall-under-Heywood,
Nr Church Stretton,
Shropshire SY6 7DS
Tel: 01694 771771
Fax: 01694 771772
info@mullockmadeley.co.uk
www.mullock-madeley.co.uk

SOMERSET

Clevedon Salerooms
The Auction Centre, Kenn Road,
Kenn, Clevedon, North
Somerset BS21 6TT
Tel: 01934 830 111
Fax: 01934 832 538
info@clevedon-salerooms.com
www.clevedon-salerooms.com

Gardiner Houlgate
The Bath Auction Rooms,
9 Leafield Way,
Corsham, Bath,
Somerset SN139SW
Tel: 01225 812912
Fax: 01225 811777
auctions@gardiner-houlgate.co.uk
www.invaluable.com/gardiner-houlgate

Lawrence's Fine Art Auctioneers Ltd
South St, Crewkerne,
Somerset TA18 8AB
Tel: 01460 73041
Fax: 01460 74627
enquiries@lawrences.co.uk
www.lawrences.co.uk

STAFFORDSHIRE

Potteries Specialist Auctions
271 Waterloo Rd, Cobridge,
Stoke-on-Trent,
Staffordshire ST6 3HR
Tel: 01782 286622
Fax: 01782 213777
www.potteriesauctions.com

Richard Winterton
School House Auction Rooms,
Hawkins Lane, Burton-on-Trent,
Staffordshire DE14 1PT
Tel: 01283 511224

Wintertons
Lichfield Auction Centre
Fradley, Lichfield, WS13 8NF
Tel: 01543 263256
Fax: 01543 415348
enquiries@wintertons.co.uk
www.wintertons.co.uk

SUFFOLK

Diamond Mills
Orwell Hall, Orwell Rd,
Felixstowe, Suffolk IP11 7BL
Tel:01473 218 600
diamondmills@btconnect.com
www.diamondmills.co.uk

Neal Sons & Fletcher
26 Church St,
Woodbridge,
Suffolk IP12 1DP
Tel: 01394 382263
Fax: 01394 383030
enquiries@nsf.co.uk
www.nsf.co.uk

SURREY

Barbers
The Mayford Centre,
Smarts Heath Rd,
Woking, Surrey GU22 0PP
Tel: 01483 728939
Fax: 01483 762552
www.thesaurus.co.uk/barbers

Clark Gammon
The Guildford Auction Rooms,
Bedford Road, Guildford, Surrey
GU1 4SJTel: 01483 880915
Fax: 01483 880918
fine.art@clarkegammon.com
www.clarkegammon.co.uk

Ewbank Auctioneers
The Burnt Common Auction
Rooms, London Rd,
Send, Woking,
Surrey GU23 7LN
Tel: 01483 223101
Fax: 01483 222171
www.ewbankauctions.co.uk

Dreweatt Neate (Formerly Hamptons)
Baverstock House, 93 High
Street, Godalming GU7 1AL
Tel: 01483 423 567
Fax: 01483 426 392
godalming@dnfa.com
www.dnfa.com/godalming

EAST SUSSEX

Burstow & Hewett
Lower Lake, Battle,
East Sussex TN33 0AT
Tel: 01424 772 374
www.burstowandhewett.co.uk

Dreweatt Neate (Eastbourne)
46-50 South St,
Eastbourne,
East Sussex BN214XB,
Tel: 01323 410419
Fax: 01323 416540
eastbourne@dnfa.com
www.dnfa.com

Gorringes
Terminus Rd, Bexhill-on-Sea,
East Sussex TN39 3LR
Tel: 01424 212994
Fax: 01424 224035
www.gorringes.co.uk

Gorringes
15 North St, Lewes,
East Sussex BN7 2PD
Tel: 01273 472503
Fax: 01273 479559
www.gorringes.co.uk

Raymond P. Inman
The Auction Galleries, 98A
Coleridge Street,
Hove BN3 5 AA
Tel: 01273 774777
Fax: 01273 735660
r.p.inman@talk21.com
www.invaluable.com/raymondin
man

Wallis & Wallis
West St Auction Galleries,
Lewes, East Sussex BN72NJ
Tel: 01273 480208
Fax: 01273 476562
auctions@wallisandwallis.co.uk
www.wallisandwallis.co.uk

TYNE & WEAR

Anderson and Garland
Anderson House, Crispin Court,
Newbiggin Lane, Westerhope,
Newcastle upon Tyne NE5 1BF
Tel: 0191 430 3000
andersongarland@aol.com
www.andersonandgarland.com

Corbitts
5 Mosley St, Newcastle-upon-
Tyne, Tyne and Wear NE1 1YE
Tel: 0191 232 7268
Fax: 0191 261 4130
collectors@corbitts.com
www.corbitts.com

WARWICKSHIRE

Locke & England
18 Guy Street,
Leamington Spa CV32 4RT
Tel: 01926 889100
Fax: 01926 470608
valuers@leauction.co.uk
www.leauction.co.uk

WEST MIDLANDS

Bonhams, Knowle
The Old House,
Station Rd, Knowle,
Solihull, B930HT
Tel: 01564 776151
Fax: 01564 778069
knowle@bonhams.com
www.bonhams.com

Fellows & Sons
Augusta House,
19 Augusta St, Hockley,
Birmingham,
West Midlands B186JA
Tel: 0121 212 2131
Fax: 0121 212 1249
info@fellows.co.uk
www.fellows.co.uk

WEST SUSSEX

John Bellman
New Pound Wisborough Green,
Billingshurst,
West Sussex RH14 0AZ
Tel: 01403 700858
Fax: 01403 700059
enquiries@bellmans.comuk
www.bellmans.co.uk

Denhams
The Auction Galleries,
Warnham, Nr Horsham,
West Sussex RH123RZ
Tel: 01403 255699
Fax: 01403 253837
enquiries@denhams.com
www.denhams.com

Rupert Toovey
Spring Gardens, Washington,
West Sussex, RH20 3BS,
Tel: 01903 891955
auctions@rupert-toovey.com
www.rupert-toovey.com

WILTSHIRE

Finan & Co
The Square, Mere,
Wiltshire BA12 6DJ
Tel: 01747 861411
Fax: 01747 861944
post@finanandco.co.uk
www.finanandco.co.uk

Henry Aldridge & Sons
The Devizes Auctioneers,
Unit 1, Bath Rd Business
Centre, Devizes,
Wiltshire SN10 1XA
Tel: 01380 729199
Fax: 01380 730073
www.henry-aldridge.co.uk

Woolley & Wallis
51-61 Castle St,
Salisbury,
Wiltshire SP1 3SU
Tel: 01722 424500
Fax: 01722 424508
enquiries@woolleyandwallis.co.uk
www.woolleyandwallis.co.uk

WORCESTERSHIRE

Andrew Grant
St Mark's House,
St Mark's Close,
Cherry Orchard,
Worcester WR5 3DJ
Tel: 01905 357547
Fax: 01905 763942
fine.art@andrew-grant.co.uk
www.andrew-grant.co.uk

**Gloucestershire Worcestershire
Railwayana Auctions**
'The Willows',
Badsey Rd, Evesham,
Worcestershire WR117PA
Tel: 01386 760109
www.gwra.co.uk

Phillip Serrell
The Malvern Saleroom,
Barnards Green Rd, Malvern,
Worcestershire WR143LW
Tel: 01684 892314
Fax: 01684 569832
www.serrell.com

EAST YORKSHIRE

Dee, Atkinson & Harrison
The Exchange Saleroom,
Driffield,
East Yorkshire YO25 6LD
Tel: 01377 253151
Fax: 01377 241041
exchange@dee-atkinson-
harrison.co.uk
www.dahauctions.com

NORTH YORKSHIRE

David Duggleby
The Vine St Salerooms,
Scarborough,
North Yorkshire YO11 1XN
Tel: 01723 507111
Fax: 01723 507222
www.davidduggleby.com

Tennants
The Auction Centre, Leyburn,
North Yorkshire DL8 5SG
Tel: 01969 623780
Fax: 01969 624281
enquiry@tennants-ltd.co.uk
www.tennants.co.uk

SOUTH YORKSHIRE

A. E. Dowse & Sons
Cornwall Galleries, Scotland
Street, Sheffield S3 7DE
Tel: 0114 2725858
Fax: 0114 2490550
aedowes@aol.com
www.aedowseandson.com

BBR Auctions
Elsecar Heritage Centre,
5 Ironworks Row, Wath Rd,
Elsecar, Barnsley,
South Yorkshire S748HJ
Tel: 01226 745156
Fax: 01226 361561
www.onlinebbr.com

Sheffield Railwayana
43 Little Norton Lane,
Sheffield, S8 8GA
Tel: 0114 274 5085
ian@sheffrail.freeserve.co.uk
www.sheffieldrailwayana.co.uk

WEST YORKSHIRE

Andrew Hartley Fine Arts
Victoria Hall Salerooms, Little
Lane, Ilkle,
West Yorkshire, LS29 8EA
Tel: 01943 816363
info@andrewhartleyfinearts.co.uk
www.andrewhartleyfinearts.co.uk

SCOTLAND

Bonhams Edinburgh
65 George St,
Edinburgh EH2 2JL
Tel: 0131 225 2266
Fax: 0131 220 2547
edinburgh@bonhams.com
www.bonhams.com

Loves Auction Rooms
52-54 Canal St, Perth,
Perthshire, PH2 8LF
Tel: 01738 633337
Fax: 01738 629830

Lyon & Turnbull
33 Broughton Place,
Edinburgh EH1 3RR
Tel: 0131 557 8844
Fax: 0131 557 8668
info@lyonandturnbull.com
www.lyonandturnbull.com

Lyon & Turnbull
4 Woodside Place,
Glasgow G3 7QF
Tel: 0141 353 5070
Fax: 0141 332 2928
info@lyonandturnbull.com
www.lyonandturnbull.com

**Thomson, Roddick & Medcalf
Ltd.**
44/3 Hardengreen Business
Park, Eskbank, Edinburgh,
Midlothian EH22 3NX
Tel: 0131 454 9090
Fax: 0131 454 9191
www.thomsonroddick.com

WALES

Bonhams Cardiff
7-8 Park Place, Cardiff,
Glamorgan CF10 3DP
Tel: 02920 727 980
Fax: 02920 727 989
cardiff@bonhams.com
www.bonhams.com

Peter Francis
Curiosity Salerooms, 19 King
St, Carmarthen, South Wales
Tel: 01267 233456
Fax: 01267 233458
www.peterfrancis.co.uk

Welsh Country Auctions
2 Carmarthen Road, Cross
Hands, Llanelli,
Carmarthenshire SA14 6SP
Tel: 01269 844428
Fax: 01269 844428
enquiries@welshcountryauctions
.com
www.welshcountryauctions.com

IRELAND

HOK Fine Art
4 Main St, Blackrock, Co
Dublin, Ireland
Tel: 00 353 1 2881000
fineart@hok.ie
www.hokfineart.com

Mealy's
The Square, Castlecomer,
County Kilkenny, Ireland
Tel: 00 353 56 41229
/41413
Fax: 00 353 56 41627
info@mealys.com
www.mealys.com

CLUBS, SOCIETIES & ORGANISATIONS

ADVERTISING

Antique Advertising Signs
The Street Jewellery Society, 11
Bowsden Ter, South Gosford,
Newcastle-Upon-Tyne NE3 1RX

AUTOGRAPHS

Autograph Club of GB
gregson@blueyonder.co.uk
www.acogb.co.uk

BAXTER PRINTS

The New Baxter Society
c/o Reading Museum & Art
Gallery, Blagrave St, Reading,
Berkshire RG1 1QH
baxter@rpsfamily.demon.co.uk
www.rpsfamily.demon.co.uk

BANK NOTES

**International Bank Note
Society**
43 Templars Crescent, London,
N3 3QR

BOOKS

The Enid Blyton Society
93 Milford Hill, Salisbury,
Wiltshire SP1 2QL
Tel: 01722 331937
www.enidblytonsociety.co.uk

The Followers of Rupert
www.see.ed.ac.uk/~afm/followers

BOTTLES

Old Bottle Club of Great Britain
2 Strafford Avenue,
Elsecar, Nr Barnsley,
South Yorkshire S74 18AA
Tel: 01226 745 156

CERAMICS

**Carlton Ware Collectors'
International**
The Carlton Factory Shop,
Copeland St, Stoke-upon-Trent,
Staffordshire ST4 1PU
Tel: 01782 410 504
cwciclub@aol.com
www.lattimore.co.uk/deco/carlt
on.htm

Chintz World International
Tel: 01525 220272
Fax: 01525 222442
www.chintzworld-intl.com

Clarice Cliff Collectors' Club
Fantasque House, Tennis Drive,
The Park, Nottingham NG7 1AE
www.claricecliff.com

Goss Collectors' Club
Tel: 01159 300 441
www.gosschina.com

**Hornsea Pottery Collectors' &
Research Society**
128 Devonshire St, Keighley,
West Yorkshire BD21 2QJ
hornsea@pdtennant.fsnet.co.uk
www.easyontheeye.net/hornsea
/society.htm

M.I. Hummel Club (Goebel)
Porzellanfabrik, GmbH & Co. KG,
Coburger Str.7, D-96472
Rodental, Germany
Tel: +49 (0) 95 63 72 18 03
Fax: +49 (0) 95 63 9 25 92

Keith Murray Collectors' Club
Fantasque House, Tennis Drive,
The Park, Nottingham NG7 1AE
www.keithmurray.com

Lorna Bailey Collectors' Club
Newcastle Street,
Dalehall, Burslem,
Stoke-on-Trent ST6 3QF
Tel: 01782 837 341

Mabel Lucie Attwell
Abbey Antiques,
63 Great Whyte, Ramsey,
Huntingdon PE26 1HL
Tel: 01487 814753

Moorcroft Collectors' Club
Sandbach Rd, Burslem,
Stoke-on-Trent,
Staffordshire ST6 2DQ
Tel: 01782 820500
Fax: 01782 820501
cclub@moorcroft.com
www.moorcroft.com

Pendelfin Family Circle
Cameron Mill,
Howsin St, Burnley,
Lancashire BB10 1PP
Tel: 01282 432 301
www.pendelfin.co.uk

Poole Pottery Collectors' Club
The Quay, Poole,
Dorset BH15 1RF
Tel: 01202 666200
Fax: 01202 682894
www.poolepottery.co.uk

**Potteries of Rye Collectors'
Society**
22 Redyear Cottages,
Kennington Rd, Ashford,
Kent TN24 0TF
barry.buckton@tesco.net
www.potteries-of-rye-society.co.uk

**Royal Doulton International
Collectors' Club**
Minton House,
London Rd,
Stoke-on-Trent,
Staffordshire ST47QD
Tel: 01782 292292
Fax: 01782 292099
enquiries@royal-doulton.com
www.royal-doulton.com/collectables

**Royal Winton International
Collectors' Club**
Dancers End, Northall,
Bedfordshire LU6 2EU
Tel: 01525 220 272
Fax: 01525 222 442

The Shelley Group
38 Bowman Road,
Norfolk,
Norwich NR4 6LS
shelley.group@shelley.co.uk
www.shelley.co.uk

Susie Cooper Collectors' Group
Panorama House,
18 Oaklea Mews,
Aycliffe Village,
County Durham DL5 6JP
www.susiecooper.co.uk

The Sylvac Collectors' Circle
174 Portsmouth Rd, Horndean,
Waterlooville, Hampshire
admin@sylvacclub.com
www.sylvacclub.com

Novelty Teapot Collectors' Club
Tel: 01257 450 366
vince@totallyteapots.com
www.totallyteapots.com

**Official International Wade
Collectors' Club**
Royal Works, Westport Rd,
Stoke-on-Trent, Staffs ST6 4AP
Tel: 01782 255255
Fax: 01782 575195
club@wade.co.uk
www.wade.co.uk

**Royal Worcester
Collectors' Society**
Severn Street,
Worcester, WR1 2NE
Tel: 01905 746 000
sinden@royal-worcester.co.uk
www.royal-worcester.co.uk

CIGARETTE CARDS

Cartopulic Society of GB
7 Aldenham Avenue, Radlett,
Herts WD7 8HL

COINS

British Numismatic Society
c/o The Warburg Institute,
Woburn Square,
London WC1H 0AB
www.britnumsoc.org

Royal Numismatic Society
c/o The British Museum,
Dept of Coins and Medals,
Great Russell Street,
London WC1B 3DG
Tel: 020 7636 1555
RNS@dircon.co.uk
www.users.dircon.co.uk/~rns

COMMEMORATIVE WARE

**Commemorative Collectors'
Society**
The Gardens,
Gainsborough Rd, Winthorpe,
nr Newark NG24 2NR
Tel: 01636 671377
chris@royalcoll.fsnet.co.uk

COMICS

**Association of Comic
Enthusiasts**
L'Hopiteau, St Martin du
Fouilloux 79420, France
Tel: 00 33 549 702 114

Comic Enthusiasts Society
80 Silverdale, Sydenham,
London SE26 4SJ

**Beano & Dandy Collectors'
Club**
www.phil-
comics.com/collectors_club.html

COSTUME & ACCESSORIES

**British Compact
Collectors' Club**
PO Box 131, Woking,
Surrey GU24 9YR

Costume Society
St. Paul's House, Warwick Lane,
London EC4P 4BN
www.costumesociety.org.uk

Hat Pin Society of GB
PO Box 74, Bozeat,
Northamptonshire NN29 7UD

DISNEYANA

Walt Disney Collectors' Society
c/o Enesco, Brunthill Road,
Kingstown Industrial Estate,
Carlisle CA3 0EN
Tel: 01228 404 062
www.wdccduckman.com

DOLLS

Barbie Collectors' Club of GB
117 Rosemount Avenue, Acton,
London W3 9LU
wdl@nipcus.co.uk'

British Doll Collectors Club
'The Anchorage', Wrotham Rd,
Culverstone Green, Meopham,
Kent DA13 0QW
www.britishdollcollectors.com

Doll Club of Great Britain
PO Box 154, Cobham, Surrey
KT11 2YE

**The Fashion Doll Collectors'
Club of GB**
PO Box 133, Lowestoft,
Suffolk NR32 1WA
Tel: 07940 248127
voden@supanet.com

FILM & TV

James Bond 007 Fan Club
PO Box 007,
Surrey KT15 IDY
Tel: 01483 756007

**Fanderson - The Official Gerry
Anderson Appreciation Society**
2 Romney Road,
Willesborough, Ashford,
Kent TN24 0RW

GLASS

The Carnival Glass Society
P.O. Box 14, Hayes,
Middlesex UB3 5NU
www.carnivalglasssociety.co.uk

The Glass Association
1, White Knobs Way
Caterham, Surrey CR3 6RH
geoffctim@btinternet.com
www.glassassociation.org.uk

Isle of Wight Studio Glass
Old Park, St Lawrence, Isle of
Wight, PO38 1XR
www.isleofwightstudioglass.co.uk

Pressed Glass Collectors' Club
4 Bowshot Close, Castle
Bromwich B36 9UH
Tel: 0121 681 4872
www.webspawner.com/users/
pressedglass

KITCHENALIA

National Horse Brass Society
2 Blue Barn Cottage,
Blue Barn Lane,
Weybridge,
Surrey KT13 0NH
Tel: 01932 354 193

**The British Novelty Salt &
Pepper Collectors Club**
Coleshill,
Clayton Road, Mold,
Flintshire CH7 15X

MARBLES

Marble Collectors Unlimited
P.O. Box 206
Northborough,
MA 01532-0206 USA
marblesbev@aol.com

MECHANICAL MUSIC

**Musical Box Society of
Great Britain**
PO Box 299,
Waterbeach,
Cambridge CB4 4PJ

**The City of London
Phonograph and Gramophone
Society**
2 Kirklands Park,
Fyfe KY15 4EP
Tel: 01334 654 390

METALWARE

Antique Metalware Society
PO Box 63, Honiton,
Devon EX14 1HP
amsmemsec@yahoo.co.uk

MILITARIA

Military – Crown Imperial
37 Wolsey Close, Southall,
Middlesex UB2 4NQ

Military Historical Society
National Army Museum,
Royal Hospital Rd,
London SW3 4HT

**Orders & Medals Research
Society**
123 Turnpike Link,
Croydon CR0 5NU

PAPERWEIGHTS

Paperweight Collectors Circle
P.O. Box 941,
Comberton,
Cambridgeshire CB3 7GQ
Tel: 02476 386 172

PENS & WRITING

The Writing Equipment Society
wes.membershipsec@virgin.net
www.wesoc.co.uk

PERFUME BOTTLES

**International Perfume Bottle
Association**
396 Croton Road, Wayne,
PA 19087 USA
www.ipba-uk.co.uk

PLASTICS

Plastics Historical Society
31a Maylands Drive,
Sidcup, Kent DA14 4SB
mail@plastiquarian.com
www.plastiquarian.com

POSTCARDS

**The Postcard Club of Great
Britain**
34 Harper House,
St. James' Crescent,
London SW9 7LW

POTLIDS

The Pot Lid Circle
Keith Mortimer
Tel: 01295 722 032

QUILTS

**The Quilters' Guild of the
British Isles**
Room 190,
Dean Clough, Halifax,
West Yorks 3HX 5AX
Tel: 01422 347 669
Fax: 01422 345 017
info@quiltersguild.org.uk
www.quiltersguild.org.uk

RADIOS

**The British Vintage
Wireless Society**
59 Dunsford Close,
Swindon,
Wiltshire SN1 4PW
Tel: 01793 541 634
www.bvws.org.uk

RAILWAYANA

Railwayana Collectors Journal
7 Ascot Rd, Moseley,
Birmingham B13 9EN

SEWING

**International Sewing Machine
Collectors' Society**
www.ismacs.net

The Thimble Society
1107 Portobello Rd,
London W11 2QB
antiques@thimblesociety.co.uk
www.thimblesociety.co.uk

SMOKING

Lighter Club of Great Britain
Richard Ball
richard@lighter.co.uk

SPORTING

**International Football Hall of
Fame**
info@ifhof.com,
www.ifhof.com

British Golf Collectors Society
anthonythorpe@ntlworld.com
www.britgolfcollectors.wyenet.co.uk

STAMPS

Postal History Society
60 Tachbrook Street,
London SW1V 2NA
Tel: 020 7545 7773
john.scott@db.com

Royal Mail Collectors' Club
Freepost, NEA1431,
Sunderland, SR9 9XN

STANHOPES

The Stanhope Collectors' Club
jean@stanhopes.info
www.stanhopes.info

STAINLESS STEEL

The Old Hall Club
Sandford House, Levedale,
Stafford ST18 9AH
Tel: 01785 780 376
oht@gnwiggin.freeserve.co.uk
www.oldhallclub.co.uk

TEDDY BEARS & SOFT TOYS

British Teddy Bear Association
PO Box 290
Brighton, Sussex
Tel: 01273 697 974

**Merrythought International
Collectors' Club**
Ironbridge, Telford,
Shropshire TF8 7NJ
Tel: 01952 433 116

Steiff Club Office
Margaret Steiff GmbH,
Alleen Strasse 2, D-89537
Giengen/Brenz, Germany

TOYS

Action Man Club
PO Box 142,
Horsham, RH13 5FJ

The British Model Soldier Society
44 Danemead, Hoddesdon,
Hertfordshire EN119LU
www.model.soldiers.btinternet.co.uk

Corgi Collectors' Club
PO Box 323, Swansea, Wales
SA1 1BJ

Hornby Collectors Club
PO Box 35, Royston,
Hertfordshire SG8 5XR
Tel/Fax: 01223 208 308
hsclubs.demon.co.uk
www.hornby.co.uk

**The Matchbox Toys
International Collectors'
Association**
P.O. Box 120, Deeside,
Flintshire CH5 3HE
kevin@matchboxclub.com
www.matchboxclub.com

**Historical Model Railway
Society**
59 Woodberry Way,
London E4 7DY

**The English Playing Card
Society**
11 Pierrepont St, Bath,
Somerset BA1 1LA
Tel: 01225 465 218

Train Collectors' Society
P.O. Box 20340,
London NW11 6ZE
Tel: 020 8209 1589
tcsinformation@btinternet.com
www.traincollectors.org.uk

**William Britain
Collectors Club**
P.O. Box 32,
Wokingham RG40 4XZ
Tel: 01189 737080
Fax: 01189 733947
ales@wbritaincollectorsclub.com
www.britaincollectorsclub.com

WATCHES

**British Watch & Clock
Collectors' Association**
5 Cathedral Lane, Truro,
Cornwall TR1 2QS
Tel 01872 264010
Fax 01872 241953
tonybwcca@cs.com
www.timecap.com

COLLECTING ON THE INTERNET

■ The internet has revolutionised the trading of collectables. Compared to a piece of furniture, most collectables are easily defined, described and photographed. Shipping is also comparatively easy, due to average size and weight. Prices are also generally more affordable and accessible than for antiques and the Internet has provided a cost effective way of buying and selling, away from the overheads of shops and auction rooms. Many millions of collectables are offered for sale and traded daily, with sites varying from global online marketplaces, such as eBay, to specialist dealers' websites.

■ When searching online, remember that some people may not know how to accurately describe their item. General category searches, even though more time consuming, and even purposefully misspelling a name, can yield results. Also, if something looks too good to be true, it probably is. Using this book to get to know your market visually, so that you can tell the difference between a real bargain and something that sounds like one, is a good start.

■ As you will understand from buying this book, colour photography is vital – look for online listings that include as many images as possible and check them carefully. Beware that colours can appear differently, even between computer screens.

■ Always ask the vendor questions about the object, particularly regarding condition. If there is no image, or you want to see another aspect of the object – ask. Most sellers (private or trade) will want to realise the best price for their items so will be more than happy to help – if approached politely and sensibly.

■ As well as the 'e-hammer' price, you will probably have to pay additional transactional fees such as packing, shipping and possibly regional or national taxes. It is always best to ask for an estimate for these additional costs before leaving a bid. This will also help you tailor your bid as you will have an idea of the maximum price the item will cost if you are successful.

■ In addition to well-known online auction sites, such as eBay, there are a host of other online resources for buying and selling, such as fair and auction date listings.

INTERNET RESOURCES

Live Auctioneers
www.liveauctioneers.com
info@liveauctioneers.com
A free service which allows users to search catalogues from selected auction houses in Europe, the USA and the United Kingdom. Through its connection with eBay, users can bid live via the Internet into salerooms as auctions happen. Registered users can also search through an archive of past catalogues and receive a free newsletter by email.

invaluable.com
www.invaluable.com
sales@invaluable.com
A subscription service which allows users to search selected auction house catalogues from the United Kingdom and Europe. Also offers an extensive archive for appraisal uses.

The Antiques Trade Gazette
www.atg-online.com
The online version of the UK trade newspaper, comprising British auction and fair listings, news and events.

Maine Antique Digest
www.maineantiquedigest.com
The online version of America's trade newspaper including news, articles, fair and auction listings and more.

La Gazette du Drouot
www.drouot.com
The online home of the magazine listing all auctions to be held in France at the Hotel de Drouot in Paris and beyond. An online subscription enables you to download the magazine online.

Auctionnet.com
www.auctionnet.com
Simple online resource listing over 500 websites related to auctions online.

AuctionBytes
www.auctionbytes.com
Auction resource with community forum, news, events, tips and a weekly newsletter.

Auction.fr
www.auction.fr
Online database of auctions at French auction houses. A subscription allows users to search past catalogues and prices realised.

Auctiontalk
www.internetauctionlist.com
Auction news, online and offline auction search engines and live chat forums.

Go Antiques/Antiqnet
www.goantiques.com
www.antiqnet.com
An online global aggregator for art, antiques and collectables dealers who showcase their stock online, allowing users to browse and buy.

eBay
www.ebay.com
Undoubtedly the largest and most diverse of the online auction sites, allowing users to buy and sell in an online marketplace with over 52 million registered users. Collectors should also view eBay Live Auctions (www.ebayliveauctions.com) where traditional auctions are combined with realtime, online bidding allowing users to interact with the saleroom as the auction takes place.

INDEX

A

A
Accessocraft 229
accessories see costume and accessories
Acme Studios 247
Acme Toys 533
Acorn 492
Adidas 462, 477
Adler 490
advertising 13-16
  Art Deco 20
  Babycham 14
  buttons 505
  Coca-Cola 13
  figures 475
  Guinness 15
  signs 350
  standees 505
Afors Glasbruk 303
African
  beads 24, 25
  tribal art 557
agate 17, 24
Aiglon 54
aircraft, toy 521, 526-7, 530
airline posters 370
Aitron 437
Akro Agate Company 327-30
Aladin, Tamara 299, 300
Alberius, Olle 142
albums, photograph 332
Alchimia 129
Alcock, Martyn 57
Alexander, Madame 255, 257, 258
Allcocks & Co. 457
Alley Agate Company 330
Allner, Hazel 119
Almond, David 29
Alsterfors 302, 303
American
  advertising 13
  Art Deco 19, 20
  Bakelite and plastics 359-62
  cameras 55
  ceramics 106-7, 179
  character collectables 181
  chocolate moulds 187-8, 190, 191
  clocks 19
  coins 196
  costume jewellery 247
  Disneyana 250-4
  dolls 256-60
  dolls' houses 261
  eyewear 262-5
  glass 275-6, 279, 288, 313, 314
  handbags 218-24
  lighters 442-3
  marbles 329
  mechanical music 331, 332
  militaria 333
  natural history 335
  pens 338-42, 347
  posters 367, 370, 371, 382
  powder compacts 390, 392, 395
  Sixties and Seventies 425, 431, 434, 436
  soft toys 453, 454
  sport 478
  technology 490
  teddy bears 493, 501
  toys 533-4, 537
  trains 531, 532
  watches 564, 565
  wine and drinking 569-72
  writing equipment 348, 349
American Character Doll Co. 255
Amis, Martin 29
Amstrad 492
Ancora 347
Anderssen, John 144
Andrews, Denise 92
Anglo-Indian chess sets 551
animals
  Beswick 56-66
  black cat collectables 27
  bulls 111, 180, 453
  Carlton Ware 70
  cats 62, 94, 104, 141, 149, 189, 235, 433, 451, 454
  cheetahs 62
  chocolate moulds 187-9
  commemorative ceramics 212
  costume jewellery 235, 238
  cows 60
  deer 176
  Disneyana 251
  dogs 61, 70, 94, 110, 141, 177, 212, 235, 238, 434, 443, 450-1, 454, 552
  elephants 94, 175, 235, 348, 454, 552
  foxes 488
  giraffes 434
  goats 60
  hippopotamuses 104
  horses 58-9, 141, 189, 475
  Italian ceramics 104
  leopards 62
  lighters 443
  lions 62, 433
  Lladró 110
  Lotus Pottery 111
  monkeys 175, 443, 454
  Noah's arks 553
  pigs 60, 332
  rabbits 187-8, 453, 454
  Royal Doulton 94
  Scandinavian ceramics 141
  Sixties and Seventies 433, 434
  soft toys 450-4
  squirrels 488
  studio pottery 149
  taxidermy 488
  teddy bears 493-505
  tigers 94
  tortoises 189
  Wade 164
  see also birds; figures; fish
Anker Drolly 502
Annabel 431
Anne, Princess Royal 422
annuals 51, 271, 273
Anthony, Piers 43
Apple 489
Arabia 139, 144
Armani, Giorgio 214
Arnold 537
Arnold Print Works 256, 454

Art Deco 18-20
  ashtrays 445
  Bakelite and plastics 358, 359, 361-3
  ceramics 175, 180
  clocks 19
  cocktail shakers 571
  costume jewellery 242, 245
  figures 18-19
  glass 276-9, 323, 324
  lighters 443
  perfume bottles 351-3
  powder compacts 390, 393
  trophies 472
  watches 559, 562
Art Metal Wares 443
Art Nouveau
  inkwells 348
  powder compacts 395
Aseda 303
Ashmor 334
Ashtead Pottery 148
ashtrays 350
  advertising 14, 15
  Bakelite and plastics 363
  Clarice Cliff 74, 76, 77, 80
  Fornasetti 95
  glass 279, 282, 284, 295, 445
  Honiton Pottery 177
  railwayana 405
  Sixties and Seventies 428, 430
  studio pottery 152
Asian lighters 446
Asprey 569
Associated Biscuits 428
Atkinson's 390
atomisers 353
Atterberg, Ingrid 145
Attwell, Mabel Lucie 147
Australian posters 373
Austrian
  cameras 54
  costume jewellery 236, 238
  Pez dispensers 354
  powder compacts 392, 393
autographs
  rock and pop 409, 410
  sporting memorabilia 459, 462, 467, 475
A.V.e.M. 293
Avon 229
Aynsley 420, 422
Ayres, F.H. 465

B

Babycham 14
Backhausen, Noomi 143
badges
  Disneyana 254
  sporting memorabilia 472, 473, 476, 477
Bagley 274, 276, 277, 279
bags
  handbags 218-24
  paper 269
  Sixties and Seventies 436, 439
Bahnsen, Frode 144
Bailey, Lesley 247
Bailey, Lorna 175
Bakelite and plastics 358-63

costume jewellery 240-6
Balimann, Hans 133
balloon pumps 434
balls
  football 462
  golf 467-8
Bandai 536
Bandalasta ware 361
Bang, Arne 139
Bang, Jacob 296, 301, 302
Bang, Michael 301
bangles 225, 232, 234, 239-41
banknotes 22-3, 470
Banville, John 29
Barbie dolls 183
Baret Ware 429
Barker, Pat 29
Barlow, Hannah 85
Barlow, Robert 165
Barnes, Julian 29
Bartlett, Nick 308
baseball 477
basketry, tribal art 555
baskets, ceramic 79
Bassett, Robert 43
Bassett Lowke 531, 532
Bassett's Liquorice Allsorts 180
Batchelor, Denzil 45
Bateman, J. 364
Bates, Brown-Westhead & Moore 385
Bates, Elliot & Co. 385
Batman 181
bats, cricket 479
Baume & Mercier 563
Baxter, Geoffrey 280, 286, 316-21
Bay Keramik 170
beach outfits 216
beads 24-5
beakers
  Bakelite and plastics 361
  commemorative ceramics 417-19, 422
  glass 297
  Sixties and Seventies 432
  sporting memorabilia 471
bears
  Paddington Bear 81
  polar bears 500
  Rupert Bear 63
  teddy bears 493-505
  The Beatles 391, 406-8
Beetem, Geoffrey 308
Belgian
  lighters 443
  teddy bears 503
Bellow, Saul 29
bells
  ceramic 476
  table 473
Benbros 527
Bennett, Avril 160
Bennett, Cynthia 124
Bennett, Harold 175
Benney, Gerald 482, 483
Berliner, Emile 331
Bernatowitz, Teo 163
Bernhard, Lucian 382
Bernières, Louis de 31
Bertrandt, Andrzej 383

Beswick 14, 56-66, 266
Beusmans, John 149
Bexley 347
Bianconi, Fulvio 293, 294
bicycling 26
Bienen-Davis 218
Biggs, David B. 85
bikinis 217
Bilton's Ironstone 428
Bing 331, 493
Bing & Grøndahl 175
birds
  Beswick 56-7
  costume jewellery 235
  glass 291, 294, 295
  Italian ceramics 104
  Lotus Pottery 111
  Royal Doulton 94
  soft toys 452
  studio pottery 152
  taxidermy 485-6
Birmingham Tool Co. 506
biscuit barrels 74, 75, 267
biscuit tins 16, 428, 429
Bishop, Rachel 115
bisque dolls 255
Bitossi 103-4, 129
Björnquist, Karin 140
Black, Montague B. 369
Black, Penny 161
black cat collectables 27
Blake, Donald 364
Blangy 362
Blass, Bill 214
blotters 360
Blue Ribbon Playthings 502
Blyton, Enid 51
board games 553
Boccasile, Gino 369
Le Boeuf pens 342
Bogan 218
Bohemian
  beads 24
  glass 279, 283
Bond, Michael 48
Bond, Myrtle 120
bonds and shares 28
bone china 212
book covers 435
bookends 20, 473
bookmarks 248
books 29-51
  annuals 51, 271, 273
  Art Deco 19
  character collectables 184
  children's 48-50
  film and TV 271
  modern first editions 29-38
  paperbacks 39-47
  rock and pop 406, 409
  sporting 469-70
  teddy bear 505
Borgstrom, Bo 303
Bortnyik, Bereny 367
bottle stoppers 249
bottle tops 14
bottles
  ceramic 131, 134, 170
  glass 298, 300, 303, 306, 312, 314, 319
  see also perfume bottles
Bourjois 395
Bovey Pottery 419
Bowie knives 333
Bowler, Tim 29
bowls
  agate 17

Briglin Pottery 67
Burleigh ware 175
Carlton Ware 68, 69
Cinque Ports Pottery 138
Clarice Cliff 72, 75, 76, 78, 79
  commemorative ceramics 210, 212, 421
Crowan Pottery 83
Crown Devon 84
Fifties 266
  glass 278, 280, 284, 287, 289, 291, 304-6, 311-13, 323
Italian ceramics 103
Moorcroft 115
Poole Pottery 120, 123, 124, 126, 127
Royal Copenhagen 136
Ruskin Pottery 137
Scandinavian ceramics 140-3, 146
  sporting memorabilia 471
  studio pottery 148-50, 153
  tribal art 555
Wade 165
Wedgwood 167
West German ceramics 170
Bowser, Larry 434
boxes
  agate 17
  Bakelite and plastics 358-9
  cigarette 358-9, 446, 472
  commemorative ceramics 423
  fly 458
  jewellery 359
  powder 358, 359
  Sixties and Seventies 429, 430
  toy 522
  Wedgwood 167
  writing 350
Boyd, William 30
bracelets 230, 232, 239, 242
braces (tools) 508, 511
Bracewell, Michael 30
Bradbury, Arthur 122
Bradbury, Ray 30
Bradley & Hubbard Mfg. Co. 473
Brambly Hedge 91
Brandon, D. 210
Branzi, Andrea 179
brass
  ashtrays 405
  beads 24
  fishing reels 455-7
Brémond, B.A. 332
Bretby 175
Brett, Ronald 365
Breyen, Beth 135
Bridgwood 405
Brier, Amanda 150
Brigden, Alison 160, 162
Briglin Pottery 67
Britains 527, 539-42
Broadhurst Bros 175
brochures, shipping memorabilia 249
Brockwitz 274
bronzes, sporting 475
brooches 243-4, 247, 407
  see also pins
Brookes & Adams 361
Brosi, Manfredo 293
Brougham, Reginald 463
Brown, Fredric 39

Brown, Karen 128
Brown, P. Irwin 367
bubble gum cards 409
Buch, Bodil 135
Buckland, Ray 43
Buckle, Claude 364
bud vases
  Art Deco 20
  black cat collectables 27
  glass 318
  Royal Doulton 85
  stainless steel 481
Budd 512
Bulova 562
Bunnykins 92-3
Burato, Michele 293
Burbank 259
Burger King 182
Burleigh ware 175, 266
Burnham 343
Burroughs, Edgar Rice 46
buses, toy 520, 552
Bush, Thelma 123, 124
busts
  ceramic 108, 176, 210, 211, 416
  glass 313
  Sixties and Seventies 433
buttons, teddy bear 505
Buzzi, Daniele 372

C
cache pots 159
Cadbury's 16
Caithness Glass 322
cake stands 112, 481
calculators 490
calendars
  Art Deco 19
  Disneyana 253-4
  film and TV 273
  rock and pop 406
Cambridge Glass Co. 275
cameras 52-5, 252
Campbell Kid 257
Canadian
  coins 196
  pens 338, 339, 341, 342
  posters 367, 369
  wine and drinking 572
candleholders
  glass 307
  Myott 118
  Sampson Hancock & Sons 177
Scandinavian ceramics 142, 146
  Sixties and Seventies 432
  stainless steel 482, 483
candlesticks
  Clarice Cliff 73, 74, 79
  glass 281, 299
  Italian ceramics 104
  Rosenthal 137
  stainless steel 481
candy containers 27
Cantonese chess sets 550
Capon Heaton & Co. 467
Capp, Al 186
caps, sporting 477
car mascots 473
carafes 122
Carbis, Colin 161
Cardew, Michael 148
Cardin, Pierre 262-4, 563
cards

bubble gum 409
character collectables 181
  greeting 271
  playing cards 249
  postcards 183
  Valentine 182
Carlshutte 279
Carlton Ware 68-70
  advertising 15
  animals 70
  bowls 68, 69
  coffee sets 70
  dishes 69
  ginger jars 68
  jardinières 68
  jugs 70, 249
  money boxes 427
  royal commemoratives 423
  salt and pepper shakers 427
  teapots 70
  vases 68
Carn Pottery 149
Carnaby Street 428
Carnac, Carol 39
Carnegie, Hattie 229
Carpet Bags of America 222
Carruthers Gould, Francis 213
cars
  character collectables 185
  toy 252, 363, 513-17, 523-30
Carstens 171
Carter, Ashley 39
Carter, Truda 119
Carter Stabler Adams 119-20
Cartier 442, 446
Cartier, Louis 227
Cartwright, Justin 45
Carvacraft 360
cased glass 301-2
Casio 489, 490
Caskin, W. 508
Cassandre 364
Casson, Sir Hugh 112, 114
cast iron inkwells 348
Caswell, Shane 308
Catalá, Francisco 109
Catalin
  cigarette boxes 358
  clocks 360
  dice 363
  pencil sharpeners 360
  plaques 363
  salt and pepper shakers 361
  sculpture 363
catalogues, sporting 478
cats
  Beswick 62
  black cat collectables 27
  chocolate moulds 189
  costume jewellery 235
  Italian ceramics 104
  Royal Doulton 94
  Scandinavian ceramics 141
  Sixties and Seventies 433
  soft toys 451, 454
  studio pottery 149
Cavally, Frederick L. Jr 505
Caverswall 211
celluloid dolls 258
centrepieces
  ceramic 179
  glass 275-6
ceramics 56-180
  Art Deco 19, 180

ashtrays 445
Bernard Rooke 130-1
Beswick 56-66
bicycling 26
black cat collectables 27
Briglin Pottery 67
Carlton Ware 68-70
character collectables 181
chess sets 548, 549
Clarice Cliff 71-80
Coalport 81
commemorative 210-13,
416-23
costume jewellery 244
Crowan Pottery 83
Crown Devon 84
Disneyana 251-3
Fifties 266-7
Fornasetti 95
Hazle Ceramics 96
Hummel 98-102
inkwells 348
Italian 103-5
Josef Originals 106-7
Lladró 108-10
Lotus Pottery 111
Louis Hudson 97
marbles 330
Midwinter 112-14
Moorcroft 115-16
Myott 117-18
Poole Pottery 119-28
Postmodern 129
pot-lids 384-9
railwayana 405
Rosenthal 132-3
Royal Copenhagen 134-6
Royal Doulton 85-94
Ruskin Pottery 137
Rye Potteries 138
Scandinavian 139-46
Shelley 147
shipping memorabilia 248-9
Sixties and Seventies 425-7
sporting memorabilia 471,
475, 479
studio pottery 148-53
Susie Cooper 82
Swid Powell 154-5
teapots 156
tobacco jars 444
Tremaen 157
tribal art 555
Troika 158-63
Wade and Wade Heath 164-
5
Wedgwood 166-7
West German 168-73
Chad Valley
diecast toys 527
soft toys 450, 453, 500
teddy bears 493, 498
trains 531
Challinor 210
Chambers, Philip 39
chambersticks 282
champagne glasses 482
champagne taps 571
Champion Agate Company
328, 329
Chance 322
Chance, W.M. 89
Chanel 214-16, 222, 229,
244
Chaplins 507
character collectables 181-6
Batman 181

Disneyana 250-4
Magic Roundabout 184
Popeye 183
Smurfs 447-9
Snoopy and Peanuts 184
Superman 182
Character Doll Co. 259
character jugs 211
Charbens 527, 545
chargers
Clarice Cliff 78
glass 291, 319
Poole Pottery 123, 124,
126
Scandinavian ceramics 139
studio pottery 150, 151
Wedgwood 166
Charles, Prince of Wales 423
Charteris, Leslie 45
Chase, James Hadley 39
Chase Metalware Company
20, 360
Chatwin, Bruce 30
cheese dishes 133
Chein, J. 533, 534
Chelsea China 212
Chenet 478
Cherilea 545
chess 548-51
Chevalier, Tracey 30
Chihuly, Dale 311
Child, Lee 30
children's books 48-50
Chiltern Toys 453, 493, 497
Chilton pens 342
china see ceramics
Chinese
chess sets 550
chocolate moulds 190
coins 196
chintz ware 426
chocolate moulds 187-92
chokers 231, 234
Chown 417, 420, 423
Christensen, Kari 134-6
Christensen Agate Company
327-30
cigar cases 446
cigarette boxes 358-9, 446,
472
cigarette cases 446
cigarette dispensers 446
C.I.J. 528
Cinque Ports Pottery 138
Clappison, John 177-8, 425
Clavell, James 30
Cleverly, Barbara 30
Cliff, Clarice 71-80, 213
clips, costume jewellery 244
clocks
Art Deco 19
Bakelite and plastics 360,
362
character collectables 181
glass 279
railwayana 404
clothes see costume and
accessories
cloud glass 281-2
clubs, golf 463-6
coaches, toy 520
Coalport 81, 418, 422
coasters 429
coat hangers 407, 436
coat hooks 432
coats 215, 216
Coca-Cola 13

cocktail sets 572
cocktail shakers 569, 571
Codge 270
coffee cans 85, 177
coffee pots
Clarice Cliff 71
Crown Devon 84
Midwinter 113
Sixties and Seventies 426
stainless steel 480, 481,
483
studio pottery 153
coffee services
Carlton Ware 70
Fifties 266
Susie Cooper 82
Cohn, T. 533
coins 193-7
English 193-5
foreign 196-7
sporting memorabilia 477
Cole, D. 84
Cole, Edward 374-6
Cole, Jack 138
Cole, Walter 138
Colfer, Eoin 48
collars, dog 573
Colledge, Glynn 151
Collett, Glenna 469
Collins, Enid 220
Collins, Peter 365
comics 198-209, 475
commemorative ceramics
210-13, 249, 416-23
Commodore 490
compacts, powder 390-5
Compagnie Française de
Photographie 52
comport stands 472
comports 166, 274
composition dolls 257
Compton & Woodhouse 420
Compton Pottery 149
computer games 491
computers 492
condom holders 179
Conklin 342
Conklin, Teri 308
Connett, Catherine 127
Conran, Terence 113, 114
Constantinidis, Joanna 149
Continental
militaria 334
tobacco jars 444
Conway, Randall 43
Conway Stewart 343, 347
Cooke, S.E. 457
cookie jars 176
Cooper, Austin 365
Cooper, Joseph 508
Cooper, Susie 82
Copeland
royal commemoratives 417,
418
sporting memorabilia 471,
479
Coper, Hans 148
copper
Art Deco 20
costume jewellery 239
saucepans 405
Corgi 184, 513-15
corkscrews 569-71
Coro 226-7
Corocraft 226
Coronet Pottery 422, 423
corsets 217

Cortendorf 267
Costelloe 365
costume and accessories
214-24
advertising 13
character collectables 185
hats 405, 436, 558
sporting 461, 474, 475,
477
tribal art 555-6
costume jewellery 225-47
Coty 16, 390, 391, 395
Crace, Jim 31
crackers 184
cravats 217
Creak's 528
Creative Accessories Ltd 181
Crescent 528
cricket 479
Crompton, Richmal 48
Crowan Pottery 83
Crown Derby 421, 423
Crown Devon 84
Crown Ducal 176, 428
Crown Staffordshire 418
cruet sets 177, 361
see also mustard pots;
pepper shakers; salt pots and
shakers
cruise liner and shipping
memorabilia 248-9
posters 368-9
Crummles 423
Cryer, Marjorie 120
Culliford, Pierre 447
Cummings, Keith 311
Cuneo, Terence 364, 366
cup holders 182
cups and saucers
character collectables 183
Clarice Cliff 74
commemorative ceramics
416, 423
Crowan Pottery 83
Disneyana 253
Fifties 266
glass 288
Midwinter 113
railwayana 405
Shelley 147
Sixties and Seventies 425
Swid Powell 154
SylvaC 179
Curr, Tom 369
Curtis, Honor 158, 160-2
Curtis, Kimberley 92, 93
cushions 431, 432, 435
Cusk, Rachel 31
cut glass 280
Cutler, Carol 124-7
cutlery, stainless steel 483
Cybiko 492
Cyren, Gunnar 303
Czech
cameras 54
ceramics 180
chess sets 549
costume jewellery 238, 242
glass 274, 276-9, 283-5
perfume bottles 351-3
posters 383

D
da Ros, Antonio 293

Dadd, Caroline 92, 93
Dahl, Roald 48
Dahl-Jensen 175
Dailey, Dan 311
Dakin, R. & Company 250
Dalisi, Riccardo 179
Dallmeyer 52
Dalrymple, W. 469
"The Dandy" 200
Danish
  ceramics 134-6, 175
  glass 296, 303
  pens 344
  Sixties and Seventies 430
  stainless steel 483
  see also Scandinavian
Dansk Design 303
Dartington glass 286-7
Dartington Pottery 150
Daum 322
Davidson, George & Co. 281-2
Davies, Linda 31
Davies, Margaret 86-8, 90
Davis, Harry 83
Daws, Frederick 94
Dawson, Jill 31
De La Renta, Oscar 216
De La Rue 343
De Lucchi, Michele 247
De Rouen, Reed 43
Dean's Rag Books 453
Debón, Salvador 108, 109
decanters
  amethyst glass 324
  Caithness Glass 322
  ceramic 572
  cut glass 280
  Dartington glass 287
  Fifties 572
  Murano 295
  Scandinavian glass 296,
303
  Whitefriars 317, 318
Decimo 490
Deighton, Len 31
Deka Plastics Inc. 425
Denberg, J.J. 230
Denby 176
Denys Fisher 270
Depression glass 288
Derneys 395
desk bases 349
desk.lamps 363
desk tidies 430
Devlin, Stuart 482
Diana, Princess of Wales 423
diaries, rock and pop 407
dice 363
Dick, Philip K. 43
diecast toys 525-30
Diem 502
Dinky 516-22
dinner services 82, 114
Dior, Christian
  costume 214, 215
  eyewear 262, 264
  jewellery 230
dishes
  advertising 16
  Bakelite and plastics 361
  Carlton Ware 69
  Crowan Pottery 83
  Fifties 267
  Fornasetti 95
  glass 16, 282, 288, 290,
297, 298, 306, 319
  Italian ceramics 105

Moorcroft 115, 116
Poole Pottery 122-4, 126,
128
  Rosenthal 132
  Royal Copenhagen 135
  Scandinavian ceramics
139-40, 142, 145, 146
  shipping memorabilia 249
  Sixties and Seventies 426
  stainless steel 482, 483
  studio pottery 148, 150,
151
  Troika 163
  Wade 165
Disneyana 250-4
  action figures 272
  Pez dispensers 354
  sand pails 533
  tinplate toys 536
  Wade figures 164
display stands 350
Distler 531
Ditchfield, John 311
Doctor Who 270-1
Dodge, David 39
Dodo 438-9
dog collars 573
Dollcraft 186
dolls 255-61
  Barbie 183
  bisque 255
  celluloid 258
  character collectables 183,
185, 186
  composition 257
  Disneyana 251
  fabric 256-7
  plastic 258-60
  tribal art 557
dolls' houses and accessories
261
Dom Watch & Cie 473
Donald Duck 250-3
doorstops 27
Doubleday, Tina 159
Doughty, Louise 31
Douglass 473
Doulton 26, 348, 417
  see also Royal Doulton
Dowd, Leo 366
Dowler 570
dresses 215-16
drinking straws 253, 431
drums, tribal art 556
Dubarry 391
Dubois 371
dumb waiters 573
Dumler & Breiden 171
Dunhill 349, 440-2, 445, 563
Dunlop 468, 473
Dunn 342
Dunne-Cooke, H.J. 306
Dupin, Leon 376
Durable Toy and Novelty Corp.
331
Durham 252
Dutch
  chocolate moulds 191, 192
  posters 367
Dux 537
d'Ylen, Yves 376-8

E

Eagle, John 39

earrings 225, 228, 230-4,
236, 238, 239, 241, 245, 247
earthenware see ceramics
Eastman, P.D. 49
Eastman Kodak 55
Easton, L.P. 45
Eaton, Seymour 505
Eclipse 342
Edenfalk, Bengt 306
Edison, Thomas 331
Edward VII, King 418
Edward VIII, King 419
Edwards, L. & M. 219
Effanbee 257
egg cups 249, 418
Elgin 392, 560
Eligor 528
Elizabeth, Queen Mother 420
Elizabeth II, Queen 421-2
Elkington 348
Ellery, Peter 157
Ellison, Harlan 40
Ellson, Hal 40
Elmer, Violet 68
Elsden, Leslie 126
enamel
  lighters 442
  powder compacts 390
Enfield 334
Engman, Kjell 298
Eppelsheimer 187-8, 190
Ernemann 55
ES-Keramik 171
Essevi 176
Esterbrook 343
Estrava 217
Ethiopian beads 24
evening gowns 214
Ewart, Peter 369
eyewear 262-5

F

fabric dolls 256-7
Falcucci, Robert 373
Falkner, John 43
Fallows 537
fans, golf 473
Farmer, Arthur 40
Farnell
  soft toys 450, 454, 500
  teddy bears 493, 496
fashion
  Sixties and Seventies 436-7
  see also costume and
accessories
Faulks, Sebastian 31
Felsen, Henry Gregor 40
Fenton 276
Fenton, Harry 85
Ferrari, G. 475
Fforde, Jasper 31
Fielding, S. & Co. 84
Fielding's Crown Devon 176
Fifties 266-9
  ceramics 266-7
  sculpture 268
figures
  advertising 14, 15, 475
  Art Deco 18-19
  character collectables 182,
184, 186
  commemorative ceramics
423
  Disneyana 251

film and TV 270, 272, 273
  glass 276, 278
  Hummel 98-102
  Josef Originals 106-7
  lead 539-46
  Lladró 108-9
  militaria 334
  Paddington Bear 81
  Rosenthal 133
  Royal Doulton 86-93
  Rupert Bear 63
  Shelley 147
  Sixties and Seventies 433
  Smurfs 447-9
  sporting memorabilia 478
  Star Wars 547
  studio pottery 148
  tribal art 556-7
  Wade 164
  see also animals; birds
Fillerys Toffees 16
film and TV 270-3
  character collectables 181
  posters 383
Finney, Jack 40
Finnish
  glass 297, 299-300, 305
  see also Scandinavian
Fischer, Georg 535
fish
  ceramic 62
  chocolate moulds 189
  costume jewellery 235
  glass 324
  taxidermy 487
Fisher, Steve 40
Fisher Price Toys 186
fishing 455-8
Flammeche, Pierre 40
flask-holders 431
Fleming, Ian 45
Flisak, Jerzy 383
Florenza 230
Florida 223
flower pots 138, 252
flower sets 280, 281
fly boxes 458
Flygfors 304
Fohr 172
Foley 266, 471
Folkard, Mr 58
food-related posters 374-6
football 459-62
Forbes, Max 373
Forgan, R. 463, 464
forks, stainless steel 483
Fornasetti 95
Forsyth, Frederick 32
fossils 335-6
Fowles, John 32
frames, Art Deco 20
Franck, Kaj 139, 305
Franckhauser, Etienne 276
Frankhart Inc. 473
Franklin Mint 528
Fraser, George McDonald 35-6
Frayn, Michael 32
Freemo 267
Fremund, Richard 383
French
  ashtrays 445
  bicycling 26
  cameras 52, 54, 55
  chocolate moulds 189, 192
  coins 196
  corkscrews 569-71
  costume jewellery 239, 244

dolls 258
eyewear 262-5
glass 279
handbags 222
inkwells 348
lighters 442
mechanical music 332
pens 339, 341, 347
perfume bottles 351-3
posters 367, 369-71, 373, 376-8
powder compacts 391-4
sand pails 534
soft toys 453, 454
toys 519, 520, 553
watches 563, 565
weird and wonderful 573
French, Nicci 32
Freudenreich, Marek 383
Friberg, Berndt 141
Frith, David 150
Fritts, Drew 308
Frost, Norwich 507
fruit bowls 165
Fry, W.A. 379
Funke, Cornelia 48
furniture, dolls' house 261
Fuss, Albert 369

G

Gaiman, Neil 32
Galgut, Damon 32
Galuszka, Julie 177
games see toys and games
Games, Abram 370, 380
García, Fulgencio 108, 110
Gardner, Erle Stanley 40
Gardner, John 45
Garland, Alex 32
Garon, Marco 45
gauges, tools 509
Gavin, Jamila 48
Gaylene 221
Gee, P. 87, 88
Gellerstedt, Staffan 305
General Electrics 431
George V, King 418
George VI, King 420
George, Herbert & Co. 252
George, Muriel Joseph 106
German
  black cat collectables 27
  cameras 54, 55
  ceramics 98-102, 129, 132-3, 156, 168-73, 180
  chess sets 549
  chocolate moulds 187-92
  cigarette boxes 446
  coins 196-7
  commemorative ceramics 417
  corkscrews 570
  dolls 255-8
  glass 274-9, 307, 323
  inkwells 348
  lighters 443
  marbles 327
  match stands 445
  mechanical music 331-2
  pens 344, 346
  perfume bottles 351, 353
  posters 369, 371
  powder compacts 394
  Sixties and Seventies 432,

433
  technology 490
  teddy bears 493-5, 502-4
  toys 535-6, 553
  trains 531, 532
Giambone, Donni 434
Gibson 464
Gibson, H.P. & Sons 553
Gilbert, A.C. 272, 552
Gilbert, Alfred 149
Gilco 545
Giles, F. Kenwood 375
Gillies, Stephen 311
Gilman, George G. 45
Gilroy 15
Gilt 177
ginger jars
  Carlton Ware 68
  Crown Devon 84
  Scandinavian ceramics 144
  Shelley 147
Giotto 129
Girard, André 377
Glasform 311
glass 274-324
  ashtrays 445
  Babycham glasses 14
  beads 24-5
  British cut glass 280
  character collectables 182
  cloud glass 281-2
  Czech 283-5
  Dartington 286-7
  Depression glass 288
  dishes 16, 282, 288, 290, 297, 298, 306, 319
  Fifties 269
  goblets 280, 303, 304, 312
  inkwells 348
  Isle of Wight 290-2
  Langham Glass 289
  marbles 309, 327-30
  Mdina 290
  Murano 293-5
  perfume bottles 292, 313, 314, 351-3
  pressed glass 274-9
  Scandinavian 296-306
  Schott Zweisel 307
  shot glasses 285
  Sklo Union 283-4
  spheres 308-10
  studio glass 311-14
  vases 277-8, 280-7, 289-307, 311-24
  Whitefriars 316-21
Glass, Leo 230
glasses see eyewear
Glevum 405
Glinto, Darcy 40
Gliori, Debi 48
globes 419
goblets
  glass 280, 303, 304, 312
  stainless steel 482
Goebels, W. 177
Goerz, C.P. 54
gold
  cigarette cases 446
  coins 194, 197
  lighters 442
  watches 559-65
Golding, Richard 313
Golding, William 32
Goldscheider 19
Goldschmidt, Brigitte 67
golf 463-73

Gossard 217
Gouda 177
Gough, J. 375
Goulart, Ron 43
Gozo Glass 322
Grafton, Sue 33
Graham, Caroline 33
Graham, Jack 33
gramophones 331-2
Grandstand 491
Granoska, Jan 94
Grapinoix 351
Graves, Michael 154
gravy boats 70, 483
Gray, A.E. & Co. 82
Gray, George 138
Gredington, Arthur 56-62, 64-6
Green, Henry 33
Greenaway, Kate 16
Greene 365
greeting cards 271
Grey, Harry 41
Griffiths, E.J. 86, 89
Grimwades 156
Gruen 564
Grundig 492
GTP 535
Gucci 215, 218, 222
Guerriero, Alessandro 129
Guinness 15
Guldsmeds Aktie Bolaget 571
Gull, Ivar 373
Gullaskruf 304
Günthermann 537
Gurnah, Abdulrazak 33
Gustavsberg 139-41
gutta percha marbles 330
Gwenda 391
Gyatt, Richard 421

H

Haas, Rudolf 502
Hadeland 304
Hadid, Zaha 154
Hafner, Dorothy 133
hairdryers 185
Haji 536
Halcyon Days 422
half dolls 261
Halier, Carl 136
Hall, Dinny 230
Hallam, Albert 57, 62, 64-6, 92
Hallam, Arthur 14
Hallen, Jessie 164
Hamilton 561-2
hammers 511
Hammersley 419
Hammond, David 280
Hammond, Ingrid 125
Hampton, Hilda 119
handbags 218-24
handkerchiefs 254
Hands, David 64
Har 230-1
Harcuba, Jiří 283, 285
Hardy, Dudley 382
Hardy Bros 455-6, 458
Harper, W.K. 89, 90
Harrachov Glassworks 284
Harradine, Leslie 86-90
Harris, Michael 290-1, 323
Harris, Muriel 374

Harris, Timothy 290, 292
Hartley Wood 322
Hasbro 434
Haskell, Miriam 231
Haskins, Gwen 122
Hastings Pottery 150
Hatchard, Anne 120
hats
  railwayana 405
  Sixties and Seventies 436
  tribal art 558
Hauptmann, Arthur 371
Haussmann, Robert and Trix 155
Hayward, Walter 92
Hazel Atlas Glass Co. 288
Hazeldine, Rosetta 348
Hazle Ceramics 96
Hazzard, Shirley 33
heaters 20
Heather 395
Hecla 501
Hedger, Donald 245
Heeley, James and Sons 570
Heinrich Handwerck 255
Heinze 371
Heinze & Pedreff 372
Heller, Zoë 33
Henie, Sonja 257
Henriette 394
Henry, John 463
Herapath, Edith 348
Herkomer, K. 369
Herman, Sam 311
Hermann 493
Hermanova Glassworks 283
Hermès 218, 221
Herrick 366
Herring, John Frederick Sr 474
Hewitt, Jan 370
Hicks, W. 374
Higgins, Jack 33
Hill, John 543
Hill, Tobias 34
Him, George 370
Hirst, Henry & Son 553
Hitt, Steve 308
Hlava, Pavel 283, 284
Hobb, Robin 34
Hodgson, William Hope 46
Hoffman 278
Hoffman, Mary 48
Hogan, James 283, 318
Höganäs 144
Hoglund, Eric 284
Hohnlein 190
Holden, Wendy 34
Holder, Margaret 120
Holiday, Billie 46
Holl, Steven 155
Holland, John 342
Holland Studio Craft 186
Hollycraft 231
Holmegaard 296, 301
Holzman 218
homeware, Sixties and Seventies 429-32
honey pots 78
Hongell, Goran 297
Honiton Pottery 177
Hornby 531, 532
Horner, George W. & Co. 444
horns
  hunting 479
  powder 334
Hornsea Pottery 177-8, 425, 426

horse racing 474-5
Howard, Josh 309
Hoyrup 430
Hudnut, Richard 395
Hudson, Louis 97
Huerta, Juan 108-10
Hughes, A. 86, 88
Hughes-Lubeck, Amanda 59, 60
Hugon, Roland 367, 371
Hulet, Dinah 308
humidors 444
Hummel 98-102
Hungarian posters 367
Hunter, Evan 41
Hunter, Robert 469
hunting horns 479
Huntley & Palmer 16
Hutchison, John 463

I

I was Lord Kitchener's Valet 428
ice buckets 361, 572
Icelandic ceramics 177
Iden Pottery 138
Ihagee 55
Ihnatowicz, Maria 383
Iittala 297
Illinois 564
Illsley, Lesley 158
Indian
chess sets 551
coins 197
militaria 333
Ingber 220
inkwells 348, 472
Inuit art 556
Irish
ceramics 178
chess sets 548
teddy bears 503, 504
iron inkwells 348
ironstone 248, 425, 428
Irving, John 34
Ishiguro, Kazuo 34
Ising 54
Iskin, Harry 231
Isle of Wight glass 290-2
Isle of Wight Pottery 153
Italian
cameras 54
ceramics 95, 103-5, 176, 179
chess sets 549
cigarette dispensers 446
dolls 257, 261
eyewear 265
glass 293-5
handbags 219
pens 347
perfume bottles 351, 353
posters 369, 372
Sixties and Seventies 430, 436
Itera 26
ivory chess sets 548, 550, 551

J

jackets 215
Jacobsen, Arne 482, 483

Jacobsen, Bengt 134
Jacobson, Howard 34
Jacques, Brian 49
Jaeger Le Coultre 563
jam pots 120
James, Dorothy 120
James, P.D. 34
Jamieson, Mark 152
Janson, Hank 41, 43
Japanese
ashtrays 445
black cat collectables 27
cameras 54
ceramics 179
chess sets 550
cocktail shakers 571
Fifties 267
lighters 442, 443
pens 345, 347
posters 367
powder compacts 390, 392
technology 490
toys 527, 536, 538, 552, 553
jardinières
Carlton Ware 68
Clarice Cliff 75
glass 284
Moorcroft 116
jars
advertising 15
Crown Devon 84
Fifties 267
Fornasetti 95
ginger 68, 84, 144, 147
glass 284
Scandinavian ceramics 144
Shelley 147
Sixties and Seventies 426
tobacco 444
Troika 160
Jasba 172
jasperware 471
Jeanette Glass Co. 288
jeans 217
Jefferson, R. 87
Jefferson, Robert 123
Jelinek, Vladimir 285
Jenkins, Sheila 120
Jerome, Bobbie 221
Jersey Pottery 151
Jewelerama 231
jewellery
costume jewellery 225-47
rock and pop 407
tribal art 558
see also necklaces; pins
jewellery boxes 359
JIE 267
jigsaw puzzles 272, 405, 434
Jinks, Louise 158, 160, 163
Jobling 274-8
Johanfors 304
Johansson, Willy 304
Johilco 543
Johnen, Wilhelm 46
Johns, Capt. W.E. 49
Jones, Bobby 469
Jones, Cooper W. & Co. 509
Jones, Kate 311
Jones of New York 217
Jonteel 392, 395
Jopeko 172
Jopi 502
Josef Originals 106-7
Jourdain, Charles 222
J.P.M. 454

JRM Design 429
jugs
advertising 16
Burleigh ware 175
Carlton Ware 70
character jugs 211
Clarice Cliff 74-6, 78
commemorative ceramics 210-13, 416-19
Crowan Pottery 83
Disneyana 253
Doulton 85
glass 288, 301
Italian ceramics 105
Midwinter 112, 114
musical jugs 70, 164
Myott 117-18
Postmodern 129
puzzle jugs 180, 471
Royal Doulton 85
Royal Winton 180
Ruskin Pottery 137
Rye Pottery 138
shipping memorabilia 249
Sixties and Seventies 426
sporting memorabilia 471, 475, 479
stainless steel 480
studio pottery 148, 150, 151, 153
Susie Cooper 82
Toby jugs 85, 213, 419
Wade Heath 164
West German ceramics 169
72
Jurnikl, Rudolf 284

K

Kadin 220
Kage, Wilhelm 139
Kahn, Charles 224
kaleidoscopes 184
Kalmar (A.B.) Glasbruk 304
Karhula 297
Karston Co. 465
Kastrup 296, 301, 302
Kay Displays Inc. 13
Kedelv, Paul 304
Keeley, E.V. 379, 380
Keeley, Pat 366
Keelor, Arthur 381
Kelloggs 256
Kells, Susannah 34
Kelly, Jerry 309
Kelly bags 221
Kennedy, Jacqueline 258
key rings 408, 449
Khahn, Emmanuelle 262
Kiffa beads 25
Kigu 390
Kilburn, Simone 162
Kilrush Pottery 178
King's Lynn Glass 289
Kinnaird, Alison 312
Kirton, Irene 125
Kjartansson, Ragnar 177
Klee, Paul 161
Knickerbocker 501
knives
militaria 333
stainless steel 483
Knox, Archibald 149
Koefoed, Inge-Lise 135
Kornbluth, C.M. 44

Kosan 349
Kosta 298
Krajewski, Andrzej 383
Kramer 231
Kruger, Murray 218
Kruse, Käthe 257
Kuchler, Wilhelm 307

L

La Mode 390, 392
Labino, Dominick 311
Lacoste, G. 381
lacquer desk bases 349
Lacroix, Christian 214, 215
lady head vases 267
Lady Jane 428
Lagerfeld, Karl 214, 231
Laholm Keramik 144
Lalique
glass 274
perfume bottles 351
plastics 359
powder compacts 395
lampbases
Bernard Rooke 130-1
glass 305, 314
Italian ceramics 103
Louis Hudson 97
Scandinavian ceramics 142
Tremaen 157
Troika 162
see also lighting
lampshades
character collectables 184
Disneyana 253
Lander, Robert K. 46
Lane, Kenneth Jay 225
Langham Glass 289
Langley 151, 178
Lanvin 232
Lapidus, Ted 264
Larson, Lisa 140, 141
Laug, Andre 215
Lauren, Ralph 222
Lawrence, Caroline 35
Layton, Peter 312
Le Coultre 563
Leach, Bernard 83, 148, 150, 152
Leach, David 83, 150, 151
lead figures 539-46
Leaper, Eric 151
Lee, Terri 255
Leete, Alfred 375
Lefebure & Cie 351, 352
Lehmann 536, 538
Leiber, Judith 218, 221, 222
Leica 53
lemonade sets 479
Lenci 176, 257
Lenthérique 395
Lesney 525
Lester, Jo 153
Letang Fils 189
letter racks 350
Letts, Barry 271
Leuchovius, Sylvia 142
Levi's 217
Levy, Andrea 35
Lewenstein, Eileen 67
Leyendecker, J.C. 378
Libensk, Stanislav 283
Libochovice Glassworks 284
Lichtenstein, Roy 133

lighters 430, 440-3, 446
lighting
    advertising 15
    Art Deco 20
    Bakelite and plastics 363
    bicycle lamps 26
    glass 279, 281, 301
    railwayana 403
    Sixties and Seventies 430
    sporting memorabilia 462
    see also lampbases;
    lampshades
Lilo Product 533
Lindberg, Stig 139-41
Lindstrand, Vicke 298
Lindstrom Corporation 331
Linnemann-Schmidt, Per 144-5
Lionel 532
Lipofsky, Marvin 311
Lisner 232
lithographs 474
Litt, Toby 35
Little Legion 546
Littleton, Harvey 311
Lladró 108-10
Llangollen Pottery 152
Llewelyn 223
Loewy, Raymond 133
Loffelhardt, Heinrich 307
Logan, Ian 429
Logan, Maurice 367
Londi, Aldo 103-4
London Stereoscopic Co. 52
Lone Ranger 186
Lone Star 529
Longines 561, 563
Longmate 368
Looney Tunes 355
Lorenzl, Josef 18
lorries, toy 519, 529, 530
Lotus Pottery 111
Louvic 564
loving cups 421, 423
LPs, rock and pop 406-15
Lucas, Joseph 26
Lucinda 232
Lucite
    boxes 358, 359
    costume jewellery 241,
    244, 246
    desk ornaments 360
    eyewear 265
    handbags 219, 223-4
    perfume bottles 352
Lumley, Savile 379
Lunch At The Ritz 232
Luntoy 552
lustre ware 248
Lütken, Per 296, 301
Lyttleton, David 63, 66, 89

M

Mabie, Todd & Co. 343
McCarthy, Cormac 35
MacDonald, John D. 41
McEwan, Ian 36
McIntyre, James 115
McKie, Roy 49
MacLean, Alistair 35
McNeilly, Wilfred 46
MacNiven & Cameron 350
Maer, Mitchell 230
magazines 272, 325-6

Magic Introduction Co. 442
Magic Roundabout 184, 514
Magnor 305
Majestic 505
majolica 156
Makeig-Jones, Daisy 68, 167
Malavia, José Javier 110
Malayan militaria 333
Malevich, Kasimir 180
Maltby, John 152
Manchester Components
Company 26
manicure sets 437
mannequins, shop display
439
Manning-Bowman 19
mantel clocks 19, 279
Maori art 558
Mapplethorpe, Robert 155
Marble King Inc. 329
marbles 309, 327-30
Margaret, Princess 420, 422
Marks & Spencer 429
Marples, William 508
Marquez, Gabriel García 35
Marseille, Armand 255
Marshall & Aitken 333
Martens, Dino 293
Martin, H.B. 469
Martínez, Vincento 108, 109
Marvella 232
Marx 537
Marx Toys 252, 270, 537
Mary, Queen 418
Mascitti-Lindahl, Francesca
144
masks
    tribal art 556-8
    Troika 163
Maslankowski, Alan 66
Massarella, Nicola 128
Masudaya 536, 538
match holders 471
match stands 445
Matchbox Toys 525
Matheson, Richard 41, 44
Mattel 183, 491
Matthews, Mark 308
Matura, Adolf 283, 284
Maugham, William Charles
469
Max, Peter 435
May, J. & J. 419
Mayer 385-9
Mayes, Reginald 381
Mazer Brothers 232
Mazoyer, Albert 323
Mdina 290
Meaking, J. & G. 178
measures, tools 509
meat plates 113
mechanical music 331-2
medals, sporting 462, 472,
473
Meech, Annette 312
Mego 272
Meissen 549
Melba China 419
Melbourne, Colin 56, 60, 84,
178
Melissa 391
melon scoops 17
Memphis 129, 247
menus 249, 470
Meopta 54
Mercian China 421
Mermod Frères 332

Merrythought 450, 493, 502
Messenger, Shawn 309
meteorites 337
Mettoy 529, 552
MGM 354
Michelin 15
Mickey Mouse 250-4
Midwinter 112-14, 426
Midwinter, Eve 112, 114, 426
Mikli, Alain 262
militaria 333-4
milk jugs
    advertising 16
    Burleigh Ware 175
    Crowan Pottery 83
    Doulton 85
    glass 288
    Midwinter 112, 114
    Royal Winton 180
    Sixties and Seventies 426
    sporting memorabilia 479
    stainless steel 480
    Susie Cooper 82
Miller, Paul 289
Millers 506
Millership, Jean 125
Mills, Magnus 36
Mills, Vera 120
Milwards 457
Mimi Di N 232
miniature cameras 54
Minox 54
mirrors
    advertising 13
    character collectables 181
    Sixties and Seventies 437
Mitchell, William 348
Mogensen, Jørgen 136
money
    banknotes 22-3, 470
    coins 193-7, 477
money boxes and banks
    character collectables 185
    Disneyana 250
    Fifties 269
    Rye Pottery 138
    Sixties and Seventies 427,
    428, 433
Montblanc 344, 346
Montegrappa 347
Montgomery, James 380
Moorcroft 115-16
Moore, Simon 312
Morel, Joseph 314
Morell, Dustin 309
Morelli, Spike 41
Morestone 529
Morris, Tony 123
Morris, William 311
Morris, William II 509
Morton's 348
Moser of Karlsbad 285
Moskiwitz, Morris 222
moulds, chocolate 187-92
Movado 564
Mugler, Thierry 215
mugs
    character collectables 182,
    185
    commemorative ceramics
    210-12, 417-23
    Disneyana 253
    Fornasetti 95
    Royal Copenhagen 135
    Sixties and Seventies 425,
    428
    Smurfs 449

sporting memorabilia 471
Swid Powell 155
Troika 163
Wade 165
Mukaïdé, Keïko 312
Müller, Franz Heinrich 134
Muppets 186
Murano 293-5
Murray, Keith 166, 280
music
    mechanical 331-2
    musical jugs 70, 164
    musical tankards 421
    rock and pop 406-15
    mustard pots 70, 266
Myles Originals 223
Myott 117-18

N

Nagel 432
Naipaul, V.S. 36
Namco 491
name plates, railwayana 400
Namiki 345, 347
Napco 267
Napier 232, 245
Nason, Ben 367
Native American tribal art
554-6
natural history 335-7
Navajo art 554
Nazeing 323
necklaces
    costume jewellery 225,
    227, 229-34, 238-9, 245-6
    rock and pop 407
    Sixties and Seventies 437
    tribal art 558
Neolithic beads 24
New Zealand posters 375
newspapers, rock and pop
406
Next Interiors 178
Nicky Toys 529
Nicol, Gordon 364
Nicoll, M. 89
night lights 177
nightdress cases 500
Nintendo 491
Noah's arks 553
Noke 381
Noke, Charles J. 85, 92-4
Nomura 538
Nordbruch, Karl 313
Noritake 178-9
Norris 507
Norwegian
    glass 304, 305
    posters 373
    see also Scandinavian
Nourot, Michael 313
Novy Bor 284
nursery ware
    bicycling 26
    commemorative ceramics
    210
    Shelley 147
    Wade 165
Nuutajärvi Nöstjo 305
Nylund, Anita 267
Nylund, Gunnar 142, 144
Nymølle 144, 146

O

O'Brian, Patrick 36
O'Broin, Domhnall 322
O'Donnell, Peter 41
O'Farrell, Maggie 36
Officine Galileo Di Milano 54
Ogden, James 457
Ogilvy, Ian 49
Ohio Art Co. 429, 533
Okkolin, Aimo 299, 300
Olabuenaga, Adrian 247
Old Hall 480-1
Olivetti 350
Olonetzki, B. 382
Olympics 476-7
OMAS 347
O'Meara, Geraldine 125
Omega (teddy bears) 503
Omega watches 565
O'Neil, Rosie 533
ornaments, Sixties and Seventies 433
Orup, Bengt 304
Orwell, Graham 65, 66
Oshkosh B'Gosh 217
Otto Keramik 172

P

P&O 249
Padden, Daphne 368
Paddington Bear 81
pails, sand 533-4
paint boxes 253
paintings, railwayana 405
Palitoy 259, 270
Palm, Rolf 144
Palma, Paola 129
Palme Konig 285
Palshus 139, 144-5
Panasonic 431
pandas 500
panels, glass 312
Panorama Studios 422
paper
    bags 269
    clothing 216
    dolls 260
paper clips 478
paperbacks 39-47
paperweights 292, 315
papier-mâché animals 433
Paragon 420-3
Pardoe, Geoffrey 41
parian busts 211, 416
Park, W. 463, 464
Parke, Kris 309
Parker
    desk sets 349
    pens 338-9
    shop display stands 350
Parker, Tony 309
Parsons, Pauline 86
Pascoe, Marilyn 160
Patrick, D.M. 463
Patterson, James 36
Paveley, Ruth 119, 120, 122
Payne, Mark 257
Peanuts 184
pearlware 26, 248
Peceny, Frantisek 283
Pedigree 255, 259-60
Peggy Davies Ceramics 419
Pelham Puppets 552

Pelikan 346
Pelli, Cesar 247
Peltier Glass Company 327-9
Pemberton, Rene 69
pen holders 360
pen racks 350
pencil sharpeners 360, 449
pencils, black cat collectables 27
pendants 24
    costume jewellery 225, 227, 229, 230, 233, 234, 245, 247
    rock and pop 407
Penfold 468
Pennell, Ronald 313
penny-farthing bicycles 26
pens 338-47
Pentagram 430
penwipes 349
pepper shakers
    Bakelite and plastics 361
    Briglin Pottery 67
    Fifties 267
    Midwinter 112
    Sixties and Seventies 427-8
Pepsi 182
Percy, Arthur Carlsson 304
perfume bottles 292, 313, 314, 351-3
Perry & Co. 348
Persian writing equipment 350
Peter Jones China 422
Peters, Ellis 37
Petitcolin 258
Petz 503
pewter
    chess sets 548
    cigarette boxes 472
Pez dispensers 354-7
Pflueger 457
PG Tips 15
phenolic
    boxes 358, 359
    perfume bottles 353
Phoenix Glass 432
photograph albums 332
photographs
    rock and pop 410
    sporting memorabilia 462, 474
photography, cameras 52-5
pictures
    railwayana 405
    Sixties and Seventies 432
Pierce 565
Pierre, D.B.C. 37
Piko Spielwaren 553
pilgrim bottles 131
pill boxes 17, 423
Pilot 345
pin trays 123
pins
    character collectables 183, 186
    costume jewellery 225-37, 247
    film and TV 272, 273
    rock and pop 406, 408-13, 415
    sporting memorabilia 476, 477
    teddy bear 505
    see also brooches
pitchers, glass 288, 294
Piver, L.T. 395
Pixie Toys 503

planes (tools) 506-7, 511
planters, character collectables 181, 183
plaques
    advertising 15
    Bakelite and plastics 363
    commemorative ceramics 212
    glass 324
    Hazle Ceramics 96
    Poole Pottery 122
    Royal Copenhagen 135
    Scandinavian ceramics 142, 146
    shipping memorabilia 249
    Sixties and Seventies 438-9
    sporting memorabilia 477
    studio pottery 149, 152
    Wade 164
plaster figures 18
plastics 358-63
    dolls 258-60
    Sixties and Seventies 425
plates
    character collectables 181, 184
    Clarice Cliff 71-80
    commemorative ceramics 210-12, 416-23
    Fornasetti 95
    glass 282, 288
    Midwinter 112-14
    nursery ware 26
    Poole Pottery 123-4, 126, 128
    Postmodern 129
    railwayana 405
    Rosenthal 133
    shipping memorabilia 248
    Sixties and Seventies 425, 428
    sporting memorabilia 471, 479
    stainless steel 481
    Swid Powell 154-5
    Troika 163
    Wedgwood 166, 167
platinum watches 562
Platt, Marc 271
Platt, Warren 65
platters 82
Playboy magazines 325
playing cards 249
PMI 529
Pohl, Frederik 44
polar bears 500
Poli, Flavio 293
Polish
    ceramics 175
    militaria 333
    posters 383
    teddy bears 504
political commemorative ceramics 210-11
Polyphon 332
Polypops 429
Poole Pottery 118-28
pop see rock and pop
Popeye 183
porcelain see ceramics
Porsgrund 145
Portmeirion 179
Portuguese chess sets 549
postal scales 350
postcards 183
posters 364-83
    airline 370

bicycling 26
cruise liners 368-9
film 383
food related 374-6
product 377-8
railway 364-7
skiing 371
theatrical and performance 382
tourism 372-3
wartime 379-81
Postmodern ceramics 129
posy vases 116
pot-lids 384-9
Potter, Beatrix 65-6
pottery see ceramics
Pottinger, Sue M. 128
powder boxes 278, 358, 359
powder compacts 390-5
powder horns 334
Powell, Addie 154
Powell, Harry 318
Powell, James 318
Prangnell, Eileen 119, 120
Pratchett, Terry 32, 49
Pratt 384-9
preserve pots
    Clarice Cliff 72, 73, 76
    commemorative ceramics 420
    Shelley 147
Presley, Elvis 406, 409
pressed glass 274-9
Preston 507, 511
Price & Kensington 156, 211
Price Bros. 156, 426
prints, sporting 474
Prinztronic 490
Procope, Ulla 139
programmes
    film and TV 273
    rock and pop 413
    sporting memorabilia 13, 460, 462, 470, 476
Promenade Pottery 152
Psion 492
Pucci, Emilio 215-17, 220, 262, 263
Pukeberg 305
Pullman, Philip 49-50
punchbowls 179
puppets 496, 552
Purbeck Pottery 152
Purfleet and Erith 472
purses 436, 437
puzzle jugs 180, 471
puzzles, jigsaw 272, 405, 434
Pygmalion 394

Q

Quant, Mary 216, 233, 437

R

Rabbit telephones 492
rackets, tennis 478
Radi, Giulio 293
radios 431, 437
railwayana 396-405
    posters 364-7
Ramos, Antonio 110
Randsfjord 305
Rankin, Ian 37
Rankine, John 44

Ravenhead 323
Ravenswood 330
Ray-O-Vac 431
Raybert 262
Read, Alfred 122
Read, Ann 122
records, rock and pop 406-15
Reekie, David 313
reels, fishing 455-7
Reeve, Philip 50
Reich, S. & Co. 282
Reiche, Anton 187-92
Revere 569, 571, 572
Revere Clock Co. 19
Revie, Alistair 46
Revlon 259
Reynolds 546
Rhead, Charlotte 176
Rhead, Frederick 175
Rialto 223, 224
Richards, Cliff 434
Richardson, Cathy 310
Rickard, Jesse Louisa 19
Riddell, Chris 50
Ridgway Potteries 266, 419
Rie, Lucie 148, 152
Riihimaën Lasi Oy 299-300
Riken 54
ring holders 178
rings 233, 246
Rion, Hanna 505
Ritzenhoff 323
Roanoid 363
Robert Originals 233
Roberts, Geo. 68
Robinson, Kim Stanley 37
Robinson & Leadbeater 416
Robson, Kenneth 46
rock and pop 406-15
    The Beatles 406-8
    Elvis 409
rocks 337
Roddy 257
rods, fishing 458
Rogers, Phil 153
Roig, José 109
Rolex 559
rollerskates 182
Ronay 220
Ronneby, F.M. 305
Ronson 430, 440
Rooke, Bernard 130-1
Rorstrand 142
Rosenstein, Nettie 218, 219
Rosenthal 132-3, 323
Roth Keramik 172
Roubícek, René 283
Rouch, W.W. & Co. 474
Rowling, J.K. 50
Roy, Arundhati 37
Royal Albert Crown China 420
Royal Brierley 280
Royal Cauldon 175
royal commemoratives 416-23
Royal Copenhagen 134-6
Royal Doulton 85-94
    animals 59, 94, 212
    Brambly Hedge 91
    Bunnykins 92-3
    coffee cans 85
    figures 86-90
    jugs 85
    royal commemoratives 420,
423
    sporting memorabilia 471
    tea caddies 85
    vases 85

    see also Doulton
Royal Dux 176
Royal Norfolk 178
Royal Stafford 422
Royal Winton 180
Royal Worcester 180
Roydon 546
rubbish bins 432
Rudd 376
Rudolstadt 471
Ruiz, Julio 110
rules 509
Rupert Bear 51, 63
Ruscha 173
Rushdie, Salman 37
Ruskin Pottery 137
Russ Berrie & Co. 433
Russian
    ceramics 211
    posters 373
    powder compacts 392
    sporting memorabilia 477
Ryall, Phyllis 119
Rye Pottery 138

S

Sabino 279
Sable, Josh 310
St Ives Pottery 150-1
Saint Laurent, Yves 214
St Mungo Mfg. Co. 468
Salazar, David 308, 310
Salco 546
Sales, Harry 63, 91
salt pots and shakers
    Bakelite and plastics 361
    Briglin Pottery 67
    Clarice Cliff 73
    Crown Devon 84
    Fifties 267
    Lotus Pottery 111
    Midwinter 112
    Sixties and Seventies 427-8
salt-glazed stoneware 153
Salto, Axel 136
Salviati 293
Samco 265
Sampson Hancock & Sons
177
sand pails 533-4
Sandor 233
sandwich trays 72
Sapir, Richard 47
Sarpaneva, Timo 297
Sarreguemines 212
Sarto, Ben 42
Sasha dolls 260
sauce boats 152, 266
saucepans 405
saucers see cups and saucers
Saville, Malcolm 50
saws (tools) 510
Saxbo 139, 145
Sayer, Derek 377
Sayers, Ben 465
Sayers, Fanny 348
scales, postal 350
Scandinavian
    ceramics 139-46
    glass 296-306
    see also individual countries
scarves 254, 474
scent bottles see perfume
bottles

Scheurich 168-70
Schiaparelli, Elsa 233, 244
Schildkrait 393
Schildkröt 258
Schlossberg 173
Schmid International 179
Schoenau & Hoffmeister 255
Schott, Otto 307
Schott Zweisel 307
Schuco 454, 493, 499, 535-7
Schultz, Charles 185
scissors 183
Scott, Sir Peter 114
Scott, Septimus Edwin 375
Scottish
    coins 197
    pens 343
    tools 506, 507
scraps 424
sculpture
    Bakelite and plastics 363
    Fifties 268
    glass 290, 294, 295, 298
    Sixties and Seventies 433
Secor 531
Seeney, Enid 266
Sega 491
Seguso 293
Seiro 233
Selman, Robert 42
services see coffee services;
dinner services; tea services
Sessions 19
Seventies see Sixties and
Seventies
sewing kits 432
Seymour Mann Inc. 437
Shackleton 529, 530
shares and bonds 28
Sharp 490
Sharp, David 138
Sharp, Margery 50
Sheaffer 350
Shelley 147, 418, 419
Shep 366
Sheringham, George 366
Shine, P. 365
shipping posters 368-9
Shire, Peter 129, 247
shirts 461
shop display mannequins 439
Shoreham 223
Shorter 211
signs
    advertising 13, 350
    railwayana 396-402
    Sixties and Seventies 439
Silberstein, Alain 565
silver
    beads 24
    chocolate moulds 188
    costume jewellery 226,
227, 238-9, 245
    medals 472
    perfume bottles 353
    powder compacts 390, 393
    sporting memorabilia 472
    trophies 475
    watches 559, 563
Silver King 468
silver plate
    bottle stoppers 249
    dog collars 573
    inkwells 472
    sporting memorabilia 472
    tea sets 20
Simak, Clifford D. 44

Simenon, Georges 42
Simpson, J.&A. 465
Simpson, R. 463, 464
Simulsen, Mari 145
Sinclair 489
Sirota, Benny 158
Sixties and Seventies 425-39
    Carnaby Street 428
    ceramics 425-7
    Dodo 438-9
    fashion and style 436-7
    homeware 429-32
    ornaments 433
    Peter Max 435
    toys 434
    skiing posters 371
Skipworth, Michael and
Elizabeth 111
skittles 256
Sklo Union 283-4
Skrdlovice Glassworks 285
Skruf Glasbruk 306
Slazenger 468, 479
Smalandshyttan 306
Smale, Claude 122
Smartt, John 470
Smith, Guy N. 44
Smiths 362
smoking accessories 440-6
Smurfs 447-9
Snoopy 184
soda siphons 13
soft toys 450-4
    character collectables 185,
186
    Disneyana 250
    teddy bears 493-505
Søholm 143
Solido 530
Solingen 458
Sommerfelt, Ros 126, 127
Sommet 187, 189
Sony 489
Sottsass, Ettore
    ceramics 129, 154
    costume jewellery 247
    glass 323
    letter racks 350
soup bowls
    Carlton Ware 70
    Crowan Pottery 83
    Modernist style 180
    shipping memorabilia 248
    Swid Powell 154
South African
    posters 374
    toys 434
Sowerby 275, 276, 278, 281
Spalding 468
Spanish posters 373, 377,
381, 382
Spara Keramik 173
spectacles see eyewear
spelter
    figures 18, 478
    inkwells 348
spheres, glass 308-10
Spiers 506, 507
Spillane, Mickey 42
Spillers Homepride 15
spirit containers 164
Spode 211, 471
spoons, stainless steel 483
sporting memorabilia 455-79
    fishing 455-8
    football 459-62
    golf 463-73

horse racing 474-5
Olympics 476-7
tennis 478
spy cameras 54
Stabler, Harold 480
Stabler, Phoebe 90, 148
Staehr-Nielsen, Eva 145
Staffordshire
commemorative ceramics 416
mugs 425
sporting memorabilia 479
stainless steel 480-3
Stålhane, Carl-Harry 142
stamps 484
Standard Mill Co. 465
standees 505
Stankard, Paul 308
Stanley 506, 507
Star Wars 547
Starck, Philippe 322
Staunton, Jaques 548
Steiff
Disneyana 250
dolls 256
soft toys 450-2, 500
teddy bears 493-5
Steinbeck, John 42
Stelton 482, 483
Stennett-Willson, Ronald 286, 289, 315
Stern, Anthony 313-14
Steuler Keramik 173
stevengraphs 248
Stevens, Irene 280
Stevens & Williams 280
Stewart, Paul 50
stickers 436
Still, Nanny 299, 300, 305
stirrup cups 279
stockings 407
stoneware see ceramics
stools 451
storage jars 267, 426
Stratton 391, 393
straws, drinking 253, 431
string holders 426
Strobel, David 308
Strom, Per Olaf 302, 303
Stromberg, Gerda 306
Strombergshyttan 306
Strunz 503
Stuart 280, 323
Stuart, W.J. 44
studio glass 311-14
studio pottery 148-53
Studio Seven 365
Styron, William 38
Suetin, Nikolai 180
sugar bowls 266
sugar sifters
Clarice Cliff 71, 73, 74, 76, 77, 80
Crown Devon 84
Lotus Pottery 111
Portmeirion 179
Royal Winton 180
suits 215, 216
Sundell, Britt-Louise 140
sunglasses 262-5, 436
Superman 182
Surjan, Valerie 314
Surrey Ceramics 425
Sutcliffe 536
Suzuki Optical Co. 54
Swarovski 233
Swatch 265, 566-8

sweatshirts 13
Swedish
bicycling 26
cocktail shakers 571
Fifties 267
glass 302-6
see also Scandinavian
Swid, Nan 154
Swid Powell 154-5
Swift, Graham 38
Swiss
chess sets 549
golf scorers 473
lighters 442
mechanical music 332
posters 371-2
toys 552
watches 561, 564, 565
Sydenham, Guy 122, 123
Sykes, Wm. 478
SylvaC 179
Symphonion 331, 332

T

table bells 473
Tailyodo Koki 54
Tait, Jessie 112-14
Taj, Jesse 308, 310
Tan, Amy 38
Tangee 395
tankards
commemorative ceramics 212, 421
Wedgwood 166
Tanner, Maureen 266
tape measures 478
Tara Toys 500, 503
Tarot 179
Tate, Christine 125
taxidermy 485-8
Taylor, Edward Richard 137
Taylor, Elizabeth 260
Taylor, F.G. 545
Taylor, G.P. 50
Taylor, J.H. 470
Taylor, Linda 158
Taylor, William Howson 137
Taylor & Barrett 546
Taylor-Tunnicliffe 471
Tchalenko, Janice 148, 150, 178
tea caddies 85
tea cups see cups and saucers
tea services
Art Deco 20
Bakelite and plastics 361
Shelley 147
Teague, Walter Dorwin 55
teapots 156
Carlton Ware 70
Clarice Cliff 71, 72
commemorative ceramics 417, 418, 421, 422
Crown Pottery 83
Doulton 85
Grimwades 156
Langley 178
Midwinter 113, 114
Postmodern 129
Scandinavian ceramics 144, 145
Shelley 147
sporting memorabilia 477
stainless steel 480

studio pottery 150
Susie Cooper 82
Troika 163
technology 489-92
calculators 490
computer games 491
pocket televisions 489
teddy bears 493-505
Tekno 526
telephones 492
television see film and TV
televisions, pocket 489
Tell, I.C. 511
tennis 478
Terry, William J. 454
Texas Instruments 490
textiles, tribal art 554, 558
theatrical posters 382
thermometers 348, 362, 433
Thermos 182, 361
Thompson, D.C. 199-201
Thompson, Eric 184
Thompson, Jan 158
Thompson, Jim 42
Thorens 440, 446
Thorndike, Russell 47
Thornton-Pickard 52
Thorsson, Nils 134, 136
Thrower, Frank 286-7
Thun, Clare 372
tickets, sporting 459, 476
ties 185, 217
tiles 142
Till 156
Timpo 544
tinplate toys 535-8
tins
biscuit 16
Sixties and Seventies 428, 429, 430
toast racks
Bakelite and plastics 361
ceramic 178
Fifties 266
tobacco jars 444
Toby jugs 85, 213, 419
Toikka, Oiva 305
toiletry sets 437
Tomasello, Beth 310
TomyTronic 491
Tongue, Graham 57, 59, 62, 64-6, 91
Tonka 530
tools 506-12
toothpick holders 361
Topper 528
Topps 181
torches 431
Torquay Pottery 153
Torrijos, Regino 110
Toso, Ferdinando 293
tourism posters 372-3
Townsend, Dennis 138
Toy Biz Co. 182
toys and games 513-53
advertising 13
cars 252, 363
character collectables 185
chess 548-51
computer games 491
Corgi 513-15
diecast 525-30
Dinky 516-22
Disneyana 250-4
lead figures 539-46
railwayana 405
sand pails 533-4

Sixties and Seventies 434
soft toys 185, 186, 250, 450-4
Star Wars 547
tinplate 535-8
trains 531-2
Tri-ang 523-4
TPS 538
trains
railwayana 396-405
posters 364-7
toy 531-2
Traub, David 314
trays
Poole Pottery 122, 123
rock and pop 406
Scandinavian ceramics 140
Sixties and Seventies 425, 428, 429, 435
sporting memorabilia 477
studio pottery 151
Tremaen Pottery 157
Tremar 153
Tressa 565
Trevor, William 38
Tri-ang 259, 523-4, 532, 552
tribal art 554-8
African 557
the Americas 554-6
Trifari 228
trinket boxes 430
trinket sets 282
trio sets
Broadhurst Bros 175
commemorative ceramics 419
glass 288
Midwinter 112, 113
Susie Cooper 82
Trix 532
Troika 158-63
Trolle, Anne Marie 135
Trompf 373
trophies, sporting 472, 475
Tsosie, Gladys 554
Tubb, E.C. 44
Tudor Oyster 559
Tuffin, Sally 115, 128
tumblers 316, 479
Turner, Thomas 508
TV see film and TV
tygs 26, 417
Tynell, Helena 300
Tyson, Keith 482, 483

U

U-Keramik 173
Unica 503
Upsala, Ekeby 145
Urquhart, R.L. 464
US Metal Toys 533, 534

V

Vacchetti, Sandro 176
Valentine cards 182
Vallauris 426
Vallence, Sylvia 159
Vallien, Bertil 303
vampire protection kits 573
van Shaak, Martin 219
Van Wyck Mason, F. 47
Vannicola, Carlo 129

vans, toy 518-19
Vaseline glass 276
vases
  Art Deco 20, 175
  Bernard Rooke 131
  black cat collectables 27
  Briglin Pottery 67
  Carlton Ware 68
  character collectables 185
  Clarice Cliff 71, 72, 75-80
  commemorative ceramics 211, 418
  Crown Devon 84
  Crown Ducal 176
  glass 277-8, 280-7, 289-307, 311-24
  Gouda 177
  Hornsea 178
  Italian ceramics 103-5
  Kilrush Pottery 178
  lady head 267
  Lotus Pottery 111
  Louis Hudson 97
  Midwinter 113
  Moorcroft 115, 116
  Myott 118
  Poole Pottery 119-20, 122, 125-8
  Postmodern 129
  Rosenthal 132-3
  Royal Copenhagen 134-6
  Royal Doulton 85
  Ruskin Pottery 137
  Rye Potteries 138
  Scandinavian ceramics 139-46
  Sixties and Seventies 426
  sporting memorabilia 471
  stainless steel 481
  studio pottery 149-53
  Tremaen 157

Troika 158-63
Wade 164
  Wedgwood 166-7
  West German ceramics 168-72
  vehicles, toy 13, 513-20, 523-30
Vendome 234
Venetian beads 24, 25
Venini 293, 294
Venini, Paolo 294
ventriloquist dummies 573
Venturi, Robert 154-5
Verne, Jules 44
Versace 214
Versanto, Erkki 297
vests, tribal art 555-6
Viard 351, 352
Victoria, Queen 416-17, 429
Viladot, I.G. 381
Vilhelmsson, Eskil 286
Viners 482-3
Vinolia 390
Visconti 347
Vista Alegre 549
Vitro Agate Company 329
Vízner, Frantisek 283
Voice Organiser 492
Volupte 394
von Nesson, Walter 20
Vormenfabriek 191, 192
Vyse, Charles 153

W

Waddingtons 553
Wade 156, 164-5, 350
Wade Heath 164
Wagenfeld, Wilhelm 307
Wahl-Eversharp 342, 349
Wain, Louis 378

Walker, William 290
wall plaques see plaques
Wallace, Edgar 47
wallets 254
Walter, H. 187, 190, 191
Waltham 565
Walther, Conny 139, 146
Walther & Sohn 274-9, 282
war commemorative ceramics 212-13
Ward, Rowland 488
Warff, Goran 298
Warner 234
Warner Bros. 355
Warren Telechron Co. 362
wartime posters 379-81
wash bags 436
Washington Potteries 425
watch fobs 13
watches 559-68
  Disneyana 254
  Swatch 566-8
  watch pins 237
water jugs 85, 137
Waterman's 340-2, 347
Waters, E.J. 368
Watson 52
Watts, Mary 149
weapons, militaria 333
weaving, tribal art 554
Webb Corbett 280
Wedgwood 166-7, 421-3
Wedgwood Glass 289, 315
Weinberg, Frederick 268
weird and wonderful 573
Weisner 224
Weiss, H. 377

Weissmuller 503
Welch, Robert 480-1
Weldon, William A. 572
Weller 471
Wellings, Norah 257
Wells Brimtoy 530
West Bend Aluminum Co. 572
West German ceramics 168-73
Westwood, Vivienne 214, 234
Wheeler, Peter 318, 319
Whieldon, Thomas 156
White, Alan 126, 128
White, E.B. 50
White, Robert 465
Whitefriars 280, 283, 316-21
Whiting & Davis 234
Wiggin, J. & J. 480
Wigston, J.E. 405
Wiinblad, Bjørn 132, 146, 323
Wilardy 223-4
Wilkes, Beverley 116
Wilkinson Ltd 179, 213, 418
Williams-Ellis, Susan 179
Williamson, Alexander Hardie 323
Wills, Julie 126
Wilson, William 318
Winchcombe Pottery 148
wine and drinking 569-72
Winkle, Kathie 175
Winkworth Scott 466
Winnie the Pooh 64
Winterhalder and Hofmeier 19
Winterson, Jeanette 38
Winton 418
Wirkkala, Tapio 133, 297, 300, 306
Wittnauer 565

Wolf & Co. 13
Wolverine 538
Wood, Arthur & Sons 267, 426, 427, 471
Woodman, Rachel 314
Woolnough 501
Worcester 180
Wren, Percival Christopher 38
Wright, Russel 178
wristwatches 254, 437, 559-68
writing equipment 338-50
  desk bases 349
  inkwells 348
  pens 338-47
Wupper Design 434
Wurlitzer 362
Wyburgh, Angela 125
Wyndham, John 38
Wyon, Allan C. 148

Y

Yamamoto, Koichiro 314
Yorke, P.H. 368
Young, Ellsworth 381
Yugoslavian Pez dispensers 354

Z

Zalloni, Cari 173
Zanetti, Licio 294
Zanetti, Oscar 294
Zanini, Marco 247
Zast 394
Zeiss 55
Zeiss, Carl 307
Zelique Studio 314
Ziegfeld 393